Trade Shocks in Developing Countries

SPONSORS

The funding for this project was provided by:

Oxford Institute for Energy Studies
International Centre for Economic Growth [ICEG]
World Bank
The Dutch Government

Trade Shocks in Developing Countries

Volume 1: Africa

PAUL COLLIER

AND

JAN WILLEM GUNNING

AND

ASSOCIATES

OXFORD

UNIVERSITY PRESS

OXFORD
UNIVERSITY PRESS

Great Clarendon Street, Oxford OX2 6DP

Oxford University Press is a department of the University of Oxford.
It furthers the University's objective of excellence in research, scholarship,
and education by publishing worldwide in

Oxford New York

Athens Auckland Bangkok Bogotá Buenos Aires Calcutta
Cape Town Chennai Dar es Salaam Delhi Florence Hong Kong Istanbul
Karachi Kuala Lumpur Madrid Melbourne Mexico City Mumbai
Nairobi Paris São Paulo Singapore Taipei Tokyo Toronto Warsaw
with associated companies in Berlin Ibadan

Oxford is a registered trade mark of Oxford University Press
in the UK and in certain other countries

Published in the United States
by Oxford University Press Inc., New York

British Library Cataloguing in Publication Data

Data available

Library of Congress Cataloging in Publication Data

Trade shocks in developing countries / Paul Collier and
Jan Willem Gunning and associates.
p. cm.
Includes bibliographical references and indexes.
Contents: v. 1. Africa—v. 2. Asia and Latin America.
ISBN 0–19–829338–0 (Volume 1)
ISBN 0–19–829463–8 (Volume 2)
1. Buffer stocks—Prices—Developing countries. 2. Buffer stocks—
Prices—Africa. 3. Buffer stocks—Prices—Asia. 4. Buffer stocks—
Prices—Latin America. 5. Commodity control—Developing countries.
6. Commodity control—Africa. 7. Commodity control—Asia.
8. Commodity control—Latin America. I. Collier, Paul.
II. Gunning, Jan Williem.
HF1428.T72 1999 332.6′09172′4—dc21 98-47376

1 3 5 7 9 10 8 6 4 2

Typeset in Palatino
by Best-set Typesetter Ltd., Hong Kong
Printed in Great Britain
on acid-free paper by
Biddles Ltd
Guildford & Kings Lynn

PREFACE

This book is the outcome of a project involving many individuals and institutions. Core funding for the project was provided by the International Centre for Economic Growth (ICEG) and the World Bank. The Oxford Institute for Energy Studies funded the case studies of two oil shocks. The Dutch government funded the Asian case studies and two of the workshops. Without this support the project would not have been feasible.

The study grew out of our earlier work on the coffee boom in Kenya. The authors of the country studies were asked to adopt the methodology of the Kenyan study with respect to the estimation of windfall savings rates and the disaggregation into private and public behaviour. The methodology was discussed with the country teams at launch workshops in Washington, DC, Oxford and Colombo (Sri Lanka). Subsequent workshops in Amsterdam and Oxford were used to discuss draft chapters. Interim results of the project were published in *Trade Shocks in Developing Countries* (Institute for Contemporary Studies, for ICEG, 1994) and were presented at the European Economic Association Annual Conference of 1992 (published in the *European Economic Review*, 1993) and the Royal Economic Society Annual Conference of 1996. We would like to thank Angus Deaton for extensive comments on a previous draft.

Paul Collier and Jan Willem Gunning

Washington, January 1998

CONTENTS

Volume 1

Volume 2

1

Trade Shocks: Theory and Evidence

PAUL COLLIER AND JAN WILLEM GUNNING

1.1. Introduction

Many developing countries are prone to temporary trade shocks. Shocks have long been seen as a problem, either because they have produced booms and busts in which private agents have misallocated resources through myopia, or because they have lured governments into huge fiscal errors. To date there have been three phases in the debate on appropriate policy responses. In the first the problem was seen as inappropriate private responses to which the solution was public action at the international or domestic level. Public action at the international level sought to reduce fluctuations in the international prices of commodities. The main instrument envisaged for this was the buffer stock, financed by international collaboration. In the 1970s this led to the proposal of a common fund involving buffer stock operations for each of the major commodities. Although some of these were established, by the 1990s they had collapsed. As argued by Newbery and Stiglitz (1981), buffer stock schemes are inherently problematic: they involve substantial storage costs, they may trigger speculation by private stockholders, and to be viable they must lower the price over the long term. Public action at the domestic level sought to shield domestic producers from world price volatility by means of stabilising export taxes. Implicit in this advice was the belief that the government should play a custodial role, saving temporary windfalls which would otherwise be consumed by the private sector.

The second phase of the debate reversed the diagnosis of the first phase: now the problem was incompetent public handling of windfalls and the solution was to leave them with rational, well-informed, private agents. On the one hand the capacity of the government to handle a windfall was questioned. Gelb *et al.* (1988) showed that the oil-producing countries had handled the oil windfalls of the 1970s extremely badly. On the other hand, Bevan *et al.* (1987, 1989a,b, 1990) showed that in Kenya, where export taxation had been avoided, private agents had had a high windfall savings rate and so appeared not to have been myopic. Between them these studies suggested that private windfalls were best left with the private sector.

This critique of public action has in turn given rise to a third phase of debate which questions the underlying premiss that shocks are undesirable. Mash (1995) argues that price volatility can be welfare enhancing, giving producing countries the opportunity of shifting resources into activities which have temporarily high returns. Deaton and Miller (1996) investigate the effects of price shocks in Africa and conclude that there is no evidence that volatility has been detrimental: positive shocks have strongly increased output.

The present study was inspired by our earlier work on the effects of the 1976–79 coffee boom in Kenya (Bevan *et al.* 1987, 1989a, 1990, 1993b), a summary of which is presented in Chapter 2. That work has defined the methodology used in the twenty-three country studies of external shocks which constitute this two-volume book. As in the Kenya study, authors distinguish between responses of private agents and of the government, calculating windfall savings rates, determining the effect of a trade shock on both foreign and domestic assets, and assessing to what extent the domestic effects of a shock were changed by the control regime. Based on these twenty-three cases we reach the following conclusions. First, we find that public responses to external shocks have been remarkably diverse. The same shock has produced both increases and decreases in taxation, both financial liberalisation and financial tightening, and both trade liberalisation and trade restrictions. This policy incoherence has even extended to international agencies. For example, during the 1994 world coffee boom the International Monetary Fund was giving precisely contrary advice to the two most coffee-dependent African economies: it was recommending windfall taxation in Uganda and opposing it in Ethiopia. Second, we find that shocks have been problematic: although, during the shock, output is enhanced, this tends to be reversed in the post-shock period, which is often characterised by fiscal crisis. Third, we find support for the proposition that private agents respond appropriately to shocks: the Kenyan evidence appears to be generalisable. Powerful corollaries are developed from this evidence: the role of the government is to share information with the private sector on the nature of the shock; the appropriate fiscal response is to *reduce* rather than to raise taxation; and once the windfall is left with the private sector there is a complex task for the public sector in accommodating the changing demand of the private sector for financial assets, so that the maintenance of price stability requires an active monetary policy. Finally, we do not find support for the proposition that governments fail to save public windfalls. In general, governments are found to have high savings rates out of their windfalls, although they have tended to invest these savings badly.

Our cases consist of twelve African, five Latin American and six Asian country studies. The choice of country was determined partly by the adequacy of data and partly by the need for a spread over different types of shock. The cases are listed and classified in Table 1.1. The first four African shocks originate from the beverage boom of the late 1970s: coffee for Kenya, cocoa for Ghana, both for Côte d'Ivoire, and tea (together with tobacco) for Malawi. In Ghana and Côte d'Ivoire agricultural pricing policies were such that in the first instance most of the windfall accrued to the government, but in Kenya and Malawi it largely accrued in the first instance to farmers. Mauritius experienced a brief sugar boom. The case of Sénégal combines two shocks: a groundnuts boom and a phosphates boom, the former predominantly private, the latter predominantly public. The remaining African shocks all involve minerals: copper in Zambia, diamonds in Botswana, uranium in Niger and oil in Cameroon, Nigeria and Egypt, all of these being predominantly public. However, Egypt also experienced a remittance boom as a result of temporary migration to Saudi Arabia during the oil boom, and this accrued to private agents.

Table 1.1. The case studies

Country	Sector of shock	Recipient agent	Sign
Africa			
Kenya	Agriculture	Private	Positive
Ghana	Agriculture	Public	Positive
Côte d'Ivoire	Agriculture	Public	Positive
Malawi	Agriculture	Private	Positive
Mauritius	Agriculture	Private	Positive
Sénégal	Agriculture/Mining	Private/Public	Positive
Zambia	Mining	Public/Private	Positive/Negative
Botswana	Mining	Public	Positive/Negative
Niger	Mining	Public/Private	Positive
Cameroon	Mining	Public	Positive
Nigeria	Mining	Public	Positive
Egypt	Remittances/Mining	Private/Public	Positive
Latin America			
Colombia	Agriculture	Private/Public	Positive
Costa Rica	Agriculture	Private	Positive
Bolivia	Mining	Private/Public	Negative
Venezuela	Mining	Public	Negative
Mexico	Mining	Public	Positive
Asia			
Thailand	Multiple	Private	Negative
Sri Lanka	Import Prices	Private	Negative
Philippines	Import Prices	Private	Positive
Bangladesh	Remittances/Aid	Private/Public	Positive
Malaysia	Mining	Public	Positive
Indonesia	Mining	Public	Positive/Negative

The Latin American studies include two coffee booms, in Colombia and Costa Rica, the former accruing in part directly to the government owing to stabilising tax policy. The other three Latin American studies cover mining shocks: tin and gas in Bolivia, and oil for Venezuela and Mexico. The Asian studies include three in which the shocks were predominantly driven by changes in import prices, these being Thailand, Sri Lanka and the Philippines, though the Thai shocks were of multiple sources. Bangladesh benefited from a remittance boom and aid. Finally, the chapters on Malaysia and Indonesia are studies of mining shocks.

The sample is thus fairly evenly balanced between agricultural and mining shocks, and between public and private shocks. It is skewed towards positive shocks, but this reflects the pattern of commodity price movements, which are characterised by short, high peaks and long, shallow troughs (Deaton and Laroque 1992).

In this book we follow a case-study approach in which outcomes are compared with an explicit counterfactual which is constructed by an extrapolation of pre-shock trends. The studies use a common approach for this extrapolation, imposing pre-shock average savings and investment propensities and incremental capital–output ratios (ICORs). Obviously, this approach has both the virtues and the limitations of simplicity and uniformity. An alternative to the case-study approach is the econometric approach exemplified by Deaton and Miller (1996). While the econometric approach has some obvious advantages, it currently has difficulty in handling 'episodes' such as a multi-year price shock for which agents might have sufficient information to regard it as a single event. For short time-series it is often not possible econometrically to distinguish between trend-stationary and difference-stationary processes. Indeed, Leon and Soto (1995) go so far as to argue that previous econometric work has incorrectly classified some commodity price series as difference stationary because of a failure to allow for structural breaks. Using very long time-series, namely for the period 1900–92, they propose that nineteen out of twenty-four commodity price series are trend stationary. Even if this critique is not accepted (and there are objections to the introduction of structural breaks), there is wider agreement that conventional analyses have been overly inclined to classify price shocks as persistent when in fact they have a high reversionary component (Deaton and Miller 1996). Potentially, the case-study approach is too inclined to characterise prices as trend stationary, by treating as an episode something which can only be recognised as such with the benefit of hindsight. In an attempt to correct for this, all of the country studies discuss both the information available to agents at the time and the interpretations which agents gave to that information. Further, of the seven commodities in this study which are also covered by Leon and Soto, six are found to be trend stationary, namely cocoa, coffee, copper, sugar, tea and tin. The exception is tobacco, which is covered in only one of our studies, Malawi; but even here the tobacco shock was combined with a tea boom.

In this synthesis chapter we discuss the evidence from the country studies in the organisational terms of the analytic framework which underpins the studies. Section 1.2 sets out the analytic issues. Although it is conventional to deploy the theory of Dutch Disease to analyse shocks (for example, Neary and van Wijnbergen 1986), we devote more attention to intertemporal aspects, notably the savings responses of private and public agents and their consequences for asset acquisition. The next two sections discuss the evidence from the case studies on savings responses (Section 1.3) and asset choices (Section 1.4). Section 1.5 investigates the consequences of this asset behaviour for the growth of output in the case-study countries. In Section 1.6 we focus upon the 'control regime'. Public policy can affect private responses to shocks partly according to which regulations and taxes are in place at the start of the shock, and partly according to how they are modified in response to the shock. The section covers both the theory of public policy during shocks and the case-study evidence. Finally, in Section 1.7 we pull together the implications of the study for public policy towards external shocks.

1.2. Theories of Dutch Disease, Windfall Savings and Construction Booms

In Dutch Disease theory favourable external shocks shift resources out of the non-boom tradable sector. This is largely the result of the 'spending effect': as the extra income is seen as permanent, consumption will rise to the full extent of the increase in income. This extra spending will tend to push up the relative price of non-tradables and thereby induce resource shifts out of the non-booming tradable sector. This is only a 'disease' if particular assumptions are added to the standard analysis. For example, if the shock turns out to be temporary but this is not realised at the time then those resource shifts which are costly to reverse will be excessive. However, it is hardly surprising that an economy would do better if there were perfect knowledge of the future and there is no reason to believe that resource-allocation errors would be any greater in response to external shocks than to any other innovation. Arguments based on learning-by-doing in the non-boom tradable sector, or any other externalities generated in the sector, are not really shock specific: they constitute a case for favouring the sector in all circumstances rather than for shielding it from Dutch Disease effects.

The Dutch Disease approach needs to be augmented because price shocks should usually be treated as having intertemporal implications. Some price shocks are clearly temporary, such as the coffee booms induced by Brazilian frosts. For this type of shock part of the income increase will be seen as transient. Under most utility functions this provides an incentive to save in order to smooth consumption. In fact, it may be optimal to save most of the windfall, in which case the Dutch Disease emphasis on the change in consumption spending is misplaced. However, most price shocks, even if temporary with the benefit of hindsight, do not occur in a context in which the duration of the shock can be readily discerned. Given the high degree of uncertainty about the persistence of a price shock, the response then depends in part upon whether there are asymmetries between the consequences of errors of optimism and pessimism. For example, if the costs of erroneous optimism exceed those of pessimism then caution would be appropriate. There are, therefore, two rather different justifications for high savings rates in response to positive external shocks: that based on a belief that the shock is temporary, and that based on uncertainty coupled with asymmetric costs of errors.

An increase in savings implies an increased demand for assets. Private agents can save by acquiring claims on other agents, including the government. In aggregate, however, saving requires net acquisition of foreign assets or domestic real capital formation. In many developing countries the domestic rate of return exceeds the world deposit rate of interest. In these circumstances holding foreign assets can be optimal, but only temporarily. Were all capital tradable, windfall savings would be invested domestically until the rate of return had fallen to the deposit rate of interest. Thereafter savings would be used to acquire foreign assets since these offer an escape from diminishing returns. After the boom the foreign assets would be repatriated.

1.2.1. *Construction Booms*

The theory of construction booms combines the Dutch Disease disaggregation into tradables and non-tradables with the intertemporal analysis which disaggregates into consumer goods and assets. Above, we have argued that a positive external shock induces a disproportionate increase in the demand for assets. Some of these assets are non-tradables, such as buildings and infrastructure. Hence, the rise in demand for consumer non-tradables is weaker than that predicted within the framework of Dutch Disease theory (with a boom fully treated as temporary it might be close to zero), while the rise in demand for non-tradable capital goods may be very substantial. The sector which produces these goods, namely the construction sector, is therefore a major beneficiary of external shocks.[1] Indeed, the construction boom could be much more pronounced than the primary export boom which induces it. Since capital is partly non-tradable, the price of capital goods now rises as a result of the increase in investment. This provides a disincentive to bunched investment. Foreign assets then offer the advantage of protecting the real value of windfall savings: they can be held abroad and returned when capital prices have fallen. If these effects are sufficiently strong, as with a large but brief windfall, it will be optimal to continue investing domestically after the end of the commodity boom. Repatriated foreign assets are then used to stretch the investment boom over a longer period than the savings boom, thereby raising the efficiency of domestic investment. This role of foreign assets is one of the central propositions of the theory.

However, a counter to the efficiency of investment stretching can be based on the differential externalities generated by tradable and non-tradable capital goods. De Long and Summers (1991) argue that investment externalities accrue from equipment investment, which is tradable, but not from structures investment, which is non-tradable, since only the former embodies technical progress. This argument has two implications. First, to the extent that a commodity boom results in a higher relative price of non-tradable capital goods, substitution effects will favour equipment investment. Thus, investment externalities would be at their peak during a boom and this would at least qualitatively offset any decline in the private efficiency of investment. Second, by stretching investment, the rise in the relative price of non-tradable capital goods is mitigated, as a result of which the economy would forgo some of the investment externalities. Hence, although stretching would raise the private efficiency of investment, it might lower the social efficiency.

It should be noted that there will be a construction boom even in the case of a permanent shock. If capital is sector specific then in the case of a boom the spending effect raises the marginal productivity of capital in the production of non-tradable consumption goods, and when investment requires non-tradable capital goods this will be reflected in a construction boom.[2] (Note that in the case of a negative shock also there is an incentive to invest, but now in the importables sector.)

We can abstract from such wealth-induced investment by assuming that only tradables are consumed. This brings out the importance of the perception of the nature of the shock and of the country's access to a world capital market very clearly. For if the shock is seen as permanent there is now no reason to invest in response to it. If it is seen as temporary there will be windfall savings but no construction boom to the extent that savings are invested abroad. However, if there is no access to a perfect world capital market, so that in steady-state equilibrium the domestic rate of return exceeds the deposit rate of interest, then part of the windfall savings will be invested domestically.

As in the static case, the resulting construction boom does not represent a disease provided the nature of the shock is correctly perceived and agents are free to adjust their portfolio of foreign and domestic assets. These ideas are illustrated in the optimisation model described in the appendix to this chapter. Access to the world capital market raises welfare. It enables domestic investment to be postponed until the price of non-traded capital goods has fallen.

1.2.2. *Private Versus Public Saving*

Various arguments have been advanced in the literature for a custodial role for the government during external shocks. To execute such a role the government must either own the sector affected by the shock or tax and subsidise the private agents to whom the shock accrues. We now consider five arguments for a government custodial role.

The first is that the government is more likely to save a temporary windfall than are private agents. This was the argument advanced in the 1970s and 1980s. One reason for this is that private agents (for example, smallholders producing export crops) may wish to dissave because of a high discount rate, but normally be unable to do so because they are credit constrained. In such an environment a windfall would be fully consumed (Deaton 1990, 1991). This only establishes a case for windfall taxation to the extent that society wishes to override the savings decisions of its households. It does not rely upon differences between private and social discount rates but upon differences between private and public information. Smallholders, having little education, may miss information which indicates that the windfall may not be permanent, whereas the government has a much more sophisticated capacity to collect and interpret such information. However, there is an offsetting argument which suggests that private agents may have a higher savings rate out of windfalls. In order for the government to save a windfall it needs to abstain from current spending. This requires coordination among many spending ministries. Each spending ministry faces a free-rider problem: its own decision to transfer spending to the future might be frustrated by the increased spending of other ministries.

The second argument for a custodial role is that during windfalls the social cost of taxation may be atypically low. The rationale for this is that since the income is unanticipated, its taxation is not distortionary. There are two counters to this argument. First, if the government repeatedly taxes commodity price increases, then private agents will recognise this policy, anticipating that windfalls will be taxed even though they will be unable to predict when the windfalls will occur. This has an implication for investment: for example, coffee farmers may plant fewer trees even in years when there is no tax. In principle, governments could avoid this effect by using the revenue from windfall taxation to subsidise prices in other years. However, such a tax-cum-subsidise strategy removes the incentive for farmers to organise their production in such a way as to benefit from flexibility, shifting resources into whichever crop currently has a high world price. For example, during a windfall farmers should use more fertiliser and labour. Hence, over the long run, national income will be reduced by a tax-cum-subsidise strategy even if average output is not reduced. The volatility of world prices is advantageous if private agents increase output when prices are high and reduce it when prices are low, but private agents will not be induced to do this if domestic prices are smoothed.[3] The second counter is that the social cost of windfall taxation, far from being atypically low, may be atypically high. This is the case if private investment is initially socially sub-optimal (as is the case in many developing countries) and if the private propensity to invest is higher out of windfall income than out of normal income. Windfall taxation would then have an abnormally high opportunity cost in terms of private investment forgone.

The third argument for a custodial role is that if windfall income is allowed to accrue to the private sector the result will be inflationary. Whether this is the case depends upon exchange rate policy. Under a fixed exchange rate policy a windfall will indeed result in an increase in the price level. However, with a flexible exchange rate and no central bank intervention this is not the case: the demand for money will increase, but with no increase in supply the exchange rate will appreciate, thereby *lowering* the price level. The demand for money will increase for two reasons. First, the transactions demand will rise in line with the increase in real income. Second, the asset demand for money will rise temporarily because agents will initially hold their windfall savings as money balances, before converting them into real assets. Thus, under a flexible exchange rate there is no need for concern about the inflationary consequences of temporary windfalls.

The fourth argument for the custodial role of the government is that it is necessary to avoid temporary Dutch Disease. As with the first argument, the private sector is assumed to have an inferior capacity or inclination to forecast, though now the focus is the relative price of non-tradables. In the absence of government intervention the private sector will over-invest in the non-tradable sector, because of the failure to anticipate the reversal of the price change. However, even if the government has an informational advantage with respect to relative prices, intervention is problematic. The only way that the government can avoid any appreciation in the relative price of non-tradables is by permanently adding the windfall to its foreign exchange reserves. In most developing countries the domestic rate of return on capital is far above the return on foreign exchange reserves so that such a strategy would forfeit most of the potential gains from the windfall. However, if the windfall is only temporarily held in reserves the appreciation in the real exchange rate is simply shifted into the future. If the underlying problem is the risk that the private sector will fail to grasp that the appreciation is temporary, this may actually be accentuated by postponing the appreciation. This is because if the appreciation is synchronised with the windfall then the private sector can utilise the same information about duration for both the windfall itself and its relative price consequences. By contrast, if the appreciation is shifted by public intervention, the private sector will need to predict policy towards the reserves and its consequences for relative price changes.

The final argument for a custodial role for government is that the public sector has the advantage of not being constrained by its own rules. In particular, in economies with exchange controls it is the only agent legally able to acquire foreign assets and repatriate them. If foreign exchange controls have the effect of preventing the economy from acquiring temporary claims abroad during a private windfall then there is an unambiguous loss in welfare: windfall investment is compressed into the period of the income windfall. Even if the public sector normally has a lower return on investment than the private sector it may have a higher return upon windfall investment than the private sector because of being able to stretch the investment windfall over a longer period. However, exchange controls need not have this effect on the private sector. If the government or the central bank sells claims upon itself to the private sector while acquiring offsetting claims abroad, then private agents hold foreign assets indirectly. Although this offsets the effect of exchange control it is not equivalent to capital account convertibility. Inconvertibility enables the government to depress domestic interest rates below world rates, thereby imposing an implicit tax on financial assets. Many developing countries have been characterised by such financial repression, so that financial assets have offered very unattractive returns. The choice of financial instruments available to smallholder producers of agricultural exports has often been limited to currency and Post Office deposits with high transaction costs and negative real interest rates. This reduction in the real return on financial assets induces both higher consumption and an excessively rapid conversion of windfall savings into real assets. The social inefficiency introduced into private sector responses by foreign exchange controls is in one sense a second-best argument for a custodial role since the government always has the option of removing the underlying cause of the problem. However, foreign exchange controls might themselves be a response to divergences between private and social benefits. For example, fears of political instability might, in the absence of controls, induce capital outflows which increase the risk of the political events which motivate them.

The theoretical arguments on the relative efficacy of public and private portfolio responses to external shocks are thus ambiguous. The issue must therefore be resolved empirically, turning upon two questions. First, are public and private savings rates out of windfalls markedly different? If, for example, private savings rates are much lower than public rates then there is some basis for a public custodial savings role. Second, are public and private rates of return on windfall investment markedly different? The custodial case is at its strongest if the private sector not only has low savings rates, but also low returns on windfall investment as a consequence of being lured into excessive investment in the non-tradable sector. Such a view has underpinned the case for a custodial role. However, in principle either public or private agents could be more adept at handling windfalls. It is therefore an open question whether, if an automatic transfer mechanism is needed for windfalls, it should be designed to convert private windfalls into public, as is the intention of stabilising taxation, or to convert public windfalls into private. While the former has been the subject of much analysis, the latter has not received attention. We return to this in Section 1.7.

1.3. The Case Study Evidence on Savings Responses

We begin with the identification of the shocks: in what sense were there *ex post* episodes and were these identifiable *ex ante*? Generally, the greatest difficulties were with the mineral price shocks. Clearly, for the oil economies there were very large price shocks which *ex post* proved temporary. There was some basis for regarding them at the time as temporary, since the history of cartels suggests that they rarely persist; however, there was no way of knowing how temporary they might be, and in the late 1970s and early 1980s the central forecasts of the oil price had it continuing to rise in real terms. Another example is the copper shocks in Zambia, where World Bank price forecasts turned out to be highly inaccurate. Mineral quantity shocks were also common. Most oil producers had large quantity shocks in the form of discoveries. These ranged from the discovery of (in practical terms) limitless supplies (Venezuela) to supplies that were expected to be exhausted over a period of only ten to fifteen years (Cameroon).

This seems to have been fairly typical of mineral extraction: price shocks which were very hard to interpret, but quantity shocks which were much easier to read. In between were quantity shocks induced by pricing policy. For example, in 1980 the de Beers diamond cartel suspended purchases so as to defend the price and this caused a temporary but substantial negative shock in Botswana. In 1981 Nigeria drastically reduced oil exports in an attempt to defend the premium price of its oil over North Sea crude. In both these cases, while the quantity change could reasonably be seen as temporary, there was uncertainty over whether the strategy would succeed in its objective: in Botswana it did and in Nigeria it did not. The broad picture on mineral shocks is that the price shocks are often long lasting and hard to read, the quantity shocks related to discoveries are long lasting, while the quantity shocks related to cartel behaviour give rise to periods of high uncertainty. By contrast, agricultural price shocks seem rather easier to read. Price shocks such as the beverage booms of the late 1970s are reasonably interpretable as temporary since they can be traced to climatic shocks such as frosts. Not all frosts cause price shocks: for example, the stockholding position might be such that a temporary fall in supply can be fully accommodated by de-stocking. However, if the stockholding position is such that a frost causes a price increase, it is reasonable to expect that as supply recovers the price will tend to revert to its previous level.

1.3.1. The Aggregate Savings Response

It is not a straightforward matter to calculate windfall savings rates because it is necessary to specify counterfactual income. Even *ex post* this is fairly arbitrary, and we have no way of knowing how agents viewed their likely incomes *ex ante*.

Recall that Leon and Soto (1995) find that there is a strong reversionary component in commodity price series, most being trend stationary. Uncertainty is predominantly not about whether prices will revert but about when. Obviously, the longer the expected period of the shock the lower should be the windfall savings rate. If the expectation is that the duration will be very long, then temporariness has little implication for savings rates. However, in our sample of nineteen positive shocks, in two-thirds of the cases the duration is in the range 3–8 years. If agents were to expect that the duration would lie within this range, then even with no further information they would be likely to adopt savings rates out of windfall income considerably higher than those out of permanent income. This is corroborated by the evidence of our sample (see Table 1.2). The beverage booms were potentially recognisable as events which would last only three or four years. In Kenya, where the government explained the cause of the price increase (a Brazilian frost) to farmers through the cooperative movement, the aggregate savings rate out of the windfall was around 60%. In Côte d'Ivoire the rate for the same shock was 44%, in Colombia 48%, in Costa Rica 46% and in Ghana 85%. Other agricultural shocks could sometimes be recognised as temporary. The sugar boom of 1975 was such an event, and in the sugar-dependent economy of Mauritius the savings rate from the windfall was around 50%. In Chapter 5, Harrigan estimates that the windfall savings rate out of the tea and tobacco boom in Malawi was over 90%. The groundnuts boom in Sénégal produced a savings rate of 31%. Hence, in all of the eight positive agricultural shocks the aggregate savings rate was unusually high.

Since the positive mineral shocks were harder to interpret *ex ante* as

Table 1.2. Savings rates in response to shocks (%)

Country	Aggregate	Public		Private	
		Direct	Indirect	Direct	Indirect
Positive agricultural shocks					
Kenya	60	—	around 0	60	—
Côte d'Ivoire	44	44	—	—	33
Colombia	48	—	>100	33	—
Costa Rica	46	neg.	—	around 100	—
Ghana	85	55	—	—	94
Mauritius	50	—	15	over 50	—
Malawi	90	—	24	57	—
Sénégal	31	v. low	—	33	—
Positive mineral shocks					
Niger	73	high	—	high	—
Zambia	67	67	—	—	—
Malaysia	neg.	neg.	—	—	—
Mexico	33	around 0	—	—	around 30
Indonesia	60–74	high	—	high	—
Cameroon	64	70	—	—	neg.
Egypt	74	high	—	n.e.	n.e.
Nigeria	50–90	50–90	—	—	—
Botswana	73	73	—	—	—
Other positive shocks					
Philippines	high	—	neg.	41	—
Bangladesh	neg.	neg.	—	+/−[a]	—
Negative shocks					
Bolivia	57	n.e.	—	—	n.e.
Zambia	high	high	—	n.e.	n.e.
Botswana	73	73	—	—	—
Indonesia	52	neg.	—	—	n.e.
Venezuela	high	high	—	—	—
Sri Lanka	44	n.e.	—	52	—
Thailand	>100	—	—	>100	—

[a] See text
n.e. = not estimated; neg. = negative

temporary, we would expect a lower savings response. In fact, savings rates were usually remarkably high. The seven-year uranium boom in Niger produced a 73% windfall savings rate. The ten-year copper boom produced a 67% windfall savings rate in Zambia. The six oil booms ranged from a heavily negative savings rate in Malaysia, through 33% in Mexico, 60–74% in Indonesia, 64% in Cameroon, 74% in Egypt (1974–81) and estimates for Nigeria of between 50% (Oyejide in Chapter 12) and 90% (Bevan *et al.* 1992). The diamond boom in Botswana was composed of a prolonged series of discoveries. In Chapter 9, Hill and Knight use an econometric approach to estimate the windfall savings rate at 73%. One explanation for these high savings rates is that the windfalls accrued largely to the public sector. Governments may face collective-action problems which reduce their capacity, relative to private agents, to plan and implement savings responses to shocks. While such a collective-action problem might lead to insufficiently high savings rates out of those shocks which might reasonably be seen as temporary, it might also lead to excessive savings out of windfalls reasonably seen as long-lasting. For example, the dramatic nature of large public windfalls may encourage grand strategies which elevate the place of capital formation on public spending agendas. However, while the overall tendency of the mineral windfalls to have savings rates which are too high to be explicable in terms of their likely transience is consistent with such an interpretation, the differences within the case studies are not. In particular, in one of the nine positive mineral shocks, Malaysia, the windfall savings rate was negative. In Chapter 23, Greenaway and Pillay show that the Malaysian government projected massive continuing increases in the real price of oil. The dissaving could therefore be interpreted as a rational response to a shock whose duration was seriously misperceived. Perhaps large public windfalls generally lead to public investment booms. While these give some presumption of increased public savings, this can be offset by sufficiently optimistic expectations about the duration of the windfall, encouraging external borrowing.

The remaining two positive shocks have mixed informational structures. The boom in Bangladesh was generated partly by private remittances from the Middle East, which households might have seen as a long-term improvement in income opportunities, and partly by an aid boom. As a consequence of the high profile given to the catastrophic floods, donors became much more aware of the severe long-term poverty problems faced by the country. The increase in aid could therefore be interpreted either as a temporary response to media attention or as a permanent shift in donor awareness. The combined booms produced an overall negative savings rate. The boom in the Philippines was the result of a fall in import prices. While this may have made the shock difficult to interpret, it does appear to have resulted in a high windfall savings rate. The savings rate is difficult to calculate in this case because of the extreme variability in the savings rate prior to the shock. Because of these difficulties Fabella and Jayasuriya (Chapter 21) also analyse savings behaviour in response to the terms of trade over a forty-year period and show that the savings rate rises significantly in response to positive trade shocks.

Full-blown crashes in commodity prices are less common than booms (Deaton and Laroque 1992) and this was reflected in our sample, with only eight episodes of negative shocks: two in Venezuela and one each in Zambia, Botswana, Bolivia, Thailand, Sri Lanka and Indonesia. There were two cases of negative price shocks in metals, tin in Bolivia and copper in Zambia. The duration of such price shocks is highly uncertain *ex ante*. In Bolivia the dissavings rate from the negative shock was 57%. Although Aron (Chapter 8) does not estimate a rate for Zambia, the economy clearly dissaved very heavily, the investment rate collapsing from above 30% to around 10% and international indebtedness accumulating to reach the highest ratio of debt to GDP in the world. The negative diamond shock in Botswana was not a price shock but rather a quantity shock arising from defensive cartel behaviour. De Beers suspended purchases of diamonds to maintain the price. *Ex ante* it was unclear whether this strategy would succeed, in which case the shock would be brief with permanent income largely unaffected, or whether this was a prelude to the collapse of the cartel, in which case there would be a catastrophic collapse in permanent income. In the event Botswana had a high dissavings rate of 73%.

The study included three negative shocks for oil producers. In Indonesia the dissavings rate in response to the price crash was 52% during 1986–88. In the case of Venezuela, Hausmann (Chapter 17) analyses two negative oil shocks. That of 1982–85 was a quantity shock and that of 1986–88 a price shock. In both cases there was very substantial dissaving, although precise rates are not calculated. The negative shock in Sri Lanka was the result of a rise in import prices. The dissavings rate is estimated at 44%. Finally, Thailand suffered a series of shocks which were in aggregate negative. Simple counterfactuals suggest a dissavings rate in excess of 100%. Hence, in all eight negative shocks there was a high rate of dissaving. This is despite the fact that many of the shocks might reasonably have been regarded as long lasting.

To summarise, in all but one of the twenty-seven shock episodes analysed in the case studies savings or dissavings rates were high. Further, the one exception is explicable: the failure to save out of the Malaysian oil boom was the result of grossly optimistic price forecasts used by the Malaysian government in its budgets.

An implication of these high savings and dissavings rates is that the consumption effects of shocks will be muted whereas the investment effects will be pronounced. Hence, the Dutch Disease framework both exaggerates the importance of consumption changes and misses asset demand effects. Indeed, in the numerous cases of very high windfall savings rates we would expect that the spending effect of Dutch Disease would be virtually absent. There might, nevertheless, be increases in the relative price of non-tradable consumer goods *vis-à-vis* tradables, but this would be the by-product of a construction boom attracting resources from the sector rather than the result of an increase in the demand for its output.

1.3.2. Public Versus Private Responses

We now turn to the evidence on public and private savings rates. First, the agent to whom the windfall accrues need not be the agent who eventually benefits from it. If the oil industry is owned by the government then obviously an oil windfall accrues to the government in the first instance. The government may then choose to spend this income itself. In this case private agents may benefit, but through the gain in utility from increased supply of goods and services. However, private agents may additionally benefit if their income increases as a result of changes in relative prices owing to government expenditure on non-tradables. For example, workers would gain from increased expenditure on public works even if they attached no utility to the output if wages were bid up in the process. In the case studies we ignore such transfers. While in principle they can be quantified using computable general equilibrium modelling, it was not feasible to use this approach given the large number of studies.[4]

Alternatively, the government may choose to transfer purchasing power to private agents by means of tax reductions, subsidies, public sector wage increases or transfer payments.

Similarly, a windfall which initially accrues to private agents might either be retained by them or transferred to the public sector. Such indeed is the intention of stabilising taxation of exports. However, a transfer to the public sector might even occur inadvertently, through the non-neutrality of the tax system with respect to external shocks. Many governments in developing countries rely heavily upon trade taxes. For example, during the coffee boom of 1976–79 the Kenyan government ended up with around half of the windfall even though it had virtually no tax on coffee itself. This was because it taxed imports heavily and imports increased substantially as a result of higher export income. The inadvertent 50% public share of windfall income contrasts with an average share of government revenue in GDP of around 20%.

Finally, there might be transfers in both directions between the public and private sectors, so that a windfall ends up with the agent to which it initially accrued but only after a transfer to and then back from the other agent.

1.3.3. Windfalls Received by the Public Sector

In our sample many of the windfall gains and losses initially accrued to the government; however, some were at least partially transferred to the private sector. In those cases in which the government both received and spent the bulk of the windfall, the aggregate savings rates reported above are largely attributable to government behaviour. This applies to Nigeria, Zambia, Malaysia, Niger, Côte d'Ivoire, Venezuela and Botswana. Recall that, with the exception of Malaysia, these governments all realised high windfall savings and dissavings rates, ranging between 44% and 90%. The Malaysian government heavily dissaved by borrowing abroad. This reflected optimistic assumptions about the price of oil, which was projected to rise by 16% per annum in real terms, and slow responses to the failure of these expectations to be realised. In two further cases the boom had multiple sources and part of the windfall accrued to the public sector, which then retained it. These two public windfalls were the phosphates boom in Sénégal and the aid boom in Bangladesh. In the former the public windfall savings rate was very low. In Bangladesh the government could not borrow abroad commercially and so the aid boom could not be geared up by further borrowing. The government savings response therefore depended upon its choice between investment and consumption. In the event the government switched resources into consumption, halving its savings rate.

There are six cases in which the shock was received by the government but indirectly transferred in part to the private sector, these being Mexico, Ghana, Bolivia, Cameroon, Indonesia and Egypt. In Mexico although the entire windfall was received by the government it used an extensive variety of mechanisms to transfer it to the private sector. These included a domestic energy subsidy and a large food subsidy. In total Gavin (Chapter 18) estimates that these transfers amounted to slightly more than the entire windfall. The oil boom made extravagance temporarily sustainable. President Lopez Portillo declared 'we have freed expenditure from the slavery of revenues'. Despite an intention to save, the government completely failed to do so. Although there was a large public investment programme, it was entirely financed by foreign borrowing. Thus, Mexico is an example of negative stretching.

In Ghana the government transferred about three-quarters of the windfall to enterprises and households, although this was mainly in the form of transfers to publicly owned firms. If these are treated as private agents (which Wetzel does in Chapter 3, owing to data constraints) the government had a 55% savings rate out of its remaining share of the windfall. In Bolivia the government passed on part of the negative windfall to the private sector by means of tax increases and employment reductions, but also borrowed heavily abroad. In Cameroon the government passed on some of the oil windfall to private agents through subsidies and other transfer payments. However, it retained most of the windfall, from which it achieved a savings rate of around 70%. Spending pressures were resisted by keeping funds offshore, by keeping control over the funds with the President's Office rather than with spending ministries, and also by keeping the magnitude of the windfall secret even from the Ministry of Finance. In Indonesia behaviour differed between the positive and negative oil shocks. During the positive shocks there were substantial transfers to the private sector by means of a range of subsidies. However, the public sector accounted for a substantial portion of the high aggregate savings response. During the negative shock the government actually increased its own investment so that the aggregate dissaving during this episode is accounted for by private dissaving. For Egypt it is not possible to disaggregate the savings responses because of the multiple nature of the shocks. However, it appears that the public sector contributed fairly substantially to the aggregate savings response.

Hence, we have fifteen cases in which the initial recipient of the windfall was the government, in seven of which it retained essentially all of revenue, in two of which only part of a multiple windfall accrued to it, and in six of which some, all, or more than all of the windfall was transferred to the private sector. In eleven of the fifteen there was a fairly high savings rate. This should to an extent be qualified. In several of the public windfalls, public expenditure increased only gradually but then proved persistent in the face of a downturn in revenue. When belatedly public expenditure was reduced, it tended to be disproportionately capital expenditure. Hence, were savings rates measured over longer periods they would usually tend to be lower. For example, Deaton (1992) finds for a sample of thirty-five African countries that government expenditure had a much higher degree of persistence than the other components of expenditure. Three years after a single-year rise in export prices government expenditure was the only component of expenditure which was still higher.

Theory suggests that the four countries which did not have high savings rates during booms would differ from the eleven that did in having shocks which were *ex ante* much more likely to be perceived as long lasting. While the oil shocks which generated the Mexican and Malaysian booms were essentially similar to those which generated the booms in Nigeria, Cameroon and Indonesia, the governments of Mexico and Malaysia do appear to have held distinctive expectations as to the duration of the price boom. In Chapter 12, Oyejide shows that the government of Nigeria regarded the oil shocks as temporary, whereas, as noted above, the Malaysian government extrapolated the price increase. Similarly, the aid flow to Bangladesh might reasonably have been perceived as long lasting in view of the acute structural poverty.

Thus, with reference to the custodial capacity of governments, the evidence thus far is that there is a hazard that the government will completely fail to save the windfall, but in our sample this applies to only four countries. The majority achieved high savings rates whether or not such behaviour was *ex ante* appropriate.

1.3.4. Windfalls Received by the Private Sector

We now turn to private savings behaviour. As we have just seen, there were seven cases in which the private sector received through transfers part or all of a windfall initially accruing to the public sector. In Mexico since the government both dissaved and transferred slightly more than the entire windfall to the private sector, the aggregate savings rate of 33% is attributable entirely to the savings behaviour of private agents, whose savings rate was therefore around 30%. In Ghana the private sector had a 94% savings rate from its share of the windfall. In Cameroon the private sector *dissaved* from its share of the oil windfall. Devarajan suggests in Chapter 11 that the reason for this private response was that the government conveyed misleading information. The government both concealed information about the true extent of the windfall and disseminated a false impression as to its scale. Its expansive rhetoric suggested that the boom was larger than it actually was. In Côte d'Ivoire the private sector received the windfall in part through a reduction in taxation, the coffee price increase itself being largely taxed away by the government. The private savings rate was approximately 33%. For Indonesia, Egypt and Bolivia country authors were unable to construct estimates of private savings rates. However, in both Indonesia and Egypt there is sufficient information to infer that windfall savings rates were significantly positive.

There are fourteen cases in which private agents directly received at least part of the shock. In six of these the recipients were predominantly farmers: coffee farmers in Kenya, Costa Rica, and Colombia, groundnut farmers in Sénégal, sugar farmers in Mauritius, and tea and tobacco farmers in Malawi. The Kenyan private sector had a windfall savings rate of around 60%. Kenyan coffee farmers, whose savings behaviour could be observed through survey evidence, saved around 70% of their windfall. The Kenyan government made special efforts through the coffee marketing cooperatives to explain to farmers that the price increase was caused by a frost in Brazil and was therefore unlikely to persist. In Costa Rica, where as in Kenya there was no coffee tax, the private sector received 90% of the windfall and did not raise its consumption in response. Hence, as in Kenya, the private windfall was very largely saved.

In Colombia the private sector had a lower savings rate, 33%. One reason why the private savings rate might have been lower in Colombia than in Kenya is that information differed. Colombian coffee farmers might have been confused as to the nature of the price increase. During 1977 not only was the world coffee price high, but within Colombia the price to farmers rose because the former government marketing monopoly was liberalised, allowing private coffee marketing firms to buy at close to world prices. This was probably a response to the fact that the 1978 elections were to be the first genuinely contested elections for many years, so that rural votes now mattered.[5] It is thus possible that coffee farmers attributed much of the price increase to a change in market structure driven by the switch to contested elections. In this case they would have interpreted much of the increase in income as permanent rather than transient and so rationally have chosen a lower savings rate.

In Sénégal the private savings rate was again only 33%. As in Colombia, the increase in world prices coincided with a reform of the domestic market, the 'True Prices Operation', which raised local prices. This was introduced after a long period of confrontation with the government, and farmers may well have interpreted the passing on of world price increases as a political victory, generating a structural and therefore long-lasting improvement in their position quite unrelated to the boom. In Mauritius, where the case for high savings was evident because of the obviously temporary nature of the sugar price increase, the private savings rate was between 50% and 80% depending upon the period over which behaviour is measured. Finally, in Malawi the tea and tobacco boom produced a private savings rate of 57%.

Hence in the six agricultural windfalls there is a clear pattern. In the four cases where the government did not make structural changes to pricing policy during the windfall the private sector had a very high savings rate in the range 50–100%. In the two cases in which the windfall coincided with price increases attributable to structural marketing changes the savings rate, though still well above normal levels, was substantially lower, namely 33%. This is consistent with an interpretation based on private information about the duration of the shock.

The remaining eight cases in which windfalls directly accrued in part to the private sector are the remittance booms in Bangladesh and Egypt, the fall in import prices in the Philippines, the uranium boom in Niger, the mining shock in Bolivia, the Zambian copper boom, and the negative terms of trade shocks in Sri Lanka and Thailand. In Bangladesh, those households in receipt of remittances saved, whereas those not in receipt of them actually dissaved. In Chapter 22 Azam and Shahabuddin interpret this as showing that the former group recognised that they were benefiting from a temporary windfall, while the latter were borrowing or depleting assets on the anticipation of remittances, both of these responses being appropriate. For Egypt no satisfactory partitioning of the private and public shocks could be undertaken, although the private sector savings rate appears to have been positive. In the Philippines the oil windfall produced an increase in the savings rate but the difficulty in specifying counterfactual savings rates precludes quantification, simple procedures producing rates too high to be credible. In Niger the private uranium mining companies responded to the price increase by postponing extraction, so that saving took the form of uranium being stored in the ground. It was in the interest of the mining companies to postpone extraction until prices were expected to peak. Hence, a large increase in output occurred at the very end of the boom. This strategy resulted in a high private savings rate. In Sri Lanka, in response to the increase in import prices, the private sector dissaved substantially. For both the Philippines and Sri Lanka the country authors supplemented the simple counterfactual approach with long-run time-series-econometrics estimates of the private savings response. The private savings rate in response to terms of trade income shocks was 52% in Sri Lanka and 41% in the Philippines. In Thailand the private sector dissaved heavily in response to the negative terms of trade shocks, simple counterfactuals suggesting dissavings in excess of 100%.

We now summarise the nineteen shocks which accrued to private agents, in fourteen directly and in five indirectly through government transfers. In eight of the fourteen cases of direct accrual in which shocks could reasonably be perceived as temporary, private savings rates could be measured. In all these eight cases windfall savings or dissavings rates were very high. In three of the four cases of measured indirect private windfalls, savings rates were markedly lower than in any of these eight. Indeed, in Cameroon private saving was negative during a substantial boom which should have been regarded as temporary due to resource exhaustion. Two possible explanations for the lower savings rates in the case of transfers are either that private agents believe that the government is saving on their behalf, or that transfers destroy information. In the first case, because the government is intermediating the windfall, private agents may not raise their own savings rate because they expect that the government will build up assets with the part of the windfall which it retains. At least in Mexico such a belief would have been inaccurate. Further, even in those cases in which the government did have a high savings rate, this could be a poor substitute for private saving, either because the return on public assets is low or because the output which they generate is not a close substitute for private consumption. In the second case the transfer would make it more difficult for private agents to recognise the temporariness of the shock because they lose sight of its origin.

Loss of information might also occur for another reason, namely when there are other changes affecting the income of private agents unrelated to the trade shock. In these circumstances they might find it difficult to attribute the changes in their income to permanent and temporary sources. The structural pricing changes which occurred in Sénégal and Colombia may thus have accounted for the substantially lower savings rates found in these two cases than in any of the other eight directly received private windfalls.

Thus, as far as the evidence permits, it suggests that private agents respond in a cautious and far-sighted way to shocks as long as they have uncontaminated information. This cuts away the main rationale for domestic stabilising taxation policies. The government does not need to play a custodial role, but it does need to take care not to interfere with the crucial information on which private agents can base their interpretation of the shock.

Although the private sector often directly received the windfall, part of it frequently accrued to the government, either because of direct taxation of the windfall or because of the effect of other taxes. These cases are Kenya, Malawi, Mauritius, Colombia, Niger and the Philippines. In Kenya the public sector acquired around half of the windfall through import and sales taxes. Despite policy statements that the resources were to be used for capital expenditure, in the outturn the public savings rate was low. During the boom itself the government had a windfall savings rate of 20%. However, this masks an initially high rate which decreased as recurrent expenditure increased. By the end of the boom recurrent expenditure was high and persisted, while capital expenditure was reduced in order to pay for it. If allowance is made for this during the three post-boom years before the budget was restored to its pre-boom configuration, then the overall public windfall savings rate is slightly negative: the boom rephased public investment but did not overall increase it.

In Malawi the government achieved a 24% savings rate out of its share of the windfall. In Mauritius the public sector savings rate out of its share of the sugar boom windfall was around 15%. In Colombia the initial reaction of the government to the coffee boom windfall, which it shared with private agents, was to reduce its own expenditure in order to dampen what it expected would be the inflationary pressure of increased private expenditure, thereby initially producing a public savings rate in excess of 100%. Public savings responses were highly formalised through the coffee fund, which had a long history of complex procedures for dealing with windfalls (since, unlike most of the other coffee growing countries in our sample, Colombia was not a new entrant). There are two disappointing features of the Colombian windfall management during this period. First, although the coffee fund chose to accumulate assets, a major asset which it chose to acquire was coffee. By holding on to coffee stocks well beyond the price peak, the policy dissipated rather than deferred the boom. Second, after the 1978 election, the new president, an enthusiastic spender, was able to spend the accumulated savings on public consumption. That is, the institutionalised savings rules proved impotent against a determined president.

We have noted that in Niger the mining companies retained the entire uranium windfall until near the end of the boom by deferring extraction. Hence, the government received its part of the windfall only once the mining companies had realised this accumulation. Possibly this concentration of the public windfall in a brief period made it more readily recognisable as temporary. The government achieved a high savings rate out of this windfall. In the Philippines the government acquired part of the windfall from the fall in the price of imported oil and used this to reduce its external debt. However, such were the demands of its creditors that it had little option but to use its share of the windfall in this way.

Recall that in the fourteen cases where the public sector received the windfall directly, the government responded with high savings rates in all but four cases. By contrast, in the six indirect public windfalls the savings response is more varied. In Kenya, Mauritius and Malawi public savings rates were low. In the Philippines the rate was high, but this was not a choice of the government but rather of its creditors, who insisted upon debt repayment. In Colombia, although the savings rate was initially very high, it rapidly turned negative as in Kenya. In view of the limited number of cases we can only speculate on possible reasons for this difference. When the government receives a direct windfall it is an easy matter for the government to calculate the windfall. For example, a world price increase would immediately be translated into a rise in revenue from an export tax. When there are no reasons to expect a change in supply the government then knows with complete accuracy the transient part of its revenue. In practice there will be some degree of uncertainty owing to the unknown extent of induced supply increases, but this is likely to be a small proportion of the windfall. By contrast, it is much more difficult when government revenue is raised indirectly by a trade shock for the extent of the revenue windfall to be calculated. For example, during a commodity boom revenue from import duties will rise, but this is commonly not attributed by governments to the price shock. The lack of transparency of estimates of indirect revenue windfalls may make it more difficult for technocrats to convince spending ministries that extra revenue should not be spent.

1.3.5. *Savings Responses to Positive* versus *Negative Shocks*

Having considered the disaggregation of behaviour between public and private agents we now compare behaviour during positive and negative shocks.

Potentially, dissavings rates out of negative shocks might be lower than savings rates out of positive shocks of the same duration because of the asymmetry created by borrowing constraints. However, this does not appear to be the case: in our sample savings and dissavings rates appear similar.

Of the seven negative shocks, in six cases governments attempted to defer and smooth the shock. The exception was Sri Lanka, where the government actually amplified the private shock by increasing its own savings. There is a good case for government smoothing of negative shocks, where it is feasible, since private agents are less able to smooth negative shocks than positive shocks because they will encounter credit constraints. However, a policy of government dissaving can only succeed if it is credible. If private agents see it as a loss of control they will speculate against it in the anticipation that the crisis will eventually be resolved through devaluation or trade restrictions. Indeed, in three cases government dissaving provoked speculation and crisis. In the first of the Venezuelan negative shocks, in 1982, private agents reacted to the government's failure to adjust through capital flight (switching US$6.5bn of financial assets into foreign currency) and by stockpiling imports. (In Chapter 4, Ghanem finds similar behaviour in Côte d'Ivoire during the downturn in the early 1980s.) During the second negative Venezuelan shock, 1986, a new multiple exchange rate regime curtailed capital flight. Instead, there was hoarding of domestic production and a move into non-traded capital goods. In Zambia the government was able first to run down its assets and then to become the most indebted country in the world relative to GDP by borrowing from public agencies. This unsustainable strategy eventually led to private speculation and crisis in the mid-1980s.

There were four cases of sustainable government dissaving during negative shocks, Botswana, Bolivia, Indonesia and Thailand. In each case public dissaving was quite substantial (Botswana had a dissaving rate of 73%) yet it did not produce speculation of policy reversal. Why were these stabilisations credible? First, in all four cases governments either had good fiscal reputations built up over the long run or they signalled fiscally prudent behaviour during the shock. The Thai and Indonesian governments had a long history of fiscal prudence, the former having expenditure elasticities less than unity. They were therefore well placed to borrow without undermining confidence in macroeconomic management. In both Botswana and Bolivia the governments cut public expenditure substantially and swiftly. This made it less likely that the dissaving policy could be construed as a loss of control over public spending, or simply as policy inertia. Second, dissaving was clearly sustainable for a long time: Botswana had enormous reserves, while Bolivia and Thailand had access to external capital, the former through having just agreed sweeping policy reforms with donors and Thailand through its strong reputation.

1.3.6. Savings Behaviour: A Summary

The savings behaviour, aggregated and disaggregated by sign, agent and source was summarised in Table 1.2. Three broad conclusions have emerged from our discussion. First, aggregate savings rates out of shocks are almost invariably high. Agents behave as though they saw shocks as having a substantial temporary component. A corollary is that Dutch Disease effects should be weak, whereas we would expect powerful investment effects. Second, the key disaggregation of savings behaviour appears to be neither public versus private, nor positive versus negative, but rather direct versus indirect. Where shocks are received directly, both public and private agents have almost uniformly high savings rates. Where shocks are received indirectly, both public and private agents have lower and more varied savings rates. We have suggested above that this reflects the information loss which occurs when windfalls are transferred. Indeed, the only exceptions to the high private savings rates out of directly received windfalls reinforce the importance of clear information. In Sénégal and Colombia private agents faced the task of disentangling a price increase caused partly by a temporary change in world prices and partly by a structural change in domestic marketing policy. Third, this suggests that the important role for the government is not to impose stabilising taxation on intrinsically private windfalls but rather to ensure that private agents receive clear information.

1.4. Evidence from the Case Studies on What Assets are Acquired

If windfalls are largely saved, then the next question concerns the composition of the assets which are acquired. As discussed above, agents can either invest domestically, which in aggregate can only be in real assets, or acquire foreign assets. The acquisition of foreign assets enables the domestic investment boom to be stretched if these assets are subsequently repatriated.

Consider first the acquisition of foreign assets. The country evidence is summarised in Table 1.3. In the case of positive shocks the vast majority of countries accumulated foreign assets. In the table we distinguish between those countries which repatriated assets before the end of the boom and those which succeeded in stretching the boom, returning foreign assets after the end of the boom. In some cases the assets were never repatriated, so that the foreign asset acquisition was permanent. There were also a few cases in which there was no change in foreign assets, or where countries actually borrowed rather than accumulated during the boom. In the latter case the boom was thereby amplified. For negative shocks in principle a similar classification can be used, with foreign assets being decumulated and repaid during the shock, after it, or never. Also, as before, a country could leave its foreign assets unchanged or amplify the shock by accumulating foreign assets. However, it can be seen from the table that in our sample there are no cases of shock amplification or of debt being repaid before the end of the shock.

The extent to which foreign assets were acquired as part of an investment-stretching strategy usually depended upon the government

Table 1.3. Changes in foreign assets

During boom	After	Never	Boom amplified	No change
(a) Positive shocks: assets accumulated and returned				
Kenya	Ghana	Sénégal	Malaysia	
Costa Rica	Egypt	Philippines	Mexico	
Mauritius	Indonesia	Botswana	Malawi	
Niger	Zambia		Côte d'Ivoire	
Nigeria			Bangladesh	
Colombia				
Cameroon				
(b) Negative shocks: assets decumulated and repaid				
	Botswana	Zambia		Venezuela
	Thailand	Bolivia		
	Sri Lanka	Indonesia		

because either it was the only recipient of the windfall or it was the only agent allowed to hold foreign assets. Public windfalls were temporarily placed abroad and repatriated after the windfall by four governments: Zambia, Indonesia, Ghana and Egypt. In Zambia foreign assets were built up during the period 1965–70 and used subsequently to finance a sustained high rate of domestic investment in the period 1971–74. In Indonesia the operation was made politically feasible by being shrouded in obscurity, foreign assets not being reported in published figures. During the post-1981 downturn in oil income public investment was sustained by repatriation and external borrowing. Private investment declined, but less rapidly than savings, so that to a lesser extent private investment was also stretched beyond the windfall. In Ghana the windfall was predominantly private and restrictions on consumer imports forced an exceptionally high savings rate. However, asset choices were also limited: private agents were not allowed to acquire foreign exchange directly and the policy environment was hostile to domestic investment. Private agents therefore chose to acquire claims on the banking system, which became much more liquid during the boom, and the government built up foreign exchange reserves as a counterpart to this liability.

However, in the case of Ghana, when the assets were repatriated they were used for consumption rather than for investment. The stretching of the boom therefore did not raise post-boom consumption permanently. This provides an important counter-argument to the investment-stretching benefits of foreign asset accumulation. The two desirable responses to a brief windfall are that the windfall is committed to asset accumulation and that investment should not be crowded into the boom period. Unfortunately, these two desiderata conflict. Domestic assets, being in aggregate real investment, cannot rapidly be liquidated: depreciation is gradual and sale to foreigners is usually infeasible. Hence, the decision to invest the windfall domestically is irreversible. By contrast, foreign assets can be sold: indeed, this is a necessary feature of their use as an investment-stretching device. An implication is that when savings are in the form of foreign assets the economy is not locked into the savings decision since the liquidated foreign assets can be used to finance consumption instead of investment, as in Ghana.

The need to lock in the savings decision may differ between public and private agents. Whereas the time-horizon of a multi-generation household is intrinsically long, that of governments is not so much short as variable. As revealed by the very high savings rates out of most of the public windfalls, governments are fully capable of taking the long view. However, there are also occasions when political pressures drastically shorten the horizon. For example, Schuknecht (1994) shows that there is a pronounced increase in deficit financing in developing countries prior to elections. In the absence of lock-in a government which prudently saves a windfall risks transferring it to its imprudent successor.

Seven governments, those of Kenya, Colombia, Nigeria, Cameroon, Costa Rica, Mauritius and Niger, failed to stretch the investment boom because they repatriated foreign assets while the boom was still in progress. In three cases, Kenya, Colombia and Nigeria, early repatriation of foreign assets reflected political change. In Kenya, as in Ghana, the private sector initially acquired claims against the government. However, unlike in Ghana, the environment was not hostile to domestic investment. Since the claims against the government bore negative real interest rates, private agents had an incentive to repatriate foreign assets rapidly to convert them into domestic investment. Additionally, the government lost control of its own recurrent expenditure during the boom and this also contributed to a rapid switch from current account surplus to deficit. Thus, there were two reasons for the early repatriation of foreign assets. Private agents were repatriating into investment and the government was repatriating into consumption. The death of President Kenyatta during the middle of the boom and the need for his interim successor to establish himself on a more permanent basis may constitute an example of a temporary drastic shortening of the public time-horizon.

A similar political change occurred in Colombia at the same stage in the coffee boom. The new president switched public policy from accumulation to public consumption despite the elaborate rules ostensibly governing the coffee stabilisation fund. In Nigeria the switch from a military to a civilian government during the oil boom coincided with a radical switch from foreign asset accumulation to decumulation. Although the civilian government ostensibly used some of these repatriated funds for public investment, as discussed below it might be more accurate to regard much of this expenditure as consumption. Hence, in these three cases of early repatriation, the use of foreign assets by a prudent government enabled its imprudent successor to reverse the original savings decision.

In Cameroon foreign assets were initially accumulated. As in Indonesia this process was shrouded in secrecy. The decision was taken and implemented entirely in the Office of the President, so that not even the Ministry of Finance knew the scale of the accumulation. However, the asset accumulation policy was reversed in the last three years of the boom, the entire amount being repatriated and used to finance domestic investment. As a result, although domestic investment was sustained at a high level during the boom, it fell abruptly as the windfall ended. In Costa Rica foreign assets were accumulated during the first three years of the boom but entirely repatriated in the remaining two years. Repatriated assets were used for domestic investment. In Mauritius the boom only lasted two years. In the first the government accumulated some foreign assets but these were repatriated the next year to finance investment.

In Niger foreign assets were accumulated in a way completely different from the other six cases. Recall that the mining companies decided to postpone extraction until the price of uranium peaked. As a result, their storage of a tradable good, uranium, was a foreign asset acquisition strategy. However, intrinsic to this strategy was that this foreign asset had to be liquidated during the boom. At the time of this liquidation the windfall was to a large extent transferred to the public sector through taxation. Hence, the government had the decision between foreign and domestic assets. It chose domestic investment. Hence, in combination the private and public choices were equivalent to a repatriation of foreign assets for domestic investment during the boom.

Three governments accumulated foreign assets which were never repatriated: Sénégal, the Philippines and Botswana. The government of Sénégal implemented a policy which in effect constituted an irreversible acquisition of foreign assets. It used the windfall to nationalise foreign-owned firms with compensation. In addition to its direct effects, this policy presumably also discouraged new foreign investment. The policy thus not only precluded the stretching of investment beyond the income boom, but actually reduced it post-boom. The asset behaviour of the government of the Philippines was involuntary: heavily indebted, it had no choice but to use the boom to repay part of its debt. In Botswana the policy of foreign asset acquisition was at first highly obscure as in Indonesia and Cameroon. A vast amount of government revenue appeared in the budget only as a single line item euphemistically entitled. However, thereafter the Botswanan government became more open about its policy and conducted a campaign of education and persuasion. The salutary example of the misuse of a temporary windfall in neighbouring Zambia was put to good use. It may also have helped that since the population are historically pastoralists in near-desert conditions, they are well-used to the notion that the accumulation of assets during favourable conditions is appropriate. Over several years the Botswanan government was able to accumulate one of the highest ratios of reserves to GDP in the world. The decision not to repatriate foreign assets was a consequence of the requirement that domestic investments should meet rate-of-return criteria and the limited absorptive capacity of the economy. Although this policy rule maximised the return on windfall savings, a corollary was that the government was never able to lock in the asset accumulation. Therefore, the conversion of the windfall into permanent income depended upon continuous far-sighted behaviour on the part of the Botswanan government.

Five governments chose to amplify the boom by borrowing abroad rather than accumulating assets: Malaysia, Mexico, Côte d'Ivoire, Malawi and Bangladesh. As discussed above, the Malaysian government expected the oil price to continue to rise rapidly and therefore saw its current income during the boom as being substantially below its permanent income. Government expenditures were raised accordingly and maintained when oil prices declined. The borrowing was largely used to finance domestic public investment. In Mexico, while the government passed on more than the entire windfall to the private sector, it increased public investment substantially, this being financed entirely through foreign borrowing. Overall 63% of Mexican windfall investment was financed by foreign borrowing. In Chapter 18, Gavin explains borrowing during the boom in terms of the increased incentives for investment generated by the way in which the government passed on the windfall to private agents: the overvalued exchange rate cheapened imported capital, and the conjunction of input subsidies and the protection of firms in the domestic market made domestic investment artificially profitable. Thus, the deployment of the windfall created incentives to borrow to finance investment. In Côte d'Ivoire there was a massive increase in public investment, rising from 8% to 23% of GDP in three years, and this was in part financed by foreign borrowing. For Malawi it is difficult to estimate windfall foreign borrowing because of the erratic path of foreign assets in the decade prior to the boom. However, a range of counterfactuals all imply increased foreign borrowing during the boom. This was used almost exclusively to finance public investment. Hence, the Malawian case is similar to that of Côte d'Ivoire. In Bangladesh the government borrowed more as the boom improved its creditworthiness. This was used to finance increased government consumption.

In two countries, Egypt and Bangladesh, the public windfalls discussed above coincided with private remittance booms. Remittance booms are distinctive in two respects. First, even when governments impose foreign exchange controls, since the windfalls accrue abroad migrants can evade them should they choose to do so: the government has no means of preventing savings being held in the form of foreign assets. Indeed, because this was so apparent, and the sums involved were so large, both governments modified their control regimes in response. Foreign-currency-denominated assets were introduced which could be purchased with remitted money. In both cases there was a high rate of acquisition of foreign financial assets on the part of remitting households. However, the second respect in which remittance booms are distinctive is that because migration is usually seen as temporary, the income windfall is manifestly temporary for the household, whereas for the economy as a whole it may not be. In retrospect, even in aggregate these two remittance booms had a substantial temporary element because of the collapse of Middle East oil receipts from the mid-1980s. Hence, even at the aggregate level there was some reason for high savings. However, the case at the aggregate level was much less strong than that at the level of the individual households involved. Correspondingly, the case for stretching the investment windfall by means of the temporary acquisition of foreign assets was far weaker at the aggregate level than at the level of the individual households. The latter clearly wished to delay investment, not owing to temporary macroeconomic circumstances, but because it was sensible to delay until migration was completed, enabling an investment in housing or business which could be used by the agent.

Hence, in these peculiar circumstances the role of foreign financial assets is somewhat perverse. Whereas when the shock is temporary at the aggregate level there is a good case for deferring some investment by means of such assets, when it is temporary only at the level of each currently migrant household, the ideal would be for the resulting savings to be invested within the economy immediately. When this is not done, it may reflect the lack of confidence in, or absence of, domestic financial markets which could intermediate these private savings. If the government is sufficiently credible it is therefore indeed sensible for it to sell foreign currency liabilities to migrants, as in Bangladesh and Egypt: public action is needed both to bring forward what would otherwise be an unwarranted deferral of windfall investment and even to transform some of these (private) savings into (public) consumption. In effect, the government by borrowing the remittances is able to consume on behalf of those households which have higher permanent incomes than current incomes because they will at some future date send a migrant to the Middle East, but are unable to dissave since the prospect is not creditworthy at the household level. If the remittance boom were secure, then public action to switch the income from savings to consumption would be appropriate for the entire amount. However, the two remittance booms in our sample were essentially indirect oil booms and so savings behaviour somewhat similar to that in the direct oil booms was appropriate.

We have already discussed dissaving during negative shocks. Because domestic investment is irreversible in the short run, dissaving will be closely linked with foreign borrowing. This is a potential asymmetry between positive and negative shocks. Venezuela is the only case in which there was substantial dissavings without foreign borrowing, the dissaving being achieved by a collapse in previously high investment rates. However, even here there was heavy public foreign borrowing. In Chapter 17, Hausmann argues that private agents regarded the public response as incredible and responded by accumulating the foreign assets in the anticipation of devaluation. This represented substitution between domestic and foreign private assets.

Overall, although foreign assets were utilised during booms, this was seldom sufficiently pronounced to prevent the substantial windfall savings effects found in the previous section from translating into substantial investment effects: windfalls usually gave rise to investment booms. This is consistent with Deaton's (1992) study of the consequences of shocks in thirty-five African export price series. He finds that by far the most powerful impact of an export price shock is on investment and that nearly all of this effect is exhausted in the year following the shock.

In summary, there are only a few countries which succeeded in stretching the investment boom (Egypt, Indonesia and Zambia) or which kept windfall savings permanently as foreign assets (Sénégal, the Philippines and Botswana). By far the most common response is to repatriate foreign assets before the end of the boom.

The evidence on the composition of these investment booms is summarised in Table 1.4. The table shows four aspects of the composition of investment. Investment booms are predominantly public: of the seventeen booms that can be classified, in twelve the public sector was the major or even the only investing agent. This is more pronounced than differences in savings behaviour. In Egypt, Côte d'Ivoire and Cameroon, although the private sector received and saved part of the windfall, it acquired foreign assets at the same time as the public sector was making an opposite portfolio choice: investing more than it was saving by acquiring foreign debts.

Devarajan *et al.* (1994) compare the productivity of public investment in developing and developed countries. They find that, whereas in developed countries public investment significantly raises growth rates, in developing countries there is no such effect. This does not necessarily imply that the return on public investment is zero, but that it is no higher than the growth generated by the private expenditures which it displaces. Since most of these displaced expenditures will normally be consumption, an implication is that the return on public investment is much lower than that on private investment. As we have already discussed, since during windfalls private savings rates are atypically high, this would suggest that

Table 1.4. Investment booms

Country	Source	Destination	Agent	Relative price effect?
Positive agricultural shocks				
Kenya	mostly K_t	various	75% private	yes
Côte d'Ivoire	mostly K_t	n.a.	public	yes
Costa Rica	K_n	manufacturing	public	yes
Mauritius	mostly K_n	housing and export processing zone	private	yes
Malawi	K_n	agriculture and infrastructure	91% private	yes
Sénégal	K_t	manufacturing	public	no
Positive mineral shocks				
Niger	mostly K_n	non-tradable capital and cattle	mostly public	n.a.
Zambia	mostly K_t	manufacturing and construction	67% public	yes
Malaysia	both	infrastructure	public	n.a.
Mexico	both	n.a.	public	yes
Indonesia	both	infrastructure and agriculture	public	yes
Cameroon	mostly K_n	no change	public	yes
Egypt	mostly K_t	infrastructure and manufacturing	public	yes
Nigeria	mostly K_t	manufacturing and services	public	yes
Botswana	mostly K_t	n.a.	mostly public	no
Other positive shocks				
Philippines	mostly K_t	housing	private	yes
Bangladesh	n.a.	manufacturing	private	n.a.

Notes: K_n, K_t = non-tradable, tradable capital; n.a. = not available

the opportunity cost of public investment in terms of growth is higher than normal during booms. In addition, the return to public investment might fall absolutely rather than only relative to opportunity cost during booms. For example, in Malawi the government used the opportunity of its windfall to implement projects which had previously been turned down by donors because estimated rates of return were too low. Hence, while the country case studies do not usually estimate rates of return on windfall investment, there is some presumption that boom-induced investment would be less productive than normal arising from the differentially public sector nature of windfall investment.

This may be offset by a change in the composition of investment between equipment (tradable capital) and structures (non-tradable capital).

There is a presumption that during investment booms there will be a bias towards equipment: structures require time to plan and construct and in aggregate must compete for limited non-tradable supply, whereas equipment can be imported. This compositional change is potentially important since de Long and Summers (1991) find that equipment investment is more effective in generating growth than structures investment. They explain this in terms of the learning effects embodied in equipment. Table 1.4 disaggregates windfall investment between equipment and structures. Although there is indeed a preponderance of equipment investment this is less than might have been expected: in five cases investment was disproportionately in structures. This unexpectedly high share of structures during investment booms may be accounted for by the disproportionate involvement of the public sector as noted above, since public investment is frequently in infrastructure. In four of the five cases the investment boom is public. The remaining case, Mauritius, is one where private investment was largely in housing. Residential construction booms indeed occurred in three of four private investment booms, the others being Kenya and Philippines. This may reflect the limited extent of financial intermediation when the windfall is received by households.

1.4.1. Construction Booms

In reviewing the theory of responses to windfalls we discussed the phenomenon of construction booms, whereby expenditures on non-tradable capital goods raise their relative price. Two features of the actual responses to windfalls identified above imply that constructions booms would be pronounced. First, whereas theory stressed the desirability of stretching investment booms beyond the period of the income boom, in practice windfalls reveal little stretching. Second, whereas *a priori* one would expect windfall investment to go disproportionately into imported equipment, the combination of the predominance of public infrastructure and private residential property induces investment in structures. This should reinforce the tendency for windfalls to raise the price of non-tradable capital goods relative to that of non-tradable consumer goods: construction booms should be more powerful than Dutch Disease.

The final column of Table 1.4 reports on this relative price change. Generally, data are weaker on changes in relative prices than on quantities; however, for fourteen of the case studies it was possible to measure changes in the relative price of non-tradable capital goods. Usually this was relative to non-tradable consumer goods, which is the measure implied by the previous theory. Sometimes authors measured the price of non-tradable capital goods relative to GDP or tradable capital goods, and although less than ideal these measures were still treated as usable.

In twelve of the fourteen cases the relative price of non-tradable capital goods rose during the investment boom and fell thereafter. The two exceptions were Sénégal and Botswana. In Sénégal no relative price effect would be expected because the investment boom was entirely on tradable capital. In Botswana there was considerable expenditure upon construction but no change in its relative price. This reflected the peculiar circumstance that construction activity in Botswana is very largely imported from major South African construction companies and so is virtually indistinguishable from equipment in terms of its tradability. In the remaining twelve cases the boom caused the price on non-tradable capital goods to be bid up, thereby dissipating part of the windfall investment expenditure in the higher unit costs of capital rather than an increased quantity of investment. This provides a further mechanism whereby the returns to investment would be atypically low during investment booms.

1.4.2. Destination of Domestic Investment

The final disaggregation which we consider is investment by sector of destination. There is no clear pattern, although manufacturing, infrastructure and housing are between them the main destinations. However, a notable omission is export sectors, whether the boom sector itself or export diversification. Sometimes there was investment in the boom sector, such as coffee in Kenya, but only in Bangladesh and Mauritius were the booms used to diversify exports. Partly, this choice of sector was determined by the government since it dominated windfall investment. Infrastructure is a natural domain of government and the choice of manufacturing probably reflected the import-substituting industrialisation strategies common at the time. The combination of subsidies and protection afforded to the manufacturing sector created a divergence between private and social rates of return. An extreme instance of this, discussed by Gavin in Chapter 18, is the use of the Mexican windfall for manufacturing investment with low social returns.

1.5. Evidence on the Effects of Booms on Output and the Return on Investment

So far we have identified four mechanisms by which a windfall which induces a high savings response might yet fail to translate into a sustained increase in income. First, agents might fail to lock into the savings decision, acquiring liquid foreign assets which are then converted into consumption after the boom, an example being Ghana. Second, the windfall investment might be undertaken only by the government, choosing low-return prestige infrastructure projects, an example being Malawi. Third, the investment windfall might be skewed heavily towards structures, thereby reducing the return on investment both because structures lack the growth externalities of equipment and because the unit cost of structures rises. An example of this effect would be Cameroon. Finally, the investment windfall might be biased away from export diversification into protected import substitution, yielding social returns below their private returns, an example being Mexico. Additionally, as we have seen, most countries failed to acquire foreign assets for other than a very brief period. This is detrimental even if all capital is importable for two reasons. If windfall savings are sufficiently large then if these are all invested domestically the return on capital will decrease simply through diminishing returns to capital. Further, even if the increase in capital is not so large as to cause substantial diminishing returns *per se*, if it is installed over the brief period of the boom the efficiency of investment may fall due to congestion. Whereas all the above effects would imply that the social return to investment is atypically low during investment windfalls, the de Long and Summers effect suggests the opposite: the rate of return would be higher to the extent that investment favours tradable capital.

We now test the relationship between investment and growth on the nineteen positive shocks in our sample. We use annual data for the period 1964–91, these being the limits of International Financial Statistics data on the complete set of countries. The dependent variable is the annual growth rate in per capita GDP at constant prices. The first independent variable is the ratio of investment to GDP at constant prices, lagged one year (IR). The shock is introduced with a series of dummy variables: the variable $SHOCK$ taking the value of unity for each of the shock years; and the variables $POST_1$, $POST_2$ and $POST_3$ taking the value of unity in the first, second and third year, respectively, after the shock. Finally, we account for a lagged effect of investment in the boom period with the variables IP_1, IP_2 and IP_3, which take the value of the average investment ratio in the boom period (again calculated as the ratio of investment to GDP, both in constant prices) in the first, second and third years of the boom. The results of this regression are shown in Table 1.5.

The regression implies that the impact of a shock upon growth works through four different channels. First, to the extent that the investment ratio rises during the boom, if the rate of return on investment is maintained, then the effect of this is measured by the coefficient upon IR for each year of the boom. In our sample the mean duration of a boom is 5.5 years and the investment rate increases by 3.1% of GDP. Hence, the effect of this is cumulatively to raise the level of output by 2.0%. This estimate is evidently biased downwards, since a more reasonable ICOR of 3 would imply an increase of around 6%. Second, the shock has a direct effect on output independent of a change in the rate of investment. This is

Table 1.5. Investment and growth: regression results

Variable	Coefficient	t-statistic
Constant	−0.006601	0.924
IR	0.111993	3.057
SHOCK	0.017892	3.065
$POST_1$	−0.026769	2.074
$POST_2$	−0.036636	2.833
$POST_3$	−0.039756	3.010
IP_1	0.155544	0.589
IP_2	−0.403705	1.525
IP_3	−0.574617	2.163
adjusted R^2	0.1038	
F	7.266	

measured by the variable *SHOCK*, which is positive and significant. Taking into account the mean duration of a boom the cumulative effect on the level of output is an increase of 10.3%. This is consistent with Deaton and Miller (1996), who study the effect of export price shocks on output for a sample of thirty-five African countries. They find that an export price increase significantly raises output in the year of the shock. However, the coefficients on the three post-shock years, all of which are significant, cumulatively imply that this gain in output does not persist: the output loss in these three years is 9.9%. This is not a surprising result since output gains which do not reflect increases in the capital stock—for example those resulting from an increase in labour supply owing to temporarily higher real wages—are liable to be reversed. The final effect is the lagged effect of investment during the boom, measured by the variables IP_1, IP_2 and IP_3. Two of these are significant, both being negative. Cumulatively, the three imply a loss in output of 18%. Note that we already control for changes in the rate of investment, so what this effect measures is a reduction in the return on investment during boom periods. Were the non-boom ICOR 3, this would imply that during booms the return on investment was approximately halved.

The overall effect of the typical positive shock in this sample is eventually substantially to reduce output, despite the effect being strongly positive at the time of the shock.[6] This suggests that the de Long and Summers effect is swamped by the various other negative effects discussed above. Clearly, a positive shock to which the response is a high savings rate should be capable of augmenting output. That it appears not to have done so on average in our sample suggests that either the initial policy regime or the policy response is often problematic. This is the subject to which we now turn.

1.6. The Control Regime and Policy Response: Theory and Evidence

The domestic effect of trade shocks is determined in part by the pre-shock policy stance (the control regime) and in part by changes in policies adopted in response to the shock. We first set out the underlying theory and then turn to the evidence from the case studies.

1.6.1. *Fiscal Policy During a Private Shock*

We have already discussed the arguments concerning windfall taxation: *a priori* it is ambiguous whether the rate of taxation of windfalls should be higher or lower than that of normal income. The actual rate of windfall taxation is determined partly by the fiscal response to the shock, notably the imposition of windfall taxes on the export sector, but also by the initial structure of taxation. The former has received much more attention than the latter but may often be less important. In many developing countries the government relies heavily for its revenue upon import taxes. An external windfall can ultimately only be used to increase imports.[7] Hence, in countries with high taxes on imports, the government will automatically capture much of a private windfall even with unchanged policies. That is, the government will tax windfall income more highly than normal income unless it actively reduces tax rates. Import taxes are equivalent to export taxes in their incidence (the Lerner Equivalence Theorem). Hence, even if the windfall is not explicitly taxed through an export tax on the booming commodity, exporters as a group bear the burden of the indirect taxation of the windfall. However, should the government wish to avoid the abnormally high taxation of a windfall implied by its tax structure it faces a difficulty. Clearly, it must temporarily reduce tax rates. While the objective may be to maintain the same tax rate of the windfall as that on normal income, the private sector may interpret the conjunction of an external windfall and a tax reduction as two windfalls with distinct probabilities of persistence. If the tax windfall is seen as permanent, then that part of income attributed to the tax reduction will not be saved. In this example, a fiscally neutral policy stance (keeping constant the share of income taken in taxation) requires sufficiently confusing policy changes that the private sector is misled into insufficient savings. Thus, even if there is otherwise a good case for leaving private windfalls with private agents, the interventions needed to achieve this may substantially weaken the case. In turn this would constitute an argument against a heavy reliance upon import taxes: one cost of such a tax structure would be the inefficient utilisation of windfalls.

The principle underlying public expenditure responses to windfalls is the same as that for expenditure as a whole. That is, to the extent that the price of non-tradable capital goods is temporarily driven up during the investment boom, and that investment implementation deteriorates because of congestion, some expenditures should be deferred until prices have reverted. However, while the principle is the same, the magnitude of its application is likely to be quite different. The composition of public capital formation is typically heavily skewed towards non-tradable goods, whereas private capital formation has a higher component of equipment. Hence, for a given investment rate it would be appropriate for the public sector to defer a larger proportion of its expenditures. However, the deferral of public expenditures may be problematic because of the free-rider problem discussed above. Each spending ministry must take the decision to defer its own expenditures in the knowledge that it has no control over the resources thereby released: other ministries may be the beneficiaries of its expenditure restraint. Underlying this is an important legal difference between private agents and spending ministries. Firms and households can defer expenditure by the acquisition of financial assets. By contrast, because of budget rules, a ministry cannot accumulate savings and transfer them across fiscal years. The government as a whole often has access to a range of financial assets superior to that of private agents since it is not subject to foreign exchange controls. By contrast, the individual ministries which face the temporary price increases in non-tradable capital goods have fewer options for intertemporal substitution.

1.6.2. Monetary Policy During a Private Shock

A trade shock which accrues to private agents affects the demand for money in two ways. First, as discussed above, the savings rate out of a windfall will usually be higher than that out of normal income, so that there is an increase in the demand for assets. The time-path of asset acquisition will in turn involve an initial phase in which the predominant additional assets are financial, and a subsequent phase in which these get converted into real assets. The private sector in aggregate can only increase its financial assets either by increasing its claims on the government or by acquiring claims abroad. The latter are often precluded, either by exchange controls or by prohibitive transactions costs: for example, farmers will not have direct access to foreign financial assets. Hence, the predominant financial assets for the private sector are claims on the government, and in most developing countries much the most important of these claims is base money. Hence, the asset response of private agents implies that there will be an initial phase in which the demand for base money increases, and a subsequent phase in which it declines. This makes monetary targeting during a boom particularly problematic since the expectation must be that the velocity of circulation will fall and then rise again, though by an uncertain amount. Were the government to target the money supply based on the presumption of a constant velocity, then neither would it achieve its objective of a stable price level, nor would private agents achieve their portfolio-management objectives. Since the private sector can always achieve its desired real money balances through changes in the price level, the changes in money demand would first drive down the price level and then raise it. This would have the effect that in the phase of falling velocity the private sector would acquire claims on the government by virtue of the greater real value of the government's nominal monetary liabilities, whereas in the phase of rising velocity the government would in effect default on these additional claims as prices reverted. Thus, in aggregate, the private sector would not succeed in using the temporary acquisition of financial assets to facilitate the more gradual acquisition of real assets.

Second, the transactions demand for money will rise since real expenditures rise and non-tradables prices increase. This is referred to by Eastwood and Venables (1982) as the 'liquidity effect'. This demand in one sense reinforces the temporary increase in the asset demand for money, but is distinct in that, whereas the asset demand can only be satisfied in aggregate by an increase in base money, the additional transactions demand could be met either by an increase in base money or by an expansion of credit. How the increase in the demand for base money is accommodated depends upon exchange rate and fiscal policies. With a floating exchange rate without government intervention, the central bank does not augment base money and so private agents bid up the exchange rate, lowering the price level. With a fixed exchange rate the government meets the increased demand for base money. The government then has a choice as to whether to offset this increase in base money through sterilisation, that is the sale of other assets to private agents. An expansion in base money increases credit to the extent that banks are able to lend the extra deposits and so potentially creates a much larger increase in the total money supply. Hence, a second point of decision for the government is whether to restrict bank lending through an increase in the minimum liquidity ratio of the banking system.

Remaining with the case of a private windfall with a fixed exchange rate, consider the implications for credit. Suppose that the primary recipients of the windfall, exporters, wish to save it since they see it as temporary. If they are subject to exchange controls they convert their export income into domestic currency and deposit it with the banking system. If the latter has been constrained in its lending by its liquidity ratio, it will now increase lending. Other private agents who had wished to consume or invest but had been constrained from doing so by credit rationing will now borrow. The economy thus experiences a temporary financial quasi-liberalisation. That is to say, since bank liquidity rises, the market-clearing interest rate falls and may fall below the official maximum so that both the liquidity ratio and the interest rate controls become slack. For likely initial ratios of M_0/M_2 and M_0/GDP, the supply of credit will increase relative to real income. There is thus a case either for sterilising a part of the foreign exchange inflow through sales of government debt, or for temporarily raising the minimum liquidity ratio of the banking system, each mechanism having the objective of preventing the boom-induced expansion in credit from being proportionately greater than the boom-induced increase in real income. However, it should be stressed that given exchange controls the only way in which the private sector can stretch a windfall is by increasing its claims upon the public sector, which in many economies can only be done through increasing M0 since there is no significant market in public debt. This increase in M0 is not itself inflationary since the private sector wishes to hold it as an asset. What can be inflationary is the expansion in credit which it permits.

1.6.3. Trade and Exchange Rate Policies During a Private Shock

Agents not only want to increase their money holdings, they also want to increase their expenditure upon goods, and this introduces a further government decision concerning trade policy. At one extreme all imports are controlled by quantitative restrictions which are maintained throughout the windfall. A corollary is that the price of importables will rise: that is, there is an increase in the implicit tariff. At the other extreme the government either reduces actual tariffs or so relaxes quantitative restrictions that the implicit tariff rate falls. We refer to this as an 'endogenous' trade policy. This policy rule is a corollary of a fixed exchange rate regime in which imports are rationed by the availability of foreign exchange. In between these active trade policies, policy could be neutral in the sense that tariff rates are kept constant.

These three different trade policies have different implications for saving. To the extent that the shock is recognised as temporary private agents have an incentive to save as discussed above. There is an additional reason for intertemporal substitution when changes in consumer prices induced by the shock are recognised as temporary. This is inevitably the case for prices of non-tradables. During a boom the price of non-tradable consumer goods is temporarily high, so there is a case for the postponement of consumer expenditure analogous to the postponement of investment expenditure while construction prices are high. However, this effect can be compounded or offset by changes in trade policy. Calvo (1987) has shown that a temporary trade liberalisation will reduce the incentive to save. Conversely, maintaining quantitative restrictions will increase savings since the resulting increase in the domestic price of importables will be recognised as temporary.

Not only does an endogenous trade policy rule reduce the incentive to save and increase the incentive to hoard imports, it precludes investment-stretching behaviour. Even if the private recipients of the windfall choose to save it they must cash in their foreign exchange for a claim on the government. The government now sells the foreign exchange to other private agents who are initially rationed, driving down the implicit tariff rate. The structure of claims is thus that the windfall recipients have a claim on the government and the government has a reduced liability to other private agents. Although the private agents who purchase the foreign exchange might use it for investment, so that the savings rate of the economy need not be reduced, there is evidently no foreign asset accumulation since the policy rule implies that reserves are constant.

The greater fall in the relative price of importables under an endogenous trade policy than under floating has a further consequence. As Calvo (1988) has shown, if agents anticipate a reversal of trade liberalisation they have an incentive to hoard imports. If, therefore, the private sector judges that a windfall is temporary (and their savings behaviour suggests that they usually do), and if they know the policy rule, they can be expected to hoard imports. An endogenous trade policy rule is usually so transparent that the agents who regularly import are bound to recognise it. In a country like Tanzania, where for many years the reserves covered less than a week's supply of imports while the exchange rate was fixed, it was evident that the central bank simply sold such foreign exchange as came in. In both Tanzania and Kenya there is evidence that during the coffee boom there was substantial hoarding of durable imports.

We now turn to exchange rate policy. The government faces two regime choices: whether the exchange rate is fixed or floating, and whether the currency is convertible or inconvertible. Under both a fixed and a floating exchange rate a positive shock will increase the demand for real money balances. With a fixed rate this will give rise to a phase of current account surplus and a rising price level, whereas under a flexible rate regime the rate will appreciate, lowering the price level. Thus, if the government wishes to prevent the shock from changing the price level it will have both to allow the exchange rate to appreciate and also to intervene in the market to prevent it appreciating as much as would otherwise occur. Such an intervention would be in addition to the required monetary intervention discussed above.

As we have mentioned above, exchange controls constitute a potential restraint on the windfall savings strategies of the private sector, the severity of which depends upon the degree of domestic financial repression. However, exchange controls not only introduce a constraint upon the private sector, they also weaken a restraint upon the government. In particular, the presence of exchange controls facilitates government misuse of windfall foreign exchange reserves. With convertibility, if a government adopts a spending strategy which is payments incompatible, then private speculation will rapidly shift ownership of the foreign exchange reserves into private hands. With exchange controls the government is able to implement a payments-incompatible spending plan, running down the reserves to finance its expenditures. The private sector may still anticipate exchange rate collapse by increasing imports, but this is both slower and more costly than capital transactions and so provides a weaker discipline on public action. In turn, if the private sector recognises this weakening of restraints on the government, claims on the central bank will be less attractive under exchange controls than with convertibility. This reinforces the incentive effects of exchange controls, further reducing windfall savings and accelerating the acquisition of real assets.

The choice of exchange rate regime will legitimately be influenced by many considerations other than responses to external shocks. However, a shock-prone country is better suited, other things being equal, to a floating exchange rate combined with central bank intervention to stabilise the price level, and to capital account convertibility.

1.6.4. Policy During a Public Shock

Now consider the policy implications of a windfall which initially accrues to the government. Since the government is receiving foreign exchange its first decision concerns exchange rate policy. One possibility is to have a floating exchange rate and sell the foreign exchange as it comes in. Superficially, such a policy is very like an endogenous trade policy with a fixed exchange rate, since in both cases the government sells all its foreign exchange to the private sector as it receives it. However, the consequences turn out to be quite different. A policy of selling foreign exchange as it comes in tends to stabilise public revenue under a floating exchange rate. By contrast, it has no advantages in the context of a fixed exchange rate with an endogenous trade policy. If the government sells more foreign exchange the implicit tariff rate will fall. The volatility of government revenue in domestic currency is therefore not reduced at all; private rents in the trade sector will either be stabilised compared with government revenue or even be counter-cyclical, while other private agents will suffer just as much volatility as under floating. Hence, the costs of instability generated by intra-private transfers are incurred as with floating without any offsetting benefits. This suggests that if a government starts with this policy configuration (fixed exchange rate and rationing of imports) and itself owns the boom sector, then either it should alter the control regime or attempt to stabilise by means of accumulating foreign exchange. For reasons which take us beyond the scope of this study, attempting permanently to liberalise a control regime during a boom may not be good timing, since it is likely to be seen as a response to the boom and therefore temporary. Hence, governments caught with a windfall and a control regime may be best advised to try to save the windfall rather than transfer it.

1.6.5. Evidence on Fiscal Policy

The evidence on the control regime and policy responses is summarised in Table 1.6. As shown there, fiscal responses varied widely. In some countries tax rates were reduced during booms. For example, in Côte d'Ivoire and Sénégal tax collection declined during the period of the windfall so that part of it was transferred in a highly indirect form to the private sector. In Kenya and Malawi precisely the opposite happened: taxes were increased during the boom. However, part of the increase in tax revenue was automatic in that the structure of taxation, notably the heavy reliance upon import taxes, increased the share of revenue in GDP even with unchanged tax rates. The Bangladesh experience is particularly interesting in that there were coincident public and private windfalls so that in principle the transfer could have been in either direction. In the event the government chose to make net transfers to the private sector by means of reduced taxation. Hence, the private sector received both its own remittance windfall and a share of the aid windfall. The Philippine government already had a stabilisation scheme in place prior to the fall in the price of imported oil but chose to relax it in response to the fall in the world oil price of 1986.

We also note some interesting findings of a study by Schuknecht (1997) of fifteen coffee-boom countries in Africa and Latin America. First, he found that the rate of taxation of the windfall significantly affected private savings rates during the windfall. On average, a 10% higher rate of taxation depressed private savings during the windfall by 0.8% of GDP. Dividing his sample according to whether the tax rate on coffee was above 30%, in the six low-tax countries private savings rose during the boom by 3.9% of GDP whereas in the nine high-tax countries private savings actually fell slightly.

Recall that overall during the windfall public savings rates were high, so that expenditure did not rise proportionately with revenue. However, from Table 1.3 we have seen that it was rare for these savings to be held for long in financial assets: before the end of the boom the foreign financial assets acquired during its early stages were typically fully depleted. This has a counterpart in the path of public expenditure: during the booms both capital and current expenditures rose, but in the post-boom period current expenditures were difficult to reduce, giving rise either to large fiscal deficits or to reductions in public investment. Schuknecht finds the

Table 1.6. The control regime and policy responses to shocks

Country	Trade/ exchange	Monetary	Fiscal	Capital account
Kenya	ETP	liquidity up	taxes up	closed
Côte d'Ivoire	ETP	banks lent abroad	taxes down	open
Colombia	ETP	credit tightened	no change	liberalised
Costa Rica	ETP	credit favours government	no change	open
Ghana	some ETP	credit tightened	taxes down	closed
Mauritius	controls stay	liquidity up	taxes up	closed
Malawi	uncontrolled	liquidity up	taxes up	closed
Sénégal	reverse ETP	monetary loosening	taxes down	open
Niger	n.a.	credit tightened	taxes down	open
Zambia	ETP	liquidity up	taxes up in slump	closing
Malaysia	open	n.a.	no change	open
Mexico	ETP	n.a.	taxes down	open
Indonesia	reverse ETP	liquidity up	balanced budget rule	open
Cameroon	controls stay	n.a.	taxes down	open
Egypt	ETP	capital outflow	taxes down	opening
Nigeria	ETP	liquidity up	taxes down	closed
Botswana	open	credit tightened in slump	no change	open
Philippines	n.a.	no change	taxes down	closed
Bangladesh	liberalised	n.a.	taxes down	opening
Bolivia	open	monetary tightening	taxes up	open
Venezuela	ETP	relaxed in slump	no change	open/ closed
Sri Lanka	ETP	credit tightened	no change	closed
Thailand	n.a.	n.a.	no change	open

Notes: ETP = endogenous trade policy (see text); n.a. = not available; 'taxes' refers to taxes other than taxation of the booming commodity

same pattern in his coffee-boom sample. Additionally, distinguishing between the high-tax and low-tax countries, he finds that the fiscal deficit increased much more in the former group both during and after the boom: extra tax revenue did not, except in the short run, lead to higher public savings.

Throughout the period in which these shocks occurred the academic and international institution consensus was largely favourable towards stabilising taxation. The wide range of actual tax responses suggests that policies might have been influenced more by local political factors than by international policy advice. However, windfalls did disproportionately accrue to the public sector, largely through ownership of the boom sector or the initial bias of the tax structure towards imports. Thus, the public sector was commonly the main custodian of windfalls even where there was no explicit export taxation. However, the expenditure response suggests that there was considerable deviation from the model envisaged by advocates of stabilising taxation. Although on average during a windfall governments had high savings rates, the fiscal position was typically deteriorating into a dissavings phase in the later years of the boom and after it. Far from governments stabilising the economy in the face of shocks, the shocks appear to have destabilised the budget.

1.6.6. Evidence on Monetary Policy

We now turn to base money and credit policies. As discussed, the impact of an external shock on the financial sector will in the first instance depend upon whether it accrues to the public or private sector. Since base money is a claim by the private sector on the public sector, a public windfall reduces the money supply because the government sells at least part of the foreign exchange to the private sector, thereby reducing its net liability. When the windfall accrues to the private sector the initial effect depends upon whether the government is operating a floating or a fixed exchange rate: with the latter there is an automatic mechanism for an increase in the supply of base money and this enables an expansion in credit. At the outset of the shock financial repression was common: most governments in the sample had in place maximum interest rates. Hence, a private windfall under a fixed exchange rate lowers the market-clearing interest rate towards or below the ceiling interest rate and so temporarily floats the economy off financial repression.

In most of the cases of private windfalls under fixed exchange rates this temporary financial liberalisation took place: Kenya, Côte d'Ivoire, Mauritius, Malawi, Sénégal and Egypt. For example, in Kenya the banks became unable to find borrowers even at interest rates below previous levels and so the liquidity of the banking system rose to a peak of 37%. Indeed, the inability of the banking system to find borrowers was a common feature of both public and private windfalls. In Ghana the banking system reached 80% liquidity and in Zambia it ran for long periods with liquidity in excess of 50%. Prior to the shocks, interest rate ceilings created shortages of deposits, but even when deposits increased enormously as a result of shocks short-term lending to the government was more attractive than private lending. Where there was an open capital account as in Côte d'Ivoire and Egypt, the banks used the increase in deposits for the acquisition of foreign assets.

While credit expansion during booms (and contraction during slumps, as in Bolivia and Botswana) was common, in two cases, Colombia and Niger, the government more than offset the tendency to liberalisation so that credit became more restricted. In each case this was sufficient to produce an overall reduction in private investment despite the windfall, probably a sign that the policy was carried too far. The investment response during shocks may be sensitive to the monetary response because much of the initial saving of the primary recipients may be financial. For example, in Kenya in the first two years of the coffee boom about half of the windfall received by farmers was saved as bank deposits which were gradually depleted over the next few years and converted into fixed investment. Much of the initial investment boom thus depended upon financial intermediation. We do not know whether the increased investment by agents other than coffee farmers was induced by the increase in real incomes and then financed by the banking system because funds happened to be available, or whether it was directly induced by the extra finance in the sense that projects which firms would have wished to undertake anyway now became financeable. The experience of Colombia and Niger suggests that financial liberalisation is at least the handmaiden of an investment boom during a trade shock.

1.6.7. *Evidence on Trade and Exchange Rate Policy*

We now consider trade and exchange rate policy. Many governments in our sample liberalised trade policy during a windfall and reversed it during the subsequent slump or, equivalently, temporarily tightened policy during a slump. Such an endogenous trade policy (ETP) was adopted in Colombia, Kenya, Côte d'Ivoire, Costa Rica, Mexico, Egypt, Nigeria, Bangladesh, Venezuela, Sri Lanka and Zambia. However, in two countries the government did exactly the opposite: Indonesia and Sénégal. In Indonesia the government was concerned about the effect of Dutch Disease on manufacturing and devalued the exchange rate to offset it, a policy known as 'exchange rate protection'. In Sénégal the government had similar objectives but, being a member of the Franc Zone, lacked the exchange rate as a policy instrument. Instead it used trade policy, raising tariffs and lowering export taxes and thereby simulating a devaluation. Ghana illustrates the difficulty in interpreting trade policy when protection takes the form of quantitative restrictions. The government liberalised quantitative controls to a limited extent, tightening them again after the boom. For example, imports of cars increased by about 50% between 1976 and 1978 and then declined again. However, this small relaxation was probably insufficient to prevent the boom from increasing implicit tariff rates. Indeed, the premium on the parallel exchange rate increased from around 100% prior to the boom to over 400% during it.

Hence, while the government might have thought that it was liberalising trade, in price terms trade policy was considerably tightened. As discussed above, price increases when recognised as temporary will induce savings and this may well explain why Ghana has the highest windfall savings rate in our sample. The remaining countries varied as to the extent to which trade was restricted but did not use trade policy actively during the shock.

We now compare the consequences of the four different policy reactions observed in the sample: the ETP rule, exchange rate protection, increased trade restrictions and a neutral trade and exchange rate policy. The policy-neutral response permits private agents to acquire foreign assets without government intervention in the foreign exchange market and keeps tariff rates constant. To the extent that private agents choose to stretch the investment windfall over a longer period than the savings windfall their choice will dampen the appreciation in non-tradables prices. Policy interventions can either further dampen or amplify these relative price changes. Exchange rate protection, as pursued in Sénégal and Indonesia, dampens the increase in the relative price of non-tradables by inducing additional foreign asset accumulation. By contrast, an endogenous trade policy amplifies relative price changes compared with policy neutrality, whether the windfall is saved or spent. An endogenous trade liberalisation causes more income changes at a disaggregated level: all the windfall must be spent under an ETP rule and the boom sector gets an additional windfall from trade liberalisation at the expense of the import-competing sector. The difference between the ETP rule and the other policy stances is larger the greater the proportion of the windfall which is saved. The demand shock diminishes as savings increase under floating but not under an endogenous trade policy. Hence, if private agents receive a windfall and save it, but the government operates an endogenous trade policy, there will be much more income volatility than under a floating rate. In such circumstances the government might easily conclude that it was necessary to have stabilising taxation to prevent social disruption. This would be a serious misreading of the problem, which is caused by the government's excessive liberalisation of imports.

An endogenous trade policy thus gives rise to two problems. First, changes in relative prices are amplified, and consequently income volatility is increased, owing both to transfers which compound the initial windfall and an inability to acquire foreign financial assets. Second, there is liable to be a speculative accumulation of imports. By contrast, exchange rate protection is a strategy of inducing the private sector to increase its foreign assets by more than it would otherwise choose. The consequent temporary protection of the import-substitute sector is not necessarily welfare enhancing. It is efficient for there to be a temporary contraction of the sector if thereby resources are released for the boom export and construction sectors, whose activities need to increase for an economy to make the best use of a temporary windfall. The accumulation of foreign assets is better seen as being justified by the increased efficiency resulting from a stretching of the investment boom. That is, it is the capacity of the economy to absorb investment rather than the need to prevent temporary contractions of some sectors which should determine the foreign asset, and hence the exchange rate, path of the economy. To justify exchange rate protection even if there was no difficulty in absorbing investment, there would need to be substantial external costs to reversed contractions in the non-boom tradable sector.

Finally, consider the Ghanaian policy of increasing implicit tariff rates by the failure to relax quantitative restrictions. Unless the volume of exports falls to offset the price increase, binding import quotas entail an improvement in the balance of payments. In turn the latter implies an increase in the supply of base money. Cocoa farmers might be willing to accept this increased money supply for two reasons. First, as in our preceding analysis, private agents might choose to have high savings rates out of windfall income and wish to hold these savings in liquid form. However, even if the chosen savings rate is zero, farmers will still choose to export in exchange for an increased supply of domestic currency since by spending it they can increase their consumption. In aggregate the increased monetary expenditure without increased imports will be inflationary. Exporters thus inflict a negative pecuniary externality on other private agents; that is, other agents lose through an erosion of their real money balances. Hence, the government receives the entire cocoa windfall by means of the inflation tax. Within the private sector there is only redistribution: cocoa farmers could benefit from the windfall only at the expense of other private agents. An analogy is the economics of a gold rush. Individuals who discover gold mines benefit, but this is entirely at the expense of other agents through a rise in the price level. However, the expenditure of cocoa farmers will bid up the price of non-tradables, so that it is possible that the relative price of cocoa will actually fall. In that case the redistribution is in the other direction: producers of non-tradables gaining at the expense of cocoa farmers. This indeed happened in Ghana: in real terms the price of cocoa to producers fell by 16% during the cocoa boom and cocoa output fell sharply, although some of this will have been the result of smuggling.

This is obviously a highly inefficient way of benefiting from an external windfall since the resource shifts are the opposite of those that would be needed to take advantage of it. Given the difficulty of monitoring implicit tariffs, a government which uses a lot of quantitative restrictions on trade cannot even be sure whether it is liberalising or tightening trade policy (as defined by implicit tariff rates) in response to a shock. If it is neutral in the sense of keeping the controls constant it will have an increase in implicit tariffs, which we have seen might be highly inefficient. If it is neutral in the sense of passively selling whatever foreign exchange is available, it will have an endogenous trade liberalisation. It therefore has to be very active and skilful in order to be neutral in the sense of keeping implicit tariffs constant. Given the lack of information and skill, it is therefore highly likely that if the government starts with quantitative restrictions on trade it will inadvertently either endogenously liberalise or endogenously tighten. Any active trade policy is strictly dominated by a floating exchange rate policy. Hence, the conclusion is, first, that countries prone to external shocks should not have quantitative restrictions on trade, and second, that if a country with quantitative restrictions faces a windfall, it should focus upon the question of appropriate foreign asset acquisition, deriving its trade policy from that. It is not a good time to undertake a trade liberalisation. Even the more modest step of converting quotas to equivalent tariffs will produce a transfer to the government (in the form of tariff revenue) at just the time when it is likely to be least able to use it productively.

An implication of this is that one may observe a high aggregate savings rate even if private agents choose not to save out of the windfall. What is observed is the saving by the government, in the form of foreign exchange reserves financed out of the inflation tax. Since the inflation tax is not counted as part of government revenue, there will appear to be a 100% private savings rate. Hence, what is in fact public savings will be attributed to the private sector. However, even this is somewhat misleading since the saving is an inadvertent consequence of the failure to relax trade policy. In Ghana, although quantitative restrictions were slightly relaxed, the above mechanism might well explain why we observe an apparently much higher private sector savings rate for the Ghanaian private sector than for any other windfall in our sample.

Finally, we consider exchange controls. In only three countries did the policy response include changes in capital account restrictions. Both Egypt and Bangladesh liberalised such restrictions in an attempt to attract the foreign assets of migrants. Zambia, in response to declining terms of trade, tightened exchange control. The other countries maintained their pre-shock regime. In seven countries (Kenya, Ghana, Mauritius, Malawi, Nigeria, the Philippines and Sri Lanka) this involved exchange control, so that private agents could accumulate foreign assets only indirectly.

1.7. Conclusion: Implications for Policy

The policy debate concerning external shocks has usually focused upon how governments should respond to them. However, appropriate policy response is itself contingent upon the policy environment in place prior to the shock. In this conclusion we consider both the appropriate policy regime for a shock-prone economy and the policy responses appropriate during a shock.

Because large external shocks usually persist for less than a decade, the appropriate response will be an atypically high savings rate. The evidence of our case studies suggests that both public and private agents usually raise their savings rates sharply in response to positive shocks. Thus, in most countries the initial policy regime was not so deficient as to prevent private agents saving. This is not surprising since private agents normally have three distinct asset options—foreign assets, domestic financial assets and domestic real assets—and only in extreme policy environments will all three be closed off. More typically, governments have closed off one or other of the three asset choices, by enforcing foreign exchange controls, by domestic financial repression or by reducing the return on private investment.

Such partial closures appear to have affected the composition of savings more strongly than their level, since private windfall savings rates have typically been high. However, governments can frustrate private savings responses not only by closing off asset choices but by obscuring the informational content of price changes on which private agents must base their savings decisions. In two of our case studies, Colombia and Sénégal, private savings responses were unusually low and this is likely to have been the result of confused price information. In both countries the government synchronised a policy change (reducing taxation of the boom commodity) with the boom. Thus, private agents were faced with two windfalls with potentially quite different durations. In each case the private savings rate was high by normal standards but low in comparison with other windfalls. One interpretation of these results is that savings rates out of windfalls are most likely to be high when recipients are clear about their true source. The policy implication is that the government should attempt to enhance the quality of information available to private agents rather than transfer private windfalls to itself in order to play a custodial role. One way to do this is to broadcast world prices to private agents. This may be particularly important in the case of peasant farmers with limited access to world news. During the 1976–79 coffee boom the Kenyan government used the network of coffee cooperatives to explain to farmers that prices were temporarily high. The Ethiopian government during the coffee boom of 1994–95 broadcast auction prices on the radio.

Thus, in a shock-prone economy the ideal policy regime for a private savings response is one in which none of the three asset options is closed and in which the information concerning world price changes is not contaminated by synchronised policy changes. With such a policy regime there is no case for a government custodial role based on the assumption that the private sector will not save the windfall. There is potentially a second-best case for a government custodial role if the initial policy regime departs sufficiently from this ideal.

We now consider whether windfall savings are transformed into productive investment. Despite the high savings rates out of windfalls, both the individual case study evidence and our econometric analysis of the full sample of windfalls suggests that the eventual returns to investment during boom periods have typically been low. This may derive from several distinct effects. In the case of public investment, rapid increases in expenditure may lead to a deterioration in standards of control and accountability. Further, returns may decline because of a bias in favour of structures rather than tradable capital. In the case of private investment returns may reflect the constraints imposed by the control regime, in particular by exchange control, financial repression and endogenous changes in trade policy. That windfalls should often lead to an eventual reduction in output is an indication of substantial policy error.

Some of the windfall savings will often need to be held temporarily abroad in order to avoid a sharp decline in the return to domestic investment. If there is capital account convertibility the private sector can do this directly. If not, then the same effect can be achieved if the central bank offers attractive domestic financial assets, temporarily building up foreign reserves to match its increased liabilities. Additionally, as in any economy, a whole range of other policies will affect whether private savings can be productively invested. If the policy environment is highly unattractive for private investment then there is a second-best case for a government custodial role, although the first-best would presumably be to reform the policy environment. However, in an environment in which private investment is unattractive, the return on public investment is also liable to be low, so that the best use of the windfall may be to hold it abroad until policies are reformed. Private capital flight would in this case perform the custodial role, protecting the windfall from being dissipated.

The appropriate response to an external shock involves inter-sectoral as well as inter-temporal decisions. The transformation of private windfall savings into productive investment is thus dependent upon the sectoral allocation of windfall investment. There is often concern that the allocation of investment to the booming export sector will be excessive. This might arise either because of insufficient financial intermediation or because the windfall price change is erroneously regarded as persistent.

The former case may arise when the windfall savings made by agents specialised in the boom sector are invested directly in the sector because of a lack of opportunities for financial intermediation. During the period covered in our case studies this was a problem in most countries, although with the widespread liberalisation of financial markets during the 1990s it will presumably be less of a problem in the future. Because in shock-prone economies there is a periodic large and systematic divergence between sectoral savings and sectoral investment opportunities, such economies have a greater need for liberalised financial markets. However, even in those countries in which financial markets have been very restricted, there has often been scope for windfall investment to be allocated outside the boom sector, because in many cases the recipients are peasant households engaged in multiple activities.

The latter case is when overinvestment in the export sector is the result of agents overestimating the duration of the price boom. However, this problem is unlikely to be as severe as the early development literature supposed: the circumstances in which private agents save the windfall are those in which they recognise its temporary nature. Relatedly, it has sometimes been argued that windfall export taxation is unanticipated and thus has no disincentive effects, so that its costs are lower than the taxation of normal income. We have argued by contrast that the costs of windfall taxation are atypically high. First, while agents do not anticipate a particular instance of a shock, they do recognise that shocks will occur, so that a policy of windfall taxation will deter investment. Second, since the investment rate out of windfall income is much higher than that out of normal income, windfall taxation has a disproportionate opportunity cost in terms of private investment, which is the component of expenditure which most governments most desire to see increased.

Since private agents appear to be able to handle windfalls satisfactorily (conditional upon a suitable policy environment) there might appear to be a case for transferring public windfalls to the private sector. In effect, in contrast to windfall taxation, this would be a policy of windfall subsidy of the private sector. However, windfall subsidy would encounter many of the problems of windfall taxation. In particular, there is liable to be loss of information concerning the likely duration of the windfall as it is transferred to the private sector, so that savings rates out of transferred windfalls may be much lower than desirable. On the criterion of savings response it may therefore be best to leave windfalls with their primary recipients.

Although the thrust of policy advice has been for governments to increase taxation during windfalls, there is a better case for taxation to decrease as a share of GDP. As we have seen, the costs of taxation are likely to be atypically high during a windfall. The effects of a windfall on the benefits of expenditure are, however, ambiguous. For example, if public investment in infrastructure is complementary to private investment then there is a case for increasing it during the boom. Offsetting this, such expenditures will amplify the construction boom. Thus, while the arguments on the effect of a windfall on the benefits of public expenditure could go either way and cannot realistically be measured, the effect on the cost of taxation is an unambiguous increase. Hence, to the extent that such theory is any guide to windfall taxation policy it suggests a decrease in taxation rather than an increase. By contrast, if the tax structure is unaltered then even without explicit windfall taxation the share of revenue in GDP will rise because of the disproportionate dependence of most developing countries upon import taxes for revenue. Hence, to the extent that the share of revenue in GDP should fall during windfalls, owing to the temporary increase in the costs of taxation relative to the benefits of expenditure, tax rates will need to be lowered.

Although many of the countries in our case studies had a high level of import restrictions, shock-prone economies are particularly unsuited to such a policy environment. As we have already argued, there is little case for a public custodial role. Hence, taxation of a private windfall is in general undesirable. Directly, this implies that windfall export taxes should be avoided. However, import restrictions replicate the fiscal effects of export taxes through two processes. The first is the Lerner Equivalence Theorem, by which an import tax is equivalent to an export tax in its effect on export incomes. Thus, for example, in Kenya, where there was an explicit decision to leave the windfall with coffee farmers by avoiding export taxation, nevertheless, because there were high import taxes, much of the windfall was taxed from coffee farmers and accrued to the government. The second process by which import restrictions tax the windfall is if the restrictions take the form of widespread quantitative restrictions. In this case, unless the quantitative restrictions are relaxed during the boom windfall spending merely drives up the price level, until the entire windfall is transferred to the government via the inflation tax. Such an inadvertent windfall tax occurred in Ghana.

If the windfall accrues to the government as a result of the inadvertent and implicit mechanisms involved in import restrictions, the government is liable to mistake the nature of its windfall. An instance of this occurred in Uganda during the 1994 coffee boom. Whereas export tax receipts were recognised as temporary and saved in a distinct account at the central bank, the much larger increase in tariff revenue attributable to the boom was treated as a part of normal revenue.

Because many countries started windfalls with high trade restrictions there was strong pressure for trade liberalisation during the boom. Such an endogenous trade policy appears to be a serious mistake, amplifying changes in relative prices, adding to volatility and encouraging welfare-reducing speculative imports. Combined with exchange control, a combination which until recently was very common in Africa, an endogenous trade policy makes foreign asset accumulation impossible. We have found, however, that an endogenous trade policy is the policy response used by most countries in our sample.

We have already suggested that shock-prone economies have a greater need for financial intermediation, so that financial repression is liable to be atypically costly. During windfalls private agents in aggregate initially require increased financial assets prior to their acquisition of investment goods, so that the central bank should temporarily increase its supply of money. However, such an increase in base money automatically expands credit, producing a temporary financial liberalisation in initially repressed systems. This is undesirable both because it is inflationary and because an initially repressed banking system will lack the skills to expand lending in a prudent and productive manner. In order to avoid inflationary effects, the central bank needs to respond to the windfall either by sterilising the increase in base money or by raising the minimum liquidity ratio. However, the temporary increase in claims by the private sector on the central bank is itself desirable.

In the past, shock-prone economies have forfeited part of the growth opportunities presented by windfalls because of inadequacies in the initial policy environment and in policy response. Generally, the two aspects of policy error interact, since appropriate responses become more complex when one starts from inadequate initial policy regimes. However, with good policies price volatility need not be the curse that policymakers think it is. In this case, not only are windfalls an opportunity for growth, but price volatility itself can become beneficial. An economy in which resource allocation is flexible can convert price volatility into the equivalent of a permanent improvement in its terms of trade by constantly shifting resources in response to price changes. Hence, rather than seeking to mitigate the effects of price instability through export diversification, policymakers in shock-prone economies should first put in place policies conducive to the efficient conversion of windfalls into investment, and then take full advantage of price shocks by enhancing resource mobility.

Appendix
A Model of Private Responses to a Temporary Shock

Consider the problem faced by a developing country which has to adjust to a temporary positive trade shock, a commodity boom. The scope for smoothing consumption is limited since the country does not have access to a perfect capital market. Indeed, we will begin by describing a country with a closed capital account and then move to the more realistic case of a developing country which faces a borrowing constraint in the world capital market.

First consider the problem

$$\max_c \int_0^\infty u(c)e^{-\rho t}dt$$

subject to

$$\dot{k} = g(k) - c + b. \tag{A.1}$$

Here c denotes consumption, $u(c)$ the instantaneous utility function, ρ the time preference rate, $g(k) = f(k) - \delta k$ output net of depreciation, and k the capital stock. We assume the functions f and u to be strictly concave. Boom income b is a positive constant during the period $(0,T)$ and is otherwise equal to zero.

Initially the economy is in steady-state equilibrium with the capital stock equal to k^* where $g'(k^*) = \rho$. The problem at time $t = 0$ is to choose an optimal consumption path taking into account that the boom will be over at time T.

Write λ for the co-state variable corresponding to the capital stock k. Conditions for an optimum include

$$\dot{\lambda} = -g'\lambda, \tag{A.2}$$

$$e^{-\rho t}u' = \lambda. \tag{A.3}$$

Differentiating (A.3) with respect to time gives

$$\rho\lambda - e^{-\rho t}u''\dot{c} = g'\lambda.$$

Hence $u''\dot{c} = (\rho - g')u'$, or

$$\dot{c}/c = \sigma(g' - \rho), \tag{A.4}$$

where $\sigma = -u'/(u''c)$ is the inter-temporal elasticity of substitution.[8] Note that $\dot{c} = 0$ implies $k = k^*$. This is shown as the vertical $\dot{c} = 0$ locus in Figure 1.A1. The Keynes–Ramsey rule implies that c falls (rises) to the right (left) of the locus, as indicated by the arrows.

The budget constraint (A.1) defines the $\dot{k} = 0$ locus.[9] For higher consumption levels the capital stock falls, while below the locus net investment is positive.

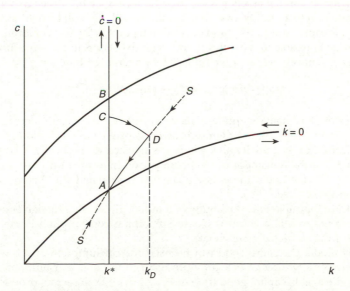

Figure 1.A1. Adjustment with tradable capital, closed capital account

There are two paths which converge to the steady-state equilibrium at A; these form the stable branch SS.

The initial equilibrium is at A, where c and k are both constant. The trade shock ($b > 0$) shifts the $\dot{k} = 0$ locus upwards. If the boom were permanent, equilibrium would shift instantaneously to B: the extra income would simply be consumed. With a temporary boom consumption will not rise to the full extent. Adjustment starts at a point such as C. This lies below the new $\dot{k} = 0$ locus, hence k increases and c falls along the path CD. When the boom ends the $\dot{k} = 0$ locus shifts back to its original position so that point D now lies above the locus. Hence, after the boom the economy moves to the left in the diagram: the capital stock falls. Note that at time T the problem reduces to the standard Ramsey model with b in equation (A.1) equal to zero. Hence adjustment in the post-boom period is along the stable branch SS, from D back to A.

Adjustment to a temporary positive shock therefore involves two phases. During the first the capital stock increases as part of the boom income is invested and in the post-boom period this investment is reversed, enabling a higher consumption level. Investment smooths consumption: instead of following a step function consumption is permanently higher than before the shock, jumping up at time $t = 0$ and then declining monotonically towards its pre-shock level.

In this model the capital account is closed so that all domestic savings are invested domestically. Now consider a developing country which has access to a world capital market, but an imperfect one: it can hold foreign assets (a) but it cannot borrow ($a \geq 0$). The world interest rate is lower than the time preference rate ($\rho > r^*$) so that at A the domestic rate of return (g') exceeds the world interest rate: there is an incentive to borrow.

Suppose that with a closed capital account investment would proceed so far that the rate of return fell below r^*: k_D in Figure 1.A1 and exceeds k^{**} where $g'(k^{**}) = r^*$. Then obviously foreign assets will be used because they offer the advantage of a higher rate of return. In this case non-human wealth (w) will be held in the form of domestic capital until $k = k^{**}$ and beyond that point in the form of foreign assets. This makes it possible to write this model with two assets in the same form as the single-asset Ramsey model. If we replace k by w and the function g by

$$h(w) = g[\min(w, k^{**})] + r \max(0, w - k^{**}),$$

then the previous analysis applies. Hence in Figure 1.A2 wealth increases in the boom period (along CE) and then returns to its pre-boom level (along the stable branch from E to A). Initially all savings are invested domestically (CD) until k^{**} is reached. For the remainder of the boom period investment is in foreign assets (DE) and after the boom these assets are first repatriated (EF) before domestic investment is reversed (FA).

Clearly, in this model the possibility of temporarily holding foreign assets raises welfare: if the capital account is closed smoothing consumption is more costly because of the restricted asset choice.

In this model the same good can be used for consumption and investment. Now consider a two-sector economy producing a tradable consumption good (t) and a non-tradable capital good (i) ('construction').[10] Both sectors produce under constant returns to scale using capital and labour and these factors are both

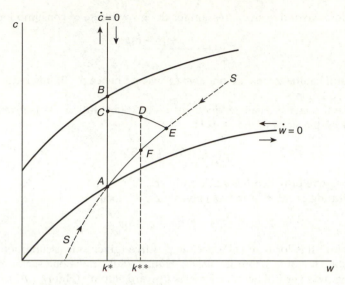

Figure 1.A2. Adjustment with tradable capital, open capital account

intersectorally mobile. Labour is in fixed supply ($\bar{l}$). We assume the construction sector to be labour intensive.

In this case the model is

$$\max_{k_t,l_i} \int_0^\infty u(c)e^{-\rho t}dt,$$

where $c = t(k - k_v, \bar{l} - l_i) + b$, subject to

$$\dot{k} = i(k_t, l_i) - \delta k. \tag{A.5}$$

This gives:

$$\dot{\lambda} = -e^{-\rho t}u't_k + \delta\lambda, \tag{A.6}$$

$$t_k = p i_k, \tag{A.7}$$

$$t_l = p i_l, \tag{A.8}$$

where p is defined as $e^{-\rho t}/u'$. The marginal productivity conditions (A.7) and (A.8) allow us to write output as a function of the aggregate capital stock and the relative price of capital goods: at an optimum $t = \tilde{t}(k,p)$ and $i = \tilde{i}(k,p)$ where because the tradable sector is capital intensive the partial derivatives satisfy

$$\tilde{t}(k,p)_k > 0 > \tilde{i}(k,p)_k$$

and

$$\tilde{t}(k,p)_p < 0 < \tilde{i}(k,p)_p.$$

We assume that $\tilde{t}_{kp}$ is non-positive.

As before we derive an expression for the growth rate of consumption:

$$\frac{\dot{c}}{c} = \frac{\tilde{\imath}_k + \dot{p} - (\rho + \delta)p}{p}\sigma. \tag{A.9}$$

Note that if capital goods are tradable ($p = 1$ and hence $\dot{p} = 0$) this reduces to the Ramsey equation.

The $\dot{k} = 0$ locus is again defined by $i = \delta k$. Substituting $i = \tilde{\imath}(k,p)$ and using $c = \tilde{\imath}(k,p) + b$ the slope of the locus is

$$\frac{dc}{dk} = \tilde{\imath}_k + (\delta - \tilde{\imath}_k)\tilde{\imath}_p \big/ \tilde{\imath} - p.$$

This is positive provided δ is sufficiently small.[11]

Substituting $\dot{c} = \tilde{\imath}_k\dot{k} + \tilde{\imath}_p\dot{p}$ in (A.9) gives the $\dot{c} = 0$ locus as[12]

$$\tilde{\imath}_k\big(1 - \dot{k}\big/\tilde{\imath}_p\big) = (\rho + \delta)p.$$

The slope of this locus in (c,k)-space is positive (given our assumption that the construction sector is labour intensive). Hence, while in the one-sector model the $\dot{c} = 0$ locus was vertical here the locus is upward sloping (Figure 1.A3).

The boom shifts both the $\dot{k} = 0$ locus and the $\dot{c} = 0$ locus upwards. If the shock is permanent the new equilibrium is at B. In the case of a temporary shock, adjustment is along CDA; as before, c declines throughout while the capital stock increases during the boom period and returns to its old value in the post-boom period.

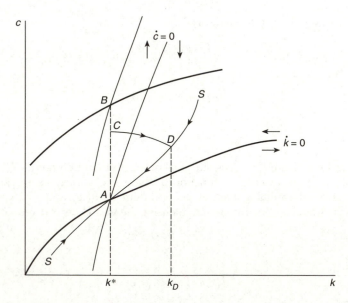

Figure 1.A3. Adjustment with non-tradable capital, closed capital account

The adjustment path is shown in Figure 1.A4 in (p,k)-space. Here both loci are upward sloping but the $\dot{k}=0$ locus is steeper than the $\dot{p}=0$ locus. In the case of a closed capital account the price of construction jumps up at the beginning of the boom and then continues to rise during the boom period along AB.[13] This implies that the domestic rate of return $r=(\tilde{l}_k+\dot{p}-\delta p)/p$ falls. If r^* is reached it is again optimal to acquire foreign assets.

In Figure 1.A5 two possibilities are shown for the case of an open capital account. In the first case there is an initial phase of domestic investment until $r=r^*$; in the second case r drops to r^* instantaneously. Once foreign assets are held $r=r^*$ by arbitrage and hence the $\dot{p}=0$ locus through F (where $\tilde{l}_k=(r^*+\delta)p$) is the relevant one. Hence p falls: in the first case once the higher $\dot{p}=0$ locus has been crossed (at C) and in the second case immediately. Unlike in the previous model, in this model there can be simultaneously foreign and domestic investment.

Since $r^*<\rho$ it is not optimal to hold foreign assets permanently. Hence foreign assets will be drawn down. Eventually $a=0$ and the $\dot{p}=0$ locus shifts back to its original position. The final adjustment phase is then again along the stable branch, from E or G back to A.

In this model investment may continue after the boom, financed by drawing down foreign assets. Alternatively, repatriated foreign assets are used after the boom to finance a higher level of consumption as in the previous model.

In either case access to the world capital market raises welfare compared with the closed capital account model. It does so in two ways. First, as in the earlier model, domestic investment is subject to diminishing returns while the interest rate on foreign assets is constant. Second, it offers the possibility of postponing investment until the price of capital goods has fallen.

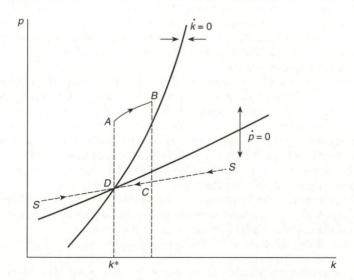

Figure 1.A4. Adjustment with tradable capital, closed capital account

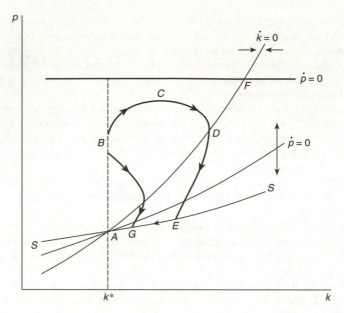

Figure 1.A5. Adjustment with non-tradable capital, open capital account

NOTES

1. It should be noted that during a construction boom the relative price of non-tradable consumer goods to tradable goods may rise even if there is no increase in consumption spending. This would be the result of resources being pulled into the construction sector at the expense of the supply of non-tradable consumer goods. In this case there would be a symptom of Dutch Disease without any spending effect.
2. If capital is mobile the outcome depends, of course, on relative factor intensities. In a three-sector model (tradables, non-tradable consumer goods and non-tradable capital goods) with a perfect world capital market, a construction boom (in the sense of an increase in the output and the price of non-tradable capital) can occur only if construction is more capital intensive than tradables (Van Wincoop 1993). This seems implausible. Observed construction booms must therefore be explained in terms of capital market imperfections or factor immobility.
3. In a static model without distortions, convexity of the profit function implies that volatility is welfare enhancing (for a mean-preserving spread of the export price) if the export is not consumed domestically.
4. For our earlier application of this approach to the Kenyan coffee boom see Bevan *et al.* (1990).
5. We would like to thank Robert Bates for this point. His work on the Colombian coffee boom is in progress.

6. This result is consistent with that of Deaton and Miller (1996), who also find a short-run positive effect but do not explicitly model a post-boom effect.
7. As we discuss below, there is one further possibility, namely that the windfall is used to reduce export volumes, as we show occurred in Ghana. However, this is a highly costly and unusual type of response and we ignore it here.
8. Equation (A.4) gives the Keynes–Ramsey rule: consumption increases (decreases) if the marginal productivity of capital exceeds (is less than) the rate of time preference. See Blanchard and Fischer (1989, ch. 2) for a recent exposition of the Ramsey (1928) model.
9. The locus is upward sloping up to the point where $f' = \delta$.
10. We ignore tradable capital goods because they can be aggregated with tradable consumption goods and we assume that only tradables are consumed to abstract from the Dutch Disease spending effect.
11. For a large δ the positive effect of a capital stock increase on consumption may be more than offset by the increase in replacement demand for capital goods.
12. Note that in equilibrium ($\dot{k} = 0$) this equates the return to one unit of tradables invested domestically (the marginal productivity minus the depreciation rate: $\tilde{t}_k/p - \delta$) to its opportunity cost in terms of foregone consumption, ρ.
13. The price p must rise since $\dot{c} = \tilde{t}_k \dot{k} + \tilde{t}_p \dot{p}$ and c falls while k increases. At time T the price drops. This ensures a jump in the production of tradables so that consumption does not drop at the end of the boom. At T, r jumps up so that the rental price rp is continuous. The post-boom adjustment path is along CD.

REFERENCES

Bates, R.H. (1981), *Markets and States in Tropical Africa*, Berkeley, Calif., University of California Press.

Bevan, D.L., P. Collier and J.W. Gunning (1987), 'Consequences of a Commodity Boom in a Controlled Economy: Accumulation and Redistribution in Kenya, 1975–1983', *World Bank Economic Review*, vol. 1, pp. 489–513.

Bevan, D.L., P. Collier and J.W. Gunning (1989a), 'Fiscal Response to a Temporary Trade Shock the Aftermath of the Kenyan Coffee Boom', *World Bank Economic Review*, vol. 3, pp. 359–78.

Bevan, D.L., P. Collier and J.W. Gunning (1989b), *Peasants and Governments: An Economic Analysis*, Oxford, Clarendon Press.

Bevan, D.L., P. Collier and J.W. Gunning (1990), *Controlled Open Economies: A Neoclassical Approach to Structuralism*, Oxford, Clarendon Press.

Bevan, D.L., P. Collier and J.W. Gunning (1992), *Nigeria: Policy Responses to Shocks, 1970–1990*, San Francisco, ICS Press.

Bevan, D.L., P. Collier and J.W. Gunning (1993a), 'Trade Shocks in Developing Countries: Consequences and Policy Responses', *European Economic Review*, vol. 37, pp. 557–65.

Bevan, D.L., P. Collier and J.W. Gunning (1993b), 'La Politique Economique face aux chocs externes dans les pays en développement', *Revue d'Economie du Développement*, vol. 1, pp. 5–22.

Blanchard, O.J. and S. Fischer (1989), *Lectures on Macroeconomics*, Cambridge, Mass., MIT Press.

Burger, K., P. Collier and J.W. Gunning (1993), 'Learning by Observing: Theory and an Application to Innovation in Kenyan Agriculture', mimeo, CSAE, Oxford.

Calvo, G.A. (1987), 'On the Costs of Temporary Policy', *Journal of Development Economics*, vol. 27, pp. 245–61.

Calvo, G. (1988), 'Costly Trade Liberalizations: Durable Goods and Capital Mobility', *IMF Staff Papers*, vol. 35, pp. 461–73.

Collier, P. and D. Lal (1986), *Labour and Poverty in Kenya*, Oxford, Clarendon Press.

Corden, W.M. (1984), 'Booming Sector and Dutch Disease Economics: Survey and Consolidation', *Oxford Economic Papers*, vol. 36, pp. 359–80.

Corden, W.M. and J.P. Neary (1982), 'Booming Sector and De-industrialisation in a Small Open Economy', *Economic Journal*, vol. 92, pp. 825–48.

Deaton, A.S. (1990), 'Saving in Developing Countries: Theory and Review', in *Proceedings of the World Bank Annual Conference on Development Economics 1989*, Supplement to the *World Bank Economic Review* and the *World Bank Research Observer*, pp. 61–96.

Deaton, A.S. (1991), 'Saving and Liquidity Constraints', *Econometrica*, vol. 59, pp. 1221–48.

Deaton, A.S. (1992), 'Commodity Prices, Stabilization and Growth in Africa', Discussion Paper 166, Research Program in Development Studies, Center for International Studies, Princeton.

Deaton, A.S. (1995), 'Data and Econometric Tools for Development Analysis', in J.R. Behrman and T.N. Srinivasan (eds.), *Handbook of Development Economics*, vol. 3, Amsterdam, North Holland, pp. 1785–882.

Deaton, A.S. and G. Laroque (1992), 'On the Behaviour of Commodity Prices', *Review of Economic Studies*, vol. 59, pp. 1–23.

Deaton, A.S. and R. Miller (1996), 'International Commodity Prices, Growth and Policies in sub-Saharan Africa', *Journal of African Economies*, vol. 5 (supp.), pp. 99–191.

de Long and L. Summers (1991), 'Equipment Investment and Economic Growth', *Quarterly Journal of Economics*, vol. 106, pp. 445–502.

Devarajan, S., V. Swaroop and H. Zou (1994), 'The Composition of Public Expenditure and Economic Growth', *Journal of Monetary Economics*, vol. 37, pp. 313–44.

Dixit, A. (1989), 'Intersectoral Capital Reallocation under Price Uncertainty', *Journal of International Economics*, vol. 26, pp. 309–25.

Eastwood, R.K. and A.J. Venables (1982), 'The Macroeconomic Implications of a Resource Discovery in an Open Economy', *Economic Journal*, vol. 92, pp. 285–99.

Edwards, S. and S. van Wijnbergen (1986), 'The Welfare Effects of Trade and Capital Liberalization', *International Economic Review*, vol. 27, pp. 141–8.

Gelb, A. and associates (1988), *Oil Windfalls: Blessing or Curse?*, New York, Oxford University Press.

Leon, J. and R. Soto (1995), 'Structural Breaks and Long Run Trends in Commodity Prices', Policy Research Working Paper 1406, World Bank, Washington D.C.

Mash, R. (1995), 'The Consequences of International Trade Prices Volatility for National Income and Welfare: Theory and Evidence', D. Phil. thesis, University of Oxford.

Mellor, J. (ed.) (1993), *Agriculture on the Road to Industrialisation*, Baltimore, Johns Hopkins University Press.

Neary, J.P. and S. van Wijnbergen (eds.) (1986), *Natural Resources and the Macroeconomy*, Oxford, Basil Blackwell.

Newbery D.M.G. and J.E. Stiglitz (1981), *The Theory of Commodity Price Stabilization*, Oxford, Clarendon Press.

Ramsey, F.P. (1928), 'A Mathematical Theory of Saving', *Economic Journal*, vol. 38, pp. 543–59.

Roemer, M. (1985), 'Dutch Disease in Developing Countries: Swallowing Bitter Medicine', in M. Lundahl (ed.), *The Primary Sector in Economic Development*, London, Croom Helm, pp. 234–51.

Schuknecht, L. (1994), 'Political Business Cycles and Expenditure Policies in Developing Countries', IMF Working Paper.

Schuknecht, L. (1997), 'Tying Governments' Hands in Commodity Taxation', mimeo, World Trade Organisation, Geneva.

Van Wincoop, E. (1993), 'Structural Adjustment and the Construction Sector', *European Economic Review*, vol. 37, pp. 177–201.

Wijnbergen, S. van (1984), 'Inflation, Employment and the Dutch Disease in Oil-Exporting Countries: A Short-Run Disequilibrium Analysis', *Quarterly Journal of Economics*, vol. 99, pp. 233–50.

2

Anatomy of a Temporary Trade Shock: The Kenyan Coffee Boom of 1976–79

DAVID BEVAN, PAUL COLLIER AND JAN WILLEM GUNNING

The Kenyan coffee boom of 1976–79 was an archetypal temporary external shock. First, it was substantial: at its peak in 1977 the barter terms of trade improved overall by 54% on their pre-boom level. Second, although the price change could not reasonably have been foreseen, it was recognisably temporary. Its main cause was a frost in Brazil which damaged but did not destroy the tree stock. Although the precise duration of the boom was uncertain, the fact that it was not a permanent event was not in dispute.

A central theme of this chapter is the extent to which assets were used to convert a large temporary shock into a small permanent shock. Sections 2.1 and 2.2 analyse the impact of the boom on the economy as a whole. We show that overall the economy achieved quite a high savings rate from this windfall. In Section 2.3 we disaggregate between private and public agents. The windfall initially accrued to private agents (coffee farmers) since, against international advice, the Kenyan government chose not to impose 'stabilizing' taxation. However, owing to the structure of expenditure and trade taxes around half of the windfall indirectly accrued to the government. We show that, whereas the private sector had a very high windfall savings rate, the government did not.

A second theme is the consequences for goods markets. The static analysis of Dutch Disease, in which the key disaggregation is between tradable and non-tradable goods, is refined by a further disaggregation into capital and consumer goods. The Kenyan coffee boom led to a massive increase in the demand for non-tradable capital goods, giving rise to a *construction boom*. In Section 2.2 we show that construction prices were pushed up substantially and in Section 2.3 we show that the timing and composition of government expenditure accentuated the construction boom. As a result, we suggest, the high windfall savings were inefficiently converted into real assets.

A third theme of the chapter is that the responses of private agents were heavily constrained by the regulatory environment, which we term the 'control regime'. Section 2.4 analyses the consequences of various components of the control regime. We suggest that, as with public expenditure, the control regime caused inefficiency in the conversion of savings into real assets.

Section 2.5 provides two assessments, one of public policy, the other of the analytic framework used to investigate the shock.

2.1. The Nature of the Shock

The coffee boom was a large, short trade shock caused by frost in Brazil. It was recognised at the time both as temporary and as exceptional. The price Kenya received for its coffee exports more than quadrupled between 1975 and the peak of the boom in 1977, this directly constituting a 38% improvement in the barter terms of trade.[1] However, the boom which Kenya enjoyed in this period was much larger: the coffee boom triggered a substantial increase in tea prices and there were other terms of trade improvements. The total increase in the barter terms of trade was 54%.[2] By 1980 the terms of trade had virtually returned to their 1975 level. Thus the boom lasted for four years, with much of the gains accruing in 1977.

We estimate that the undiscounted value of the windfall was equal to 25% of 1975 GDP. The rest of this paragraph sets out the basis for this estimate. To construct a counterfactual for the 1976–79 period we assume that without the boom the barter terms of trade would have remained constant at the 1975 level. We also take the actual export volumes as given. In fact in 1977 coffee exports were over 20% greater in volume than in 1975, and this was no doubt largely a response to the price increase: labour input on coffee rose, partly at the expense of other crops and partly at the expense of leisure. However, to count the increase in coffee output entirely as a windfall gain of the boom would be to ignore that it was achieved at a cost (and that some of it was the result of smuggling from Uganda). Since we cannot estimate the net effect, we make the conservative assumption that the trade shock had no effect on export volumes. Hence in Table 2.1, the counterfactual value of exports is obtained by dividing the actual value by the barter terms of trade index (the ratio of export and import prices). We then calculate the windfall as the difference between the actual and the counterfactual values of exports. This gives the windfall series shown in column (5) of Table 2.1. Deflating this by the import price index we obtain the real value of the boom at 1975 prices. To convert this windfall into the gain in permanent income had it been fully invested we need to know the rate of return on domestic capital formation. Since there is no reliable estimate we will use 10% to discount the real annual gains. This gives the present value of the boom in 1976 as K£232m. Again using 10%, this implies a permanent income increase of K£23m, equivalent to 2.1% of 1975 GDP.[3]

After a short period of uncertainty about the extent of the damage to the

Table 2.1. Magnitude of the coffee boom

	Value of exports (1)	Price indices		Counterfactual (4)	Windfall at current prices (5)	Windfall at 1975 prices (6)
		Imports (2)	Exports (3)			
1975	230.4	100	100	230.4	—	—
1976	335.4	136	116	286.1	49.3	42
1977	480.3	193	125	311.1	169.2	135
1978	370.0	163	132	299.6	70.4	53
1979	385.5	174	153	339.0	46.5	30
Total 1976–89					335.4	261

Notes:
Col. (1) = values in K£m (current prices), from *Statistical Abstract* 1981 (hereafter *SA 81*), p. 66
Cols. (2), (3) = price indices of exports and imports, from *SA 81*, p. 82
Col. (4) = col. (1) times col. (3) divided by col. (2)
Col. (5) = col. (1) − col. (4)
Col. (6) = col. (5) deflated by col. (3)

Brazilian coffee trees, the boom's temporariness was widely known and accepted. The Kenyan government knew it to be temporary, stating 'Coffee prices cannot be expected to indefinitely remain at present high levels'.[4] The government took steps to convey this information to coffee farmers through the cooperatives and extension services.

2.2. Behaviour of the Representative Agent and of the Economy as a Whole

2.2.1. Asset Changes and Savings Rates

A fundamental aspect of responses to a temporary shock is the extent to which it is converted into a smaller permanent shock by means of changes in assets. In Kenya around half of windfall income appears to have been saved, whereas prior to the boom the savings rate had averaged around 20%. Not only was the overall windfall savings rate thus high, but its composition was noteworthy. In the first two years of the boom aggregate windfall savings were driven by foreign asset accumulation, which was so substantial that the usual net capital inflow became an outflow. In the last two years foreign borrowing was resumed in earnest, so that over the whole period of the boom indebtedness increased, but there was an unprecedented investment boom. In outline, then, the coffee boom induced an investment boom which was lagged behind the income gain through the accumulation and decumulation of foreign assets. Indeed, as we show in Section 2.3, the repercussions of the boom extended well beyond the

Table 2.2. Counterfactual growth and capital formation

	Actuals		Counterfactuals			Windfall GFKF	
	GFKF/ income at current prices (FX) % imports (1)	Real income (GDP at 1975 prices and windfall) (2)	GFKF (3)	Real income (4)	GFKF/Y (5)	GFKF (6)	Annual (7)
1972	25.1						
1973	24.6						
1974	21.7						
1975	22.9	1,054.4	241.9	1,054.4	22.9	241.9	0.0
1976	22.8	1,143.7	259.1	1,101.2	23.5	258.8	2.0
1977	23.9	1,332.1	317.8	1,196.9	24.2	289.7	28.1
1978	28.9	1,328.8	383.7	1,273.2	24.8	315.7	68.0
1979	27.3	1,360.2	371.8	1,320.8	24.8	327.5	44.3

Notes:
Col. (1) = SA 87, table 37 (a) and corresponding tables for earlier years
Col. (2) = SA 84, table 37(b) and corresponding tables for earlier years for GDP at 1976 prices, converted to 1975 prices by the factor 0.864 (from SA 83 tables 37(a) and (b)), plus windfall at 1975 prices from Table 2.1 above
Col. (3) = col. (1) times col. (2)
Col. (4) = in 1975 and 1976 actual GDP at 1975 prices, in 1977–79 also corrects for returns on windfall investment, lagged one year
Col. (5) = linear reversion to 1972–73 average by 1979
Col. (6) = col. (4) times col. (5)
Col. (7) = col. (3) minus col. (6)

period of boom income. However, in this section we confine our estimate of windfall savings to asset changes made during the period in which income was atypically high. The rest of this section sets out the basis for this estimate, distinguishing between three components of savings: gross fixed capital formation (GFKF), inventory accumulation and foreign assets.

To estimate the savings rate from windfall income we must define a counterfactual to the observed changes in assets. For this we must specify counterfactual income and counterfactual propensities to acquire assets (domestic and foreign) out of income. First consider the propensity to acquire domestic assets in the form of capital formation (GFKF). The actual propensity to GFKF out of income (at current factor cost prices) is shown in the first column of Table 2.2. It is at once evident from this series that GFKF in 1978 and 1979 was abnormally high, whereas at the onset of the boom it was abnormally low, most likely because of the oil shock. It is difficult to determine a normal GFKF propensity because a major break in the National Accounts between 1971 and 1972 drastically reduces the number of 'normal' (i.e. pre-boom and pre-oil shock) years which can be observed.

To convert expenditure on GFKF into real terms the propensities shown in column (1) are applied to a series of real income.[5] Were there no terms of trade shock, the real income series would simply be GDP at constant (1975) prices. However, this would be to omit the windfall. Hence, real income is the sum of GDP at constant 1975 prices plus the windfall as estimated in Table 2.1: it is shown in the second column of the table. The value of GFKF at 1975 prices is, then, the propensity shown in column (1) times real income and is shown in column (3).

We now need counterfactual income and propensities. In 1975 counter-factual income would have been actual GDP at constant prices. There are three alternative methodologies for constructing a GDP counterfactual for subsequent years: extrapolation from past GDP growth, simulation through a model, or subtraction of estimated windfall growth from actual growth. The first of these approaches is unattractive because Kenyan growth has been far from steady. The second we have attempted else-where, using a CGE model (Bevan *et al.* 1990). Here we therefore adopt the third approach. We apply an assumed rate of return (10%) and a one-year gestation lag to windfall investment. Hence, in 1976 counterfactual in-come is again actual GDP. In subsequent years it is actual GDP at constant prices minus the assumed 10% return upon the cumulative windfall in-vestment of previous years. The latter is calculated as the difference between actual and counterfactual investment and for this we need a counterfactual investment propensity. The actual propensity to GFKF out of income was higher in 1972 and 1973 than during the oil shock period 1974–75. We assume that in the absence of the boom there would have been a gradual reversion to the average of the 1972–73 period by 1978. The counterfactual propensity is then linearly interpolated between the actual 1975 value and this posited 1978 value. The resulting series for windfall investment (column 7), can be checked by its implication for behaviour in 1976 and 1977. Since investment out of unplanned income is likely to be lagged, the propensity to invest in 1976 out of 1976 windfall income should be negligible. This is indeed what the counterfactual implies. Windfall income is K£42m (Table 2.1) but windfall investment is only K£2.0m. Hence, the present counterfactual yields credible implications.[6] Overall, the counterfactual implies that during the period windfall GFKF was K£142.4m at 1975 prices.

The analysis is now repeated for the propensity to accumulate foreign debt. Foreign savings at 1975 prices (deflated by the imports deflator) as a proportion of real income at 1975 prices are shown in the first column of Table 2.3. As might be expected, the period 1974–75 was atypical due to the oil shock: indebtedness was increased far more rapidly than during 1972–73. Again we assume a gradual adjustment process back to the 1972–73 average, reached by 1978. As before, the counterfactual propensity for

Table 2.3. Actual and counterfactual foreign savings

	Foreign savings propensity (%)		Foreign savings (K£m at 1975 prices)		
	Actual (1)	Counterfactual (2)	Actual (3)	Counterfactual (4)	Windfall (5)
1972	3.49				
1973	2.02				
1974	8.70				
1975	5.32				
1976		4.47	−8.7	49.2	−57.9
1977		3.61	−50.1	43.2	−93.3
1978		2.76	151.4	35.1	116.3
1979		2.76	89.2	36.4	52.8

Notes:
Col. (1): source as col. (1) of Table 2.2
Col. (2): see test
Col. (3): source as col. (1) of Table 2.2 deflated by the imports deflator
Col. (4): col. (2) times counterfactual income as given in col. (4) of Table 2.2
Col. (5): col. (3) minus col. (4)

1976–77 is a linear interpolation between the actual 1975 figure and this posited 1979 value.

Counterfactual foreign savings are then derived as this counterfactual propensity times the counterfactual income derived in Table 2.2. Cumulated over the period this constitutes a net increase in indebtedness of K£17.9m as a result of the windfall. This implies that the increase in income as a result of the coffee boom increased the perceived debt capacity of the economy.

The final component of windfall savings comes from inventory behaviour. With GFKF and foreign borrowing we have based a counterfactual upon behaviour in the years immediately preceding the boom (recall that a longer series is precluded by a break in the National Accounts). This approach is quite unsuitable for inventory behaviour because of its much greater volatility. For example, in 1975 there was heavy de-stocking which was clearly unsustainable. Since any estimate of savings owing to inventory behaviour would be highly precarious we have adopted the assumption that actual and counterfactual inventory accumulation were coincident, so that windfall savings from this source were zero. Since inventory accumulation was in fact high during the coffee boom years this probably leads to an under-estimate of the overall windfall savings rate. However, it prevents our estimate from being contaminated by an indefensible component.

We now bring the counterfactuals together and derive savings rates out of transient income. We first discount the estimates of windfall assets and transient income to present values. The discounted present value of windfall GFKF is K£117.0m and that of the changes in foreign indebtedness is −K£6.9m.[7] Windfall savings out of windfall income is, then, the sum of these less a small adjustment of K£1.7m for savings at the normal rate out of the permanent increase in income arising from windfall investment, making a total of K£122.2m.[8] Recall that the terms of trade change itself, discounted at 10%, was worth K£232m. The propensity to save out of windfall income is thus windfall savings (K£122.2m) divided by windfall income (K£232m), which is 52.7% of windfall income. We conclude that in aggregate a high fraction of the windfall was saved.[9] We will show later that this estimate masks large differences in savings rates between the private and the public sectors.

2.2.2. Goods Markets

We now turn to the impact of the boom in goods markets. An unanticipated gain in permanent income will normally lead to a rise in demand for non-tradables and hence an increase in their relative price (the *spending effect* of Dutch Disease). A transient windfall which leaves permanent income unaltered may have no spending effect, but instead lead to a 'construction boom': a rise in demand for non-tradable capital goods. Hence, the permanent/transient distinction has implications not only for savings rates as explored above, but for relative prices: specifically, for whether the boom chiefly raises the price of non-tradable consumer goods or the price of non-tradable capital goods. In this section we show that the Kenyan coffee boom gave rise to only a weak spending effect but to a powerful construction boom.

A measure of the spending effect is to estimate the price of non-tradable consumer goods relative to that of tradables. In Figure 2.1 we use sector-specific GDP deflators as proxies for this relative price. There was only a modest rise in the price of non-tradable consumer goods in the years in which windfall expenditure took place. Further, as we discuss below, this measure is probably picking up the effect of an endogenous trade liberalisation.

Now consider capital goods and in particular the construction sector. As shown in Figure 2.2, the income boom was rapidly transmitted into higher demand for traded capital goods. Already in 1977 volume was far higher than any plausible counterfactual. The boom in demand for non-tradable capital goods was markedly smaller and lagged the income windfall by some two years. This is probably because of differential implementation lags. First, windfall savings must be translated into investment plans, this lag being common to tradable and non-tradable capital goods. Second, these plans must be realised. It is easier to increase pur-

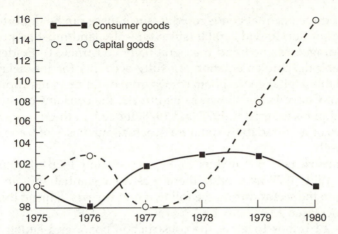

Figure 2.1. Prices of non-tradable capital and consumer goods relative to import substitutes (*1975 = 100*)

Note: The consumer non-tradable sector is here defined as electricity and water; wholesale and retail trade and restaurants and hotels; transport, storage and communications; finance, insurance, real estate and business services; other services in the monetary economy; and domestic services purchased by private households. Import substitutes are proxied by manufacturing.

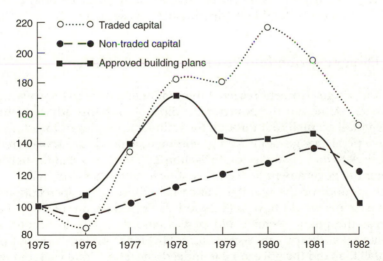

Figure 2.2. Traded and non-traded capital goods at constant prices (*1975 = 100*)

Source: *Economic Survey* (1978: tables 12.6 and 12.7; and corresponding tables for other years).

chases of traded capital goods rapidly (since these can be imported) than purchases of non-traded capital (since typically land must be purchased and buildings designed and then gradually constructed). Evidence that this differential implementation lag fully accounts for the delay in the non-tradable capital goods boom comes from building plans approved by Municipal Councils. As shown in Figure 2.2, the constant price value of approved plans jumped in 1977 and 1978. Indeed, in these years planned purchases of non-tradable capital track actual purchases of traded capital quite closely.

The construction boom thus took place during 1978–81 rather than 1976–79. With 1977 as a base, there was a substantial shift in relative output into the sector during the following four years. During this period output increased at its peak by 14% relative to GDP.

Figure 2.1 brings together the construction boom and Dutch Disease. The central prediction of construction boom theory is borne out: the price of non-tradable capital goods rose substantially relative to the price of non-tradable consumer goods during the coffee boom. Further, the path of the relative price is consistent with the different consumption and investment lags.

To conclude, as a result of the temporary terms of trade gain there were two boom sectors: the beneficiary of the primary price increase (the coffee- and tea-growing sector) and the beneficiary of the induced price increase in non-tradable capital goods (the construction sector).

2.3. Disaggregation into Private and Public Sectors

The Kenyan government received international advice to levy a windfall coffee tax. Although the government did not take this advice, some of the windfall accrued to it through the indirect tax system. Offsetting this, relative price changes and extra government expenditure transferred income back to the private sector. In Section 2.3.1 we show that the net effect was for the government to acquire just over half of the windfall.

The ground for the windfall coffee tax advice was a perception that private agents would have unduly low savings rates out of the windfall whereas the public sector could play a custodial role. In Section 2.3.2 we show that the private sector had a far higher savings rate out of its windfall than did the government. Indeed, the latter's rate was somewhat lower than the pre-boom average savings rate for the economy. Further, the public current expenditure boom persisted after the end of the coffee boom, financed in part by a squeeze on public investment. Once this induced fall in subsequent investment is included, the public sector savings rate from the windfall may well have been negative. The boom substantially changed the phasing of public capital formation rather than its total. Investment was shifted from the early 1980s to 1979–80; that is, it became powerfully pro-cyclical with the private investment boom, thereby reinforcing the construction boom.

2.3.1. *Revenue and Expenditure Transmission Mechanisms Between the Two Sectors*

The initial or impact incidence of a trade shock may accrue predominantly to either public or private sectors, depending on the division of economic activities between them and the nature of the shock. The ultimate incidence may, however, be markedly different from that at impact. The major mechanisms for transmitting gains or losses between public and private agents are changes in government revenue and changes in government expenditure. Government spending has three potential consequences for the private sector. First, it may provide services which are productive, either because they enhance private production or because they are of direct utility to private agents. Second, it will usually alter the pattern of demand and may in consequence alter the relative price of nontradables. Third, it may consist of payments to labour or other transfers which directly enhance the purchasing power of the private sector. Only if incremental public expenditure is both unproductive and confined to purchases of tradable goods will it leave the private sector's opportunities unaffected.

As regards incremental revenue, there are again three components to consider. First, there may be some direct taxation of the trade windfall itself (or a corresponding reduction in taxes when the shock is adverse). Second, there is a further increment in government revenue, associated with the increase in private disposable income and spending. Third, there may be, as in the case of expenditure, relative price changes consequent upon the structure of these incremental revenues. Analytically, it is appropriate to distinguish between increments in non-tradable taxes, direct windfall taxation, and any other incremental taxes on tradables. Whether the latter distinction is important depends on the nature of the shock. It is of least significance if the shock is of the inclusive variety and of greatest significance if it is of the exclusive, unrevised variety.

In this section we operationalise these concepts. As we have already stressed, the coffee boom was perceived to be temporary by both public and private agents. The government chose not to levy any direct windfall taxation but to allow the whole benefit to accrue to private growers. Hence, while we have categorized the boom as exclusive and unrevised, and so an appropriate target for windfall taxation, this option was not exercised by the government. There is little evidence that the government's incremental spending was productive. In time-series regressions a dummy variable for the boom years is significant in explaining total public expenditure but not for any of its productive components such as health, education, water or roads.[10] In consequence, the major transmission mechanism relevant to the Kenyan windfall is the relatively involuntary and automatic increase in revenue arising from additional private spending, which transferred part of the gain to the public sector. Additionally, there is a rise in public spending which returns part of this transfer to the private sector. Since the increase in spending exceeded the original increase in revenue, and was longer lived, it had second-round effects, necessitating discretionary increases in taxation and also exacerbating the budget deficit.

To examine the consequences of the coffee boom, it is necessary to construct a counterfactual assumption as to how fiscal policy would have evolved in its absence. It is clear that a major part of the fiscal response to the coffee boom, namely the public expenditure boom, was deferred until after 1979, so it is necessary to extend the analysis, at least until 1983.

Transmission from private income to public revenue and expenditure Table 2.4 details the changing pattern of a number of fiscal aggregates, as percentages of GDP at factor cost, over the period 1970–83. Expenditure is divided into exhaustive expenditure (public consumption and gross fixed capital formation) and transfers (domestic interest payments, foreign interest payments, and unrequited transfers). The difference between revenue and exhaustive expenditure defines the 'primary' surplus: the excess of transfers over this determines the overall deficit, which must be financed by a combination of net domestic and foreign borrowing. The rationale for this framework is the assumption that exhaustive expenditures (such as civil service salaries) have some claim to autonomy, because they are relatively hard to adjust: transfers then play, to some extent, an accommodating role, and fiscal rectification ultimately requires the government to achieve an appropriate relationship between revenue and exhaustive expenditure.

The relative size of the budget (measured by exhaustive expenditure as a percentage of GDP) increased dramatically after 1977. Hence, the coffee boom was followed by a rapid expansion in government spending. In addition the decline in the early 1980s suggests that the levels attained at the turn of the decade were perceived as an overshooting of what was appropriate or desirable, and official documents support this view.

Further, despite the intention of the government to raise capital formation following the boom, and its initial success in raising the development component of the budget relative to the recurrent component, the bulk of the increased spending was in the form of consumption. By the end of the period government capital formation was a smaller share of GDP than in 1975, while consumption was several percentage points higher.

Finally, the increases in government revenue and borrowing came from

Table 2.4. Fiscal pattern (*percentages of GDP at factor cost*)

	Total revenue (1)	Consumption (2)	GFKF (3)	Total exhaustive expenditure (4)	Primary surplus (5)	Unrequited transfers (6)	Domestic interest (7)	Foreign interest (8)	Total transfers (9)	Overall deficit (10)	Net domestic borrowing (11)	Net foreign borrowing (12)
1970	20.8	13.5	4.7	18.2	2.6	3.3	0.7	0.6	4.6	2.0	0.4	1.7
1971	22.8	15.6	5.7	21.2	1.6	2.8	0.8	0.6	4.2	2.6	1.2	1.4
1972	21.1	15.3	5.6	20.8	0.2	2.3	0.7	0.7	3.7	3.5	1.4	2.1
1973	21.6	15.1	5.3	20.5	1.1	2.4	0.8	0.7	3.8	2.7	0.8	2.0
1974	22.6	15.8	5.0	20.8	1.8	2.6	0.8	0.6	4.0	2.2	0.7	1.5
1975	23.8	18.3	5.0	23.3	0.5	2.0	1.0	0.6	3.7	3.1	0.8	2.3
1976	23.4	18.4	5.0	23.4	0.0	1.1	1.1	0.6	2.8	2.8	0.7	2.2
1977	24.1	18.1	5.0	23.1	1.0	1.0	1.1	0.7	2.8	1.8	0.3	1.4
1978	27.5	21.4	5.6	27.0	0.5	1.4	1.4	0.7	3.6	3.1	0.8	2.2
1979	28.7	22.4	6.3	28.8	-0.1	1.5	1.4	0.9	3.8	3.8	0.8	3.0
1980	29.9	23.0	6.9	30.0	-0.1	1.8	1.4	1.2	4.4	4.5	1.0	3.5
1981	28.6	24.0	5.6	29.6	-1.0	2.0	2.0	1.6	5.6	6.6	2.8	3.8
1982	27.4	23.3	4.4	27.7	-0.3	1.6	2.7	1.8	6.1	6.4	3.1	3.3
1983	26.9	21.8	3.4	26.2	0.7	1.8	3.0	2.0	6.7	6.0	2.3	3.7

Notes: Col. (4) = col. (2) plus col. (3)
Col. (5) = col. (1) minus col. (4)
Col. (9) = sum of cols. (6), (7) and (8)
Col. (10) = col. (9) minus col. (5) = col. (11) plus col. (12)
Sources: Bevan *et al.* (1989a), table 1

indirect taxation and foreign debt, respectively. The contribution of direct taxation to revenue (not shown in the table) was very stable throughout the period, varying between 7% and 8% of GDP; the rise in revenue was primarily through indirect taxation, which rose from 12.3% of GDP in 1975 to peak at 17.0% in 1981. The main increases took place in the period 1978–80, when sales taxes and some import duties were raised in order to finance the raised levels of expenditure which had been triggered by the boom. The bulk of the government's net borrowing was foreign throughout the period. This implies that the government's failure to balance its budget largely took a deferred form, building up future debt-servicing problems, rather than immediately crowding out private domestic capital formation.

In order to determine whether these fiscal changes can be attributed to the boom we construct a counterfactual case. We use the calculations of the terms of trade windfall shown in Table 2.1 and the counterfactual GDP series constructed in Table 2.2. We concentrate on revenue and exhaustive expenditure and assume that the 1975 fiscal pattern would have been maintained in the counterfactual. The 1975 fiscal pattern is then applied to the counterfactual GDP series to generate counterfactual time-series of fiscal aggregates. The differences may be considered as fiscal changes resulting from the boom and are shown in Table 2.5. This shows the powerful ratchet effect of the boom. The government does not merely spend out of its windfall income plus any continuing income accruing from windfall investment; what would be a temporary increase is trans-

Table 2.5. Fiscal changes owing to the boom (*K£m in 1975 prices*)

	Total Revenue (1)	Consumption (2)	GFKF (3)	Total Exhaustive Expenditure (4)	Primary Surplus (5)
1976	4.2	8.1	1.5	9.5	−5.3
1977	36.6	22.7	6.1	28.9	7.7
1978	48.4	41.1	7.4	48.5	0.0
1979	76.8	63.7	20.2	84.1	−7.3
1980	86.7	67.5	27.4	94.9	−8.2
1981	72.9	85.5	9.3	94.7	−21.8
1982	57.6	77.5	−8.1	69.4	−11.8
1983	52.7	58.2	−9.1	49.2	3.4

Notes: Col. (4) = col. (2) plus col. (3)
Col. (5) = col. (1) minus col. (4)

Sources: Table 2.4 and computations described in text

formed into a long-lived increase because of the relative irreversibility of government expenditure. This sustained rise in turn forces accommodating increases in taxation or borrowing, or both.

From column (5), it emerges that revenue was not raised sufficiently to match the boom-induced increase in expenditure. The cumulative deterioration in the primary surplus over the period is K£43.3m.

While caution must be exercised in interpreting any counterfactual, the implications are quite striking. Despite the lack of any serious effort to tax the windfall, government revenue rose over the period 1976–79 (relative to the counterfactual) by nearly 65% of the undiscounted value of the windfall.[11] This very high level of the government's share reflects the energy with which the authorities set out to increase discretionary revenue during the later years of the boom.

The transmission of the public expenditure on to private incomes In Kenya the principal transmission mechanism between public and private agents was clearly from the latter to the former by means of windfall government tax revenue. However, the public expenditure boom which this induced in turn transferred windfall income back to the private sector through various mechanisms. Here we consider such mechanisms, though it should be stressed that in the context of the Kenyan boom they are only of a second order of importance.

In addition to any direct benefits of public expenditure (which we have suggested were modest in this instance), there are three mechanisms which can potentially transfer windfall income to private agents as a result of a public expenditure boom. The first involves rents in the public sector labour market. If there is a wage differential in favour of the public sector, then if public sector employment increases as part of windfall expenditure, the rents from public sector employment will increase. To estimate the changes in such rents thus requires two components: quantifying the public sector wage premium, and quantifying counterfactual public sector employment growth in order to identify boom-induced increases in employment. A simple counterfactual is to assume that any boom-related change in public sector employment had been nullified by 1986. The path of actual public sector employment can then be compared with that which would have occurred had the growth rate which applied for the end-points of the period 1976–86 also applied in each year.

Between 1976 and 1986 public sector employment grew at an annual rate of 5.3%. However, during the boom years growth was more rapid. Such a counterfactual has various biases. However, there are strong grounds for regarding this transmission mechanism as unimportant because any wage premium in favour of the public sector was small. There is good evidence for this from surveys of the wage labour force in 1971

(Johnson 1971), 1977/78 (Bigsten 1983) and 1980 (Knight and Sabot 1989). All three concluded that there was no significant premium for the public sector as a whole, although there might be a small premium for the uneducated. Johnson, for example, found a 16% premium for the non-unionised unskilled. As an upper bound we adopt this 16% premium for the whole of the public sector, though it should be recognised that a more defensible figure would be zero. The rents which such a premium would imply given the magnitude of boom-induced employment expansion are small even at their peak in 1980 (K£3.7m). We have already estimated that windfall public revenue in 1980 was K£141m at current prices,[12] so that even at its peak this mechanism was transferring only 3% of the public revenue windfall back to the private sector as labour market rents.

The second transfer mechanism also works through the labour market. If wages rise as a result of the boom then existing public sector wage earners receive a boom-induced windfall. Prima facie, however, there is no boom-attributable rise in public sector wages. From 1976 onwards there is a fairly steady fall. The counterfactual is particularly problematic in this case. First, Collier and Lal (1986) show that real wages had been falling since the late 1960s and that this can be interpreted as a gradual movement to equilibrium which still had some way to go as of the mid-1970s. Second, the oil shock sharply reduced the equilibrium wage. The former effect would imply that the counterfactual is for wages to fall more rapidly in the late 1970s than in the early 1980s; the latter would imply the reverse. In fact, wages fell fairly continuously. In the peak expenditure year of 1980 they were a little below their long-run trend for 1976–85. There therefore seems to be no basis for attributing a wage increase to the coffee boom.

The final possible transmission mechanism works through the commodity market. Any boom-induced rise in the price of non-tradable goods will increase the cost of government purchases. Recall that for both consumer non-tradables and non-tradable capital goods there was a boom-induced price increase (see Figure 2.1). The former was so small that its transfer effect was negligible. The construction boom effects were, however, more powerful and are estimated in Table 2.6.

At its peak in 1980 around one-sixth of government windfall revenue was transferred back to the private sector in the form of rents on the sale of non-tradable capital goods to the public sector.

Taken together, the three mechanisms imply that by 1980 possibly around one-fifth of the public revenue boom was transferred back to the private sector in the form of rents. Since this transfer peaked well after the primary private sector windfall, government actions had the effect of somewhat stretching the private income boom beyond the income windfall to the economy, shifting private windfall income from the coffee boom years to the public expenditure boom years.

Table 2.6. Transfers via the non-tradable capital goods market

	Non-traded capital goods price premium (1)	Government expenditure on non-tradable capital (K£million, current prices) (2)	Transfer (K£million) (3)
1977	1	710.2	0.7
1978	3	381.0	2.4
1979	11	108.3	12.0
1980	16	125.2	20.0
1981	16	117.9	18.9

Notes: Parastatals are excluded from the public sector. The price premium is measured as the increase in the prices of non-traded capital goods relative to import substitutes against the 1975 level
Col. (3) = col. (2) times ((col. (1) divided by 100) minus 1)

Sources: as Fig. 2.1 and Table 2.5

2.3.2. Use of the Windfall

In estimating aggregate windfall savings rates we confined our analysis to the period of the income boom (1976–79). This has an obvious rationale: windfall savings arise out of windfall income. To decompose savings between the public and private sectors we therefore estimate public sector savings over the same period, deriving private savings residually. However, such an analysis leaves the public sector asset story only half-told. By the end of 1979, although the coffee boom was over, the public expenditure boom was in full swing and the budget in deepening deficit. During the first half of the 1980s the budget was rectified by retrenching investment. Thus, the public asset accumulation during the boom was followed by induced decumulation after the boom. Once this is allowed for, the public savings rate out of the windfall is substantially lowered.

First, we focus on decomposition of windfall assets during the boom period. The relative contributions of the public and private sectors to fixed capital formation may be assessed by bringing together the counterfactual exercises in Tables 2.2, 2.3 and 2.5.

Overall, these calculations attribute nearly one-quarter of induced capital formation during the coffee boom to the central government. Offsetting this cumulative capital formation (which, discounted at 10%, has a present value of K£28.3m) was the small cumulative deterioration in the primary surplus attributed to the boom (Table 2.5), which has a present value of K£3.8m. Public assets thus rose by only K£24.5m, whereas in total assets rose by K£122.2m (from Section 2.2), leaving as a residual an increase in private assets of K£97.7m. Recall that the present value of the windfall was K£232.5m, of which K£135m accrued to the government in increased revenues (Table 2.5). However, some of this was transferred back to the private sector through rents on government purchases of non-tradable capital goods as estimated in Table 2.6. The present value of these transfers for the period to 1979 was K£11.6m. Hence, net of this transfer, public windfall income was K£123.4m and private K£109.1m. While the overall savings rate out of transient income was 53% per cent in the boom period, that of the government was 20% and that of the private sector was 90%. While this estimate of the private rate is too high to be plausible, there are two independent reasons to believe that it was indeed very high.

First, for an important subset of private agents, peasant coffee farmers, we have direct evidence that the windfall savings propensity was indeed high. In the first year of the boom coffee farmers saved around 45% of windfall income in bank deposits. This can be concluded from a study of the coffee cooperative in Muranga (15% of all Kenyan coffee farmers). The mean bank deposit of these farmers in October 1976 was 950sh. By October 1977 it had risen to 2,970sh, thereafter gradually declining to 1,600sh by 1982. The normal annual addition to deposits was probably less than 100sh: there had been few new entrants to coffee in the decade to 1976 so the mean deposit of 950sh must have been accumulated over at least this period. Hence, during 1976–77 the mean deposit increased by 2,020sh, of which perhaps 100sh is accounted for by the pre-boom trend. Windfall coffee income per farmer in this period was 4,350sh.[13] Hence, in the first year the windfall savings rate into bank deposits was around 44% ((2,020 − 100)/4,350). These savings were subsequently spent, and we next investigate whether this was on consumption or investment.

For this we use panel survey evidence of 800 Kenyan farmers. During the boom years the mean coffee farmer in our sample received windfall income of 6,330sh. Over the period 1975–82 these farmers invested over four times as much in equipment and buildings as did farmers not growing coffee, despite having permanent incomes only 20% higher. The excess of their investment over that of other farmers (correcting for their higher permanent income) was 3,070sh, implying a propensity to invest in this form out of windfall income of 49%.[14] Coffee farmers were also significantly more likely to adopt improved livestock than other farmers during this period, and undertook substantial extra coffee planting, the two together constituting a 17% investment rate out of windfall income. Between them these identified forms of investment (which are by no means comprehensive) yield a 66% investment rate out of the windfall.[15]

The second reason to believe that the private sector savings rate was indeed very high is that there were powerful transfers in favour of profits. In effect, income was transferred from low-saving non-coffee-growing farmers to higher-saving firms supplying non-tradable goods. Potentially,

Table 2.7. Boom-induced capital formation (*K£million in 1975 prices*)

	Total	Government	Government share (%)
1976	2.0	1.5	75.0
1977	28.1	6.1	21.7
1978	68.0	7.4	10.9
1979	44.3	20.2	45.6
Cumulative 1976–79	142.4	35.2	24.7
1980		27.4	
1981		9.3	

this transfer effect can raise the aggregate private windfall savings rate in excess of 100%.

Now we extend the public asset story beyond 1979. First, the boom in public capital formation outlived the coffee boom (see Table 2.7). Boom-induced public capital formation peaked in 1980, the year in which the relative price of construction peaked (see Figures 2.1 and 2.2). Thus, the government contributed materially to causing the construction boom of 1979–81.

Second, beyond 1980 as the government retrenched upon capital formation in order to restore the budget, the impact of the coffee boom turned negative. Recurrent expenditure had been increased during the boom, and capital expenditure was reduced in order to maintain this new level of recurrent expenditure after the boom. For the period 1980–75, the NPV (discounted to 1976) of public capital formation relative to its counterfactual is −K£8.3m. Once this is included, the public sector savings rate out of windfall income falls to only 13%—that is, well below the normal savings rate for the economy.

2.4. The Control Regime

The government operated a wide-ranging control regime which had been put in place during the preceding decade. Some of these controls were a façade, others were binding. Price and wage controls were very largely a façade. A price commission notionally regulated consumer prices since the government needed to be seen to be 'doing something' about inflation. However, it did not attempt to hold prices below market-clearing levels. Wages were controlled in both directions: minimum-wage laws held wages above the supply price of labour for unskilled recruits; annual wage guidelines attempted to reduce wages in real terms. The minimum wage had tended to distort the wage structure while the incomes policy has been shown to have been slack: real wages were falling owing to market forces by more than required under the policy (see Collier and Lal 1986).

Nominal interest rate ceilings were imposed, so that real interest rates were negative. The banks were also constrained by a minimum cash-to-deposits ratio requirement set by the central bank. As a result of these controls there was financial repression: on the eve of the boom only around 15% of private sector capital formation was financed through the banking system. The government attempted to allocate bank loans to favoured sectors, but these allocations were not enforced.

The exchange rate was fixed to the SDR and was not seen as a policy instrument to be used actively. Exchange controls applied to capital movements. Although it was possible to bypass these controls through the black market or over-invoicing, penalties could be severe and the controls were vigorously enforced.

Finally, there were extensive controls over imports, usually in the form of quantitative restrictions. These had built up rapidly in response to the balance of payments crisis of 1972 and the oil crisis of 1974. Quantitative trade restrictions had become endogenous to the macroeconomic environment, accommodating monetary and exchange rate decisions. Phelps and Wasow (1972) had found that as of 1971 over 40% of consumer goods industries in the manufacturing sector had negative value-added at world prices. Between 1970 and 1976 the final output price of manufactures rose by a further 18% relative to their world prices. Hence, on the eve of the boom Kenya had a heavily protected manufacturing sector. We now consider the consequences of these controls.

2.4.1. Foreign Exchange Controls

As a result of foreign exchange controls private agents in aggregate faced a restricted choice as to which assets they might acquire with their remarkably high savings rates out of windfall income. In particular, they were denied access to foreign financial assets either as direct holders or, more likely, as indirect holders via the banking system.[16] The case for temporarily holding financial assets is that the investment boom is thereby stretched beyond the income and savings boom, enabling investment to take place when non-tradable capital goods prices are lower and returns (net of capital losses) higher. Since the private sector cannot, in aggregate, increase net financial claims against itself, the prohibition on foreign assets precludes it from acquiring financial assets unless the government permits an increase in fiat money. Hence, foreign exchange controls raise two issues. First, what would have been the rate of return on deferring investment by means of temporary foreign savings? Second, to what extent did the government permit private agents to acquire alternatives in the form of domestic financial assets? We consider these questions in turn.

The most attractive financial asset which private agents in aggregate could acquire was a claim on the government in the form of treasury bills. The relevant interest rate on these is the rediscount rate which the central bank will pay to commercial banks if they are cashed. On the world market, equivalent short-term financial assets were six-month Euro-currency deposits. Since the Kenyan currency was pegged to the SDR until 1981, the risk-minimising strategy, had private agents been free to hold such deposits, would have been to hold them in a basket of currencies corresponding to the Euro-dollar basket. We compare the return on Kenyan treasury bills with that on such a basket.[17]

First, consider windfall savings earned at the start of the boom (January 1976) and held in financial assets until the end of 1982. In Kenyan treasury bills the compound interest would have been 57%, whereas converted into foreign exchange, held in the Euro-currency market and finally reconverted, compound interest would have been 183%. The large difference between these returns represents a tax levied by the government on financial asset holding achieved by foreign exchange controls. A private agent who saved through treasury bills enabled the government to earn 183% interest and received 57%. This is equivalent to the government permitting private agents to hold foreign assets but taxing their cash-in value at 45% ($= 1 - (1.57/2.83)$). Such a high rate of implicit taxation presumably discouraged the acquisition of financial assets out of windfall income. One consequence is that the overall private savings rate out of the windfall would have been even higher in the absence of exchange controls; the other is an accelerated acquisition of capital goods, the effect of which we now quantify.

Recall that most of the windfall income accrued in 1977. Compare the return on saving income received at the end of 1977 with and without the constraint of exchange controls, if in both cases it ends up invested in non-traded capital goods. With controls it is probably best to make purchases of capital goods as soon as possible after the receipt of windfall income subject to the lags imposed by planning, purchase and construction. We will take as an example the case in which such lags amount to two years. Thus, K£100 held in treasury bills for two years would have accumulated to K£111.7 by end-1979. Without controls, shrewd private agents might have chosen to defer purchases of non-tradable capital goods until after the peak of the construction boom. Figure 2.2 shows that the boom was rapidly fading in the two years following its peak in 1980. Hence, we consider a strategy in which savings are held abroad until end-1982 and then switched into non-tradable capital goods. By this time the K£100 initially saved would have accumulated to K£251.3. Because non-tradable capital goods prices rose in nominal terms between end-1979 and end-1982 by 38%, this would have bought only K£182.6-worth of non-tradable capital goods at end-1979 prices. However, this is substantially more than the K£111.7 of such goods bought when exchange controls prevail. By using foreign financial assets to defer investment for three years the shrewd unconstrained investor ends up with 63% more capital goods. Hence, the annual real rate of return on investment which the constrained investor must earn during those three years in order to match this performance is 17.8%. This seems implausibly high even as a long-term rate of return on capital in Kenya. Further, during 1980–82, because of the investment boom, firms were presumably being forced to accept atypically low returns.

To conclude, exchange controls had effects equivalent to the government levying a 45% tax on the value of financial assets held abroad. This discouraged private agents from deferring their investment, a strategy which would have had a real annual rate of return of 17.8% between end-1979 and end-1982. Thus, exchange controls constituted a powerful disincentive to a strategy which would have yielded a very high real social rate of return.

2.4.2. Financial Repression

In an initially credit-constrained economy such as Kenya, many private agents wished to borrow more than was available prior to the boom. One side-effect of the foreign exchange controls was that the increased asset demand for domestic money gave rise to a temporary financial liberalisation. There were two possible routes by which this could come about, depending upon the initial cause of financial repression. The government used two instruments to control the banking system, the cash-to-deposits ratio and interest rate ceilings. The latter reduced the flow of savings deposits to the banks, the former restricted their capacity to make loans given their deposit flow. As we have seen, the government permitted an increase in fiat money, so that for a given cash ratio and savings behaviour, more could be lent. Additionally, as we have seen, the savings propensity rose sharply: those agents who received windfall income and wished to save it could lend it to initially rationed agents. This build-up of financial savings was disproportionately held in the form of bank deposits. The combined result was a substantial increase in the liquid assets of the banking system: more money could be lent.

The control regime included both maximum and minimum interest rates on bank loans: in 1975 these were 10% and 8% respectively (Central Bank of Kenya, *Quarterly Economic Review*, April 1988, table 1.8.2). The maximum rate was maintained constant throughout the boom[18] but the capacity of the banks to lend expanded so substantially that this regulation rapidly ceased to be a binding constraint. The minimum interest rate regulation would have become binding but was suspended from 1977 onwards.[19] Reviewing the banking system during 1977 the government commented that 'lending was a problem for some financial institutions and particularly in the middle of the year some reserves available for short-term borrowing could not find lending outlets even at near-zero rates of interest' (*Economic Survey* (1978), p. 36). The liquidity ratio, the minimum for which was set at 18%, rose from 19% at the end of 1975 (when it was presumably binding) to a peak of 37% through the third quarter of 1977. Even by the end of 1979 it had only fallen to 23%.[20] Thus, between 1976 and 1980 the maximum lending rate temporarily ceased to bind and credit was readily available at low nominal rates of interest. As we have seen in Section 2.2, the sector which undertook the dominant share of windfall investment was manufacturing industry, and we now consider the real interest rates which it faced during this period. Between 1976 and 1980 the rate of inflation for value-added in the manufacturing sector averaged 8.6%. Although there are no data as to the average interest rate paid on advances, the fact that the 8% minimum requirement had to be abandoned between 1976 and 1980, together with the government's comment concerning 'near-zero rates of interest' suggests that in real terms interest rates were significantly negative.

Since the commercial banks were unable to lend out all their available funds even at these rates, it suggests that had firms drawn up additional investment plans with positive real returns they would have been able to finance them at a profit. That firms did not do this presumably implies that such opportunities were already being exhausted by the investment boom. A crucial implication of this is that the real (private) *ex ante* rate of return upon the marginal investment project undertaken during the period was probably very low, and may well have been zero or even negative.

The temporary financial liberalisation permitted an increase in financial intermediation for investment. This can be quantified through central bank data on advances which are classified partly by sector and partly by use. From these we have constructed proxies for advances used to finance capital formation in the enterprise sector.[21] Loans outstanding at the end of each year are then deflated by the manufacturing GDP deflator[22] to 1975 constant prices. Although the annual change in the real value of these loans, which is the proxy for new lending to enterprises for investment, is rather volatile, there was a major expansion of credit during 1978 and 1979 followed by a credit squeeze in 1982–83. Indeed, so substantial was the expansion at its peak in 1978 that despite the investment boom an increased proportion of investment was financed through the banking system: 20% as opposed to only 15% during 1975–76.[23]

Financial liberalisation also enabled previously credit-constrained agents to borrow for consumption. Had this been widespread, it would have been possible for recipients of the windfall to have had a very high savings rate (as they did) while the private sector as a whole had no increase in savings. Although it is not possible to construct an adequate proxy for bank advances to finance consumption, the fact that net savings rose so substantially suggests that this effect was relatively minor.

Potentially, the temporary financial liberalisation was highly beneficial. Financial intermediation should improve the efficiency of investment allocation. By being synchronised with the investment boom, this improvement in efficiency occurred when it was of most use. However, this inference must be qualified somewhat. The banking system had been repressed for about a decade by the time of the temporary liberalisation. It may well not have had the knowledge base with which to identify appropriate borrowers. During the period of liberalisation a secondary banking fringe developed rapidly. This mainly borrowed from the deposit-taking banks and probably lent to finance construction. It cannot be assumed that private investment during the boom occurred in an allocatively efficient way.

2.4.3. Import Controls

In Kenya trade restrictions were pervasive and largely took the form of binding quotas. Faced with an influx of foreign exchange, the government had the choice of maintaining these controls or relaxing them partially or completely. The two extremes, maintenance or abolition, would each have caused severe problems. If quotas are kept constant then the only way the private sector can benefit from an improvement in the terms of trade is for export production to fall, releasing resources to the import substitute sector.[24] At the other extreme, if controls are abolished, private agents will rationally interpret this as a temporary event associated with the boom (we refer to such a policy rule as an 'endogenous trade policy'). They will then import consumer durables and intermediate goods in anticipation of subsequent controls, with the coincident temporary financial liberalisation easing the financing of this inventory accumulation.

We now investigate what actually happened to trade policy. Changes in the trade regime cannot be inferred directly from tariff schedules or tariff revenue because of the prevalence of quotas. Instead, we use two distinct measures. The first is the ratio of total private consumption to household consumption of imports. As can be seen from Figure 2.3, this ratio changes very substantially over the boom. Changes in the volume of consumer imports relative to the volume of private consumption should reflect changes in the ratio of domestic price of importable consumer goods to

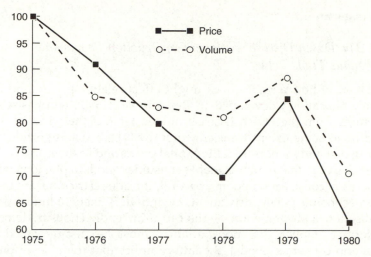

Figure 2.3. Two measures of trade policy (*1975 = 100*)

Note: Price = domestic price/world price of import substitutes; volume = volume of total private consumption/volume of household imports.

Source: Bevan *et al.* (1990: figure 5.8).

non-tradable consumer goods. Between 1975 and 1980 the exchange rate was maintained constant against the SDR, so that the principal cause of these large and non-monotonic alterations is probably changes in trade policy. Figure 2.3 then compares this with a second measure of trade policy, the ratio of an index of the c.i.f. price of imports to an index of the final output price of domestic manufactures (using as weights the share in manufacturing output). The two measures tell a similar story.

Quite clearly, trade policy changed with the windfall. In 1976–78 there was a continuous liberalisation which was reversed in 1979 as the windfall receded. Knowing the endogenous trade policy rule, private agents would then rationally anticipate the reversal of the liberalisation, making pre-emptive purchases of imports of consumer durables. A proxy for imports of private consumer durables[25] indeed shows an enormous increase: during the peak liberalisation years of 1978 and 1980 the volume more than doubled relative to 1975. However, this increase is open to another interpretation. Even were there no import controls we would expect some increase in the consumption of durables as part of the response to high transient income. We have already seen that the private sector recognised boom income as transient, since it had such high savings and investment rates. Durables are the capital goods of the household sector.

2.5. Assessment

2.5.1. *The Dutch Disease Critique: Construction Booms and Endogenous Trade Policy*

The theory of how a trade shock might affect relative prices (and hence resource allocation), developed in Bevan *et al.* (1990), emphasised two departures from the Dutch Disease model. First, if the windfall is perceived as to some extent transient, there will be a disproportionate increase in demand for non-tradable capital goods and so their price is likely to rise relative to that of non-tradable consumer goods: a phenomenon we refer to as a 'construction boom'. Second, if trade restrictions are used as a macroeconomic policy instrument, a windfall is likely to induce a trade liberalisation: a phenomenon we refer to as an 'endogenous trade policy'. The former implies that non-tradables must be disaggregated (into capital and consumer goods), the latter implies that tradables should be disaggregated (into protected and unprotected). Each of these propositions has found support in our analysis of the Kenyan coffee boom. By contrast, the spending effect of Dutch Disease, which predicts a rise in the price of non-tradable consumer goods relative to non-boom tradables, was found to be negligible. Hence, using the Dutch Disease disaggregation into tradables and non-tradables in the case of the Kenyan coffee boom adds nothing significant to working with a single-aggregate model of the economy, while missing powerful effects which become apparent only with further disaggregation.

2.5.2. *The Public Sector*

As an agent in its own right The government correctly assessed the nature of the shock and elected to allow the benefits to accrue to producers. Even so, it received a substantial lagged share of the proceeds through the operation of the existing tax system and the temporary liberalisation of imports which the boom made possible and which we have argued was a rational response by government. Given the nature of the shock, it would probably have been optimal to have saved the bulk of this revenue gain: the long-run addition to permanent national income, and hence the desirable increase in the size of the public sector, were bound to be small. Hence, it was probably a mistake to attempt a rapid increase in public capital formation, even disregarding the danger of thereby inducing long-run increases in current expenditure, as proved to be the case. In addition, the presence of foreign exchange controls tended to exacerbate the construction boom which the windfall would in any case have induced. In these circumstances, the decision to invest was a mistake, albeit a very natural one. The failure to save sufficiently to cover this incremental investment, and hence the increase in the overall deficit, were also inadvisable, even within the boom period 1976–79 itself. Later, in the period 1980–85, public performance deteriorated still further, with capital investment and saving markedly down, and a widened deficit. Thus, the relatively small increase in saving in the first subperiod was wholly reversed in the second, and the entire increase in public capital formation over the period was ultimately financed by borrowing. To caricature the situation, the government should have saved but not invested: instead, it invested but did not save.

The regulatory framework Prior to the boom the government had enacted a wide-ranging control regime. In analysing the boom two aspects of this regime deserve emphasis: first, it had powerful repercussions on the capacity of private agents to utilise the windfall, and second, the government made relatively little attempt to modify the controls during the course of the boom. To take the latter point first, the fixed exchange rate was held constant, exchange controls were maintained constant and nominal interest rate ceilings were maintained constant. There were small modifications to the cash ratio requirement on banks and there were some relaxations of import quotas.

We have established reasonable grounds for concluding that this regulatory framework reduced the private windfall savings rate, accelerated the conversion of savings into local investment, thereby inefficiently amplifying the construction boom, induced a surge in imports of consumer durables and increased the price level. Foreign exchange controls operated like a 45% tax on the cash-in value of savings temporarily held in foreign assets. As such, they must surely have discouraged the saving of windfall income and induced a more rapid transformation of that part which was saved into real investment. We have shown that without exchange controls, had private agents taken advantage of foreign financial assets to defer investment by three years, they and the economy would have achieved around an 18% annual real return on savings so utilised. Exchange controls forced private agents into accepting returns which were probably very much lower than this. We have shown that there are good grounds for regarding the real rate of return on domestic investment as being zero at the margin during the boom period. Exchange controls thus seriously impaired the capacity of the economy to convert a temporary windfall into permanent income. Since a disproportionately large amount of an economy's savings take place during favourable temporary shocks, this effect can be serious even if such shocks are rare. The temporary liberalisation of import controls on consumer durables probably induced hoarding in anticipation of subsequent re-tightening: by 1978 such imports were more than double their 1975 level, falling back sharply in 1979. The hoarding of imported consumer durables is not a socially efficient form of saving. Finally, the fixed nominal exchange rate prevented what might otherwise have been a modest appreciation: on the black market the currency appreciated by 7%. It seems likely that such an appreciation would have reduced the price level.

In summary, it is hard to avoid the conclusion that if private agents could be trusted to recognise windfall income as transient, the Kenyan government was operating a control regime quite unsuited to a country prone to temporary favourable external shocks.

2.5.3. *The Private Sector*

Quite clearly private agents did recognize windfall income as transient. Our estimates for the entire private sector imply that the private savings rate out of windfall income was around 90%. While this is surely exaggerated, a high savings rate probably compounds two effects: not only was there conscious saving out of income perceived as transient, but there was a redistribution in favour of profits. However, the latter effect is certainly not the sole explanation: survey evidence shows coffee farmers to have had a windfall savings rate in excess of 66%. The private sector translated these savings into investment, disproportionately skewed towards the tradable sector of the economy and, in particular, import-substitute manufacturing. Inadvertently, this investment contributed to a powerful trade liberalisation in the early 1980s as the demand for imports fell even more rapidly than import volumes were reduced.

2.5.4. *The Public Sector's Role as Custodian*

This leads to a paradox. Given the lack of faulty perceptions or apparently irrational behaviour in the private sector, the main argument for custodial intervention by the public sector rests on the existence of controls operated by the public sector which interfere with private responses. However, the major weapon for such intervention would be compensatory taxation, and the track record of the government in handling the non-discretionary increase in revenues does not generate confidence that it would have handled a discretionary increase much better. Indeed, if discretionary changes had led to incremental expenditure consequences similar to those occasioned by non-discretionary ones, then government intervention would almost certainly have worsened the situation, notwithstanding the presence of controls.

NOTES

1. Import prices rose by 25% between 1975 and 1977 and coffee accounted for 16.4% of the value of exports in 1975.

2. Although coffee thus accounted for only 70% of the 1977 gain, we will refer to the entire terms of trade gain as the 'coffee boom'.

3. In relative terms this estimate is quite sensitive to the choice of discount rate; the permanent income gain is 1.1% of GDP for a 5% discount rate and 3.0% of GDP for a 15% discount rate. However, in all three cases the permanent income gain is small relative to GDP.

4. *Economic Survey* (1977, published in June 1977), p. 8.

5. Note that the resulting series does not show the volume of GFKF since it does not allow for changes in the relative price of capital goods to GDP. Rather, it shows the value of expenditure on GFKF in units of GDP at 1975 prices.

6. Since it would be implausible that windfall income in 1976 actually reduced investment, this places a bound upon the speed of recovery of the GFKF propensity to its 1972–73 average. Were we to assume a faster recovery (restoration by 1977 instead of 1978) then implied windfall GFKF in 1976 would be negative. A slower recovery than we have assumed would increase the estimate of windfall GFKF. Hence, our estimate of the windfall savings propensity is a lower bound.

7. That is, although undiscounted there is a rise in indebtedness of K£17.9m, because this occurs late in the period, the discounted present value of the changes is negative.

8. Our estimate of the 'normal' savings rate is the GFKF propensity minus the foreign indebtedness propensity. In 1979, for example, the sum of the two propensities is 22.0% and income from windfall GFKF is K£9.8m (Table 2.2). Hence, such savings amount to K£2.2m. The net present value of these savings over the period is only K£1.7m. Deducting this component of savings leaves windfall savings estimated at K£122.2m.

9. This result is insensitive to the discount rate. Repeating the calculation with discount rates of 5% or 15% we find windfall savings rates change by less than 3 percentage points.

10. These results are reported more fully in Bevan *et al.* (1989a).

11. By K£166.0m. This was skewed towards the end of the boom. In 1976 windfall revenue was only 11% of the value of the windfall to the economy and in 1977 only 27%.

12. Table 2.5 gives incremental revenue in 1980 as K£86.7m at 1975 prices, and the implicit GDP deflator for 1980 is 162.9, based to 1975.

13. The difference between actual coffee payments and those which would have been made had the volume of sales been the same but the price that of 1975 adjusted by inflation.

14. The survey was also conducted in Tanzania, where the coffee boom was taxed, so that farmers received virtually no windfall. The investment propensity of Tanzanian coffee farmers was 2.7%, not significantly different from nongrowers in either Tanzania (3.0%) or Kenya (2.8%). Hence, the very much higher investment propensity of Kenyan coffee farmers cannot be attributed to coffee farmers having inherently different behaviour from non-growers.

15. The details of this and the other calculations are set out in Bevan *et al.* (1989a).

16. That is, farmers for example might have had claims on banks denominated in domestic currency which the banks could have used to acquire foreign currency assets.

17. Until 1981 the SDR basket was a highly complex and varying basket of many currencies for some of which there was no Euro-currency market. In 1981 a simplified basket of five major currencies was adopted. Throughout, our calculations are based upon this latter basket.
18. In 1980 it was raised to 11%.
19. It was briefly reintroduced in 1980.
20. The statutory minimum was briefly raised to 20% in 1978.
21. Our proxy is commercial bank loans to enterprises in agriculture, mining, manufacturing, construction, electricity and water, and transport, and non-bank financial intermediary loans to agriculture, manufacturing and construction.
22. This deflator is chosen since manufacturing was the dominant sector to which loans were made.
23. New loans in 1975 were K£29.1m and in 1976 were K£16.1m. Converting the latter figure to current prices gives K£18.5m. Hence, at current prices new loans totalled K£47.6m. Private GFKF at current prices in those years was K£309.8m, so 15% of GFKF was loan financed. In 1978 new advances were K£48m at constant prices, K£64.3m at current prices, and GFKF was K£320.6m, so 20% of GFKF was loan financed.
24. This is brought about as follows. With fixed quotas importables behave as non-tradables at the margin. Increased demand drives up their price until it has risen relative to the export good, for only then will resources be induced to reallocate into the sector enabling the extra demand to be met. This is obviously highly inefficient, especially since the economy should use the period of high prices to increase export production.
25. The proxy is the sum of cars and televisions as reported in *SA*86 table 58(b) and *SA*81 tables 61(a) and (b), weighted at 1975 values in imports.

REFERENCES

Bevan, D.L, P. Collier and J.W. Gunning (1987) 'Consequences of a Commodity Boom in a Controlled Economy: Accumulation and Redistribution in Kenya 1975–83', *World Bank Economic Review*, Volume 1, Number 3.
—— (1989a) 'Fiscal Responses to a Temporary Trade Shock: The Aftermath of the Kenyan Coffee Boom', *World Bank Economic Review*, Volume 3, Number 4.
—— (1989b) *Peasants and Governments: An Economic Analysis*, Oxford: Clarendon Press.
—— (1990) *Controlled Open Economies: A Neoclassical Approach to Structuralism*, Oxford: Clarendon Press.
Bigsten, A. (1983) *Education and Income Determination in Kenya*, Aldershot: Gower.
Collier, P. and D. Lal (1986) *Labour and Poverty in Kenya: 1900–1980*, Oxford: Clarendon Press.
Harris, J.R. and M. Todaro (1970) 'Migration, Unemployment and Development: A Two Sector Analysis', *American Economic Review*, 60, 126–42.

Johnson, G.E. (1971) 'The Determination of Individual Hourly Earnings in Kenya', Discussion Paper 115, Nairobi: IDS.

Knight, J.B. and R.H. Sabot (1989) *Education, Productivity and Inequality*, Oxford: Clarendon Press.

Phelps, M.E. and Wasow, B. (1972) 'Measuring Protection and its Effects in Kenya', Working Paper 37, Nairobi: IDS.

3

Ghana's Management of a Temporary Windfall: The Cocoa Boom of 1976–77

DEBORAH WETZEL

The production and export of cocoa has been an integral part of the Ghanaian economy since the turn of the century. Until recently cocoa production accounted for about 10% of GDP and 60% of exports. The government has also relied on the cocoa export tax as a major source of revenue. With the exception of the early 1980s and very recent years, it has provided between 25% and 40% of total government revenues annually. For many years Ghana was the world's largest producer and exporter of cocoa. During the 1970s, however, (official) cocoa production declined dramatically, despite a quadrupling of world prices from 1975 to 1977. During this period, the economy entered a downward economic spiral from which it did not begin to recover until the mid-1980s.

In this chapter, we consider the effects on the Ghanaian economy of the cocoa boom in the context of recent developments in the theory of temporary trade shocks set out in earlier chapters. Given the importance of cocoa in Ghana, one would have expected that the quadrupling of world prices would have been a major boon to the economy. We have found that it only helped to mitigate economic decline. In Section 3.1, we assess the positive shock to the terms of trade resulting from the rise in cocoa prices in 1976–77 and estimate the magnitude of the windfall to the Ghanaian economy. Section 3.2 considers the response of the overall economy to the shock in terms of asset changes and savings rates, as well as relative prices, output and factor markets. Section 3.3 focuses on the response of the public sector to the shock and in particular on the government's management of the windfall income. Finally, Section 3.4 considers how the control regime that existed at the time prevented the economy from reaping the benefits of an extraordinary increase in the price of its principal export commodity. Note that, given the problems of data collection and extensive black-market activity during this period, the estimates made throughout this chapter should be viewed as indicators of orders of magnitude rather than as precise figures.

3.1. The Cocoa Boom and the Terms of Trade

Figure 3.1 shows the substantial increase and subsequent fall in the world price of cocoa that took place in the latter half of the 1970s. World market prices for cocoa reflect changes in the supply of cocoa, because of a low elasticity of demand for cocoa and cocoa products. Following the reduction of world inventories of semi-processed cocoa products in the early 1970s[1] and a decline in the world output of cocoa beans in 1976 and 1977, world market prices of cocoa more than quadrupled between 1975 and 1977; the average yearly price rose from 723 pounds sterling per metric ton in 1975 to 1,399 pounds sterling in 1976 and to 2,944 pounds sterling in 1977. The sharp decline in world output was largely the result of poor weather conditions, including a protracted drought from 1975 to 1977 in the West African producing countries.

Data from the Cocoa Marketing Board (CMB), which controls the purchase and sale of cocoa, show a slight increase in cocoa prices in 1977 and a substantial increase in 1978. Figure 3.2 shows price indices for cocoa beans and for total exports from 1975 to 1982.[2]

Both indices rise gradually in 1977, sharply in 1978, peak in 1979 and drop off after 1980, with the cocoa price falling more rapidly than that of total exports. The increases that occur in 1978 and 1979 in both indices are at least partly the result of the devaluation of the cedi in 1978 and 1979.[3] However, the increase in cocoa prices is the primary factor behind the rise in the overall index.

The explanation for the lag in cocoa price increases until 1978 lies in the seasonal pattern of cocoa production in Ghana. The cocoa crop is

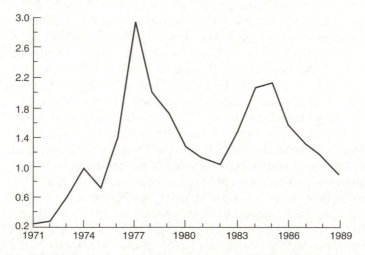

Figure 3.1. World price of cocoa, 1971–89 (*nominal, £'000 sterling/metric ton*)

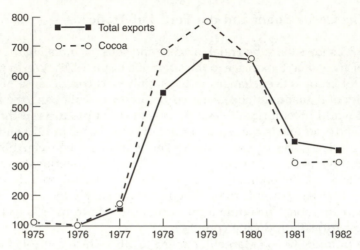

Figure 3.2. Export price indices, 1975–82 (*1976 = 100*)

harvested mostly during October–December and is shipped for export by the middle of the next year, with shipments reaching a peak during January–March. A large part of the cocoa crop is sold through forward contracts starting in April and continuing through October, and calling for delivery to Ghanaian ports within three to six months or longer. With these forward contracting arrangements, there is often a divergence between average realised unit values and world spot prices. Given the structure of the world cocoa market and this seasonal pattern of exports, the rise in prices that occurred between mid-1976 and mid-1977 in the world market was reflected in Ghana's exports in 1977 and 1978.

Despite the rise in the price of cocoa during this period, the volume of official cocoa exports continued to decline, falling from 342 metric tons in 1976 to 221 metric tons by 1979. A number of factors contributed to this decline. Both nominal and real producer prices fell during the 1960s, leading to little incentive for replanting; new plantings virtually stopped after 1964. In 1966 subsidies for spraying and the control of capsids were dropped (they were restored in 1972). The Alien Compliance Act of 1969 forced many foreign workers to leave the country, inducing labour shortages. Thus maintenance of plants also declined dramatically, leading to a rising incidence of plant disease. Owing to the production cycle of cocoa,[4] these policies of the 1960s affected cocoa output in the 1970s. Also, unremunerative prices for cocoa farmers (see Figure 3.5 below) led many producers to switch into food crops or to smuggle their cocoa into neighbouring countries where the real producer price was higher. All of these factors contributed to the dramatic drop in the volume of cocoa production and official exports during this period.

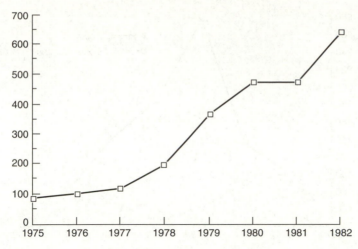

Figure 3.3. Import price index, 1975–82 (*1976 = 100*)

While cocoa and cocoa products dominate the movement of export prices (together their share in total exports was 63% in 1976), the prices of some of Ghana's other exports peaked in 1980. The price of gold exports (9% of total exports in 1976) increased by 96% in 1978, 88% in 1979, and 174% in 1980. It then fell by 30% over the next three years. The price of timber and log exports (8.4% of total exports in 1976) reached a peak in 1980 after falling dramatically in 1978. After 1980, the prices of all exports other than manganese and bauxite (2.1% and 0.4% of total exports, respectively) fell sharply. Although all of the price changes contributed to the total export price series, given the large weight of cocoa and cocoa-product exports in total exports, the terms of trade gain discussed below will be referred to as the cocoa boom.

Figure 3.3 shows import prices over the period of the cocoa price boom. Import prices increased by 367% from 1977 to 1980. They levelled off during 1981, but increased again in 1982 by 36%. As in many other countries, the largest contributing factor to the rise in import prices is the increase in the price of oil. Owing to the lack of data it is not possible to separate out the effect of oil price increases on the total import price index. Import prices were also affected by the devaluation of the cedi.

Dividing the export price index by the import price index gives us the terms of trade, which is presented in Figure 3.4 as the line marked with boxes. The increase in the terms of trade in 1977 was 34%.[5] The terms of trade peaked in 1978, 106% higher than in 1977. They then fall off sharply and by 1982 are only about 55% of the 1976 level.

In order to assess the magnitude and the effects of the cocoa boom, we must construct a counterfactual representing what would have occurred

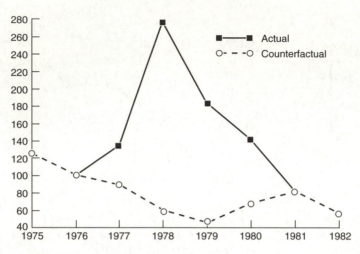

Figure 3.4. Terms of trade, 1975–82 (*1976 = 100*)

had the boom in cocoa prices not taken place. In its Five Year Development Plan, covering 1975/76–1979/80, the government states: '[Over the
plan period], the average price of cocoa is expected to stagnate' (Supreme-
Military Council 1977, p. 69). In setting out its plan, the government
assumed that the cocoa price would remain at its 1976 price throughout
the period. In the counterfactual we thus recalculate the export price index
keeping cocoa at its 1976 price throughout the boom period. The counterfactual terms of trade are then the counterfactual export price index divided by the actual import price index. In calculating the windfall
resulting from the cocoa boom, it is assumed that the increase in the terms
of trade did not affect *official* export volumes—as discussed above, official
export volumes were declining (we discuss the effect of the cocoa boom
on unofficial exports below). We also assume that import prices remain
the same in the counterfactual. The difference between the actual terms of
trade and the counterfactual terms of trade provides us with a measure of
the official windfall owing to the rise in cocoa prices.

Table 3.1 estimates the real value of the boom in 1976 prices.[6] This was
260.4 million cedis in 1977, 1,056.6 million cedis in 1978, 631.1 million
cedis in 1979, and 351.6 million cedis in 1980. The total windfall in 1976
prices (undiscounted) was 2,299.7 million cedis or 35.2% of 1976 GDP.
This figure includes only the official component of the windfall due to the
boom.

The large increase in cocoa prices combined with low producer
prices led to a substantial increase in smuggled cocoa during this period.
Those smuggling cocoa would also experience a windfall owing to the
boom in cocoa prices. One of the principal functions of the CMB is to

Table 3.1. Magnitude of the official boom (*millions of cedis*)

	Actual Export Value	Actual Export Volume Index	CFT Export Price Index	CFT Export Value Index	CFT Export Value	Windfall (current prices)	Import Price Index	Windfall (1976 prices)
	(1)	(2)	(3)	(4)	(5)	(6)	(7)	(8)
1976	710.4	100	100	100	710.4	0.0	100	0.0
1977	911.2	83	104	86	609.9	301.3	116	260.4
1978	2,664.4	69	119	82	580.9	2,083.6	197	1,056.6
1979	3,041.7	64	164	105	746.8	2,295.0	364	631.1
1980	3,217.1	69	320	222	1,574.7	1,642.5	467	351.6
1981	1,711.8	64	375	241	1,711.8	0	468	0.0
Total						6,322.3		2,299.7

Notes: CFT = Counterfactual
(1) Values in millions of cedis (current prices) from CMB (World Bank Report (1989): 154 for cocoa and QDS, June 1987: 60 for all other export
(2) Column (1) divided by Export Price (see data annex) and indexed so 1976 = 100
(3) See text
(4) Column (2) multiplied by column (3) divided by 100
(5) Percentage change of (4) applied to actual value in 1976, and to counterfactual export values thereafter
(6) Column (1) minus column (5)
(7) QDS, June 1984 and June 1987
(8) Column (6) deflated by column (7)

determine the price to be received by cocoa farmers for each year's crop. This price is announced at the beginning of the season (September/October). Figure 3.5 shows the real producer price paid to Ghanaian cocoa farmers over the period. While the world price received by the CMB increased substantially during this period, the price paid to producers declined in real terms in every year except 1979 and was well below its level in the early 1970s. Hence the CMB did not pass any of the official boom along to cocoa farmers; they experienced a fall in prices in the official market. This encouraged many cocoa producers to smuggle their cocoa into neighbouring countries where the producer price was higher.

There have been a few studies that have tried to estimate the amount of smuggling that has taken place in Ghana (see Franco 1981; May 1985; Stryker 1990). May (1985) estimates cocoa smuggling using the following explanatory variables: production capacity, real producer prices, rainfall and the ratio of producer prices in Ghana and the neighbouring country. He derives estimates for smuggling in the Brong-Ahafo region. Dividing his estimates by the share of the Brong-Ahafo region in total production gives us a proxy for total smuggling, which is set out in column (1) of

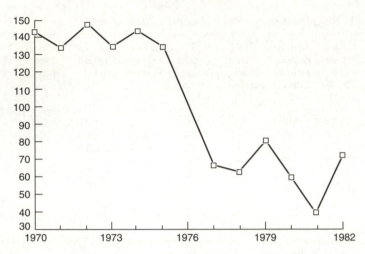

Figure 3.5. Real producer price for cocoa, 1970–82 (*1976 = 100*)

Table 3.2.[7] We use May's work to estimate the unofficial windfall from the cocoa boom.[8]

This unofficial windfall was largest in 1978 and 1980, at 134.4 and 175.1 million cedis, respectively. The total windfall to smugglers over the period in 1976 prices (undiscounted) is 616 million cedis or about 9% of 1976 GDP (adjusted to incorporate cocoa smuggling).

Putting the official and unofficial windfalls together, we estimate that the Ghanaian economy experienced a windfall (in 1976 prices) of 332.7 million cedis in 1977, 1,190.4 million cedis in 1978, 734.4 million cedis in 1979, 526.6 million cedis in 1980 and 131.0 million cedis in 1981—a total windfall in 1976 prices of 2,915.7 million cedis or 44.3% of 1976 GDP adjusted to incorporate smuggling.

In order to determine the gain in permanent income had all of the windfall been invested (which it was not), an assumption must be made about the rate of return on domestic capital formation. Unfortunately, there are no estimates for the rate of return in Ghana during this time-period, so we will use 10% to discount real annual gains.[9] This gives a present value of the boom of 1,954.5 million cedis, a permanent income increase of 195.4 million cedis or 2.9% of GDP (adjusted in 1976 prices).[10]

The degree to which the boom is invested depends in theory on how much of the windfall is taken to be permanent income, which in turn depends upon expectations regarding the price shock. It is clear from the cocoa price forecasts up to 1977 that the sharp increase in cocoa prices that occurred between mid-1976 and mid-1977 was not expected. Bateman (1971) forecast cocoa prices from 1971 to 1985. He explored four cases based on differing assumptions concerning Ghanaian production, rest of

Table 3.2. Magnitude of the unofficial cocoa boom (*millions of cedis*)

	Estimated smuggled cocoa ('000MT) (1)	CFT smuggled cocoa ('000MT) (2)	Smuggling from boom ('000MT) (3)	Actual BM cocoa price (C'000/MT) (4)	CFT BM cocoa price (C'000/MT) (5)	Windfall at current prices (6)	Import price index (7)	Unofficial windfall at 1976 prices (8)
1976	35.0	35.0	0	1,557	1,557	0.0	100	0
1977	64.3	48.8	15.5	4,260	3,893	83.9	116	72.3
1978	60.8	37.4	23.4	7,731	5,487	264.8	197	134.4
1979	56.0	32.1	23.9	10,972	7,433	375.8	364	103.2
1980	61.5	38.2	23.3	21,866	13,803	817.5	467	175.1
1981	46.3	27.3	19	20,338	12,034	613.1	468	131.0
Total						2,155.1		616.0

Notes: CFT = counterfactual, BM = black market, MT = metric tons
(1) Estimates of May (1985): 79 divided by share of Brong-Ahafo region in total production of cocoa (see data annex)
(2) See data annex
(3) = (1) minus (2)
(4) Actual Côte d'Ivoire producer price converted into cedis using black market rate see May (1985)
(5) Counterfactual assuming that Côte d'Ivoire producer price rose at its 1976 rate in 1977 and 1978 and at its actual rate thereafter.
(6) = (3) times (4) + (2) multiplied by (4) minus (5).
(7) QDS, June 1984 & June 1987.
(8) = column (6) deflated by (7).

world production, and world consumption of cocoa. In the case that Bateman chose as his most likely scenario,[11] the price forecast rose fairly sharply in 1972/73 and 1973/74, reached its peak in 1974/75, and fell gradually thereafter. The World Bank's *Country Economic Memorandum* for 1975 stated the following: 'Most recent Bank forecasts indicate that the spot Ghana, N.Y. prices for 1975 and 1976 will be about 69 cents/lb. and 79 cents/lb., respectively, and will improve only marginally in the following years' (World Bank 1975, App.: 3). A study by Singh *et al.* (1977: 100) stated: 'The highest prices reached in 1974 are not expected to be sustainable in the years ahead, partly as a result of their impact on final demand and partly because of a moderate increase in production'. As discussed above, the government clearly stated in its development plan that it expected prices to stagnate. Expectations concerning the cocoa boom can thus be categorised as exclusive because the boom in cocoa prices was not consistent with expectations.

It is more difficult to classify whether expectations were revised or not. The principal cause of the rise in prices was the continuing drought that reduced world cocoa supplies. To the extent that this drought was perceived as a once-and-for-all event, expectations would remain unrevised. Other causes, however, such as the reduction in inventories and structural factors that reduced Ghana's cocoa output would imply that price expectations should be revised upwards.

A distinction should be made, however, between economic agents. The public sector (including the CMB) faced a price boom. Given a history of substantial fluctuations in cocoa prices, one would guess that these agents were familiar with sharp increases and decreases in cocoa prices and would consider the enormous increase as a once-and-for-all event. Discussions with some members of the Cocoa Marketing Board indicate that in fact the CMB did revise its expectations. In the first year of the boom, when the price topped 1,000 pounds per metric ton, marketing agents of the CMB still felt that the price was too good to last. By 1977, when the price was approaching 3,000 pounds per metric ton, their expectations had been revised and, despite the forecasts, they expected (and hoped) it would reach 4,000 pounds per metric ton. As one fellow put it, 'after the first year of increases, they got greedy'.[12] Thus one could say that the public sector's expectations were exclusive, unrevised in the first year of the boom, but then switched to exclusive, revised in the second year and thereafter.

In the official cocoa market, producers faced a drop in prices—the producer price had and would continue to be set by the Cocoa Marketing Board. Producers presumably saw that the official price was declining in real terms and would continue to do so. With respect to the official market, the expectations of cocoa producers must have been inclusive.

In contrast, producers smuggling cocoa across the border did experience a price increase. They may have realised that the price increase was a once-and-for-all event; alternatively they may have revised their expectations about the prices to be received across the border. It is difficult to tell *a priori*.

In practice it is likely that the boom gave rise to a change in both permanent income and transient income and hence would have had some impact on savings and investment. We turn to this in the next section.

3.2. Behaviour of the Economy as a Whole

We first consider the effect of the boom on investment and savings. Then we turn to relative prices and factor markets.

3.2.1. Asset Changes and Savings Rates

In order to estimate the actual rate at which windfall income was saved, a counterfactual to the observed changes in assets needs to be constructed. Counterfactual income and counterfactual propensities to acquire domestic and foreign assets must be specified to create this counterfactual. First, we consider the propensity to acquire domestic assets in the form of gross fixed capital formation (GFKF). In column (1) of Table 3.3, the actual

Table 3.3. Actual and counterfactual growth and capital formation

	Actuals			Counterfactuals			Windfall GFKF		
	GFKF/ GDP (%)	GDP	GFKF	GDP	GFKF/ GDP (%)	GFKF	Annual	Cumulative	Return at 10%
	(1)	(2)	(3)	(4)	(5)	(6)	(7)	(8)	(9)
1976	9.8	6,580	645	6,580	9.8	645	0.0	0.0	0.0
1977	9.4	7,264	683	7,264	9.4	683	0.0	0.0	0.0
1978	5.1	8,857	452	7,239	5.1	369	82.5	82.5	82.5
1979	6.7	8,328	558	7,002	6.7	469	88.9	171.4	17.1
1980	6.1	8,816	538	6,993	6.1	427	111.2	282.6	28.3

Notes: GFKF = Gross Fixed Capital Formation
(1) From QDS, various years. Both GFKF and GDP in current prices
(2) GDP in 1976 prices from QDS data adjusted to include value of estimated smuggling (column (1) Table 2) plus total official and unofficial windfall in 1976 prices
(3) = (1) multiplied by (2)
(4) In 1976 and 1977, actual GDP at 1976 prices, in 1978–81 corrects for (i.e. subtracts) returns on windfall investment as shown in column (9), lagged one year
(5) same as (1)
(6) = column (4) multiplied by column (5)
(7) = column (3) minus column (6)
(8) = column (7) summed
(9) = column (8) multiplied by 0.1

propensity to acquire GFKF out of income (the ratio of GFKF to income) is shown for the cocoa boom period. The data indicate that the propensity to invest in Ghana is low even for a developing country. Investment in Ghana was highest in 1960 and 1961, at about 20% of GDP. By 1976 it had fallen to 9.8% of GDP. Thereafter investment collapsed, falling to 6.1% of GDP by 1980 and eventually reaching a low of 3.5% of GDP in 1982.

The low and falling level of investment in Ghana during this period can largely be attributed to the extensive control regime and to considerable economic and political uncertainty that existed at the time (World Bank 1977: 4). The shortage of imports that resulted from the import licensing regime was one of the principal reasons for reductions in investment. Shortages of spare parts and raw materials created widespread excess capacity (utilisation rates at the time were about 25%)—any plans for expansion were postponed until capacity utilisation improved. Numerous changes and widespread corruption and bribery in the import licensing regime augmented uncertainty with regard to investment inputs. Large budget deficits, financed by the Bank of Ghana, led to a quadrupling of credit to the government—most of which was used to finance increasing consumption. The use of money creation to finance the deficit led to high inflation rates. This, combined with interest rate controls, implied negative real interest rates. Throughout the 1976–81 period there were continuous strike actions—many of which immobilised the country. The government changed hands continuously, with a series of three military (and one civilian) takeovers between 1976 and 1981. The combined effects of the control regime, macroeconomic mismanagement and political instability precipitated the investment collapse.

Table 3.3 estimates windfall investment (column 7).[13] The results show that windfall investment was 82.5 million cedis out of a windfall of 1,190.9 million cedis in 1978. In 1979, windfall investment was 88.9 million cedis out of a windfall of 734.3 million cedis. Finally, in 1980 it was 111.2 million cedis out of a windfall of 526.6 million cedis. Overall the counterfactual implies that windfall investment was 282.6 million cedis in 1976 prices (9.6% of the total windfall).

A similar analysis is repeated for the propensity to accumulate foreign assets.[14] Over the period there was an overall decrease in foreign savings of −1,416 million cedis as a result of the windfall, implying an increase in foreign asset holdings by Ghanaians. The increase in foreign assets amounted to about 49% of the total windfall.

If we combine the investment and foreign savings counterfactuals, we find that the acquisition of domestic capital assets combined with the increase in foreign assets represents an increase in assets of 1,698.7 million cedis. In order to derive the rate of saving of the windfall, we subtract the present value of windfall foreign savings (−949.3 million cedis) from the present value of windfall GFKF (189.4 million cedis). From this we must

Table 3.4. Actual and counterfactual foreign savings (*millions of cedis*)

	Actuals		Counterfactuals		
	Foreign savings/ GDP (%)	Foreign savings	Foreign savings/ GDP (%)	Foreign savings	Windfall foreign savings
	(1)	(2)	(3)	(4)	(5)
1975	2.36	159	—	—	—
1976	3.45	227	3.45	227	0.0
1977	0.10	7	0.0	0	−7
1978	−9.56	−737	0.0	0	−737
1979	−4.73	−360	0.0	0	−360
1980	−3.74	−312	0.0	0	−312
Total	—	—	—	—	−1,416

Notes:
(1) Foreign savings (imports minus exports deflated by import price index) divided by GDP in 76 prices. Data on imports and exports from CMB (World Bank, 1989) for cocoa and from QDS for all others
(2) As (1)
(3) Assumes foreign savings propensity falls to 0 in 1977 and remains there
(4) = (3) multiplied by counterfactual GDP as in column (4) of Table 3.3
(5) = (2) minus column (4)

also subtract the present value of the savings that arise out of extra permanent income, which is estimated by applying the difference between GFKF and foreign savings propensity (the domestic savings propensity) to each year's additional permanent income (from Table 3.3). This gives a present value of savings of 1,136.5 million cedis (189.4 + 949.3 − 2.2), or 58.1% of windfall income (1,136.5/1,954.7). Thus, the savings rate of windfall income was 58.1% and the bulk of this was through accumulation of foreign assets.

3.2.2. Relative Prices

According to both Dutch Disease theory and construction boom theory, expenditure resulting from the boom will have an impact on relative prices in the economy. Dutch Disease theory predicts a rise in the price of non-traded prices relative to tradable prices as the result of the boom. Given that the windfall was largest in 1978 and 1979 we would expect non-tradable prices to rise relative to tradable prices in 1978, 1979 and 1980, if Dutch Disease theory holds.

Figure 3.6(*a*) and (*b*) presents two proxies of this price. The first is the ratio between the non-traded goods price index and the price index of import substitutes (NT/IS). The second is the ratio between the non-

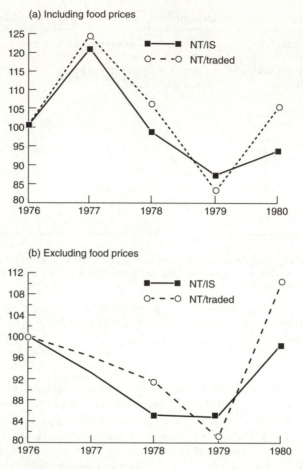

Figure 3.6. Relative price of non-traded to traded goods, 1976–80 (*1976 = 100*)

traded goods price index and the traded goods price index (NT/Traded). (See the Appendix for details on the construction of these indices.) In Figure 3.6(*a*), both indices increase sharply in 1977, and then fall in 1978 and 1979. They both rise in 1980.

The sharp increase in relative prices in 1977 is in part the result of a sharp increase in food prices owing to the drought in 1976. Figure 3.6(*b*) presents the same indices excluding the food component and we see that for both indices the relative price of non-traded to traded goods falls in 1977, 1978 and 1979. Since over 50% of a Ghanaian household's expenditure is on food, it is difficult to discern how much of the increase in the non-tradable index in Figure 3.6(*a*) is the result of shortages resulting from the drought as opposed to increased expenditure on food owing to windfall income. Given that a sizeable proportion of windfall income was held

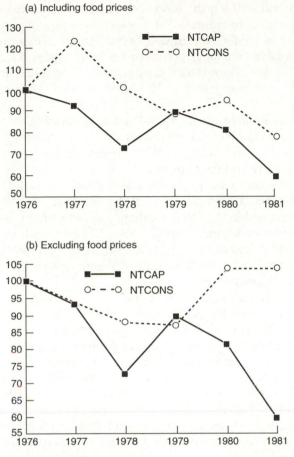

Figure 3.7. Prices of non-traded capital and consumer goods relative to import substitutes, 1976–81 *(1976 = 100)*

as foreign assets and that the increase in income resulting from investment was small, we would not expect strong upward pressure on the prices of non-traded goods, especially in an environment of collapsing investment. It is thus not surprising that we do not find a Dutch Disease effect.[15]

In order to evaluate relative prices with respect to construction boom theory, we need to disaggregate non-tradable prices into prices for capital and consumer goods. As discussed above, there was a collapse in investment during this period, hence we would not expect there to be an increase in demand for capital goods nor an increase in the price of non-traded capital goods relative to non-tradable consumer goods.

Figure 3.7 decomposes non-tradable goods into capital and consumer goods (with and without the food sector) relative to import substitutes (see the Appendix). In Figure 3.7(*a*), non-tradable capital goods prices fall in every year but 1979. Non-traded capital goods prices are also lower than non-tradable consumer goods prices in all years other than 1979. Although the price of non-traded capital goods is greater than the price of non-tradable consumer goods in 1979, both indices are lower than their 1976 values.

Figure 3.7(*b*) removes food prices from non-tradable consumer prices and we see that non-tradable consumer prices are still higher than non-tradable capital prices, except for 1979. Thereafter, the non-traded capital index falls sharply and the non-traded consumer index rises sharply. As anticipated, the cocoa boom shows no evidence of having produced a construction boom. Given that most of the windfall was initially held as foreign assets, combined with the collapse in investment, we would not expect a rise in non-traded capital prices. The increase in non-traded consumer good prices in 1980 suggests that, as foreign assets were repatriated in the years after the boom, they were spent on consumer goods rather than investment.

Figure 3.8 takes a closer look at the decomposition of non-tradable consumer goods (see the Appendix). The series presented are for the relative prices of the food sector (agriculture and livestock), the distribution sector (wholesale and retail trade), and the residual sectors (transport, storage and communications, and finance, insurance and business). As expected in the food sector we see a sharp rise in 1977 and a reduction thereafter. The relative price of the distribution activities increases dramatically after 1979. Indeed, the distribution sector experiences a bonanza during this period as a result of price controls and chronic shortages. With access to manufactures at controlled prices, the distribution sector sold

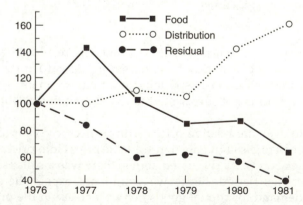

Figure 3.8. Relative price of non-traded consumer goods to import substitutes by sector, 1976–81 (*1976 = 100*)

them at black-market prices, thus gaining substantial rents. The relative price of the residual sectors, in contrast, declined steadily from 1977.

3.2.3. Output

The changes in output that occurred over the period are presented in Table 3.5.[16] There is no increase in output of the tradable boom sector, cocoa production and marketing. The reasons for this were discussed above. The output of the non-boom tradable sector, including forestry and logging, fishing, mining and quarrying and manufacturing, declined over the period from 23.1% of GDP in 1976 to 16.4% of GDP in 1981. Manufacturing experienced the greatest decline in output within this group. Output of non-tradable consumer goods including agriculture and livestock and the services increased from 56.8% of GDP in 1976 to 71.1% of GDP in 1981. This increase reflects the substantial increase of the agricultural and

Table 3.5. Sectoral composition of GDP, 1976–1981 (*% of GDP, constant prices*)

	1976	1977	1978	1979	1980	1981
Agriculture	49.0	45.8	50.0	53.1	54.2	54.5
Agriculture and livestock	26.2	26.0	32.5	36.1	35.8	37.2
Cocoa	15.2	12.2	10.5	10.1	11.4	10.3
Forestry and logging	5.9	5.7	5.4	5.3	5.4	4.9
Fishing	1.6	1.9	1.7	1.5	1.6	1.7
Industry	21.0	21.2	18.1	16.0	15.9	14.0
Mining and quarrying	1.9	1.7	1.5	1.3	1.3	1.2
Manufacturing	13.7	13.7	12.2	10.4	10.2	8.6
Electricity and water	0.7	0.7	0.6	0.7	0.8	0.9
Construction	4.7	5.1	3.9	3.5	3.7	3.2
Services	30.6	33.6	33.3	32.4	31.3	33.9
Transport, storage and communication	3.3	3.6	3.2	3.4	2.9	3.3
Wholesale and retail trade	11.6	11.5	10.3	10.9	9.9	10.1
Finance, insurance and business	5.7	6.2	6.3	6.4	6.6	7.2
Government and other	10.0	12.3	13.6	11.6	11.9	13.3
Boom sector[a]	15.2	12.2	10.5	10.1	11.4	10.3
Non-boom traded sector 2[b]	23.1	23.0	20.8	18.5	18.5	16.4
Non-traded consumer goods 3[c]	56.8	59.6	65.8	68.5	67.1	71.1
Non-traded capital goods 4[d]	5.4	5.8	5.5	4.2	4.5	4.1

Note: Based on sector output and GDP at constant (1975) prices
  [a] Cocoa production and marketing, adjusted to include value of smuggled cocoa at 1975 prices
  [b] Foestry and logging, fishing, mining and quarrying and manufacturing
  [c] Agriculture and livestock and services
  [d] Electricity and water and construction

Source: Quarterly Digest of Statistics, various years

livestock output as a percentage of GDP—as economic conditions in the country deteriorated resources moved into food production.[17]

Finally, output of the non-tradable capital or 'construction' sector (construction and electricity and water) as a percentage of GDP declined from 5.4% in 1976 to 4.1% in 1981.

3.2.4. Factor Markets

As seen in Table 3.5, the share in total GDP of the booming sector, the construction sector and the non-boom tradable sector declined. In contrast, the non-tradable consumer sector grew substantially. Such changes could not have occurred without some reallocation of capital and labour.

Data on investment by sector are not available for Ghana, so we must rely on evidence on the classification of loans and advances by sector that is provided to the Statistical Service by the central bank. Although the data are provided in a similar classification to that of GDP by sector, no breakdown of credit to the agricultural sector is given. Cocoa marketing advances[18] are not included in the data, and it is not possible to determine how much credit is going to the non-traded agricultural sector as opposed to the traded agricultural sector. Credit guidelines were in force throughout the period and, although they are generally considered to have been ineffective,[19] they undoubtedly had some influence on credit allocation. Finally, informal credit markets are extensive in Ghana and the official statistics will not reflect the allocation of informal credit, so we may not be attaining a completely accurate measure of credit allocation using the official statistics. They will, however, provide us with some information on changing patterns in official credit allocation.

Table 3.6 sets out the share of the various sectors in total lending in 1976 prices. Manufacturing obtains the majority of credit and its share continues to increase over the period. The share of credit to agriculture fell in 1977, but increased substantially in the last two years of the period.[20] Construction received about 14% of total credit and its share rose substantially in 1979 (to 18.5% of all credit), only to fall sharply in 1981. The 'other' category of commerce and finance also received a sizeable share of credit; its credit jumped to 16% of total credit, but fell to 6% by 1981.

Table 3.7 indicates that lenders favoured the non-traded sector. Between 25% and 30% of the total value of lending went to the traded sector and between 70% and 75% to the non-traded sector. Within the non-traded sector, consumption sectors were favoured over capital sectors.

In Table 3.7, a counterfactual credit allocation is created to help assess the impact of the boom on credit allocation. The counterfactual is created by subtracting annual windfall investment in 1976 prices (Table 3.3) from the actual level of credit and applying the 1976 shares of credit to the traded (26.6%) and non-traded (73.4%) sectors. When the counterfactual is

Table 3.6. Classification of loans and advances by sector, 1976–1981 (*% of total value, 1976 prices*)

	1976	1977	1978	1979	1980	1981
Agriculture, forestry and fishing	17.6	15.1	18.5	15.9	22.1	30.3
Mining and quarrying	3.9	6.5	6.2	3.7	3.3	6.9
Manufacturing	22.6	22.2	23.1	21.3	25.9	28.5
Construction	13.8	13.7	14.4	18.5	10.3	7.8
Electricity, gas and water	0.3	0.3	1.0	0.2	4.2	0.5
Commerce and finance						
Import Trade	5.0	2.8	3.3	2.2	1.1	0.9
Export Trade	3.0	2.8	2.1	2.9	9.8	6.6
Other	14.3	16.4	16.0	14.2	9.2	6.1
Transport and Communication	9.9	9.0	7.5	12.0	7.7	6.2
Services	9.9	6.6	4.8	5.6	3.6	3.5
Miscellaneous	5.7	4.6	3.2	3.4	2.8	2.8
Total	100	100	100	100	100	100

Notes: Includes loans and advances from both primary and secondary banks. Excludes staff loans, unpaid interest, and cocoa marketing advances. Agriculture, forestry, and fishing; mining and quarrying; and manufacturing deflated by the traded capital price index. All other categories deflated by the non-traded capital price index (see Appendix Table 3)

Traded capital index used for the agriculture category despite the fact that agriculture (largely food production) is treated as non-traded because investment is likely to be in traded capital (machines, equipment, etc.)

Source: *Quarterly Digest of Statistics*, June 1984

subtracted from the actual credit allocation, we see that the boom-induced credit allocation favoured traded goods, despite the fact that in 1976 the share of credit going to non-traded goods heavily outweighed the share going to traded goods. The counterfactual also shows that credit to non-traded goods also increased as a result of the boom, though not as much as credit to the traded sector.

The most reliable data on the distribution of labour come from the information collected as part of the census (see Table 3.8).[21] Because these data have only been collected in 1960, 1970 and 1984, they will not provide us with a precise indication of changes in employment patterns over the specific span of the boom period. Rather, they will provide us with a broad view of employment patterns over the decades.[22]

In all industries except agriculture and commerce, the share in total employment dropped from 1970 to 1984. The data do not provide a classification for the cocoa sector, but Stryker (1990) points out that there was a shift during this period away from cocoa production and into the production of food crops and other informal activities. At the foot of the table we see that the share of employment in traded production[23] rose to 13.0% of total employment by 1970, but then fell to 11.4% in 1984.

Table 3.7. Actual and counterfactual credit allocation (*% and millions of cedis, 1976 prices*)

	1976	1977	1978	1979	1980	1981
Actual						
Traded Sectors (%)	26.6	28.7	29.3	25.0	29.2	35.3
Non-Traded Sectors (%)	73.4	71.3	70.7	75.0	70.8	64.7
Traded Sectors (level)	202.1	214.7	213.5	99.6	155.0	205.9
Non-Traded (level)	558.3	532.3	515.9	298.8	376.0	376.7
Counterfactual						
Traded Sectors (%)	26.6	26.6	26.6	26.6	26.6	26.6
Non-Traded Sectors (%)	73.4	73.4	73.4	73.4	73.4	73.4
Traded Sectors (level)	202.1	198.7	172.1	82.3	111.7	155.0
Non-Traded (level)	558.3	548.3	474.8	227.2	308.1	427.6
Difference (level)						
Traded Sectors	0.0	16.0	41.4	17.2	43.3	50.9
Non-Traded Sectors	0.0	−16.0	41.0	71.7	67.9	−50.9
Total Difference						
Traded Sectors						168.9
Non-Traded Sectors						113.7

Notes: Traded includes mining and quarrying and manufacturing. Non-traded includes all other categories. Agriculture, forestry and fishing poses some difficulty because some components (cocoa, forestry and fishing) are traded and others (agriculture and livestock) are not. The data do not provide a breakdown between these groups. Given that agriculture and livestock dominate the category in output terms, we assume that the category is non-traded. Our estimates of credit to the non-tradable sector will thus be slightly overestimated

Source: Data from Table 3.6. The counterfactual is created by subtracting annual windfall investment in 1976 prices (column (7), Table 3.3) from the actual level of credit and applying the 1976 shares of traded (26.6%) and non-traded (73.4%)

Table 3.8. Distribution of employment by industry (%)

	1960	1970	1984
Agriculture	61.8	57.2	61.6
Mining and quarrying	1.9	1.0	0.5
Manufacturing	9.1	12.0	10.9
Construction	3.5	2.3	1.2
Utilities	0.6	0.4	0.3
Commerce	14.5	13.9	14.6
Transport and communication	2.6	2.7	2.3
Services	6.0	10.5	9.2
Total employment	2,559,383	3,133,042	5,422,480
Traded sectors	11.0	13.0	11.4
Non-traded sectors	89.0	87.0	88.6

Sources: For 1960 and 1970, Ewusi (1978); for 1984, Statistical Service, *1984 Population Census: Demographic and Economic Characteristics*

Employment in non-traded production fell to 87% of total employment in 1970, but then increased to 88.6% of total employment in 1984. There was thus a shift in employment out of traded goods (mining and manufacturing) and into non-traded goods (mostly agriculture and commerce) in the period between 1970 and 1984.

To summarise, our analysis of the economy as a whole suggests that the economy responded to the windfall income of the cocoa boom by saving a large portion of it, about 58%. However, the bulk of this was not saved domestically and used to finance investment; rather, it was held abroad in foreign assets. This behaviour is consistent with the discussion of expectations during the boom. In the first year of the cocoa price rise (1978), agents assumed that the rise was temporary and saved it abroad. In subsequent years agents changed their expectations and began to act as though high cocoa prices were permanent.

Relative prices (after taking the effect of drought into consideration) do not show either Dutch Disease or construction boom effects, but this comes as no surprise. Given that much of the windfall was held as foreign assets, and given the low and falling rate of investment during the boom period, we would not expect to find such price effects. Because investment was falling over the period, there was no increase in the demand for non-traded capital goods and so their prices did not rise relative to non-tradable consumer good prices.

Treating the economy as a whole masks the different behaviour of the public and private sectors. The majority of the windfall went directly to the government in the form of the export tax on cocoa. It is therefore of interest to see how the government made use of this windfall. We now turn to a disaggregation of the public and private sectors and focus in particular on the government's response to the boom.

3.3. Disaggregation into Public and Private Sectors

In assessing the private/public breakdown of the windfall we first consider the allocation of the windfall, its effect on fiscal patterns and the transmission of the windfall to the private sector via public expenditure.[24] We then consider the uses that the public sector made of the windfall in terms of investment and savings, as well as the allocation of labour between the public and private sectors.

3.3.1. Allocation of the Windfall and Its Effect on Fiscal Patterns

As seen in Section 3.2, windfall from the boom can be broken down into the official and unofficial windfall. The official windfall (2,299.7 million cedis in 1976 prices) went to the public sector in the form of the export duty. The export duty received by the government is the difference between Cocoa Marketing Board receipts from cocoa exports and what it pays out to farmers plus a percentage to cover its costs. As discussed above, real producer prices to cocoa farmers had been declining relative to the pre-boom period, so private farmers received none of the official windfall. They did, however, receive the unofficial windfall that resulted from smuggling cocoa across the border, which amounted to 616.0 million cedis in 1976 prices. Because this unofficial windfall was the result of smuggling, it was not taxed by the government and went entirely to the private sector. Hence, in the first instance, about 79% of total windfall income accrued to the public sector and about 21% to the private sector.

Table 3.9 sets out the actual fiscal patterns of the central government for the years 1969/70 to 1983. The period prior to the boom, 1975/76 to 1977/78, was one of very high central government deficits. The overall deficit peaked at 15.2% of GDP in 1975/76. During the years of the cocoa price boom the economy had already entered a downward spiral. Whereas in most countries trade booms lead to an increase in revenue and expenditure above the pre-boom level, in Ghana the windfall income that accrued to the government served only to temporarily assist a fiscal regime that was rapidly deteriorating.

Gross fixed capital formation, which was at its highest in 1975/76 and 1976/77, fell by 2.6% of GDP in 1977/78 and then even further in 1978/79. The fall in government investment thus contributed to the overall collapse in investment. Consumption rose in 1977/78, but fell sharply after 1978/79. Combined consumption and investment expenditure are referred to as 'exhaustive' expenditure. Considering revenue minus exhaustive expenditure, we see a reduction from the mid-1970s.

Transfers were substantial in 1976/77 and 1977/78, though they were not as great as in 1975/76. In 1978/79 these expenditures fell. Interest payments were low and fairly stable throughout the period.

In 1976/77 consumption was cut sharply, but from 1977/78 gross fixed capital formation bore the brunt of the government's efforts to reduce expenditure. Transfers were cut more gradually than other expenditures, reflecting their importance as a means of providing political patronage and rewards during this period.

Another sign of the deterioration in the fiscal regime during this period is the sharp decline in tax revenues, despite the increase in income from the cocoa boom windfall. During 1975/76 central government revenue was 13.8% of GDP. This fell sharply during the cocoa boom period to 5.7% of GDP in 1980/81.

The conventional deficit peaked in 1975/76, but remained very high in the following two years: 12.7% of GDP in 1976/77 and 10.9% of GDP in 1977/78. It dropped to 8.8% of GDP in 1978/79, 5.0% in 1979/80 and then went back up to 8.2% of GDP in 1980/80. Without the windfall income of

Table 3.9. Fiscal patterns (% of GDP)

	Revenue (1)	Consumption (2)	GFKF (3)	Exhaustive expenditure (4)	Exhaustive surplus (5)	Transfers (6)	Interest (7)	Deficit (8)
1969/70	10.6	8.6	2.6	11.2	5.4	8.8	1.5	4.9
1970/71	20.2	10.4	3.8	14.2	6.0	3.8	1.7	−0.5
1971/72	16.1	10.3	3.4	13.7	2.4	6.2	2.2	6.0
1972/73	12.5	9.5	2.6	12.1	0.4	5.1	1.8	6.5
1973/74	14.2	10.4	2.8	13.2	1.0	4.5	1.7	5.1
1974/75	16.2	12.2	4.3	16.6	−0.4	7.8	1.5	9.6
1975/76	13.8	13.0	5.9	18.9	−5.1	8.4	1.7	15.2
1976/77	12.2	9.7	6.0	15.7	−3.5	7.1	2.0	12.7
1977/78	9.6	9.3	3.7	13.0	−3.4	6.0	1.5	10.9
1978/79	8.9	8.4	2.5	9.9	−1.0	4.7	2.1	8.8
1979/80	8.5	6.3	1.2	7.5	1.0	3.9	2.0	5.0
1980/81	5.7	6.7	1.6	8.3	−2.6	3.7	1.8	8.2
1981/82	5.7	5.3	0.9	6.2	−0.5	2.9	2.5	5.9
1982	5.4	5.2	0.9	6.1	−0.7	3.2	2.5	6.3
1983	5.6	3.9	0.9	4.5	1.1	2.5	1.2	2.7

Notes: Data covers central government only and excludes capital expenditure financed through project lending
(1) Total revenue including grants divided by current GDP
(2) Expenditure on consumption: includes current expenditure on wages, goods and services, military and rent
(3) Capital expenditure minus capital transfers and other capital payments
(4) = (2) + (3)
(5) = (1) − (4)
(6) Transfers includes current and capital transfers, net lending (net loans and advances granted and net investment in public boards, corporations, institutions and companies, classified as transfers because these were rarely repaid)
(7) Domestic plus external
(8) = Columns (4) + (6) + (7) minus (1)

Source: Quarterly Digest of Statistics, various years

the cocoa boom, there is little doubt that the deficit would have been even higher.

Once again, in order to assess how the boom has contributed to fiscal patterns it is necessary to construct a counterfactual. The counterfactual assumes that the boom did not change the overall deficit.[25] During this period the government was completely constrained by lack of access to finance and by a falling revenue base. The boom did not alleviate these constraints: credit was sufficiently tight that no additional borrowing was possible and revenue was falling so dramatically that there was no intention of running a reduced deficit.

Table 3.10 sets out the fiscal changes resulting from the boom. It is constructed by applying counterfactual shares of revenue, consumption and GFKF to counterfactual GDP. Changes resulting from the boom are then derived by subtracting the counterfactual from actual fiscal patterns. Interest payments and the overall deficit are assumed not to have been altered by the boom. Transfer payments are then calculated as a residual.[26]

The boom increased revenue over the period by 2,229.7 million cedis (in 1976 prices), with the biggest gains in 1977/78 and 1978/79. The increase in expenditures associated with the boom income was on consumption expenditure (1,078.4 million cedis or 47% of the windfall), GFKF (279.8 million cedis or 12.1% of the windfall) and on transfers (941.6 million cedis or 40.9% of the windfall). We now consider the extent to which these expenditures transferred the windfall back to the private sector.

3.3.2. *The Transmission of Public Expenditure to Private Incomes*

There are a number of ways in which the government transmits income back to the private sector. One mechanism is through direct transfers to the private sector. We have seen that transfers increased as a result of the boom and we shall consider the distribution of these transfers below. A second mechanism by which the government can transfer income back to the private sector is through rents in the public sector labour market. If public sector employment increases as a result of the windfall, and if there is a wage differential in favour of the public sector, then the rents from public sector employment will increase. Another rent to the private sector may result from a boom-induced increase in wages. A final transfer mechanism works through the commodity market. A boom-induced rise in the price of non-tradable goods will increase the cost of government purchases and thus provide a rent to the private sector. In this section we consider whether rents were transmitted to the private sector during the cocoa boom period via any of these mechanisms.

Table 3.11 presents a decomposition of actual transfers over the 1976/77–1980/81 period. Current transfers are divided into domestic transfers and transfers abroad. Domestic transfers are further disaggregated into

Table 3.10. Fiscal changes resulting from the boom (*millions of cedis, 1976 prices*)

	Revenue (1)	Consumption (2)	GFKF (3)	(2) + (3) (4)	(1) − (4) (5)	Transfers (6)	Interest (7)	Deficit (8)
1976/77	130.2	52.6	0.0	52.6	77.6	77.6	0.0	0.0
1977/78	658.5	224.7	84.8	309.6	348.9	348.9	0.0	0.0
1978/79	843.9	253.1	69.5	322.3	521.3	521.3	0.0	0.0
1979/80	491.4	181.0	32.1	213.1	278.3	278.3	0.0	0.0
1980/81	175.7	366.9	93.3	460.2	−284.5	−284.5	0.0	0.0
Total	2,299.7	1,078.4	279.8	1,358.4	941.6	941.6	0.0	0.0

Notes:
(1) Actual revenue minus counterfactual tax rate times counterfactual GDP. Counterfactual tax rate equals actual revenues minus official windfall income (Table 1) divided by GDP
(2) Actual consumption minus counterfactual consumption share applied to counterfactual GDP. See text for discussion of counterfactual
(3) Central government investment propensities assumed to be unaffected by the boom. Actual propensities are applied to counterfactual GDP after 1977
(4) = (2) + (3)
(5) = (1) − (4)
(6) = (8) + (1) − (4) − (7)
(7) and (8) See text

Table 3.11. Decomposition of actual transfers (*% of total transfers*)

	1976/77	1977/78	1978/79	1979/80	1980/81
Current transfers	51.7	65.0	70.6	86.7	80.0
Domestic sector	50.3	64.5	69.6	84.8	78.8
to public enterprise and local government	NA	49.5	59.6	70.5	64.4
to households	NA	15.0	10.0	14.3	14.4
Abroad	1.4	0.5	1.0	1.9	1.2
Capital Transfers	8.6	6.3	7.9	5.0	9.2
to public enterprises	NA	NA	6.8	4.1	8.6
to local government	NA	NA	1.1	0.9	0.6
Net lending[a]	39.7	28.7	21.5	8.3	10.8

[a] Net lending consists of net loans and advances granted to Public Boards, Corporations, Institutions and Companies. It is classified as a transfer because it was rarely paid back

Source: *Quarterly Digest of Statistics*, various years

those going to public enterprises and local government and those going to households. Capital transfers are also provided. These went solely to public enterprises and local government. Net lending is also included in transfers because it largely went to public enterprises and was rarely repaid. The table shows that on average only 13% of total transfers went directly to households. The remaining transfers went either to public boards, public enterprises or to local government. Local government was relatively weak in Ghana during this period, so the large part of these transfers was to public enterprises.

In Table 3.12 we use this decomposition to show the changes in expenditure on transfers that resulted from the boom. Our counterfactual is created by applying the 1976/77 decomposition of transfers to counterfactual total transfers, which were determined above.[27] Windfall transfers are then determined by subtracting the counterfactual from actual transfers.

Of the transfers that resulted from the boom 87.3% went to public enterprises and local government, 11.9% went to households, and 0.8% went abroad. In order to be consistent with the public/private disaggregation used above, transfers to public enterprises should be classified as transfers to the private sector. The 822.3 million cedis (in 1976 prices) that went to the public enterprises represent 35.8% of the total official windfall income. The 112.2 million cedis that went to households is 4.8% of total official windfall income. If we combine this with the unofficial windfall income of 616 million cedis (Table 3.2), the private sector windfall including direct transfers from the government is 1,550.5 million cedis or 53.2% of the entire windfall.[28]

Table 3.12. Windfall transfers (*million cedis, 1976 prices*)

	Public enterprises and local government	Households	Abroad	Total
1976/77	65.0	11.5	1.1	77.6
1977/78	296.8	52.4	−0.3	348.9
1978/79	461.1	54.8	5.4	521.3
1979/80	233.5	39.0	5.8	278.3
1980/81	234.1	−45.5	−4.9	−284.5
Total	822.3	112.2	7.1	941.6

Note: Actual transfer expenditure shares multiplied by actual expenditure on transfers (see Table 3.11) minus 1976/77 expenditure shares multiplied by counterfactual transfer expenditure. Transfers to households are assumed to be 15% in 1976/77

A less direct method of transmitting income to the private sector is through rents in the public sector labour market. Although public sector employment increased during the boom period, average monthly earnings were larger in the private sector than in the public sector (*Quarterly Digest of Statistics*, Dec. 1983: 44). Since there was no wage premium for working in the public sector, no transfer of income to the private sector would have occurred via this mechanism.

Rents to the private sector may also result from a boom-induced increase in government wages. Given the collapse in revenue that occurred during the period, central government wages were in fact reduced. Central government wages fell from 5.1% of GDP to 3.5% of GDP in 1979/80, one of the peak years of the boom. In real terms, central government wages had fallen 40% by 1979/80 and would fall to only 25% of their 1976/77 level by 1983. Because there were no boom-induced increases in government wages, no rents accrued to the private sector through increased wages.

The final transfer mechanism to be considered works through the commodity market. A boom-induced increase in the price of non-tradable goods increases the cost of government purchases and transfers income to the private sector. Figures 3.6 and 3.7 showed that non-tradable prices other than food fell during the boom period relative to 1976. We thus would not expect to find any positive rents being transmitted to the private sector through increases in non-tradable prices.

The transmission of the public windfall to the private sector thus occurred largely through direct transfers to public enterprises (which, owing to poor data, must be considered as part of the private sector) and to households. The estimated windfall that was ultimately in the hands of the private sector comprised: the windfall of 616.0 million cedis (in 1976 prices) from unofficial smuggling, the 822.3 million cedis transmitted directly to public enterprises as part of transfers and the 112.2 million cedis transmitted directly to households. The total windfall ultimately transferred to the private sector was thus about 1,550.5 million cedis (in 1976 prices) or 53.2% of the total windfall (both official and unofficial). The public sector (central government) windfall was ultimately about 1,365.2 million cedis or 46.8% of the total windfall.

3.3.3. Use of the Windfall

Table 3.13 considers the contribution of windfall gross fixed capital formation of the central government to total fixed capital formation. Column (1) shows total annual windfall capital accumulation from Table 3.3 (column 7 adjusted to fiscal years). Column (2) shows windfall investment by the central government from Table 3.10 (column 3). In all years other than 1979/80, most windfall investment was carried out by the central government. In 1979, there was a coup and investment expenditure (as well as other expenditure) was cut back sharply. This may be at the root of the sudden drop in government windfall capital formation in that year.

In Section 3.2, we found that the economy as a whole saved 58.1% of windfall income. Because most of the capital formation that resulted from the boom was undertaken by the government, the savings rates of the central government and the private sector will differ.

In the public sector, the change in assets resulting from the boom will equal boom-induced capital formation of the central government or 279.8 million cedis in 1976 prices.[29] Private assets changed by that part of boom-induced investment not attributable to the public sector (Table 3.13) minus the increase in foreign assets (Table 3.4) giving: $(282.6 - 279.8) - (-1,416) = 1,418.8$ million cedis in 1976 prices.[30]

Table 3.13. Boom-induced capital formation (*millions of 1976 cedis*)

	Total (1)	Central government (2)	Government share (%) (3)
1976/77	0.0	0.0	0.0
1977/78	41.3	84.8	205.3
1978/79	85.7	69.5	81.1
1979/80	100.1	32.1	32.0
1980/81	55.6	93.3	167.8
Total	282.7	279.7	99.0

Notes:
(1) = Column (7) of Table 3.3 adjusted to give fiscal year
(2) = Column (3) Table 3.10
(3) = Share of (2) in (1)

The total value of the windfall, as seen in Section 3.2, was 2,915.7 million cedis. Of this, 2,299.7 million cedis or 78.8% went in the first instance to the government, while 616.0 million cedis or 21.1% went directly to the private sector. However, some of the government windfall was transferred to the private sector, so that 1,365.2 million cedis remained with the central government and 1,550.5 million cedis were passed on to the private sector. These figures allow us to calculate the savings rate of the public and private sectors. After making transfers, the public savings rate *of windfall income* is estimated to be 20% (279.8/1,365.2) and the private sector savings rate *of windfall income* is 91.5% (1,418.8/1,550.5).[31]

These divergent savings rates may appear extreme but given the circumstances at the time in Ghana they may be sensible. This was a period of great instability with very high prices, an extremely overvalued exchange rate, rapid expansion of the black market and a series of different governments, which must have had very short time-horizons. This would have encouraged government consumption of windfall income, especially as expectations regarding the windfall changed. A relatively low savings rate of windfall income is therefore not surprising. The private sector also faced great uncertainty and instability. Under such uncertain conditions it would be reasonable to expect individuals to hold on to any incremental windfall gains. It would also be reasonable, given high inflation and negative interest rates, to expect individuals to want to hold their savings in the form of foreign assets rather than as domestic savings.

3.4. Rules and Their Consequences: The Control Regime

At the time of the cocoa boom the Ghanaian economy was dominated by an extensive control regime that had been created in the early years of Ghana's independence. The relationship between the control regime and the cocoa boom is complex. On the one hand, the control regime completely dominated the use of the windfall. Rather than the windfall going directly to cocoa farmers, it went to the central government and was then transferred predominantly to public enterprises. Had the cocoa farmers received the boom, they might have increased their investment. However, given the rapid deterioration of the economy, which was at least partly due to rigid economic controls, it seems unlikely that they would have invested much. On the other hand, the cocoa boom did lead to a slight alleviation of the strength of controls for a short period of time. There was a slight increase in the real producer price in 1978 and import restrictions appear to have been slightly liberalised as the result of the boom. In contrast, financial controls were made more restrictive during the period of the windfall. We now consider the interaction between the control regime and the boom with respect to the major components of the control regime: price controls, the nominal exchange rate, import restrictions and the financial system.

3.4.1. Price Controls

The single most important effect of the control regime was that the system of price controls meant that the majority of windfall income went directly to the government rather than to the producers of cocoa. The system of price controls had developed over the years, largely as the result of the fiscal system. Since before independence, the government had counted on the cocoa export tax to finance the country's development plans. This was fine so long as cocoa revenues were high. When they began to fall, rather than develop other sources of revenue, the government continued to squeeze the producer price of cocoa. With the fall in revenue from cocoa exports and continuous increases in expenditure, deficits skyrocketed. The only way to finance them was by borrowing from the central bank, which proved highly inflationary. The government's response was to impose price controls in order to keep inflation down. We consider each of these price controls in turn.

The producer price to cocoa farmers Producer prices and the purchasing and marketing of cocoa have historically been controlled by the Cocoa Marketing Board (CMB). Under the arrangements of the CMB, the official producer price was determined by the government and announced before each buying season. The buying agencies received a fixed allowance per metric ton to cover all expenses from the buying point to the ports plus a profit margin which varied with the price. The surplus (CMB receipts minus payments to producers and the costs of the buying agents) was originally intended to offset CMB deficits when world prices were low. In practice the government, through the use of the export tax, used CMB surpluses as its principal source of revenue. It thus had a direct incentive for keeping the producer price low.

Figure 3.5 showed the real producer price of cocoa (deflated by the rural CPI) from the early 1970s onwards. The year 1975 was the beginning of a long plunge in real producer prices which did not reach bottom until 1983, when the real producer price was only 34% of its level in 1972. In 1977, the year of huge increases in world cocoa prices, the real producer price fell by 16%. It increased slightly in 1978, but then fell sharply in 1979 and 1980. Only in 1985 was there a significant increase in the real producer price (Stryker 1990: 102). The share of farmer income in total sales also varied over the period. In 1964–65 farmers earned 81% of sales, but only 36% in 1969–70 after world market prices had recovered. During the boom years this share fell to about 26%.

As discussed in Section 3.2, the decline in producer prices encouraged cocoa producers either to switch into the production of other food crops or to smuggle cocoa into Côte d'Ivoire, where prices were favourable at the black-market exchange rate. Hence, rather than seeing a movement into the original booming sector as we might expect, the official figures indicate a movement away from this sector. As seen above, there was also a substantial increase in smuggling.

In effect the government's control of producer prices led to lower official output of cocoa when the world price would have encouraged increased output. In doing so it not only eliminated the gains in the formal market which cocoa producers might have made as the result of the windfall, but also reduced the public sector gains that would have resulted from increased export volumes during the boom period. The large amount of effort that went into smuggling and into its control resulted in reduced government revenues and a substantial waste of resources. It also contributed to bribery, corruption and a general undermining of the government's authority.

Other price controls The government consistently attempted to dampen inflation by controlling the prices of certain consumer goods, such as milk, sugar and fish, as well as some capital goods, such as cement. It also limited the approved outlets in which such goods could be found. In general the government was only able to maintain price controls in the formal sector manufacturing enterprises found in the major cities. These controls provided huge incentives for rent-seeking, for once these manufactured goods left the factory they could be sold at an enormous profit. Controls on imports also provided substantial rent-seeking opportunities.

Figure 3.9 sets out the price indices of ex-factory manufactures: manufactures at their controlled price level, the domestic price of import substitutes, and the price level of the wholesale and retail sectors (see the Appendix). The difference between the distribution sector price level and the ex-factory manufacturing price level, and the difference between the distribution price level and the domestic price of imports reflect the magnitude of these two sources of rents. Although these rents were not sizeable during the early years of the boom they grew to be substantial by 1980 and 1981. In the early years, an increase in imported goods (particularly in 1978) helped to keep these rents down. Thus, even though price controls were not completely effective, they provided a strong incentive for rent-seeking behaviour.

There was no change in the actual system of price controls as a result of the boom. Implementation of price controls may have weakened during the boom years, but this cannot be said to be a direct result of the increase in windfall income. Rather it was a result of the deterioration of the government's authority and an increase in corruption. To the extent that increased corruption resulted from the increase in cocoa prices, the boom

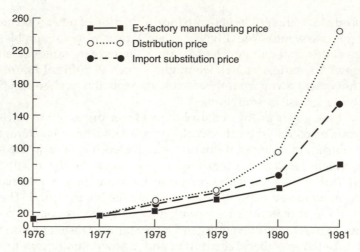

Figure 3.9. Rents to the distribution sector, 1976–81 (*1976 = 100*)

can be said to have indirectly contributed to a deterioration in the implementation of price controls. In 1979, Rawlings took drastic measures to reimpose price controls, but these were only short-lived.

3.4.2. *Exchange Rate Policy*

The nominal exchange rate was not constant throughout the entire boom period. The cedi was pegged to the US dollar at 1.15 cedis per dollar in 1976 and 1977. It was devalued to 1.51 cedis per dollar in 1978 and was devalued again in 1979 to 2.75 cedis per dollar. In spite of these devaluations the currency remained overvalued throughout the period.

A boom in the context of a fixed or managed exchange rate is likely to be inflationary. In theory, during the windfall the demand for money rises as a result of the 'asset effect' (in which the demand for foreign assets is likely to be increased) and the 'liquidity effect' owing to the increase in real expenditure associated with the windfall. In a freely floating regime, the increase in demand for domestic currency leads to an appreciation in its value. The extra transactions demand for money is thus accommodated by a fall in the price of tradable goods. With a fixed or managed exchange rate, these changes are not accompanied by a reduction in the price of tradable goods; instead the money supply increases. Hence the fixed exchange rate case implies more inflation than the floating exchange rate case.

In most years there was a gap between the fixed official exchange rate and the floating black-market exchange rate. The black-market premium is a measure of this gap and an indicator of the degree of overvaluation of the currency. In 1977, the black-market rate was eight times the official rate. With the windfall in 1978, the premium fell, indicating that the constraint on foreign exchange had at least in part been alleviated; though at six times the official rate the black-market premium indicated that the currency remained substantially overvalued. After a period of rapid appreciation between 1972/73 and 1977/78, the real exchange rate stabilised until 1981/82. Although the foreign exchange inflows which resulted from the boom could not address the fundamental overvaluation of the currency, they did help to stabilise both the premium and the real exchange rate for a short period.

3.4.3. Import Controls

During the period of the boom, imports were programmed. Table 3.14 sets out the planned imports for the boom period. In real terms,[32] programmed imports increased in 1977, but fell every year thereafter.

As Table 3.14 shows many more licences were issued than were incorporated into the initial programme. Letters of credit established by banks and approvals for goods on a collections basis became the *de facto* method of import-licence allocation. The actual value of licences still exceeded the programmed amount, but followed the same pattern of peaking in 1977 and falling thereafter. The issuing of licences thus shows a liberalisation of quotas in 1977 and 1978, with a tightening of quotas in the following years.

It makes sense for the government to have loosened controls in response to a foreign exchange windfall. During this period manufacturers of import substitutes were all but incapacitated owing to shortages of inputs and spare parts. Had the government maintained constant restrictions, demand could only have been met through the expansion of the import substitute sector. In theory, this would have come at the expense of the booming export sector. In practice, as we saw in Table 3.5, the output

Table 3.14. Import licenses issued and letters of credit established, 1976–1981 (*in millions of 1976 cedis*)

	1976	1977	1978	1979	1980	1981
Initial program for licenses	554.0	970.7	812.2	668.1	364.5	386.8
Actual licenses issued	978.4	1,698.2	1,192.7	931.9	415.2	540.8
Letters of credit established	865.4	933.7	600.5	406.0	226.6	—
Approvals on collection	52.0	143.1	275.1	91.3	148.4	—
Sum of LOC and approvals	917.4	1,076.8	875.6	497.4	375.0	—

Sources: Central Bureau of Statistics, *Economic Survey, 1977–1980* for 1976–1980. Jebuni *et al.* (1990) for 1981

of the cocoa sector was declining despite the boom. Indeed, even with the slight liberalisation in 1978, production of import substitutes (manufacturing) declined. Production in all sectors other than the non-tradable consumer goods sector (including food) contracted.

There is also evidence that, had import controls been completely abolished, private agents would have responded by hoarding consumer goods with the assumption that controls would be reimposed. As an example, consider imports of passenger cars during the boom period. In 1976, 6,197 passenger cars were imported. In 1977 the number was 7,646. With the liberalisation in 1978, the number jumped to 10,094, and with the reimposition of restrictions it fell in 1979 to 8,769. In 1980, the number fell even further, to 8,109. By 1983 the number of passenger cars imported had fallen to 2,328.[33] Previous liberalisation experiences, frequent balance of payment difficulties, and high black-market premiums indicate that there was substantial pent-up demand for imported (particularly consumer) goods.

One explanation for the reimposition of import controls was that the rents provided by import licences were critical instruments in the government's allocation of patronage. Distributing import licences had long been a means of maintaining political support. As the economy deteriorated, the government had fewer and fewer rents at its disposal, with more opponents to appease. Thus, while continued liberalisation would likely have provided the greatest benefits to the economy during the boom, it was politically unfeasible.

3.4.4. Financial Repression

The Ghanaian financial system consists of the central bank, three large commercial banks (the Ghana Commercial Bank, Barclays Bank of Ghana, and the Standard Bank of Ghana) known as the 'primary banks', two small commercial banks (the Social Security Bank and the National Savings and Credit Bank) and various specialised banks, including rural banks.

Foreign exchange restrictions implied that any income received by the private sector would either be used for consumption or held as domestic assets. However, we saw above that a large portion of the windfall was held as foreign assets. This implies that individuals either moved assets overseas by evading restrictions or, alternatively, that foreign assets were acquired indirectly, in that the windfall was deposited in the banks and the banks (and the government) increased their holdings of foreign assets.

The government used a number of instruments to control the banking system, including the cash-to-deposits ratio, interest rate ceilings and direct credit allocation. The low rates of saving and investment in the

Ghanaian economy are in part the result of heavy intervention in the financial system by the government. Prior to and during the period of the boom, government efforts were focused on preventing any inflationary effects the boom might have. Consequently, the government's response to the boom with respect to the financial sector was to tighten controls.

Interest rate controls were in place throughout the period. The nominal deposit rate was increased from 8% to 13% in 1978. This may have been an attempt to draw windfall income into deposits. It may also, however, have been a response to the jump in inflation in 1977. The nominal rate was again increased, to 19%, in 1981. Given high inflation rates none of these increases was sufficient to provide positive real interest rates. In 1977 the real deposit rate was −35.5%. It improved to −18.6% in 1979, but by 1981 had fallen to −31.0%. Nominal lending rates were also increased in 1978, from 12.5% to 18.5%. They remained at 18.5% until 1982. As with real deposit rates, real lending rates were also negative throughout the boom period.

The government also used cash and liquidity ratios to counter the inflationary effects of the boom. For several years prior to 1977, banks were very liquid and most banks held reserves far beyond the required amount. At the same time commercial banks were refusing to take new savings and time deposits were paying no interest on savings above 10,000 cedis.

During the windfall period, the government substantially raised the required liquidity ratio, in an attempt to control domestic credit and to slow down money creation. Liquidity ratios rose from 50% to 90% between 1977 and 1979 for the commercial banks and from 45% to 70% for the secondary banks. The actual ratios were below the required ratios for 1977, 1978 and 1979. Required ratios then dropped and, once again, the banks held well beyond the required rate of both cash and other liquid assets—with actual reserves held at about 80% of total deposits (Bank of Ghana, *Economic Bulletin*, various years).

The final and main instrument of control over the banking system was the credit guidelines established by the central bank. Table 3.6 indicated that the level of credit during the boom period declined, but that credit would have been even lower had the boom not occurred. Traditionally, priority sectors for credit allocation were agriculture, export trade, manufacturing, mining and quarrying, and transport, communications and storage. While credit to agriculture was a priority before the boom, it received even greater emphasis in the allocations after the boom. The guidelines were expressed as an allowed percentage increase over the previous year's credit. For example, credit to agriculture and the export trade was allowed to increase by 100% over the previous year's level.[34] Credit to manufacturing was allowed to increase by 44% and that to mining and quarrying by 30%. Of the non-priority sectors (construction, commerce and finance, services and import trade) only construction was allowed any increase at all (15%).

In practice, however, credit to priority sectors did not increase at the rates set out in the credit guidelines. For the June 1978–June 1979 period, for example, credit to agriculture increased by 5.7% and that to export trade by 10.9%. Credit to manufacturing increased by 42.8%, 1% under its allotted increase. During this period credit to electricity, water and gas grew by 1,075%, compared with the 25% increase provided in the credit guidelines. In the non-priority sectors, credit to construction increased by 17.8%, 2.8% more than the allocated amount. Credit to services increased by 3.7%, whereas credit to the import trade fell by 18.1%; the guidelines made no provision for changes to credit in these sectors. Without sanctions or the proper incentives for the banks the credit guidelines were generally ineffective.

The combined effect of these financial controls during the boom was to create an environment in which the banks were flush with funds but there appeared to be a capital shortage. In the boom years, the massive increase in required liquidity ratios prevented banks from lending out funds for investment. After 1979, bank liquidity was again high, but interest rate controls biased the composition of bank lending towards low-risk, low-return projects. The fact that credit allocation guidelines were not met implies that there were simply not enough low-risk projects for banks to lend to. This also implies that the real (*ex ante*) rate of return to the marginal investment project must have been zero or negative.

An additional direct intervention on the part of the government contributed to financial disintermediation during the boom period. In March 1979 the government attempted to mop up excess currency in the system, sabotage black-marketeers and strengthen tax enforcement through a currency exchange. It can be argued that the cocoa price boom resulted both in increased currency in the system and in an increase in black-marketeers, and hence that the currency conversion can at least in part be viewed as a response to the effects of the cocoa boom.

After the currency exchange the non-bank financial institutions substantially increased their recourse to the banks because of increased withdrawals by depositors following rumours of a possible government move to attach individual accounts until an explanation was provided about how individual wealth was acquired. From 1979 onwards the public increasingly shifted from holding deposits in the formal financial sector to holding currency and real assets and to participating in informal financial markets.[35]

Table 3.15 sets out the monetary survey between 1976 and 1981. Net foreign assets tripled in 1978 and remained high in 1979. In 1980 they fell back to their pre-boom level. The government's foreign exchange reserves also tripled between 1976 and 1978, remained high in 1979 and began falling in 1980.

Table 3.15. Monetary survey, 1976–81 (*end of period stocks as % of GDP*)

	1976	1977	1978	1979	1980	1981
Net foreign assets	0.5	0.5	1.4	1.1	0.4	−0.3
Domestic credit	37.2	34.5	30.8	26.2	22.2	20.5
Central government	24.1	24.9	21.5	17.4	15.2	14.0
Public enterprises	6.0	3.8	5.3	5.8	4.6	4.5
Private sector	5.9	5.0	3.5	2.8	2.3	1.8
Other financial institutions	1.2	0.8	0.4	0.3	0.2	0.1
Money	21.9	21.4	19.7	16.6	14.2	12.5
Quasi-money	7.2	5.8	4.8	4.5	4.3	3.5
Restricted deposits	2.3	2.3	2.3	2.3	1.1	0.9
Other items (net)	6.2	5.4	5.3	4.0	3.0	3.4
Forex reserves (US$million)	84.0	136.3	264.8	271.1	180.4	144.9

Source: International Monetary Fund

Table 3.15 also highlights that, although credit to the public sector in the boom period fell, the government continued to receive the lion's share of formal credit in the financial system. Credit to the private sector (including public enterprises) fell from 12% of GDP in 1976 to 6.3% in 1981; however, the bulk of this credit went to the public enterprises.

On the liability side, we see that, despite the boom, the money supply fell in 1978 and 1979, and continued to do so in the years that followed.

In sum, despite some small increases in producer prices and slight trade liberalisation (which was shortly reversed), the Ghanaian control regime was not fundamentally altered by the cocoa boom. Indeed, the cocoa boom may in fact have helped the control regime last even longer than it might have had the boom not occurred. Radical reform began in Ghana in 1983, when the economy had ground to a halt. One of the principal reasons for adopting the reform programme was that the only available sources of foreign assistance were conditional upon reform programmes and the government had no hope of improving the economic situation without foreign assistance. To the extent that the windfall from the cocoa boom made things better than they would have been otherwise, the boom may have put off the 'breaking-point' of the economy and the government by a few years. One might speculte that, had the boom not occurred, the reform programme would have begun sooner.

3.5. Conclusion

The 1970s were a period of substantial economic deterioration in Ghana. So much so that the large increase in the terms of trade during 1977–79 is never referred to in analyses of this period. Rather, attention has focused on the sharp drop in the terms of trade that occurred after the cocoa boom and its contribution to the economic deterioration of the time. Ghana did in fact receive a windfall as a result of the increase in cocoa prices, which is estimated to have totalled 2,915.7 million cedis in 1976 prices or 44.3% of 1976 GDP (2,299.7 million cedis of which were an official windfall and 616 million cedis of which were the windfall to smugglers). The mismanagement that was creating economic difficulties was extended to the cocoa windfall. As a result, the boom served mostly to mitigate economic decline rather than improve matters.

Our analysis suggests that the bulk of the windfall went to the central government and that a good portion was passed on to the public enterprises in the form of transfers. We estimate that, of the portion of the windfall that remained with the central government, about 20% was saved. Of the windfall that went to the private sector, which includes the public enterprises, about 90% was saved. Very little of the windfall was saved domestically. Most was used to acquire foreign assets.

A first feature that stands out is that only a small proportion of the windfall was invested domestically. There seem to be two possible explanations for this. The first is that the investment environment during the period was very poor, largely as a result of macroeconomic mismanagement combined with the control regime. Investment was hindered by shortages of imported inputs and uncertainty with respect to the import control regime, which was constantly changing. Low capacity utilisation implied that utilisation would be expanded before new investment would take place. Public sector credit requirements crowded out the private sector, and financial sector controls made the mobilisation of savings and credit allocation highly inefficient. On top of this, political instability led to substantial uncertainty. All of these factors discouraged domestic investment of the windfall.

The second explanation for the low level of domestic investment of the windfall concerns expectations with respect to the shock. In the initial year of the boom, Cocoa Marketing Board officials assumed that the price rise was a short-term, one-off event. Their expectations were thus exclusive, unrevised and any windfall income would be viewed as transient, hence saved, but saved abroad. In the following years, these officials began to take high prices for granted and thus revised their expectations—they expected the increases in price to continue. Windfall income was now assumed to be permanent and hence consumed.

The collapse in investment which occurred during the boom period and the low levels of investment imply that there would be no construction boom effect as a result of the windfall. The empirical analyses of Section 3.3 confirm this. The shifts in relative prices which would occur in the event of a construction boom do not occur because there is no increase in the demand for non-tradable capital goods as a result of the windfall since domestic investment does not increase.

The second notable feature of the Ghanaian case is the fiscal situation and the government's allocation of the windfall. By 1975/76, the government had reached an unsustainable fiscal position. This, combined with severe deterioration in the economy, implied that both revenues and expenditures fell dramatically during the period of the boom. Hence rather than leading to a clear-cut increase in revenues and reduction in the deficit, the windfall income in Ghana prevented revenue from falling as sharply as it would have had the boom not occurred. With respect to expenditures, the windfall was mostly spent on increases in consumption and transfer payments.

The central government's allocation of the windfall is also of interest. Boom-induced fiscal changes showed that the majority of transfers to the private sector were made directly through transfers. Transfers worth 36% of the official windfall were made to public enterprises and transfers worth 5% of the official windfall were made to households. There was no evidence of transfers owing to increased employment, a wage effect or commodity prices. Unusually, it seems that transfers were the one area of the budget subject to relatively gradual reductions, while other expenditures, particularly capital expenditures, were being cut sharply. The substantial transfers to public enterprises makes sense in light of the importance of political patronage and the significant political uncertainty which existed during this period.

Finally, the Ghanaian case highlights the two-way relationship between the windfall and the control regime. Economic controls affecting the cocoa sector, particularly producer price of cocoa, led to drastic reductions in the production of cocoa and substantial increases in cocoa smuggling. This implied a much lower windfall than would have occurred had the control regime not had such a bias against cocoa production. Hence, the control regime effectively had a part in determining the size of the windfall.

As mentioned above, the control regime also created an environment which discouraged investment. Indeed the control regime was at the heart of the collapse in investment. The regime thus influenced the use of the windfall as well.

In turn, the windfall had minor effects on the control regime, though it did not alter the regime substantially. In 1978, the government increased real producer prices, but only slightly. They were still well below the prices of the early 1970s. There is also some evidence of a short-lived trade liberalisation in 1978. There appears to be little evidence of financial liberalisation. The government's reaction to the boom was to increase interest rates and to increase liquidity ratios in an effort to control domestic credit and the money supply.

Appendix:
Data Sources

Figure 3.1. The London spot prices for cocoa for 1971–78 are from the Central Bureau of Statistics, *Economic Survey 1977–80*. From 1978 data are from the *Quarterly Digest of Statistics (QDS)*, various years.

Figure 3.2. The data on export prices vary significantly depending on the series for cocoa that is used. The export price used in Figure 3.2 is calculated as the value-weighted average of the unit value (e.g. price) indices of cocoa, gold, diamonds, bauxite, manganese and timber and logs as shown in Table 3.A1.

As discussed in note 2, data from the Cocoa Marketing Board (the ones used in Table 3.A1) indicate a larger increase in the cocoa price than do the trade data. Discussions with Ghanaian economists and the Director of Research at the Cocoa Marketing Board suggested that this difference is likely to be due to delays in updating cocoa prices on the part of customs officials. It was suggested that the Cocoa Marketing Board series would be the more appropriate one to use. Thus, Cocoa Marketing Board data for a given crop year, say 1976/77, are incorporated as the cocoa series for 1977. This is because the crop year and Cocoa Board accounts begin in October of each year and end in the September of the following year. The export price series based on the *QDS* trade data and that using the Cocoa Marketing Board data are presented in Table 3.A2 for comparison.

Figure 3.3. Data on the import price index are from the *QDS* for June 1984 and June 1987.

Figure 3.4. The actual terms of trade series used in this chapter (as opposed to the counterfactual series) is calculated by dividing the export price index using CMB

Table 3.A1. Price indices of exports *(1976 = 100)*

	Cocoa	Gold	Diamonds	Bauxite	Man-ganese	Timber and logs
	(1)	(2)	(3)	(4)	(5)	(6)
1976	100	100	100	100	100	100
1977	170	110	135	113	107	117
1978	681	216	369	179	155	104
1979	785	408	542	285	244	281
1980	658	1,118	554	278	280	344
1981	307	936	433	345	286	342
1982	310	789	367	380	163	275

Notes: Columns (1), (2), and (5) based on cedi/metric ton unit values. Column (3) based on cedis' 000 gram unit values; (4) on cedi/carat unit values and column (6) on cedi/cubic metre value-added. Data on volume and value of aluminum and electricity exports not available. Data on cocoa from Cocoa Marketing Board as cited in World Bank (1989: 154). Data on other exports from *Quarterly Digest of Statistics*, June 1984 and June 1987.

Table 3.A2. Export price series with different cocoa price data

	Using *QDS* trade data	Using CMB data
1976	100	100
1977	154	155
1978	256	546
1979	528	668
1980	591	654
1981	415	375
1982	317	351

Notes: *QDS* series calculated as a value-weighted average of export prices using the data for all exports in the June 1984 and June 1987 issues. Series using CMB data calculated as in note to Table 3.A1.

data by the import price index presented in Figure 3.3. The counterfactual shown in Figure 3.4 is then constructed by recalculating the 'CMB' export price index assuming that the cocoa price remains at its 1976 level throughout the boom period and dividing by the import price index (see discussion in text).

Figure 3.5. Real producer price of cocoa from Stryker (1990: 308), deflated by the rural consumer price index from the *QDS* and indexed to 1976.

Table 3.2. Column (1) of Table 3.2 is based on May's (1985: 79) estimates of smuggled cocoa divided by the share of the Brong-Ahafo region in the total production of cocoa (see Stryker 1990: 266). May's estimation is as follows:

$$Q_{CMBBR} = 2.596 + 0.234 PCAP + 0.306 P(-1) + 0.140 R_{BR}(-1) + 0.295 P_{SIC},$$

$$(2.06) \qquad (1.32) \qquad (1.10) \qquad (1.56) \qquad (2.35)$$

$$R^2 = 0.656, \text{ F-statistic} = 7.630, \text{ Rho} = 0.404, \text{ D.W.} = 2.036,$$

where Q_{CMBBR} is the total supply of the Brong-Ahafo region to the CMB; $PCAP$ is production capacity, $P(-1)$ is the real producer price lagged one period, $R_{BR}(-1)$ is rainfall in the Brong-Ahafo region lagged one period, and P_{SIC} is the ratio of the producer price in Ghana to the producer price in the Côte d'Ivoire multiplied by the black-market exchange rate. The amount smuggled is then calculated as $Q_s = ((1-s)/s) Q_{CMB}$, where s is a fraction of cocoa sales to the Cocoa Marketing Board out of total production and is determined as $s_t = (P_{SIC_t})^{\varpi 4}$, where s_t is equal to the ratio of the producer price in Ghana to the producer price in the Côte d'Ivoire to the power of estimated coefficient on the ratio of the producer price variable (see May 1985: 75). Column (2) re-estimates May's equation employing a counterfactual producer price for cocoa in the Côte d'Ivoire. The counterfactual Côte d'Ivoirian producer price is based on the assumption that the producer price in Côte d'Ivoire rises at its 1976 rate in both 1977 and 1978 and at its actual rate thereafter. The results of this estimation using the counterfactual producer price differential, called $P_{SIC}(2)$, are as follows:

$$Q_{CMBBR} = 1.896 + 0.305PCAP + 0.473P(-1) + 0.150R_{BR}(-1) + 0.247P_{SIC}(2),$$
$$(1.69) \quad (1.68) \quad\quad (2.07) \quad\quad\quad (1.25) \quad\quad\quad (1.63)$$

$R^2 = 0.6269$, F-statistic = 4.71, Rho = 0.463, D.W. = 2.22.

The figures derived using the same method as described above are presented in column (2).

Figure 3.6. The data used to construct the non-traded goods index (NT), and traded goods index (TRADED) are from the national accounts data in current and constant prices presented in the *QDS*, various years. Indices are calculated as a weighted average of the quotient of the current and constant series. The non-traded goods price index includes the following sectors: agriculture and livestock (domestic food production, which is by and large non-traded); electricity and water; construction; transport, storage and communications; wholesale and retail trade; and finance, insurance and business. Note that in Ghana some electricity is exported to Togo, but it is not possible to separate electricity and water, so both have been included as non-traded goods. The traded goods price index includes: cocoa production and marketing; forestry and logging; fishing; mining and quarrying; and manufacturing. Ordinarily, the deflator of the manufacturing sector would be used as a proxy for the domestic price of importables; however, during this period these prices are subject to controls. The index for import substitutes (IS) is constructed as a weighted average of the CPI indices for beverages and tobacco, clothing and footwear, and furniture and furnishings using data from the *QDS* (see Table 3.A3).

Figure 3.7. The non-traded capital goods index is calculated as a weighted average of the quotients of the current and constant price series for buildings, other construction and land improvement available in the *QDS* table entitled 'Gross capital formation by type of good'. Non-traded consumer goods include agriculture and livestock (non-traded food production); transport, storage and communication; wholesale and retail trade; and finance, insurance and business from *QDS*

Table 3.A3. Price indices (*1976 = 100*)

	Traded	IS	NT	NT w/out food	NT CAP	NT CONS	NT CONS w/out food	NT food	NT DIST	NT RES
1976	100	100	100	100	100	100	100	100	100	100
1977	143	147	178	137	136	182	137	211	148	124
1978	278	298	295	254	216	298	261	309	329	179
1979	448	429	374	363	383	375	372	366	456	268
1980	569	639	602	631	517	604	661	562	916	366
1981	701	1,508	1,157	1,454	886	1,163	1,553	962	2,433	606

Sources: Calculated from *Quarterly Digest of Statistics* data, as discussed above

national accounts data. The import substitute index is calculated as discussed above for Figure 3.6 (see Table 3.A3).

Figure 3.8. The food price index is calculated as the quotient of the current to constant price of the agriculture and livestock sector of the national accounts from the *QDS*. Distribution consists of the wholesale and retail trade sector. The residual index includes transport, storage and communication and finance, insurance and business categories. Import substitutes are calculated as for Figure 3.6 (see Table 3.A3).

Figure 3.9. Indices for ex-factory manufacturing and distribution are calculated as the quotient of current to constant sector value-added from the national accounts data presented by the *QDS*. Domestic prices of imports are proxied by a weighted average of CPI indices of beverages and tobacco; clothing and footwear; and furniture and furnishings, also from the *QDS*.

NOTES

1. From 1972 to 1974 the average stocks maintained by manufacturers were sufficient for less than two-and-a-half months of grindings. Previously stocks were kept at a level sufficient for five months of grindings (Singh *et al.* 1977: 96).
2. The data from the Cocoa Marketing Board indicate a much larger increase in price than do the official trade statistics. This is likely to be due to the fact that the official trade statistics are based on customs data and although the prices used by customs officials are supposed to be updated weekly, they often go for long periods without being updated. We thus use data provided by the CMB for cocoa. Data on all other exports comes from the trade statistics. See the Appendix to this chapter for details.
3. From 1972 to 1977 the official value of the cedi was 1.15 cedis to the US dollar (period average). It was devalued to 1.51 cedis per dollar in 1978 and to 2.75 cedis per dollar in 1979. The cedi remained fixed at this rate until 1983.
4. A cocoa tree does not bear fruit until five years after it is planted. It reaches maximum yield at about eight years and continues to produce for twenty to twenty-five years.
5. The terms of trade in Figure 3.4 have been directly calculated from the Cocoa Marketing Board data and Ghana's trade statistics. They differs somewhat from other estimates of the terms of trade in Ghana. See the Appendix for details.
6. The counterfactual value of exports is determined by multiplying the counterfactual export price index (column 3) by the actual export volume index (column 2) to derive the counterfactual export value index (column 4). This is then applied to the actual value in 1976 and to counterfactual values thereafter. The windfall is then calculated by subtracting counterfactual exports

from actual exports (column 6). Deflating the value of the boom by the import price index gives the real value of the boom in 1976 prices.

7. We choose to base our estimates on May's work because he incorporates the Ghana/Côte d'Ivoire price differential into his equation and because his work provides us with enough detail to re-estimate his equations. Franco (1981) covers too short a time-period for our purposes and Stryker (1990) chooses to use a rule of thumb for his estimates which obviates any effect that the price differential might have.

8. In order to construct a counterfactual for cocoa smuggling we have re-estimated May's equation (see the Appendix for details). We assume that, if the boom in cocoa prices had not occurred in 1977, the Côte d'Ivoire producer price would not have increased as dramatically as it did in 1977 and 1978— hence we assume that the price paid to producers increased by its 1976 rate in both 1977 and 1978; thereafter the producer price increases at its actual rate. This assumption gives us a counterfactual of the price differential faced by Ghanaian farmers had the cocoa boom not occurred. We use this new differential in re-estimating May's equation and derive a counterfactual for cocoa smuggling. Column (3) in Table 3.2 subtracts counterfactual smuggling from 'actual' smuggling to give us an estimate of the amount of smuggling that occurred as the result of the cocoa boom (or rather, as the result of the increased price differential that resulted from the cocoa boom). If we multiply the volume of cocoa smuggling resulting from the boom by the black-market price in thousand cedis, we arrive at the value in current prices of one component of the windfall to cocoa smugglers. In addition to the extra cocoa smuggled as a result of the boom, smugglers of cocoa will receive a windfall as a result of the increased price they receive for what they would have smuggled anyway. This is calculated as normal (non-boom) cocoa smuggling (column 2) times the differential in boom and non-boom prices (column 4 minus column 5). Adding the two components together and deflating this by import prices (column 7) gives us the total unofficial windfall in 1976 prices.

9. The interest rate on treasury bills during this period averaged 10%. This figure of 10% is also a frequently assumed discount rate in economies such as Ghana's.

10. The same calculations were done using a discount rate of 5% and 15%. The permanent income gain (in 1976 prices) using 5% was 119.4 million cedis or 1.8% of GDP; using 15% the gain was 240.0 million cedis or 3.6% of GDP.

11. In this case, growth in Ghanaian production was assumed to be low (2%), growth in rest of world production was assumed to be high (4.25% to 1974/75 and 4.5% thereafter), and growth of world consumption was assumed to be moderate.

12. Personal communication with Research Manager, Cocoa Marketing Board.

13. In Table 3.3 the actual investment propensities (column 1) are applied to a series of real income which includes the windfall (column 2), since the windfall can be taken to augment GDP. This gives the value of GFKF in 1976 prices (column 3). In constructing the counterfactual value of GFKF we need to specify counterfactual GDP and counterfactual investment propensities. In 1976 and 1977 counterfactual income would have been actual GDP at 1976 prices (assuming a one-year gestation lag between investment and its returns).

In subsequent years, GDP is calculated as actual GDP minus the assumed 10% return upon windfall investment. This return is calculated as the difference between actual and counterfactual investment (hence, the calculations are iterative). With regard to counterfactual propensities to acquire GFKF, we assume that these do not change. Given the dramatic drop in investment that was occurring, it seems that the domestic economic and political environment dominated the shock in terms of affecting decisions concerning investment. A number of counterfactual investment propensities were considered, and in every case counterfactual investment values were negative. It does seem implausible that investment would decline as the result of the boom; it is thus assumed that the boom had no effect on investment propensities.

14. Foreign savings in 1976 prices as a proportion of GDP is shown in column (1) of Table 3.4. The foreign savings propensity was 2.36% in 1975 and 3.45% in 1976, but then fell very sharply to −9.56% of GDP by 1978. We assume that without the boom the foreign savings propensity would have fallen to zero in 1977 and remained zero for the rest of the period. This reflects Ghana's lack of access to foreign credit during this period. We apply our counterfactual foreign savings propensity to counterfactual GDP to obtain counterfactual foreign savings in 1976 prices. Windfall foreign savings are then derived as the difference between actual and counterfactual foreign savings.

15. Note that the sharp drop in the series that occurs in 1979 may be explained by a very strong re-imposition of price controls during this year as part of the first Rawlings government. These strong controls were short-lived and became largely ineffective when Limann came to power in September of the same year.

16. Note that output figures have been adjusted to include smuggling estimated from Table 3.2 in cocoa production and marketing.

17. This large increase in the food-production sector reflects the movement of cocoa farmers out of cocoa and into food production given the rapidly declining real producer price. It also reflects a movement out of the cities and into subsistence farming in rural areas that occurred at the time (see Stryker 1990.)

18. Each year the Cocoa Marketing Board receives advances at the beginning of the crop season in order to pay producers. These advances are repaid when payment for cocoa exports has been received.

19. See Aryeetey *et al.* (1990) and the discussion in Section 3.4 on credit controls.

20. Note that the majority of credit to the agriculture sector is from the Agricultural Development Bank, rather from the first tier of commercial banks (whose lending to agriculture is about 6% of their portfolio).

21. The Central Bureau of Statistics provides data on recorded employment on a yearly basis. This data is collected through surveys of businesses and industries in various regions of the country. While these data have the advantage of being available on a yearly basis, they have the disadvantage of incomplete coverage. Because of the nature of the survey, agriculture and private sector industries are underrepresented and services are overrepresented. It also appears that in the 1970s, when the economic crisis deepened, the coverage of the survey was reduced. Consequently we have chosen to use the census data.

22. Also note that owing to the deterioration of the economy during this period,

a substantial number of Ghanaians left the country to work elsewhere in Africa and abroad.

23. Note that because we cannot separate out cocoa employment from total agricultural employment, we have considered all of agricultural employment as non-tradable. This implies that non-tradable employment is overestimated and tradable employment is underestimated.

24. There are insufficient data on public enterprise accounts during this period to allow us to construct the accounts of the complete public sector. Hence, the term 'public sector' here refers to the central government and the 'private sector' incorporates public enterprises unless explicitly stated otherwise.

25. Our counterfactual draws on the government's Five Year Development Plan for 1975/76 to 1979/80, which sets out the government's planned revenues and expenditures. It is clear from the development plan that the government did not anticipate the substantial drop in revenues that occurred in the mid–late 1970s. It estimated that revenue would be 17.3% of GDP in 1975/76, 16.0% of GDP in 1976/77, 15.1% in 1977/78, 14.5% of GDP in 1978/79 and 14.2% of GDP in 1979/80. In the event, revenues were on average 5% of GDP lower than the government had planned. For our revenue counterfactual, however, we must consider what government revenues would have been had the cocoa boom not occurred. In this case revenues would have been even lower than they in fact were. Thus for our revenue counterfactual we use actual revenue minus the revenue that went directly to the government (in the form of the export tax) as the result of the boom.

In constructing our expenditure counterfactual we also consider the government's planned expenditure. Actual consumption and capital expenditures were less than the government had set out in its plan—indicating that these areas were the ones that suffered cuts even during the boom period. We keep these expenditures at their actual share of GDP in the counterfactual because it is unlikely that they could have been cut any further. In contrast, transfers were a much larger proportion of GDP in practice than was set out in the development plan. Revenue from the boom thus appears to have been used for increased transfer payments. In the counterfactual, it is assumed, given Ghana's limited access to foreign credit during this period, that interest payments did not change as a result of the cocoa boom. Counterfactual transfer payments are determined as the residual given the above assumptions and the assumptions concerning the effect of the boom on the deficit.

26. Note that because budgetary data are in fiscal years we have converted the windfall into fiscal years in order to calculate fiscal changes resulting from the boom.

27. Because our disaggregation of domestic transfers only goes back to 1977/78, we have made the assumption that current transfers to households in 1976/77 were 15% of total transfers, as in 1977/78; thus current transfers to public enterprises and local government are assumed to be 35.3% of transfers.

28. If transfers to public enterprises and local government are excluded from private transfers, total transfers to the private sector are 112.2 million cedis (4.7% of the official windfall). This combined with the unofficial windfall of 616.0 million cedis implies a total windfall to the private sector of 728.2 million

cedis or 25.0% of total windfall income and a total windfall to the public sector of 2,187.5 million cedis or 75.0% of the total windfall.

29. Note that because we have assumed no change in the overall deficit, government net assets other than fixed capital formation are assumed not to have been affected by the boom.

30. This assumes that all foreign asset accumulation was undertaken by the private sector, which was in fact not the case. Unfortunately there are insufficient data to determine how much of foreign savings was public sector and how much was private sector. The estimate given here provides an upper bound to private savings.

31. If transfers to public enterprises and local government are not included as transfers to the private sector the public savings rate of windfall income is 50.4% (279.6 + 822.3)/2,187.5 and the private sector savings rate of windfall income is 81.9% (2.9 − 822.3 + 1,416.0)/728.2.

32. Nominal programmed imports deflated by the import price index.

33. See the *Quarterly Digest of Statistics*, June 1987: 67.

34. The commercial banks were required to have at least 20% of their loan portfolios directed to the agricultural sector (see Aryeetey *et al.* 1990: 24; data from IMF).

35. Aryeetey and Gockel (1990) estimate that on a household level between 20% (urban) and 50% (rural) of incomes are not consumed but saved either in the form of real assets or with the informal financial system.

REFERENCES

Aryeetey, E.Y. and F. Gockel. 1990. 'Mobilizing Domestic Resources for Capital Formation in Ghana: The Role of Informal Financial Markets'. Research Paper 3. Nairobi: African Economic Research Consortium.

Aryeetey, E.Y., Y. Asante, F. Gockel and A. Kyei. 1990. 'Mobilizing Domestic Resources for African Development and Diversification: A Ghanaian Case Study'. Research Report presented at a workshop of the International Development Centre, Queen Elizabeth House, Oxford University, 16–20 July 1990.

Bank of Ghana. various years. *Quarterly Economic Bulletin*. Accra.

Bateman, Maurice. 1971. 'Ghana's Cocoa Prospects, 1971–1985'. Unpublished mimeo for the World Bank.

Beckman, Bjorn. 1976. *Organizing the Farmers: Cocoa Politics and National Development in Ghana*. Uppsala: Scandinavian Institute of African Studies.

Bevan, David, Paul Collier and Jan Gunning. 1990. *Controlled Open Economies*. Oxford: Clarendon Press.

Central Bureau of Statistics, Republic of Ghana. 1962. *1961 Statistical Yearbook*. Accra.

——1968. *1967–68 Statistical Yearbook*. Accra.

——1981. *Economic Survey, 1977–80*. Accra.

Corden, W.M. 1984. 'Booming Sector and Dutch Disease Economics: Survey and Consolidation'. *Oxford Economic Papers*. 36: 359–80.

Corden, W.M. and Peter Neary. 1982. 'Booming Sector and De-industrialization in a Small Open Economy'. *The Economic Journal*. 92(December): 825–48.

Ewusi, K. 1978. 'The Size of the Labour Force and Structure of Employment in Ghana'. ISSER Technical Publication No. 37. Legon: Institute of Social, Statistical and Economic Research.

Franco, K.G. 1981. 'The Optimal Producer Price of Cocoa in Ghana'. *Journal of Development Economics*. 8: 72–92.

Frimpong-Ansah, Jonathan. 1991. *The Vampire State in Africa: The Political Economy of Decline in Ghana*. London: James Curry.

Jebuni, C.D., A.D. Oduro and K.A. Tutu. 1990. 'Trade and Payments Liberalization and Economic Performance in Ghana'. Paper presented at African Economic Research Consortium Workshop, Abidjan, Côte d'Ivoire, 9–14 December 1990.

Jebuni, C.D., N.K. Sowa and K.A. Tutu. 1991. 'Exchange Rate Policy and Macroeconomic Performance in Ghana'. Research Paper 6. Nairobi: African Economic Research Consortium.

Little, I.M.D., Richard Cooper, W.M. Corden and Sarath Rajapatirana. 1993. *Boom, Crisis and Adjustment: The Macroeconomic Experience of Developing Countries*. Washington, DC: Oxford University Press for the World Bank.

May, Ernesto. 1985. 'Exchange Controls and Parallel Market Economies in Sub-Saharan Africa: Focus on Ghana'. World Bank Staff Working Paper 711. Washington, DC: World Bank.

Neary, J.P. and Sweder van Wijnbergen. 1986. *Natural Resources and the Macroeconomy*. Oxford: Blackwell.

Singh, S.J., J.C.L. Hully de Vries and P. Young. 1977. 'Coffee, Tea and Cocoa: Market Prospects and Development Lending'. World Bank Staff Occasional Paper 22. Washington, DC: World Bank.

Statistical Service, Republic of Ghana. various years. *Quarterly Digest of Statistics*. Accra: Statistical Service.

——1987. *1984 Population Census of Ghana*. Accra: Statistical Service.

Stryker, J. Dirck. 1990. 'Trade, Exchange Rate and Agricultural Pricing Policies in Ghana'. In A. Krueger, M. Schiff and A. Valdes. eds. *The Political Economy of Agricultural Pricing Policy*. Vol. 3. Baltimore, MD: Johns Hopkins University Press.

Supreme Military Council. 1977. *Five Year Development Plan, 1975/76–1979/80*. Part I. Accra.

van Wijnbergen, Sweder. 1984. 'Inflation, Employment, and the Dutch Disease in Oil Exporting Countries: A Short-run Disequilibrium Analysis'. *Quarterly Journal of Economics*. 99: 232–50.

World Bank. 1975. *Fiscal and Balance of Payments Aspects of Ghana's Development*. Report No. 638a-GH. World Bank Internal Publication. 19 May 1975.

——1977. *Ghana: Economic Position and Prospects; Prospects for Exports of Processed Products; Financial Structure—A Flow-of-Funds Approach*. Report No. 1533a-GH. World Bank Internal Publication. 29 June 1977.

——1981. *Ghana: Report on Domestic Resource Mobilization*. Report No. 3072-GH. World Bank Internal Publication. 18 February 1981.

——1985. *Ghana: Towards Structural Adjustment.* Report No. 5854-GH. World Bank Internal Publication. 7 October 1985.

——1987. *Ghana: Policies and Issues of Structural Adjustment.* Report No. 6635-GH. World Bank Internal Publication. 30 March 1987.

——1989. *Ghana: Structural Adjustment for Growth.* Report No. 7515-GH. World Bank Internal Publication. 23 January 1989.

——1991. *Ghana: Progress on Adjustment.* Report No. 9475-GH. World Bank Internal Publication. 16 April 1991.

4

The Ivorian Cocoa and Coffee Boom of 1976–79: The End of a Miracle?

HAFEZ GHANEM

4.1. Introduction

From independence, in 1960, to 1975 the Ivorian economy grew at an average annual rate of around 6.5%, in real terms. This remarkable growth was achieved while maintaining internal and external equilibria. The Ivorian 'miracle' was mainly due to the country's vast natural resources, its political stability and the inflow of cheap labour from neighbouring sahelian countries. Economic policies were conservative; they emphasised fiscal and monetary restraint while maintaining administratively determined agricultural producer prices at levels that encouraged the expansion of production, especially that of cocoa and coffee. Government policy changed markedly as a result of the cocoa and coffee boom of the mid-1970s. Expenditures were increased to unprecedented levels. Adjusting to the end of the boom in 1980 proved to be a daunting task. Thus, the 1980s were a period of deep crisis for the Ivorian economy, with negative GDP growth and soaring fiscal and current account deficits, except for a brief respite during 1985–86, when another temporary improvement in the terms of trade occurred.

In this paper I analyse the behaviour of the Ivorian economy during the boom period. I show that the commodity boom has led to an investment boom and a sharp decline in the returns to capital. This behaviour of the economy as a whole can be explained by the control regime: all of the initial windfall gain was captured by the government, which launched a massive public investment programme. If the full windfall had been passed to private agents the outcome would probably have been different.

The paper is divided into eight sections. After this introduction, Sections 4.2 and 4.3 describe the control regime and the nature of the shock. Section 4.4 analyses the behaviour of the representative agent, and Section 4.5 describes the evolution of relative prices and tests whether there was a construction boom. Sections 4.6 and 4.7 study the impact of the control regime on the economy's behaviour during the boom, with Section 4.6 looking at fiscal policy and Section 4.7 analysing monetary policy and the role of the financial sector. Finally, my overall assessment and conclusions are presented in Section 4.8.

4.2. The Control Regime

Membership in the West African Monetary Union (Union Monétaire Ouest-Africaine, UMOA) is the most important feature of Côte d'Ivoire's macroeconomic policies. Between the mid-1950s and 1994 the union's common currency, the CFA franc, was pegged to the French franc at a fixed exchange rate (1 FF = 50 CFAF). Thus, the exchange rate was not considered to be an instrument of national economic policy during the period analysed here. The CFA franc is convertible and the capital account open. This convertibility is guaranteed by the French Treasury, which finances the balance of payments deficits of Franc Zone members through a special operations account. In return, reserves are deposited with the French Treasury, and monetary policy is managed by the Union's Central Bank (the Banque Centrale des Etats de l'Afrique de l'Ouest), which controls the money supply to achieve its balance of payments targets. Fiscal deficits cannot be monetised, since there is a limit on government borrowing from the BCEAO. The stock of government debt to the BCEAO in any given year cannot exceed 20% of the previous year's tax revenues.

During the period under study (1975–80), the BCEAO's policies presented a typical example of financial repression: all interest rates were administratively determined and negative in real terms, credit allocation was controlled and preferential lending rates to 'priority' activities were in place. The financial sector was relatively underdeveloped, with four commercial banks accounting for some 90% of deposits. The banks relied heavily on the BCEAO for refinancing, with BCEAO refinancing accounting for about 35% of the financial system's liabilities. As a result of this set-up and the underdevelopment of the domestic financial system, an important portion of financial intermediation was carried out abroad, mainly in France, with depositors sending their money abroad and foreign banks lending directly to the Ivorian private and public sectors.

The marketing of export crops was completely controlled by the state through the Marketing Board (the Caisstab). This is a system under which all the risk (windfall losses and gains) is borne by the Government. The Caisstab fixed farm-gate prices as well as all marketing costs (transport, storage, interest payments, various profit margins, etc.), which were guaranteed to licensed exporters. Exporters could not sell their products without the agreement of the Caisstab, which monitored the CIF price and the quantities sold. The difference between the actual export price and guaranteed costs constituted Caisstab revenues.

The rest of the economy was also highly controlled. In 1969, Côte d'Ivoire introduced a complicated system of price controls which covered virtually all domestically produced and imported goods. Imports were also controlled through quantitative restrictions and reference prices. Labour market regulations were pervasive, with limits on hiring and firing and minimum wages for different categories of workers.

4.3. The Nature of the Shock

The cocoa and coffee boom was a short term of trade shock caused by weather conditions in Brazil. The price which Côte d'Ivoire received for its cocoa (in CFAF) increased by 204% between 1975 and 1977, and the price of robusta coffee increased by 250%. This certainly led to a large increase in windfall income; especially since those two commodities represented 42% of the value of Côte d'Ivoire's exports (FOB). Thus, the country's barter terms of trade improved by some 85% between 1975 and 1977.

Figure 4.1 shows the evolution of Côte d'Ivoire's barter terms of trade between 1975 and 1983. It indicates that the boom started in 1976, reached a peak in 1977 and ended in 1980–81, when the terms of trade were more or less at the same level as in 1975. The shock was very sharp but did not last for a long time: the terms of trade quickly returned to their long-term trend.

One method of measuring the magnitude of the boom is to calculate its impact on Gross Domestic Income (GDY) and show by how much this

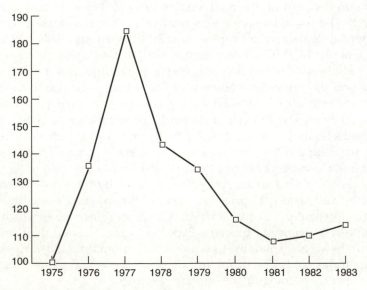

Figure 4.1. Barter terms of trade, 1975–83.

deviated from GDP. First a terms of trade adjustment, measured as the difference between exports deflated by the MPI and exports deflated by the XPI, is calculated. GDY is then defined as GDP in constant CFAF plus the terms of trade adjustment. The deviation between GDY and GDP can then be used as a measure of the impact of the trade shock. This calculation is presented in Table 4.1 and shows that the windfall gains from the boom amounted to 11% of GDP in 1976, 26% in 1977, 20% in 1978, 14% in 1979 and 9% in 1980 as the boom was reaching its end.

Another method of calculating the magnitude of the boom consists of estimating the value of windfall exports in nominal terms, which is simply obtained by multiplying the terms of trade adjustment by the import price index. The present value of the windfall was calculated using a discount rate of 10%. This yielded a value of 764 billion CFAF, or 92% of 1975 GDP.

In order to classify the Ivorian cocoa and coffee boom it is necessary to consider whether it was expected and whether it led economic agents to revise their expectations of future prices. Given the magnitude of the boom it is difficult to believe that the Ivorian producers and government had expected the boom. Coffee and cocoa have been grown in Côte d'Ivoire, mainly by smallholders, since before independence and

Table 4.1. The magnitude of the boom (*billion CFAF*)

	1975	1976	1977	1978	1979	1980
Exports in current prices (goods and NFS)	306.50	465.00	656.10	651.10	673.00	744.10
Export price index	100.00	135.71	208.07	195.34	197.20	194.41
Import price index	100.00	105.24	115.71	120.45	136.41	152.62
Exports in constant 1975 CFAF	306.50	342.63	315.32	333.31	341.27	382.75
Terms of trade adjustment	0.00	99.23	251.70	207.25	152.10	104.81
GDY in constant 1975 CFAF	834.50	1,029.63	1,216.92	1,265.08	1,231.00	1,308.93
GDP in constant 1975 CFAF	834.50	930.40	965.22	1,057.83	1,078.90	1,204.12
GDY/GDP	1.00	1.11	1.26	1.20	1.14	1.09
Windfall exports (billion current CFAF)		104.43	291.24	249.63	207.48	159.96
Present value of windfall exports	764.19					
Present value of windfall/1975 GDP	91.57					

fluctuations in their prices had occurred in the past, but never had they been so sharp. Hence, it seems unlikely that the agents' subjective probability distribution allowed for such an event, and I conclude that the shock was exclusive. The probability of such a sharp increase in cocoa and coffee prices reoccurring is quite remote, since the weather conditions in Brazil which led to the increase were highly unusual. It was clear that the terms of trade had returned rapidly to their long-run trend. Therefore, it seems that there was no reason for economic agents to change their price expectations; that is, the shock was unrevised. Classifying the shock as exclusive and unrevised implies that it was a pure windfall: permanent income only rose inasmuch as this windfall was invested. It should be noted that this classification differs from that of Nowak (1994), who argues that the boom led to a change in agents' future expectations.

4.4. Behaviour of the Representative Agent

In order to analyse the behaviour of the economy as a whole during the boom period it is necessary to construct a counterfactual with which the actual outcome can be compared. I have, therefore, constructed a consistent set of counterfactual national accounts and balance of payments for the boom period, under the assumption that the terms of trade remain at their 1975 level. This counterfactual scenario was constructed as follows:

1. It was assumed that the propensity to consume out of permanent income remained constant and equal to its average level during 1971–75, and permanent income was defined as being equal to the value of output at 1975 relative prices. Thus, a series for counterfactual consumption (C) was obtained.
2. Ideally, gross fixed capital formation (GFKF) would be determined so that, at the margin, the rate of return on investment is equal to the cost of foreign borrowing. However, to derive such a series a much more sophisticated model than the one used here would be needed. Instead, I assumed that the level of GFKF prior to the boom relative to the capital stock was optimal. Thus, using GDP as a proxy for the stock of capital, I fixed the ratio of GFKF to GDP to its average during 1971–75—admittedly a very rough approximation.
3. Counterfactual GDP at time t was defined as GDP at time $t-1$ plus GFKF at time $t-1$ divided by the average value of the incremental capital–output ratio (ICOR) for the period 1971–75.
4. Counterfactual real exports were obtained by maintaining the share of exports in GDP constant at its 1971–75 level.
5. Counterfactual GDY was set equal to GDP since the terms of trade were assumed fixed at their 1975 level.

6. The counterfactual resource gap (RG) was calculated as the sum of counterfactual C and investment less counterfactual GDY.
7. Thus, counterfactual imports were calculated as the sum of the counterfactual resource gap and counterfactual exports; and counterfactual gross domestic savings (GDS) were obtained by subtracting the counterfactual resource gap from counterfactual investment.
8. The treatment of the stock of foreign debt posed some problems. The change in a country's stock of debt from one year to the next is, in theory, exactly equal to the current account deficit. However, available debt data cover medium- and long-term debt only and hence do not satisfy this condition. Therefore, I constructed a 'hypothetical' debt series by taking the earliest reliable estimate of the stock of Ivorian debt (1977) and calculating a debt series by adding (subtracting) the current account deficit to obtain a debt figure for the following (preceding) years.
9. The average interest rate on the debt is then defined as actual interest payments divided by this 'hypothetical' debt series.
10. The counterfactual balance of payments was then constructed by multiplying counterfactual exports and imports by the import price index (to maintain constant terms of trade) to obtain a counterfactual resource balance. To obtain a counterfactual current account balance, counterfactual exports and imports of factor services were assumed to be the same as their actual values, except for the interest on the foreign debt. This was calculated by applying the average actual interest rate to the counterfactual stock of debt defined as the past year's debt plus the past year's counterfactual current account deficit.

Table 4.2 shows the results of these calculations for GFKF and GDP. It indicates that the terms of trade improvement was accompanied by an important increase in domestic investment, with windfall GFKF representing about 56% of windfall GDY. The increase in investment was accompanied by a decline in its efficiency. The incremental capital–output ratio increased rapidly. The average ICOR during the period 1976–81 was 60% higher than during the period 1970–75. Despite this apparent decline in the return to investment, output was higher as a result of the commodity boom, with windfall GDP in 1981, at the end of the boom, amounting to 102 billion CFAF, or 8.4% of actual GDP.

The behaviour of consumption and savings is shown in Table 4.3. Since the shock was classified as exclusive and unrevised, it left permanent income unchanged except inasmuch as the windfall was invested. Hence, consumption should not have changed as a result of the terms of trade shock and the entire windfall should have been saved. In fact, this did not happen, and the increase in savings was less than windfall income. The propensity to save out of the windfall, defined as the ratio between

Table 4.2. Actual and counterfactual investment and growth *(billion 1975 CFAF)*

	1975	1976	1977	1978	1979	1980	1981
Actuals							
GDP	834.50	930.40	965.22	1,057.83	1,078.90	1,204.12	1,218.46
GDY	834.50	1,029.63	1,216.92	1,265.08	1,231.00	1,308.93	1,260.39
GFKF	183.90	226.92	324.67	395.88	357.15	359.22	323.73
GFKF/GDP	22.04	24.39	33.64	37.42	33.10	29.83	26.57
GFKF/GDY	22.04	22.04	26.68	31.29	29.01	27.44	25.68
Counterfactuals							
GDP	834.50	876.66	920.02	965.53	1,013.29	1,063.42	1,116.02
GDY	834.50	876.66	920.02	965.53	1,013.29	1,063.42	1,116.02
GFKF	183.90	189.17	198.53	208.35	218.66	229.47	240.82
GFKF/GDP	22.04	21.58	21.58	21.58	21.58	21.58	21.58
GFKA/GDY	22.04	21.58	21.58	21.58	21.58	21.58	21.58
Windfall GFKF	0.00	37.75	126.14	187.53	138.50	129.75	82.91
Windfall GDP	0.00	53.74	45.20	92.30	65.61	140.70	102.44
Windfall GDY	0.00	152.97	296.89	299.55	217.71	245.51	144.37
Windfall GFKF/windfall GDY		24.68	42.49	62.61	63.62	52.85	57.43

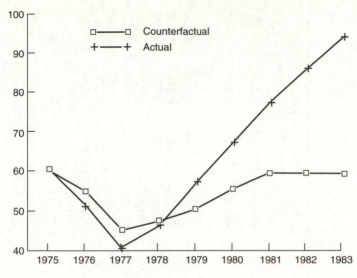

Figure 4.2. Actual and counterfactual debt/GDP, 1975–83

Table 4.3. Actual and counterfactual consumption and savings (*billion 1975 CFAF*)

	1975	1976	1977	1978	1979	1980	1981
Actuals							
Consumption	646.00	736.20	795.17	881.69	907.84	1,006.52	937.56
GDS	188.50	293.43	421.74	383.39	323.16	302.41	322.83
C/GDP	77.41	79.13	82.38	83.35	84.14	83.59	76.95
C/GDY	77.41	71.50	65.34	69.69	73.75	76.90	74.39
GDS/GDP	22.59	31.54	43.69	36.24	29.95	25.11	26.50
GDS/GDY	22.59	28.50	34.66	30.31	26.25	23.10	25.61
Counterfactuals							
Consumption	646.00	664.56	697.43	731.93	768.14	806.13	846.01
GDS	188.50	212.10	222.59	233.60	245.16	257.28	270.01
C/GDP	77.41	75.81	75.81	75.81	75.81	75.81	75.81
C/GDY	77.41	75.81	75.81	75.81	75.81	75.81	75.81
GDS/GDP	22.59	24.19	24.19	24.19	24.19	24.19	24.19
GDS/GDY	22.59	24.19	24.19	24.19	24.19	24.19	24.19
Windfall consumption	0.00	71.64	97.74	149.76	139.70	200.38	91.54
Windfall GDS	0.00	81.33	199.15	149.78	78.00	45.12	52.82
Windfall GDS /windfall GDY		53.17	67.08	50.00	35.83	18.38	36.59

Table 4.4. Actual and counterfactual balance of payments and debt (*billion current CFAF*)

	1975	1976	1977	1978	1979	1980	1981	1982	1983
Actuals									
Exports of goods and non-factor services	306.50	465.00	656.10	651.10	673.00	744.10	856.10	938.00	940.00
Imports of goods and non-factor services	305.30	403.80	559.20	667.40	732.50	864.60	892.10	945.00	917.00
Resource balance	1.20	61.20	96.90	−16.30	−59.50	−120.50	−36.00	−7.00	23.00
Interest on the foreign debt	11.70	17.70	24.10	37.50	50.30	69.20	103.50	153.80	190.00
Worker remittances (outflow)	38.00	69.20	84.70	103.40	120.00	151.20	138.60	152.00	129.00
Other (outflow)	17.60	20.20	23.50	31.40	32.20	37.00	28.20	23.90	32.90
Net factor income	−67.30	−107.10	−132.30	−172.30	−202.50	−257.40	−270.30	−329.70	−351.90
Net transfers	−2.20	−5.20	−7.10	−13.30	−30.50	−9.30	−3.40	0.10	−24.10
Current account balance	−68.30	−51.10	−42.50	−201.90	−292.50	−387.20	−309.70	−336.60	−353.00
Current account/GDP	−8.18	−4.59	−2.76	−11.32	−15.04	−17.43	−13.33	−13.50	−13.31
Stock of debt (hypothetical)	506.10	574.40	625.50	827.40	1,119.90	1,507.10	1,816.80	2,153.40	2,506.40
Debt/GDP	60.65	51.56	40.64	46.41	57.58	67.83	78.20	86.38	94.48
Average interest rate	3.50		4.20	6.00	6.08	6.18	6.87	8.47	8.82

Counterfactuals

Exports of goods and non-factor services	306.50	356.86	411.78	449.85	534.66	627.78	771.87	918.51	1,070.66
Imports of goods and non-factor services	305.30	341.52	399.37	420.68	511.64	619.13	754.08	892.22	1,000.98
Resource balance	1.20	15.34	12.42	29.17	23.02	8.65	17.79	26.30	69.68
Interest on the foreign debt	11.70	17.70	24.18	40.03	47.22	57.29	75.32	108.16	131.69
Worker remittances (outflow)	38.00	42.44	48.97	53.50	63.58	74.66	91.79	109.23	127.32
Other (outflow)	17.60	20.20	23.50	31.40	32.20	37.00	28.20	23.90	32.90
Net factor income	−67.30	−80.34	−96.65	−124.92	−143.00	−168.95	−195.31	−241.29	−291.92
Net transfers	−2.20	−5.20	−7.10	−13.30	−30.50	−9.30	−3.40	0.10	−24.10
Current account balance	−68.30	−70.20	−91.33	−109.05	−150.48	−169.60	−180.92	−214.90	−246.34
Current account/GDP	−8.18	−6.69	−6.23	−6.70	−8.24	−8.64	−8.50	−8.62	−8.47
Stock of debt	506.10	576.30	667.63	776.69	927.17	1,096.77	1,277.69	1,492.59	1,738.93
Debt/GDP	60.65	54.90	45.51	47.73	50.76	55.89	60.05	59.89	59.81

windfall savings and windfall income, averaged around 44% during the boom period.

Figure 4.2 and Table 4.4 compare actual and counterfactual balance of payments and debt accumulation. Looking at the actual figures it is interesting to note that the propensity to invest out of the windfall was higher than the propensity to save, except in 1976 and 1977. The difference between windfall investment and windfall savings was financed through increased foreign borrowing. After an initial reduction in 1976–77, the current account deficit jumps to 13.3% of GDP in 1978, 5 percentage points above its 1975 level, and continues to rise, to 15% in 1979 and 17% in 1980. As a result, by 1981 the debt to GDP ratio reached 78%, some 18 percentage points above its 1975 level. The counterfactual scenario is more stable: the current account deficit remains at around 6–8% of GDP and the stock of debt at the end of the boom remains at more or less the same level, relative to GDP, as in 1975.

4.5. The Construction Boom and Relative Prices

Considering the change in the structure of demand and output during the period 1975–81, it seems clear that the commodity boom led to a construction boom. The share of investment in GDP at market prices rose from 22% in 1975 to a peak of 29.7% in 1979 before falling again to 22.5% in 1982. The rise and fall in investment corresponds exactly to the evolution of the terms of trade with a one-year lag. Consumption behaviour was exactly the opposite: the share of consumption in GDP fell from 77% in 1975 to 66% in 1977, before rising again to 76% in 1982. This indicates that the demand for non-traded capital goods should have risen proportionally more than the demand for non-traded consumer goods.

The increased investment demand was associated with a change in the structure of output. The share of construction in GDP at factor costs rose from 7% in 1975 to 10% in 1978 then fell again to 7% in 1981, mirroring the commodity boom (Figure 4.3). The share of other non-traded goods and services in GDP moved in the opposite direction; falling from 47% in 1975 to 45% in 1978 and then rising again to 47% in 1981. That is, the boom was not associated with a change in the structure of output in favour of non-traded goods in general, but rather it specifically led to a greater output of non-traded investment goods—construction.

Before analysing movements in relative prices it is necessary to consider the effects of import and price controls. Import controls would, at the margin, lead to tradable prices moving in the same direction as non-tradable prices, since the supply of traded goods becomes nearly as inelastic as that of non-tradables. Hence, one would expect the domestic price of tradables to rise during the boom as a result of the increased demand, and

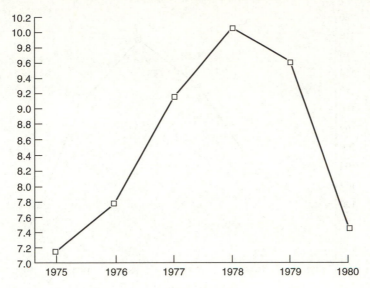

Figure 4.3. Share of construction in GDP, 1975–80

then fall again once the boom is over. If price controls are effective, those price movements would not be observed, and quantity rationing would occur. In fact, owing to administrative weaknesses and some flexibility in applying existing regulations, price controls have not been effective in Côte d'Ivoire except for goods produced by a monopoly (so there is only one seller to control) or goods which are considered to be politically sensitive necessities so the administration seriously tries to enforce the fixed price (oil, rice, bread, gasoline, etc.). The data indicate that import restrictions were more effective than price controls. Comparing the domestic price of manufactured goods and the import prices, it is noted that the index of the ratio between the two rose from 100 in 1975 to 118 in 1978 before falling to 96 in 1980 (Figure 4.4).

If import controls were completely fixed (that is, supply elasticity is zero) then imported goods would have to be treated as non-traded and one would not expect to observe an appreciation of the real exchange rate as predicted by the Dutch Disease literature. In fact, this did not turn out to be the case in Côte d'Ivoire. Import restrictions were somewhat relaxed during the boom period. Thus, imports of manufactured goods, the most heavily protected sector in the economy, grew (in real terms) by about 60% between 1975 and 1988, before falling again to about their 1975 level in 1980–81. That is, although the supply of imports was not totally elastic—as is indicated by the fact that domestic prices of imported goods increased faster than world prices during the boom—the controls them-

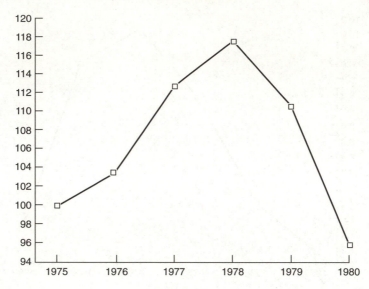

Figure 4.4. Ratio of the domestic price of manufactures to import prices, 1975–80 (*1975 = 100*)

selves seem to have been endogenous, so that the supply of imported goods did increase in response to the higher demand.

Thus, the movement in the real exchange rate (defined here as the ratio between the prices of non-tradables and tradables) predicted by the Dutch Disease literature was observed in Côte d'Ivoire; although it would probably have been more pronounced had there been no import or price controls. The real exchange rate index rose from 100 in 1975 to 125 in 1977 and then fell again to 101 in 1980 after the boom was over (Figure 4.5). This result is similar to that of Nowak (1994).

In order to check whether the conclusion of the construction booms theory (that the price of non-tradable investment goods will rise faster than that of other non-tradables) holds in the case of Côte d'Ivoire, I compared the evolution of the construction deflator with that of the deflators for other non-tradable sectors, services. This goes beyond the work of Nowak (1994), who looks only at the relative price of tradables to non-tradables. Comparing the price index for construction with that for services yields the result predicted by the theory of construction booms: the ratio of those two indices rises during the boom (from 100 in 1975 to 140 in 1978 and 160 in 1979) and then starts falling again as the boom subsides (to 130 in 1981, Figure 4.6). The fact that the construction boom lasted longer than the commodity boom is not surprising. Investment continued growing after the terms of trade returned to their trend level since it was financed through increased foreign borrowing.

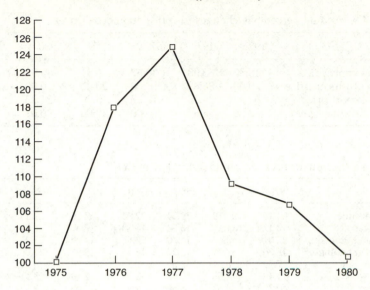

Figure 4.5. Real exchange rate, 1975–80 (*1975 = 100*)

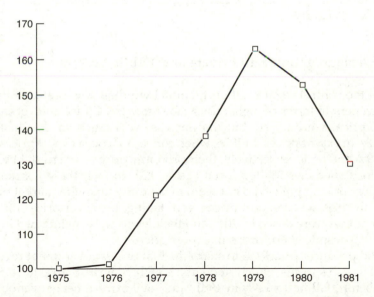

Figure 4.6. Ratio of the price of construction to public services, 1975–81
(*1975 = 100*)

Table 4.5. Annual percentage changes in coffee and cocoa prices

	1976	1977	1978	1979	1980	1981
Coffee export price	118.82	63.00	−30.67	6.81	−9.94	−18.03
Coffee producer price	20.00	38.89	0.00	20.00	0.00	0.00
Cocoa export price	64.56	84.75	−10.27	−3.09	−21.23	−19.96
Cocoa producer price	2.86	38.89	0.00	20.00	0.00	0.00

Table 4.6. Summary fiscal accounts (*percentage of GDP*)

	1975	1976	1977	1978	1979	1980	1981
Total revenue	24.18	20.18	33.24	32.98	32.16	27.23	25.73
Caisstab	2.17	n.a.	16.54	10.40	7.37	4.01	1.40
Tax and others	22.01	n.a.	16.70	22.58	24.79	23.23	24.33
Current spending	18.36	17.79	15.22	18.45	20.96	21.06	22.53
Wages bill	7.59	6.34	7.09	7.34	8.08	8.31	8.90
Interest	1.40	1.59	1.57	2.10	2.59	3.11	4.46
Others	9.37	9.87	6.56	9.01	10.29	9.63	9.18
Government saving	5.82	2.39	18.02	14.53	11.20	6.17	3.19
Capital spending	8.05	14.77	21.69	22.94	21.53	18.09	14.36
Fiscal surplus	−2.23	−12.38	−3.66	−8.41	−10.33	−11.92	−11.16
Primary surplus	−0.83	−10.79	−2.10	−6.30	−7.74	−8.80	−6.71

Note: n.a. = not available

4.6. Disaggregation into Private and Public Sectors

Given the control regime, all of the initial windfall was captured by the government in terms of higher Caisstab surpluses. Coffee and cocoa producer prices were raised, but that increase was much smaller than the increase in export prices. In 1976, when coffee and cocoa export prices rose by 119% and 65%, respectively, their producer prices were raised by only 20% for coffee and 3% for cocoa (Table 4.5). In fact, the government's producer pricing policy did not seem to have any link with market prices. Thus, in 1979, when export prices were falling, producer prices for both commodities were raised by 20%, and their levels were maintained in 1980 and 1981 despite sharp drops in export prices.

Rigid producer prices led to sharp fluctuations in government revenue. The Caisstab surplus, which stood at 2% of GDP in 1975, rose to 16.5% in 1977 before falling to 1.4% in 1981, and total government revenue rose from 24.2% of GDP in 1975 to 33% in 1977 and 1978, before falling back again to 25.7% in 1981, when the marketing surpluses had virtually disappeared (Table 4.6). This increase in total revenue during the boom period occurred despite a reduction in tax and other non-tax revenues. The boom was correlated with a fall in revenue-collection efforts. Thus, non-Caisstab revenues fell from 22% of GDP in 1975 to 16.7% in 1977, but they rose again quickly as the Caisstab surpluses started dwindling.

Higher revenues led to some increase in government current spending, but this increase was in line with GDP growth (which itself was temporarily high owing to the boom), so that the ratio of current spending to GDP remained more or less constant. Thus, government saving soared from 5.8% of GDP in 1975 to 18% in 1977 and 14.5% in 1978.

Yet, the increase in saving was accompanied by a rise in the fiscal deficit owing to the boom in public investment. Government capital expenditures rose from 8% of GDP in 1975 to about 23% in 1978—nearly a threefold increase. As a result, the fiscal deficit rose from 2.2% of GDP in 1975 to 8.4% in 1978 and 10.3% in 1979. Owing to the UMOA rules and the underdevelopment of the financial system, most of those deficits were financed abroad, with net domestic financing being negative up to 1979.

Part of the windfall was transferred, directly or indirectly, to the private sector via three mechanisms: higher agricultural producer prices, lower tax collections and higher government spending. The data do not indicate an increase in private spending comparable to the public spending boom. Private consumption fell from 60% of GDP in 1975 to 53% in 1977 and 55% in 1978. Private investment rose slightly, from 13% of GDP in 1975 to 15% in 1977 and 16% in 1978, but quickly returned to its pre-boom level in 1979.

Table 4.7 divides windfall GFKF and consumption into their public and private components. Counterfactual public and private GFKF were calculated using the same methodology as in Section 4.4. The table indicates that the terms of trade shock had a greater impact on capital expenditures than on consumption expenditures: windfall GFKF represented on average more than 33% of total GFKF during the boom period, while windfall consumption represented 14% of total consumption. The table also shows that windfall spending by the public sector was proportionately higher than windfall private spending. Windfall public GFKF represented on average more than 50% of total public GFKF during the boom, while windfall private GFKF represented 14% of total private GFKF. Similarly, windfall public consumption averaged 23% of total public consumption during the boom, while windfall private consumption averaged 11% of total private consumption.

4.7. The Role of the Financial Sector

Initially, the private sector used a portion of its windfall to increase its holding of domestic and foreign financial assets. Thus, the ratio of M2 to GDP rose from 29.5% in 1975 to 34.2% in 1977 (Table 4.8). Concomitantly,

Table 4.7. Public and private investment and savings

	1975	1976	1977	1978	1979	1980	1981
Actuals (billion 1975 CFAF)							
GFKF	183.90	226.92	324.67	395.88	357.15	359.22	323.73
Public GFKF	76.90	96.79	135.53	178.25	176.22	189.39	131.18
Private GFKF	107.00	130.13	189.14	217.64	180.94	169.83	192.55
Consumption	646.00	736.20	795.17	881.69	907.84	1,006.52	937.56
Public consumption	141.80	165.29	178.09	212.59	229.90	236.00	223.90
Private consumption	504.20	570.91	617.08	669.10	677.94	770.52	713.66
Counterfactuals (billion 1975 CFAF)							
GFKF	183.90	189.17	198.53	208.35	218.66	229.47	240.82
Public GFKF	76.90	63.12	66.24	69.52	72.96	76.57	80.35
Private GFKF	107.00	126.05	132.29	138.83	145.70	152.91	160.47
Consumption	646.00	664.56	697.43	731.93	768.14	806.13	846.01
Public consumption	141.80	140.27	147.20	154.49	162.13	170.15	178.56
Private consumption	504.20	524.29	550.23	577.45	606.01	635.99	667.45
Windfalls (billion 1975 CFAF)							
Windfall GFKF	0.00	37.75	126.14	187.53	138.50	129.75	82.91
Windfall public GFKF	0.00	33.67	69.29	108.73	103.26	112.83	50.82
Windfall private GFKF	0.00	4.08	56.85	78.81	35.24	16.92	32.08
Windfall consumption	0.00	71.64	97.74	149.76	139.70	200.38	91.54
Windfall public consumption	0.00	25.03	30.89	58.11	67.78	65.85	45.34
Windfall private consumption	0.00	46.61	66.85	91.66	71.93	134.53	46.21
Windfall as a percentage of actual realisations							
GFKF		16.64	38.85	47.37	38.78	36.12	25.61
Public GFKF		34.79	51.12	61.00	58.60	59.57	38.74
Private GFKF		3.14	30.06	36.21	19.47	9.96	16.66
Consumption		9.73	12.29	16.99	15.39	19.91	9.76
Public consumption		15.14	17.34	27.33	29.48	27.90	20.25
Private consumption		8.16	10.83	13.70	10.61	17.46	6.47

Table 4.8. Summary monetary situation (*percentage of GDP*)

	1975	1976	1977	1978	1979	1980	1981
Net foreign assets	0.28	−0.23	2.33	2.47	−1.89	−9.40	−15.04
Domestic credit	32.21	33.40	34.54	33.14	34.85	37.58	44.25
M2	29.49	31.55	34.21	32.74	29.11	26.18	27.54
Other liabilities	3.00	1.62	2.65	2.87	3.85	1.99	1.67

demand for foreign financial assets also increased and private unrequited transfers (net) more than doubled, going from 38 billion CFAF in 1975 to 82 billion CFAF in 1977.

The initial increase in money holdings was not correlated with a large increase in domestic credit, which remained at around 33% of GDP up to 1978. Thus, the banking system also raised its holdings of foreign assets. Net foreign assets of the banking system increased from 0.3% of GDP in 1975 to 2.5% in 1978.

From 1978, the monetary situation changed markedly with the decline in the terms of trade. Holdings of domestic financial assets fell rapidly, so that by 1980 the ratio of M_2 to GDP was 3 percentage points below its 1975 level. This occurred because, as the boom ended and private saving returned to its pre-boom level, private transfers abroad continued to increase. Net private unrequited transfers, which stood at 82 billion CFAF in 1977, reached 149 and 132.5 billion CFAF in 1980 and 1981, respectively. Private agents started switching from domestic to foreign financial assets, a phenomenon with two possible explanations. First, the interest rate differential between France and Côte d'Ivoire increased since the BCEAO did not raise sufficiently the administratively determined interest rates when international rates started increasing. Between 1975 and 1979 the domestic deposit rate (deposits were, for all practical purposes, the only domestic interest-bearing asset) was fixed at 6%; it was raised to 6.25% in 1980 and 1981. During the same period, the yield on French government bonds, which fluctuated between 8.9% and 9.5% during the period 1975–79, rose from 9.5% in 1979 to 13% in 1980 and 15.8% in 1981. Second, by 1979 it became clear that the government's financial situation, with soaring deficits and a rapid accumulation of foreign debt, was unsustainable, which increased the perceived riskiness of domestic assets.

The fall in deposits after 1979 was not accompanied by a decline in domestic credit. Domestic credit, which stood at 33.1% of GDP in 1978 actually increased to 34.9% in 1979, 37.6% in 1980 and 44.3% in 1981. Thus, the net foreign asset position of the banking system deteriorated rapidly, from 2.5% of GDP in 1978 to −1.9% in 1979, −9.4% in 1980 and −15% in 1981.

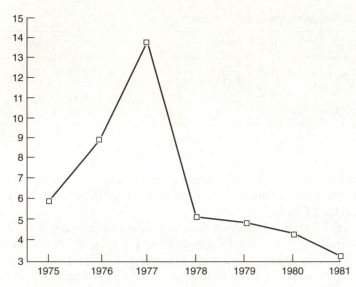

Figure 4.7. Ratio of the change in credit to the private sector to GDP, 1975–81

The increase in domestic credit after 1979 was the result of higher government borrowing from the banking system. Figure 4.7 shows the change in credit to the private sector (net lending flow) as a ratio of GDP. It indicates that, while credit to the private sector increased when the terms of trade were improving, it stagnated and then fell slightly, as a ratio to GDP, after 1978. The monetary system's net credit to the government increased from −114 billion CFAF in 1979 to −54.7 billion CFAF in 1980 and 61.5 billion CFAF in 1981.

4.8. Assessment and Conclusions

In this chapter I have argued that the Ivorian commodity boom of the mid-1970s was exclusive and unrevised. The economy reacted to the boom by increasing domestic savings as well as somewhat increasing consumption; however, domestic investment increased faster than domestic saving. The commodity boom led to a construction boom with an appreciation of the real exchange rate and a rise in the price of non-traded investment goods relative to non-traded consumption goods.

The private sector, which received a portion of the windfall through higher agricultural producer prices, lower tax collection and higher government purchases of domestic goods, reacted conservatively to the boom. It increased its GFKF and consumption, but also raised its holdings of domestic and foreign financial assets.

The government, which received most of the windfall owing to its producer pricing policy, reacted differently. It raised its capital expenditures to unprecedented levels and resorted to heavy foreign borrowing instead of accumulating foreign assets. Its investment programme was not particularly productive: high-rise office buildings in downtown Abidjan and sparsely used superhighways. Even when it entered into productive sectors (e.g. investing in sugar and oil-palm factories), the results were discouraging—the public companies which produce those two goods do so at a cost which is nearly double world prices. As a result, the overall return to investment fell during the boom period. A comparison of average ICORs between 1970–75 and 1976–81 indicates a 60% decline in the efficiency of investment.

The BCEAO's failure to raise interest rates sufficiently after 1978 led to a continued rise in foreign asset holdings by the private sector, which occurred at the expense of domestic deposits. Moreover, by allowing the government and public enterprises to increase their borrowing from the banking system after 1978, it let the country's net foreign asset position deteriorate dramatically. The erosion of the deposit base and the rise in public debt, which soon became non-performing, were reflected in the banks' balance sheets. They soon started facing serious liquidity and solvency problems (five banks had to be liquidated) which threatened the whole system's stability.

In 1975 the Ivorian economy was growing steadily, its fiscal and current accounts were more or less balanced and it had a manageable foreign debt. It was considered a model African economy and people spoke of the 'Ivorian miracle'. All of this ended as a result of the public spending spree which accompanied the commodity boom. During the 1980s and early 1990s the economy has been in crisis, with negative GDP growth, fiscal and current account deficits that exceed 10% of GDP and a stock of foreign debt of around 100% of GDP.

NOTE

The views presented in this chapter are the author's. They do not necessarily reflect the views of the World Bank.

REFERENCES

Bevan, D.L., P. Collier, and J.W. Gunning (1987) 'Consequences of a Commodity Boom in a Controlled Economy: Accumulation and Redistribution in Kenya 1975–83', *The World Bank Economic Review*, 1 (3): 489–513.

Corden, W.M. (1984) 'Booming Sector and Dutch Disease Economics: Survey and Consolidation', *Oxford Economic Papers*, 36 (3): 359–80.

Edwards, S. (1984) 'Coffee, Money and Inflation in Colombia', *World Development*, 12 (11/12): 1107–17.

Ministry of Finance (1990) 'Momento économique de la Côte d'Ivoire', Abidjan.

Nowak, J.J. (1994) 'Le Boom du café et du cacao en Côte d Ivoire: une étude de cas du syndrome neerlandais', *Revue d'Economie du Developpement*, 4: 51–75.

Van Wijnbergen, S. (1984) 'The Dutch Disease: A Disease After All?', *Economic Journal*, 94: 41–55.

World Bank (1987) 'The Côte d'Ivoire from Adjustment to Self-Sustained Growth', Washington, DC: World Bank.

5

Malawi's Positive 1977–79 Trade Shock

JANE HARRIGAN

5.1. Introduction

Malawi's brief, temporary (1977–79) positive trade shock provides an interesting case study of an African trade shock since it illustrates how the public sector response is crucial in determining the outcome of the shock even in an economy which was not excessively interventionist and where the shock occurred in the private sector. Although the windfall income initially accrued to the private sector it was rapidly transferred to the public sector via discretionary and automatic government revenue increases. The public sector therefore played the lead role in fuelling the construction boom which resulted from the trade shock. The evidence suggests that the public sector carried out its role as custodian of the trade shock windfall poorly.

Windfall public investments were characterised by low rates of return and so did little to fulfil the trade shock's potential to increase the economy's permanent income.[1] An inappropriate control regime was also maintained which suppressed the investment and construction boom in a manner which further reduced the permanent income gain. Most important of all, the fiscal responses triggered by the boom led to a severe destabilisation of the budget deficit. Hence, rather than increasing permanent income, the long-run effect of the positive trade shock was a need to undertake a painful and protracted stabilisation and adjustment process during the 1980s.

5.2. The Nature of the Shock

In 1977 Malawi's terms of trade registered a 19% rise over their 1976 value. This improvement followed a period of steady decline. By 1980 the terms of trade had returned to levels dictated by the trend decline of the 1971–76 period (Figure 5.1). Malawi's temporary trade shock was caused by three distinct factors: a halt in 1978 in import price increases; a sharp (53.7%) increase in the 1977 price of tea exports, tea accounting for over one-fifth of the total value of 1976 exports; and an acceleration in

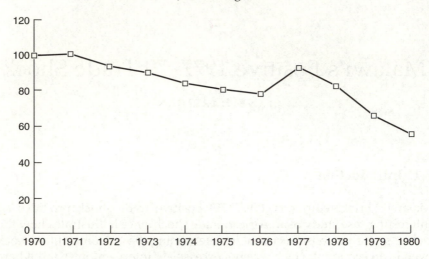

Figure 5.1. Terms of trade, 1970–80 (*1970 = 100*)

Source: Malawi Statistical Yearbook 1980 and 1984.

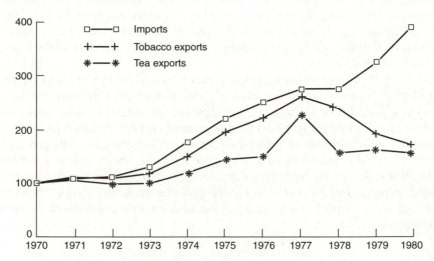

Figure 5.2. Import and export price indices, 1970–80 (*1970 = 100*)

Source: Malawi Statistical Yearbook 1980 and 1984.

the increase in tobacco export prices, which rose by 18.8% in 1977, tobacco accounting for almost half of the total value of 1976 exports (Figure 5.2).

In order to measure the impact of this positive shock on the Malawian economy a counterfactual scenario must first be specified. To construct a counterfactual terms of trade series for 1977–79 we can assume that in the absence of the 1977–79 tea, tobacco and import price instability the terms of trade would have continued to decline at a steady rate towards the actual 1980 value. Simple linear interpolation between the actual 1976 and 1980 values therefore provides the counterfactual terms of trade series given in Table 5.1. If we also assume that the terms of trade improvement had no effect on export volumes, then actual export volumes can be used in the counterfactual.[2] Hence, the counterfactual value of exports can be derived simply by deflating actual export values by the ratio between the actual and the counterfactual terms of trade indices. This results in the counterfactual export value series shown in column (6) of Table 5.1. Deducting this series from the actual values of exports gives the terms of trade income windfall in current values, which can be deflated by the import price index to obtain the real value of the windfall in 1976 prices. This is done in Table 5.1, which shows that the windfall accrued over three years, 1977, 1978 and 1979, and was relatively small, namely, Malawi Kwacha (MK) 72.1 million in constant value terms.

In the absence of reliable estimates of the rate of return on domestic capital formation, the windfall has been converted into a permanent income gain by taking real annual gains (assuming all the windfall is invested) and discounting by 10%. The resulting 1977 present value of the terms of trade boom is MK 67.9 million, implying a permanent income increase of MK 6.79 million, or 1.2% of 1976 GDP.

Because the 1977–80 terms of trade deviation from the trend decline resulted from changes in tea, tobacco and import prices, specification of the shock's informational properties in terms of price expectations requires reference to these distinct components of the shock. The 1978 halt in rising import prices followed a seven-year period of steady increase and was caused by a temporary fall in the price of two import categories— 'building materials' and 'other industrial inputs'. Since price indices for these two categories had, prior to 1978, increased steadily, it can be assumed that the 1978 import price component of the terms of trade shock was exclusive to the prior expectations of all agents. Given previous trends, and the fact that 1979 and 1980 witnessed a resumption in import price increases, unrevised expectations can also be assumed for this component of the shock.[3]

The sharp increase in 1977 tea prices resulted from reduced global output caused by drought in Sri Lanka and India in the mid-1970s and from increased demand following the massive increase in coffee prices caused by a Brazilian drought. In view of these unpredictable climatic causes this component of the overall 1977–79 terms of trade shock is also assumed to be exclusive to prior expectations. The temporary nature of this price increase appears to have been well understood by both plantation producers and government agencies responsible for disseminating information to smallholder tea producers (Government of Malawi

Table 5.1. Magnitude of the positive terms of trade boom (*MKm*)

	Export price index (1)	Import price index (2)	Barter terms of trade (3)	Counterfactual terms of trade (4)	Value of exports (5)	Counterfactual value of exports[a] (6)	Windfall (current (7)	Windfall (1976 prices)[b] prices) (8)
1976	100.0	100.0	100.0	100.0	151.6	151.6	0.0	0.0
1977	132.0	111.0	119.0	93.0	180.3	140.9	39.4	35.5
1978	119.0	111.0	106.0	86.0	155.7	126.3	29.4	26.5
1979	108.0	127.0	85.0	79.0	181.7	168.9	12.8	10.1
1980	112.0	155.0	72.0	72.0	228.0	228.0	0.0	0.0
Total							81.6	72.1
								(discounted at 10% = 67.9)

Notes:
[a] col. (5) × (col. (4)/col. (3))
[b] deflated by import price index

Source: Malawi Statistical Yearbook 1980 and 1984; Pryor (1988, table F-2a)

Table 5.2. Expectational properties of the terms of trade shock

	Private sector	Public sector
Import prices	Exclusive, unrevised	Exclusive, unrevised
Tea prices	Exclusive, unrevised	Exclusive, unrevised
Tobacco prices	Inclusive, unrevised	Exclusive, revised

Economic Report, 1976–85 issues, ch. 6 'Commodity Markets'). Unrevised expectations are therefore assumed for this component of the shock.

The 1977 increase in tobacco prices followed a four-year period of significant price increases, hence it is likely that private tobacco producers incorporated a 1977 price increase into their expectations. This is supported by the fact that between 1975 and 1977 the total acreage devoted to tobacco increased by 32%. Government statements, however, suggest that the 1977 tobacco price increase was exclusive to public sector expectations. The *Economic Report 1977*, for example, makes the following observation in relation to the predicted 1977 tobacco market: 'The short-term outlook indicates relative abundance with remarkable build-up of stocks . . . This is likely to depress prices in a number of auction markets' (p. 31).

By the following year, the same publication indicated a revision of public sector expectations regarding tobacco prices in the light of the unanticipated 1977 price increase. This suggests discrepancy between private and public sector expectations regarding the tobacco price component of the 1977–79 terms of trade boom, with private sector expectations being of the inclusive and unrevised type, and public sector expectations being exclusive and revised. Table 5.2 summarises the expectational properties assigned to the various components of the 1977–80 terms of trade shock and shows that exclusive unrevised expectations dominated.

5.3. Behaviour of the Economy as a Whole

5.3.1. *Asset Changes and Savings Rates*

If the expectations assumptions underlying Table 5.2 are correct, the theory of construction booms predicts a high level of windfall savings in the economy as a whole since four of the six cells in the table indicate a large positive transient income savings effect. These predictions are supported by the evidence presented in this section, where the economy-wide propensity to save from windfall income is estimated to be slightly below unity.

In order to derive the propensity to save out of windfall income the windfall-induced change in both domestic and foreign asset accumulation must be calculated. For domestic assets, actual gross fixed capital formation (GFKF) can be compared with a counterfactual GFKF. Actual GFKF at constant 1976 prices is given in column (3) of Table 5.3. To calculate counterfactual GFKF we first need to estimate counterfactual income and the counterfactual GFKF propensity.

Counterfactual income can be calculated by deducting the shock and shock-induced growth from actual GDP.[4] The resulting counterfactual real income series is given in Table 5.3 column (4).[5] The counterfactual GFKF propensity can be derived from an analysis of changes in the actual propensity prior to the trade-shock period. Such an exercise suggests that it is plausible to assume that the counterfactual GFKF propensity would have remained at the 1976 level of 23.4% throughout the terms of trade boom period of 1977–79. Combining this counterfactual GFKF propensity with the counterfactual income series yields the estimate of counterfactual GFKF and windfall-induced investment shown in columns (6) and (7) of Table 5.3.

As one would expect, the results which emerge from Table 5.3 show that most of the windfall-induced investment out of unanticipated windfall income is lagged by at least a year. Overall, the counterfactual implies that windfall GFKF was MK 140.6 million at 1976 prices, or MK 124.5 million in discounted present value terms.[6]

In order to ascertain the net effect of the terms of trade shock on asset accumulation, the windfall-induced change in foreign savings/debt must be added to the above estimate of windfall-induced GFKF. The actual foreign savings propensity for the terms of trade boom period is given in Table 5.4. A counterfactual series for the foreign savings propensity can be derived by extrapolating from the three- to four-year cyclical trend displayed by the actual 1968–76 series (Pryor 1988, table E-1).[7] The resulting counterfactual foreign savings propensity and the estimate of windfall-induced foreign asset accumulation are given in Table 5.4. The terms of trade boom gave rise to an MK 65.14 million increase in foreign debt, with the bulk of the windfall increase in foreign debt occurring two years after the onset of the unanticipated boom.[8]

The above estimates suggest that over the period 1977–79 windfall GFKF amounted to MK 140.6 million, while the windfall increase in foreign debt amounted to MK 65.14 million. To derive the net change in assets generated from transient income, the windfall GFKF stream and the windfall foreign debt stream need to be discounted, resulting in asset changes of MK 124.5 million and MK −53.5 million respectively. The MK 4.9 million-worth of savings generated from extra permanent income (i.e. from the return on windfall-induced investment) must also be deducted.[9] Windfall asset accumulation out of transient income therefore amounted to MK 66.1 million (124.5 − 53.5 − 4.9). Dividing this windfall asset

Table 5.3. Domestic capital formation: actual, counterfactual and windfall

	Actuals			Counterfactuals			Windfall GFKF		
	GFKF/income (%)	Real income (MKm)[a]	Real GFKF (1976 prices)	Real income (1976 prices)[b]	GFKF/income (%)	GFKF (1976 prices)	Annual	Cumulative	Return (at 10%)
1976	23.4	622.5	145.7	622.5	23.4	145.7	0.0	0.0	0.0
1977	23.6	686.4	162.0	650.9	23.4	152.3	9.7	9.7	0.97
1978	33.3	742.3	247.3	714.8	23.4	167.3	79.9	89.6	8.96
1979	29.5	763.8	225.3	744.7	23.4	174.3	51.0	140.6	14.1
								(discounted present value at 10% =124.5)	

[a] GDP at 1976 prices plus windfall income
[b] in 1976 and 1977 actual GDP at 1976 prices; 1978–79 also deducts returns on windfall-induced investment

Source: Pryor (1988); Gulhati (1989)

Table 5.4. Actual and counterfactual changes in foreign assets

	Actuals		Counterfactuals		Windfall foreign saving (1976 prices MKm)
	Change in foreign assets (1976 prices MKm)	Foreign savings propensity (%)	Foreign savings propensity (%)	Change in foreign assets (1976 prices MKm)	
1976	−45.90	−7.37	−7.37	−45.90	0.00
1977	31.60	4.90	4.60	29.90	1.70
1978	−17.80	−2.50	−2.63	−18.80	0.96
1979	−56.00	−7.40	1.58	11.77	−67.80
Total					−65.14

Source: Pryor (1988, Tables L-4a, G-1 and E-1)

accumulation by the MK 67.9 million transient windfall income produces a savings rate of 97%.[10] This propensity to save out of windfall income for the economy as a whole is extremely high compared to the historical average savings propensity.

5.3.2. Goods Markets

In response to a positive terms of trade shock, construction boom theory predicts not only a rise in the price of non-tradables relative to tradables but also a rise in the price of non-tradable capital goods relative to the price of non-tradable consumer goods. The former price-ratio change occurs in response to increased demand for non-tradables caused by the 'spending' and 'resource movement' effects which are common to both the Dutch Disease and the construction boom theories. The latter price-ratio change, a key prediction of the dynamic construction boom theory, occurs in response to the investment effect of a positive trade shock, which increases the demand for capital goods relative to consumer goods. Rigorous empirical testing of construction boom theory therefore requires analysis of expenditure patterns, relative prices and factor movements according to the following commodity aggregates: tradable consumer goods, non-tradable consumer goods, tradable capital goods and non-tradable capital goods.

Data-availability for Malawi limits the ability to conduct such an analysis. National Accounts do not report capital formation by type of asset or consumption expenditure by type of good. It is not possible, therefore, to break down total expenditure according to the relevant commodity aggregates. Budgetary data can, however, be used to disaggregate public sector capital expenditure between tradables and non-tradables. The results are given in Figure 5.3. The income boom resulted in an immediate increase in

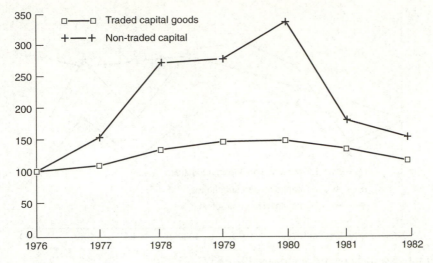

Figure 5.3. Public sector demand for traded and non-traded capital, 1976–82 (*1976 = 100*)

Source: World Bank (1985: statistical appendix, tables 7.04 and 7.06).

the public sector demand for both tradable and non-tradable capital goods, with demand peaking in 1980. The increase in demand for non-traded capital goods was much larger than that for traded capital goods. A construction boom is, therefore, clearly evident in the public sector. The fact that this construction boom occurred over the period 1978–80 indicates that the public sector investment boom was not stretched beyond the income boom years.

Malawi's Composite Retail Price Index can be used to derive the relative price indices needed to test construction boom theory.[11] The price index of items listed under the heading 'Other' (which consists mainly of school fees, personal services, entertainment and travel) in the Composite Retail Price Index has been used to proxy the price of non-traded consumer goods. Owing to the limited coverage of goods it is not possible to use disaggregated data from the Composite Retail Price Index to create a price index for non-tradable capital goods. Instead, the change in the unit value of buildings (residential, industrial, commercial and miscellaneous) completed in the two main cities is used as a proxy.

The resulting relative price indices (Figure 5.4) provide evidence of construction boom effects in the Malawian economy. The first year of the terms of trade boom, 1977, witnessed a rise in the price of non-tradable consumer goods relative to both the price of import substitutes and the price of non-tradable capital goods. This initial relative price effect is not unexpected given the different implementation lags required for

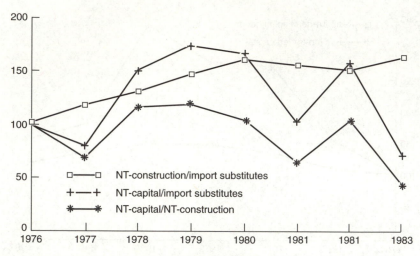

Figure 5.4. Relative price indices, 1976–83 (*1976 = 100*)
Source: Malawi Statistical Yearbook 1980, tables 10.7 and 10.8.

consumption and investment expenditure to become effective. Following this initial one-year lag, 1978 and 1979 witnessed a rise in the price of non-traded capital goods relative to both the price of non-traded consumer goods and import substitutes. This supports the price predictions of construction boom theory. By 1980, the direction of change had been reversed, with the price of non-tradable capital falling relative to both non-tradable consumer goods and import substitutes, suggesting that the economy as a whole, as with the public sector, did not extend the investment boom beyond the terms of trade windfall period.

5.3.3. Factor Markets

The above analyses of public sector expenditure patterns and relative price changes indicate that, in addition to the primary tea and tobacco boom sectors, a secondary boom in the construction sector was created by the effects of windfall-induced investment. One would expect, therefore, to find evidence of mobile resources being attracted into the boom sectors from other lagging sectors of the economy.

The sectoral allocation of capital, in the form of GFKF, over the period 1976–80 is shown in Figure 5.5. The allocation clearly favoured the two boom sectors, agriculture and construction, at the expense of the rest of the economy.[12] After the first year of the terms of trade windfall the dynamics of a construction boom are evident. Following the initial fall in the price of non-traded capital goods relative to non-traded consumer goods (Figure 5.4), and the consequent increase in GFKF in the services

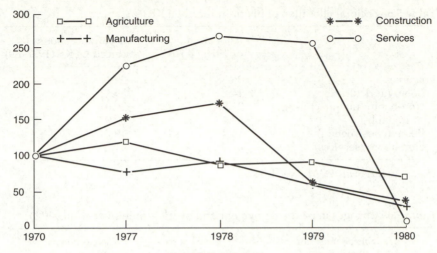

Figure 5.5. Sectoral allocation of GFKF, 1976–80 (*1976 = 100*)

Source: Malawi Statistical Yearbook 1984, table 9.3.

sector (Figure 5.5), the relative price of non-traded capital goods rises. In response, GFKF in both non-boom sectors (services and manufacturing) declines, while GFKF in the two boom sectors continues to increase sharply. This investment increase is both more pronounced and of a longer duration in the primary boom sector (agriculture) than in the secondary boom sector (construction), but in both cases the investment boom, as measured by GFKF allocation, is not stretched beyond the terms of trade income-boom period.

The above evidence of a construction boom in the Malawian economy during the trade shock years is based on the allocation of total GFKF in 400 large establishments. Further evidence will be provided if the allocation of windfall-induced, as opposed to total, GFKF displays similar trends. In order to analyse the sectoral allocation of windfall-induced GFKF a counterfactual must first be specified. We have already calculated a counterfactual real GFKF stream in Table 5.3. Hence we can assume that in the absence of the terms of trade windfall the total GFKF series which we are using to analyse sectoral allocations would have increased by the same percentage per annum as this Table 5.3 counterfactual. We will also assume that the 1976 sectoral allocation pattern remained constant throughout the period. The resulting estimates of the sectoral allocation of counterfactual and windfall-induced GFKF are summarised in Table 5.5.

Confining the disaggregation to 'tradables' and 'non-tradables' the allocation of boom-induced investment is similar to the pre-boom (1976) allocation pattern. But if each sector is further disaggregated to its boom and non-boom components we find the allocation of windfall GFKF

Table 5.5. Sectoral allocation of boom-induced GFKF (%)

	Allocation of 1976 GFKF	Allocation of boom-induced GFKF (1977–80)
Tradables	36.6	39.1
Boom (agriculture)	14.8	59.1
Non-boom (manufacturing)	21.8	−20.0
Non-tradables	63.4	60.9
Boom (construction)	16.4	19.7
Non-boom (services)	47.0	41.2

Source: Malawi Statistical Yearbook 1984

Table 5.6. Changes in paid employment and average monthly earnings (%)

	Tradable boom sector (agriculture)		Non-tradable boom sector (construction)		Whole economy	
	Employment	Av. earnings	Employment	Av. earnings	Employment	Av. earnings
1977	29.0	12.6	5.4	7.5	3.7	−1.6
1978	9.1	17.0	35.6	7.5	9.9	17.0
1979	7.8	0.8	5.7	1.0	6.1	5.3
1980	−0.6	9.4	−1.8	24.7	2.0	16.6
1981	−16.6	18.6	−25.3	−4.5	−10.9	12.9

Source: World Bank (1982) and (1985, statistical appendices tables 6.01 and 6.02)

clearly favouring the boom sectors—over half of windfall investment was allocated to the primary boom sector (agriculture), whereas this sector received only 14.8% of total GFKF in 1976. The result is less dramatic, but nevertheless significant, for the secondary boom sector (construction), which received one-fifth of windfall GFKF, compared to 16.4% of GFKF in 1976. By contrast, both non-boom sectors suffered in the allocation of windfall-induced GFKF relative to their 1976 shares.

Table 5.6 shows the percentage change in paid employment and in average monthly earnings in the primary and secondary boom sectors relative to the whole economy.[13] In the early years of the terms of trade income windfall both the primary and secondary boom sectors attracted labour from other sectors. By 1980 a reversal of the labour transfer into the two boom sectors was under way. The data for average monthly earnings suggest that, with the possible exception of the primary boom sector in the second year of the boom, no increase in relative wages was necessary to induce the observed increase in employment shares in the two boom sectors.

We are now in a position to summarise the results of the analysis of the economy-wide response to the positive trade shock. The windfall income savings propensity is estimated at 97%. This suggests that most agents treated the terms of trade shock as temporary and the income windfall as transient, since virtually the entire windfall was saved. This supports the expectational properties assigned in Table 5.2 to the various components of the terms of trade shock, according to which the overall shock is predominantly characterised by exclusive unrevised expectations. These expectational properties lead one to predict dynamic construction boom effects in response to the positive trade shock. The analysis of goods and factor markets bears out this prediction.

Goods and factor markets provide evidence of Dutch Disease effects in the first year of the boom—the relative price of non-tradable consumer goods rises and both capital and labour are drawn into this sector. Following the first year of the income windfall, however, the dynamics of a construction boom are evident, with the high savings rate stimulating investment. In the public sector, at least, there is a sharp increase in the demand for non-tradable capital goods. The price of non-tradable capital goods rises relative to import substitutes and, more importantly in the context of construction boom theory, relative to non-tradable consumer goods. Reacting to the relative price changes, labour and capital are drawn into both the primary boom sector (agriculture) and the secondary boom sector (construction) from the lagging manufacturing and services sectors.

Evidence from goods and factor markets suggests that the construction boom was modest in both magnitude and duration. The primary boom sector, agriculture, experienced a longer and much larger boom, in the form of the transfer of capital resources, than the construction sector. In addition, the duration of the construction boom was not stretched beyond the period of the terms of trade income windfall. The sharp increase in public sector demand for non-traded capital goods, for example, was confined to the 1978–80 period, as was the increase in the relative price of non-tradable capital goods, and the transfer of capital and labour to the construction sector occurred only in 1977 and 1978. This suggests a suboptimal response to the income windfall. The crowding of GFKF into the windfall years, evident in the public sector, intensified the rise in the relative price of non-tradable capital, which, in turn, will have lowered the return to both private and public sector investment. The sharp increase in the public sector's expenditure on construction during the economy's income boom years also suggests the possibility of pre-emptive use of private agents' windfall savings. This possibility will be investigated in Section 5.4 below, where we disaggregate the economy-wide response to the shock into the private and public sector response.

5.4. Disaggregation of Private and Public Sectors

5.4.1. *Transmission from Private Income to Public Revenue and Expenditure*

The initial impact of the positive terms of trade shock accrued predominantly to the private sector (defined here to include the relatively autonomous parastatal sector). Tobacco and tea production were private sector activities, conducted by both smallholders and estates. The only direct impact gain to the public sector consisted of a reduction in the public sector import bill owing to the import price component of the terms of trade boom. The government did not levy any direct taxation on the commodity-specific components of the terms of trade gain by increasing taxes specifically in the tea and tobacco sectors,[14] even though the tea price component of the income boom, being characterised by exclusive unrevised private sector expectations, was an appropriate target for windfall taxation.

Although the initial incidence of the income boom was felt mainly in the private sector, there was a significant resource transfer to the public sector via two revenue-transmission mechanisms: the automatic increment to government revenue induced by the increase in private disposable income and spending; and the conscious decision by government to increase both direct and indirect tax rates in the context of the buoyant economic environment. The resulting increase in government revenue in turn affected government expenditure.

The actual trends in key fiscal aggregates (as a percentage of GDP) presented in Table 5.7 indicate a significant increase in government revenue during the terms of trade income boom period. Between 1976 and 1979 revenue as a percentage of GDP increased from 18.2% to 28.2%. In absolute terms, revenue doubled from MK 94.93 million to MK 187.0 million. This government revenue increase was one of the most remarkable macro effects of Malawi's positive terms of trade shock. To what extent was it the result of automatic revenue increases caused by the buoyancy of the tax system and to what extent was it the result of a conscious government decision to tax away the income windfall from the private sector as a whole via discretionary tax increases?

A crude estimate of the automatic and discretionary components of the central government revenue increase can be obtained by applying revenue elasticity coefficients to the appropriate tax bases in order to derive an estimate of automatic increases. The discretionary component can then calculated as a residual. The results are summarised in Table 5.8. Of the MK 91.84 million central government revenue increase which occurred between 1976/77 and 1979/80, 31% can be attributed to automatic tax increases and 46% can be attributed to discretionary tax increases.[15]

Table 5.7. Fiscal pattern as a percentage of factor cost GDP

	Total revenue[a]	Consumption	GFKF	Total exhaustive expenditure	Primary surplus	Interest and debt repayment	Overall deficit	Domestic borrowing	Foreign borrowing	Balancing item
1970	20.9	13.2	8.6	21.9	−1.0	2.9	14.4	2.1	13.7	−1.4
1971	18.2	12.1	6.3	18.4	−0.2	2.8	9.9	2.1	7.4	0.3
1972	18.9	11.7	6.2	17.9	1.1	3.2	8.1	1.8	6.1	0.2
1973	19.8	11.1	8.0	19.1	0.7	3.1	7.2	1.8	6.2	−0.8
1974	18.5	11.2	8.5	19.7	−1.2	3.2	7.9	3.1	5.7	−0.9
1975	20.4	10.9	13.7	24.7	−4.3	2.9	10.7	2.7	7.4	0.7
1976	18.2	10.1	8.6	18.8	−0.6	2.7	7.7	0.7	4.9	2.1
1977	19.4	10.1	10.5	20.6	−1.3	2.5	7.7	2.3	6.9	−1.6
1978	23.5	12.5	15.6	28.0	−4.5	2.7	10.6	1.9	9.0	−0.3
1979	28.2	14.0	15.7	29.8	−1.6	4.7	10.1	1.7	6.2	2.3
1980	26.9	14.2	17.2	31.4	−4.5	6.3	15.5	1.1	6.9	7.5
1981	26.3	15.5	12.5	27.8	−1.5	9.3	13.4	16.8	10.3	−13.7
1982	25.0	14.4	11.4	25.8	−0.9	6.9	12.1	1.4	6.6	4.1
1983	24.7	14.2	12.3	26.5	−1.8	6.3	10.6	4.0	8.7	−2.0

[a] Does not include foreign and domestic borrowing

Source: Pryor (1988, tables E-2, K-1a and K-2b)

Table 5.8. Automatic and discretionary increases in government revenue 1977–80 (*MKm*)

	Revenue 1976/77	Revenue increase 1976/77–1979/80	Automatic revenue increase 1976/77–1979/80	Discretionary revenue increase 1976/77–1979/80
Direct taxation				
Personal and company	34.43	24.54	17.14	7.4
Indirect taxation				
Domestic surtax	7.5	35.8	2.6	33.2
Import surtax and duties	23.5	8.9	8.07	0.83
Excise duties	4.2	2.1	0.9	1.2
Other	1.5	1.1	n.a.	n.a.
Non-tax revenue	23.8	19.4	n.a.	n.a.
Totals	94.93	91.84	28.71	42.63

Source: Malawi *Monthly Statistical Bulletin* Jan. 1987, tables 2 and 15; World Bank (1982, table 7 and appendix table 7.08) and (1985, appendix table 2.01)

There is a clear behavioural distinction between direct tax revenues and indirect tax revenues. The bulk, 83%, of the discretionary revenue increase was achieved via the indirect tax system. By contrast, 60% of the automatic revenue increase occurred via the direct taxation of both individuals and companies. In summary, nearly half of the government revenue increase which occurred during the terms of trade shock period was caused by discretionary tax increases which were heavily concentrated on indirect taxes.

Part of the massive transfer of income to the government was passed back to the private sector via an increase in public sector expenditure. Between 1976 and 1979 public sector exhaustive expenditure (consumption plus GFKF) increased from 18.8% of GDP to 29.8% of GDP. The expenditure increase was particularly sharp for GFKF, which almost doubled as a percentage of GDP. In view of the fact that a large proportion of the increased public sector GFKF was expressed as demand for nontraded capital goods (Figure 5.3), this suggests that the public sector played an important role in fuelling the construction boom.

The increase in total exhaustive government expenditure exceeded the increase in total revenue in both magnitude and duration. Consequently, the primary deficit deteriorated from 0.6% of GDP at the onset of the boom to 4.5% of GDP in 1980. The overall deficit also increased dramatically, from 7.7% of GDP in 1976 to 10.1% in 1979 and 15.5% in 1980 (Table 5.7).

The public sector expenditure 'overshoot' during the terms of trade boom years set in motion several adverse medium-term fiscal trends. Although both the primary and the overall deficit were successfully reduced to pre-boom levels by 1983, this was achieved by a sharp reduction in public sector GFKF, while public sector consumption as a percentage of GDP was retained at its increased boom level. Deficit reduction was also achieved by discretionary tax increases, which kept the revenue/GDP ratio above pre-boom levels. The ratchet effect operating on consumption may be explained by the fact that exhaustive consumption expenditure partly consists of wages and salaries,[16] which are politically harder to cut than GFKF expenditure, which can be cut by postponing or cancelling planned investment projects.

The above trends suggest that an overshooting of public sector expenditure during the income boom years can have adverse effects over and above the pre-emptive use of private sector savings. If part of the overshoot consists of a ratchet-type increase in exhaustive consumption, the necessary post-boom reduction in the budget deficit will need to be effected by a reduction in public sector GFKF and/or discretionary tax increases. Both measures potentially reduce the economy's ability to stretch the investment and construction boom beyond the income-windfall years—the former directly prevents the public sector from drawing out the investment boom and the latter reduce the private sector's ability to save and invest in the post-boom period. The dynamic predictions of construction boom theory show that such a scenario will reduce the economy's ability to translate a transient windfall income gain into an increase in permanent income and hence consumption.

Table 5.9 shows the changes in the tax and revenue burdens which arose in the boom and post-boom period compared to the pre-boom fiscal year 1976. Combining Tables 5.7 and 5.9, several significant trends are evident. First, although both tax and non-tax revenue increased as a percentage of GDP during the boom years, the actual share of these

Table 5.9. Sources of government revenue as a percentage of total revenue

	1976	1977–79	1980–83
Income tax, companies	16.2	14.4	10.2
Income tax, individuals	9.6	6.4	7.5
Import duties	8.8	9.7	12.0
Excise duties	2.8	2.2	2.4
Domestic surtax	12.0	12.7	13.4
Other	1.0	0.9	1.1
Total tax revenue	47.2	46.2	46.6
Non-tax revenue	15.9	13.4	9.3
Domestic borrowing	2.7	7.3	15.6
Foreign borrowing	18.9	25.1	19.0
Grants and other	15.4	8.1	9.6

Source: World Bank (1985, statistical appendix table 7.07)

revenue sources in total government revenue declined, while foreign borrowing both as a percentage of GDP and as a share in total revenue increased dramatically. This indicates that increases in public sector domestic revenue were not adequate to cover the increased public expenditure of the boom years. Consequently, part of the increase resulted in a growing overall deficit and part was covered by recourse to extra foreign borrowing. In general, a foreign-borrowing strategy, which is often facilitated by the perceived increase in an economy's foreign debt capacity during a positive shock, is likely to exacerbate the adverse post-boom fiscal trends outlined above, since it will result in subsequent increases in debt-servicing obligations which intensify the budget deficit problem. Because the debt-servicing obligations fall on the current account they also restrict the flexibility to cut consumption expenditures and therefore increase the downward pressure on public sector GFKF needed to rectify the post-boom deficit.

In order to maintain the higher level of public sector revenue as a percentage of GDP in the post-boom period, discretionary indirect tax increases were necessary, since the slow-down in the economy reduced the contribution of both income taxes and non-tax revenue to total revenue. Most of the increased indirect tax burden fell on tradables—with import duties, excise duties and the domestic surtax all increasing. Despite this adjustment of post-boom tax burdens from direct to indirect taxes, the overall contribution of tax revenues to total revenue remained constant. In addition, as the economy's foreign credit-worthiness deteriorated in the post-boom period, government reliance on foreign borrowing was reduced. The brunt of post-boom fiscal adjustment on the revenue side therefore occurred through a dramatic increase in the government's domestic borrowing, which reached 16.8% of GDP in 1981 (Table 5.7) and averaged 15.6% of total post-boom public sector revenue, compared to 7.3% in the boom period and 2.7% in the pre-boom year (Table 5.9). The resulting post-boom crowding-out of private domestic capital formation in order to sustain the excessive boom-induced level of public consumption expenditure placed a further restriction on the private sector's ability to stretch investment expenditure beyond the income boom.

The above analysis of fiscal trends is based on changes in actual fiscal variables. In order to assess the extent to which such changes are attributable to the positive trade shock, boom-induced fiscal changes need to be analysed using a counterfactual fiscal scenario. We can assume that the fiscal counterfactual is characterised by maintenance of the 1976 fiscal pattern as given in Table 5.7.[17] Applying these patterns to the counterfactual GDP stream (from Table 5.3) provides an estimate of counterfactual revenue, consumption, GFKF and the primary surplus. Deducting the above from the actual value of these aggregates results in the estimate of boom-induced fiscal changes shown in Table 5.10.

Table 5.10. Boom-induced fiscal changes (*MKm, 1976 prices*)

	Total revenue	Consumption	GFKF	Total exhaustive expenditure	Primary surplus
1976	0.0	0.0	0.0	0.0	0.0
1977	13.5	3.0	15.5	18.5	−5.0
1978	46.9	21.9	55.9	77.8	−30.9
1979	80.8	32.2	56.4	88.6	−7.8
1980	71.6	34.2	68.3	102.5	−30.9
1981	61.4	39.9	29.5	69.4	−8.0
1982	49.6	31.3	20.4	51.7	−2.1
1983	49.2	31.3	28.0	59.3	−10.1
Total	373.0	193.8	274.0	467.8	−94.8

Table 5.10 indicates that the boom-induced fiscal changes coincided, to a large extent, with the actual fiscal trends observed in Table 5.7. The boom gave rise to a substantial increase in public sector revenue. Despite this additional revenue, the windfall-induced increase in expenditure was such that the boom-induced primary deficit deteriorated by MK 94.8 million over the period 1976–83. A ratchet effect operated on the boom-induced expenditure increase, particularly in the case of consumption expenditure, with strong effects on the latter still evident in 1983. Accommodating post-boom revenue increases are also apparent.

During the terms of trade boom period, 1977–79, 70% of the boom-induced increase in public sector expenditure was devoted to GFKF. It is important to assess whether or not such investments helped to increase the economy's permanent income. Comparing government investment outlays (current prices) in the pre-boom period with outlays in the 1977–80 period (Table 5.11) we see that the most dramatic increases occurred under the headings of 'Transport' and 'Other services', where expenditures increased by MK 126.8 million and MK 121.1 million, respectively. Much of this increase was accounted for by projects which were personally promoted by President Banda for political and strategic, rather than economic, reasons. Such projects included continued up-grading of the road along Lake Malawi in order to improve access to the politically troublesome northern region; improving the operation of the newly constructed railway to Nacala port in Mozambique; building a new airport, which absorbed over half of the 1977–80 expenditure increase under the 'Transport' heading; expanding the facilities offered to the armed services; and shifting the centre of government from Zomba in the South to Lilongwe in the Chichewa-speaking central region, which provided the basis of Banda's political support. Government and army buildings

Table 5.11. Central government development account expenditure (*MK m, current prices*)

	1973–76 total	1977–80 total	Increase
Agriculture	48.8	73.4	24.6
Transport	70.8	197.6	126.8
Aviation	1.9	70.2	68.3
Railways and lakes	35.5	58.8	23.3
Roads	33.4	68.6	35.2
Post and	9.6	11.6	2.0
telecommunications			
Social services	12.3	33.9	21.6
Other services	55.5	176.6	121.1
Gov. buildings	19.8	28.9	9.1
Army buildings	3.6	57.4	53.8
Miscellaneous	2.1	23.9	21.8

Note: 1976 stands for fiscal year 1976/77 and so forth

Source: World Bank (1985, appendix table 7.05)

together accounted for over half of the increased expenditure under 'Other services', while civil service housing accounted for much of the rest. Most of these projects had earlier been refused aid finance on the grounds that they were uneconomical with unacceptably low rates of return in terms of both financial and social prices.[18]

Since all of the above investments had such low rates of return that they were ineligible for donor finance, they are the very projects which can be regarded as non-fungible windfalls: the large increase in public sector revenues during the terms of trade boom and the government's increased willingness to use foreign debt on hard terms enabled the public sector substantially to increase investment in poorly conceived, politically motivated projects with very low rates of return. Hence, most of the windfall-induced public sector GFKF was far from productive and did little to increase the country's permanent income.

As a result of ratchet effects operating on consumption expenditure increases, combined with poorly chosen boom-induced capital expenditures, the legacy of the boom was a substantial expansion of the public sector, which was left presiding over an increasingly unproductive range of projects.

5.4.2. Transmission of the Public Expenditure Boom on to Private Incomes

A boom-induced increase in public expenditure has the potential to transfer resources back to the private sector through a number of channels, namely, the provision of productive or utility-enhancing services to private agents, the transfer of payments through the public sector labour market and the transfer of rents via government purchases of non-tradables.

It is difficult to quantify the first of these transfers, the magnitude of which depends on the composition of the additional public sector expenditure. The part of increased expenditure which was not fungible, in the sense of being a candidate for donor finance, was the sharp increase in expenditure on administration, government and army buildings, defence and debt-servicing. This boom-induced increase in public exhaustive expenditure was largely unproductive and so would have transferred little utility to the private sector.

A boom-induced public expenditure increase can also potentially transfer income back to the private sector via two distinct channels in the labour market. Public to private sector income transfers will result from any boom-induced increase in public sector employment if the public sector labour market is characterised by a rent-creating positive wage differential. This transfer mechanism did not operate in Malawi, since the wage premium favoured the private sector. A labour market income transfer from public to private sector will also arise if the boom induces an increase in public sector wages, so providing existing public sector employees with a boom-induced windfall. Following a seven-year period of steady decline, 1978, the second year of the terms of trade boom, witnessed a sharp 30% increase in public sector real average earnings (Table 5.12) which was made possible by the significant 1977 and 1978 boom-induced increase in government revenue.

In order to quantify the magnitude of this transfer a counterfactual must be specified. Between 1970 and 1977 average real earnings in the public sector displayed a trend decline of 6.5% per annum. It is assumed that, in the absence of the boom, real public sector wages would have been held constant at the 1977 average level of MK 614 per annum through to 1983. Using this assumption we can derive an estimate of the public sector wage windfall, which constitutes an income transfer from the public sector back to the private sector (Table 5.12). Between 1976 and 1983 this transfer amounted to MK 20.8 million.

Commodity markets also served as an important channel for the transmission of the public expenditure boom on to private income. The boom-induced increase in the price of non-tradables increased the cost of government purchases and so transferred rents to the private sector. Tables 5.13 and 5.14 provide estimates of the resulting rents. Over the 1978–80 period of rising relative non-tradable capital goods prices (Figure 5.4), the rental transfer via the non-tradable capital goods market amounted to MK 44.1 million in current–price terms, and over the 1978–83

Table 5.12. Boom-induced transfers via public sector labour market rents

	Real av. sector earnings (MK p.a.)	Counter factual real av. public sector earnings (MK p.a.)	Public sector employment ('000)	Total public sector wage bill (MKm p.a.)	Counter factual total public sector wage bill (MKm p.a.)	Public sector wage windfall (MKm p.a.)
1976	600	680	70.0	47.6	47.6	0.0
1977	614	614	68.6	42.1	42.1	0.0
1978	796	614	68.4	54.5	42.0	12.5
1979	722	614	69.5	50.2	42.7	7.5
1980	651	614	76.5	49.8	47.0	2.8
1981	603	614	76.0	45.8	46.7	−0.9
1982	631	614	77.1	48.7	47.4	1.3
1983	585	614	79.9	46.7	49.1	−2.4
Total						20.8

Source: Pryor (1988, table H-2); Gulhati (1989, table A-4) *Malawi Statistical Yearbook* (various issues, table 7.1)

Table 5.13. Public to private rent transfers via non-tradable capital goods market

	Non-traded capital goods inflation index (1976 = 100)	Gov. expenditure on non-traded capital goods (MKm, current prices)	Rent transfer (MKm)
1978	135	28.8	10.1
1979	155	32.3	17.8
1980	143	37.7	16.2
Total			44.1

Source: *Malawi Satistical Yearbook* (1980, tables 10.7 and 10.8); Pryor (1988, table G-1)

period of non-tradable consumer goods inflation there was an MK 68.4 million public to private sector rent transfer.[19]

In summary, the analysis of revenue transmissions has shown that an MK 373 million boom-induced increase in public sector revenue (Table 5.10) resulted from both autonomous and discretionary revenue increases over the 1977–83 period. During the same period MK 133.3 million (i.e. 35.7%) of this boom-induced increase in public sector revenue was transferred back to the private sector—30.2% via commodity markets and 5.5% via the labour market. MK 72.9 million of this revenue transfer occurred in

Table 5.14. Public to private rent transfers via non-tradable consumer goods
market

	Non-traded consumer goods inflation index (1976 = 100)	Gov. expenditure on non-traded consumer goods (MKm, current prices)	Rent transfer (MKm)
1978	117	23.2	3.9
1979	131	27.7	8.6
1980	139	32.1	12.5
1981	131	39.4	12.2
1982	133	43.9	14.5
1983	133	50.7	16.7
Total			68.4

Source: World Bank (1985, statistical appendix table 7.01)

Table 5.15. Public sector share of boom-induced GFKF

	Total (MKm)	Public sector (MKm)	Public sector share (%)
1977	9.7	15.5	160
1978	79.9	55.9	70
1979	51.0	56.4	111
Total	140.6	127.8	91

Source: Tables 5.3 and 5.10

the post-boom 1980–83 period. Hence, commodity and labour market
rents did little to compensate for the adverse effects of fiscal policies
which transferred boom income to the public sector and helped to restrict
the construction boom to the terms of trade income-boom years.

5.4.3. Public and Private Sector Assets and Expenditure

Table 5.15 presents the public sector's share of boom-induced GFKF and
shows that, during the income-boom years, most of the induced GFKF
increase occurred in the public sector. Figure 5.3 and Table 5.15 together
suggest that the public sector was the lead contributor to the construction
boom. Not only was 90.9% of boom-induced GFKF attributable to the
public sector, 82% of the resulting public sector demand for capital goods
was directed towards non-tradables (Figure 5.3). The lead public sector
role is further evidenced by the fact that the period in which the relative
price of non-tradable capital goods was forced up and capital and labour
resources drawn into the non-tradable capital goods sector (Figures 5.4

and 5.5; Table 5.7) coincided with the peak years of public sector boom-induced GFKF (Table 5.10) and with the sharp increase in public sector demand for non-tradable capital goods (Figure 5.3).

In Section 5.3.1 the economy-wide savings rate out of transient income was found to be 97%. Given that the boom resulted in large revenue transfers to the public sector such that the bulk of windfall-induced GFKF took place in the public sector, diversity in public and private sector savings rates can be expected. To calculate separate windfall savings rates for the public and private sectors, the boom-induced increase in the primary deficit must be taken into consideration. Deducting the increase in the deficit (i.e. MK 43.7 million over 1977–80; Table 5.10) from the MK 127.8 million increase in public sector capital formation (Table 5.15) gives an increase in public sector assets of MK 84.1 million. Over the same period the increase in private sector assets consisted of that part of boom-induced GFKF not attributable to the public sector plus the value of the boom-induced deterioration in the primary deficit minus the induced increase in foreign debt (MK 140.6 − MK 127.8 + MK 43.7 − MK 65.14 = MK − 8.64 million).

In order to calculate disaggregated private and public sector savings rates for the terms of trade boom period, any sector-specific induced rents which were created during 1977–79 must be included as part of the relevant sector's windfall income. Such rents consist of incomes derived indirectly from the boom in the form of rents created by boom-induced expenditure on non-tradables and by boom-induced changes in labour markets.[20]

The derivation of total boom transient income in Section 5.3.1 produced an estimate of MK 67.9 million. Since the boom induced an MK 141.2 million increase in public sector revenue over 1977–79 (Table 5.10) it would appear that none of the direct windfall income gain remained in the hands of the private sector. Consequently, we can discount the possibility of any windfall rents having been created by private sector expenditures. Rental income transferred back to the private sector via boom-induced public sector wage increases amounted to MK 20.0 million over the period 1977–79 (Table 5.12). Public to private sector rent transfers via the non-traded capital and non-traded consumer goods markets are estimated in Tables 5.13 and 5.14 and amount to MK 27.9 million and MK 12.5 million, respectively, over the same period. Hence, out of the boom-induced MK 141.2 million increase in public sector revenues, a total of MK 60.4 million was transferred back to the private sector, leaving net public sector windfall income at MK 80.8 million. Net private sector windfall income consisted of the entire direct terms of trade windfall (i.e. MK 67.9 million) minus the MK 141.2 million induced increase in public sector revenues plus the MK 60.4 million reverse transfer in the form of induced rental incomes, giving a negative net private sector windfall of MK −12.9 million.

The above calculations can be used to compare the public and private sector savings behaviour in response to each sector's windfall income. The public sector saved MK 84.1 million out of its MK 80.8 million income windfall, giving a public sector savings rate of 104%. By contrast, the private sector dissaved MK 8.64 million in response to its negative net windfall income of MK −12.9 million. Trends in total private sector savings provide further evidence of the sector's dissaving. As can be seen from Figure 5.6, total private sector savings, which had steadily increased since 1973, declined from 1978 onwards.

In calculating the separate private and public sector savings rates, the MK 65.14 windfall-induced increase in foreign debt has been treated as a private sector liability. However, effective foreign exchange controls existed during the late 1970s such that, with the exception of parastatals and certain multinational companies, the private sector was not in a position to accumulate its own foreign debt. Hence, we can conclude that much of the non-budget foreign debt was due to parastatals. Since data for the parastatal subsector are scant for the period, it has been treated throughout this study as part of the private sector. It is interesting, nevertheless, to see what happens if we assume that all the non-budget boom-induced foreign debt was due to parastatals and remove the parastatals from our definition of the private sector. In this case boom-induced private sector

Figure 5.6. Private sector savings, 1973–82 (*current MK m.*)

Note: Savings from large enterprises including parastatals.

Source: World Bank (1985: statistical appendix, table 2.04).

savings become positive and instead of dissaving MK 8.64 million the newly defined private sector accumulated MK 56.5 million-worth of assets. On the other hand, the public sector, now including parastatals, accumulated only MK 18.96 million of assets instead of MK 84.1 million. If we assume that the reclassification does not affect each sector's boom transient income, then the public sector's transient income savings propensity falls from 104% to 24%. The importance of these results is that the non-parastatal private sector does appear to have saved in response to the boom. However, as we will see in Section 5.5 below, the government's control regime was such that the non-parastatal private sector had little scope to pursue an optimal policy of deferring investment out of its MK 56.5 million of windfall assets.

The marked differences in public and private sector savings behaviour, with the private sector (including parastatals) dissaving, can be explained by the expectational properties which characterised the various components of the terms of trade shock (Table 5.2) in conjunction with the government's fiscal response to the windfall (Tables 5.7 and 5.10). Private sector expectations regarding the tobacco price component of the shock were inclusive. This anticipated windfall transient income, however, failed to materialise, since fiscal policy transferred all of the windfall to the public sector and the private sector found its income reduced by MK 12.9 million as a net result of the entire terms of trade boom. The unexpected windfall from tea and import price changes did not, therefore, compensate for the failure of tobacco prices to produce the income increase expected in the private sector. As a consequence, income in the private sector fell relative to expectations, despite the positive terms of trade shock.

The high public sector savings rate of 104% is also compatible with public sector expectations regarding the various components of the terms of trade shock. Each component was exclusive to expectations (Table 5.2), yet the income boom resulted in a massive transfer of resources to the public sector, with neither the tea nor the import price component of this boom giving rise to a revision of public sector expectations.

We are now in a position to summarise the disaggregated private and public sector response to the temporary positive trade shock. Most of the windfall income from the trade shock initially went to the private sector. Although the government made no attempt to tax the resulting income at source it was rapidly transferred to the public sector via both automatic and discretionary revenue increases. The boom induced an MK 141.2 million increase in public sector revenue over 1977–79. MK 60.4 million of this was transferred back to the private sector via rents created in the labour and non-tradable goods markets. The public sector's savings propensity out of its windfall transient income was 104%, whereas the private sector dissaved MK 8.64 million in response to a negative net windfall of

MK −12.9 million. This result is highly sensitive to the fact that parastatals are included within the private sector. If parastatals are counted as part of the public sector the latter's savings propensity falls to 24%, whereas the private sector saves MK 56.5 million as a result of the boom.

The boom-induced increase in government revenues triggered an excessive increase in public sector expenditures, which led to a sharp deterioration in the budget deficit. Owing to a ratchet effect which operated on the consumption component of the expenditure increase, the government was forced to resort to reductions in public sector investments, an increase in the tax burden and excessive domestic borrowing in order to cure the deficit in the immediate post-boom years. All of these actions inhibited the economy's ability to extend the construction boom beyond the trade shock period.

Over 90% of boom-induced GFKF during the trade shock years occurred in the public sector, which played a lead role in fuelling the construction boom. Yet most of the public sector's windfall investment projects were poorly chosen with low rates of return and so did little to increase the economy's permanent income.

5.5. Rules and Controls

5.5.1. *Government Regulations*

Of the three types of rules and controls which affect agents' capacity to respond to a windfall—namely, government regulation of private agents, private agents' regulation of each other, and regulations imposed by foreign agents—only the former type was of importance in Malawi during the terms of trade boom years.

Rules imposed by private agents, via interest groups such as trade unions, to govern collective behaviour were virtually non-existent, and rules imposed by foreign agents in international finance and commodity markets do not appear to have restrained the economy's response to the terms of trade windfall. Access to the international tea and tobacco markets was unconstrained, and foreign credit, both commercial and concessional, was not in tight supply during the 1970s.

Throughout the late 1960s and 1970s the Malawi government used a wide range of controls to regulate private sector economic activity. Interventions included extensive price controls on a large number of consumer and intermediate goods and on producer prices of smallholder agricultural output. Statutory minimum wage rates were set and incomes policies gave rise to a steady decline in real wage rates in both the private and public sectors. Between 1975 and 1984 the Malawi kwacha was pegged to the SDR with infrequent downward adjustments. In addition to control of the exchange rate, capital movements were restricted via barriers to the transferability of the kwacha. Extensive controls also existed in the domestic finance market. The Reserve Bank of Malawi set maximum deposit rates, minimum lending rates and minimum liquidity ratios for the commercial banking system. A major objective of interest rate controls was to minimise the cost of funds to the government. The controlled rates were adjusted infrequently and were negative in real terms throughout much of the 1970s. Physical controls were also used to allocate credit to favoured sectors. Moderate controls were exercised over imports. Import tariffs ranged from 5% to 35%, with the highest rates on consumer goods, but quantitative import restrictions were only binding in times of severe balance of payments pressure.

5.5.2. The Effects of Exchange Controls and Fiscal Policy

Although foreign exchange controls prevailed during the terms of trade boom period their effect on private agents' asset choice set was overridden by the fact that private sector windfall income was rapidly transferred to the public sector. As a result of fiscal policy the private sector dissaved during the boom period. The adverse effects of fiscal policy in conjunction with exchange controls can, nevertheless, be assessed by comparing the government's actual use of the windfall with a counterfactual scenario under which the windfall income remained in the private sector and was freely convertible into foreign financial assets.

Table 5.10 shows that over the period 1977–80 boom-induced revenue accruing to the public sector amounted to MK 212.8 million and boom-induced public sector GFKF amounted to MK 196.1 million. The public sector, therefore, made no attempt to defer investment. In 1978, the first boom year in which substantial boom-induced revenue accrued to the public sector and resulted in significant boom-induced GFKF, MK 100 of windfall income transferred to the public sector and spent immediately on non-tradable capital goods would have procured an equivalent value of goods, i.e. MK 100. By contrast, MK 100 accruing to the private sector at the start of 1978 and held in foreign financial assets until the end of 1981, when the construction boom as measured by the relative price of non-tradable capital goods was over, would have accumulated to MK 154.[21] The price of non-tradable capital goods had also fallen in absolute terms by 14% between 1978 and 1981, so that the MK 154 would have purchased MK 179-worth of non-tradable capital goods at 1978 prices. The policy option of deferred investment (by either the private or public sector) in the absence of exchange controls would therefore have enabled MK 100 of windfall income to procure 79% more non-tradable capital goods compared to the actual fiscal strategy adopted. The real annual social rate of return from the optimal deferred-investment strategy over the period 1978–81 would have been 15.7%.

The foregone social return calculated above was a direct result of the fiscal policy adopted in response to the boom, namely, a policy which increased government revenues and spent them immediately. Had a minimalist fiscal strategy been combined with a monetary policy which permitted private agents in aggregate to acquire domestic financial assets (but not foreign assets) as a means of deferring investment, a second-best outcome would have resulted. Taking the re-discount rate on treasury bills to represent the rate of return on domestic financial assets, MK 100 of private windfall income held in this form between the start of 1978 and the end of 1981 would have accumulated to MK 135. This would have purchased MK 157-worth of non-tradable capital goods at 1978 prices as opposed to MK 179-worth under the optimum strategy of deferring investment via the holding of foreign financial assets. This second-best strategy, compared to the optimum, results in a foregone social return of 3.35% over the period 1978–81.

5.5.3. *The Effect of Controls in the Finance Market*

In the two years immediately prior to the terms of trade income boom financially repressive government controls in the money market had contributed to private sector credit constraints. The years 1974–76 witnessed a sharp slow-down in the accumulation of private financial resources. This restricted the ability of the banking system to provide investment funds while maintaining an adequate level of international reserves, particularly since the banks were constrained by government-controlled interest rates. The resulting tightening of the liquidity position was reflected by a falling commercial bank liquidity ratio (Figure 5.7).

Despite the fact that Malawi's positive trade shock occurred in the context of a credit-constrained private sector with restrictions on the holding of foreign financial assets, it did not result in significant endogenous financial liberalisation. This is not surprising since fiscal policy transferred the bulk of the income windfall to the public sector, which rapidly spent it on consumption and the acquisition of capital goods while the private sector dissaved. A large boom-induced increase in the asset demand for money did not, therefore, occur. There was, nevertheless, a relaxation of credit constraints facing certain favoured sectors of the economy during the terms of trade boom years, but this was the result of factors which were exogenous to the trade shock.

The first year of the terms of trade boom witnessed a recovery in private sector commercial bank deposits. This was followed by more moderate increases in 1978 and 1979. This was the result of an increase in the average savings propensity caused by factors unrelated to the trade shock, namely, the reversal of the factors which had contributed to the earlier slow-down in private sector domestic financial asset accumulation,[22]

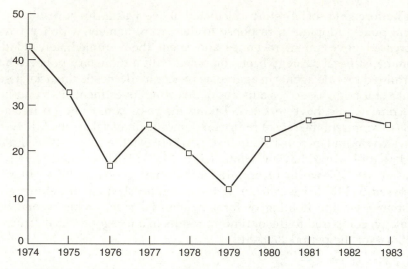

Figure 5.7. Commercial bank liquidity ratio, 1974–83 (%)
Source: Reserve Bank of Malawi.

rather than of a high marginal propensity to save out of windfall income. The increase in private sector deposits combined with a rapid growth in the money supply (M_1 rising from MK 58.5 million in 1976 to MK 92.5 million in 1980) increased loanable resources available to the domestic banking system, and in 1977 the commercial bank liquidity ratio recovered from its low point of the previous year (Figure 5.7).

The marked 1977 rise in the liquidity of the domestic banking system prompted an excessive increase in net bank credit, most of which was channelled to the central government and to politically favoured tobacco estates within the private sector. Between 1976 and 1979 commercial bank credit to the public sector increased from MK 35.9 million to MK 55.7 million. Credit to the private sector increased from MK 71.7 million to MK 170.6 million, 66% of which went to the agricultural sector—mainly to tobacco estates owned by politicians and bureaucrats (Table 5.16).

Although the tobacco subsector was part of the primary boom sector the large increase in financial resources made available to the subsector did not represent an efficient resource allocation. Most of the new and expanding estates were highly geared (being capitalised with what were effectively bank overdrafts), were poorly managed and had high capital import demands. Consequently, investment returns were low and by the early 1980s many of the estates faced bankruptcy—to an extent which threatened the viability of the domestic banking system. The banks, however, were powerless to resist the political pressure to allocate finance to the estates.

Table 5.16. Allocation of commercial bank credit to private sector (%)

	1975	1976	1977	1978	1979	1980	1981	1982	1983
Tradable boom sector (primary)	24.6	38.9	35.0	44.5	48.0	53.8	49.7	51.8	52.5
Non-tradable boom sector (secondary)	0.9	2.5	0.7	2.3	2.1	0.9	0.7	0.6	0.3
Tradable non-boom sector	11.0	10.7	14.7	11.2	5.8	4.1	3.4	3.5	4.1
Non-tradable non-boom sector	63.5	47.9	49.6	42.0	44.1	41.2	46.2	44.1	43.1

Source: Reserve Bank of Malawi *Financial and Economic Review* (various issues)

The politically motivated physical controls on credit allocation during the boom years help to explain why the construction boom was relatively moderate compared to that in the primary boom sector. Between 1976 and 1980 commercial bank credit to the construction sector fell both absolutely and as a percentage of total credit (Table 5.16). This undoubtedly suppressed both GFKF and employment expansion in the construction sector.

The allocation of credit to the favoured public sector and the tobacco subsector during the boom years gave rise to credit scarcity not just in the construction sector but in most other non-public and non-tobacco sectors. This is evidenced by numerous official statements. The *Economic Report 1979*, for example, draws attention to the 'shortage of liquidity in the business community', and the *Economic Report 1981* comments on the 'tight liquidity conditions in the economy that have characterised the most recent three years'.

Political intervention in the finance market, in addition to suppressing the construction boom and inflating the boom in the primary boom sector during 1977–80, also prompted a tightening of controls by the monetary authorities. The excessive expansion of bank credit to favoured sectors and government in 1978 and 1979 was such that the liquidity position of the commercial banks, which had briefly recovered in 1977, again deteriorated (Figure 5.7). By 1979 the liquidity ratio had fallen below the statutory 25% minimum. In response to this overextension of the commercial banking system the monetary authorities attempted to restrict credit by placing monthly limits on the growth of commercial bank credit, raising the minimum liquidity ratio to 30% and raising the minimum bank lending rate from 10.0% to 11.5%. The maximum deposit rate was also raised in 1979 and 1980 in an attempt to increase the supply of bank funds. This tightening of credit controls in 1979 had the desired effect of reducing the growth of credit to government and the private sector. In response GFKF by both government and private enterprises declined dramatically. The investment boom and the suppressed construction boom were therefore abruptly truncated by monetary policy in a manner which prevented their extension beyond the income boom period.

5.5.4. Import Controls

The positive terms of trade shock was associated with a relaxation of controls on consumer imports. Import duty rates on consumer durables fell in 1978, 1979 and 1980, and rates on non-durables fell in 1979 and 1980 (Table 5.17).

Since quantitative import restrictions were not generally binding in the pre-boom years, changes in import duty rates provide an adequate measure of consumer import liberalisation. As a further check, however, Figure 5.8 presents an alternative proxy measure in the form of the ratio of consumer imports to total consumption. Between 1976 and 1979 this ratio increased substantially. Since the exchange rate over this period was constant (in terms of the SDR to which it was tied) it is likely that the increase in the volume of consumer imports relative to total consumption reflects a liberalisation of consumer imports. The two measures of import control show a re-tightening of controls in the post-boom period.

The loosening of import controls is a rational policy response to a positive trade shock since it enables increased consumption demand arising from the foreign exchange influx to be met via imports rather than via the expansion of import substitutes at the expense of exports. Table 5.18 compares actual export performance with a counter-factual which is based on the assumption that in the absence of the terms of trade shock exports would have grown in line with GDP.[23] With the exception of 1978, export performance exceeds the counterfactual, with actual exports increasing by 48% over the 1976–80 period, compared to a 7% increase in counterfactual performance. This significant boom-induced expansion in exports indicates that consumer import liberalisation was sufficient to

Table 5.17. Import duty rates, by end use (*as a percentage of import c.i.f.*)

	1976	1977	1978	1979	1980	1981	1982	1983
Consumer durables	19.5	20.9	19.2	17.0	16.8	18.1	19.0	20.9
Consumer non-durables	15.7	15.9	17.8	16.0	13.9	17.5	17.3	17.1

Source: National Statistical Office

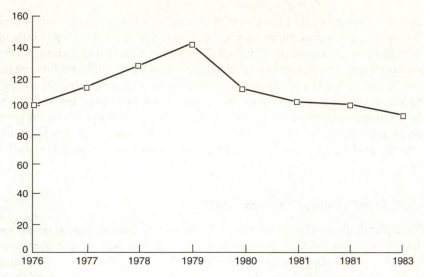

Figure 5.8. Index of consumer imports to total consumption, 1976–83
(1976 = 100)

Source: Malawi Annual Statement of External Trade.

Table 5.18. Actual and counterfactual exports[a]

	Actual	Counterfactual	Boom-induced change
1976	100	100	0
1977	86	80	6
1978	91	97	−6
1979	131	111	20
1980	148	107	41

[a] Quantum index of actual and counter-factual exports deflated by the unit-value index of total exports.

Source: Pryor (1988, table F-1)

prevent importables behaving as non-tradables at the margin and so drawing resources from the export sector in response to increased demand for importables.

There is some evidence that the liberalisation of import controls may have been excessive. Between 1977 and 1979 the index of imports of private consumer durables increased by 61%. This increase coincided closely with trade liberalisation as measured by changes in import duty rates on consumer durables (Table 5.17) and by the consumer import ratio (Figure 5.8). The magnitude of the increase in consumer durable imports suggests hoarding actions on the part of rational private agents who correctly viewed trade liberalisation as a temporary phenomenon associated with the positive trade shock. To the extent that hoarding occurred, liberalisation was excessive in that it prompted an inflated demand for consumer imports in excess of that which could be sustained by increased permanent income and therefore gave rise to a pre-empting of foreign exchange which may otherwise have been used to finance investment in the booming sectors of the economy. The rapid rise in consumer imports following liberalisation also led to a marked increase in import duty revenue and so increased the public sector's share of transient windfall income.

5.5.5. Fixed Nominal Exchange Rate

Throughout the 1977–79 terms of trade boom period the nominal exchange rate was held constant at MK 1.00 = SDR 0.9487. In the context of a positive trade shock such a policy is likely to be inflationary compared to the outcome under a freely floating exchange rate regime. Under the latter, the boom-induced expenditure increase and the associated rise in the transactions demand for money will cause an appreciation in the value of domestic currency and hence a fall in the domestic currency price of tradables. Whether or not the fixed nominal exchange rate induced inflation relative to the counterfactual scenario of a freely floating rate during the boom period can be assessed by analysis of movements in the freely floating black-market exchange rate.

Figure 5.9 shows movements in the black-market exchange rate, de-

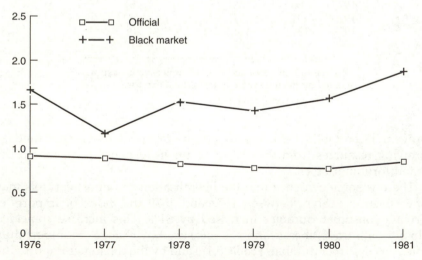

Figure 5.9. Official and black-market exchange rate, MK/US$, 1976–81
Source: Pryor (1988: table G-2).

nominated in Malawi kwacha to the US dollar, and compares this to movements in the official kwacha to dollar rate (the official rate was held constant in terms of the SDR, hence there is some movement in the official kwacha to dollar rates). In 1977, the first year of the income boom, the black-market rate appreciated by 30%, with a further small (6%) appreciation in 1979. These movements in the black-market rate suggest that a freely floating exchange rate would likewise have appreciated during the terms of trade boom period. Hence, it would appear that the policy of retaining a fixed exchange rate during the positive trade shock was inflationary in 1977 and 1979. Since inflation increases the attractiveness of holding real assets relative to financial assets, control of the exchange rate may well have provided a further disincentive to a deferred investment strategy by either private or public agents.

5.5.6. Price Controls

Throughout the 1970s the government exerted effective controls over the prices of a large number of intermediate and final consumption goods. Prices of mass-produced homogeneous products considered of national importance, such as cement, fertiliser and petroleum products, were regulated, as were prices of goods which figured prominently in the consumption of low-income groups. By the late 1970s, 56 items were subject to formal price control and a large number of goods were also subject to informal, but equally effective, controls. Virtually the entire output of the domestic manufacturing sector, which was almost exclusively orientated towards the home market, was subject to rigorous price control, with prices set on a 12–18% cost-plus basis.

The existence of a cost-plus pricing system meant that prices tended to respond more to changing supply-side conditions than to changing demand conditions. This inhibited the ability of relative price signals to respond to the changing demand pressures brought about by the positive terms of trade shock. Such price responses are central to both Dutch Disease and construction boom theory.

It is not possible, without a computable model, to measure the changes in relative prices which would have occurred over the 1977–79 period in the absence of price controls. The evidence presented in Section 5.3.2. indicates that, even under the controlled regime, price ratios moved in the directions predicted by both Dutch Disease theory and construction boom theory: in accordance with the former the price of non-tradables (both capital and consumer) rose relative to non-boom tradables (import substitutes); in accordance with the latter the price of non-tradable capital goods rose relative to non-tradable consumer goods (Figure 5.4). Malawi's price control regime, however, contained several asymmetries of direct relevance to the empirical assessment of the two trade-shock theories.

The commodity aggregate subject to the greatest price controls was domestic manufacturing, i.e. import substitutes (the non-boom tradable sector of Dutch Disease theory). The fact that prices in this sector were suppressed by controls to a much greater extent than the prices of the non-tradable commodity aggregates helps to explain why Dutch Disease price effects appear, on the basis of Figure 5.4, to be much stronger than construction boom price effects. Furthermore, the prices of non-tradable consumer goods (i.e. services) were subject to very little, if any, control, whereas the prices of many non-tradable capital goods were controlled. In particular, the price of cement, a key item in any construction price index, was rigorously controlled. This second price control asymmetry also contributed to the relative weakness of construction boom price effects.

Since tea and tobacco prices were freely determined on the auction floors, the price of non-tradable capital was also suppressed relative to output prices in these two primary boom sectors. This helps to explain why the boom in the latter, as measured by sectoral allocation of GFKF (Figure 5.5), was so much greater than that in the construction sector (although this was also the result of the fact that the tobacco subsector received extensive credit allocations from the commercial banking system).

Another effect of price controls was to limit the transfer of windfall income from the public sector back to the private sector via rents created by government expenditure in the non-traded capital goods markets. The limiting of this transfer reduced the amount of transient windfall income which ultimately ended up in private hands.

We can now summarise the impact of the public sector's control regime on the economy's response to the positive trade shock. The government's control regime had a significant impact on the dynamics of the construction boom. The overall effect of government intervention in domestic pricing exacerbated Dutch Disease symptoms (the rise in the non-tradable/tradable price ratio; the consequent decline in the tradable non-boom sector, i.e. manufacturing; and the expansion of the primary boom sector) and suppressed the relative price signals normally associated with a construction boom. Physical controls in the domestic finance market resulted in the primary boom sector (agriculture) and the central government receiving excessive favoured credit allocations at the expense of all other sectors, including construction. This also helped to suppress the construction boom. The resulting overextension of the domestic banking system led to a tightening of monetary controls in the immediate post-boom period which inhibited the economy's ability to extend the investment and construction boom beyond the trade-shock years. There is evidence that the fixed nominal exchange rate had an inflationary effect during the shock period which encouraged investment in physical assets and so inhibited the stretching of the investment boom. Although import controls were relaxed, the liberalisation was excessive, leading to import hoarding which diverted foreign exchange resources away from the booming sectors. If windfall income had remained in the private sector, the existence of foreign exchange controls, by preventing optimum private sector investment deferral through the holding of foreign assets, would have resulted in a forgone social return of between 3.35% and 15.7%. Overall, therefore, the effect of the government's control regime was to suppress both the magnitude and duration of the construction boom.

5.6. Summary and Conclusions

5.6.1. Indications of a Construction Boom

The behaviour of the Malawian economy in response to the 1977–79 terms of trade income windfall supports the central propositions of construction boom theory. The high (97%) economy-wide savings propensity out of windfall income indicates that the windfall was viewed as transient. Following a positive trade shock which is perceived as temporary, construction boom theory predicts an increase in the demand for, and the price of, non-tradable capital relative to non-tradable consumer goods. Both trends were evident in Malawi over the 1977–80 period.

Although it is not possible to disaggregate total expenditure into demand for non-tradable capital goods and demand for non-tradable consumer goods, disaggregation for the public sector shows a sharp increase in public sector demand for non-tradable capital following the income windfall. The economy-wide relative price ratio between non-traded capital and non-traded consumer goods also increased following the income windfall. Mobile factors of production responded to this relative price change, with the allocation of boom-induced GFKF favouring not just the primary boom sectors (tea and tobacco) but also the secondary, construction boom sector. Both sectors also attracted labour from other parts of the economy, although increased relative wages were not necessary to induce this labour transfer. Taken together, these trends in expenditure patterns, relative prices and factor movements provide strong evidence that the positive trade shock gave rise to a construction boom.

5.6.2. Assessment of Dutch Disease and Construction Boom Models

A notable feature of the Malawian construction boom was its modest size. The change in the key construction boom price ratio between non-tradable capital and non-tradable consumer goods was much smaller than the increase in the relative price ratio between non-tradables as a whole and import substitutes (Figure 5.4). Also, the allocation of capital favoured the primary boom sector at the expense of non-boom tradables (manufacturing) to a much greater extent than it favoured the construction sector at the expense of non-tradable consumer goods (Figure 5.5).

In terms of size, therefore, relative price changes and relative factor movements appear to have favoured the commodity aggregates of the Dutch Disease model to a greater extent than those of the construction boom model. This, however, was largely the result of government controls. Asymmetries in the government's price control regime suppressed the relative price changes normally associated with a construction boom and inflated those associated with the Dutch Disease model. Interventions in the domestic finance market also ensured that credit allocations favoured the primary boom sector at the expense of the construction sector. In the absence of such controls Malawi's construction boom would probably have been much more marked.

5.6.3. *The Dynamics of the Construction Boom*

A second notable feature of Malawi's construction boom is its limited duration. The boom did not stretch beyond the period of the income windfall. By 1980 the price of non-tradable capital relative to both import substitutes and non-tradable consumer goods had returned to its pre-boom level, the transfer of both capital and labour to the construction sector had ceased, and demand for non-tradable capital goods (measured only for the public sector) was falling back towards pre-boom levels. The economy-wide failure to defer investment suggests a suboptimal response to the transient income windfall, with the crowding of investment into the 1977–79 period lowering returns and reducing the permanent income gain from the windfall.

5.6.4. *The Role of the Public Sector as an Agent in Its Own Right*

The public sector, both as an agent in its own right responding to the windfall and as the regulator of the private sector response, played a lead role in ensuring that the construction boom was confined to the income-windfall years.

Although the windfall initially accrued to the private sector, it was ultimately transferred to the public sector via both automatic and discretionary increases in public sector revenue. Rather than saving the additional unexpected revenue the government immediately spent it on both consumption and GFKF. Since a large percentage (Figure 5.3) of public sector GFKF was expressed as demand for non-tradable capital goods, public sector expenditure played a major part in amplifying the construction boom in the 1977–79 period. Indeed, over 90% of boom-induced GFKF occurred in the public sector.

Not only did the public sector fail to save and defer investment, the immediate increase in public sector expenditure was excessive, leading to deterioration in the budget deficit and necessitating extensive foreign borrowing. Owing to a ratchet effect operating on increased public sector consumption, the post-boom deficit was brought under control by a reduction in public sector GFKF and by an increase in the overall tax burden. Excessive foreign borrowing during the boom period also forced the government to resort to domestic borrowing in order to finance the post-1980 deficit. These post-boom fiscal trends, set in motion by the fiscal response during the 1977–79 period, restricted the economy's ability to stretch the investment boom beyond the income windfall years: the government was forced to cut back on GFKF, while the private sector found itself crowded out of the domestic credit market and facing a greatly increased tax burden, both of which inhibited its ability to invest in the post-boom period.

The social cost of the government's fiscal response to the terms of trade boom was high. The policy of increasing public sector revenues and spending them immediately resulted in a forgone social return of 15.7% per annum compared to the optimum strategy of deferring investment expenditures through foreign asset accumulation until the end of 1981. The fiscal response alone, however, cannot be blamed for the entire forgone return. Had windfall income remained in the private sector, the existence of foreign exchange controls would have resulted in a forgone return of between 3.35% and 15.7% over the 1978–81 period, the exact magnitude depending on the impact of monetary policy on the private sector's ability and willingness to hold domestic financial assets.

5.6.5. Effects of the Control Regime

The nature of the government's extensive control regime compounded the effects of fiscal policy in confining the construction boom to the income-windfall years. The fixed nominal exchange rate had an inflationary impact which reduced the attractiveness of holding financial assets relative to real assets and so discouraged investment deferral. Interventions in the domestic credit market led to an overextension of the domestic banking system and necessitated credit-restraint measures in the post-boom period, which, in turn, abruptly truncated the investment and construction booms.

The only part of the control regime which the government correctly adjusted in response to the income windfall was the regulation of foreign trade. Import restrictions were relaxed, mainly through tariff reduction, so that endogenous trade liberalisation prevented increased consumption demand from drawing resources from the export sector. There is evidence, however, that liberalisation was excessive, giving rise to hoarding of imported consumer durables and so causing a pre-empting of foreign exchange which may otherwise have been used to finance investment in the booming sectors.

Overall, it is hard to avoid the conclusion that the government handled the 1977–79 income windfall extremely badly both in its direct fiscal response and in its failure to adjust the control regime appropriately. Price control asymmetries suppressed the construction boom and exacerbated Dutch Disease effects, and interventions in the credit market resulted in inefficient resource allocations which excessively favoured the primary boom sector and inflated the boom in that sector at the expense of the construction sector. In addition fiscal, exchange rate and monetary policy all contributed to the economy's inability to extend the investment and construction boom beyond the income-windfall period. The dynamics of construction boom theory show that such a failure reduces an economy's ability to translate a transient income windfall into an increase in permanent income and hence consumption.

Suboptimal public sector responses to positive trade shocks were characteristic of the entire 1966–81 period and as such reduced Malawi's long-term growth potential:

Historically Malawi had experienced considerable export instability and had not succeeded in insulating the domestic economy. Windfall gains in years of good exports were not ploughed into reserves; instead they were used to purchase extra imports. Simulation exercises for the period 1966–81 showed that import instability could have been reduced by 53 percent if reserves had been managed contra-cyclically. (Gulhati 1989, p. 7)

Indeed, the 1977–79 income windfall was handled so poorly by the public sector that many analysts have characterised the late 1970s as a period of negative trade shocks. Rather that viewing the sharp 1977 improvement in the terms of trade as a positive shock which gave rise to a three-year positive deviation in the terms of trade from their trend decline, the fall in the terms of trade from their 1977 peak is stressed (without regard for historical trends) as a negative shock. Such an interpretation is understandable in view of the fact that many commentators mistakenly view Malawi as a highly market-orientated economy (Acharya 1981) and so require adverse exogenous shocks to explain the macroeconomic deterioration of the late 1970s and early 1980s. Once, however, the extent of the inflexible government control regime is fully appreciated, the existence of a positive trade shock and the subsequent deterioration in macroeconomic performance are no longer incompatible, since the public sector's handling of the income windfall was one of the main contributory factors in the economic decline.

5.6.6. *Private Sector Potential*

On the basis of the evidence available from the 1977–79 income-windfall period it is difficult to judge whether the private sector would have responded more efficiently to the windfall than did the public sector had the windfall income remained in private hands and had the control re-gime been adjusted appropriately. The private sector dissaved during the boom period. Given private sector expectations, particularly the inclusive expectations regarding the tobacco price component of the terms of trade shock, and given the negative private sector windfall-income effect caused by fiscal policy, such dissaving was not an irrational response. This, however, does not provide an adequate basis from which to judge the potential of an unfettered private sector to respond rationally to a large unexpected income windfall following a positive trade shock.

NOTES

1. Calculations later in the chapter indicate that the windfall had the potential to increase permanent income by 1.2% of 1976 GDP.
2. This simplifying assumption is based on the fact that the sharp 1977 increase in tea prices had no positive effect on tea export volumes, and although 1978–80 saw a significant increase in tobacco exports, much of this can be regarded as a continuation of the 1970–77 export expansion. Part of the increase in tobacco exports was, however, in response to the 1977 price improvement, but since it is not possible to estimate the opportunity cost of this component of the increase it has not been treated as an effect of the trade shock.
3. This latter view is supported by government statements prepared during 1978 and disseminated to the private sector in the *Economic Report 1979*, in which predicted increases in import prices were identified as two key factors in determining the economic outlook.
4. This method has been chosen in preference to extrapolation from past GDP growth, since both the incremental capital–output ratio and growth rates over the 1966–77 period were highly unstable.
5. The counterfactual income series is calculated by taking actual GDP at con-stant prices and deducting the return on any windfall-induced investment. It is assumed that such investment yields a 10% return after a one-year lag.
6. The domestic savings propensity results are surprising in that the 1978 pro-pensity exceeds unity, while total windfall GFKF amounted to MK 140.6 million out of a total windfall income of only MK 72.3 million. Various alter-native specifications of the counterfactual were investigated but all produced similar results. The root of the problem lies, not in the specification of the GFKF counterfactual, but in the fact that the actual 1978 and 1979 propensities are extraordinarily high compared to previous levels.
7. It is assumed that the cycle continues under the counterfactual scenario, with the counterfactual peak and trough values calculated using three-year moving averages.

8. Despite the boom-induced increase in foreign debt a positive trade shock was not needed to increase the perceived foreign debt capacity of the Malawian economy since the country had not been credit constrained before the boom. The terms of trade boom increased the need, rather than the ability, to borrow. As shown below this increased need for foreign borrowing was the result of a public sector expenditure overshoot triggered by the fiscal response to the trade boom.

9. Assuming that the savings rate out of this extra permanent income is equal to the counterfactual savings rate (i.e. col. (5) of Table 5.3 plus col. (3) of Table 5.4) gives the following savings stream: MK 0.28 million in 1977; MK 1.86 million in 1978; and MK 3.55 million in 1979. The 1977 present value of this stream (using a 10% discount rate) is MK 4.9 million.

10. Including the entire discounted value of windfall income as transient income ignores the fact that private sector expectations of tobacco prices were inclusive, so that this component of the windfall should be seen as permanent rather than transient income. As shown in section 5.4.1, however, most of the private sector windfall income was rapidly transferred to the public sector, where expectations were exclusive.

11. Since the National Accounts do not use sector-specific deflators, value-added deflators cannot be used to derive relative price indices for commodity aggregates.

12. The adverse capital-allocation effect on services, the non-tradable non-boom sector, is delayed. In the first year of the income windfall GFKF in the services sector actually increases. This, however, accords with both the static predictions of Dutch Disease theory and the predictions of construction boom theory regarding the impact effect of an income boom: both point to an initial spending effect which will raise the price of non-tradable consumer goods hence drawing mobile resources into the services sector. Even under the extreme assumption that the entire terms of trade windfall is characterised by exclusive and wholly unrevised expectations such that all windfall income is regarded as transient and saved, construction boom theory will still predict an initial spending effect since rational agents will respond to an increase in permanent income arising from the anticipated return on windfall savings.

13. The data upon which Table 5.6 is based suffers from several limitations: paid employment excludes self and own-farm employment, the earnings data only cover the formal sectors, and the classification of the entire 'Agriculture, Forestry and Fishing' sector as the primary boom sector ignores intra-sectoral labour transfers and changes in earnings between the tobacco and tea subsectors and other agricultural activities.

14. A high implicit tax was levied on smallholder tobacco producers by ADMARC, the monopsonistic state marketing board. This implicit tax, estimated at 280% in 1977 (World Bank 1982) took the form of a large differential between the producer price offered by ADMARC and the farm-gate export parity price. The increase in ADMARC's profits contributed to significant sector-specific financial liberalisation and GFKF, with ADMARC funds channelled through the commercial banks to fund investment in the politically favoured tobacco boom sector. These transfer mechanisms will be examined in Section 5.5.1.

15. The remaining MK 20.5 million consisted of non-tax revenue increases and it has not been possible to disaggregate this into automatic and discretionary components.

16. The role of public sector wages and salaries in the government consumption expenditure increase was large. Between fiscal years 1976/77 and 1980/81 central government current consumption increased by MK 51.6 million (current values). Of this increase 43% can be attributed to public sector wage and salary increases (Table 5.12).

17. The 1976 fiscal pattern for primary surplus aggregates is fairly similar to patterns observed for the previous seven years, despite the fact that this period contained the first oil shock. Hence, the oil shock does not appear to have had a major impact on government expenditure and revenue patterns as a percentage of GDP. It seems reasonable, therefore, to base the counterfactual, which contains a second oil shock, on 1976 revenue and expenditure patterns.

18. Although many of the projects had been initiated earlier in the 1970s, they became candidates for continued and expanded investment during the boom period.

19. Unlike transfers in the capital goods markets, a large part of the rent transfer through the consumer goods market occurred in the post-boom years.

20. Rents were not included as part of the windfall income in the calculation of the aggregate economy-wide savings rate in Section 5.3.1 since, being transfers, such rents net out at the aggregate level.

21. The kwacha was pegged to the SDR during this period. It is assumed that the rational investor holds assets in a basket of currencies corresponding to the SDR basket. Since the latter was a complex basket of sixteen currencies prior to 1981, the calculations have been simplified by assuming that the rational investor's portfolio is based on the post-1981 five-currency SDR basket. Annual returns are calculated using London Interbank Offer rates on six-month deposits for the five currencies and creating a weighted average return using the SDR currency basket weights. The final return is based on compound interest over the four-year period.

22. These factors included the desire to acquire import stocks owing to fear of supply disruptions in the face of political disturbances in neighbouring countries and rapid inflation which created negative real rates of interest. These made real assets more attractive relative to the holding of financial assets in the immediate pre-boom years.

23. This is a plausible assumption on which to base the counterfactual. Between 1970 and 1976 the average annual growth rate in export volumes was 6.7%, while the average annual GDP (constant factor prices) growth rate was 7.0%.

REFERENCES

Acharya, S.N., 1981. 'Perspectives and Problems of Development in Sub-Saharan Africa', *World Development* vol. 9, no. 2.

Government of Malawi, 1976 to 1985. *Economic Report*, Government Printer, Zomba.

Government of Malawi, 1976 to 1984. *Malawi Statistical Yearbook*, National Statistical Office, Zomba.

Government of Malawi, 1976 to 1985. *Monthly Statistical Bulletin*, National Statistical Office, Zomba.

Government of Malawi, 1982. 'National Accounts Report 1973–78', Government Printer, Zomba.

Gulhati, R., 1989. 'Malawi: Promising Reforms, Bad Luck', Economic Development Institute of the World Bank, Washington, DC.

Pryor, F., 1988. 'Income Distribution and Economic Development in Malawi: Some Historical Statistics', World Bank Discussion Papers, Washington, DC.

World Bank, 1982. 'Malawi, Growth and Structural Change: A Basic Economic Report', Report No. 3082a-MAI, Washington, DC.

World Bank, 1985. 'Malawi, Economic Recovery: Resource and Policy Needs. An Economic Memorandum', Report No. 5801-MAI, Washington, DC.

6

Private and Public Sector Responses to the 1972–75 Sugar Boom in Mauritius

DAVID GREENAWAY AND ROLAND LAMUSSE

6.1. Introduction

Mauritius is a small island located in the Western Indian Ocean. It has a population of just over one million, with a current GDP per capita of over US$3,000. Mauritius is almost unique among Sub-Saharan African countries in terms of its recent economic performance: it has unequivocally undergone a successful stabilisation and structural adjustment programme; diversified its industrial and export base; and embarked on a path of rapid and sustained growth in real GDP and real GDP per capita. Moreover, all of this has been achieved in a relatively short space of time, basically between the late 1970s and mid-1980s. The speed and extent of adjustment implies a degree of flexibility and responsiveness to economic stimuli which is unusual in the Sub-Saharan African context. The reasons for this impressive performance have been explored elsewhere (Greenaway and Milner, 1991) and are not the core of this chapter. Instead, our interest is in the impact of a major trade shock, in the mid-1970s, on the Mauritian economy in general and the process of adjustment in the aftermath of the shock.

In the 1970s, Mauritius was very heavily dependent on sugar exports, indeed so much so that it could reasonably be thought of as having a monocrop economy. In 1972–73, world prices increased sharply and increased even more dramatically in 1974 and 1975. They fell back in 1976; rose again sharply in 1980, only to fall in 1982. The first of these shocks was externally generated, manifestly temporary and sharp. Our purpose is to investigate the reaction of private and public sector agents to that shock and to elaborate how, if at all, they impacted on the adjustment process. The second shock was driven to a much greater degree by domestic cyclone damage and will not figure prominently in the analysis. Moreover, as we shall see, a variety of factors meant that the 1980–81 shock had a muted impact on the economy.

The chapter is structured as follows. Section 6.2 sets the context by reviewing price shocks in general and evaluating the background to the

1972–75 sugar boom. In Section 6.3 we trace the impact of the boom on the private sector and in Section 6.4 we assess public sector responses. Section 6.5 examines relative price changes across sectors, Section 6.6 reviews the evolving policy regime and Section 6.7 concludes.

6.2. An Overview of the 1974 Sugar Boom

There have been three clear sugar price booms which have affected Mauritius—1963, 1972–75 and 1980–81. Of these the most marked was that in 1972–75 (see Figure 6.1 and Table 6.1). The 1963 boom was sharp in that domestic sugar prices increased significantly. Although the 1980–81 spike in world sugar prices was also a very sharp one, from the Mauritian standpoint the shock was relatively unimportant—in part because export diversification had reduced the relative importance of sugar, but more importantly because by this time the Sugar Protocol of the Lomé Agreement ensured that some 80% of total production was subject to guaranteed prices. The impact of this is shown very clearly in Figures 6.1 and 6.2, where, as we can see, both domestic sugar prices and the Mauritius terms of trade are largely unaffected by the shock.

By contrast the 1972–75 shock was dramatic. Between 1972 and 1975, the domestic sugar price increased almost fourfold (in constant prices). The boom was externally generated, stimulated partly by demand factors

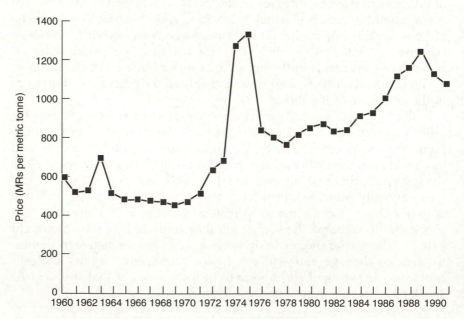

Figure 6.1. Sugar Prices 1960–1991, at constant (1972) prices

Table 6.1. Domestic price 1960–1991 and sugar production

Year	Price Rs./metric tonne	Production/metric tonnes
1960	503.87	—
1961	438.25	—
1962	445.21	—
1963	570.89	—
1964	433.13	—
1965	409.32	—
1966	421.50	561,762
1967	424.40	638,322
1968	428.39	596,549
1969	445.27	668,672
1970	471.70	576,000
1971	522.64	621,087
1972	641.43	686,366
1973	790.21	718,464
1974	1,877.59	676,786
1975	2,256.11	468,256
1976	1,617.03	689,932
1977	1,678.36	665,435
1978	1,742.01	665,219
1979	2,144.28	688,383
1980	2,319.48	475,494
1981	2,710.37	574,526
1982	2,868.54	687,940
1983	3,067.24	604,730
1984	3,583.21	575,617
1985	3,896.55	645,797
1986	4,212.61	706,839
1987	4,807.39	691,134
1988	5,399.04	631,224
1989	6,526.13	586,301
1990	6,714.32	624,302
1991	6,883.80	611,340

Source: Mauritius Chamber of Agriculture, Annual Reports

and partly by supply factors. On the demand side, sugar prices, like most commodity prices, had been stimulated by strong demand in industrial countries and had risen in the early 1970s. In 1974/75 some re-stocking was underway in the USA and Western Europe and served to reinforce upward pressures on price. More importantly, on the supply side, Cuba suffered a major shortfall as a result of a very poor harvest. Aside from the shortage on the world market which this created it also encouraged Russia, its key consumer, to purchase on the open market. This interven-

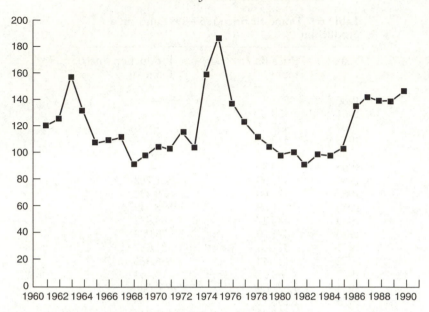

Figure 6.2. Terms of trade in Mauritius, 1960–1991

tion served to raise expectations of price increases in what is a relatively thin market.

At the time of the price shock, Mauritius could reasonably be thought of as a monocrop economy, with sugar and sugar-related products accounting for in excess of 80% of total exports (Table 6.2). At around 10% of total government revenues, sugar was also a major source of government funding. Agricultural sugar output and industrial sugar output accounted for close to 30% of GDP and some 40% of total employment. Clearly, sugar and sugar-related activities played a predominant role in economic activity, so that a major price shock, which was translated into a terms of trade shock (see Figure 6.2), could be expected to have a non-negligible impact on economic activity.

It should be noted that two other possible shocks impacted on the Mauritian economy during the boom period, which could influence the interpretation of events. The first was the setting-up of the Export Processing Zone (EPZ) in 1970. This offered incentives to both indigenous and overseas investors to produce for export markets. It is true that this did stimulate some initial increase in investment. However, the magnitudes are such that we need not worry unduly about it complicating our analysis. Foreign direct investment, which amounted to a negligible 9 million Mauritius rupees in 1970 only increased to MRs 24 million by 1976. The other event to be noted is the 1973–74 oil shock. This impacted adversely

Table 6.2. Sugar exports as a share of total exports

	%		%
1960	92.0	1976	72.0
1961	91.9	1977	66.9
1962	93.0	1978	62.9
1963	95.2	1979	61.8
1964	94.4	1980	60.6
1965	92.2	1981	49.6
1966	91.8	1982	56.5
1967	93.4	1983	57.8
1968	86.4	1984	46.0
1969	85.1	1985	41.0
1970	86.0	1986	38.0
1971	82.7	1987	36.3
1972	85.3	1988	32.2
1973	78.3	1989	31.8
1974	83.0	1990	28.2
1975	81.0	1991	27.0

on most developing countries. A priori it could be expected to counteract to a degree the effects of the sugar boom. Interestingly, however, even at that time Mauritius had a limited dependence on imported oil, since the bulk of its energy requirements were met by the burning of bagasse (the residue left after sugar cane has been crushed). Imports of petroleum and petroleum-related products amounted to 7.8% of total imports before the first oil shock and 9.1% afterwards. Thus, the increase in world oil prices is unlikely to complicate the analysis of the sugar shock.

The sugar boom presents a very clearly defined episode—a distinct and unambiguously temporary trade shock. We will evaluate in detail the impact of the shock on different groups of agents in the economy. For the moment we trace in broad outline apparent private and public sector responses.

As we shall see, the shock was a significant one, having a present value equivalent of 6% of GDP. Even without any change in rules, public sector revenues would of course have increased. However, government levied a special 15% surcharge on corporate taxes and individual taxes and increased sugar export taxes, ostensibly to cover the cost of rice subsidies, but manifestly to reclaim part of the windfall. The fact that this was explicitly a special levy implies that the windfall was perceived to be temporary. Government policy in resisting pressures from elsewhere in the Commonwealth to withdraw from the Sugar Protocol also signals a belief that the shock was a temporary one.

The bulk of the windfall, as we shall see, accrued to the private sector. In the mid-1970s there were pervasive controls on exports of financial assets and taxes on the export of capital; quantitative restrictions were fairly tight and there were tight regulations relating to import deposit schemes. Furthermore, no stock market existed and ceilings were applied to interest rates. Against this backdrop, most of the windfall appears to have gone into construction in general and construction in the tourist industry in particular. Superficially, therefore, the impact on expenditure and income appears to be consistent with that documented by Bevan *et al.* (1987) for the Kenyan coffee boom.

6.3. Private Sector Responses

Although the most marked increase in sugar prices occurred in 1974, significant increases also occurred in 1972, 1973 and 1975. For purposes of analysis, therefore, it will be assumed that the boom began in 1972 and lasted until 1975. Inspection of the constant price series reveals a clear break in 1972 in an upward direction (which in fact turns out to be statistically significant). Prices continue to rise until 1975 and decline sharply in 1976. Although the 1976 price level is almost a third greater than the 1971 price, the decline is sufficiently marked to signal the end of the boom. Moreover, in 1975 there was a sharp supply shock—with cyclone damage reducing the sugar crop by one-third. What were the effects of the price shock on the private sector?

6.3.1. Total Windfall Income

The value of the windfall arising from the price shock depends upon several factors, in particular the change in price and change in output relative to expected values. Take output first of all Figure 6.3 charts actual sugar output for the period 1966–91. Two things are notable; first 1975 and 1980 are clear outliers, when output declines to around 470,000 tonnes. Both were years when cyclones devastated the crop. Second, with the exception of these observations, output fluctuates in a relatively narrow range, with a mean value of 642,000 tonnes and a standard deviation of 50,115. The acreage under cane is fairly stable and relatively little takes place by way of short-run substitutions across crops. To simplify computation of the windfall we will therefore assume that output is exogenous.

In price-setting, Mauritius is a classic small open economy, with world prices exogenously determined. However, a complicating factor is that the market is regulated through the Sugar Protocol of the Lomé Agreement. The guaranteed prices which this offers pertain to around 80% of

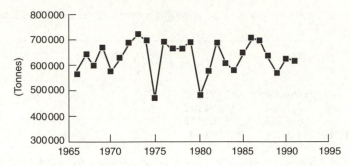

Figure 6.3. Sugar output, 1966–1991

the 'normal' output and offer a considerable degree of insulation from adverse world price changes (see Woldekidan and Weisman 1993). This will clearly influence medium- to long-run supply responses. Fortunately, from the standpoint of this study, the Sugar Protocol only became effective in 1975. At the time of the boom, therefore, it can plausibly be argued that agents had not adapted to the change in the regime. Moreover, the boom took sugar prices well above guaranteed levels. For purposes of calculating the windfall we can safely assume that the sugar protocol arrangements do not create any major problems.

In order to calculate a windfall gain, some counterfactual needs to be framed. The strategy followed by Bevan *et al.* (1992), and in the derivative studies of trade shocks in Africa and Latin America, is to take the pre-boom price as the assumed reference price and calculate the price shock as the difference between this and the boom price. This implicitly assumes that no updating occurs from one year to the next. In the case of a short, sharp boom, this is admissible. It is possible that when one is dealing with a price shock which persists for several years some updating occurs and this needs to be allowed for, however crudely.

Our methodology is as follows. We take the domestic reference price of sugar (P_t) to be that prevailing in the final pre-boom year, MRs 523 per tonne (in constant 1972 prices). This is taken as the 'farmgate' price, that is, the price actually received by growers. Anything in excess of this is assumed to be windfall income. Since output is assumed to be exogenous, the windfall (W_1) for any given year is defined as

$$W_1 = P_t Q_t - P_{1971} Q_t = (P_t - P_{1971}) Q_t. \tag{6.1}$$

The results of the windfall calculations using this methodology are presented in Table 6.3. They indicate that in 1972–73 the windfall was worth 6–8% of GDP (in constant 1972 prices). It peaked in 1974 at 25% of GDP, and despite a production shortfall in 1975 owing to the cyclone, still

Table 6.3. Estimated private sector windfall revenue from the 1972–75 sugar price shock (*MRs*)

	P_t	Q_t	W_1	W_1/GDP (%)	W_2	W_2/GDP (%)
1972	641	686,366	80,991,188	5.9	80,991,188	5.9
1973	696	718,464	124,294,272	8.0	39,515,520	2.5
1974	1,281	696,786	528,163,788	25.2	407,619,810	19.5
1975	1,342	468,256	383,501,644	19.3	28,563,616	1.5

Notes: The 1971 reference price is MRs 523 per tonne; all values are in constant 1972 prices

amounted to 19% of GDP. This is clearly a very significant windfall. For pedagogic purposes, another way of looking at it is to convert the windfall into permanent income. For this purpose we use a discount rate of 8%, this being the after-tax rate of return realised by the large sugar estates at that time. Viewed in permanent income terms at a discount rate of 8%, the windfall has a present value which is equivalent to 5% of GDP. Clearly this is a discount rate which, from a social standpoint, is likely to be on the high side—the rate on long-term government debt being around 5% at the time. We regard it as appropriate, however, since most of the windfall accrued to the private sector and because if anything it leads us to under-estimate the present value.

It could be argued that a possible source of overstatement of the wind-fall is the fact that we allow for no updating of expectations. By way of a simple sensitivity analysis an alternative set of calculations was completed assuming static expectations. In other words, the current price is assumed to be next year's price, again with output treated as exogenous. This defines the windfall as

$$W_2 = P_t Q_t - P_{t-1} Q_t = (P_t - P_{t-1}) Q_t. \tag{6.2}$$

This yields estimated windfalls of 6% and 2.5% of GDP, respectively, in 1972 and 1973, a peak windfall equivalent to 19.5% of GDP in 1974 and a windfall of 1.5% of GDP in 1975. W_2 and W_1 are obviously identical in 1972, but thereafter W_2 is less than W_1. The largest margin between the two occurs in 1975, 19.3% for W_1 and 1.5% for W_2. The present value equivalent of the total accumulated windfall (again at an 8% discount rate), is 3.2% of GDP—about two-thirds of that associated with W_1. Even if we take this as a lower-bound estimate, therefore, we are still dealing with a significant price shock. Thus, whether we calculate the magnitude of the shock in current price, or present value terms, we are dealing with a major perturbation.

6.3.2. *Private Sector Savings*

From Figure 6.4 we can see that the savings ratio changes markedly in response to the sugar boom. Prior to the shock, the average propensity to save ranges from 0.12 to 0.18; for the eight years following the boom it also lies broadly within this range, only showing a trend increase to over 0.20 after 1984, when export-oriented growth was sustained. For the price shock years, however, savings ratios range from 0.19 to 0.34, the lower ratio being recorded in the first year of the boom, the highest ratio being recorded in 1974, when windfall income peaked. Note that although the savings ratio declines in 1975 and 1976, it is still above trend, despite the cyclone of 1975. It seems clear, then, that the windfall resulted in a significant increase in savings rather than consumption. This is certainly consistent with the price shock being perceived as temporary by private sector agents. Figure 6.5 superimposes the savings ratio on the terms of trade, showing a clear co-movement.

6.3.3. *Private Sector Investment*

Figure 6.4 provides details of the investment ratio from 1950 to 1991. The series shows a clear upward trend, growing at 2.8% per annum (significant at 1%) over the period. Clearly, however, the series breaks down into two distinct subseries, 1952–71 and 1972–91. For the earlier period the mean investment ratio is 0.18, with a standard deviation of 0.03 and a range of 0.13 to 0.23. By contrast, in the latter period the respective summary statistics are 0.28, 0.6, 0.7 and 0.38. The only year for which the ratio is less than 0.20 is 1972. The series shows a discrete jump during the sugar

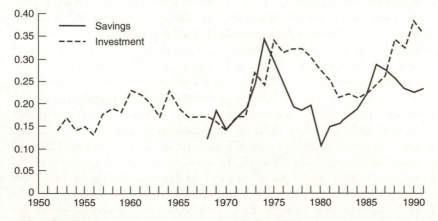

Figure 6.4. Savings and investment rates, 1952–1991

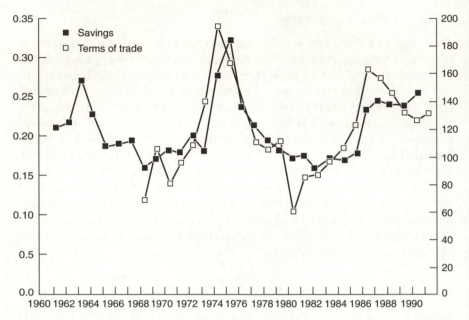

Figure 6.5. Terms of trade and savings, 1961–1991

shock, with a local maximum of 0.34 in 1975. Thereafter there is a steady decline to 0.21 in 1984 and a further rapid rise thereafter. This latter change was associated with the successful adjustment of the economy and a sustained period of export-led growth, sustained in large measure by the expansion of the EPZ.

The investment boom of the mid-1970s is clearly contemporaneous with the sugar price shock and lags the changes in windfall and savings. Figure 6.6 plots the co-movement of the investment and terms of trade series. Not only is the close correlation evident, the lagged effect on investment is notable after the 1972–75 shock, as investment stretching occurs to prolong the impact of the boom. Inspection of individual sector trends reveals that the boom was not associated with reinvestment in sugar, but rather with reinvestment in the then nascent EPZ and, more importantly, in private residential construction and residential construction for the tourist industry. The former attracted government subventions; the latter was (correctly) perceived as a good long-term bet. Data on construction activity are limited. However, one revealing source of information is that on the issue of permits for new buildings and their floor area. Unfortunately this series only dates from 1972. Nevertheless, as Figure 6.7 shows, the trend in both residential and non-residential approvals is illuminating. The series for non-residential approvals shows a

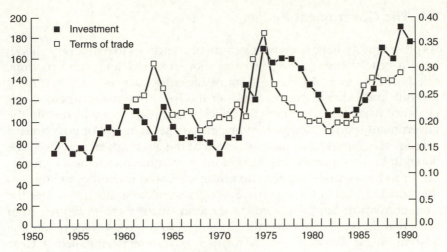

Figure 6.6. Terms of trade and investment, 1952–1991

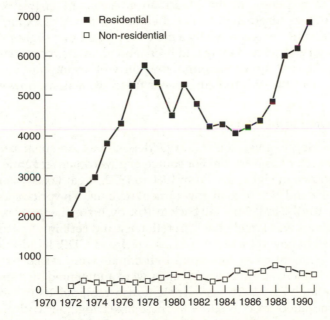

Figure 6.7. Annual construction permits issued, 1972–1991

very slow, upward drift, with no obvious breaks. By contrast that for residential approvals shows a sharp increase post-1972, peaking in the late 1970s, declining somewhat through the 1980s and only rising sharply again in 1988/89.

6.4. The Government Budget

As other studies have shown, government responses to temporary shocks have a crucial bearing on both the short-run and long-run economic effects of the shock. Before we examine the consequences for government revenue and expenditure we consider the issue of whether there is any evidence which indicates how the shock was initially perceived—did the government see it as temporary or permanent? A range of government actions/statements leads us to believe that the government perceived the boom to be a temporary one. First of all, government statements encouraged producers to desist from diverting increased quantities of sugar to the world market at the expense of longer-term commitments under the Commonwealth Sugar Agreement. Second, there were pressures from elsewhere in the Commonwealth for sugar producers to renegotiate the nascent Sugar Protocol—the Mauritian government signalled a clear intention that it would not do so. Finally, as we shall see in the next section, the initial policy signals indicated the perception of a temporary boom. The responses of the Mauritian government in this regard are perhaps not so surprising. As noted earlier, in terms of export dependence, the country was essentially a monocrop economy; sugar prices are a long-memory series and there had been a boom in the recent past (that in 1963–64). Against this background, the policy of urging caution is understandable. Did the government's deeds match its actions, however?

6.4.1. Government Revenue

Not surprisingly, given the country's dependence on sugar production, the sugar sector has been a major source of government revenue for some time, as shown in Figure 6.8. From 1960 to 1972, sugar taxes accounted for between 6% and 12% of total government revenue. The price shock raised this share to 17% in 1974; it fell back to 10% by 1976. The increase in sugar tax collections was largely non-discretionary and certainly contributed to an increase in government revenue as a share of GDP. In addition, however, government collections from individuals were raised by a special levy of 15% and corporate income taxes were augmented by a special 10% surcharge in 1973/74. The government also replaced its 6% export tax with a graduated tax of 6% to 9%. These taxes, together with the expansion of the tax base, account for the peak in government revenue as a share of GDP in 1975. This was a limited, though quite deliberate, attempt on the part of the government to absorb part of the windfall.

Thus, owing to a combination of both discretionary and non-discretionary fiscal policy government revenue increased, both in nominal terms and as a share of GDP. However, the increase was not as

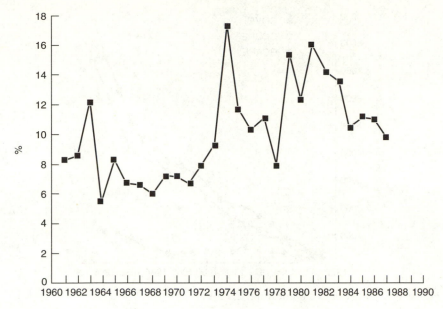

Figure 6.8. Sugar tax revenues as a percentage of total revenue, 1961–1987

marked as that recorded in the aggregate savings ratio, nor as sustained. Government tax policy towards the windfall is therefore certainly consistent with a perception that it was a temporary phenomenon.

6.4.2. Government Expenditure

As we saw in the previous section, government revenue increased as a consequence of the sugar boom; so too did government expenditure, both in absolute terms and as a share of GDP (Fig. 6.9 and Table 6.4). The increase was sharp and, to a degree, boom induced. Moreover, the bulk of the increase was recorded in current rather than capital expenditure. Capital expenditure did show a modest increase but this seems to have been a consequence of a prior commitment to increased support for the Development Works Corporation and the Export Processing Zone. Current expenditure increased to provide additional financing for rice and flour subsidies which amounted to over MRs 108 million, or 30% of current expenditure in 1973–74. In addition public sector emoluments increased substantially, by an average of 30%. This followed the publication in 1973 of the Sedgwick Report. The Bank of Mauritius estimated that this added MRs 47.5 million in fiscal year 1973–74, as well as MRs

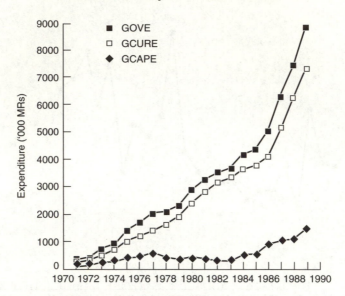

Figure 6.9. Goverment expenditure, 1971–91

Table 6.4. Government revenue and expenditure

Financial year	Revenue			Expenditure			
	Current	Capital	Total	Current	Capital	Total	Net revenue
1971–72	294.1	130.3	424.4	283.2	100.8	384.0	40.4
1972–73	349.7	156.4	533.1	326.4	127.4	453.8	79.3
1973–74	575.4	130.1	645.0	354.8	244.9	779.7	−134.7
1794–75	744.9	412.0	1,156.9	734.3	259.0	993.3	163.6
1975–76	1,075.7	344.3	1,420.0	1,071.0	123.4	1,494.4	−74.4
1976–77	1,210.7	255.7	1,496.4	1,261.0	485.4	1,476.4	20.0
1977–78	1,260.8	458.0	1,718.8	1,441.3	645.9	2,087.2	−368.4
1978–79	1,456.4	718.9	2,205.3	1,770.0	669.3	2,439.9	−234.0
1979–80	1,863.9	730.4	2414.3	2,016.4	886.0	2,902.1	−487.8
1981–82	2,220.9	—	2,220.9	2,892.2	444.0	3,336.2	−1,115.3
1982–83	2,806.6	—	2,802.6	322.6	3,650.4	2,583.0	219.6
1983–84	3,069.8	—	3,069.8	3,393.7	349.5	3,743.2	−673.4
1984–85	3,396.2	—	3,396.2	3,691.3	555.2	4,276.5	−907.5
1985–86	4,128.3	—	4,128.3	3,843.4	304.5	4,444.9	−316.6
1986–87	5,202.6	—	5,202.6	4,246.6	978.4	5,125.0	77.6
1987–88	6,466.8	—	6,466.8	5,257.2	1,119.5	6,376.7	82.9
1988–89	7,630.5	—	7,630.5	6,297.6	1,185.2	7,482.8	147.7
1989–90	8,884.8	—	8,884.8	7,384.0	1,495.9	8,879.9	4.9
1990–91	10,150.9	—	10,150.9	8,254.2	1,725.8	9,979.5	171.4

Data from 1980–81 includes capital grants and net lending to parastatal organisations. These items do not appear in similar cases on government financial statistics.

Source: CSO Bi-annual and Annual Digest of Statistics Surplus Deficit

12.5 million by way of increases in pension and other social security benefits—in total a 12% augmentation of recurrent commitments, at 1973 prices. To the extent that the wage increases were stimulated by the Sedgwick Report, they can be seen as independent of the boom. However, insofar as the improved public finances associated with the latter provided the means for implementation it can reasonably be seen as a boom-induced increase in expenditure. As we shall see later these, more than any other expenditure commitments, were responsible for the fiscal constraints of the late 1970s.

6.5. Relative Price Changes in the Tradable and Non-Tradable Goods Sectors

Trade shocks theory, whether in its Bevan, Collier, Gunning or Dutch Disease form, predicts that relative prices between tradables and non-tradables change. Specifically, theory predicts that a boom in the tradables sector will raise the price of non-tradables *vis-à-vis* tradables. Crudely this follows because the shock raises the demand for assets relative to consumption, both because inter-temporal substitution occurs (boom stretching) and because the control regime constrains consumption possibilities. The resultant excess demand for real assets, especially in the construction sector, drives up the relative price of non-tradables.

As we have already seen, there is evidence to suggest that an increase in construction activity did indeed follow the savings boom. How did this impact on relative prices? It is possible to disentangle the consumer price index into five categories of expenditure—three tradables (food and alcoholic beverages, tobacco, and clothing), one semi-tradable (fuel and light) and one non-tradable (housing). All of the series increase sharply in the mid-1970s with the general increase in inflation which followed the boom. However, the series for housing and housing services increases more sharply than the others.

Figure 6.10 reports detailed information on the ratio of a composite price index for non-tradables to a price index for tradables. These indices are taken from Greenaway and Milner (1986) with a range of representative products from each category. Unfortunately the series is a short one. However, the data are monthly and cover the period 1969–76, the period in which we are interested. We can see that the series is fairly stable until 1974, at which point it increases sharply. The increase is then sustained through to the end of the series in 1986. This is not inconsistent with a boom-induced increase in the relative price of non-tradables. Thus, whether we take individual price series or aggregate price series, relative prices move in a fashion consistent with the Bevan, Collier, Gunning trade shocks theory.

6.6. The Policy Regime

Mauritius has undergone remarkably successful stabilisation and structural adjustment programmes dating from the early 1980s (for details see
World Bank 1989, 1992). Over the past ten years significant trade liberalisation has occurred, combined with extensive financial deregulation. A
credible case can be made to the effect that these changes in the policy
environment were a key enabling factor in the diversification and (manufactures) export-led growth of the past seven years. In the mid-1970s, at
the time of the sugar boom, however, the policy environment was rather
different.

Broadly speaking the post-independence trade policy regime was characterised by pervasive import controls and relatively high levels of import
protection. Nominal tariffs were relatively high, with a fairly wide disper-
sion, and effective tariffs were even higher. A range of hidden tariffs were
in place and there were relatively high export taxes on sugar. In addition,
extensive reliance was placed upon quantitative restrictions. The overall
effect of these measures was to install a strong anti-export bias in relative
incentives (see Greenaway and Milner 1986). From independence, the
exchange rate was fixed against sterling and there were extensive controls
on exports of financial assets. Domestic interest rates were administered
by the central bank, which maintained a regime of interest rate ceilings
and applied differential rates to priority sectors.

It was against this background that the boom occurred and given the
strong anti-export bias and very limited options for investment it is not

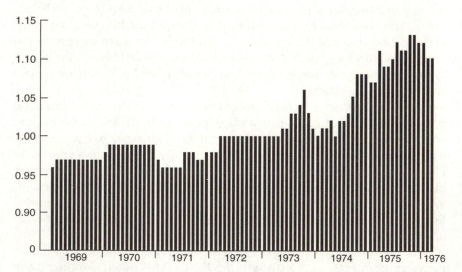

Figure 6.10. The relative price of non-tradables to tradables by month, 1967–1976

surprising that the windfall resulted in a construction boom. This is consistent both with Bevan *et al.* (1992) and with the experiences of a number of other developing countries. Agents had few alternatives in terms of investment instruments and, as we have seen, a large part of the windfall was channelled into non-residential construction. What is interesting is that a significant proportion was clearly channelled into the emerging tourist sector, with a large number of new hotels being constructed. Anecdotal and limited documentary evidence indicates that most of the windfall of some of the larger sugar plantations went directly into this sector.

Unlike the cases of a number of other developing countries, the control regime was not, however, markedly affected by the sugar boom or subsequent construction boom. In other words trade policy became no less restrictive. There was no endogenous trade policy response. Indeed in the late 1970s it became ever more restrictive as controls were extended and new tariffs introduced (see Greenaway and Milner 1989). When sugar prices declined post-1976 and government revenues with them, a growing shortfall in the government current account emerged. The new financial commitments through its current expenditure account made by the government in response to the initial increase in revenues could not be sustained. As can be seen in Table 6.4 this culminated in a fiscal crisis in 1979. At one point in that year, the government had only two weeks' import cover of foreign exchange reserves. Since tariff revenue constituted a major source of government revenue, new tariffs and surcharges were introduced in 1977, 1978 and 1979—ultimately to no avail: the fiscal position continued to deteriorate and the incentive system became ever more distorted. It was only with the new credits attached to the IMF stabilisation and World Bank structural adjustment programmes, and with the programmes themselves, that the situation was brought under control. The emergence of a fiscal crisis shortly after a boom is not an uncommon characteristic of other countries' experiences (see Bevan *et al.* 1993). It emerged in Mauritius for much the same reasons as it emerged elsewhere—the government used its windfall revenues as if they were a permanent increase in the revenue stream. What is interesting about the Mauritian case, however, is that we have circumstantial evidence to indicate that the government initially correctly perceived the boom as temporary.

As for other areas of policy the fixed exchange rate with sterling was broken in 1976 and replaced with a peg to the SDR. This, however, had much more to do with sterling weakness than Mauritius rupee strength. The government was concerned with excess liquidity during the boom but its only policy innovation was the flotation of new development stock in an attempt to mop up some of the liquidity—an experiment which was not very successful. It was only in the post-adjustment regime of the mid-1980s that serious liberalisation and deregulation were initiated in Mauritius.

6.7. Concluding Comments

In this chapter we have offered an evaluation of the impact of a trade shock in a small open economy. Analytically it is an especially interesting case study since in 1972–75 when the sugar boom occurred, Mauritius was very heavily dependent on the sugar sector; indeed it could be described at that time as a monocrop economy.

The sugar boom was sharp, temporary and relatively short-lived. Judging from the reaction of private savers, it was correctly perceived as temporary. Although various government actions at the start of the boom implied a perception of a temporary shock, subsequent government usage of the revenue windfall was more in tune with a response to a permanent shock. In other words, the government windfall was dissipated on increased expenditure, and largely current expenditure at that. Private savings served to fuel an investment boom centred on the construction sector and since much of this was in setting up a tourism infrastructure, it left a rewarding legacy.

The legacy of increased government expenditure was, however, growing fiscal constraints, culminating in the fiscal crisis of 1979. This 'boom–bust' sequence of events has been recorded elsewhere. In other cases it has led to a downward cycle. Fortunately, in the Mauritian case it stimulated a series of credible and sustained reforms which laid the foundations for impressive growth and diversification performance from the mid-1980s onwards. In short, the characteristics of the boom mark it out as a classic temporary shock. What is strikingly different in the Mauritian case compared with other episodes in Sub-Saharan Africa is the aftermath. In part this was conditioned by the windfall, in that some went into the EPZ and tourist sectors, thereby helping to provide the infrastructure for the export-led boom of the second half of the 1980s. The latter, however, had more to do with the marked change in the policy environment in the first half of the 1980s, than with 'boom-stretching' investment.

REFERENCES

Bevan, D., Collier, P. and Gunning, J.W. (1987) Consequences of a Commodity Boom in a Controlled Economy, *World Bank Economic Review*, Vol. 1, pp. 489–513.

Bevan D.L., Collier, P. and Gunning, J.W. (1992) 'Anatomy of a Temporary Trade Shock: The Kenya Coffee Boom of 1976–9', *Journal of African Economies*, 1, 2, pp. 271–305.

Bevan, D., Collier, P. and Gunning, J. (1993) Trade Shocks in Developing Countries, *European Economic Review*, Vol. 37, pp. 557–65.

Collier, P. (1993) Trade Shocks, Consequences and Policy Responses: Theory and Evidence from African, Asia and Latin America (mimeo, CSAE).

Greenaway, D. and Milner, C.R. (1986) Estimating the Shifting of Protection Across Sectors: An Application to Mauritius, *Industry and Development*, Vol. 16, pp. 1–22.

Greenaway, D. and Milner, C.R. (1989) Nominal and Effective Tariffs in a Small Industrialising Economy: The Case of Mauritius, *Applied Economics*, Vol. 21, pp. 995–1010.

Greenaway D. and Milner, C.R. (1991) Did Mauritius Really Provide a 'Case Study in Malthusian Economics'?, *Journal of International Development*, Vol. 3, pp. 325–38.

Woldekidan, B. and Weisman, E. (1993) Impact of EC Sugar Trade Liberalisation on the Mauritian Economy: A CGE Simulation (mimeo).

World Bank (1989) *Mauritius: Managing Success* (Washington, DC: World Bank).

Wold Bank (1992) *Mauritius: Expanding Horizons* (Washington, DC: World Bank).

7

The Groundnut and Phosphates Boom in Sénégal, 1974–77

JEAN-PAUL AZAM AND GÉRARD CHAMBAS

Sénégal is a West African country classified as falling in the bottom group of middle-income countries. Its GNP per capita in 1988 is estimated at US$630 (World Bank 1990). It has poor achievements in terms of education and health relative to other less developed countries with similar income. Sénégal's primary school enrolment ratio was 60% in 1987, against 104% on average for middle-income countries, and its life expectancy at birth is 48, against an average of 65 for the countries of this income class.

It is a small country, both in terms of area (less than 200,000 km^2) and in terms of population (fewer than 7.1 million inhabitants in 1988). It has extensive access to the Atlantic Ocean, thanks in particular to the remarkable port of Dakar, the capital city. The Gambia makes an English-speaking enclave inside the Sénégalese territory and to some extent separates the region of Casamance from the rest of the country.

Sénégal is regarded by many observers as a sort of political and cultural model for francophone Africa. It is a rather democratic society, with several political parties, free elections, limited violence and powerful trade unions. Its first president, Leopold Sedar Senghor, is regarded as an important writer and poet, known for his works on 'La négritude' (Blackhood) and African socialism.

Except for the Casamance region, located south of The Gambia, the country has a sahelian climate, with many rather dry regions, and repeated droughts (1973, 1978, 1980, 1981, 1984). The whole economy has often been heavily affected by climatic shocks. At the same time, the country receives a lot of aid: US$30 of concessional aid per capita in 1976 (World Bank 1979a). The 1973 drought would have resulted in a famine without international aid. In 1979, it received US$56 per capita of aid, compared with an average for Sub-Saharan Africa of below US$27 (World Bank 1979b). This above-average position for aid has even improved recently: the corresponding figures for 1987 are US$96.4 for aid received by Sénégal and US$30.5 for Sub-Saharan Africa as a whole.

Dakar was the capital city of the Afrique Occidentale Française (AOF,

French West Africa) and has inherited two peculiarities from this past role. First, before independence in 1960, the Sénégalese economy was largely built around the production and processing of one export crop, namely groundnuts. Until 1968, France was buying the whole crop at a preferential price, above the world market price. In 1975, the share of the world groundnut market held by Sénégal was 21.3%. Despite many efforts aiming at diversifying the economy in favour of other crops and other activities such as fishing and tourism, and the continuing problems of the groundnut sector, it remains essential for the economy of Sénégal. Its importance derives equally from the various downstream activities it entails. At independence, groundnut processing accounted for 42% of the total turnover of Sénégalese industry (Caswell 1983). Moreover, Sénégal's stock of infrastructure (roads, railways, ports, etc.) was better developed than that of its neighbours.

But at independence Sénégal inherited an oversized administration which was meant to manage the whole of the AOF. Many civil servants all over the AOF were of Sénégalese origin and returned home at independence. At the same time, many civil servants from other francophone West African countries, and particularly from Upper Volta (now Burkina Faso), were based in Sénégal and went back home, but this does not change the main result. Similarly, Sénégal's industrial sector had sold its products on the regional market, but this started shrinking as many neighbouring countries adopted inward-looking policies.

These facts help to explain Sénégal's poor economic performance: during the 1960s, GDP per capita grew very little, at an average rate of about 0.2% per annum, and in the 1970s it decreased on average by 0.7% per annum. Leaving aside the drought years 1978 and 1980, which were very bad for agriculture, the average rate of decline of GNP per capita was 0.5% in 1970–77.

Moreover, Sénégal faced serious macroeconomic imbalances at the end of the 1970s, leading its government to adopt a program of stabilisation and structural adjustment. The first austerity measures were adopted as early as 1978, but they had little initial impact.

These problems occurred, paradoxically, just at the end of a period when Sénégal benefited from two positive external shocks which are often regarded as having been particularly mismanaged (see e.g. Devarajan and de Melo 1987). However, we find that some policy measures were in fact going in the right direction. Without anticipating too much the results to be presented below, we can say that in response to the external shocks the government tried to implement relatively well-directed policies in the field of relative prices (taxes, subsidies, tariffs, etc.) but pursued a rather detrimental portfolio strategy regarding its foreign assets and liabilities and its control over productive firms.

There was a groundnut boom in 1974–77, with the price of raw groundnut oil increasing by 135% in 1974, and a boom in phosphates, whose price increased by 274% in the same year (Youm 1986). Groundnut products and phosphates accounted for about 50% and 10% of export revenues, respectively, in 1977, when a second groundnut price hike occurred. Both booms were over by 1978, when a drought crystallised the underlying macroeconomic problems. But in the meantime, the government enjoyed a fiscal bonanza.

We analyse in this chapter the macroeconomic consequences of these two booms. We examine the nature of these shocks in 1974–77 and analyse how the various economic agents, including particularly the peasants and the government, reacted to them. Then we try to show the various result-ant impacts on the structure of the economy, including the changes in the relative weights of the different sectors, and the relative prices. We emphasise the role of government policy in bringing about these changes.

7.1. The Nature of the Shock

In 1972, which can be regarded as a normal year for groundnut produc-tion (see Table 7.1), groundnut products and phosphates accounted, re-spectively, for 52.9% and 10% of FOB merchandise exports. In 1974, the world price of groundnut oil (both raw and refined) more than doubled compared to the 1973 price, and the prices of phosphates and phosphate-based fertilisers were multiplied by approximately four and two, respec-tively. The price of groundnuts underwent a second hike in 1977, when it nearly reached its 1974 level.

Since these two booms of 1974 occurred simultaneously with the oil shock and the increase in the prices of various products imported by Sénégal, the terms of trade improved in 1974 by just 24.3% (World Bank 1990). (Note that Sénégal is an exporter of refined petroleum products, from the Société Africaine de Raffinage (SAR).) The terms of trade re-turned to their previous level in 1978, after four years of improvements.

In Table 7.2, we compute the windfall gain from these booms by apply-ing the method used in the Chapter 2. We compute counterfactual export revenues by taking the export volume as given and assuming that the terms of trade would have been unchanged since 1973 had there been no shock. The windfall gain each year is then defined as the difference be-tween actual and counterfactual export revenues. We can see that there is a significant windfall gain so computed in 1974. It amounts to 19.2% of export revenues and 8.2% of GDP that year.

If we discount all these windfall export gains over the four years back to 1974, using 10% as the discount rate (for lack of precise information), and translate the resulting present value in terms of a permanent increase in exports, it comes to 5% of 1974 actual export revenues and about 2.1% of

Table 7.1. Data on agriculture

	1970	1971	1972	1973	1974	1975	1976	1977	1978	1979	1980
1. Groundnut producer price											
1.1. bn current CFAF	17.5	18.5	22.0	22.0	24.0	40.0	40.0	40.0	40.0	40.0	43.0
1.2. bn 1970 CFAF	17.5	17.7	18.5	17.9	16.7	21.2	20.7	18.8	18.2	16.7	16.5
2. Groundnut output (1,000 Tons)	789	583	989	570	675	980	1,412	1,208	511	1,061	650
3. Acreage sown in groundnuts (1,000 ha.)	953	1,049	1,060	1,071	1,026	1,052	1,203	1,345	1,113	1,179	
4. Relative millet/ groundnut price	92	79	74	74	98	72	72	84	84	100	
5. Acreage sown in millet (1,000 ha.)	1,037	976	975	936	1,094	1,154	963	895	943	1,055	968
6. Acreage (3) + (5)	1,990	2,025	2,035	2,007	2,120	2,206	2,166	2,240	2,056	2,234	
7. Acreage index (100 = 1973)	99	101	101	100	106	110	108	112	102	111	
8. Rainfall (mm)	660	684	607	349	565	583	645	593	415	600	482
9. Groundnut money income (bn CFAF)	10.2	7.3	17.1	8.4	13.5	29.3	44.9	37.7	13.3	32.5	20.7
10. Total money income in agriculture (bn CFAF)	12.1	8.1	18.8	10.1	16.0	34.5	49.0	41.5	16.0	38.5	24.0
11. Groundnut money income (bn 1971 CFAF)	10.6	7.3	16.2	7.1	9.8	16.1	24.5	18.5	6.3	14.0	8.2
12. Agricultural GDP (bn CFAF)	33.9	25.2	36.8	27.6	37.6	72.6	82.8	72.1	45.3	83.1	59.0

Sources: computed from BCEAO, 'Notes d'information et statistiques' and Duruflé (1985)

Table 7.2. Counterfactual and windfall exports

	Export revenues (bn current CFAF)	Export price index	Import price index	Terms of trade	Counterfactual export revenues (bn current CFAF)	Windfall (bn current CFAF)	Windfall (bn constant 1974 CFAF)[a]
1973	79.2	100.0	100.0	100.0	79.2	0.0	0.0
1974	144.6	188.1	152.2	123.7	116.9	27.7	27.7
1975	148.6	173.4	149.8	116.0	128.1	20.5	18.4
1976	177.6	164.4	147.0	112.0	158.6	19.0	16.2
1977	209.2	177.7	160.7	110.7	189.0	20.2	16.5

[a] deflated by GDP deflator

Sources: computed from Duruflé (1985) and World Bank (1990)

1974 GDP. Hence, we should not expect too much in the way of permanent aggregate impact from these booms.

However, they had important effects on the Sénégalese economy because of the redistribution of income flows that they entailed, and because of the changes in the structure of production that resulted. The main point is that they helped the state to establish greater control over the economy. The policy response of the government played a large part in determining the final impact. The groundnut windfall, which resulted mainly from two price hikes in 1974 and 1977 on the world market, turned into a fairly large and sustained boom because the government increased the real producer price, which remained relatively high for four years after the 1974 external shock.

There was a sizeable supply response from groundnut growers, which implied a windfall gain for the government. In the phosphates sector, there was no noticeable supply response. It seems that the mines could not increase production because of the constraints imposed by the extraction technology and the existing transport facilities.

7.2. The Reactions of the Government and the Peasants

The groundnut boom had a significant impact on the rural sector and on government behaviour. The relationships between the two are the result to some extent of the institutional organisation of agriculture, where the state plays a large part.

7.2.1. The Role of the State in Agriculture

Since independence, the organisation of the agricultural sector has undergone many reforms which have tended to give the state an increasing role.

In 1966, the Office National de Coopération et d'Assistance au Développement (ONCAD, the national board for cooperation and development assistance) was created, turning out to be much more than a standard marketing board for groundnuts (Caswell 1983). The following year, there was no authorised private trader of groundnuts left in the country.

The only legal route for the peasants to sell groundnuts was through cooperatives, which then sold the crop to ONCAD. Some exceptions were allowed for the *gros producteurs* (big producers)—often at the same time religious authorities—who could sell directly to ONCAD, with a price premium. ONCAD was therefore a monopsony for groundnuts, and some other crops, and had a monopoly on the sale of most inputs to peasants, including credit. It also had some control over the transport network during the crop season by virtue of being the largest contractor and owning a large fleet of trucks of its own, which enabled it to compete with private transporters. Thus, cooperatives were mainly used as distribution points for inputs, including seeds, credit and fertilizers, and as collection points for outputs of groundnut production (Caswell 1983). ONCAD also controlled the marketing of other crops.

The workings of the sector offered very little room for peasant initiative, with ONCAD and the cooperatives acting like a straightjacket on the farmers. Inputs were sold on credit at a subsidised price and rationed in a rather bureaucratic way. For example, groundnut seeds were distributed according to rigid quotas, men receiving 100 kg and women 50 kg each. Seeds were to be repaid in kind at harvest time with 25% interest. Moreover, all kinds of fraud by agents of the cooperatives and of ONCAD have been reported, making the overall levy on the peasants even heavier (Caswell 1983).

Nevertheless, some flexibility was kept in the system by various mechanisms. First, the peasants were often in a position to exert pressure on ONCAD by their collective behaviour, for example, by refusing to repay their debts, or to use fertilizers or the seeds. Through this type of conflictual attitude, they managed to retain some influence on the behaviour of the sector.

Second, some parallel trade for inputs and outputs existed, both internally and externally. There are estimates of the amount of groundnuts smuggled through the border with The Gambia—around 10% of the crop—but this figure is controversial. Moreover, there are examples of private trade of inputs among regions, including redistribution from favoured farmers to less favoured ones, and distress sale of the seeds by poor families. Lastly, farmers had a strong incentive to try to store some of their output as seeds for the next season, since the delivery by ONCAD was uncertain and not always timely.

ONCAD was dismantled in 1980, with a level of debt reaching 94 billion

CFAF—about 15% of GDP, or 67.5% of the total fiscal revenues for 1980. By that time, it had gone out of control and had become a means for distributing political patronage, with overmanning and rent-seeking at all levels. But it was only after 1982 that some attempts at liberalisation were made (Marodon 1987).

The second main organ of state control over the agricultural sector was the Caisse de Péréquation et de Stabilisation des Prix (CPSP, the price equalization and stabilization fund). Its role was theoretically to ensure, by a combination of taxes and subsidies, an equal price for the crop across the country and to stabilise the producer price over time. But in fact its tasks were much wider, including taxing or subsidising input prices and consumer prices (for rice, sugar, groundnut oil, flour, etc.), as well as funding the *programme agricole* (the delivery of inputs and organisation of the agricultural season) and absorbing some of the peasants' debt cancellations. Such cancellations occurred on several occasions, including the boom year 1976/77 (for seeds) and the drought year 1978. Some of CPSP's surpluses ended up in the general budget of the central government.

Table 7.3 presents the flow of transfers within the stabilisation fund in order to characterise its behaviour and its reactions to the boom. One can observe that the levy on groundnut producers has always been positive, and that it was especially high in the boom year 1974, and in 1977, when the world price swung up again by 30%, close to the 1974 level. This CPSP levy is not the only levy on groundnut production, since the state collects other taxes, including an export tax which contributes directly to the budget, as will be seen below. Some of this CPSP levy is returned to

Table 7.3. Transfers within the CPSP (*bn CFAF*)

	1971/72	1972/73	1973/74	1974/75	1975/76	1976/77	1978
Levies on producers	3.4	2.7	14.3	−1.2	−2.5	4.9	0.5
Groundnuts	3.8	4.8	14.3	2.9	3.4	14.5	5.2
Cotton	0.1	0.3	1.2	0.1	—	—	−0.8
Agricultural programme (mainly fertilisers)	−0.5	−2.4	−1.2	−4.2	−5.9	−9.6	−3.9
Levies on Consumers	−1.8	−3.2	−11.1	−4.7	4.7	3.2	1.4
Rice	—	—	−5.0	−1.7	5.1	3.8	3.2
Sugar	−0.2	−0.5	−1.7	−1.1	2.4	1.0	2.2
Groundnut oil	−1.6	−2.7	−4.4	−0.6	−0.4	−1.6	−4.7
Flour	—	—	—	−1.3	−2.4	—	0.7
Balance	1.6	−1.5	3.2	−5.9	2.2	8.1	1.9

Note: negative figures are subsidies

Sources: World Bank (1979, p. 20); see also Caswell (1983, p. 26)

farmers as subsidies on inputs within the *programme agricole*. But the net levy on producers was negative only in 1975 and 1976.

On the consumer side, we observe two distinct subperiods. Until 1975, the CPSP subsidised consumer prices significantly, and hence, to some extent, the real incomes of urban dwellers. After 1975, it started to tax them. The table allows for a description of the CPSP response to the boom in 1974. This sheds some interesting light on the overall mismanagement of the boom, referred to above, and provides some elements to qualify this judgement.

In 1974, the CPSP taxed away the windfall from the producers and used the proceeds to subsidise consumers. This was more a mechanical application of the usual CPSP assignment than a real policy decision. In the following year, the CPSP passed the price increase on to the producers and reduced the consumer subsidies. This move was known as the 'Opération Vérité des Prix' (the true prices operation, discussed in greater detail below). It was regarded as a major policy decision and widely publicised as such. During the last two years of the boom (1976–77), the CPSP taxed consumers, and producers as well, but returned part of the proceeds to the latter, with large inputs subsidies.

As a result of this policy, the groundnut boom was delayed for the producers but lasted longer in real terms than we saw above. The real producer price remained above its 1974 level up to 1979, when it fell back to its original level (Table 7.1). Consumers benefited first from the windfall gain, but for only two years. This fairly sustained real producer price increase for groundnuts entailed a large supply response, to which we now turn.

7.2.2. The Supply Response of Groundnut Growers

Peasants responded strongly to the spectacular price increase (by 66% in money terms and 26.9% in real terms) which occurred in 1975. This can be checked by looking at the output row or the acreage row in Table 7.1.

One may observe that there seems to be a lag in the supply response. This is especially noticeable for acreage, and less so for output. Hence, it seems that the initial response in 1975 was through an increase in yields, which recovered the level reached in 1972, followed the year after by a large increase in acreage sown. Similarly, leaving aside the drought year 1978, one may observe that the fall in output lagged one year behind the real price drop of 1979. This is partly the result of the cumbersome organisation of the *programme agricole*, which is such that farmers have to order their inputs more than six months in advance, long before the producer price is known (Caswell 1983). This undermines to a large extent the *raison d'être* of the stabilisation fund, which is supposed to be a device for reducing the uncertainty faced by farmers when they make planting

decisions. The announcement of the price by CPSP can only affect planting decisions for the following year, and only by providing the peasant
with a nominal floor for the price, since there is no historical example of
the nominal price of groundnuts going down, except in 1968. Moreover,
the delivery of the ordered inputs is to some extent conditional on the
creditworthiness of each cooperative, itself assessed mainly by looking at
production figures in the recent past. This reinforces the sluggishness of
the supply response. This might partly explain why the classic Nerlove
model of peasant supply response performs reasonably well for
Sénégalese groundnut production (Nascimento and Raffinot 1984).

Hence, the announcement of the price can affect yields mainly when it
is made, and this is evident from the data in Table 7.1. The area planted
responded very strongly the year after. Taking as a benchmark the average acreage planted over the period 1970–74 (1,032,000 ha.), we see that
the increase in the area planted, relative to the benchmark, is 20,000 ha. in
1975, 171,000 ha. in 1976, 313,000 ha. in 1977, and 81,000 ha. in 1978.

Assuming that exports increased in proportion to the increase in acreage, this supply response is equivalent to an increase in export revenue
worth 0.77 billion CFAF in 1975, 9.16 billion CFAF in 1976 and 17.62
billion CFAF in 1977, representing respectively 0.52%, 5.43% and 8.25% of
actual export revenues. Although this cannot be counted as a windfall
gain for the country as a whole, since it is acquired at a cost, it can be
regarded as a welcome gain in foreign currency. Moreover, since it was
obtained by removing price distortions, and in particular by cutting consumer subsidies, we may assume that the foreign currency gain was larger
than estimated above, since some imports were probably curtailed as well.

Hence, as will be seen below in more detail, the Opération Vérité des
Prix constituted a good policy response to the boom, producing some of
the effects of a depreciation of the real exchange rate. Adopted after the
main groundnut shock, but during the phosphates boom, and while the
world price of groundnuts was still high, it may be regarded as an 'Anti-
Dutch Disease' device, akin to the devaluation in Indonesia during the
second oil shock (Pinto 1987). But many other measures worked in the
wrong direction. As will be seen below, the groundnut expansion can also
be regarded a public finance bonanza.

The question arises of whether the peasants regarded this real producer
price increase as permanent or transitory. Since there was obviously no
opinion poll on this question at the time, we have to guess the answer
from indirect evidence.

First, we can look at the political background of the price increase. The
Opération Vérité des Prix, which enabled the CPSP to increase producer
prices while simultaneously reducing consumer subsidies, was widely
publicized and looked like a major change of policy. It occurred after a
long period of peasant disillusionment and more or less passive resistance

in the 1960s, which was called at the time the *'malaise paysan'*. It probably started when, in 1968, France withdrew its commitment to purchase the whole Sénégalese crop at a subsidised price, which led to a 16% producer price cut. But, it was wider than a question of price and encompassed many conflictual aspects of the relationship between the state and the peasants. The latter resisted debt repayment, made difficult by the drought, and this prompted some initially violent reactions by the state, including corporal punishment (Caswell 1983). Moreover, the peasants accused the agents of corruption and fraud.

The Opération Vérité des Prix was launched at nearly the same time as some 2 billion CFAF of farmers' debts were written off (World Bank 1979a). Hence, the farmers benefited from a capital transfer which probably had a positive impact on their permanent income. These moves may have been regarded by the farmers as a political victory, and as a U-turn in government policy, breaking for good with a long period of downward drift in the real producer price and of exploitative relationships in favour of urban dwellers. Had the farmers held these views, they would have been to some extent vindicated by what happened subsequently. The CPSP carried on taxing consumers after 1978, to subsidize the producers. The main levy was on imported rice, especially in 1979, 1980 and 1982. The *'programme agricole'* was again heavily subsidised in 1979–80–81, and groundnut products were subsidised in 1980 and, more highly, in 1982 and 1983.

On the other hand, evidence regarding the opportunity cost of this increase in acreage sown in groundnuts points in the other direction. It appears that when farmers started to increase the area devoted to groundnuts, they simultaneously increased the area devoted to millet and sorghum, the main subsistence crops in the groundnut-growing areas. Taking as a benchmark the average acreage devoted to these two staples over the period 1970–74 (1.004 million ha.), there was an increase of 150,000 ha. above the benchmark in 1975, followed by a drop by 41,000 ha. below the benchmark in 1976, and by 119,000 ha. in 1977. The overall response of acreage devoted to groundnuts and millet and sorghum combined is thus positive. Although it is known that cross-price effects can be quite complicated (Braverman and Hammer 1986), one may suppose that the initial increase in the total acreage devoted to both groundnuts and the main staples was taken not merely from other crops, but from fallow.

If this observation is right, then it reveals an inter-emporal substitution of crops now for crops later, typical of a response to a price increase regarded as temporary. The subsequent reduction in the acreage devoted to the staples in 1976–77 might be a response not to a change of expectations, but to the type of effect studied by Hammer (1986): when inventories of grains are large (e.g. after an exceptionally good crop), farmers will tend to reduce cultivation of these crops and turn to other crops or to leisure, independently of any price effects. Since the area devoted to millet and sorghum was exceptionally high in 1975, and rainfall was not especially low in 1975 and was quite high in 1976, one may assume that granaries were full in 1976 and 1977, reducing the incentive to produce staples, which faced fairly difficult marketing conditions, owing in part to ONCAD again.[1] Thus the exceptionally large supply response of acreage devoted to groundnuts in 1977 could be due in part to the bumper food crop of 1976, amplifying the positive effect of the price increase.

Pushing this reasoning one step further, one may hypothesise that the large increase in the acreage devoted to millet and sorghum in 1975 was the response of the farmers to the increased price of groundnuts, filling granaries in anticipation of a large increase in the area planted with groundnuts next year, which would leave less labour time and less acreage available for staples.

Therefore, we have found arguments pointing in both directions for determining whether the real price increase was regarded by farmers as temporary or permanent. Hence, we will have to wait for further evidence to give a definitive answer.

7.2.3. Government Reactions

The Sénégalese state gets two different kinds of levy from the groundnut sector: the CPSP levy, which we have analysed above, and an export tax. As can be seen from Table 7.4, the latter made a substantial contribution to the government budget in 1976 and 1977, when groundnut production was at its highest.

Table 7.5 provides a more complete view of the impact of the external shock on central government public finance. Besides groundnut taxation, we can see that phosphates made a significant contribution to the central government budget in 1975, and especially in 1976 and 1977. The government owns the majority share in the assets of the three main mining firms. Moreover, it has obtained from the mining firms agreements to the effect that it gets 80% of the incremental profits.

In 1976, these two types of levy accounted for 23.3% of current revenues, whereas they accounted for only 3.4% in 1973. Despite this, the ratio of current revenues to GDP was not particularly unstable. But one can observe a gradual increase of this ratio in 1977 and 1978, which seems to reveal that the state increased its control over the economy. This seems especially true for the drought year 1978, when the groundnut-cum-phosphates bonanza was over—but this is partly an artefact resulting from the well-known lag in tax collection combined with the decrease in GDP owing to the drought. Nevertheless, Table 7.5 shows that current revenues carried on increasing while the groundnut export tax and the phosphates revenues went down. The compensation came from increased

Table 7.4. Taxation of groundnuts (*bn* CFAF)

	1971–72	1972–73	1973–74	1974–75	1975–76	1976–77	1977–78	1978–79	1979–80
1. CPSP levy on groundnuts	3.8	4.8	14.3	2.9	3.4	14.5	5.2	4.6	–2.6
2. Groundnut export tax	3.1	1.2	1.7	3.1	9.0	7.1	2.0	4.4	2.5
3. Total public levy on groundnuts	6.9	6.0	16.0	6.0	12.4	21.6	7.2	9.0	0.1
4. Public transfer to producers	n.a	n.a	0.6	1.4	5.1	8.3	7.5	4.9	9.2
5. Net levy on groundnut producers	n.a.	n.a.	15.4	4.6	7.3	13.3	–0.3	4.1	–9.1

Sources: World Bank (1979) and CERDI (1981)

Table 7.5. Central government finance, special accounts included (*bn CFAF; percentages in parentheses*)

	1973	1974	1975	1976	1977	1978
1. Current revenue	55.1	55.4	77.3	87.2	104.8	112.1
(Ratio to GDP)	(19.8)	(16.3)	(19.0)	(19.1)	(21.6)	(22.7)
1.1. Groundnut export tax	1.2	1.7	3.1	9.0	7.1	2.0
1.2. Phosphate revenues	0.7	0.7	5.2	11.3	10.0	1.2
1.3. (1.1) + (1.2)	1.9	2.4	8.3	20.3	17.1	3.2
2. Current expenditure	50.8	49.7	67.5	84.1	90.3	104.4
(Ratio to GDP)	(18.3)	(14.7)	(16.6)	(18.4)	(18.7)	(21.1)
3. Central gov. saving,	4.3	5.7	9.8	3.1	14.5	7.7
(1–2) (Ratio to GDP)	(1.5)	(1.7)	(2.4)	(0.7)	(3.0)	(1.6)
4. Central gov. investment and participations	9.6	25.8	12.9	17.1	23.7	12.4
4.1. Investment	5.1	8.2	7.5	9.7	16.5	9.4
4.2. Participations and loans	4.5	17.6	5.4	7.4	7.2	3.0
5. Budget deficit	−5.3	−20.1	−3.1	−14.0	−9.2	−4.7
(Ratio to GDP)	(−1.9)	(−5.9)	(−0.8)	(−3.1)	(−1.9)	(−1.0)

Source: World Bank (1979a)

import taxes. There was in particular a 5% increase in the customs duties on goods imported from Europe, which had benefited before from preferential treatment.

On the expenditure side, we observe a gradual increase in public consumption, above its 1970–72 average (15.2%). Again, one should take into account the fact that this ratio was above normal during the drought years (1973 and 1978). The rate of public saving shows some increase during the boom—in 1974, and mainly in 1975 and 1977, with a temporary fall in 1976. This is discussed in more detail below.

Public investment by the central government increased roughly in line with central government saving, with an average saving to investment ratio of 82.6%. This ratio fluctuated quite widely in 1974–76, but one should not overemphasise these swings, which tend to compensate each other quite rapidly and might be due simply to such factors as small delays in the completion and recording of some projects. The overall picture is that of a reasonable strategy regarding the level of investment, which follows to some extent the performance of public saving.

One gets a wider picture of public saving and investment by looking at Table 7.6, which takes a more encompassing definition of government. A remarkable figure is the level of public saving in 1976–77, which is twice the 1973–74 figure, and three times the 1975–76 one. This table shows in

Table 7.6. Public saving and capital expenditure (*bn CFAF*)

	1972–73	1973–74	1974–75	1975–76	1976–77	1977–78
1. Central government saving	4.3	5.7	9.8	3.1	14.5	7.7
2. Other public saving	2.4	7.2	0.3	4.8	10.2	3.6
3. Interest on public debt	0.5	0.8	1.7	3.9	4.0	4.7
4. Public saving, (1) + (2)	6.7	12.9	10.1	7.9	24.7	11.3
5. Debt amortisation	−1.3	1.7	2.3	4.8	9.0	12.1
6. Participations and loans	4.5	17.6	5.4	7.4	7.2	3.0
7. Central government investment	5.1	8.2	7.5	9.7	16.5	9.4
8. Other public investment (including extra-budgetary foreign aid)	11.0	21.0	27.5	30.7	32.0	37.0
9. Total public investment, (7) + (8)	16.2	29.2	35.0	40.4	48.5	46.4

Source: World Bank (1979a)

addition the role of debt servicing, which increased mainly after 1977, creating a major problem for the subsequent period.

Row 6, participations and loans, is quite interesting, since it shows an important aspect of the government's industrial strategy. In 1973 it started a policy of 'Sénégalisation' of the capital of the modern sector which continued until 1976. Thanks to the funds collected from the external shock, the government was in a good financial position. This could be amplified by borrowing on the world capital market, since Sénégal was then perceived as offering good collateral. The government used its financial strength to take large stakes in many modern sector firms in order to strengthen its control of the economy. In particular, in 1975 it took 50% of the shares of the three main mining companies; and in 1976, it created SONACOS, a company linked to ONCAD which had a monopoly on processed groundnut products, with 65% of its assets owned by the state. It also took 50% of the capital of a bank and numerous stakes in hotels (7 billion CFAF from 1973–74 to 1976–77). Foreign shareholders generally received fair compensation and were often only too happy to be thus able to divest from firms whose profitability had been crippled by price controls, excessive labour costs and rigidities, and loss of competitiveness entailed by inward-looking policies. Thus the government organised to some extent the export of foreign capital, and the private net capital flows had a sizeable negative impact on the balance of payments in 1973–74–75 (World Bank 1979a).

Hence, the government used part of the windfall to buy foreign assets, thus reducing the country's liability to foreign investors. Using foreign assets as a temporary store of purchasing power is an appropriate strategy for a country facing a temporary external shock, since it thus avoids detrimental bunching of investment, as shown in Chapter 1. However, the foreign assets purchased by the Sénégalese government were not as liquid as the theory would prescribe. The probability of a profitable resale of the shares in the Sénégalised firms was slight. This move did not help to smooth the investment path, as the purchase of liquid foreign assets would have done; instead it precluded the use of the windfall gain for future investment. By 1976, firms in which the state had direct or indirect participation produced about 43% of modern sector output (World Bank 1979a). This participation policy cost the government a large share of its current and future revenues. In 1974, the amount spent in participations was roughly equivalent to the windfall CPSP levy on the groundnut sector, as can be seen by comparing Tables 7.4 and 7.5. As might be guessed from the ONCAD experience described above, this policy of increasing state control did not in general result in an improvement in productivity. Overmanning and excessive wage increases were soon to develop in these firms.

One of the reasons why governments in Franc Zone member countries are often so eager to increase their control over many firms is that it enables them to circumvent to some extent one of the constraints which the rules of the monetary union impose on them. In principle, governments cannot borrow from their domestic banking sector more than 20% of the previous year's fiscal revenues. This is a device for preventing the growth of the money supply from accelerating too fast. But such a rule does not apply to publicly owned firms, which can borrow as much as they want from the banking sector. It is easy for them to borrow in order to fill in financial gaps, especially if the banks are themselves controlled by the state. (This was largely the case in Sénégal at that time, since the government controlled directly or indirectly around 50% of the capital of the ten banking institutions of the country.) Then, to close the circle, the state can overburden these firms with various levies and transfers to the state, with the accumulation of arrears on their bills, and so on (see World Bank 1979a, p. 64). In other words, the government can obtain compulsory credit from publicly owned enterprises, which themselves obtain large credits from publicly controlled banking firms to tide them over. The banks can only accommodate this indirect credit to the government budget by restricting the distribution of credit to the private sector, since they must comply with credit ceilings imposed on them by the BCEAO.

The government likewise used its improved financial position to increase its share of the labour market. Before 1974, the growth rate of the number of civil servants was roughly in line with that of the population. Then it increased to 5.1% in 1975 and jumped over 7% in 1976 and 1977. Table 7.7 represents the growth of the number of civil servants,

Table 7.7. Number of civil servants

Category	Dec. 1971	Dec. 1972	Dec. 1973	Dec. 1974	Dec. 1975	Dec. 1976	Jan. 1979
A	838	975	1,058	1,207	1,350	1,536	2,049
B	4,013	4,604	5,094	5,494	6,237	7,163	9,664
C	6,261	6,902	7,359	7,854	9,724	9,937	10,267
D	7,640	7,580	7,695	7,776	11,528	12,812	13,768
E	538	476	430	541	2,940	3,396	3,503
Other	13,336	12,868	12,628	12,366	4,812	3,808	4,350
Subtotal	32,626	33,405	34,264	35,238	36,591	38,652	43,593
Army and police	5,043	5,045	5,460	5,377	6,080	7,220	9,138
Total	37,669	38,540	39,724	40,615	42,671	45,672	52,731

Source: Direction de la Statistique

disaggregated by category. One observes that growth is particularly fast in the A category, the highest-ranking one.

On the other hand, the government's wage policy was pulling in the other direction in terms of income distribution. For example, during the Opération Vérité des Prix, the government granted large wage increases to civil servants in order to compensate them partly for the cuts in consumer subsidies. But these wage increases were devised as a move for equalizing incomes, with an increase of 82% at the lower end of the scale and a near stagnation at the top of the scale, where the increase was limited to 3% (Youm 1986). This egalitarian policy was probably not particularly productivity enhancing either. As a result of inflation, and despite the increase in the share of public employment in the labour market, the share of the public wage bill in GDP remained roughly equal to its 1970–72 average level (11.3%).

In Sénégal, labour laws and regulations are deemed to be well respected because of the existence of powerful trade unions with extensive political connections. These unions already existed in colonial times and were the origin of violent strikes in the late 1940s. Sénégal has had a minimum wage since 1925. In the 1930s it imported all the labour laws created by the left-wing Front Populaire, which governed France for two years from 1936. The minimum wage (*salaire minimum interprofessionel garanti*, SMIG) is thus an important determinant of labour costs, at least in the urban sector and in the modern rural sector.[2] Table 7.8 shows how it evolved over the external shock period. The second and third columns of the table represent, respectively, the real consumption wage (deflated by the African CPI) and the real production wage (deflated by the GDP deflator). We observe that the SMIG was more than doubled between 1973 and 1975 in nominal terms. This meant a 38.9% increase in its purchasing power and

Table 7.8. The minimum wage (*index*, 1973 = 100)

	Nominal	Real consumer[a]	Real producer[b]
1973	100.0	100.0	100.0
1974	115.0	98.4	97.8
1975	211.7	138.9	161.5
1976	211.7	135.0	154.0
1977	211.7	122.5	146.7

[a] deflated by the CPI
[b] deflated by the GDP deflater
Source: BCEAO

a 61.5% increase in the real cost of labour. Therefore, the government in fact used the minimum wage to offset partly some of the effects of the Opération Vérité des Prix. By combining its wage policy and its hiring policy, it engineered a kind of 'resource movement effect', made familiar by the Dutch Disease literature (Corden and Neary 1982): it reduced the available supply of labour to the private sector and increased its cost.

This runs against the results of the Opération Vérité des Prix presented above, which tended to offset Dutch Disease effects by removing some consumer subsidies, including subsidies on imported goods, and removing part of the levy on exported groundnuts.

Similarly, various measures were taken to favour tradables in the industrial sector. Besides some export-promoting measures, such as the creation of the Dakar Export Processing Zone in 1974 and the launching of the Sénégalese Foreign Trade Centre in 1977, many measures were taken to protect the sectors producing importables or import substitutes (Chambas and Geourjon 1985). The share of customs duties and internal taxes in the total value of imports increased between 1974 and 1979. Many non-tariff barriers were instituted as well. The latter probably had some effect on the market power of local firms, favouring some price increases and other monopolistic practices, according to an argument originally advanced by Bhagwati (1965; see also Helpman and Krugman 1989). All these measures worked like a policy of exchange rate protection *à la* Corden (1981), preventing the real exchange rate from appreciating. Between 1974 and 1979, the share of export industries in the total value-added of manufacturing went from 34.3% to 40.4%, while the corresponding share for domestically oriented industries decreased (Chambas and Geourjon 1985). In countries which have a credible pre-commitment not to use devaluation, like the members of the Franc Zone (Guillaumont and Guillaumont 1984), these tax-cum-subsidise measures aimed at increasing the prices of tradables relative to that of non-tradables seem to be the main possible policy choice to try to prevent Dutch Disease effects.

These policies had inflationary consequences and resulted in a real effective exchange rate appreciation, which is to be contrasted with the depreciation of the real exchange rate analysed below. This point under-lines the fact that the former is not a good measure of the latter. We now study these points in the wider context of the macroeconomic impacts of the external shocks.

7.3. Macroeconomic Impacts

We now analyse in turn money and inflation, relative prices and changes in the structure of production, and finally, aggregate saving and investment.

7.3.1. *Money and Inflation*

We have seen above that many measures adopted by the government during the external shocks period had an inflationary bias: increases in the minimum wage, cuts in consumer subsidies, increased tariff and non-tariff protection for industry. We can observe their impact by looking at the real effective exchange rate, better called the Comparative Inflation Index, presented in Table 7.9. This is the ratio of the Sénégalese CPI for African families to the weighted average of the CPIs of the top eight countries of origin of Sénégalese imports, expressed in CFAF using the official exchange rates (Guillaumont-Jeanneney 1985). The weights used in the calculation are each country's share of imports in Sénégal. It is thus akin to the real effective exchange rate according to the IMF definition. This table clearly shows that inflation was running faster in Sénégal than in its main trading partners.

Sénégal's policy changes were largely accommodated by monetary policy, which was quite expansionary. This is shown clearly by Table 7.10. In the first column of this table we see that Sénégal had a negative net foreign asset position throughout this period. It was the first country of the UMOA to reach such a position (see Guillaumont and Guillaumont

Table 7.9. Comparative inflation index

1974	100.0
1975	120.8
1976	112.6
1977	110.4

Note: calculations are explained in the text
Source: Computed from Guillaumont-Jeanneney (1985)

1984). The country was 'punished' in 1978 when the UMOA decided to lower the government's eligibility to central bank credit from 20% to 15% of the previous year's government revenue (World Bank 1979a). However, this monetary expansion was not initially due to government debt with the central bank, which increased only at the end of this period, but to total credit to the economy. Notice that the net foreign asset position became especially weak in 1975, when the CPSP started the Opération Vérité des Prix. The last column of Table 7.10 illustrates this point.

Table 7.11 helps establish a clearer idea of the causes of this monetary expansion. It shows that domestic credit growth was mainly driven by the increase in the government debt, on the one hand, and by the increase in agricultural crop credit (*crédits de campagne*), whose share in the total increased dramatically, on the other hand.

There are two elements which need to be kept in mind to understand the agricultural crop credit. First, it is not covered by the credit ceilings which the BCEAO imposes, after negotiation, on each of the member countries (Vizy 1989). Hence, it can grow with nearly no outside control. Second, crop credit came to be more and more diverted from its original use by ONCAD and the whole cooperatives system (see Section 7.2.1), which in fact used it to fill in financial gaps. This can be seen by looking at

Table 7.10. Monetary aggregates (*ratio to GDP × 100*)

	Net foreign assets	Domestic credit	Net government debt	Total credit to the economy (excl. the government)	Net foreign asset total credit
1974	−2.7	23.6	−0.4	24.1	−0.11
1975	−5.0	27.0	0.3	26.7	−0.19
1976	−4.2	30.1	1.8	28.3	−0.15
1977	−4.5	33.7	3.1	30.6	−0.15

Source: computed from BCEAO (1978)

Table 7.11. Shares of domestic credit (*average yearly percentage*)

	Government	Agricultural crop credit	Other short term	Medium and long term
1974	−1.9	4.6	81.0	16.3
1975	1.0	19.0	66.6	13.4
1976	6.0	22.5	58.0	13.5
1977	9.2	14.5	61.1	15.1

Source: computed from BCEAO (1978)

the seasonal pattern of crop credit (see BCEAO 1978, p. 12). Before 1975, crop credit outstanding used to be nil during the third quarter of the year, when no groundnuts are marketed. But after 1975, the seasonal pattern of this credit tended to flatten out, with crop credit starting to be rolled over from one season to the next. As a result, the money supply grew quite fast, pushed by domestic credit (see Table 7.10).

However, probably owing to the relative price policy sketched out above, and owing as well to an increased demand for money, described below, there were no signs of Dutch Disease for either relative prices or the sectoral distribution of GDP.

7.3.2. Relative Prices and Sectoral Distribution of GDP

There are no satisfactory data on relative prices to allow for a thorough analysis. But we can look at some partial evidence.

In Table 7.12, we have a comparison of various consumer prices, including the real price indexes for food and for clothing and the real value in terms of the CPI of the construction cost index (BCEAO 1978, p. 20). One observes that the price trends are the opposite to those expected from construction booms theory (see Chapter 1). While the real price of food is going up, the real cost of construction is going down. This is probably due to a large extent to the *Opération Vérité des Prix*, which removed consumer subsidies on such goods as rice, and to the accompanying egalitarian measures such as the increase in the minimum wage, which must have put upward pressure on the prices of some non-traded food items.

This rather unexpected diagnosis is partly confirmed by looking at the sectoral deflators presented in Table 7.13. This disaggregation structure *à la* Colin Clark is not satisfactory for the purpose at hand and can only offer some impressionistic evidence on the trends of the relative prices of tradables and non-tradables. But we can consider that the sectors are to some extent ranked according to the relative importance of traded goods

Table 7.12. Relative consumer prices (*index, 1974 = 100*)

	African CPI	Real food price[a]	Real clothing price[a]	Real construction cost[a]
1974	100.0	100.0	100.0	100.0
1975	130.6	106.8	89.7	97.0
1976	134.0	104.1	99.9	97.0
1977	148.0	105.6	98.4	96.0

[a] deflated by CPI

Source: computed from BCEAO (1978)

in them. The primary sector comprises mainly tradables, the secondary sector comprises such non-tradables as construction, and the tertiary sector is mainly made up of non-tradables.

Accepting this convention, we then find that relative prices went up for some tradables and down for some non-tradables. The secondary sector, which includes construction, presents the lowest price increase, while the primary sector, which comprises mainly tradables, had the fastest growth, for reasons explained above.

Correlatively, we observe in Table 7.14 that the sectoral distribution of GDP does not move in the direction predicted by construction booms theory over our period of analysis. We have classified separately the booming tradables sectors (agriculture and mining) and the non-booming ones. Taking as a benchmark either the average shares in 1970–72 (before

Table 7.13. Relative deflators

	Primary sector	Secondary sector	Tertiary sector	GDP deflator
1974	100.0	100.0	100.0	100.0
1975	123.3	106.6	101.9	111.2
1976	127.2	103.3	112.8	117.2
1977	130.9	110.0	120.8	122.6

Source: Duruflé (1985)

Table 7.14. Shares of GDP (*percentage*)

	1970–72 average	1974	1977
Booming tradables	13.6	17.3	17.0
Agriculture	12.5	11.1	15.3
Mining	1.1	6.2	1.7
Other tradables	27.4	27.4	29.4
Livestock	5.3	5.9	6.7
Fishery	3.5	4.6	3.7
Forestry	2.0	2.2	1.7
Industry	16.6	14.7	17.3
Non-tradables	59.1	55.2	53.6
Construction	3.9	4.0	4.4
Transportation	7.5	7.2	5.9
Commerce	27.4	24.9	23.6
Other services	9.0	8.2	7.1
Administration	11.3	10.9	12.6

Sources: World Bank (1979a, 1984)

the drought) or the shares in 1974, we observe that even the non-booming tradable sector increased its share, while the non-tradable sectors lost ground rather drastically. Hence, Sénégal offers an interesting example of exchange rate protection (Corden 1981) performed without a nominal devaluation.

We may give the credit for these anti-Dutch Disease, or anti-construction-boom, results to the relative price policies pursued, since other theoretical predictions of the construction boom theory, concerning variables unaffected by these policies, appear to be vindicated. This is the case for private saving.

7.3.3. Private Saving

We have presented in Table 7.15a the decomposition of saving into its private, public and foreign components. The data are presented as ratios to GDP (%). The private saving ratio has been calculated as a residual, using the actual data for the other components of saving and investment.

We observe that the private saving rate reacts fairly predictably to the windfall gains from the external shocks, as described in Table 7.2. We see that the ratio goes up, above its 1970–72 average value, when the windfall gain is large, in 1974. Then, it goes down when the windfall becomes smaller, and reaches a value slightly below its 1970–72 average in 1976 and 1977. But its average value over 1974–77 (11.5%) is higher than the 1970–72 average.

We observe similarly an increase in the public propensity to save above its average 1970–72 value in the boom year 1974, with a second increase in 1977, when the price of groundnuts went up again. Notice the dip in 1976 of the public propensity to save, which corresponds to the fall in central government saving, as seen in Tables 7.5 and 7.6. On average, over 1974–77, this propensity remained slightly above its average pre-boom level.

Table 7.15a. Decomposition of saving (*percentages of GDP*)

	Private		Public		Foreign net saving	Total domestic	
	Saving	Investment	Saving	Investment		Saving	Investment
Av. 1970–72	10.8	11.3	2.9	5.1	2.7	13.7	16.4
1974	14.5	14.9	3.8	8.6	5.2	18.3	23.5
1975	11.4	9.9	2.5	8.6	4.6	13.9	18.5
1976	10.0	7.7	1.7	8.8	4.8	11.7	16.5
1977	10.0	8.6	5.1	10.0	3.5	15.1	18.6

Note: all inventories accumulation is counted, as private investment

Sources: computed from World Bank (1979a, 1984)

The table also conveys an important piece of information regarding the distribution of investment between the public and private sectors. We see that the 1974 boom, which gave rise to an increase in the private saving ratio, gave rise similarly to an increase in the private investment ratio. But, as could be inferred from the participation policy described above, we can see that the relative importance of private and public investment switches in favour of the latter during the period. This is the result of the increased socialisation of industry which was the hallmark of the government's industrial policy at the time.

It is possible to reconcile the observation of an investment boom, in 1974 and 1975, with the absence of a construction boom as described above. This can be done with the help of Table 7.15b, which provides some decomposition of gross domestic investment for these two years. (Unfortunately, the corresponding data are not available for subsequent years.) This table shows that the investment boom affected mainly the import of equipment goods and stock variation, in 1974. No significant change occurred in construction. It is possible that the endogenous protection policy described above played a part in determining this orientation. The inflationary consequences of protection might have been expected by importers and traders, providing them with an incentive to increase stocks. Moreover, the expected protection of the existing manufacturing sector may have been an incentive to increase investment in equipment goods. During the period of the government's Fourth Plan (1973/ 74–1976/77), 28% of realised investment took place in the industry and energy sectors, compared with only 4% during the Third Plan (1969/ 70–1972/73) (World Bank 1984). Many infrastructural projects were conceived by the government at the time of the boom, including massive investment in the Sénégal basin, but were implemented only later, and only partly so.

Thus, the question arises of which assets private agents did buy with their savings, knowing that they invested less after 1975. We cannot provide an exhaustive answer to this question for lack of appropriate data

Table 7.15b. Gross domestic investment (*bn 1971 CFAF*)

	Investment in equipment goods	(of which imports)	Construction	Stock variation	Total gross domestic investment
Av. 1970–72	15.8	(13.5)	16.6	8.7	41.0
1974	19.8	(16.2)	17.8	11.7	48.8
1975	18.4	(14.8)	15.6	6.0	40.0

Source: World Bank (1979a)

Table 7.16. Liquidity ratio ($M2/GDP \times 100$)

1970–72	15.5
1974	22.8
1975	21.2
1976	24.7
1977	27.1

Source: BCEAO (1978)

on, for example, herd size and granaries. Nevertheless, part of the answer is probably given by Table 7.16, where the series of the liquidity ratio is represented. This is the ratio of the money supply (M_2) to GDP. We thus observe a reduction in velocity, despite the increase in inflation shown in Table 7.11. Assuming that the representative agent did not grossly underestimate inflation when forming his expectations, we can rationalise this increase in the demand for money by assuming that the marginal efficiency of capital went down drastically because of government industrial policy (described above), thus reducing the opportunity cost of holding money. Moreover, the implementation of protection measures, including quantitative restrictions and increases in custom duties, removed part of the incentive to accumulate imported goods at the end of the boom period.

Obviously, because of convertibility, there is in Sénégal the possibility of investing abroad. Guillaumont and Guillaumont (1984) discuss the issue of capital flights in the CFAF zone. As noted above, we have evidence of negative net private capital inflows for 1973–74–75. But this did not continue afterwards, suggesting that foreign assets were not massively purchased at that time. A possible explanation for this accumulation of local financial assets by the private sector may be found in the fact that most of the time the banking sector in Sénégal is supplying rationed credit at below the market rate of interest. Hence, holding deposits in local banks during periods of high liquidity may be an investment in goodwill, a way of securing priority access to rationed credit in times of hardship.

However, these series only give an aggregate description of the saving and investment ratios. We can try to shed more light on the underlying behaviour by decomposing these data into their 'normal' and 'windfall' components, as was done in the Chapter 2.

7.3.4. The Use of Windfall Income

Define windfall income as the sum of the windfall gains from the terms of trade shock and the returns to the investments induced by these windfall gains. In order to generate the latter, we need an assumption about the

Table 7.17. Windfall saving and investment (*bn constant 1974 CFAF*)

	Windfall income	Windfall investment	Windfall saving	Propensity to save windfall income (%)
1974	27.7	28.6	19.4	70.0
1975	21.3	11.2	3.6	17.1
1976	20.2	3.7	−5.0	−24.9
1977	20.8	12.1	8.4	40.2

Sources: computed from World Bank (1979a) and Tables 7.2, 7.6 and 7.15a,b

rate of return on windfall investment and an assumption about the generation of this windfall investment.

As far as the rate of return is concerned, we have assumed a rate of 10%, consistent with the discount rate used above. This has no claim to precision or realism, but it should give the right order of magnitude. Windfall investment is defined as the difference between 'normal', or counterfactual, investment and actual investment. The former is generated by applying the average share of investment in GDP over the 1970–72 period, namely 16.4%, to counterfactual GDP. This series is itself generated as the difference between actual GDP and windfall income. Hence, windfall income and windfall investment are generated recursively. They are represented as the first two columns of Table 7.17.

Then, windfall saving is defined as the difference between actual and counterfactual saving. The latter is generated by applying the average domestic propensity to save over the period 1970–72 (13.7%) to counterfactual GDP. Lastly, we compute the propensity to save windfall income as the ratio of windfall saving to windfall income. This series is represented in the last column of Table 7.17, and we find rather erratic behaviour. The figures corresponding to 1974 and 1977 (i.e. to the two peaks in the world groundnut price) are very high, as expected from the theory (see Chapter 1), but we find a strong drop in the propensity to save in 1976. As was noted above, this corresponds mainly to a fall in the central government's propensity to save. On average, we find a moderately high figure (27.6%), about one-third above the actual average propensity, 19.3%. It thus seems that the representative Sénégalese agent recognized clearly the temporary nature of the groundnut and phosphates boom and tried to save a larger than average fraction of the windfall.

In order to understand better the fall in public saving in 1976 and the overall behaviour of this series, we submit it to the same kind of decomposition into counterfactual and windfall components as the aggregate series.

We first compute counterfactual and windfall series for central government revenue, presented in Table 7.18. The counterfactual figures are

Table 7.18. Central government revenue (*bn constant 1974 CFAF*)

	Actual	Counterfactual	Windfall	Tax rate on windfall GDP (%)
1974	55.4	58.7	−3.3	−12.1
1975	69.5	65.0	4.5	21.1
1976	74.4	69.7	4.7	23.1
1977	85.5	70.6	14.9	71.7

Sources: computed from World Bank (1979a, 1984) and Tables 7.5 and 7.6

Table 7.19. Central government current expenditure (*bn constant 1974 CFAF*)

	Actual	Counterfactual	Windfall	Propensity to spend windfall revenues (%)
1974	49.7	51.9	−2.3	67.4
1975	60.7	57.5	3.3	73.1
1976	71.8	61.7	10.1	216.8
1977	73.7	62.4	11.3	75.5

Sources: computed from World Bank (1979a, 1984) and Tables 7.5 and 7.6

computed by applying the average tax rate over the 1970–72 period (18.87%) to counterfactual GDP, as presented above. The windfall series is computed as the difference between the actual and counterfactual series. The tax rate on windfall income is computed as the ratio of windfall revenue to windfall GDP. One may observe that it took some time for the Sénégalese government to capture the boom in the fiscal net. The immediate reaction, in 1974, was to relax the fiscal pressure, resulting in a negative tax rate on windfall GDP, as shown in the last column of Table 7.18. Afterwards, the pressure built up, generating a sizeable windfall revenue figure for 1977, with a windfall tax rate of 71.7%. This is another aspect of the increased control of the state over the economy which was noted above. Hence, although the whole windfall income accrued initially to the private sector, via the negative tax on windfall income, it was taxed away to a large extent by the government at the end of the boom (1977). We observe as well that this series cannot explain the fall in public saving which occurred in 1976, since we have a fairly smooth behaviour pattern.

However, a similar decomposition of central government current expenditure (Table 7.19) provides a useful clue on this question. Counterfactual expenditures were constructed by applying the 1970–72 average government propensity to spend (16.7%) to counterfactual GDP. We observe that windfall government expenditure in 1974 is negative, falling

Table 7.20. Public saving (*bn constant 1974 CFAF*)

	Actual	Counterfactual	Windfall	(of which central government)
1974	12.9	9.0	3.9	(−1.0)
1975	9.1	10.0	−0.9	(1.2)
1976	6.8	10.7	−4.0	(−5.4)
1977	20.2	10.9	9.3	(3.6)

Sources: Computed from World Bank (1979a, 1984) and Tables 7.5 and 7.6

in line with the government windfall revenue computed above. But we see that government current expenditures got completely out of hand in 1976, with a propensity to spend windfall revenue of about 217%. This propensity is defined as the ratio of windfall expenditures to windfall revenues.

In Table 7.20, we present a related series concerning public saving. The counterfactual public saving series was constructed by applying the 1970–72 average public propensity to save (2.9%) to counterfactual GDP. It turns out that windfall public saving is negative in 1975 (slightly) and (mainly) in 1976. This confirms the picture drawn above. We find a public propensity to save out of windfall revenue, defined as the ratio of windfall public saving to windfall government revenue, which is strongly negative in 1976.[3] The final column of this table represents windfall saving by the central government alone. The difference between this column and the previous one measures mainly the windfall saving by the stabilisation fund and public enterprises. These figures show that the bad public saving performance of 1976 is entirely down to the central government, which also dissipated to some extent the public saving raised outside central government in 1974. Hence, there was some sort of compensation between the two sources of public saving during the first three years of the boom, whereas they worked in the same direction during the final year.

Table 7.21 represents the contribution of the private sector and the public sector to windfall saving, as a fraction of windfall GDP. The performances of the two sectors evolved in opposite directions. Whereas the private sector was responsible for the whole of windfall saving at the beginning of the boom period, it was the public sector which saved the second groundnut shock (1977). But these saving rates cannot be interpreted as behavioural parameters, since the split of the windfall income between the two sectors changed drastically over these four years.

In order to approximate more closely to a behavioural analysis, we compute in Table 7.22 the public propensity to save windfall revenues.

Table 7.21. Windfall saving rates (*percentage of windfall GDP*)

	Total	Public	Private
1974	70.0	−14.1	55.9
1975	17.1	−4.4	21.5
1976	−24.9	−19.7	−5.2
1977	40.2	44.8	−4.6

Sources: computed from Tables 7.17 and 7.20

Table 7.22. Public propensity to save windfall revenue (*bn constant 1974 CFAF*)

	Windfall public saving	Windfall public revenue	Public propensity to save windfall revenue (%)
1974	3.9	1.6	243.8
1975	−0.9	−3.0	30.0
1976	−4.0	6.1	−65.6
1977	9.3	20.6	45.2

Sources: computed from Tables 7.18, 7.19 and 7.20

This is the ratio of windfall public saving to windfall public revenue. The latter is computed as the sum of windfall central government revenue and windfall 'other public saving' (computed following the same principles as above). It is evident from the table that this propensity is quite erratic. The very large 1974 figure is obtained despite the windfall dissaving by the central government. It mainly reflects the stabilisation fund's levy on groundnut production. It is partly spurious, since the tax cuts by the central government tend to inflate this ratio. It could be counted as an increase in expenditures with other accounting conventions. The negative propensity found for 1976 has already been commented on above. In order to aggregate these propensities into a single figure, one can compute the present value of windfall public saving and windfall public revenues, again using 10% as the discount rate. One then finds 34.9% as the public propensity to save windfall revenue. This is more than the figure which can be computed by the same method using total windfall saving and total windfall income, which is 31.3%. Therefore, the public sector did slightly better than the private sector in terms of saving the windfall. However, the difference is not very substantial, and probably not statistically significant. It is mainly due to the relatively strong discounting of the central government spending spree of 1976, compared to the high early savings that occurred despite the small windfall revenue of 1975.

Table 7.23. Private propensity to save windfall disposable income (*bn constant 1974 CFAF*)

	Windfall disposable income	Windfall private saving	Propensity to save disposable income (%)
1974	26.1	15.5	59.4
1975	24.3	4.5	18.5
1976	14.1	−1.0	−7.1
1977	0.2	−0.9	−450.0

Sources: computed from Tables 7.17 and 7.22

In order to compare more easily the public and private propensity to save windfall revenue or income, we can perform the same calculation as above for the private sector. This is done in Table 7.23. Private windfall disposable income is defined as windfall income (from Table 7.17) less windfall public revenue (from Table 7.22), and windfall private saving is defined as windfall saving (from Table 7.17) less windfall public saving (from Table 7.22). The final column represents the private propensity to save windfall disposable income, defined as the ratio of the second column to the first.

We should not pay too much attention to the value of the propensity computed for 1977, which is nearly indeterminate as the ratio of zero by zero. In this year, the benefit of the boom was completely captured by the government. We find the expected pattern of saving behaviour for the first two years of the boom, with an especially high saving propensity on windfall income near 60% in 1974. The following year witnesses a return to normal, while some dissaving occurs afterwards. Aggregating these figures over the whole boom, as done above for the public sector, we find a ratio of the present value of saving to the present value of disposable income (discounting again at 10%) of 30.2%.

Therefore, Sénégal does not provide an example of a very large private sector propensity to save a windfall gain. This is partly due to the way in which it was transferred to the private sector. In 1974, the windfall was taxed away from the producers, and part of it was handed over to the private sector through tax cuts and consumer subsidies. Nevertheless, the private sector contributed largely to a sizeable windfall saving that year. Then a widely publicised policy U-turn, the *Opération Vérité des Prix'*, occurred, with a cut in consumer subsidies and an increase in producer prices. It is, then, possible that farmers did not perceive correctly the temporary nature of the price hike, and that they regarded it as permanent. Another possible explanation for the low propensity of the private sector to save the windfall is that, on aggregate, it was quickly taxed away by the government. Thus, the possible increase in peasant saving might have been more than offset by a cut in saving by urban dwellers forced on them by the degradation of their position, which they might have regarded as temporary.

7.4. Conclusion

Sénégal had a short-lived external shock in the mid-1970s, with the increases in the prices of groundnuts and phosphates resulting in a 24.3% improvement in the terms of trade, despite the oil shock and the rises in the prices of other imported goods. There was a positive windfall in 1974, with the terms of trade moving back to their previous level by 1978.

These shocks provided the government with funds which were, roughly speaking, used in two different directions, besides a short-lived increase in current expenditure in 1976. The government adopted first a relative price policy which counteracted to some extent the Dutch Disease or construction boom effects. Taxes and subsidies were used to increase the price of tradables relative to non-tradables, that is, to depreciate the real exchange rate. This may be regarded as a move towards a greater emphasis on import-substituting industrialisation strategy. But in a more short-run perspective, this policy may be interpreted as a sort of real exchange rate protection against Dutch Disease, without devaluation. However, some of these measures, such as the creation of non-tariff barriers, paved the way for some long-run productivity problems. Their favourable effects were also partly offset by an egalitarian wage policy.

At the same time, these funds provided the government with the means to pursue an industrial policy based on Sénégalisation and socialisation of industry, and more generally to increase state control over the economy. The world capital market amplified this financial capacity of the government's, regarding the booms as good collateral. This did not much improve the position of the socialised firms, which were already facing difficult conditions when they were in the private sector because of various rigidities and state controls, notably in the labour market. Moreover, the experience with ONCAD, the big parastatal in charge of agriculture, did not allow for optimistic predictions regarding the evolution of efficiency in the newly state-controlled firms. In fact, the marginal productivity of capital probably went down quite rapidly in these firms (World Bank 1984). Moreover, these publicly controlled firms, including ONCAD in the first instance, were instrumental in pushing monetary policy in an overexpansionary direction.

These changes paved the way for the macroeconomic imbalances which led to the adoption of some drastic stabilisation and adjustment programmes in the 1980s. In particular, by purchasing illiquid foreign assets with the proceeds from a temporary positive shock, the government reduced the potential capacity of the country to invest later. Moreover, as the management of these firms changed for the worse, it is probable that the rate of return on these assets was reduced.

Hence, we can say that Sénégal avoided Dutch Disease by adopting some rather well-conceived tax-cum-subsidy policies, taking into account that, as a Franc Zone member, it was precommitted not to devalue the currency. But the economy caught a 'Public Enterprise Disease' instead, with some unpleasant after-effects in terms of lost investment and reduced productivity.

NOTES

1. Morris and Newman (1989) describe the cereals market in Sénégal, but for a more recent period.
2. See Svejnar (1984) for an analysis of modern sector earnings in Sénégal. As a cross-section study, it cannot take into account the SMIG, which is the same for everyone.
3. However, one may wonder whether this is not just a data problem. It is known that 1976 is a problematic year in this respect in the Sénégalese National Accounts. It is left as a gap in many series between the 1979 and 1984 World Bank reports on Sénégal, suggesting that little confidence was given to these data. In the 1979 World Bank report, there are inconsistencies in this respect. For example, the figure for Central Government Investments in 1976/77 is 16.5 billion CFAF on p. 58, and 13.5 billion on p. 66, a difference of about 20%. Although the problem at hand concerns only current expenditures, this inconsistency suggests that some problems exist with these data. Even in the 1989–90 edition of the *World Tables* (World Bank 1990), some gaps are left in the government accounts for that year, and in particular on the expenditure side.

REFERENCES

BCEAO (1978): *Statistiques économiques et monétaires, Sénégal*, October 1978, BCEAO: Dakar.

Bhagwati, J.N. (1965): 'On the Equivalence of Tariffs and Quotas', in R.E. Baldwin *et al.* (eds): *Trade, Growth and the Balance of Payments: Essays in Honor of Gottfried Haberler*, Rand McNally: Chicago.

Bloch, P.C. (1985): *Wage Policy, Wage Structure and Employment in the Public Sector of Sénégal*, CPD Discussion Paper No. 1985–41, World Bank: Washington, DC.

Braverman, A. and J.S. Hammer (1986): 'Multimarket Analysis of Agricultural Pricing Policies in Sénégal', in I.J. Singh, L. Squire, and J. Strauss (eds):

Agricultural Household Models: Extensions, Applications, and Policy, pp. 233–254, Johns Hopkins University Press: Baltimore.

Caswell, N. (1983): '*Peasants, Peanuts and Politics: State Marketing in Sénégal, 1966–1980*', paper presented at the International Seminar on Marketing Boards in Tropical Africa, African Studies Centre: Leiden (unpublished).

CERDI (1981): *Le STABEX au Sénégal*, Report to the EEC, CERDI: Clermont-Ferrand (unpublished).

Chambas, G. and A.-M. Geourjon (1985): 'Domestic Policies, Crisis and Adjustment in Sénégal', in T. Rose (ed.): *Crisis and Recovery in Sub-Saharan Africa*, pp. 155–165, Development Centre Seminars, OECD: Paris.

Corden, W.M. (1981): 'Exchange Rate Protection', in R.N. Cooper *et al.* (eds): *The International Monetary System under Flexible Exchange Rates: Global, Regional, and National*, Ballinger: Cambridge, Mass.

Corden, W.M. and J.P. Neary (1982): 'Booming Sector and De-industrialisation in a Small Open Economy', *Economic Journal*, 92, 825–48.

Devarajan, S. and J. de Melo (1987): 'Adjustment with a Fixed Exchange Rate: Cameroon, Côte d'Ivoire, and Sénégal', *World Bank Economic Review*, 1, 447–87.

Duruflé, G. (1985): *Déséquilibres structurels et programmes d'ajustement au Sénégal*, Ministère de la Coopération: Paris (unpublished).

Guillaumont, P. and S. Guillaumont (1984): *Zone franc et développement africain*, Economica: Paris.

Guillaumont-Jeanneney, S. (1985): 'Foreign Exchange Policy and Economic Performance: A Study of Sénégal, Madagascar, and Guinea', in T. Rose (ed.): *Crisis and Recovery in Sub-Saharan Africa*, pp. 180–98, Development Centre Seminars, OECD: Paris.

Hammer, J.S. (1986): ' "Subsistence First"—Farm Allocation Decisions in Sénégal', *Journal of Development Economics*, 23, 355–369.

Helpman, E. and P.R. Krugman (1989): *Trade Policy and Market Structure*, MIT Press: Cambridge, Mass.

Marodon, R. (1987): *Contraintes et efficacité de la politique des prix agricoles: l'exemple du Niger, du Rwanda et du Sénégal*, doctoral thesis, CERDI: Clermont-Ferrand (unpublished).

Morris, M.L. and M.D. Newman (1989): 'Official and Parallel Cereals Markets in Sénégal: Empirical Evidence', *World Development*, 17, 1895–1906.

Nascimento, J.-C. and M. Raffinot (1984): 'Politique de prix agricoles et comportement des producteurs: le cas de l'arachide au Sénégal', *Revue Economique*, 4, 779–95.

Pinto, B. (1987): 'Nigeria During and After the Oil Boom: A Policy Comparison with Indonesia', *World Bank Economic Review*, 1, 419–45.

Svejnar, J. (1984): 'The Determinants of Industrial-Sector Earnings in Sénégal', *Journal of Development Economics*, 15, 289–311.

Vizy, M. (1989): *La zone franc*, CHEAM: Paris.

World Bank (1979a): *The Economic Trends and Prospects of Sénégal*', Report No. 1720a-SE, World Bank: Washington, DC.

World Bank (1979b): *Accelerated Development in Sub-Saharan Africa*, World Bank: Washington, DC.

World Bank (1984): '*Sénégal—Country Economic Memorandum*', Report No.5243-SE, World Bank: Washington, DC.

World Bank (1990): *World Tables, 1989–90*, Johns Hopkins University Press: Baltimore.

Youm, P. (1986): 'Crise de l'endettement: le cas du Sénégal', in H. Bourguinat and J. Mistral (eds): *La crise de l'endettement international, acte II*, pp. 255–266, Economica: Paris.

8

The Zambian Copper Boom and Crash, 1964–80

JANINE ARON

8.1. Introduction

Zambia lies at one extreme of the group of less developed countries classified as highly mineral dependent, that is, where the mineral sector contributes more than 10% of GDP, or in excess of 40% of total export earnings (Nankani 1979). At independence from Great Britain in 1964, copper supplied 90% of Zambia's foreign exchange, over 60% of its tax revenues and 20% of the formal sector employment and contributed almost half of the GDP.[1] Outside the copper sector, the economy was poorly developed. Yet, despite abundant rhetoric in favour of economic diversification, mineral dependence persisted throughout the 1970s and 1980s.[2]

The extent of Zambia's mineral dependence following independence is illustrated in Table 8.1. Copper export values in constant US dollars fluctuated substantially during the boom years of 1964–74 and fell by 40% from a boom average of US$620 million, to an average of US$350 million, during 1975–80. Although the mining sector's share in GDP declined from over 50% in the boom years to 35% in 1975–80, it remained a significant proportion. With the first negative copper price shocks of the early 1970s, the mineral revenue contribution to total revenue fell sharply and all but disappeared after the major copper shock in 1974. This decline was partially compensated for by a broadening of the tax base; nevertheless, total revenue contracted. The table shows that dependence on copper for foreign exchange scarcely diminished from 1964; and when other minerals' earnings are added, the contribution of the mining sector to total foreign exchange earnings during 1964–80 was over 95%.

This degree of mineral dependence made Zambia highly susceptible to large trade shocks from fluctuating world copper prices. The pattern of world copper prices is shown in Figure 8.1. A large positive external shock occurred during the decade 1964–74, the onset of which coincided with Zambia's independence. This was punctuated by several small negative shocks in the 1970s. At the peak of the boom in 1969, the terms of trade had increased by 98% relative to their 1964 level. The boom was followed

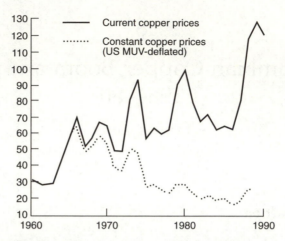

Figure 8.1. London Metal Exchange copper prices (USc/lb)
Source: IMF, *International Financial Statistics.*

Table 8.1. Zambian copper dependence

	Copper export value (1963 US$m)	Copper value (% of GDP)	Copper earnings (% of total forex)	Mineral revenue (% total revenue)
1964	407.5	59.12	88.46	—
1965	468.1	48.27	90.22	—
1966	605.0	54.31	93.31	65.13
1967	564.8	45.35	92.34	61.45
1968	675.5	48.59	94.80	57.58
1969	904.0	55.13	94.52	58.62
1970	800.4	55.89	95.30	55.50
1971	501.2	38.12	92.78	36.92
1972	501.7	36.41	90.63	18.84
1973	675.1	43.93	94.20	28.09
1974	673.9	44.43	92.68	42.32
1975	341.5	29.75	90.40	13.29
1976	443.6	36.31	91.59	2.56
1977	341.3	32.52	91.22	0.00
1978	271.4	26.55	87.02	0.02
1979	362.5	33.86	82.62	0.00
1980	323.4	28.53	85.44	5.45

Notes:
1. The deflator in col. (2) is the US Manufacturing Unit Value index
2. Mineral revenue here refers to taxation of copper, as well as metal by- and co-products, and includes mining income tax, withholding taxes and dividends

Sources: *International Financial Statistics* (IMF); *Monthly Digest of Statistics*

by a steep fall from mid-1974 in the terms of trade, which declined during 1975–80 on average to 33% of the peak level of the boom. Prices did not again recover in real terms to the pre-boom level. The decline in Zambia's economic fortunes between the positive and negative shocks was drastic, and the boom was not managed so as to smooth the transition into recessionary circumstances.

An extensive literature on the theory of the 'Dutch Disease' has examined the impact and optimal management of unexpected permanent trade shocks.[3] The object of this chapter is to employ an analytic framework derived from the dynamic extension of Dutch Disease models[4] to analyse the government's management of temporary trade shocks in Zambia in the presence of wide-ranging economic controls. Three key aspects of public policy will be examined. First, the role of Zambia's economic and political control regime in constraining the set of possible adjustments to the shocks is examined. Second, an explanation is given for Zambia's failure to achieve a sustainable diversification from excessive mineral dependence, despite this being a priority of the government, and despite the apparently abundant opportunity afforded by the copper boom. Finally, the damaging impact of revenue instability owing to mineral revenue fluctuations is explored—in particular, the potential for ratchet effects in expenditure and the loss of fiscal control without a stabilising fiscal framework.

The structure of the chapter is as follows. In Section 8.2, the nature and likely impact of the economic control regime from 1964 to 1980 are described. Using various counterfactuals, the sizes of the positive and negative shocks are quantified in Section 8.3, and an attempt is made to characterise public and private sector expectations of world copper price changes in both periods. Asset changes and savings and dissavings rates are calculated in Section 8.4, and structural changes by sector are examined. Section 8.5 evaluates the path of public finances during the shocks. Finally, Section 8.6 concludes with lessons from the Zambian experience.

8.2. Characterisation of the Economic Control Regime

After Zambia achieved independence in 1964, existing economic controls were maintained or reinforced, and new controls added. Virtually every aspect of the economy was subject to varying levels of state intervention during the next two decades, with an intensification of controls after falls in the copper price. Economic behaviour and outcomes during the copper boom, as well as choices available for public management of the boom, were profoundly influenced by the control regime. The nature of this influence is twofold, acting both through the direct economic impact of controls and via secondary behavioural responses to conditions of excess demand induced by the controls. The nature of controls in Zambia, 1964–80, is discussed in Section 8.2.1, and secondary effects in Section 8.2.2.

8.2.1. The Direct Impact of Economic Controls

The controls exerting probably the greatest influence on behaviour and outcomes during the copper boom and its aftermath were exchange rate policy, interrelated restrictions on imports and foreign exchange, and credit controls. Price and wage controls were also applied, though enforcement was patchy. Finally, although the state sector was the principal victim of price controls, it was favoured in credit, foreign exchange and import licence allocations.

Exchange rate policy in Zambia was largely passive from 1964 to mid-1976, under various fixed regimes. The kwacha was linked first to the pound sterling and then, from 1971, to the US dollar. Moreover, the kwacha appreciated against the currencies of most trading partners from 1971 to 1976 (save the Deutschmark) owing to appreciation of the floating US dollar. This exacerbated a tendency towards capital-intensive, import-substituting industrialisation and discouraged agricultural exports. From mid-1976, the dollar link was severed and the exchange rate linked to the SDR, effecting a *de facto* devaluation of 20%. There were two further devaluations until a crawling peg was installed in 1983: in 1978 (10%) and in 1983 (20%).

The fixed exchange rate was maintained in the face of copper price shocks by imposing ever-tighter capital and trade restrictions. Zambia had been the only country of the three (Zambia, Zimbabwe and Malawi) at the dissolution of the Federation of Rhodesia and Nyasaland to relax the exchange control restrictions imposed in 1961. However, these liberalisation measures were minor. In 1971, after a shock to the copper price, stringent exchange controls were imposed to protect foreign exchange reserves. These controls were further tightened after the copper price collapsed in mid-1974. Positive net foreign assets were acquired until 1970, but depleted thereafter, turning negative from 1974.

Import licensing was originally devised to avoid congestion after the closure of various transport routes in the mid-1960s, but increasingly it served to control import levels. In 1972, a more restrictive import licensing system was introduced: certain categories of imports were banned, but capital and intermediate goods imports continued to be liberally licensed. Import licensing was further tightened early in 1975. The emphasis of the licensing system, placing fewer restrictions on raw materials and capital goods than non-essential consumer goods, was reinforced by the tariff structure.[5] To illustrate the trends in trade policy, a measure is employed which captures the effects of both import quotas and tariffs. This is given by the differential between the c.i.f. value of imports (pre trade policy prices) and the retail price of domestic import substitutes (post trade policy). In Figure 8.2 the ratio of imported to retail manufacturing price indices is plotted from 1966 to 1978 (increasing trade restrictions are indicated by a movement down the y-axis).[6] Trade policy was fairly dormant until 1969,[7] but an endogenous trade liberalisation is apparent for most of the boom years (1964–74). Policy tightened following the negative price shock of 1974, and this trend persisted into the late 1970s. One impact of trade policy was the burgeoning of an import and capital-intensive importables sector during the boom, and its rapid contraction from 1974.

Also closely linked to the availability of foreign exchange were episodes of financial repression and temporary financial liberalisations. Monetary policy changes were principally effected via changes in the minimum liquidity ratio and reserve requirements, and directives to the commercial banking sector. Interest rates had virtually no role as a policy instrument. Although there were no official ceilings, interest rates were held low and constant, with real interest rates negative for most of the period. The effect of negative real interest rates was to reduce the flow of savings deposits, create a large unsatisfied demand for credit and reinforce a bias to capital-intensive production.

There were a number of episodes of temporary financial liberalisation for the private sector, governed by the prevailing copper price. During periods of high copper prices and budget surpluses (1965–70), total liquid

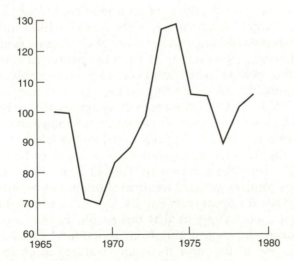

Figure 8.2. Implicit trade policy (*1966 = 100*)

Source: Author's calculations using the *Monthly Digest of Statistics* (CSO) for Zambia

assets in the banking system increased, and the fruits of the expansion in credit fell to the parastatal and private enterprise sectors. The coincidence of budget deficits with balance of payments deficits, on the other hand, saw vastly increased credit demand by the government, and credit to the private sector (particularly the non-parastatal private sector) was limited. Credit extended to the non-parastatal private sector contracted sharply in 1972/73, a move which was reversed in 1974. A sharp expansion in the afflicted (parastatal) mining companies' demand for credit further squeezed the private sector in 1975. In 1976 the minimum liquidity ratio was elevated to 30%,[8] and between 1975 and 1978, credit to the non-parastatal private sector declined by a further 20% in real terms. The trend was again reversed with more favourable copper prices in 1979/80.

In fact, the statutory minimum liquidity ratio was never binding: the actual liquidity ratio did decrease by 16 percentage points during the first phase of the boom, 1965–71, but it rose again sharply after the negative copper shocks in 1971 and 1974. The failure of commercial banks to lend sufficiently, even at negative real interest rates, has two probable explanations: supply constraints owing to the investment boom and reduced private sector confidence, for political reasons. However, there appears to be some evidence for efficient financial intermediation of loans for capital formation in the non-parastatal private sector: advances to the private sector increased synchronously with the investment boom between 1965 and 1974 (save for the rationing in 1972/73, discussed above).

Price controls were applied to three major categories of prices from independence: producer prices of agricultural goods (where prices were set well below world or border prices[9]), prices of 'essential commodities'[10] and the prices of some products of parastatal companies. The last two categories are largely synonymous, since between 1970 and 1980, over 70% of the parastatal manufacturing share of GDP came from food, beverages and tobacco. However, apart from the parastatal companies and state marketing boards, where controls were more easily enforceable, price controls for the manufacturing sector were probably only binding from the mid- to late 1970s. Price controls, set on a cost-plus basis, proved difficult to administer in periods of increasing inflation and import prices. Parastatals were particularly disadvantaged by the failure to adjust controls during the negative shock; profitability fell sharply, necessitating larger subsidies from the government. The failure to create regional variations in price controls induced frequent shortages of essential goods in rural areas (given transport costs and the low value to weight ratio); and Tanzanian experience suggests that this would have compounded the production disincentives resulting from agricultural producer pricing.[11] In retrospect, one of the most damaging features of entrenched price controls on essential goods was the political vulnerability they implied for the government. In IMF reform packages of the 1980s the last liberalising reform to be enacted was raising the maize price, invariably reneged on owing to popular protest. Subsidies to maintain price controls proved very costly for the budget.

Real wages grew strongly after independence in all sectors. The view in 1969 was that money wage increases should not exceed productivity gains, and not exceed 5% per annum; but this was unevenly enforced, and was exceeded in mining and services. The gap between mining and non-mining wages narrowed, but by 1972 average mining wages still exceeded those in most other sectors by over 60%. With the first shocks to the copper price in 1971, the government salary scale was frozen, and real wages for civil servants declined during 1972–75. An attempt was made to recoup these losses on the strength of strong copper earnings in 1973–74, with average wage increases in 1975 of 20%. Thereafter the scale was again frozen. Wage agreements with the mine workers' union in 1970 and 1973 provided rather modest wage settlements, and required a standstill on further wage claims. However, the 1973 agreement was not adhered to, and rises were granted of 7–20% in 1975 and 12% in 1976. It is possible that increased state control of the copper industry from 1973/74 rendered the government more vulnerable to mine workers' demands. Nonetheless, these increases were insufficient to raise real wages above the 1972 level.

8.2.2. *Quantifying the Secondary Effects of Economic Controls*

Apart from the direct effects of controls, there may be substantial secondary effects via profit opportunities created by conditions of excess demand. Trade and foreign exchange controls and an overvalued exchange rate provide incentives for smuggling and for the misinvoicing of foreign trade. Reported trade indices then become unreliable indicators of the true extent of trade. Further, if illegally accumulated foreign exchange was not consumed but saved, the use of reported indices will misrepresent changes in foreign assets. There is also an impact on government revenue, which will be diminished by smuggling and the underinvoicing of imports and exports, but increased by import overinvoicing.

Secondary effects were significant in Zambia during 1964–80. The rationing of foreign exchange, overvalued exchange rate and stringent trade controls enhanced the importance of black markets from independence, and illegal trade transactions flourished. The black-market premium on the official exchange rate had risen to almost 200% by 1978.

Estimates of import misinvoicing[12] using partner-country data comparisons are presented in Table 8.2. They are used to provide correction factors for the calculations of windfall income and savings (Sections 8.3 and 8.4), and to estimate the impact on government revenue. A positive percentage difference for the trade ratio, R, indicates net overinvoicing, while a negative figure indicates net underinvoicing. Trade ratios are shown for the UK and the USA (comprising on average 22% and 10% of Zambian imports, respectively), for the six main trading partners, and for the OECD (comprising 60% of imports). All four series suggest that capital flight through misinvoicing was rife during the copper boom. With the imposition of more restrictive exchange and import controls in 1971, the black-market premium doubled and overinvoicing was sustained. However, the terms of trade recovery in 1973 saw a diminution of the premium and misinvoicing. From mid-1974, with a further tightening of controls, the premium more than doubled and in tandem, misinvoicing grew. After mid-1976 and until the early 1980s, the premium fell steadily owing to a more active exchange rate policy and improved borrowing opportunities with the recovery of copper prices in 1979. Overinvoicing was negligible

Table 8.2. Percentage misinvoicing using partner-country-trade data

	UK	USA	Six major partners	OECD
1965	38.3	—	40.8	65.1
1966	13.1	12.7	8.0	8.2
1967	21.1	22.3	8.1	5.6
1968	36.9	73.8	36.0	36.3
1969	30.6	76.2	34.1	31.9
1970	36.5	64.5	29.8	29.3
1971	13.2	58.5	20.0	20.8
1972	15.9	44.4	13.2	16.9
1973	13.2	22.6	−1.1	2.2
1974	3.7	−9.4	−13.2	−16.9
1975	3.3	34.5	14.0	9.4
1976	32.8	47.7	9.7	3.0
1977	2.7	49.0	12.9	8.6
1978	12.5	8.2	7.0	6.4
1979	6.1	2.6	0.0	−4.1
1980	2.2	−21.6	−8.8	3.8

Notes:
1. The trade ratios are $R = 100(Mz - Xf)/Xf$, where Mz are Zambian recorded f.o.b. imports and Xf partner-country-recorded f.o.b. exports
2. The six main trading partners, excluding South Africa and Saudi Arabia, are USA, UK, France, Italy, Germany and Japan. South African exports are not recorded for individual African countries. Saudi Arabian trade is predominantly in oil, which, analogous with copper, is unlikely to be misinvoiced
3. No data were available before 1965; the 1965 figure for the six main trading partners is an average of five countries, excluding the USA, for which figures were unavailable. Further, OECD figures for 1965–67 were available as monthly averages only
4. Details of the method applied in calculating these figures can be found in Aron and Elbadawi (1996)

Sources: Direction of Trade Statistics (IMF); *Foreign Trade Statistics* (OECD)

in this period, and in some years the incentives due to trade policy dominated and underinvoicing is indicated.

8.3. The Nature of the Trade Shocks

Copper consumption growth was rapid after 1964 owing to the Vietnam
War and high world economic growth. However, capacity growth lagged
growth of demand, and political disturbances and strikes in several
supplier countries meant that even existing capacity was underutilised. A
protracted but discontinuous positive trade shock ensued which comprised three price maxima of decreasing magnitude, with the first two
attaining over double the 1963 copper export price (see Figure 8.1). Two
small short negative shocks were experienced after the first two price
peaks of 1966 and 1969, and a large and protracted negative shock ensued
when prices fell precipitously from the final peak in 1974. The terms of
trade are shown in Figure 8.3, with and without the misinvoicing adjustment to import values. The three small booms are apparent, with the
unadjusted maximum implying an improvement in the terms of trade of
about 50% relative to 1964.

In order to calculate the size of the positive shock, a non-shock counterfactual for the 1964–74 period was constructed by extrapolating the
pre-boom economic behaviour of the years 1959–63. These years are par-

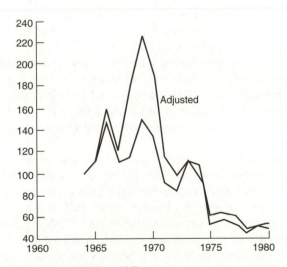

Figure 8.3. Terms of trade (*1964 = 100*)

Note: Terms of trade with and without IUV adjusted for misinvoicing.

Source: IMF, *International Financial Statistics*.

ticularly suitable as a base, since they fall within a stable subperiod for copper prices. Despite rapid growth of consumption owing to the Korean War and copper stockpiling by the USA, the price remained at a relatively low level (99 cents/lb, 1947–63, in 1983 prices). Guaranteed producer prices were close to quoted market prices throughout the subperiod. There was a period of oversupply after the 1955–56 boom years, but by 1963 market balance had been restored. However, the onset of the copper boom coincided with Zambia's independence in late 1964. Political and economic regime shifts which occurred in this period present serious difficulties for data linkage and time-series interpretation. The use of counterfactuals here is subject to this caveat.

It is not obvious which counterfactuals to employ for the negative shock period. Two contrasting bases were chosen: first, taking the norm to be the 1959–63 period; second, measuring the (greater) decline from the second phase of the boom in 1971–74.

Windfall income from the copper boom and the size of the negative shock are estimated in Section 8.3.1 using counterfactuals. Then an attempt is made in Section 8.3.2 to characterise public and private sector perceptions of the degree and duration of the price shocks.

8.3.1. The Magnitude of the Two Shocks

The windfall gain due to the protracted positive boom was estimated using price and export volume counterfactuals for the 1964–74 period. The price counterfactual assumes that the terms of trade level for 1963 would have persisted in the absence of the boom. This appears reasonable, given the relative constancy of the copper price and terms of trade in the early 1960s. The trends for misinvoicing in Table 8.2 suggest that increased demand for foreign assets during the boom (as well as political uncertainty after independence) induced substantial capital flight. Thus, the reported import unit value (IUV) series, used in calculating the terms of trade, was corrected for misinvoicing during the boom with a correction factor derived from partner-country-trade comparisons from 1966 (see Tables 8.3 and 8.4).

Two different quantity counterfactuals were constructed which give rise to upper- and lower-bound estimates for windfall gain. The first counterfactual equates actual and counterfactual volumes, by assuming that export volumes were not affected by the boom. In fact a price response in copper export volumes did occur, as evidenced by Table 8.1: on average, in peak years, export volume exceeded the 1963 level by 20%. However, the additional windfall gain due to the export price response would have to be adjusted for the costs of expanding output. Using actual volumes in the first quantity counterfactual is a conservative assumption which avoids the difficulty of estimating the net effect. It also implicitly takes account of transport and mining shocks to output in the period.[13] The counterfactual value of exports was then obtained by correcting the actual value of exports for changes in the terms of trade; thus actual volumes were divided by the (corrected) terms of trade index, set to equal 100 in 1963.

Another justification for using actual volumes in the counterfactual would be if the Hotelling Rule applied (Hotelling 1931): in this case, slower depletion would be expected in periods when the expected growth rate of the copper price exceeded the return on alternative assets, and vice versa. Following this rule would mean that both saving and dissaving would be reflected in the actual production volumes. However, although there is some evidence for inventory speculation according to this rule, the flexibility of Zambian mining companies after independence was increasingly limited. The government's budget constraint in the face of greatly increased expenditure from 1964 had fashioned an implicit resource-extraction policy of maximising production to provide tax and foreign exchange. Royalties and windfall taxes were imposed during 1960–69 to extract rents, and with partial state ownership beginning in 1969, maximising employment and production took precedence over profit-and-loss aspects.

A second approach to the quantity counterfactual is to capture and correct for the observed responsiveness of export volumes to copper prices. The first step in constructing the counterfactual was estimation of a copper supply equation. For simplicity, output expansion was assumed to be costless. Although this is partially justified by the overcapacity present in Zambian mines (and in most producing countries) in the early 1960s, which would reduce expansion costs, the resultant counterfactual is best regarded as providing an upper bound for the windfall gain.

A distinct regime shift occurred in the period. From 1960 to 1975, capacity did not present an important constraint on supply: there was adequate labour, expatriate skills and foreign exchange, and the rather dated technology was still appropriate in the prevailing mining conditions. Export volumes responded positively to a real exchange rate for copper, calculated as the current London Metal Exchange copper price corrected for royalties and the copper export tax, multiplied by the nominal exchange rate, and deflated by an index for building costs. Also strongly significant was the ratio of the copper supply in the previous period to the contemporaneous level of stocks: this ratio acts as a proportional control mechanism on supply, and displays the expected negative partial elasticity of supply.[14] Price expectations and transport shocks are also proxied by this stocks variable. Dummy variables were used for partial nationalisation and an altered tax regime in 1969 (D69), and the Mufulira mine disaster in 1972 (D72).

Table 8.3. The magnitude of Zambia's copper boom and crash

	Copper exports (Km)	EUV (1963 = 100)	IUV (1963 = 100)	IUV corrected (1963 = 100)	Terms of trade (1963 = 100)
	(1)	(2)	(3)	(4)	(5)
1. *Positive shock* (1960–63 base)					
1959	214.4	100.4	99.2	99.2	101.3
1960	239.2	105.3	96.0	96.0	109.7
1961	220.2	99.1	100.0	100.0	99.1
1962	217.6	99.6	96.0	96.0	103.7
1963	235.6	100.0	100.0	100.0	100.0
1964	296.8	106.6	103.2	103.2	103.3
1965	343.2	123.0	106.5	106.5	115.6
1966	460.6	188.1	124.2	114.3	164.5
1967	434.0	177.0	154.8	142.3	124.4
1968	516.1	196.5	164.5	105.3	186.5
1969	724.5	242.9	157.3	103.6	234.6
1970	681.4	243.8	175.8	123.4	197.5
1971	450.2	173.5	183.9	147.1	117.9
1972	490.9	169.0	195.2	169.4	99.8
1973	698.3	254.9	221.0	223.4	114.1
1974	838.5	304.9	274.2	308.7	98.8
2. *Negative shock* (1963 base)					
1974	838.5	304.9	274.2	308.7	98.8
1975	472.0	179.6	340.3	292.5	61.4
1976	688.6	226.1	379.8	343.0	65.9
1977	645.1	237.2	435.5	379.3	62.5
1978	597.7	246.9	538.7	500.7	49.3
1979	897.2	338.5	646.0	645.8	52.4
1980	872.4	442.5	806.5	877.1	50.4
3. *Negative shock* (av. 1971–74 base)					
1974	838.5	182.5	125.4	145.5	91.7
1975	472.0	214.7	155.7	137.9	57.1
1976	688.6	281.0	173.8	161.7	61.2
1977	645.1	356.2	199.2	178.8	58.1
1978	597.7	581.7	246.5	236.0	45.8
1979	897.2	899.6	295.5	304.4	48.7
1980	872.4	1,525.4	369.0	413.4	46.9

Notes:
1. $IUV_{corrected} = IUV_{63} \times (1 - sixtot/100)$; *sixtot* from Table 8.2, col. (3)
2. The copper supply correction factor is the ratio of counterfactual copper volumes (generated using equation 8.1 on p. 272) to actual copper volumes

Counterfactual copper exports adjusted for (5)	Windfall using (3) (Km)	Windfall using (3) adjusted for (4) (Km)	Copper supply correction factor	Windfall using (9) (Km)	Windfall uncorrected for overinvoicing and supply response (Km)
(6)	(7)	(8)	(9)	(10)	(11)
211.7	2.7	2.7	—	—	2.7
218.0	21.2	22.1	1.00000	22.1	22.1
222.2	2.0	−2.0	1.00000	−2.0	−2.0
209.8	7.8	8.2	1.00000	8.2	8.2
235.6	0.0	0.0	1.00000	−0.0	0.0
287.3	9.5	9.2	0.86345	47.2	9.2
297.0	46.2	43.4	0.85148	84.8	43.4
280.0	180.6	158.0	0.97775	163.5	125.9
349.0	85.0	59.7	0.97501	65.8	35.1
276.7	239.4	227.3	0.91102	250.7	51.0
308.8	415.7	401.4	0.88416	435.9	162.5
344.9	336.5	272.6	0.85640	312.8	108.1
381.7	68.5	46.6	0.91820	67.8	−14.7
491.9	−1.0	−0.6	0.93171	19.3	−38.9
612.1	86.2	38.6	0.87449	73.0	42.0
849.1	−10.6	−3.4	0.86528	33.6	30.8
849.1	−10.6	−3.4	0.86528	33.6	30.8
768.5	−296.5	−101.4	0.91384	−78.7	−124.0
,044.7	−356.1	−103.8	1.02245	−110.6	−123.3
,031.6	−386.5	−101.9	1.12539	−136.0	−123.9
,212.2	614.5	−122.7	1.20223	−171.7	−131.1
,711.7	−814.5	−126.1	1.00930	−128.6	−126.2
,729.3	−856.9	−97.7	0.95293	−88.4	−89.0
914.0	75.5	−51.9	0.86528	32.7	56.0
827.3	355.3	−257.7	0.91384	−206.0	−281.9
,124.6	−436.0	−269.7	1.02245	−285.3	−281.9
,110.5	−465.4	−260.3	1.12539	−338.2	−281.9
,304.9	−707.2	−299.6	1.20223	−411.4	−296.5
,842.6	−945.4	−310.6	1.00930	−316.2	−286.6
,861.6	−989.2	−239.3	0.95293	−218.1	−202.6

The period after 1974/75 saw an increase in state control over the copper industry and its vulnerability to political imperatives: during 1976–89, a different regime applies. No significance could be found for the copper price in the evolution of copper exports: instead, foreign exchange shortages, the increasing skills deficit, transport shocks and high taxation dominate. Foreign exchange rationing is proxied by the black-market premium; the skills shortage by the declining ratio of skilled expatriates to Zambian employees (for the most part, unskilled); transport shocks are captured by the supply/stocks ratio; and the dummy D8588 measures the impact of a temporary mineral export tax. In both regimes, the presence of lagged supply in the supply/stocks ratio captures the inertia of supply, given high fixed costs in the industry.

The determinants of copper exports in metric tonnes were estimated by non-linear least squares, using annual data from 1960 to 1989, and are given below in equation (8.1).[15]

$$\log X_t = \alpha(5.0 + 0.25 \log RER_{x_t} - 0.05 \log STOCKS_{t-1} + 0.10D69$$
$$(14.08) \qquad (4.40) \qquad\qquad (3.75) \qquad\qquad (1.77)$$
$$+ 0.12D72) + (1-\alpha)(6.11 - 0.18 \log q_t + 0.36 \log SKILLS_t$$
$$(2.25) \qquad\qquad (67.82) \quad (5.83) \qquad\qquad (7.09)$$
$$- 0.05 \log STOCKS_{t-1} - 0.17D8588), \qquad\qquad\qquad (8.1)$$
$$(3.75) \qquad\qquad (4.49)$$

where $\alpha = 1$ for 1960–75 and $\alpha = 0$ for 1976–89. $\bar{R}^2 = 0.91$; DW = 1.92; s.e. regression = 0.052; t-statistics in brackets.

Counterfactual export volumes were obtained from the fitted equation by iterative substitution (given the lag), where the 1960–63 average level of stocks and tax-corrected prices were assumed to hold in the absence of the boom or crash. The declining availability of expatriate skills was assumed to persist in the counterfactual, whereas the black-market premium was restricted to its 1970 figure of 34% (the earliest available data). The ratio of counterfactual to actual volumes then provides a correction factor which can be applied to the reported copper export values series to adjust for export price response.[16] Counterfactual copper export values were then generated as with the first quantity counterfactual, using the corrected terms of trade series.

The windfall in current prices for each counterfactual case is then the difference between actual and counterfactual export values. Deflation by the corrected import price index yields the real value of the boom in 1963 prices. In the case of the negative shock, the same procedures were followed for the two base periods of 1960–63 and 1971–74. The various windfall series are shown in Table 8.3. The constant-volume quantity counterfactual (columns 7 and 8) obviously results in a far smaller windfall than the case where export volumes are allowed to respond to prices (column 10) (this is reversed for the negative shock). For the positive shock these undiscounted windfall gains total K1,252m (column 8) and K1,554m (column 10), respectively. It is worth noting that the latter value exceeds by K1,000m the windfall gains where no corrections are made for overinvoicing and supply response (column 11).

The gain in permanent income due to the shocks, in the absence of a reliable estimate of the rate of return on domestic capital formation, is calculated with discount rates of 5%, 10% and 15% applied to the real annual gains. The results for the two different quantity counterfactuals and the various shocks are shown in Table 8.4. The present value of the boom in 1963 terms for the first quantity counterfactual, discounting at 10%, is K821m, which implies a permanent income increase over the decade of K75m, or one-fifth of the average 1960–63 GDP. The equivalent case for the negative shocks results in present values of −K519m in 1974 (using the 1963 base) and −K1,303m in 1974 (using the 1971–74 base), with permanent income decreases, respectively, of K47m and K119m.

Thus, the present value of the boom in 1963 is twice as large as the average 1960–63 GDP. The present value of the negative shocks in 1974 lies between one-quarter and three-quarters of the 1974 GDP, depending

Table 8.4. Present value of the shocks and permanent income changes

	Discount rate (%)	Present value (Km)	Permanent income change	
			(Km)	(% av. 1960–63 GDP)
1. *Positive shock* (1963 base)				
Case A	5	1,005.9	47.9	12
	10	821.2	74.7	18
	15	680.5	88.8	22
Case B	5	1,243.3	59.2	14
	10	1,015.0	92.3	22
	15	844.0	110.1	27
2. *Negative shock* (1963 base, 10% discount)				
Case A		−519.0	−47.2	12
Case B		−563.4	−51.2	12
3. *Negative shock* (av. 1971–74 base, 10% discount)				
Case A		−1,303.8	−118.5	29
Case B		−1,405.4	−127.8	31

Notes:
1. A uses the windfall corrected for overinvoicing, but assuming export volumes are unchanged
2. B uses the windfall corrected both for overinvoicing and the export supply price response, but assuming output expansion is costless

on the base employed. The huge size of these shocks is due to a combination of steep terms of trade changes and the extensive duration of the shocks.

8.3.2. *Characterisation of Copper Price Expectations*

Public and private agents' expectations concerning the incidence and the duration of both the positive price shock of 1964–74 and the subsequent negative shock are broadly classified here in terms of the Bevan *et al.* (1990b) taxonomy as 'exclusive' and 'unrevised'. This means that the incidence of both types of shock was inconsistent with prior expectations. Further, both were seen as transient phenomena. Several sources are employed here to lend support to this classification.

Expectations prior to 1974 Between 1956 and 1966, Zambian copper producers engaged in active intervention in the world copper market in order to stabilise the London Metal Exchange (LME) copper price, acting in concert with major world copper producers. Rising copper prices from 1964 were regarded with consternation by producers and government officials alike as potentially inducing substitution out of copper. Beginning in 1964, an attempt was made to stabilise the LME price, with Zambian and Chilean producers switching from LME pricing to pre-announced producer prices for their contract customers outside the USA. These were similar to the US producer price, and all were much lower than the LME price. In fact this had the effect of raising the LME price, and as the gap widened, large windfall profits were reaped by contract customers. The Chilean producer price was raised in 1966, and Zambia followed suit, in the hope of convergence on the LME price. However, an export tax of 40% on sales imposed by the government in 1966 to maximise revenue from a perceived copper windfall finally made producer pricing untenable, and it was abandoned in April of that year. In the late 1960s, supply shocks from civil unrest, strikes and transport difficulties in various producer countries caused further price rises. Once again, unsuccessful attempts were made to coordinate producers for the maintenance of price stability.

The public sector's expectations for short-term copper price changes can be gauged from disparities between realised mineral revenue and approved budgetary estimates. Up to 1973, only, budgetary estimates were based on mining companies' forecasts of profits: thus reported public expectations and those of the mining companies were coincident in this period. The period from 1959 to 1964 was one of relative stability in prices and there is no marked error of price estimation. Between 1964 and 1974 caution is apparent on the part of budget planners, who consistently underestimated the price.[17] Nevertheless, disparities between actual and estimated recurrent and capital expenditures suggest a 'ratchet effect' on government expenditure, with unsustainable rises in spending taking the form of current rather than capital expenditure.

The public sector's expectations for copper price changes over the medium term are suggested by assumptions employed in the first two National Development Plans. The First National Development Plan 1966–1970 (FNDP) based the financing of economy-wide planned investment up to 1970 on projections of copper exports, assuming an output of 800,000 long tons of copper, at a price of K600 per ton. Although production estimates were exaggerated, the shortfall in expected price compared to realised price more than compensated, and gross output exceeded plan targets. The Second National Development Plan 1972–1976 (SNDP) aimed to achieve production of 900,000 metric tons (*c.* 886 long tons) by 1976, based on investment to extend mining capacity. The SNDP price estimation, considered cautious, was K740 per tonne (15% below the realised average of the FNDP period). Once again, production was overestimated and the price underestimated.

Expectations after 1974 The World Bank's forecasts of the copper price were published from 1974 onwards; they track the expectations of external agents over the medium term and were probably influential in shaping producers' and governments' expectations. Projected and realised copper prices are compared in Table 8.5, from 1974 to 1980, and in real and nominal terms. The first series of forecasts in May 1974 are revealing in that they pre-date the precipitous fall in copper prices by one quarter. A small fall in prices was predicted for 1975, with a recovery by 1977 and a sharp increase thereafter. Although the projected prices were modified in the light of new information, successive years' predictions saw the price recovering to at least 70% of the 1964–74 real average by 1980. In fact it achieved little over 50% in real terms. The cost to Zambia of shortfalls from these predictions can be assessed for the 1975 case, using the 1974 predictions. The difference in export earnings would amount to US$690 million, a sensitivity of US$14 million per US cent shortfall.

The SNDP failed to anticipate the protracted decline in copper prices from 1974, stating explicitly that the copper price was expected to recover. This optimism was based on inflationary trends and monetary instability in Western countries, and on the increased costs of production of copper and consumption, forecast to rise by 4–5% annually. Another perspective on the Zambian producers' copper price expectations for the post-1974 period is lent by the cumulative copper stocks profile. Transport problems and inventory speculation may well be conflated in a number of these years, but there was a substantial accumulation in 1974, which suggests that the crash was unexpected.

Table 8.5. World Bank copper price projections versus actual prices
(*US cents/16*)

	1974	1975	1976	1977	1978	1979	1980
1. *Nominal price*							
Forecasts							
May 1974	110	105	107	109	117	125	135
May 1975	—	68	81	98	109	117	126
May 1976	—	—	67	80	104	112	120
May 1977	—	—	—	70	80	95	120
May 1978	—	—	—	—	62	68	85
Actual price	93	56	64	59	62	90	99
2. *Real price* (MUV deflated, 1974 prices)							
Forecasts							
May 1974	110	95	95	88	82	77	76
May 1975	—	61	72	79	77	73	71
May 1976	—	—	76	65	73	69	68
May 1977	—	—	—	57	56	59	68
May 1978	—	—	—	—	44	42	48
Actual price	93	50	57	48	44	56	55

Source: Calculated using World Bank forecasts from Gulhati (1989)

8.4. The Response of the Economy to the Trade Shocks

Various estimates of the windfall income resulting from the copper shocks
were presented in Table 8.3. In Section 8.4.1, savings or dissavings rates
out of windfall income are calculated by comparing realised rates of
saving with counterfactual rates based on extrapolation of behaviour in
the base period preceding the boom or crash. In Section 8.4.2, economic
outcomes during the boom and crash in Zambia are tested against the
predictions of temporary trade shock theory, conditional on the presence
of a control regime.

8.4.1. Asset Changes and Savings Rates

The overall savings rate is defined as the sum of rates of domestic gross
fixed asset formation and foreign asset accumulation. The calculations
are described for the case of the positive shock. Windfall investment in
domestic assets is estimated in Table 8.6 (column 7), as the difference
between actual real gross fixed capital formation (GFKF) and a counterfactual for real GFKF. The series for actual GFKF (column 3) is created by
multiplying a series for real income by actual propensities to acquire
GFKF out of income (column 1 multiplied by column 2). Real income here

Table 8.6. Actual and counterfactual capital formation

	Actuals			Counterfactuals			Windfall GFKF		
	GFKF/ income (%)	Real income (Km)	GFKF (Km)	Real income (Km)	GFKF/ income (%)	GFKF (Km)	Annual (Km)	Cumulative (Km)	Returns (Km)
	(1)	(2)	(3)	(4)	(5)	(6)	(7)	(8)	(9)
1. Positive shock (1960–63 base)									
1959	21.8	395.8	86.5	—	21.8	—	—	—	—
1960	17.8	446.7	79.7	—	17.8	—	—	—	—
1961	19.3	422.4	81.5	—	19.3	—	—	—	—
1962	18.0	426.1	76.6	—	18.0	—	—	—	—
1963	15.4	428.4	66.0	428.4	15.4	66.0	0.0	—	—
1964	15.2	494.8	75.1	485.6	15.2	73.7	1.4	1.4	0.1
1965	19.4	671.5	129.9	628.0	18.0	113.0	16.9	18.3	1.8
1966	22.9	760.7	174.5	600.9	18.0	108.2	66.4	84.7	8.5
1967	25.7	692.8	178.1	624.6	18.0	112.4	65.6	150.3	15.0
1968	27.1	876.8	237.4	634.4	18.0	114.2	123.2	273.5	27.4
1969	21.1	1,071.0	226.0	642.7	18.0	115.7	110.3	383.9	38.4
1970	27.8	964.4	267.8	653.4	18.0	117.6	150.2	534.0	53.4
1971	33.1	742.8	245.8	642.8	18.0	115.7	130.1	664.2	66.4
1972	33.0	759.7	250.8	693.9	18.0	124.9	125.9	790.1	79.0
1973	26.6	791.6	210.4	674.0	18.0	121.3	89.1	879.1	87.9
1974	26.5	800.3	212.3	715.9	18.0	128.9	83.4	962.5	96.3

Table 8.6. Continued

	Actuals			Counterfactuals			Windfall GFKF		
	GFKF/ income (%) (1)	Real income (Km) (2)	GFKF (Km) (3)	Real income (Km) (4)	GFKF/ income (%) (5)	GFKF (Km) (6)	Annual (Km) (7)	Cumulative (Km) (8)	Returns (Km) (9)
2. Negative shock (1960–63 base)									
1974	26.5	800.3	212.3	803.8	26.5	213.2	−0.9	—	—
1975	38.0	681.4	259.0	782.8	18.0	140.9	118.1	118.1	11.8
1976	23.5	724.8	170.1	816.8	18.0	147.0	23.1	141.2	14.1
1977	24.3	686.9	167.0	774.7	18.0	139.4	27.6	168.8	16.9
1978	19.4	629.2	122.2	735.0	18.0	132.3	−10.1	158.7	15.9
1979	16.9	695.4	117.6	805.7	18.0	145.0	−27.4	131.3	13.1
1980	18.2	704.7	128.4	789.3	18.0	142.1	−13.6	117.6	11.8
3. Negative shock (1971–74 base)									
1974	26.5	1,554	412.2	1,606	26.5	426.0	−13.8	—	—
1975	38.0	1,307	496.7	1,564	29.8	466.2	30.5	30.5	3.1
1976	23.5	1,386	325.3	1,653	29.8	492.5	−167.0	−137.0	−13.7
1977	24.3	1,316	320.0	1,590	29.8	473.8	−154.0	−290.0	−29.0
1978	19.4	1,203	233.5	1,532	29.8	456.4	−223.0	−513.0	−51.3
1979	16.9	1,331	225.1	1,693	29.8	504.5	−279.0	−793.0	−79.3
1980	18.2	1,364	248.6	1,683	29.8	501.5	−253.0	−1,046.0	−105.0

is the sum of real GDP in 1963 prices and a series for real windfall income (column 8 in Table 8.3). In order to calculate counterfactual GFKF (column 6), a real income counterfactual is required. This is GDP in 1963 prices, but corrected for a return on windfall investment, assumed to be 10%. A lag of one year in returns to investment of the previous year means that the first correction to real income is made in 1965, the second year of the boom.

The estimation of these returns (column 9) is by iterative substitution (given the lag) and employs a counterfactual series for the propensity to acquire GFKF out of income. The actual propensities for 1963 and 1964 were about 15%, compared with averages of 18% and 23% for 1960–62 and 1965–67, respectively. In the early 1960s, gross fixed capital formation was largely due to the government or mining companies; the dip probably reflects uncertainties and delays in the transition between the Federation (1953–63) and an independent Zambia (October 1964). Hence actual propensities for the aberrant years 1963 and 1964 were retained in the counterfactual, while the actual average propensity for 1960–62 was substituted for the boom years, 1965–74. Some support for the choice of the latter figure was obtained by the average propensities to acquire gross fixed capital for neighbouring countries: in the early post-independence years, 1965–70, average propensities were 15.9%, 16.0% and 17.1% for Tanzania, Malawi and Kenya, respectively. Given the mineral wealth endowment of Zambia, the higher figure of 18% appears plausible.

As would be expected for unplanned income, the resulting series for windfall investment during the boom displays a lagged response to positive changes in windfall income, while a lagged cut-back is apparent after the negative shocks of the early 1970s. Overall windfall investment from 1964 to 1974 was K962.5m, in 1963 prices.

The calculations for the negative shocks are identical. For the 1960–63 base, the first correction to GDP (1963 prices) for returns to windfall investment occurs in the second year of the negative shock, 1976. Using the 1971–74 base, the average annual 1971–74 propensity to GFKF out of income was employed as the counterfactual propensity for 1975–80. Here GDP is in 1971–74 average prices; the first correction for windfall investment again falls in 1976. Both windfall GFKF series display a lagged response to the fall in income, but a rapid decline thereafter. The cumulative size of windfall GFKF for 1975–80 was K117.6m, in 1963 prices, and −K1,046m in 1971–74 average prices.

The windfall in foreign assets during 1964–74, at 1963 prices, is estimated in Table 8.7 (column 5). The calculations are described for the case of the positive shock but are identical for the negative shock (adjusting for the different bases). Foreign asset accumulation (repayment of debt) is proxied by the surplus of exports of goods and services over imports of goods and services, deflated by the import price index corrected for overinvoicing. The actual propensity to accumulate foreign assets out of

Table 8.7. Actual and counterfactual foreign asset accumulation

	Foreign savings propensity (%)		Foreign savings (Km, 1963 prices)			Increase in stocks (Km)
	Actual (1)	Counterfactual (2)	Actual (3)	Counterfactual (4)	Windfall (5)	(6)
1. *Positive shock* (1960–63 base)						
1959	15.6	15.6	61.3	—	—	−2.4
1960	18.5	18.5	78.4	—	—	23.4
1961	14.2	14.2	60.2	—	—	18.8
1962	12.0	12.0	50.2	—	—	17.8
1963	17.5	17.5	74.8	74.8	—	9.0
1964	28.2	15.5	136.9	75.3	61.6	−18.8
1965	16.5	15.5	103.9	97.3	6.6	35.5
1966	17.5	15.5	105.2	93.1	12.1	50.4
1967	6.5	15.5	41.4	96.8	−55.4	48.9
1968	10.8	15.5	70.4	98.3	−28.0	56.0
1969	63.0	15.5	421.8	99.6	322.2	−39.4
1970	25.2	15.5	174.1	101.3	72.9	−11.5
1971	−2.5	15.5	−17.1	99.6	−117.0	47.4
1972	1.7	15.5	12.6	107.6	−94.9	31.4
1973	14.9	15.5	112.5	104.5	8.1	42.0
1974	7.2	15.5	57.8	111.0	−53.2	190.0
2. *Negative shock* (1960–63 base)						
1974	7.2	7.2	57.8	57.8	0.0	190.0
1975	−13.5	15.5	−106.0	121.3	−227.0	40.0
1976	3.4	15.5	28.1	126.6	−98.5	6.5
1977	−1.7	15.5	−13.6	120.1	−134.0	7.0
1978	−2.0	15.5	−15.1	113.9	−129.0	100.0
1979	4.5	15.5	37.0	124.9	−87.9	−74.0
1980	−1.8	15.5	−14.0	122.3	−136.0	55.0
3. *Negative shock* (1971–74 base)						
1974	7.6	7.6	122.6	122.6	0.0	190.0
1975	−14.3	4.9	−224.0	76.7	−301.0	40.0
1976	3.6	4.9	59.6	81.0	−21.4	6.5
1977	−1.8	4.9	−28.8	77.9	−107.0	7.0
1978	−2.1	4.9	−32.0	75.0	−107.0	100.0
1979	4.8	4.9	78.5	83.0	−4.5	−74.0
1980	−1.9	4.9	−29.8	82.5	−112.0	55.0

Source: MDOS

real income is given in column (1). A counterfactual is then constructed by substituting the average 1959–63 actual propensity for all the subsequent years 1964–74 (the 1963 figure is not aberrant relative to earlier values). Counterfactual foreign asset accumulation is the product of counterfactual real income (Table 8.3, column 6) and the constructed counterfactual.

Table 8.8. Present discounted value of windfall saving and income (*1963 prices*)

	Discount rate (%)	GFKF	Foreign assets (Km)	Permanent savings (Km)	Net saving (Km)	Total gain (Km)	(Dis)saving rate (%)
1. Positive shock (1960–63 base)							
Case A	5	720.6	140.1	139.3	721.4	1,005.9	71.7
	10	553.8	136.8	101.4	589.2	821.2	71.8
	15	435.7	130.0	75.6	490.1	680.5	72.0
Case B	5	781.3	143.8	151.6	773.4	1,243.3	62.2
	10	601.6	139.4	110.6	630.4	1,015.0	62.1
	15	474.6	131.9	82.7	523.8	844.0	62.1
Case C	5	781.3	572.2	178.3	1,175.2	1,243.3	94.5
	10	601.6	481.7	131.6	951.8	1,015.0	93.8
	15	474.6	408.8	99.3	784.1	844.0	92.9
2. Negative shock (1960–63 base, 10% discount)							
Case A		127.1	−668.6	14.7	−556.2	−519.0	(107.2)
Case B		121.0	−668.6	14.7	−562.2	−563.4	(99.8)
Case C		121.0	−583.6	16.3	−478.9	−563.4	(85.0)
3. Negative shock (1971–74 base, 10% discount)							
Case A		−763.8	−561.5	−37.1	−1,288.2	−1,303.8	(98.8)
Case B		−777.8	−561.5	−37.1	−1,302.1	−1,405.4	(92.7)
Case C		−777.8	−440.3	−36.0	−1,181.8	−1,405.4	(84.1)

Notes:
1. A uses the windfall corrected for misinvoicing, but assuming export volumes are unchanged. All illegally acquired dollars from overinvoicing are assumed to be spent abroad or on smuggled goods
2. B uses the windfall corrected both for misinvoicing and the export supply price response, but assuming output expansion is costless. Again, all smuggled dollars are spent
3. C as in B, except that all smuggled dollars are saved

The windfall is then the difference between the actual and counterfactual series (1963 prices); the series responds with a lag to windfall income. The cumulated net increase in foreign assets due to the positive shock is K135m. Total windfall assets in 1964–74 thus amount to K1,097.5m, in 1963 prices.

The equivalent figures for the negative shock period are cumulated net foreign assets of −K812.4m (1960–63 base) and −K652.9m (1971–74 base), with total windfall assets of −K694.8m (1960–63 base) and −K1,698.9m (1971–74 base).

Calculations of various windfall savings rates are shown in Table 8.8. Net windfall savings are the difference between the discounted present value of total windfall assets and the discounted present value of permanent savings out of windfall investment income. Permanent savings are calculated as the product of the overall counterfactual savings propensity (GFKF plus foreign assets) and the cumulated series of returns to investment (Table 8.6, column 9). Three different savings estimates are given for the positive shock in Table 8.8; they do not prove sensitive to the rates of discount used. Employing the windfall estimate corrected for overinvoicing, but not copper supply response, yields a savings rate of about 72% (case A). The larger windfall estimate, correcting both for misinvoicing and the copper supply response, but neglecting costs of expanding copper supply, lowers the savings rate to 62% (case B). This constitutes the lower bound for windfall savings out of Zambia's copper boom. In both cases the reasonable assumption employed is that all misinvoiced foreign exchange is spent on smuggled goods and not saved. The other boundary assumption, where all misinvoiced foreign exchange is assumed saved, raises the savings rate to over 90% (case C), an upper bound for windfall savings. It appears reasonable, therefore, to use the rate for case A when disaggregating into public and private sector savings rates (Section 8.5). The various savings rates are sizeable, lending support to the earlier characterisation of unrevised and exclusive expectations during the boom.

For the negative shock, there are very high and similar dissavings rates for both the bases employed, and all three cases considered above (where the expected reversed size order of savings rates are obtained). Here too the expectations characterisation of Section 8.3.2 is reinforced by the magnitude of dissaving relative to the income shock.

8.4.2. *Structural Change: Relative Price, Output and Factor Trends*

Dutch Disease theory predicts that the booming tradables sector will expand output and attract labour through higher wages, causing a contraction of the non-booming tradables sector. However, the mining share of real GDP in Zambia contracted steadily between 1965 and 1980. Real value-added per annum declined during the boom period (by 4.7% over 1965–70, and 0.5% over 1971–74), and fell a further 1.5% between 1975 and 1980. Annual production fluctuated between 586,000 and 748,000 tonnes in the period, but showed no upward trend (the production projections of FNDP and SNDP proved hopelessly unrealistic). A number of controls and exogenous constraints explain the deterioration in performance prior to the 1974 copper price shock. Production costs rose sharply, with increased labour costs, falling productivity and declining ore grades. The transport shock at Rhodesia's declaration of UDI caused the costly diversion of exports routes, vastly increased inventory holdings, and induced delays and shortages. A further setback was the flooding of the Mufulira mine in 1970. Moreover, frequent changes in mineral policy, including nationalisation of the mines in 1970, created an uncertain business environment.

The rate of capital accumulation in the already capital-intensive mining industry was not especially high during the boom; but a rising capital–output ratio in the face of declining output increased production costs, giving rise to an unfavourable incremental capital–output ratio (ICOR) of −2.7 (1965–73). Capital intensity continued to increase from 1974, as evidenced by rising capital–labour ratios. Where the booming sector is capital-intensive mining, the resource movement effect (RME) is likely to be small. However, employment elasticities for mining reflect positive employment growth, despite the decline in output (the ambitious employment goals of the FNDP and SNDP were met). Rapid 'Zambianisation' of the labour force, with inadequate training for the transition, was partly responsible, together with increased overhead labour. Further, state ownership of the mines from 1970 saw maintenance of excess employment imposed as one of the objectives of mineral policy. Unsurprisingly, therefore, labour–output ratios rose from 1964 to 1980 (labour productivity fell). Mining wages rose in the late 1960s (tending to drive other wage changes) but decreased in real terms after 1970. The net result was a sharp increase in labour costs.

The non-booming tradables sector is predicted to decline as the boom progresses. Conventionally this occurs by squeezing manufacturing; but in Zambia, non-mineral exports were largely agricultural. Maize, tobacco and a few manufactured goods constituted an average of 2.7% of total exports during the boom years, falling in value from K14.5m to K5.5m between 1965 and 1970, and to an average of around K5m during 1975–78 (1965 prices). It is possible that a 'Dutch Disease'-type effect was operative; but contributory were the uncertain political environment and poor business confidence in an expatriate-dominated sector with transport and pricing problems. The sectoral share of real GDP remained virtually constant from independence to 1980, with low average growth during the boom (1.7% over 1965–70, and 2.4% 1971–74) and in 1975–80 (0.8%).[18] There was little growth of employment, and real wages declined sharply after 1970. The frequent policy declarations concerning agricultural development for diversification were largely rhetorical: in fact, few resources were devoted to the sector. Further, production incentives decreased and real farming incomes fell as a consequence of government controls on producer prices for various agricultural products, set well below world or border prices. The rural–urban terms of trade thus fell to 86.6 in 1970 and 80.5 by 1976 (1965 = 100), and rapid urbanisation resulted (increasing from 20.5% to 35.3%, 1963–74). To the extent that 'Dutch Disease' was operative, migration may be indicative of a negative RME.

Far from de-industrialisation occurring, the protected importables sector, manufacturing, grew dramatically from a low base. An additional catalyst for growth was provided by the sanctions imposed against Rhodesia after UDI in 1965 (S. Rhodesia had previously supplied around 40% of Zambia's imports). During the boom, real value-added manufacturing grew at 11.2% (1965–70) and 8.8% (1971–74), turning negative in 1975–80, at −1.1%. The share of real GDP rose from 6.8% in 1965 to an average 12% over 1971–74. A strong impetus was lent to manufacturing growth by the increased public share after 1968. By 1972, parastatal manufacturing constituted 53% of total manufacturing output, largely concentrated in essential goods and natural resources.[19]

However, the nature of manufacturing growth as fashioned by economic controls ultimately did not serve the oft-stated objective of diversification. Manufacturing saw the highest sectoral rate of capital accumulation, averaging 30.5% per annum in 1965–72 (real investment quadrupled). Capital and import intensity were encouraged by zero duties on capital goods, low interest rates, favourable tax treatment (investment credit and generous depreciation allowances) and the overvalued real effective exchange rate. In consequence, the capital–labour ratio quadrupled by 1974 and continued to rise in 1975–80 (although annual real investment halved). The capital–output ratio also grew strongly, with the ICOR rising from less than 2 in 1966/67 to 3.5 by 1971/72. High ICORs are due both to capital intensity and underutilization of capacity. The firms with the highest investment (parastatals) were also the most capital intensive, and had the highest (or negative) ICORs. Capacity utilisation in parastatal manufacturing ranged between 40% and 70%, in the second phase of the boom, and was around 50% by 1980 (attributable to delays in investment and scarcity of foreign exchange).

Given that trade controls impart a certain non-tradability to the importables sector, a large RME would be expected. However, employment growth was limited by the tendency towards capital intensity, expanding at the rate of 10.3% (1965–70) and 2.8% (1971–74) during the boom, and at 2.7% in 1975–80. Real wages growth was high in 1965–70, but declined in 1970–74. Productivity rose quite dramatically from independence: by 1974, value-added per worker had increased by almost 70%. Further, the discrepancy with wages growth was less than in other sectors, so that labour costs rose less strongly. After 1974, however, despite capital deepening, productivity fell (especially in the parastatal sector). Overall manufacturing factor productivity growth during 1965–80 was −3.8.

The negative shock thus impinged on a large but capital- and import-intensive industrial sector, causing a sharp contraction. Parastatal firms experiencing falling profitability were further damaged by the maintenance of price controls, despite rapidly rising inflation.

Trends for services (the non-tradable consumption sector) confirm the theory's predictions of a rapid expansion: real sectoral GDP growth rivalled manufacturing growth, and the sectoral share increased by 50% between 1965 and 1976. Limited and poorly enforced price controls did not much constrain the expansion of non-tradables during the boom. Capital accumulation was more moderate in services, and capital–labour ratios rose modestly, save in the 1970s. The theory predicts a positive RME for services, giving an indirect impetus to contraction of the non-booming tradables sector. Indeed, the highest sectoral employment growth occurred in services, at 6.2% in the first phase of the boom, 4.2% in the second phase, and 3.4% over 1975–80. Real wages rose strongly in the first phase of the boom and fell in the second. Productivity actually rose from 1965 but failed to keep pace with wage increases, implying rising labour costs.

Relative price movements conform to predictions for the sector. In Figure 8.4, proxies for the prices of non-tradable goods are plotted relative

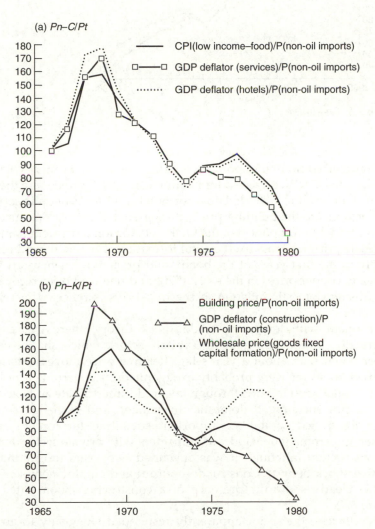

Figure 8.4. Non-tradable relative price changes (*1966 = 100*)
Source: Author's calculations using the *Monthly Digest of Statistics* (CSO) for Zambia

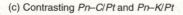

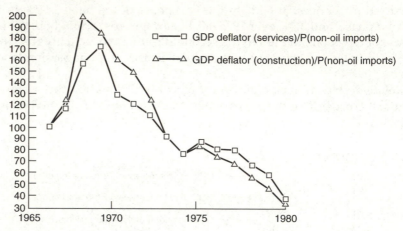

Figure 8.4. *Continued*

to a constructed non-oil import price index, corrected for misinvoicing.[20] Pt is the non-oil IUV, corrected for misinvoicing. $Pn\text{-}C$ proxies are the low-income CPI and the GDP deflators for hotels and for economic services. $Pn\text{-}K$ proxies are the building price (disaggregated and reconstructed to remove tradable components), the GDP deflator for construction and the wholesale price for gross fixed capital formation. The relative indices rise sharply in the first years of the boom, and price movements mirror the setback in copper prices in the early 1970s and renewed price recovery of 1973. Rising domestic inflation in the mid-1970s is reflected in relative price rises.

Consonant with temporary trade shock theory, there was a large construction boom (non-tradable capital sector), which shadowed the copper boom with about a year's lag. Relative price movements in the construction sector were probably exaggerated by government policies. Cheap capital good imports through tax, trade, interest rate and exchange rate policies encouraged domestic investment, and exchange controls made non-traded capital an important substitute for foreign assets. Further, government demand was coincident with private sector demand for construction (although it was sustained two years longer into the negative shock period). Construction output and employment series for Zambia clearly show the presence of a construction boom after 1963 (Figure 8.5).[21]

Nevertheless, the sector apparently responded sluggishly to government demand and created insufficient employment in the ten-year boom. Dominated by foreign firms in a climate of lowered business confidence in

(a) Employment in the construction industry

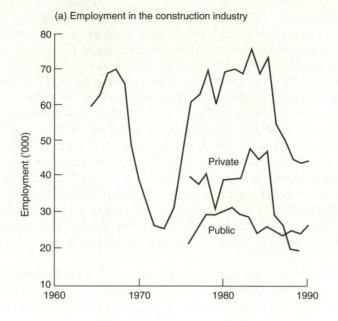

(b) Construction output of private contractors

Figure 8.5. Construction boom: output and employment trends

Note: Deflator in part (b) is the building price index.

Source: *Monthly Digest of Statistics*.

the 1960s, there was real growth of construction value-added until 1970 of 7.9%; in the second phase of the copper boom this fell to 6.3%. The government's development programme fluctuated as a function of the availability of foreign exchange and budgetary resources; thus, given the predominance of government demand in construction, investors maintained low capacity and inventories. Further, the import content of total construction costs in 1976, virtually unchanged from 1964, was about 30%. Import lags from 1965 owing to transport difficulties, and to fluctuations in the availability of foreign exchange in the 1970s, prevented a flexible response to demand. Economic controls favoured increasing capital intensity (as evidenced by pronounced increases in capital–labour ratios). This limited the expected large RME in construction, although there was positive employment growth in both phases of the boom. The growth rate of capital stock was high during the boom (18.5%), but both capital–output and labour–output ratios rose, implying declining efficiency and increased production costs. The very high ICOR for construction of 18.8 (1965–73) is attributable to the increased capital intensity and underutilisation of capacity, resulting from delays in investment and import shortages. The overall sectoral share of real GDP during 1965–80 was 6%.

Relative prices mirror the trends in construction employment and output. The price ratios of three possible proxies for non-tradable capital goods prices relative to the non-oil import price index (corrected for misinvoicing) are shown in Figure 8.4.[22] The ratio rises sharply from 1966, and begins to fall in the 1970s with a slower rate of change; the fall is attenuated in 1973/4, and thereafter the ratio falls steadily for the value-added price ratio. For the other two proxies, building price and wholesale price inflation cause a rise in relative prices to 1977, when the trend reverses. The more rapid escalation and decline of the relative prices of non-tradable capital as against non-tradable consumption are also shown in Figure 8.4. The pattern is in conformity with the specification of expectations of both shocks. Expectations of temporarily high copper prices during the boom, and of temporarily low prices in the slump, are reflected in the pronounced construction boom and its rapid fall-off relative to consumption (there is a lag). However, the relative price fall-off in the construction sector does display the expected asymmetry.

8.5. Public Management of the Trade Shocks

The copper price predictions which are implicit in the annual budgetary figures for estimated mineral revenue suggest that public sector expectations (and those of the copper companies) were 'exclusive' and 'unrevised' for both types of shock. That is, price changes appear to have been unexpected and seen as impermanent. However, despite cautious revenue predictions during 1964–74, rapid rises in public expenditure were driven by ambitious development plans and political expectations. By the early 1970s, when mineral revenue declined with lower copper prices and an altered tax regime, expenditure had significantly outpaced revenue. Thereafter, the 'unrevised' nature of expectations is manifest in the public expenditure boom from 1974, sustained largely by domestic borrowing. The fiscal pattern is discussed in Section 8.5.1, where a simple budgetary counterfactual is constructed to assess the impact of the shocks. The overall savings rate out of windfall income is disaggregated into its public and private components in Section 8.5.2.

8.5.1. *Revenue Instability and the Government Expenditure Boom*

The composition of government revenue was completely altered across the positive and negative trade shocks. The government's view was that copper prices were only temporarily high during the boom, and there was concern over the excessive budgetary dependence on mining. This resulted in a relatively successful drive to broaden the tax base after 1970, which partially compensated for the decline in mineral revenue. Table 8.9 reveals the dominant contribution to total recurrent revenue of mineral tax in the boom years and equally its substitution by sales, excise and customs taxes with the fall in copper prices. Non-mineral revenue expressed as a proportion of current GDP rose from 8.3% in 1965/66 to a peak of 25.1% in 1977, while total revenue was identical in these two years at 25.1% (columns 2 and 3). The increased contribution of non-mineral taxes from 1970 was due to improved collection, extended coverage and increased rates on various existing taxes, and to the introduction of a 10% sales tax on imports. The bulk of revenue collection fell on the tradables sector in 1964–80, where tradable revenue is defined as mineral revenue plus customs, sales and excise taxes (these taxes applied principally to importables).

Despite diversification of the tax base, instability in total revenue was not avoided. Until 1970, the system of taxing production by royalties and the copper export tax had guaranteed a basic level of revenue, which smoothed the revenue stream. In the second phase of the boom until 1974, however, revenue fluctuated by up to 10 percentage points of GDP (column 3). The tax system altered in 1970: a mineral tax on profits replaced the production-based taxes, and 100% deduction of the year's capital expenditures at cost was allowed. The new tax regime and lower copper prices caused mineral revenue to halve in 1971 and again in 1972, and the decline was compounded by slower growth of non-mineral revenue. Total revenue recovered with higher copper prices by 1974 to 34% of GDP. Thereafter there was a steady decline to 22% in 1979, a fall of 40% from the boom peak, with reduced volatility due to negligible dependence on the mineral sector.

Although revenue estimations were consistently cautious in the boom years, higher than expected copper prices nevertheless fuelled pressures

Table 8.9. The fiscal pattern at factor cost (*percentage of GDP*)

| | Revenue | | | Recurrent expenditure | | | Capital expenditure | Total expenditure | Net lending | Surplus | Financing | |
| | Mineral | Other | Total | Constitutional and statutory | Other | Total | | | | | Domestic | Foreign |
	(1)	(2)	(3)	(4)	(5)	(6)	(7)	(8)	(9)	(10)	(11)	(12)
1964/65	—	—	29.4	2.3	11.9	14.2	2.3	24.6	1.4	3.4	—	—
1965/66	16.7	8.3	25.0	4.4	10.8	15.2	5.4	20.6	0.8	3.5	—	—
1966/67	17.1	11.1	28.2	4.0	15.6	19.5	8.6	28.1	4.2	-4.1	—	—
1968	16.6	11.4	28.0	3.6	16.6	20.2	16.8	36.9	1.0	-9.9	8.1	1.9
1969	17.9	12.8	30.7	3.2	14.0	17.2	8.2	25.4	2.6	2.7	-4.3	1.6
1970	20.6	16.9	37.6	5.8	15.5	21.4	8.2	29.6	6.1	1.9	-3.0	1.1
1971	9.6	16.7	26.3	9.1	18.4	27.5	13.0	40.6	2.0	-16.4	13.3	3.0
1972	4.1	17.9	22.0	9.6	14.8	24.4	7.7	32.1	3.0	-13.1	11.9	1.1
1973	6.8	22.7	29.5	7.5	15.8	23.3	6.1	29.5	16.8	-16.7	7.5	9.2
1974	18.0	16.2	34.3	8.7	13.5	22.1	6.0	28.1	2.9	3.4	-5.3	2.0
1975	3.8	24.5	28.3	16.3	18.3	34.5	8.3	42.8	7.9	-21.5	17.8	3.7
1976	0.6	23.3	23.9	12.2	17.4	29.7	6.5	36.1	2.5	-14.2	12.7	1.6
1977	-0.1	25.1	25.1	13.2	16.3	29.5	6.0	35.5	4.4	-13.1	12.2	1.0
1978	0.0	24.7	24.7	12.2	13.4	25.6	4.1	29.7	10.3	-14.4	13.5	0.9
1979	-0.4	22.7	22.3	10.2	16.9	27.1	3.4	30.4	2.0	-9.1	3.9	5.2
1980	1.4	23.6	25.0	12.9	20.1	33.0	4.0	37.0	7.3	-18.6	9.7	8.8

Notes:
1. The financial years of 1964/65 and 1965/66 run from July to June, while the 1966/67 data were annualised from an eighteen-month period beginning in July 1966; thereafter the data are on a calendar-year basis.
2. 'Mineral Revenue' covers copper and other metals, and includes income tax, various mineral export taxes, witholding taxes and dividends
3. 'Constitutional and statutory' expenditure comprises interest payments on the public debt, defence expenditure and pensions

Sources: GFS (IMF) (1972 onwards); *International Financial Statistics* (IMF); *National Accounts* (1954–64); *Monthly Digest of Statistics*; Financial Reports (1964/65 onwards)

for expenditure increases. Overshooting approved expenditure was the norm. Striking changes in the fiscal pattern are shown in Table 8.9 (expressed as a percentage of GDP at factor cost).

The relative size of the Zambian budget, or total expenditure (column 8), almost doubled between 1965 and 1971 to 41%, although it was curtailed somewhat with the fall in revenue in the second phase of the boom. Average real annual growth of expenditure was 19.3% in 1965–70, falling to 4.8% during 1970–74. This measure of growth fell to −4.5% for 1975–80, but very high levels of expenditure persisted, the average annual size of total expenditure being 35% of GDP. Capital expenditure (column 7) bore the brunt of expenditure cuts with the revenue shocks, the major part of recurrent expenditure (column 6) not being amenable to short-term alteration. Capital formation had risen strongly from a low base in 1964, but by 1974 comprised much the same percentage share of GDP as in 1965 (column 7). By contrast, in 1975 relative consumption had doubled. The late 1970s reveal drastic reductions in capital expenditure, but continued high consumption.

The source of growth in recurrent expenditure may be shown straightforwardly by disaggregation into two components: 'constitutional and statutory expenditure' (column 4) and 'other recurrent expenditure' (column 5). The former includes pensions, defence and public debt service; the latter is predominantly civil servants' salaries, consumer subsidies, health, education, transport and other services, and non-capital development (agricultural extension services). Strong growth occurred in constitutional and statutory expenditure during the 1960s and in the 1970s. By the late 1970s, as a percentage of GDP, this category was three times larger than its 1965–70 average. Apart from the increace in defence expenditure in the midst of warring countries, the main cause was a rapid rise in government debt, compounded by higher interest rates and shortening maturity periods.

Whereas the two categories showed similar real rates of growth until 1970, other recurrent expenditure showed little growth in the 1970s (it was sustained at an average of 17% of GDP during 1975–80). Nevertheless, consumer subsidies and civil servants' salaries fell in real terms, and there were serious reductions in government services. Another component of budgetary expenditure which showed rapid growth was net lending (including short term): this has not been included under total expenditure, but as a separate item (column 9). This growth is mostly accounted for by the parastatal sector, which was aided by the state with extensive loans on generous terms (most of which were not repaid), and by increased state equity capital holdings.

The public expenditure boom, coupled with the instability of revenue, led to periodic budget crises (column 10). The country ran a budget surplus during the first phase of the boom, except for the two years following the closure of the borders after UDI, when severe transport constraints limited exports. Net foreign assets rose from 21% to 31% of GDP during 1965–70. Thereafter, except for 1974, the country ran a budget deficit. The average size of the deficit from 1971 to 1980 (excluding 1974) was 15% of GDP.

The deficits were initially financed by drawing down foreign assets, and then mainly by short-term domestic borrowing. Foreign assets fell sharply after 1970, turning negative in 1975. Limited use was made of domestic borrowing in 1965–70. However, with the imbalances in 1971 and 1972, credit to the private sector was officially constrained, and government borrowing soared. This trend was reversed with higher copper prices in 1973/74. But in the downswing, with foreign assets largely depleted, the government resorted again to the banking system. Short-term borrowing, as a percentage of total domestic borrowing, rose from 46% in 1972 to a maximum of 90% in 1978, and money supply growth increased sharply, accelerating inflation. Except for 1973 and 1979/80, foreign financing of the budget deficit remained at a low level.

Having described the fiscal pattern, it would be interesting to ascertain what proportion of the expenditure changes and induced deficit is attributable to fluctuating mineral revenue. However, there were dramatic shifts in political priorities and hence the economic policy regime with independence, which coincided with the onset of the copper boom, and these preclude the derivation of a policy-neutral counterfactual. Further, the budget received a number of positive revenue shocks quite apart from elevated copper prices. Dissolution of the Federation freed revenue worth about K20m a year. Mineral royalties, enjoyed by the British South Africa company for over thirty years, were transferred to the government a few hours before independence. These were worth K42m in 1964/65. Restructuring the tax system in 1964 increased income tax returns from large companies and private individuals and saw a huge rise in revenue from customs duties (all totalling K90m in 1964/65). Revenue also increased in April 1966 with the abandonment by the copper companies of producer pricing. Thus, although realised revenue doubled in 1967, and by 1970 was treble the 1963 figure, this was not all due to the copper boom.

Hence there is no obvious budgetary counterfactual for the transitional period, and 1963 and 1964 are best treated as aberrant years. A possible counterfactual, which suffers from the fact that the boom is already in progress, is to apply the fiscal pattern of 1965/66 to subsequent years. Presumably new political and economic priorities would be reflected in the year's spending patterns, while other revenue shocks would by then have been absorbed. A counterfactual case is constructed by applying the 1965/66 fiscal pattern to the counterfactual GDP series from Table 8.3.[23] Differences between the actual and counterfactual fiscal series may be

Table 8.10. Fiscal changes owing to the boom (*Km, 1963 prices*)

	Revenue	Consumption	Capital expenditure	Total exhaustive expenditure	Exhaustive surplus
	(1)	(2)	(3)	(4)	(5)
1965	40.4	−0.1	−18.9	−19.1	59.5
1966	40.0	17.2	8.7	25.9	14.1
1967	39.4	40.3	25.5	65.8	−26.5
1968	86.7	76.8	112.6	189.4	−102.7
1969	168.1	80.6	53.3	133.9	34.2
1970	198.9	79.1	43.8	122.9	76.0
1971	35.0	67.2	62.0	129.2	−94.2
1972	−6.0	37.7	20.6	58.3	−64.3
1973	64.9	52.4	12.0	64.4	0.5
1974	95.6	30.3	8.9	39.2	56.3
1975	21.2	50.3	19.2	69.6	−48.4
1976	−6.4	48.5	8.0	56.6	−63.0
1977	3.5	39.3	4.8	44.1	−40.6
1978	−2.9	15.7	−8.5	7.2	−10.1
1979	−20.2	41.5	−14.7	26.8	−47.0
1980	5.0	67.7	−8.8	58.9	−53.9

Notes: Government consumption is here defined as current expenditure less constitutional and statutory expenditure, which largely comprises transfers, but unfortunately also includes defence spending. Defence figures are not published throughout the period, so disaggregation was not possible. Further, net lending is not considered

regarded as resulting from the trade shocks and are shown in Table 8.10. To emphasise the relatively unmalleable nature of a large part of public expenditure, the expenditure category considered is exhaustive expenditure (public consumption and gross fixed capital formation), and transfers (domestic and foreign interest payments and unrequited transfers) are excluded. This brings out public sector spending on labour in the periods of the two shocks. The expected changes in revenue are apparent. The strong influence of the boom on capital expenditure before 1971 is seen, with sharp reductions suffered thereafter, particularly beyond 1975 (column 3). The increase in recurrent expenditure is striking, with a slow decline beyond the boom relative to that of capital expenditure (column 2). Finally, the pattern of the exhaustive surplus (column 5) is closely linked to the terms of trade.

Were there any policy measures the government could have taken to ameliorate the deterioration in the public finances? There are at least two possibilities, neither of which is uncontroversial nor without implementational difficulties. The first concerns the nature of mineral taxation, where there are two opposing schools of thought. Garnaut and

Ross (1983) oppose the taxation of production because of the disincentive effects on investment and the potentially distortionary nature of extraction, and these criticisms were recognised by commentators at the time. However, Conrad *et al.* (1990) conclude that no one revenue instrument is superior for mineral-dependent developing countries, and that as resource owner and tax collector, a government may require multiple tax instruments. Under the prevailing tax regime, which included over-generous capital allowances, mineral revenue was substantially reduced from 1970, and absolutely negligible from 1975 to 1983. Given the sustained level of non-tax revenue in this time, it is difficult to accept that more tax could not have been paid by the copper companies. A related point is that the deterioration in performance of the companies after 1975, in comparison with international competitors, was in large part due to inadequate safeguards against political manipulation under state ownership in a one-party state.[24]

A second significant failing was the lack of an institutionalised framework to stabilise volatile mineral revenue. An example of such a framework is provided by the Chilean Stabilisation Fund, instituted in 1986. Revenue is placed in the fund when world copper prices exceed the predicted base price. Only a percentage of this revenue is available to the government. If the actual price is less than the base price, the mechanism operates in reverse. One advantage of such a framework is the efficient phasing of the quantity and quality of investment. Rather than an abundance of low-yielding projects in the boom, and a paucity of high-yielding projects in years of low prices, investment is stabilised across the shocks. The process still relies on conservative estimation of the copper price, however. The case for a stabilisation fund in Zambia has been examined by Bell (1983). Again the point is made that highly accurate medium-term predictions of revenue and expenditure aggregates are required; indeed the simulations were carried out using actual financial data, implying perfect foresight on the part of the authorities. Under these assumptions, and for varying rules governing the operation of the fund, the short-term borrowing requirements were found to be smoothed from 1966 to 1981, reducing the absolute sizes of deficits and surpluses. However, every simulation saw the fund exhausted by 1981.

8.5.2. Derivation of the Public Sector Savings Rate

The overall savings rate out of windfall income can be disaggregated into public and private sector components using Table 8.10 with the boom-induced fiscal changes, Tables 8.6–8.8 on overall asset changes, and Table 8.3 on the size of the overall windfall income. First, the changes in public and private asset holdings are estimated. The total annual cumulative windfall in gross fixed capital formation during the boom was calculated as K963m (Table 8.6, column 8). Of this, the government's cumulated share was K329m or 34% (Table 8.10, column 3) less the cumulative decline in the exhaustive surplus induced by the boom, K47m (Table 8.10, column 5). Thus, public assets rose by K282m. The increase in private asset holdings is calculated as the sum of residual GFKF assets (K963m − K282m) and the cumulative reduction in indebtedness, K135m (Table 8.7, column 5), which equals K816m.

The total windfall in income is the sum of the cumulative undiscounted real windfall income, K1,253m (Table 8.3, column 8), and the cumulated return on invested windfall assets, K474.2m (Table 8.6, column 9), which equals K1,727m. The portion of this income windfall which accrued to the public sector in increased revenue is K763m (Table 8.10, the cumulated sum of column 1), or 44%. Thus, the public sector savings rate out of boom income is 37% (K282m/K763m). The private sector savings rate is derived as a residual, and is 85% (K816m/(K1,727m − K763m)).[25] Both these savings rates are exaggerated by virtue of the budgetary counterfactual employed. The choice of this counterfactual was justified in the previous section, but underestimates both the extent of the revenue increase and, probably to a greater extent, the increase in public sector gross fixed capital formation. Nevertheless, a high value of the private savings rate is expected given the perceived transient nature of the boom, and this was compounded by exchange and trade controls during the boom, which both limited consumption possibilities and enhanced the size of domestic investment. By contrast, the government's saving performance was poor. A very large part of the income gain was transferred through subsidies, salaries, pensions and low-interest loans to the government's political constituency, the core of which comprised urban consumers, the huge state-owned sector and the army. The entrenched nature of these transfers in the face of shocks ultimately contributed to macroeconomic instability.[26]

8.6. Conclusions

Zambia presents an extreme case: an undiversified and landlocked economy, exhibiting extraordinarily high mineral dependence (even by LDC standards), and subject to external shocks and transport shocks in the first decade of independence. At the same time, the prevailing socialist ideology emphasised state intervention and extensive economic controls. Nonetheless, there are some useful lessons from the Zambian experience.

The challenge facing the government at independence was managing a limited mineral resource for sustainable economic diversification, in the midst of copper price shocks. There were several reasons why it was costly to delay diversification: first, there were limited extractable reserves; second, the geology of deposits made it inevitable that mining costs would increase sharply over time; finally, copper prices were unusually buoyant from the early 1960s. This chapter has shown that the inappropriate economic control regime instituted from 1964 distorted sectoral growth and actually enhanced the vulnerability of the economy to trade shocks. Not only was dependence on copper maintained, but a short-sighted mineral policy reduced the efficiency and medium-term viability of the sector. Finally, misguided budgetary policy failed to smooth the flow of mineral revenue across the trade shocks, so that acute foreign exchange shortages were experienced during the negative shock. Political factors were influential in each case.

Diversification was limited for the following reasons. Agriculture (effectively the non-booming tradables sector) experienced a Dutch Disease-like stagnation, with a negative resource movement effect. Little support was given to the lagging sector, despite rhetoric to the contrary. Moreover, controls on producer prices, with a large premium relative to border prices, reduced incentives and incomes of farmers. Political factors were at play, since the party's political constituency lay in urban areas, which were subsidised at the expense of rural agriculture. The importables sector burgeoned behind trade barriers. However, an over-valued exchange rate and the cheap capital policies (negative real interest rates, and low tariffs and taxes on capital imports) created a capital- and import-intensive manufacturing sector, which was vulnerable to falls in foreign exchange during negative shocks. Few export incentives were provided to either sector. In addition, an inefficient foreign-exchange-dependent parastatal sector was fostered. In this sense, the copper wealth was wasted.

The non-tradables sectors boomed during the positive shock. There was a very high aggregate rate of savings out of windfall income during the temporary copper boom, and since exchange controls restricted asset choices, the demand for non-tradable capital was exacerbated. A large construction boom occurred, where a substantial component of demand was from the government. However, fluctuating government plans according to the prevailing copper price saw low capacity maintained by the sector. This fact, taken together with the simultaneous phasing of government and private investment, caused supply constraints and elevated prices. The services sector, fuelled by government demand, flourished across both shocks. But, as with the importables sector, the system of controls redirected outcomes so that relative price changes were larger than they might otherwise have been. Thus, the copper windfall was partially dissipated in higher-priced construction and services.

The damaging features of exchange rate policy, tariff, credit and price controls in the positive shock were exacerbated when copper prices fell. The exchange rate was allowed to appreciate against most major currencies between 1971 and 1976, and was devalued only in mid-1976, some years after the copper price crash. The government did allow trade liberalisation during the boom, but this was reversed completely, rather than partially, after 1974 with stringent import controls. Financial liberalisation fluctuated with the copper price (being captive to budgetary mismanagement) and intermittently induced severe credit squeezes on the private sector. The failure to ease price controls in the face of rising inflation from 1974 proved particularly damaging to parastatals, which subsequently required large government subsidies. Thus, controls were not adjusted to ameliorate the negative shock. Moreover, policy inconsistencies encouraged speculation against incredible liberalisations, while black markets burgeoned. These secondary effects caused wasteful capital flight and the diversion of scarce investment funds into imports of consumer durables and inventories.

Not only did the economic control regime fail to promote the type of growth which would have reduced dependence on the mineral sector, but public policy towards the mineral sector itself was myopic. The government failed to articulate an explicit resource-extraction policy in the 1960s and 1970s. The implicit policy was the short-term maximisation of production to increase foreign exchange earnings and tax revenue, with less concern for commercial viability. Revenue maximisation occurred at the expense of medium-term planning for efficient resource extraction (planning via the National Development Plans was unrealistic and politically motivated). Further, operational oversight was negligible through the underfunded Ministry of Mines.

Majority state ownership from 1970, and complete control of management from 1973 (by then in a one-party state), led to a further deterioration of regulation through the practice of political appointments. The companies became subject to multiple and often conflicting objectives. Costs rose with the requirement to maintain excess employment, and production in loss-making mines; further, there was considerable diversion of resources to non-mining activities. The state-owned mining companies thus faced recessionary conditions in 1974 from a weakened position, with unabated demand on them for scarce foreign exchange.

The taxation of mineral sales revenue via royalties and the export tax in the 1960s (which ignores production costs) may successfully have removed windfall rent from the sector, but probably occurred at the expense of development, exploration and new investment. Political uncertainty and the frequency of changes of taxation and regulatory policies exacerbated these effects. However, while the mineral tax regime which applied after 1970 removed the distortionary revenue taxes, the profits-only taxes yielded negligible revenue after 1974. In part this was due to over-generous tax allowances.

The undesirable sectoral outcomes resulting from the control regime and mineral policy were compounded by inadequate budgetary management. One problem was reliance on the notoriously difficult process of commodity price forecasting to establish probable revenue, which then conditioned expenditure plans. There was no institutionalised framework for fiscal stabilisation, with expenditure rules and procedures for the smoothing of volatile mineral revenue. Cautious revenue estimations during 1964–74 provided no safeguard against political pressure for increased expenditure. The result was a loss of control of expenditure, and by the early 1970s, when mineral revenue declined with lower copper prices and an altered tax regime, expenditure had significantly outpaced revenue.

Fiscal profligacy deepened the deficits that became the norm for Zambia from the early 1970s. While capital expenditure experienced sharp cutbacks during 1975–80, recurrent expenditure persisted at high levels during the negative shock. Further, net lending increased strongly. There were three contributory factors in this pattern. First, public sector expectations (conditioned by international observers) erroneously held that copper prices were only temporarily low, so that full adjustment to the income shock was not made. Second, in the absence of expenditure rules the increased recurrent expenditure exhibited a ratchet-like nature. A high proportion of this expenditure comprised civil servants' salaries, government services and consumer subsidies, and for political reasons this was obviously difficult to curtail. Finally, the government was required to prop up the large import-dependent and inefficient parastatal sector it had created, which increasingly relied on the government for scarce foreign exchange, subsidies and cheap loans. The result was that the government's savings rate out of windfall income was low, at about half the private sector's savings rate.

The consequence was that, except for 1974, the government ran a budget deficit throughout the 1970s. Initially the deficit was funded by drawing down foreign assets. However, by about 1972 these were largely depleted. Thereafter, the government resorted to expensive short-term domestic borrowing, which comprised 90% of all domestic borrowing in the late 1970s. Two damaging consequences were periodic credit squeezes on the private sector and inflationary pressures, which rose with the expanding money supply.

Thus, the nature of public management amplified both the boom and crash in Zambia, setting the stage for the necessary structural adjustment of a highly mineral-dependent and debt-ridden economy in the 1980s.

NOTES

I am very grateful to Simon Appleton of the Centre for the Study of African Economies, Oxford University, Charles Harvey of IDS, University of Sussex, and John Muellbauer, Nuffield College, Oxford for helpful discussion, and for comments from the editors.

1. Auty (1990) computes a mineral dependency index for Zambia (defined as the mean percentage contribution of mining to GDP, exports and revenue), which was high, at 67, in 1965, compared with a value for Chile of 33 in the early 1970s.
2. The monotonous nature of official pronouncements on diversification, from as far back as the 1930s, is emphasised in King (1987).
3. Surveys include Neary and Van Wijnbergen (1986) and Corden (1984).
4. Contributions include Bevan *et al.* (1987b, 1990a,b), Harberger (1983), Edwards and Aoki (1983), Bruno and Sachs (1982) and Buiter and Purvis (1982).
5. In 1969 the Zambian tariff system was based around three rates: 50% for luxury goods, 30% for non-essential consumer goods, 15% for consumer goods for low-income groups. Capital and intermediate goods were not subject to tariffs. In the mid-1970s, rates were raised on luxury goods and certain goods competing with domestic production. A 5% levy on capital goods was introduced and a 10% sales tax on all imports.
6. Pt/Pm is the ratio of a constructed import unit index (IUV) for manufacturing to the wholesale price (WP) for manufacturing (the pattern was confirmed with the GDP deflator for manufacturing as denominator). The IUV (manufacturing) was constructed using domestic weights (from the wholesale price index) for categories of imports also manufactured in Zambia (chemicals, and manufactures by material) and is corrected for misinvoicing using data in Table 8.2. The WP combines the same manufacturing categories as the IUV, weighting in 1966. In both cases, categories 'food, beverages and tobacco' and 'non-metallic mineral products' are excluded: dominated by parastatals (in 1972, 75% and 66%, respectively), they were subject to strictly enforced price controls.
7. The apparent sharp rise in trade policy during 1967–68 reflects the leap in misinvoicing for the six main trading partners (Table 8.2), used in adjusting the import unit values from 1966. Aggregate misinvoicing estimates may be unreliable for the first years after independence.
8. The minimum liquidity ratio during the negative shock (30% in 1976) can be contrasted with 18% for Kenya in the same year.
9. A World Bank study in 1974 showed that the border price premium for seven important agricultural products was on average 28%.
10. The spectrum of essential commodities with controlled prices reflects the political concerns of the party in catering to its urban constituency. In 1973 these were: margarine, sugar, condensed milk, candles, cooking oil, soaps, detergents, tinned food, soft drinks, charcoal, locally made clothes, cigarettes, blankets, reflective number plates, opaque beer, bicycles, cabbage, tomatoes, onions, bananas, rice, maize meal and fish.
11. In Bevan *et al.* (1987a), perverse responses to raised agricultural producer prices were linked to shortages of consumer goods in rural areas.

12. Underinvoicing of exports is unlikely to be a significant component of capital flight, given the predominance of metals trading at known world prices in the composition of exports. This has been confirmed by Yeats (1990), where export discrepancies between Zambia and industrial countries in the 1982–83 period were in the range of transport correction factors.

13. Rhodesia's unilateral declaration of independence (UDI) in 1965 resulted in closure of the border between the two countries; ensuing transportation problems induced an export shortfall in 1966 and 1967 of 75,000 and 45,000 tonnes, respectively, from the 1965 level. The Mufulira mine flooded late in 1970, substantially reducing the quantity of exported copper in 1970 and 1971.

14. In the absence of suitable data, these stocks were proxied by the cumulative difference between production and exports in each year. This assumes quite reasonably that domestic consumption is negligible.

15. The equation is drawn from Aron and Elbadawi (1996). The regime shift, and value for α, were accepted by the data in a single-equation non-linear OLS estimation.

16. The reported annual copper export value series is derived from finely sampled price and quantity data, and takes account of differing contract types. The lack of disaggregated data implies the unavoidable assumption that monthly output price response is identical within a particular year.

17. Faber and Potter (1971) emphasise the unexpected nature of copper price behaviour up to 1970, pointing out that successive external marketing experts quoted a long-term copper price at £234, £240, £280, £300, £330, £350 and £450 per ton. Apparent overestimation in 1971 was due to falling copper prices and the flooding of Mufulira mine.

18. Domestic requirements for food and raw materials were not met by the sector, despite rich land resources (over a quarter of marketed food was imported during the boom).

19. Net assets of the holding company for parastatal manufacturing firms increased from K16.6m in 1969/70 to K100.2m in 1975/76, and employees from 5,300 to 22,300.

20. The direct effect of oil price rises is separated out, though its indirect effect as an input to other tradable goods will remain.

21. The employment series extends back to the 1950s, when another temporary copper boom and parallel construction boom occurred.

22. Pn-K proxies are the building price (disaggregated and reconstructed to remove tradable components), the GDP deflator for construction, and the wholesale price for gross fixed capital formation.

23. The counterfactual GDP series for the positive shock, with base 1963, is used, but extended to 1980 (extension not shown in Table 8.3). Thus both trade shocks are considered relative to the 'pre-boom' norm.

24. Both these issues are explored in depth in Aron (1992).

25. The overall savings rate is 63% ((K816m + K282m)/(K1,727m), and is less than the aggregate rate of around 70%, calculated in Section 8.4.1. Owing to the difficulty of ascribing windfall investment to public or private sectors, the current calculation adds windfall investment to terms of trade income, and

does not subtract permanent savings in the numerator. Further, the rate in Section 8.4.1 used discounted present values.
26. This is well documented for other LDCs (see Floyd *et al.* 1984).

REFERENCES

Aron, J. (1992). Regulatory Capture in a Mining Parastatal: Zambia Consolidated Copper Mines Limited. Working Paper, Center for International Development Research, Duke University.

Aron, J. and Elbadawi, I. (1997). The Parallel Market Premium and Exchange Rate Unification: A Macroeconomic Analysis for Zambia, chapter 8 in Miguel Kiguel, J. Saul Lizondo and Stephen O'Connell (eds.), *Parallel Exchange Rates in Developing Countries*, London: Macmillan and New York: St Martin's.

Auty, R. (1990). Mineral Exporter Response to Price Volatility: The Early-1970s Pre-conditions, Working Paper 91, Lancaster University.

Bell, M. (1983). Government Revenue Stabilisation in Primary-Producing Countries: A Model for Zambia, *Journal of Modern African Studies*, 21, 1, 55–76.

Bevan, D., Bigsten, A., Collier, P. and Gunning, J. (1987a). East African Lessons in Trade Liberalization, London: Trade Policy Research Centre.

Bevan, D., Collier, P. and Gunning, J. (1987b). Consequences of a Commodity Boom in a Controlled Economy: Accumulation and Redistribution in Kenya 1975–83, *World Bank Economic Review*, 1, 489–583.

Bevan, D., Collier, P. and Gunning, J. (1990a). Economic Policy in Countries prone to Temporary Trade Shocks, in M. Scott and D. Lal (eds.) *Public Policy and Economic Development: Essays in Honour of Ian Little*, Oxford: Clarendon Press.

Bevan, D., Collier, P. and Gunning, J. (1990b). *Controlled Open Economies: A Neo-Classical Approach to Structuralism*, Oxford: Clarendon Press.

Bruno, M. and Sachs, J. (1982). Energy and Resource Allocation: A Dynamic Model of the 'Dutch Disease', *Review of Economic Studies*, 44, 845–59.

Buiter, W. and Purvis, D. (1982). Oil, Disinflation and Export Competitiveness: A Model of the 'Dutch Disease', in J. Bhandari and B. Putnam (eds.), *Economic Interdependence and Flexible Exchange Rates*, Cambridge, MA: MIT Press.

Conrad, R., Shalizi, Z. and Syme, J. (1990). Issues in Evaluating Tax and Payment Arrangements for Publicly Owned Minerals, World Bank Policy Research Working Papers, No. 496, Washington, DC: World Bank.

Corden, W. (1984). Booming Sector and Dutch Disease Economics: Survey and Consolidation, *Oxford Economic Papers*, 36, 359–80.

Edwards, S. and Aoki, M. (1983). Oil Export Boom and Dutch Disease: A Dynamic Analysis, *Resource and Energy*, 5, 219–242.

Faber, M. and Potter, J. (1971). *Towards Economic Independence: Papers on the Nationalisation of the Copper Industry in Zambia*, Cambridge: Cambridge University Press.

Floyd, R., Gray, C. and Short, R. (1984). 'Public Enterprise in Mixed Economies: Some Macroeconomic Aspects', International Monetary Fund.

Garnaut, R. and Clunies Ross, A. (1983). *Taxation of Mineral Rents*, Oxford: Clarendon Press.

Gulhati, R. (1989). Impasse in Zambia: The Economics and Politics of Reform, *EDI Policy Case Studies*, 2, Washington, DC: World Bank.

Harberger, A. (1983). Dutch Disease—How Much Sickness, How Much Boon? *Resources and Energy*, 5, 1–20.

Hotelling, H. (1931). The Economics of Exhaustible Resources, *Journal of Political Economy*, 39, 137–75.

King, B. (1987). From Dutch Disease to Dutch Auction, mimeo, Washington, DC: World Bank.

Nankani, G. (1979). Development Problems of Mineral Exporting Countries, World Bank Staff Working Paper no. 354, Washington, DC: World Bank.

Neary, J. and van Wijnbergen, S. (eds.) (1986). *Natural Resources and the Macroeconomy*, Oxford: Blackwell.

Yeats, A. (1990). On the Accuracy of Economic Observations: Do Sub-Saharan Trade Statistics Mean Anything? *World Bank Economic Review*, 4, 2, 135–56.

9

The Diamond Boom, Expectations and Economic Management in Botswana

CATHARINE HILL AND JOHN KNIGHT

9.1. Introduction

Botswana has acquired a mineral economy over the last two decades. Mining and quarrying account for over half of GDP, and diamond exports for over two-thirds of total exports. Mineral revenues of one sort or another make up more than two-thirds of government recurrent revenue. Botswana is now the highest value producer of diamonds in the world. But diamonds are potentially a risky, uncertain commodity, and so this heavy dependence on diamonds poses macroeconomic management problems.

Many developing countries experiencing export booms have used their gains to increase government spending and even to borrow against future expected export receipts. Various countries whose export booms proved to be temporary then faced painful adjustment problems. However, Botswana seems to have avoided such problems—possibly because it was luckier and possibly because it adopted more appropriate macroeconomic policies.

The Botswana government's policy on trade shocks is well stated in the 1979–85 National Development Plan, the stress being on prediction and caution:

Government's judgements on external and internal balance must be fairly long-sighted. There are serious costs to the economy if adjustments to restore balance have to be sudden and sharp. A sudden credit squeeze when the balance of payments worsens, for example, should if possible be avoided by planning a smooth path of credit expansion that anticipates balance of payments trends. Similarly, if the level of resources available to Government suddenly increases, it is better to plan a steady but sustainable increase in expenditures than to go on a short-lived spending spree that inevitably exceeds domestic production capacities and results mainly in increased imports. Regular revision of economic forecasts and anticipation of the trends they show can make a stop-go cycle much less likely. (Republic of Botswana 1980, p. 67)

Despite fluctuations in its export proceeds Botswana has not experienced balance of payments crises. The government has avoided the excessive expansion of public expenditure during commodity booms. Instead it has built up international reserves and government balances at the central bank. It has apparently followed a consumption and saving path consistent with the permanent income hypothesis. It has encouraged diversification despite the diamond boom, by preventing the real exchange rate from appreciating and running a balance of payments surplus—even a trade surplus from 1982/83 onwards. This case study of Botswana therefore provides helpful insights into the successful management of trade shocks.

The control regime in force in Botswana can be characterised as non-interventionist. There have been no exchange, price or import controls. Indeed, until 1976 Botswana did not even have its own currency, being part of the Rand Monetary Area. The public sector is necessarily important in an economy with only an incipient capitalist sector but the major forms of government intervention have been the basic ones: exchange rate, interest rate, budgetary and wage policies. However, another important function of government has been the management of relations with foreign companies and governments. Each of Botswana's main exports is sold on a regulated market in which negotiation has been needed to secure a good deal, and Botswana's economic relations with South Africa have been subject to periodic negotiations. There is relative freedom for resources to move in response to price signals, not only internally but also internationally. The controls which blunt the operation of macroeconomic management in many developing countries are absent. Botswana has a very open economy: non-tradables probably account for less than 40% of GDP, possibly only one-quarter. Non-tradables have a weight of 25% in the official cost-of-living index, domestic tradables 30% and imported tradables 45%.[1] However, this openness to external influences intensifies the need for domestic macroeconomic management.

Botswana has one of the fastest growing economies in the world. We have data on GDP and its components at constant prices for the period from 1973/74 to 1989/90.[2] The growth of GDP was fairly constant over that period, averaging over 10% per annum. Mining production grew in spurts according to the opening or expansion of mines but it averaged no less than 20% growth per annum over the fifteen years. Even the growth of non-mining production exceeded 7% per annum.

With population growth of some 3.5% per annum, output per unit of labour input in the economy grew at a remarkable rate. This reflects the vent-for-surplus nature of mining expansion in Botswana. Capital, management, technology, expertise and mining equipment could all be imported. The promising investment opportunities and the availability of foreign exchange from exports, together with the open nature of the Botswana economy with respect to imports of goods and capital, meant that neither a saving nor a foreign exchange constraint was binding. The effective constraint on the economy was probably skilled labour. In the long term its relaxation depended on public expenditure on education and training. In the short term its relaxation required the use of skilled expatriates, and this in turn involved a policy decision on the number of relatively expensive expatriates to be allowed in.

We start with a discussion of the mining sector and the nature of the trade shocks that Botswana experienced during the 1970s and 1980s (Section 9.2). This brings out the unusual and idiosyncratic features of export fluctuations in Botswana, which differentiate our methodological approach and analysis from those for other economies subject to shocks. Section 9.3 analyses the economic response to these fluctuations, covering four effects: on construction, on the government budget, on economy-wide consumption and on the real exchange rate. By comparing counter-factual forecasts in the numerous National Development Plans with actual outcomes, we can measure various economic responses to shocks defined as unanticipated fluctuations. In Section 9.4 we examine Botswana's one negative shock in greater detail, and pose the counterfactual question: 'What if the diamond recession had not occurred?' Section 9.5 concludes by attempting to explain the relatively successful economic management in Botswana and drawing both local and general lessons.

9.2. The Nature of the Botswana Shocks

The theoretical framework within which this comparative research project is set requires us to distinguish between permanent and temporary shocks, and to concentrate on the latter. The project is therefore concerned with short-run dynamics rather than comparative statics. The term 'shock' itself implies that the trade fluctuation was unpredicted. We therefore make a distinction between those changes that could be forecast and those that were truly 'shocks'. Shocks can result from changes in the random error term or in other terms of the predictive equation. Changes in the former can be regarded as inclusive shocks, consistent with prior expectations and therefore having only a small effect on permanent income. Unforeseen changes in the latter—for instance, a new variable in the equation or a change in a parameter—referred to as exclusive shocks, are inconsistent with prior expectations and more likely to produce a significant revision of permanent income. A third distinction can be drawn between private shocks, in which the initial gain or loss accrues mainly to the private sector, and public shocks, in which it accrues mainly to the public sector. We proceed in two stages: first, we describe and explain actual fluctuations and, second, we classify the Botswana shocks according to the criteria above.

There are three diamond mines in Botswana: the Orapa mine, discovered in 1967, opened in 1971 and expanded in 1978; the Letlhakane mine, discovered in 1971 and opened in 1976; and the Jwaneng mine, discovered in 1973, reported to the government in 1976, starting production in 1982 and expanded in 1983 (De Beers, *Annual Reports*). As each mine was opened or expanded, diamond production increased by a large step. Most spectacularly, the opening of the Jwaneng mine in 1982 more than doubled total diamond production. There has been a series of diamond booms, involving sharply increased rates of growth and then a levelling-off. They offer scope for examining the management and effects of positive shocks in the 1970s and the 1980s.

These indivisibilities in production are one source of instability. Another concerns the quality of diamonds produced by the mines. A third arises from the diamond market, in the form of price fluctuations and quota restrictions on sales. An understanding of this requires a knowledge of the idiosyncratic arrangements for marketing world diamond production. These arrangements, in place since the 1930s, reflect the peculiar characteristics of the diamond as a non-renewable natural resource and a durable, non-standardised good whose value depends on fashion, status considerations and confidence (Knight, forthcoming).

All three diamond mines are joint ventures between the Botswana government and De Beers, each of which has a half share in the producer company, Debswana. The entire output of Debswana is sold through the trading arm of De Beers, known as the Central Selling Organization (CSO). The diamond cartel, run by the CSO, might be regarded as the most successful cartel of the twentieth century.[3] It is maintained through De Beers's near-monopoly of the distribution of natural diamonds. The CSO enters long-term contracts with all the major producers, including Botswana. The inducement it offers is guaranteed sales at stable prices.

Producers in turn are expected to accept quota restrictions in times of recession in demand, and there is an 'exclusive dealing' clause. De Beers has by these means and by judicious stocking policy been able to keep market prices stable in dollars in the short term and rising on a steady trend at about the nominal rate of interest in the long term. This is precisely the behaviour that exhaustible resource theory would predict.

There are two parts to the diamond market, gems and industrial diamonds. Gems account for 20% of the market by volume and for 80% by value. Botswana's production is of gems, and high-quality gems at that. The cartel was seriously tested in the late 1970s and early 1980s. In the late 1970s there was a speculative upsurge in demand for gems in the retail and secondary wholesale markets. De Beers wished to maintain its buying and selling prices on their steady long-run trend path, but pressures from the producers—who sought to benefit from the boom—forced the CSO to raise its prices rapidly. This was the main source of dollar price instability over the period under consideration. However, the price of Botswana diamonds, being a unit value index in pula, has also fluctuated for two other reasons. There have been changes in the quality composition of Botswana sales and there have been changes in the exchange rate between the pula and the dollar. The import-purchasing power of diamonds is of course affected by the exchange rate between the dollar and the composite currency, dominated by the rand, reflecting the composition of Botswana's imports.

The speculative boom in the gem market in the late 1970s led to a serious recession in the market in the early 1980s, exacerbated by the recession in industrial countries and the high rates of interest that then prevailed. To weather the storm, the CSO imposed quota restrictions on all members of the cartel. Botswana was especially hard hit because the demand fell particularly for the high-quality gems that Botswana mainly produces. It continued production but was unable to sell the highest-quality gems during the period 1981–83 and had to stockpile them. This episode provides an opportunity for examining the management of a negative shock, the duration of which was uncertain.

Figure 9.1 (explained in Table 9.1) shows diamond production, measured in thousands of carats, by mine (depicted additively, so that the top curve gives total production). We see the opening of the Orapa mine in 1972 and its expansion in 1979 and 1980. The contribution of the Letlhakane mine is understated because of the high quality of its gems: value is extremely sensitive to quality. We also see the build-up of Jwaneng production in the years 1982–84. Despite the implementation of cartel quotas during this period, Botswana was allowed to expand production and sales because it had previously been agreed that Jwaneng would be accommodated within the cartel.

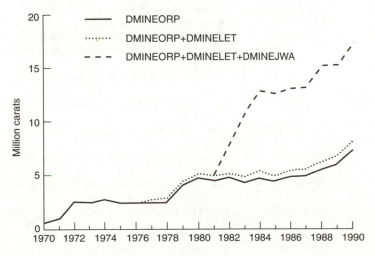

Figure 9.1.

Table 9.1. Notation used in the figures

Figure [9.x]	Notation	Description
Passim	LN	Natural logarithm of the variable
Passim	R	Constant prices (normally 1990 pula)
1	DMINEORP	Diamond production of Orapa mine
1	DMINELET	Diamond production of Letlhakane mine
1	DMINEJWA	Diamond production of Jwaneng mine
2, 19	GDP	Gross domestic product
2, 6	M	Mining
2, 6	N	Non-mining
2	MCPI	Implicit mining sector price deflator
3	DIAMPROD	Diamonds, value of production
3	CARATS	Diamonds, volume of production (carats)
3	DUNITVAL	Diamonds, implicit unit value
3, 20	GDPFLAT	GDP deflator
4	PULAER	Pula/dollar exchange rate
4	DIAPIP	Botswana diamond price index in pula
4	DIAPID	Botswana diamond price index in dollars
4	DIAPICSO	CSO cartel-wide diamond price index in dollars
5	TOTRD	Terms of trade (export/import unit values)
5	RANDER	Rand/dollar exchange rate
6	GFKF	Gross fixed capital formation
7	SASUPPLY	South African supply price of construction
7	BUCOST	Building plans: unit cost
7	BFLOOR	Building plants: floor area
8, 22, 23	SURPLUS	Government overall surplus
8, 22, 23	RECSURP	Government recurrent surplus
9, 10, 21	MINREV	Mineral revenue
9	MINNDP3	Mineral revenue predicted in NDP3
9	MINNDP4	Mineral revenue predicted in NDP4
9	MINNDP5	Mineral revenue predicted in NDP5
9, 10	MINMTR5	Mineral revenue predicted in MTR5
10	MINNDP6	Mineral revenue predicted in NDP6
10	MINMTR6	Mineral revenue predicted in MTR6
10	MINNDP7	Mineral revenue predicted in NDP7
11, 12	REXPEND	Government recurrent expenditure
11	REXNDP3	Government recurrent expenditure predicted in NDP3
11	REXNDP4	Government recurrent expenditure predicted in NDP4
11	REXNDP5	Government recurrent expenditure predicted in NDP5
11	REXMTR5	Government recurrent expenditure predicted in MTR5
12	REXNDP6	Government recurrent expenditure predicted in NDP6
12	REXMTR6	Government recurrent expenditure predicted in MTR6
12	REXNDP7	Government recurrent expenditure predicted in NDP7
13, 14	DEXPEND	Government development expenditure
13	DEXNDP3	Government development expenditure predicted in NDP3

Table 9.1. *Continued*

Figure [9.x]	Notation	Description
13	DEXNDP4	Government development expenditure predicted in NDP4
13	DEXNDP5	Government development expenditure predicted in NDP5
13	DEXMTR5	Government development expenditure predicted in MTR5
14	DEXNDP6	Government development expenditure predicted in NDP6
14	DEXMTR6	Government development expenditure predicted in MTR6
14	DEXNDP7	Government development expenditure predicted in NDP7
15	AGDERAT	Percentage share of agriculture in development expenditure
15	ECDERAT	Percentage share of economic services (including agriculture) in development expenditure
15	EDDERAT	Percentage share of education in development expenditure
15	GENDERAT	Percentage share of general services in development expenditure
15	SOCDERAT	Percentage share of social services (including education) in development expenditure
15	TRDERAT	Percentage share of transfers in development expenditure
16	TAXES	'Other revenues and grants'
16	PTAXES	Projection of 'other revenues and grants'
16	TAXDIF	Windfall difference between actual and projected 'other revenues and grants'
17	CON	Total consumption
17	PRIVCON	Private consumption
17	GOVCON	Government consumption
18	SRATE	Total saving rate as a percentage of GDP
18	SPRATE	Private saving rate as a percentage of GDP
18	SGRATE	Government saving rate as a percentage of GDP
19	RER1	Real exchange rate, import-weighted
19	RER2	Real exchange rate, trade-weighted (excluding diamonds)
19	RER3	Real exchange rate, pula/rand
19	AVMW	Average minimum wage
20	BOOMTP	Boom traded goods price
20	NONBTP	Non-boom traded goods price
20	NONTP	Non-traded goods price
21	REVENUE	Government revenue
21	EXPEND	Government expenditure
21	GOVSAV	Government saving
21, 22, 23	CF	Counterfactual

Sources: The data are derived largely from official statistics, taken from Bank of Botswana, *Annual Reports*; Republic of Botswana, Central Statistics Office, *Statistical Bulletin*; IMF, *International Financial Statistics*; and the various National Development Plans.

Production is not the same as sales. A discrepancy arose between the two series, beginning in 1981. The value of production exceeded export revenue over the period 1981–84: Debswana's diamond stocks accumulated. The stocks were gradually sold off from 1985 onwards, but especially in 1987 as a result of a deal between De Beers and the Botswana government. Although the full terms of the deal are not available, De Beers took over Debswana's diamond stocks in return for De Beers shares and cash. Implicit stocks appeared to become negative in 1987. This, however, was due to an accounting convention. For statistical purposes the stockpiled diamonds were valued at production cost, which was a small fraction of the price at which they were selling before the diamond recession. Reported sales, on the other hand, reflected actual sales prices.[4] The stockpiled diamonds were eventually sold at prices that were no doubt much higher than their production cost.

The price index for mining sector unit values (Figure 9.2) and for diamond production unit values (Figures 9.3 and 9.4) are subject to various other influences, one being De Beers's purchase prices (Figure 9.4)—a cartel-wide index—and another the quality composition of Botswana's diamond sales. This was partly a matter of differences among mines: because average quality at Jwaneng exceeded that at Orapa, Jwaneng's expansion may have raised the unit value. Price was also dependent on the quality of the stockpile: it was particularly the large, high-quality gems for which the market collapsed. *Ceteris paribus*, this depressed the unit value of diamond sales during the period of stockpiling and contributed to its rise as the stocks were depleted.

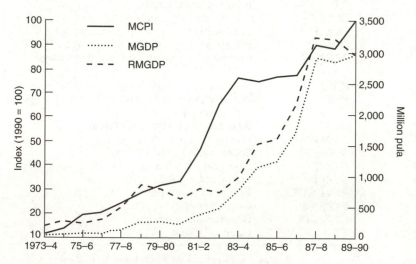

Figure 9.2.

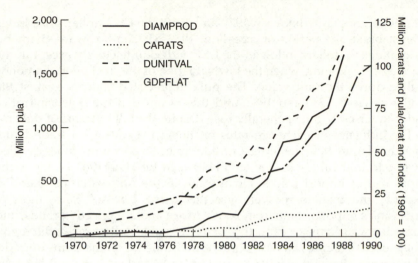

Figure 9.3.

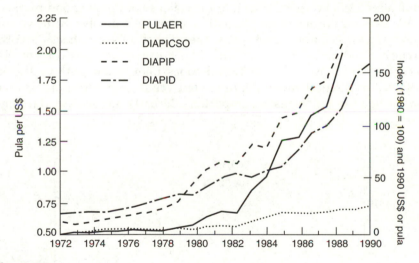

Figure 9.4.

A final influence on the pula value of diamond proceeds is the exchange rate. Diamond purchase prices are set in US dollars, reflecting the major market, and the pula/dollar exchange rate has varied. Figure 9.4 shows this exchange rate, both the pula and dollar prices of Botswana's diamonds, and the CSO's diamond purchase price index (potentially inaccurate for Botswana owing to compositional differences). Having risen in the 1970s, especially between 1977 and 1980, the CSO dollar price index was stable in the period of recession, 1980–85. The Botswana diamond price index in dollars followed the CSO index quite closely except in the period of stockpiling, when the low valuation of the stockpiled diamonds pulled down the unit value. The pula depreciated sharply against the dollar between 1980 and 1985, and this meant that the Botswana price index in terms of pula generally rose despite the fall in terms of dollars.

The influence of exchange rates on Botswana's terms of trade is depicted in Figure 9.5. The terms of trade series (export unit values divided by import unit values) is seen to fall between 1980 and 1983, owing to the rapid rise of import prices and the fall in the unit value of diamond exports, and then to recover over the period 1985–87. Since most of Botswana's imports come from South Africa and are priced in rands, and since Botswana's major exports have fairly stable dollar prices, the rand/ dollar exchange rate can have a powerful influence on the terms of trade. The appreciation of the dollar against the pula, and even more against the rand, after 1980 should have improved the terms of trade: Botswana could obtain more rands for the dollars that it earned. This was not apparent until after 1985, however, owing to the collapse of the diamond market.

Whereas the normal trade fluctuations commonly involve inclusive and unrevised expectations of export values, Dutch Disease shocks involve exclusive and revised expectations. The Botswana shocks contain elements of both. Over the last two decades unexpected positive shocks occurred as three diamond deposits were discovered and mines started production (we ignore, as less important, the early discovery and mining

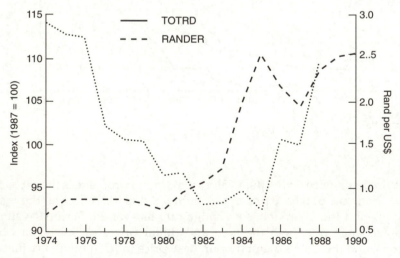

Figure 9.5.

of copper–nickel). The 'news' would come with the discovery of a deposit. It could then be expected that this would lead to production with a lag of x years, and that production would continue for at least y years, where y is a large number (x is about 5 and y may be 50). These shocks were thus exclusive, revised and permanent but, once the investment decision had been taken, they were expected. Further revisions in expected export values would occur as the quality and quantity of diamonds from a mine became evident and as the prospects for the diamond market were perceived to change.

Botswana is partly shielded from the normal export price shocks that beset most primary commodities by the stabilising effect of the diamond cartel on diamond prices and producers' sales. The long-term contracts and guaranteed purchases have normally stabilised diamond exports. Annual fluctuations in export unit values owing to compositional changes in the quality of diamonds have occurred, but they were not predictable and they did not lead to revised expectations unless, as with the opening of a mine, there was a trend. The only important negative shock that Botswana has experienced since it became a mineral economy occurred when the demand for gem diamonds collapsed in the early 1980s, selling quotas were implemented and Botswana was unable to sell its production for a period. Owing to the severity of the recession—this was the biggest slump in the diamond market since the 1930s—expectations at that time, which would otherwise have been inclusive and unrevised, may have contained exclusive and revised elements.

Clearly, some of these influences on income from the sale of diamonds could be better forecast than others. At one end of the scale is the long-term development of mines once discovered and at the other the discovery of mines and the vagaries of the foreign exchange and diamond markets. Some of the diamond shocks have been permanent in nature and some temporary (the distinction between production and price, or demand, shocks is important in this regard). Botswana has experienced only one important shock that was expected probably to be temporary. Many interesting aspects of the Botswana diamond boom do not fall neatly into the framework of most temporary trade shocks.

The Botswana experience is nevertheless worth examining in the context of short-term dynamics, for various reasons. First, however clear a theoretical distinction can be made between exclusive and revised expectations with significant effects on permanent income, on the one hand, and inclusive and unrevised expectations with only windfall effects being significant, on the other, in practice the distinction is blurred. Economic agents are often poorly informed and have to peer into an uncertain future when they take their decisions. 'Keynes uncertainty' is common, and it is generally easier to classify shocks *ex post* than *ex ante*. For instance, at the time of the temporary slump in demand there was a fear in some quarters that the diamond cartel would collapse, with incalculable consequences for the diamond market in the future. Second, many governments appear to have treated a temporary positive shock as though it were permanent, possibly because their decisions were influenced by poorly informed pressure groups or electors. By contrast, we shall argue that the Botswana government appears to have treated part of a permanent positive shock as though it were temporary, in the sense that it has generally underestimated the effect on permanent income. The political economy of economic management in Botswana is potentially interesting.

The Botswana shocks were essentially public shocks in that they were initially experienced mainly by the exchequer and by Debswana, the only local owner of which was the government. The effect of the shocks on government revenue and expenditure, expectations and behaviour is central to our story.

The inclusion of three diamond discoveries as well as one diamond recession over a period of some twenty years means that the case study is rather less specific and less well directed than it would be if it were the analysis of a single episode. It is arguable that the diamond shocks have been either too big or too small to be amenable to counterfactual simulation analysis. On the one hand, the big question—'What if diamonds had not been discovered at all?'—cannot be answered satisfactorily by means of necessarily simple and mechanical simulations. On the other hand, the single negative shock, which forms the basis of our conventional counterfactual analysis, was limited in its effects and small in relation to a nearly concurrent positive shock, and it affected the timing rather than the quantity of diamond sales. However—if economists are permitted a third hand—the forecasts contained in the frequently revised National Development Plans can themselves be regarded as the appropriate counterfactual, in that they enable us to examine various economic responses to unanticipated fluctuations. In these respects our study differs from others in this volume.

9.3. Responses to the Diamond Shocks

Our initial concern is to examine the appropriateness and adaptability of the standard Dutch Disease model to the analysis of diamond shocks in Botswana. In that model an expansionary trade shock should produce a resource movement effect and an expenditure effect. We shall argue that the resource movement effect has been insignificant and the expenditure effect important only in certain respects.

Consider first the resource movement effect. The enclave nature of the diamond sector in Botswana has meant that there has been little transfer of resources from the non-boom to the boom sector. Mining investments occurred as a result of resource discoveries. Since most of the finance for these projects came from outside Botswana, there was little diversion of funds from the non-boom sectors. The amount of labour employed in the new mines was largely determined by the size of the diamond pipes and the amount of capital invested. Once the optimal extraction strategy had been decided and the construction stage completed, mining production and employment were technologically determined and remained fairly constant. Diamond production is extremely capital intensive and very little labour is required in relation to value-added. Employment in mining and quarrying has not exceeded 9% of total paid employment (1977) nor 7,500 people in total (1988), even when diamonds accounted for between 13% (1976/77) and 44% (1987/88) of formal sector GDP. The additional mining employment was not sufficiently large to have a market impact on wage levels in the Botswana economy, and no relationship is ascertainable between the diamond booms and sectoral wage relativities. Thus, the diamond sector appears to operate as an enclave with respect to both labour and capital markets.

The spending effect of the diamond shocks requires closer scrutiny. In theory, the spending effect arises if an export boom generates increased demand for non-tradable goods, which in turn raises their price and thus appreciates the real exchange rate. We examine four effects: on construction, on the government budget, on economy-wide consumption and on the real exchange rate.

9.3.1. Construction Booms

Construction booms interact with export booms. Thus, the discovery of a profitable diamond pipe attracts mining investment, which with a lag raises diamond production. This in turn generates an investment boom beyond the mining sector. Figure 9.6 shows fluctuations in real investment in mining, in non-mining and in the economy as a whole. We see the heavy investment in the Jwaneng mine in the period 1978/79–1981/82. The capital cost of the Jwaneng project came to P280 million—more than 10% of GDP for that period. Mining investment peaked in 1979/80, whereas non-mining investment boomed until 1981/82 and then fell in the wake of the recession in the diamond market and the consequent monetary and fiscal restraint. The investment boom of 1984/85 in the non-mining sector was probably brought on mainly by a lumpy water and electricity project rather than by the 1983/84–1984/85 recovery in the quantity and price of exports.

The hypothesis we wish to test is that investment booms cause inflation in non-tradable investment goods and services. However, the implicit deflator for gross fixed capital formation as a whole and our calculated deflators for machinery and equipment (a tradable component of

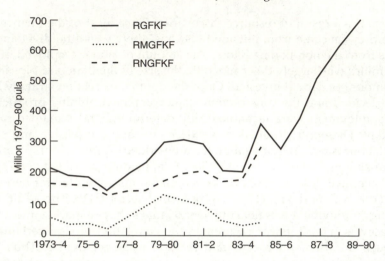

Figure 9.6.

investment) and for building and construction (which might be non-tradable) kept very close together during the period 1974–95. The best test is to examine the construction boom that lasted from 1979/80 to 1981/82. Between 1978/79 and the final year of the boom, the price index of building and construction rose by 36% and that of machinery and equipment by 45%. There is no indication of a rise in the price of non-tradable investment goods relative to that of tradable investment goods; nor even relative to the price of consumer goods, since the retail price index rose by 60%. Moreover, Figure 9.7, which shows the quantity and unit cost of building plans approved, indicates an inverse relationship: unit cost actually fell in 1980 and stayed low in 1981. Only for the construction boom beginning in 1987 is a positive relationship suggested by these data: construction costs rose rapidly during the period 1987–89.

An explanation might be found in the open nature of the Botswana economy. Botswana is unusual in being able to import construction capacity relatively quickly and easily from across the border with South Africa. Machinery, management and skilled labour can all be transferred fairly costlessly. In that sense all investment expenditure is tradable. The supply curve of the construction sector in Botswana is elastic. This is particularly true of construction in Gaborone, the capital city, and the other main centres close to the borders with South Africa and Zimbabwe. It may be less true of the hinterland, however: transport costs within Botswana cause construction costs to escalate and may deter foreign tenders.

Given that South Africa is the dominant source of additional construction capacity, the most likely determinant of change in the supply price is

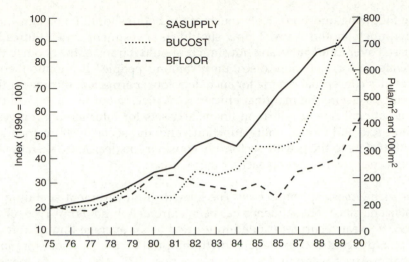

Figure 9.7.

change in the relevant South African price level and in the pula/rand exchange rate. The South African supply price (the implicit deflator for gross fixed capital formation in South Africa adjusted for the gradual appreciation of the pula against the rand after depegging in 1976) is shown in Figure 9.7. The foreign supply price continued to rise during the construction boom: between 1978 and 1981 it increased by 49%. It cannot therefore provide an explanation for the limited rise, or indeed the fall, in the price of Botswana building and construction services during that boom. Figure 9.7 does provide an alternative explanation for the rise in building costs after 1987. The sharp increase between 1987 and 1990 was almost matched by the increase in the South African supply price. At the least, therefore, the existence of potential foreign competition could not prevent domestic construction prices from rising in response to the boom.

The main conclusions of this subsection are twofold. First, construction booms have both preceded and followed export booms in Botswana: causation can and does run both ways. Second, there is little evidence for Botswana that construction booms have raised the relative prices of construction services; construction activity appears to be in elastic supply and may well have a large tradable component.

9.3.2. Government Revenue and Expenditure

Government gained directly from the diamond booms as a result of its ownership of mineral rights and part-ownership of Debswana, and indirectly through its ability to tax mining profits. It therefore had to answer the following questions. How much of the boom should it consume and how much should it save? How should its investment expenditures be phased over time? How, and how much, should it transfer the boom to the private sector, and how distribute it among people? Economic theory provides conceptual criteria for such decisions: permanent income for the saving decision; the marginal efficiency of investment in relation to the international rate of return on financial assets for inter-temporal investment; and individual utility functions and the social welfare function for transfers to the private sector. We consider the decisions taken by the Botswana government on each of these issues.

The saving/consumption decision The growth in government spending in Botswana since independence has been extremely high. From 1966/67 to 1986/87, real recurrent expenditure grew at an average annual rate of 11.5%. By contrast, average growth in public consumption for Sub-Saharan Africa was only 4.9% over the period 1973–1983. Over the period 1966/67–1986/87, real development expenditures in Botswana grew even faster, at an average annual real rate of 12.6%. Despite these high rates, expenditure growth has been consistently less than revenue growth. Whereas before 1976 revenue growth was led by customs revenue and mineral revenues equally, after 1976 mineral revenues accounted for 60% of revenue growth (Harvey and Lewis 1990, p. 195). Moreover, other forms of government revenue also depended on diamonds in that the diamond boom raised income in other sectors and raised imports. In 1986/87, mineral revenue accounted for 72% of tax revenue and customs revenue from imports for 16%. Thus, in the second decade after independence, government income depended crucially on diamonds.

Figure 9.8 demonstrates how the government has saved an increasing proportion of its income as its revenues have expanded. The government had converted a recurrent deficit at independence into a recurrent surplus by 1972/73. Thereafter, government funded an increasing share of its development programme from its own resources until its overall budget moved into surplus in 1983/84. Thereafter the government's net acquisition of financial assets was positive.

By funding deficits from concessional external loans and grants, the government incurred no domestic debt. Indeed, it built up substantial deposits with the domestic banking system, which by 1987/88 were equivalent to over one-and-a-half years of government expenditure. These assets largely represent the sterilisation of the substantial net foreign assets earned from diamonds. Net foreign assets reached P4.4 billion by the end of 1988, or roughly twenty-four months of import cover.

In principle those changes in diamond proceeds that are already expected have already been taken into account by government and private

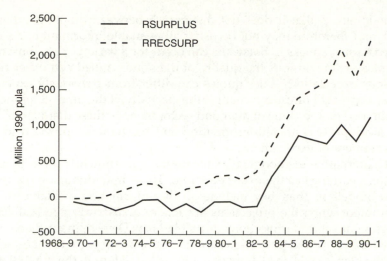

Figure 9.8.

agents in their economic decisions. It is, then, unexpected changes that require adjustments to be made in public and private behaviour, such as spending and saving. These are the true 'shocks'. We therefore develop a methodology to examine the response to shocks defined in this way.

Income from diamonds in Botswana can be measured by mining GDP, diamond exports or government revenues. To quantify shocks we need to have some measure of the previously expected level of diamond income with which to compare actual income. Previous work on measuring shocks in Botswana (Hill 1991a; Cuddington and Hill 1991) has adopted two alternative methodologies. One assumes that diamond sector earnings can be represented by a univariate time-series model. Expected earnings equal the fitted values from the time-series regression while the innovations or residuals represent the new information or unexpected earnings in the sector. The second methodology takes the government's projections as the expected values of the earnings variable. The shocks are therefore the difference between the actual values and the government's projections. Both methodologies have advantages and disadvantages.

The econometric time-series models are useful in that the regressions can be used to revise the future expected path of the variable, given the innovations or new information at each point in time. In other words the results, both the estimated model and the residuals, can be used to draw conclusions about the permanence of booms and busts. It is possible to calculate the effects of new information on permanent income, rather than just current income, which is what is needed in order to decide whether the expenditure response to booms is appropriate. A problem with this methodology is that it does not distinguish between different types of shock and therefore may not be using all available information. As discussed earlier, shocks in Botswana can occur for a variety of reasons: new mines can come on line, the quality of diamonds mined can differ from previous expectations, sales quotas can differ from previously expected levels, and world prices can change unexpectedly. If the time-series model is estimated on the value of diamond sector income, these distinctions are lost: it adopts a restricted-information and mechanical approach to the measurement of expectations.

The alternative methodology is to use the government's projections of diamond earnings as the expected value. These may dominate the time-series models in that they include all the information available to the government when the projections are made. A disadvantage is that the government reports projections in its National Development Plans only every few years. The projections are therefore the expected values at the time the plan is published, but not the expected values in the immediately preceding time-period. Projections revised by the government on an annual basis would dominate use of the projections reported in the National Development Plans but are not publicly available. The absence of up-to-date projections makes it difficult to infer how an outturn different from the expected value affects future expectations. Does the new information lead the government to revise its expectations?

As it turns out, the two methodologies yield very similar estimates of the difference between expectations and actuals. Given this, Cuddington and Hill (1991) examine the effects of booms, using the econometric estimates, on total consumption, government consumption and government recurrent expenditure. A version of the Hall test (Hall 1978) is used to see whether consumption is smoothed over time. The results suggest that boom income is primarily saved and does not lead to increases in either total or public consumption. This is taken as evidence in favour of the permanent income hypothesis and as evidence that the government has regarded booms as temporary rather than permanent.

In this chapter we use information about government expectations of both revenue and expenditure contained in successive development plans in order to construct a data series of revenue and expenditure innovations by matching expected against actual values. This differs from previous work in that it analyses the effects of new developments in the diamond sector on actual government expenditures relative to previously planned levels, as represented by the government's projections. This avoids the problem mentioned above of projections not being updated annually. What are examined here are the effects of revenue innovations—that is, deviations of actual government revenues from projections made in the past (RI)—on expenditure innovations—that is, deviations of actual government expenditures from projections made at the same time in the past

(*EI*). The analysis of this relationship offers evidence on the government's propensities to spend and to save out of unanticipated revenue.

In the post-independence period, the Botswana government has published seven National Development Plans and two Mid-term Reviews.[5] Government has taken planning very seriously: the plans contain projections of national income as well as detailed projections of government revenues. Given these projections, total government expenditure has been decided upon and different areas of expenditure prioritised. Spending ministries have been expected to remain within the limits set. Until 1979 the plans were overlapping, so that a new five-year Plan was produced after three years of the previous plan had passed. Six-year plans were introduced in 1979, with a comprehensive mid-term review carried out after three years. These plans afford us a frequently, if not annually, updated insight into the expectations of the Botswana government concerning its own income and a serious statement of its expenditure intentions.[6]

The history of actual and expected mineral revenues is charted in Figures 9.9 and 9.10.[7] The early 1970s were a period of mineral revenue boom, which was curtailed in 1975/76. Government moved from an underestimation in NDP2, caused by a pessimistic estimate of the likely revenues from the newly opened Orapa mine, to an overestimation in NDP3, caused by an optimistic forecast of the likely opening date of the copper–nickel mine at Selebi-Phikwe. The period 1976/77–1980/81 saw an extremely powerful boom develop. Figure 9.9 shows how the forecasts of NDP4 and the first two years of NDP5 substantially underestimated

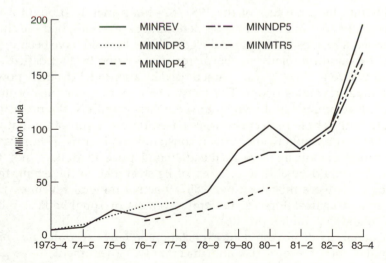

Figure 9.9.

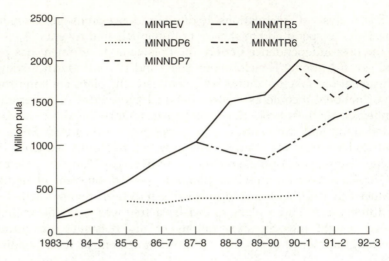

Figure 9.10.

mineral revenues. The NDP4 forecasts were based on the assumption of 9.6% real GDP growth per annum, including a spectacular 23% growth in diamond exports. Nevertheless, NDP4 underestimated both the quality of diamonds produced by the Letlhakane mine and the speculative surge in diamond prices that occurred towards the end of the 1970s. This surge also meant that even the updated forecasts of NDP5 (which made a substantial revision, as Figure 9.9 shows) were underestimating mineral revenues at the beginning of that plan period.

Although the first year of the 1981/82 slump merely brought actual mineral revenues in line with projected mineral revenues, had the slump continued into subsequent years the government would have been forced to cut expenditure relatively sharply or face a rising budget deficit. The period 1983/84–1989/90 was characterised by a second, extremely power-ful mineral revenues boom. The fact that this was a completely unex-pected development is shown by the comparison with NDP6 projections (Figure 9.10). These projections were based on the assumption that dia-mond export receipts would remain constant in real terms. There was no expectation of any increase in the diamond price in dollars, nor that Botswana would be able to sell any of its stockpile. In the event, these assumptions were mistaken: by 1988/89 actual mineral revenues were P1.5 billion against forecast mineral revenues of roughly P0.4 billion (NDP6) and P0.9 billion (MTR6).

This analysis of government expectations relative to outcomes high-lights the importance of risk and uncertainty. Governments have great difficulty in making accurate forecasts of revenues from commodities. In

Botswana's case, the mistakes have arisen from four different sources: the timing of mine openings, the volume of production, the quality of production and prices. Expectations of revenue in period t are likely to be revised and improved right up until period t has arrived, and they will still be wrong.

When a mistake in forecasting has been made, the government must decide whether the deviation in actual revenue is permanent or temporary, with consequent implications for the expenditure response. Although this decision might appear to fall into a simple categorisation whereby output shocks are permanent and price shocks are temporary, in reality matters are less clear. The opening of a mine is clearly a permanent shock: diamond mines are normally expected to produce for many years. It is less clear whether a rise or fall in income resulting from a change in quality composition is temporary or permanent. Similarly, price movements, which can occur as a result of changes both in the diamond price in dollars and in the pula/dollar exchange rate, are not easily classified. There is much statistical evidence that commodity prices in general show strong inter-temporal dependence (Gersovitz and Paxson 1990). Commodity price shocks are frequently not temporary but persist long into the future, even if eventually reverting to the previous level. With time, classification becomes *ex post* and easier, but an *ex ante* evaluation is unreliable.

In response to these uncertainties the Botswana government has adopted an essentially cautious strategy. It has sometimes chosen to incorporate relatively pessimistic expectations of mineral revenues into its development plans. For example, in the assumptions underlying NDP5 the government prepared two scenarios, namely, rapid and slower mineral growth. Whereas the GDP projections in the plan were based on the former, the government revenue forecasts were based on the latter.

The behaviour of the Botswana government is grounded in its response to genuine uncertainty, a response which involves comparing the costs of different types of mistake (Hill 1991a). On the one hand, misperceiving a temporary boom as permanent and responding accordingly involves a subsequent government retrenchment and the cost of having endured a contraction in the non-boom tradables sector which must then be reversed. On the other hand, misperceiving a permanent boom as temporary and acting accordingly merely implies a temporary rise in saving until the true nature of the boom is perceived. The costs in the latter case will generally be far less than the costs in the former. A cautious government, when faced with uncertainty as to the nature of the boom which it is experiencing, may well choose to save rather than spend.

In order to examine the relation between innovations in revenue and innovations in expenditure, we have constructed a data series for recurrent expenditure innovations (*REI*) equivalent to that constructed for mineral revenue (*MRI*). This can be seen in Figures 9.11 and 9.12, equivalent to Figures 9.9 and 9.10. Deviations of actual from expected recurrent expenditure, assumed to represent consumption, are substantially smaller than those for mineral revenue innovations, suggesting that positive mineral revenue shocks do not lead to additional recurrent expenditure and are instead saved. Furthermore, there was a far smaller revision of recur-

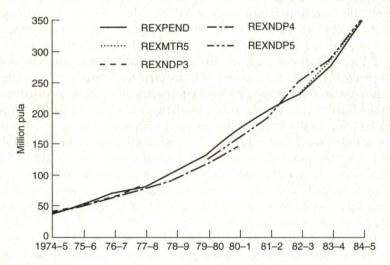

Figure 9.11.

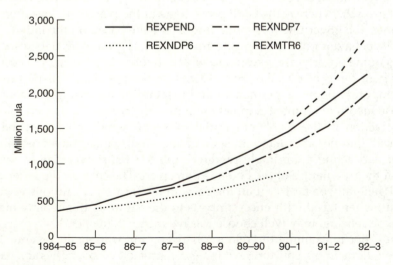

Figure 9.12.

rent expenditure plans across development plans than there was for expected mineral revenue.

Since the two data series have been constructed analogously, there is a recurrent expenditure innovation figure for each mineral revenue innovation figure, that is, for each year of each development plan forecast.[8] In order to measure the extent to which real mineral revenue innovations have caused real recurrent expenditure to rise above planned levels, the following regression was run:

$$REI = a + bMRI.$$

The results are reported in Table 9.2 (equation 1). Because the size of the revenue boom in 1986–90 was so large, the sample was truncated so as to eliminate the impact of this boom (Table 9.2, equation 3). The two regressions produce essentially the same results. In each case the coefficient on the innovation in mineral revenue, though significantly different from zero, is low. Equation (1) implies a savings rate out of the unexpected mineral revenue of 70% and equation (3) an even higher rate of 86%.

Equations (2) and (4) use the innovation in total revenue (RI) rather than in mineral revenue. The results remain substantially unchanged. The savings rate appears to be marginally higher because the total revenue innovation is fairly consistently larger than the mineral revenue innovation. Equations (5) and (6) repeat equations (1) and (2) using only the most recent projection for each year. The results are unchanged.

Table 9.2. The effects of mineral and total revenue innovations on recurrent expenditure innovations

	Equation							
	1	2	3	4	5	6	7	8
Constant term	−7.04	−0.74	4.99	4.86	5.14	10.09	12.66	14.12
MRI	0.30**		0.14*		0.20**		0.23**	
MRI_{-1}							−0.08	
RI		0.22**		0.10**		0.16**		0.17**
RI_{-1}								−0.05
$!^2$	0.89	0.90	0.23	0.22	0.57	0.49	0.62	0.51
SER	50.5	43.9	26.3	22.8	43.8	44.1	42.1	44.2
F	242.2	349.2	6.6	8.7	23.7	21.2	14.0	11.4
N	31	40	20	29	18	22	17	21
Period	1973–90	1969–90	1973–85	1969–85	1973–90	1969–90	1974–90	1970–90

** Significantly different from zero at the 1% level
 * Significantly different from zero at the 5% level

Notes:
1. The dependent variable is in each case the recurrent expenditure innovation (*REI*)
2. Equations (1) and (2) include all available observations, equations (3) and (4) exclude the years 1986–1990, and equations (5)–(8) include only the observations based on the most recent forecasts for each year
3. Innovations are measured in real levels

These results are not altogether surprising. Since revenue innovations are known only with a lag and public expenditure cannot be altered rapidly, one would expect only a small response in concurrent expenditure. We therefore transformed the data in order to include a one-period lag in the regression. For instance:

$$REI = a + bMRI + cMRI_{-1}.$$

The results, reported in equations (7) and (8) of Table 9.2, are again very similar. The unlagged coefficients remain small but positive and significant, and the lagged coefficients are slightly negative but not significantly so. The addition of a two-year lag (not shown) produced similar results. The sums of the current and lagged coefficients suggest a savings rate of 85% out of unexpected mineral revenue and 88% out of unexpected total revenue. This we regard as relatively strong evidence that the government of Botswana has indeed chosen to save a substantial part of its unexpected mineral revenue.

The investment/financial asset decision Since the government has saved a large proportion of unexpected mineral revenues, it has had to decide how to allocate that saving. Possible allocations include increasing domestic investment (for example, in the form of increased government development expenditure or increased private investment), increasing holdings of foreign assets and reducing foreign debts. The appropriate choice among these types of saving depends on their relative rates of return.

Figures 9.13 and 9.14 (analogous to Figures 9.11 and 9.12) show actual

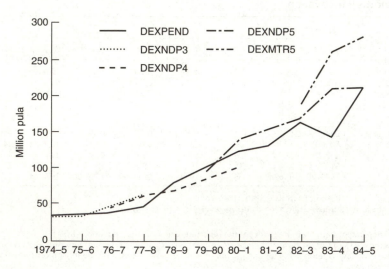

Figure 9.13.

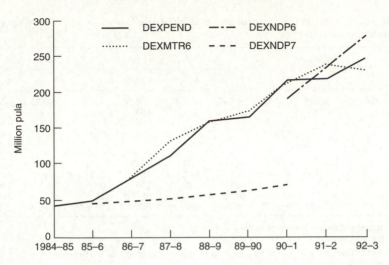

Figure 9.14.

and projected levels of government development expenditure. The innovations in development expenditure (*DEI*) are somewhat larger than those in recurrent expenditure. In particular, we see that development expenditure over the period 1980–84 fell below what had been projected in NDP5 and MTR5, on account of the diamond recession. However, over the later period 1986–90 development expenditure soared above NDP6 projections.

To see whether mineral revenue innovations have led to increased development expenditure beyond previously planned levels, regressions were run similar to those in the previous subsection, but with development expenditure innovations as the dependent variable (Table 9.3). The results suggest that, up to 1985, a relatively small share of mineral revenue innovations (about 15% using equations 3 and 4) was allocated to increased development expenditure above previously planned levels. After 1985 a substantially larger share was allocated in this way. Using NDP6 numbers, the ratio of the development expenditure innovation to the mineral revenue innovation equals 33% in 1986 and approximately 45% in each year from 1987 to 1990. For the first time development expenditure responded sharply to government windfalls.

Revenue innovations had a notable, and in one case significant, lagged positive effect on development expenditure (Table 9.3, equations 7 and 8). Moreover, the introduction of a one-year lag made the unlagged coefficients slightly negative. However, government development expenditure, more so than most recurrent expenditure, may well take longer than a year to adjust fully to revenue innovations. An attempt was therefore

Table 9.3. The effects of mineral and total revenue innovations on development expenditure innovations

	Equation							
	1	2	3	4	5	6	7	8
Constant term	−64.10*	−47.95*	−39.45	−37.45*	−32.50	−33.27	−47.53	−38.34*
MRI	0.40**		0.13		0.03		−0.03	
MRI_{-1}							0.15	
RI		0.29**		0.15		0.04		−0.01*
RI_{-1}								0.13*
$\bar{r}^2$	0.70	0.72	−0.02	0.05	−0.05	−0.02	0.09	0.15
SER	123.5	109.0	71.1	68.2	82.8	76.1	78.9	69.4
F	71.42	98.75	0.68	2.39	0.16	0.55	1.83	2.80
N	31	40	20	29	18	22	17	21
Period	1973–90	1969–90	1973–85	1969–85	1973–90	1969–90	1974–90	1970–90

** Significantly different from zero at the 1% level
 * Significantly different from zero at the 5% level

Notes: As for Table 9.2, except that the dependent variable is in each case the development expenditure innovation (*DEI*)

made to introduce two-year, as well as one-year, lagged independent variables into the equations (not shown). To avoid implausibly linking innovations across NDPs, the lagged relations were examined within development plans. The coefficients on two-year lagged variables were small and not significant. In summary, we were able to discern some evidence of delayed response, the length of the delay being no more than a year.

There was concern that the rapid increase in development expenditure above previously planned levels had been too rapid, reducing the rate of return on projects undertaken. There was also concern that it would be difficult to cut back the growth rate of development expenditure should mineral revenue stop growing rapidly. According to the Mid-term Review of NDP6 (para. 94, p. 36) in 1988:

The issue of how much of its reserves Government should invest today rather than in the future is largely an issue of what the rate of return on such investment would be in the future. Given the real constraint of implementation capacity, perhaps best measured by the difficulties in filling posts for professionals and technical personnel, it is likely that the rate of return to present investment will decline sharply as Government increases its level of domestic investment, and that Government will therefore find it best to reserve a substantial portion of its reserves for future investment.

One reason, therefore, why public development expenditure has not been expanded more quickly—and one which features strongly in government explanations—is the severe shortage of skilled labour, a legacy of the underinvestment in education in the pre-independence era. This constraint on the more rapid expansion of government, which is the most skilled-labour-intensive sector of the economy, was tightened after the decision in 1979 to share Botswana college graduates equally among central government, local government and the private sector. This decision arose from a report (Lipton 1978) which suggested that the private sector faced 'crowding out' as a result of a shortage of skilled labour, and that a more rapid growth of government would slow down the growth of the private sector. Raphaeli *et al.* (1984) stressed shortages of post-primary school graduates as a curb on training and the cause of vacancies in the public sector (14% in 1983/84). There was an elaborate system of controlling government recurrent and development expenditures, but this required that the executive capacity be in place to administer the system and ensure efficient implementation of projects (p. 27).

That part of government revenue innovations that does not go on recurrent or development expenditure is deposited in the central bank and is matched by increased foreign exchange reserves.[9] The government has simultaneously acquired foreign and domestic financial assets, deposits at the central bank and foreign reserves, and foreign financial liabilities, which have been used to pay for its development programme. Since much of this foreign debt is concessional, and since the government earns a higher (exchange rate-adjusted) rate of return on its assets, in effect the government has transferred part of the cost of development from itself to the international community. To the extent that the government of Botswana can still call on concessional assistance while increasing its own assets, saving its boom income in the form of financial assets becomes a revenue-raising policy. For instance, in the mid-1980s the government considered repaying early the Eurodollar loan that it had raised during the 1981/82 slump. After careful evaluation, it decided that the opportunity cost of using assets to pay off the loan would be greater than the cost of servicing it according to the original loan agreement.

It is very plausible that there would be asymmetry in the response to positive and negative shocks. This hypothesis was tested by re-estimating the sixteen equations in Tables 9.2 and 9.3. The method was to introduce a dummy variable (D) which took a value of 1 if the revenue innovation was negative and 0 if it was positive. Thus, for instance, in the equation

$$REI = a + bMRI + cMRI \cdot D,$$

the response to positive shocks is b while the response to negative shocks is $b + c$. We hypothesised that $c > 0$, that is, that spending is more sensitive to a bust than to a boom.

In only three of the sixteen equations was the coefficient c significantly different from zero, and in those cases (rather, three variants of the same case) it had the wrong sign. Nor did the additional interaction of D with the intercept term alter the picture. These results may simply reflect the facts that the revenue innovation is positive in the great majority of cases and that the few negative innovations are relatively tiny. The coefficient on revenue innovations in Tables 9.2 and 9.3 therefore almost entirely measures the responses to positive shocks. The single negative shock will receive a separate analysis using a different counterfactual methodology.

Transfers to the private sector The private sector has benefited from diamonds through a variety of channels. Botswana's diamond endowment allowed public consumption per capita to grow at an average annual rate of 9% per annum from 1964 to 1985. Similarly, recurrent expenditure per capita grew at 8% per annum from 1968 to 1987, while development expenditure per capita grew at 9% per annum over the same period. Largely on account of diamonds, non-mining GDP per capita grew at an annual rate of 5.5% from 1965 to 1987, while private consumption per capita grew at 5.2%. In this sense too the private sector benefited from diamonds: non-mining GDP and private consumption would have grown much more modestly in the absence of diamonds.

Consider the types of instrument used to transfer the boom to the private sector. Botswana, in contrast with other African countries, has preferred to avoid the use of price subsidies. The main subsidies in Botswana were to large-scale farmers via subsidies on beef and to civil servants via subsidies on housing. Neither of these were substantial components of government expenditure. Government has instead either made direct transfers or purchased goods and services.

The evidence above has shown that mineral revenue innovations did not lead to significant recurrent expenditure innovations. Unexpected booms were therefore not to any great extent transferred to the private sector through unplanned increases in government expenditure. Nevertheless, the planned expansion of government expenditure was rapid. As Bevan *et al.* (1989) suggest, the welfare impact on the population of government purchases of goods and services depends on their desirability and tradability characteristics. That is to say, a government purchase will affect welfare through the direct benefit of the expenditure and, in the case of non-tradables, through its rent-raising impact on domestic factor services.

We suspect that the Botswana government's purchases of goods and services have mostly been welfare-raising. Although there have been criticisms of an alleged urban bias in government expenditures, in fact it was the substantial investment in rural infrastructure which Botswana had undertaken since independence which enabled the government to distribute the Drought Relief Programme so efficiently that no deaths were recorded as a consequence of the drought and there was no statistically significant increase in malnourishment among children during the six-year period. Botswana's democratic system has made the government sensitive to the needs of voters, most of whom live in the rural areas. The government has, by comparison with other countries, placed emphasis on education, health care and other basic needs. It has avoided heavy subsidisation of parastatals providing urban services and it has avoided the extreme urban bias found in other countries. Support for the ruling party remains strong in the rural areas, whereas the party has lost some seats in the towns (Harvey and Lewis 1990, pp. 270–1).

Whereas the composition of recurrent expenditure was remarkably stable in the face of rapidly increasing total recurrent expenditure, there were greater fluctuations in the composition of development expenditure. Figure 9.15 shows the percentage shares of various components of government development expenditure. Some of the main changes have simple explanations, however. For example, spending on economic services declined after 1983/84 when the road programme drew to a close, and the peak of transfers in 1983–86 represented loans for an electricity project. The composition of government expenditure was not sensitive to trade shocks in the 1980s.

Data are not available on the tradability characteristics of government purchases. Evidence presented below shows that there was no long-term deviation of non-tradable from tradable goods prices, which might suggest that government purchases have not raised rents in the non-tradable sector. However, more disaggregated price series are needed to examine this proposition.

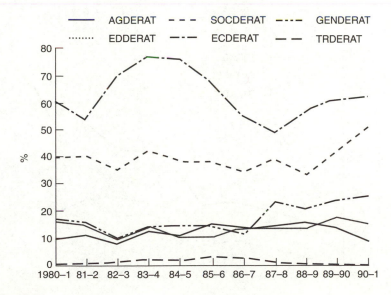

Figure 9.15.

The benefit from diamond shocks could be transferred from the public to the private sector by a reduction in the tax effort as well as by an increase in government expenditure. If tax effort is reduced when mineral revenue is unexpectedly high, other tax revenue should be below its projection. Figure 9.16 shows taxes from 'other revenues and grants' in 1979/80 prices, both actual and projected, the latter coming from NDP5 (1979/85) and NDP6 (1985/91). Far from actual revenue falling short of the projections, there was a growing windfall throughout the 1980s. Total revenue innovations were constantly larger than mineral innovations and 'other revenues and grants' innovations were positively associated with mineral innovations. It seems that mineral innovations had positive multiplier effects on other tax revenues, rather than substituting for them. There is no evidence that diamond shocks were transferred to the private sector through reduced taxation.

There is an argument that by accumulating assets from boom revenues, the government was choosing a savings path which private sector agents would have chosen were they able to. Agricultural incomes in Botswana fluctuate with the climate, which is thought to have a twenty-year cycle (fifteen years of rain followed by five years of drought). Since independence in 1966, there has been one cycle, with the drought—one of the worst in Africa—striking during the period 1981–88. Under the Drought Relief Programme the government transferred an amount which, excluding donors' food aid, totalled P358 million, equal to 45% of the agricultural GDP, over the period 1981/82–1988/89. If private agents themselves had been expected to accumulate sufficient assets in advance of the drought to

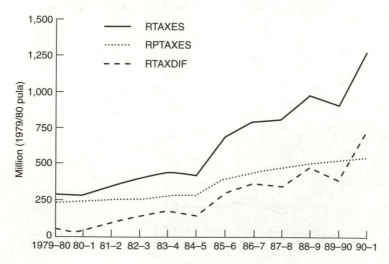

Figure 9.16.

survive it, this would have implied a savings ratio of one-third (if all income were lost) or one-sixth (if income were halved) per annum in the previous fifteen years—a heavy burden for agents with such low incomes. Rural households were saving-constrained, and the optimal policy for government required the release of that constraint through its own saving.

The drought acted as an offsetting bust to the diamond boom. Drought relief, a transfer to the private sector of some of the boom income from diamonds, would not have taken place in the absence of the drought. Was the drought relief provided on a scale sufficient to neutralise the effect of the negative shock on rural incomes? We address this question by attempting to measure the size of the shock. A comparison is made between agricultural GDP, measured in constant prices, and corresponding projections of agricultural GDP made in the development plans. The shortfall is gauged by comparing actual GDP with the pre-drought NDP5 projection: subsequent projections incorporated the shortfall resulting from the drought. The best estimate of the shortfall is obtained by extending the NDP5 projection and assumed growth rate over the remaining years of the drought (Table 9.4).

It is interesting to compare the agricultural shortfall with innovations in total and mineral revenue. The drought reinforced the diamond bust of the early 1980s, but after 1982/83 the revenue innovations were positive and much larger than the agricultural shortfall. The transfer under the Drought Relief Programme over the drought years represented 39% of the

Table 9.4. Agricultural busts and revenue innovations (*million constant 1979/80 pula*)

	Agricultural bust	Mineral revenue innovation	Total revenue innovation	Development expenditure on drought
1979/80	−1.3	12.3	−12.9	3.9
1980/81	−26.3	22.5	−1.9	2.7
1981/82	−33.3	0.3	−13.4	0.9
1982/83	−49.3	2.1	−7.9	4.1
1983/84	−63.2	22.5	32.0	7.8
1984/85	−73.6	79.6	107.6	18.4
1985/86	−73.2	116.8	171.4	25.0
1986/87	−81.7	242.7	299.6	30.3
1987/88	−79.7	278.6	331.8	44.0
1988/89	−86.6	445.9	563.3	37.2

Notes: Agricultural bust is based on NDP5 projections and assumed growth rates, projected into the later years, since the NDP6 projections include the effects of the drought. Mineral and total revenue innovations are based on NDP5 and NDP6 projections

Sources: Valentine (1993) and official statistics

agricultural shortfall (converted to current prices), of which roughly half
was funded by government. The table shows that no more than a small
share of the government windfall was transferred to the private sector
through this channel. Moreover, the regressions showing the effect of
mineral innovations on development expenditure innovations suggest
that drought relief other than food aid—primarily included in development expenditure—was not responsive to shocks.

9.3.3. Consumption and Saving in the Economy

We turn our attention from the government sector to the economy as a
whole and, by implication, to the private sector. How was consumption
affected by the fluctuations in GDP resulting from trade shocks? Have
private agents as well as government managed to smooth their consumption over time in the face of income fluctuations?

Figure 9.17 shows total GDP, non-mining GDP, and total, government
and private consumption. The measures of consumption were smooth
relative to total GDP, suggesting that the variability in diamond income
did not lead to comparable variability in consumption. Private consumption also appears smoother than non-mining GDP. Since income from
diamonds accrues to the government directly, this is the more appropriate
comparison when examining the consumption behaviour of the private
sector.

Figure 9.18 shows saving in the economy: overall saving, government
saving and private saving. Each propensity is expressed as a percentage of

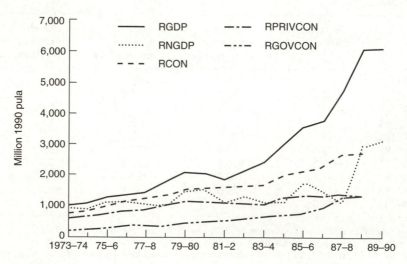

Figure 9.17.

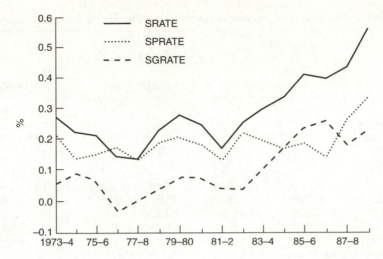

Figure 9.18.

GDP and is derived from current price data. Total saving is defined as GDP minus government and private consumption, government saving as government revenue minus government consumption, and private saving as the residual difference. We see that total saving and government saving move closely together. The interesting exception, however, is the recession year 1981/82, when government saving was maintained but total saving fell because private saving fell sharply: private consumption continued to grow despite the diamond recession.

Our hypothesis, therefore, is that consumption smoothing in the face of income fluctuations induced by trade shocks does indeed occur. It was not possible to replicate for consumption the regressions reported in Tables 9.2 and 9.3 for government expenditure, because consumption is not forecast in the National Development Plans. In order to measure the response of consumption to innovations in government mineral or total revenue, we have regressed changes (rather than innovations) in consumption (ΔC) on the income innovations as measured above. For instance:

$$\Delta C = a + bMRI.$$

Table 9.5, albeit based on small samples, suggests that consumption— whether total, public or private—does not respond in any significant way to innovations in mineral or total revenue.[10] The results remain unchanged if income innovations are allowed to affect consumption with a one- or two-year lag (equations not shown): all the coefficients on the innovations remain close to and insignificantly different from zero. This is

Table 9.5. The effects of revenue innovations on the change in consumption

	Equation					
	Total Consumption		Public Consumption		Private Consumption	
	1	2	3	4	5	6
Constant term	143.25**	138.27**	86.39**	84.81**	56.86*	53.45*
MRI	−0.10		−0.08		−0.03	
TRI		−0.07		−0.08		0.01
$\bar{r}^2$	−0.03	−0.04	−0.04	−0.01	−0.01	−0.07
SER	100.3	100.9	82.9	81.9	65.9	66.1
F	0.59	0.44	0.48	0.84	0.09	0.01
N	15	15	15	15	15	15

** Statistically significant at the 1% level
 * Statistically significant at the 5% level

Notes:
1. Only the revenue observations based on the most recent forecast for each year are used
2. The analysis covers the period 1975–89

further evidence in accordance with consumption-smoothing behaviour in Botswana.[11]

9.3.4. Exchange Rate Management

Since the positive diamond shocks improve the balance of payments they would tend to appreciate the foreign value of the currency unless the government saved all the additional income in the form of foreign assets. This in turn would harm the non-boom tradable sector, containing the non-traditional manufacturing sector which, in an agriculturally resource-poor country, is the one with the best long-term growth potential. It has been Botswana government policy to avoid harming this sector: appreciation of the real exchange rate has been prevented both through official intervention in the currency market and through overall macroeconomic management.

The goal of preventing the contraction of non-boom tradables through the avoidance of a real appreciation has been only one of the government's exchange rate objectives. Others relate to concern about inflation and policymakers' desires at certain times to effect the distribution of domestic incomes through exchange rate changes. These have worked to push exchange rate policy in different directions.

Botswana gained the option of an exchange rate policy only in 1976, when it first issued its own currency, the pula. Until then it had used the rand (as part of the Rand Monetary Area). There was a switch to a dollar peg (1977–80) and then to a basket of currencies comprising the rand and the SDR (1981 onwards). Botswana changed the nominal value of its currency both earlier and more frequently than other African countries. Whereas most of these fixed their exchange rates during the 1970s and then devalued substantially in the early 1980s, Botswana first revalued in 1977 and has made frequent, though small, changes ever since. Flexibility of exchange rate policy was assisted by the use of exchange rate 'games' for senior officials, in which different macroeconomic scenarios were presented: policymakers were well equipped to consider, and ready to make, exchange rate decisions when the need arose (Harvey and Lewis 1990).

Botswana's terms of trade are sensitive to the exchange rate between the dollar and the rand because exports tend to be priced in the former and imports in the latter currency. However, rand depreciations against the dollar are partly the result of a long-term disparity between South African and world inflation: in the medium term the terms of trade gains would be eroded by higher import inflation. Thus, one objective of Botswana's exchange rate policy has been to avoid imported inflation from South Africa by appreciating the pula.[12]

The distributional impact of exchange rate changes in Botswana could be regarded as perverse in an African context. Poor people have a higher import propensity (70%) than the better-off (40%) owing to the importation of basic foodstuffs. Thus, an appreciation of the currency is distributionally progressive in Botswana. However, the distributional impact of exchange rate changes has been explicitly cited only in the 1982 decision, when devaluation was used as a method of spreading the costs of adjustment to the diamond slump.

The authorities have been careful to avoid any dramatic appreciation of the real exchange rate (Figure 9.19). The real exchange rate can be measured in three ways: using 1980 import weights (RER1), using total 1980 trade weights excluding diamonds (RER2), and using the real pula/rand exchange rate (RER3).[13] A rise in the curve (1990 = 100) indicates a pula depreciation. There is a remarkable lack of trend from 1976 to 1983, a temporary appreciation of the pula in 1984 (especially in relation to the depreciating rand) and some real depreciation from 1985 onwards. Neither the expected nor the unexpected diamond fluctuations produced significant appreciation. The figure also contains an index of the real minimum wage. Having fallen in the 1981 recession, it showed a remarkable constancy from 1982 to 1988. In contrast to other countries which have experienced strong positive shocks, Botswana has managed to avoid Dutch Disease. It has thus managed to promote economic diversification through the encouragement of non-traditional manufactures, both production and exports. Not only have non-traditional manufactures grown

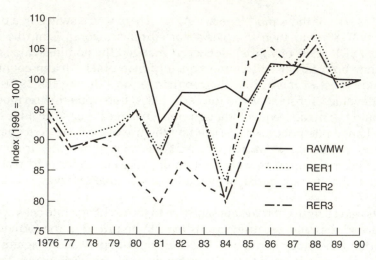

Figure 9.19.

dramatically but roughly 50% of this growth has derived from exports and import-substitution, in an economy free from import controls (Lewis and Sharpley 1988, tables 3a and 3b).

Owing to the government's policy of preventing appreciation of the real exchange rate and its restrained expenditure response to boom revenues, the price of non-tradable goods has not risen relative to the price of tradables. Figure 9.20 shows price series for boom tradables, non-boom tradables and non-tradables, derived through the arbitrary but plausible allocation of sectors to these three categories. We see the impact of the misleading mining sector (boom tradable) deflator on the GDP deflator. More importantly, we see that there has been no substantial change in the relative price of non-boom tradables and non-tradables. The only year in which the indices diverged was 1985, and this represented a slight fall, not a rise, in the price of non-tradable goods. This fall in the price of non-tradables relative to the boom and non-boom tradables was due to a nominal depreciation of the pula against all currencies except the depreciating rand.

9.4. The Diamond Recession, 1981–83

Let us examine Botswana's one negative trade shock—more properly, 'shocklet'—the recession in the gem market in the early 1980s. Owing to the fall in demand and accumulation of stocks in the wholesale and retail

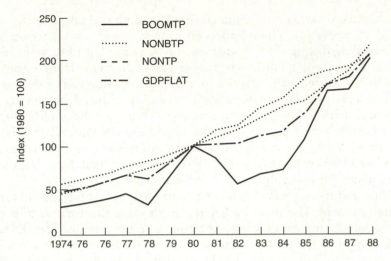

Figure 9.20.

system, the CSO imposed sales quotas on all the members of the producer cartel, particularly for high-quality gems.

From August 1981 onwards Botswana diamond exports effectively stopped. Foreign exchange reserves were falling fast. Standing at P286 million (five months of imports) in August 1981, they were projected to reach the dangerously low level of P50 million by the end of 1982 (Harvey 1985, p. 31). Nor was it clear when the diamond market would recover. Indeed, since the market for gems is maintained by confidence that they will remain a store of value, there were even some voices which questioned whether the market would recover. For the first time since the cartel had been established in the 1930s, De Beers seemed to have lost control.

The Botswana government decided that adjustment could not be postponed—that it was better to take gentle measures early rather than drastic measures later should they prove to be necessary. Government had observed the costly effects of 'import strangulation' on neighbouring countries, including Zambia. A package of policies was therefore immediately introduced, in the latter half of 1981, in order to counter the negative shock.

The policies did not include foreign exchange and import controls— the government was set against such quantitative restrictions. Nor could Botswana, being part of the Southern African Customs Union, raise import tariffs. The package unilaterally decided upon by the government included most of the orthodox policies normally insisted upon by the IMF as a condition for upper-tranche credit.

Limits were placed on commercial bank lending and interest rates were raised very sharply. There had been a rapid expansion in commercial bank lending during 1981, made possible by excess liquidity in the banking system. A ceiling of 8% was imposed on the increase from November 1981 to November 1982. The rise in interest rates—the bank rate was 6% in June 1981 and 12% in June 1982—not only reduced borrowing but switched it from local to foreign sources. We take the money supply (M_3 = currency plus demand, saving, notice and time deposits) to be the best proxy for aggregate demand in the economy. This fell in nominal terms by 14% between September 1981 and March 1982. It got back to its September 1981 real value only at the end of 1983.

Minor reductions were made in government spending and minor increases in taxes. The main budgetary effect came through wage policy. Public sector employees were expecting a large wage increase in early 1982, as part of the normal biennial review process. A rise of some 25% was needed to restore the real level established after the previous review. Government decided that there would be no public sector wage increase in 1982. Through the incomes policy, this decision was also important for the private sector. The wage-freeze policy was accepted politically and, indeed, was enduring in its effect: there was partial 'catch-up' in 1983 but the real wage regained its 1980 level only in 1984.

The main reason for the fall in government revenue between 1980/81 and 1981/82 was the fall in mineral revenue, related to diamond sales (Figure 9.21). Fiscal and financial arrangements with De Beers are not made public but mineral revenue (made up of royalties, income tax on

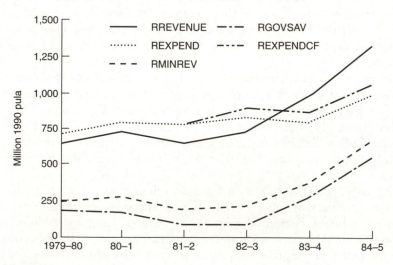

Figure 9.21.

profits, tax on remitted dividends, and dividends from government's equity holding) depends primarily on mineral profits (Harvey and Lewis 1990, p. 125). The figure shows that real government expenditure stagnated for three years. However, government saving (revenue minus government consumption) did fall in 1981/82. The figure demonstrates a remarkable similarity in the levels of government saving and mineral revenue. It is as though government decided to balance a recurrent budget from which mineral revenue was excluded and then to save mineral revenue!

The pula was devalued by 10% in May 1982 in order to improve the trade balance. The rand/pula exchange rate is the crucial one in determining import prices and the scope for import substitution. However, the pula had been appreciating against the rand over the previous year, and so the devaluation merely restored the exchange rate of May 1981. The government took out a small Eurodollar loan which had already been negotiated, and approached the IMF.

In the event it proved unnecessary to borrow from the IMF. The foreign exchange reserves shot up from P198 million in March 1982 to P301 million in June. This remarkable change was mainly in response to short-run capital movements, caused in turn by the restrictive monetary policies, but also helped by the pula depreciation and the foreign loan. The partial recovery of the gem market permitted some diamond sales, and the CSO also made purchases from the Jwaneng mine, which began production in July. Exports were up by R146 million in 1982 and imports by only R49 million; foreign exchange reserves stayed above the P300 million level.

The largely unexpected recession in the gem market thus overlapped with the scheduled opening of the Jwaneng mine. The government took its countermeasures despite the expected enormous expansion of diamond production from mid-1982 onwards. It did so because it could not be sure that the new production would be sold. In the event, the CSO purchased some Jwaneng production from the start, although it is not possible to isolate the value of sales from that source. The decision of De Beers to purchase part of the market share that had been allocated to Jwaneng was thus crucial to the outcome of this episode. Generally, the juxtaposition of a negative demand shock and a positive production shock means that the *ex post* outcome had rather limited consequences.

The crisis had proved to be short-lived. The package of measures may not have been necessary after all, although it had helped to contain imports and no doubt had bolstered expectations and confidence. The measures were easy to justify *ex ante*. Did they involve a cost *ex post*? There was a recession in non-mining investment during the period 1982–84 (Figure 9.6). At least part of this was due to the deflationary monetary policies of 1981–83 rather than the negative shock to which the policies were a response. The diamond recession had little discernible effect on real private consumption per capita. With 1980/81 as 100, the figure for 1981/82 was 103.4 and for 1982/83 104.0. There was a deceleration in the growth of central government revenue between 1980 and 1983. This appeared not to affect the growth of central government recurrent expenditure, which was steady. However, linear extrapolation suggests that it caused a loss of some 16% of development expenditure in one year, 1981/82. Moreover, we know that government employees paid at least a temporary price, in the form of a forgone wage increase, and that other wage employees also suffered.

If we pose the counterfactual 'What if there had been no recession in the diamond market?' the effects on Botswana are not easy to simulate. With no potential crisis there would have been no precautionary package of countermeasures. The recession in non-mining investment might not have occurred. However, part of this fall was due to the completion of the Jwaneng project with its large infrastructural investments. It cannot be assumed, therefore, that the recession in non-mining investment would have been entirely avoided. There would not have been a redistribution away from public sector employees. This can also be depicted in Figure 9.21: the counterfactual curve shows the implications for the government budget of a counterfactual 25% increase in the public sector wage bill in 1982/83, continuing through to 1985/86. The effect is to postpone the boom-induced movement into budgetary surplus.

To get a sense of what might have happened if the diamond recession had not occurred, two counterfactual experiments are conducted. In both cases it is assumed that, in the absence of the bust, real government revenue would have increased by a constant annual amount between 1980 and 1988 such that the simulated total government revenue for the period as a whole equalled the actual total. Thus the counterfactual is that government revenue was smooth rather than first experiencing a bust and then a boom. It seems reasonable to assume that government revenue would have been approximately the same over the period because the mines continued in production and the diamonds were not sold at low prices but stockpiled and sold at a later time. Had the recession not occurred, there would have been more exports of diamonds in the early 1980s and fewer in the late 1980s. In the actual circumstances it was a good investment to hold diamond stocks. It is not clear whether, in the absence of a diamond recession, the earlier disposal of diamonds would have yielded a higher discounted value. It is the cartel's normal pricing policy to make the timing of sales irrelevant to discounted profits. The counterfactual involves an inter-temporal reallocation of government tax revenues for which the effect on the discounted value is uncertain.

Figures 9.22 and 9.23 and Table 9.6 set out the actual outcome and two counterfactual scenarios, which differ in their assumptions about govern-

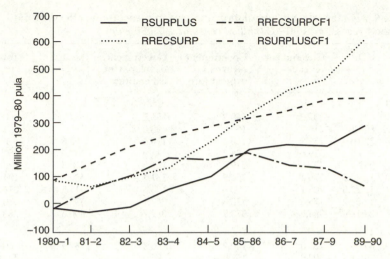

Figure 9.22.

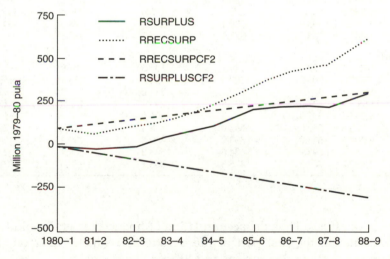

Figure 9.23.

ment spending. We saw that government spending responded little to the bust: had the recession not occurred, spending might have been much as it was. Scenario 1 (CF1, shown in Figure 9.22) assumes that recurrent and development spending followed their actual paths. The result of this assumption is that the surplus (revenue minus expenditure) of government would have been larger in the early years and smaller in the later

Table 9.6. Counterfactual simulation analysis to measure the effects of the diamond recession, 1981–83 (*million constant 1979/80 pula*)

	GDP	Government revenue	Government recurrent expenditure	Government development expenditure	Recurrent surplus	Total surplus
Actual						
1980	691.9	237.0	149.2	106.3	87.9	−18.5
1981	608.1	216.9	157.9	93.0	?	?
1982	720.0	253.8	160.2	110.0	93.6	−16.4
1983	813.8	319.6	186.2	87.9	133.4	45.5
1984	962.2	437.5	219.0	121.5	218.5	97.0
1985	1,187.1	576.4	250.9	131.4	325.5	194.0
1986	1,277.8	705.1	293.6	196.6	411.5	214.9
1987	1,504.2	778.0	320.4	247.1	457.7	210.6
1988	2,018.6	984.5	377.9	322.7	606.6	283.9
Scenario 1						
1980	691.9	237.0	149.2	106.3	87.9	−18.5
1981	790.7	303.0	157.9	93.0	?	?
1982	889.5	369.0	160.2	110.0	208.8	98.8
1983	988.3	435.0	186.2	87.9	248.8	160.8
1984	1,087.1	501.0	219.0	121.5	282.0	160.5
1985	1,185.8	567.0	250.9	131.4	316.1	184.6
1986	1,284.6	633.0	293.6	196.6	339.4	142.8
1987	1,383.4	698.9	320.4	247.1	378.6	131.5
1988	1,482.2	764.9	377.9	322.7	387.0	64.4
Scenario 2						
1980	691.9	237.0	149.2	106.3	87.9	−18.5
1981	790.7	303.0	189.9	168.7	113.1	−55.7
1982	889.5	369.0	230.7	231.2	138.3	−92.9
1983	988.3	435.0	271.5	293.6	163.5	−130.1
1984	1,087.1	501.0	312.3	356.0	188.7	−167.3
1985	1,185.8	567.0	353.0	418.4	213.9	−204.5
1986	1,284.6	633.0	393.8	480.8	239.2	−241.7
1987	1,383.4	698.9	434.6	543.2	264.4	−278.9
1988	1,482.2	764.9	475.3	605.7	289.6	−316.1

years of the 1980s. Thus the accumulation of financial assets would have been greater in the first part of the decade and smaller later on. The welfare implications are unclear and likely to be minor.

The first serious post-war diamond recession may well have provided a salutary warning of the risks and dangers of excessive expenditures and overcommitments. Had it not occurred, the large permanent positive Jwaneng shock might have induced higher spending. Both recurrent and development expenditures increased more rapidly after than before 1985. In Scenario 2 (CF2, shown in Figure 9.23) we assume that, in the absence of the bust, the more rapid rate of increase experienced after 1985 would have commenced in 1980: the same percentage growth rate is applied throughout the period. Simulated recurrent surplus (revenue minus recurrent expenditure) and total surplus figures are reported on that basis. Instead of the government accumulating financial assets from 1983 onwards, the surplus would have been negative over the entire period.

If the bust had not occurred the adjustment policies discussed earlier would not have been adopted. For example, the government would not have devalued the nominal exchange rate and would not have held down government wages—both policies adopted in response to the bust. These actions on the part of the government would have meant an appreciated real exchange rate relative to what actually occurred, a smaller current account surplus and less accumulation of net foreign assets.

Under Scenario 2, the estimate of real development expenditure in 1988 is almost twice the actual level of 1988, and the cumulative counterfactual government deficits over the nine years are approximately equal to the counterfactual GDP in 1988. Would government have behaved in the apparently profligate way implicit in this scenario? Would it have been able to do so, given the resource constraints and bottlenecks? These questions might best be answered by examining government behaviour in the 1990s, but this is outside the period of our study.

9.5. Concluding Comments

Reflecting the unusual nature of trade shocks in Botswana, this case study has differed from others not only in its conclusions but also in its methodology. The counterfactual analysis of the diamond recession in the early 1980s did not involve adjustments to the production of exports or of GDP. Rather, the simulations involved changes in the timing of export sales and of government revenue, and in the subsequent growth of government expenditure in the absence of the salutary warning provided by the diamond bust. Our methodological innovation was, by means of the National Development Plans, to define the diamond shocks in terms of unanticipated revenue fluctuations and to measure the expenditure responses to these shocks. In that sense our assumed counterfactuals were precisely the outcomes anticipated by government in its plans.

The Botswana government was able successfully to manage the shocks of the 1970s and 1980s. It adopted a cautious strategy towards the diamond boom. The persistent downward bias in the estimates of permanent income in the development plans is probably not due to the formation of adaptive instead of rational expectations. Rather, it is a consequence of the asymmetry in the costs of adjustment associated with under- and overestimation. Policies based on low estimates are less costly to correct than those based on estimates that turn out to be too high. As a result of this bias towards pessimism, by the end of 1989 the international reserves represented no less than 86% of annual GDP and twenty-two months of imports, and government deposits with the central bank represented 180% of government expenditure.

The authorities were also prudent with regard to unanticipated shocks, that is, deviations from forecasts. In the case of the one negative shock, they prepared to deal with a recession more serious and prolonged than turned out to be the case. Government had a very high marginal propensity to save unanticipated revenue (generally between 80% and 90%), and the marginal propensity to invest was low (generally between 10% and 20%). As a result, wasteful expenditures were largely avoided, at least until the late 1980s, and over time the Botswana economy became rather less vulnerable to economic setbacks.

This case study carries three general lessons for policymakers concerned to reduce the costs of export instability in poor countries. First, it is sensible to be cautious in forecasting the effects of booms on permanent income because of the asymmetry of adjustment costs. Second, there is a case for only minor adjustment to unanticipated positive shocks (in excess of forecasts), an example of which would be a low marginal propensity to spend unanticipated government revenue. Third, prudence suggests that downward divergences from forecasts be treated as potentially permanent: it may well be less harmful to adjust early and gradually than to wait until a possible crisis in the hope that it does not happen. The greater the weight attached to risk-aversion in the objective function, the more powerful are these lessons.

Various explanations can be put forward for the relatively successful economic management of trade fluctuations in Botswana (for instance, Isaksen 1981; Hill and Mokgethi 1989; Harvey and Lewis 1990). Our benchmark is of course the relative lack of success of many other governments examined in this volume.

First, Botswana had luck on its side. With one minor exception, all the shocks were positive shocks. Moreover, the rates of growth of public and private consumption (13.7% and 11.6% per annum in real terms between 1973/74 and 1985/86) made possible by the remarkable growth of output (12.3% per annum) were such that pressures for government profligacy could be resisted and contained. In different circumstances the quality of Botswana's economic management would have been more severely tested.

Second, Botswana is in a position of great vulnerability. It is semi-arid and so vulnerable to droughts. The cattle stock—before minerals the main form of wealth—has varied closely with the level of rainfall. It would not be surprising if risk-aversion had become embedded in the culture. In recent years political vulnerability has been added to ecological vulnerability. Botswana is highly dependent on South Africa for trade and transportation, and it was endangered by economic sanctions, whether they were to be imposed by South Africa or by the outside world against South Africa. Vulnerability breeds caution.

Third, the quality of leadership in Botswana has been unusually high. Since independence in 1966, there have been two presidents, both outstanding leaders. Leaders have sought and heeded economic advice. Politicians, civil servants and others in key positions have stayed in them for long periods and acquired experience. Economic success and the openness of the society have prevented the loss of key talent to international organisations. It has been said that the Botswana government is a government of cattlemen. Many politicians have therefore had commercial experience in a high-risk activity. The democratic system of government makes government responsive to citizens' opinions and to the needs of the rural majority. In principle, democracy encourages government to be excessively optimistic about positive shocks because it gives weight to the expectations of the relatively uninformed electorate rather than those of the potentially better-informed leaders. Botswana has avoided this tendency, partly because of its traditional emphasis on consultation. Moreover, the government has remained very secure and this stability has meant that it is not pliable in the hands of pressure groups.

There are signs that the quality of economic management declined somewhat after the mid-1980s. Government recurrent expenditures increased rapidly in real terms from 1984/85 to 1989/90, at an average rate of 16% per annum, on the crest of the diamond boom. Real development expenditures increased even more rapidly, by 20% per annum, until 1989/90, when capacity constraints in the economy curbed the implementation of development projects. Simultaneously a considerable cushion against adverse shocks was being built up. Nevertheless, there were reasons to believe that the remarkably rapid expansion of government expenditure in the boom years of the late 1980s was excessive in relation to capacity constraints on the efficient use of funds and the vulnerability of the economy to adverse shocks.

In 1990 the prospects for diamonds in the world market faded, the average quality of Botswana gems fell, and no further expansion of their quantity was expected. It was feared that diamond export earnings would fall and might remain depressed for years. The Bank of Botswana therefore called for real adjustments in government expenditure in the 1990s, involving not only general spending curbs but also a revision of priorities away from non-productive services, social programmes and defence (Bank of Botswana 1991, pp. 3–5).

International recession and loss of control over the diamond market forced the cartel to impose quotas in 1992, restricting Botswana sales to 75% of production capacity. The growth rate of the economy declined sharply, becoming negative in 1992/93. Although cash balances and international reserves had been accumulated precisely to deal with short-term problems of this sort, the uncertainty about the duration of the recession required firm fiscal action, which, in the view of the central bank, was not forthcoming (Bank of Botswana 1991, pp. 4–5; 1992, pp. 2, 42). Fortunately, the diamond market began to improve in 1993, and the sales quota was relaxed. The events of the early 1990s were a salutary reminder of Botswana's susceptibility to trade shocks. However, economic management in the face of a serious and prolonged diamond recession remained untested.

NOTES

We are grateful to Will Cavendish for his ideas, advice and assistance.

1. Republic of Botswana, Central Statistics Office, *Statistical Bulletin* (1992), December, 17, 4, table 5.5. Unfortunately the distinction between tradable and non-tradable price indices was introduced only in January 1990.
2. We use the IMF *International Financial Statistics* conventions: for national accounts data, 1990 refers to the fiscal year ending in 1990, and for government accounts data, 1990 refers to the fiscal year starting in 1990.
3. The mystique and secrecy which surround it may be good for the cartel but pose a problem for our study.
4. This valuation practice has implications also for the comparison of mining GDP at current and at constant (1979/80) prices (Harvey and Lewis 1990, pp. 45–6): it caused current price mining GDP to be well below its constant price equivalent until the mid-1980s.
5. These plans will be referred to as the Transitional Plan (1965/66–1970/71), NDP1 (1968/69–1972/73), NDP2 (1970/71–1974/75), NDP3 (1973/74–1977/78), NDP4 (1976/77–1980/81), NDP5 (1979/80–1984/85), NDP6 (1985/86–1990/91) and NDP7 (1991/92–1996/97), and the mid-term reviews of NDP5 and NDP6 as MTR5 and MTR6.
6. One problem encountered has been the choice of deflator to convert all the different sets of projections into current prices. On account of the misleading nature of the GDP deflator in the early 1980s, the CPI has been used, although this is not completely satisfactory.
7. As a consequence of the importance of mineral revenues in total revenues, deviations between actual and expected total revenues closely follow deviations between actual and expected mineral revenues.
8. As the development plans and mid-term reviews overlap there are two sets of data for some years.
9. A divergence between net foreign assets and government deposits emerged after 1984, in part explained by appreciation of the currencies in which the foreign assets were held relative to the pula.
10. This methodology is used in Cuddington and Hill (1991) but with the innovations based on econometric time-series models rather than on government projections.

11. If annually updated projections of future income were available it would be of interest to see whether consumption has responded to revisions of expected permanent income. However, no such projections were available from the NDP and MTR reports.

12. Appreciations for this reason occurred in 1977 (5%), 1979 (5%), 1980 (5%) and in 1989 (10%). The earlier revaluations were monitored by the Bank of Botswana to ensure that lower import prices were passed on to consumers.

13. The real exchange rate is defined in each case as $\pi(e_i p!/p)^{a_i}$ where $p!$ = foreign country i price index (CPI), p = Botswana price index, e_i = pula/foreign country i exchange rate and a_i = foreign country i weight.

REFERENCES

Bank of Botswana (1991, 1992) *Annual Report*, Gaberone.

Bevan, D.L., P. Collier and J.W. Gunning (1990) 'The Macroeconomics of External Shocks', in V.N. Balasubramanian and S. Lall (eds), *Current Issues in Development Economics*, London: Macmillan.

——(1989) 'Economic Policy in Countries Prone to Temporary Trade Shocks', in M.F. Scott and D. Lal (eds), *Public Policy and Economic Reform*, Oxford: Oxford University Press.

Colclough, Christopher and Stephen McCarthy (1980) *The Political Economy of Botswana: A Study of Growth and Distribution*, Oxford: Oxford University Press.

Corden, W. Max (1984) 'Booming Sector and Dutch Disease Economics: Survey and Consolidation', *Oxford Economic Papers*, 36, 3, 339–60.

Cuddington, J. and Catharine B. Hill (1991) 'Commodity Booms in Botswana and the Permanent Income Hypothesis', mimeo.

De Beers Consolidated Mines Limited (annual) *Annual Report*, Kimberley.

Gersovitz, M. and Christina H. Paxson (1990) 'The Economies of Africa and the Prices of their Exports', Princeton Studies in International Finance, No. 68, October.

Hall, Robert (1978) 'Stochastic Implications of the Life Cycle-Permanent Income Hypothesis: Theory and Evidence', *Journal of Political Economy*, 86, December.

Harvey, Charles (1985) 'The Use of Monetary Policy in Botswana in Good Times and Bad', University of Sussex, Institute of Development Studies, Discussion Paper 204, May.

——(1987) *Successful Macroeconomic Adjustment in Three Developing Countries: Botswana, Malawi and Papua New Guinea*, Washington, DC: Economic Development Institute, World Bank.

Harvey, Charles and Stephen R. Lewis, Jr (1990) *Policy Choice and Development Performance in Botswana*, London and Paris: Macmillan and OECD Development Centre.

Hill, Catharine B. (1991a) 'Managing Commodity Booms in Botswana', *World Development* 19, 1185–96.

——(1991b) 'A Precautionary Demand for Savings and Tests of the Permanent

Income Hypothesis in Botswana,' Williams College, Research Memorandum No. 125.

Hill, Catharine B. and D. Nelson Mokgethi (1989) 'Botswana: Macroeconomic Management of Commodity Booms', in Economic Development Institute, *Successful Development in Africa: Case Studies of Projects, Programs and Policies*, Washington, DC: World Bank.

International Monetary Fund (monthly) *International Financial Statistics*, Washington, DC: IMF.

Isaksen, T. (1981) *Macroeconomic Management and Bureaucracy: The Case of Botswana*, Bergen: Chr. Michelsen Institute, DERAP.

Knight, J.B. (forthcoming) 'Why Diamonds Should Fascinate Economists', Institute of Economics and Statistics, Oxford (processed)

Lewis, S. and J. Sharpley (1988) 'Botswana's Industrialisation', IDS Discussion Paper.

Lipton, Michael (1978) *Employment and Labour Use in Botswana*, Gaberone: Government Printer.

Neary, J.P. and S. van Wijnbergen (eds) (1986) *Natural Resources and the Macroeconomy*, Oxford: Blackwell.

Nelson, C. and C. Plosser (1982) 'Trends and Random Walks in Macroeconomic Time Series', *Journal of Monetary Economics*, 10, 139–62.

Quinn, V.M., J. Mason, M. Cohen and B.N. Kgosidintsi (1988) 'Crisis-Proofing the Economy: The Response of Botswana to Economic Recession and Drought', in G.A. Cornia, R. Jolly and F. Stewart (eds), *Adjustment with a Human Face*, New York: Oxford University Press.

Raphaeli, Nimrod, Jacques Roumani and A. C. McKellar (1984) 'Public Sector Management in Botswana: Lessons in Pragmatism', World Bank Staff Working Papers No. 709, Washington, DC: World Bank.

Republic of Botswana (1970) *National Development Plan 1970–75*, Gaberone: Ministry of Finance and Development Planning (NDP2).

—— (1973) *National Development Plan 1973–78*, Gaberone: Ministry of Finance and Development Planning (NDP3).

—— (1977) *National Development Plan, 1976–81*, Gaberone: Ministry of Finance and Development Planning (NDP4).

—— (1980) *National Development Plan 1979–85*, Gaberone: Ministry of Finance and Development Planning (NDP5).

—— (1983) *Mid-Term Review of National Development Plan Five*, Gaberone: Ministry of Finance and Development Planning (MTR5).

—— (1985) *National Development Plan 1985–91*, Gaberone: Ministry of Finance and Development Planning (NDP6).

—— (1988) *Mid-Term Review of National Development Plan Six*, Gaberone: Ministry of Finance and Development Planning (MTR6).

—— (1991) *National Development Plan 1991–97*, Gaberone: Ministry of Finance and Development Planning (NDP7).

Republic of Botswana, Central Statistics Office (CSO) (quarterly) *Statistical Bulletin*, Gaberone.

Valentine, Theodore R. (1993) 'Mineral-Led Economic Growth, Drought Relief and Incomes Policy: Income Distribution in Botswana Reconsidered', *American Journal of Economics and Sociology*, 52, 1, 31 ff.

10

The Uranium Boom in Niger, 1975–82

JEAN-PAUL AZAM

Niger is by any standards one of the poorest countries in the world, with per capita GNP in 1988 estimated to be US$310 (World Bank 1990). Moreover, its stock of human capital seems especially low, with life expectancy at birth estimated at 44.5 years in 1987, compared to an average of 54 years for low-income countries (China and India excluded), and the primary school enrolment ratio in 1986 at 29%, compared to 76% (World Bank 1990). As a result, the country was ranked last in the world according to the 1990 UNDP human development index (UNDP 1990).

Niger is a landlocked Sahelian country, and 65% of its huge territory (1.3 million km^2 for 7 million people in 1987) is part of the Sahara desert. About 10% only of its land is really useful for agriculture (see SEDES 1987). This location, on the fringe of the world's largest tropical desert, makes the country especially vulnerable to climatic shocks. After an exceptionally rainy period in 1956–65, by normal standards, it was affected by two severe droughts culminating in 1973 and 1984. The 1969–73 drought resulted in a famine (Sen 1981). Moreover, one of its traditional export crops, namely groundnuts, was so severely hit by disease in 1975, just two years after the poorest crop caused by the drought, that farmers permanently changed their production pattern in favour of cowpeas, which are more drought-resistant, and for which there is a market nearby in neighbouring northern Nigeria. But the cowpea crop contributes very little to the government budget, as opposed to groundnuts, which are heavily taxed.

Beside these natural shocks, the economy of Niger has been affected by various other shocks originating in policy reforms or external events. Charlick (1991) provides a useful account of the history of Niger, stressing its exposure to external shocks. In particular, the value of its uranium exports increased dramatically in the mid-1970s, and the macroeconomic consequences of this shock are analysed in this chapter. The uranium boom lasted until 1982–83, when the government launched an adjustment programme, supported by the IMF and later by the World Bank.

Trade shocks are essentially different when they concern mining, or the exploitation of other exhaustible resources, from the standard case where they concern reproducible products. The basic question with the former type of shock is when to extract the mineral, whereas the relevant question with the latter is simply how much to produce of the good. In other words, exploiting minerals is fundamentally a portfolio problem, and not a production problem. Mining-sector trade shocks affect the date at which the country exchanges its mineral asset for other assets, such as bonds or productive capital.

To get a sense of the importance of this shock for the economy of Niger, one can observe that exports of uranium concentrates accounted for 17.3% of official exports in 1972, 60.7% in 1975, and 84.3% in 1980. These figures do not take into account unrecorded trade, which is quite important in Niger, so that they overestimate the share of uranium in actual exports. The weight of this sector in the economy looks much less important in terms of value-added. It accounted for 5.88% of GDP in 1975, reaching a maximum of 14.24% in 1979, and decreasing gradually back to 7.65% in 1982.

This analysis is made especially interesting because Niger belongs to the franc zone (see Guillaumont and Guillaumont 1984). More precisely, it belongs to the Union Monétaire Ouest-Africaine (UMOA), with Bénin, Burkina-Faso, Côte d'Ivoire, Mali, Sénégal and Togo, and shares with these countries a common currency, the CFA franc (CFAF). The rules of this monetary union—including the pegging of the exchange rate to the French franc, automatic balance of payments support by the French treasury, and an institutional constraint on monetary financing of government budget deficits—aim at providing some monetary stability. Other African economies, outside the franc zone, often add monetary instability to the list of the possible sources of shocks to which they are subjected.

Moreover, because of these rules, franc zone member countries will not in general run the risk of facing a shortage of foreign currencies. But, as they have an institutional constraint preventing them from freely using the inflation tax, their governments have to borrow comparatively more on the world capital market than other African countries, and they can do this thanks to monetary stability and credible budgetary restraint, which enhance their creditworthiness (Mathonnat and Collange 1988).

One of the drawbacks of franc zone membership, which is due more to the French tradition than to the intrinsic logic of monetary unions, is that the favourite instrument of monetary policy is credit control. In some of the member countries, this is used in a very selective way, favouring some sectors and inhibiting the development of others. This is the case in Niger, where the distribution of credit among sectors is policy-determined (Vizy 1989). In Niger, over the period under study, the central bank used to exert some soft control on the credits extended by each bank, keeping the possibility of barring some credits (Adji 1986). Moreover, the sectoral allocation of credit had to comply with the orientations of the National Development Plan. One can find many common features of financial repression among certain of these countries, with low (often negative) real interest rates, differentiated by sector, and credit rationing.

There is no formal exchange control in the member countries of the CFAF zone, but there is a sort of *ex post* monitoring of capital flows with the rest of the world. The central bank controls the external position of the banks, and may demand the repatriation of balances held abroad by them (Adji 1986). This is not so for the non-financial firms. External financing of local projects was deterred by interest rates below the rates prevailing abroad, and in particular in France, to which many banks and firms of the modern sector are linked. It was only after 1979 that a substantial flow of private credit from France and other foreign countries occurred in Niger, by the system known as *crédits rétrocédés*, whereby local banks could lend funds borrowed from their foreign correspondents (Adji 1986).

But, although Niger is thus protected from some inflationary influences by the pegging of its currency to the French franc and by the control of its money growth, it is not protected from all exchange rate shocks. There are two possible sources of such shocks. First, the French franc fluctuates in terms of US or dollars other major currencies. Over the medium to long run, this has implied a depreciation of the CFAF in the post-war period.

Second, and more importantly, many markets in Niger are closely, although informally, integrated with markets in Nigeria (Arnoult 1983; Azam 1991a; Grégoire 1986). Hence, the exchange rate between the CFAF and the naira plays an important role in Niger. But the naira is not convertible, and it is not accepted in general by the central bank in Niger, the Banque Centrale des Etats de l'Afrique de l'Ouest (BCEAO), or by any bank of the formal sector. Only a restricted set of transactions with Nigeria is carried out at the official exchange rate. Therefore, it is the parallel market exchange rate which is relevant, and not the official exchange rate, which plays mainly an infra-marginal role (Azam and Besley 1989). It is a transmission mechanism whereby many macroeconomic shocks are transmitted from Nigeria to Niger. We must pay some attention to this variable in studying the external shocks experienced by the economy of Niger.

On the other hand, the analysis of the macroeconomic consequences of the uranium shock in Niger is made especially difficult by the existence of a large informal sector, whose importance is not known at all accurately. Only two surveys, at the firm level, have been done on this sector, in 1981–82 and 1987. The results of the latter have not yet been exploited fully to help improve the analysis of this sector in the national accounts. It is certain that the relative weight of the informal sector with respect to the modern sector changes in response to the various shocks affecting the economy (Guillaumont *et al.* 1991; Azam *et al.* 1992). Moreover, it is probable that the degree of coverage of this sector in the national accounts is not only uncertain, but changing as well. Hence, all the discussion of national account data or other official data is subject to this caveat.

The study starts in Section 10.1 by attempting to isolate the uranium shock in a complex mixture of a price shock and a resource discovery shock, which need to be distinguished. The temporary external shock in which we are interested is restricted to the deviation of the price of uranium from an initially expected path, taking into account the induced changes in behaviour relative to some initial plan. Uranium extraction started in Niger in 1971, and the big price hike hit the mining sector during the build-up phase. Then, as predicted by Hotelling's theory of the exploitation of exhaustible resources (Dasgupta and Heal 1979), the mining firms reduced the speed of extraction during the period when the price was climbing, and rushed it later, when the price stabilized, in order to reap the benefits of waiting. Therefore, part of the windfall income may be regarded as saved at the source, by comparison with a counterfactual extraction path. This is called 'pre-empted' saving in the following. The corresponding money flow, or distributed windfall, comes only later, when extraction is rushed.

Then, in Section 10.2, we try to trace the propagation of the shock to the rest of the economy. It turns out that this shock had a negligible aggregate impact on the non-mining sector. But, it had a noticeable impact on the composition of this sector, with non-tradables getting a higher share of inputs, and tradables a correspondingly smaller share. Despite some interference of economic fluctuations in Nigeria with the formation of food prices, we can observe the role of relative prices in driving this compositional change. We thus find results which agree with Dutch Disease theory (Corden and Neary 1982), and even with construction boom theory (e.g. Bevan *et al.* 1991), inasmuch as the construction and public works sector expanded relatively faster than the other tradables. However, the transmission mechanism of the shock onto the non-mining sector does not square exactly with the theory. We study the response of aggregate saving and aggregate demand in Section 10.3, showing that the driving force has been the investment expenditure of the mining sector. The latter is in turn explained by a simple forward-looking accelerator mechanism, with a variable ICOR. We find a very large average propensity to save out of windfall income, but the bulk of the saved windfall is made up of the saving pre-empted by the mining sector. Therefore, we argue that the Niger economy mishandled the shock, by failing to bank on the discounted value of the shock in order to smooth expenditures over time outside the mining sector. A public investment boom in the non-mining sector occurred only when the uranium money actually flew in at the end of the boom, with the well-known drawbacks of investment bunching (see e.g. Bevan *et al.* 1991).

Lastly, Section 10.4 is devoted to government policy. The budget deficit was on the whole reasonable, and only got out of hand at the end of the period. An investment grant boom probably helped trigger the expenditure spree. But the failure of the Niger economy to bank on the uranium boom may to a large extent be blamed on monetary policy, which was very conservative, and used selective credit control as its main instrument. Niger thus offers an interesting example of endogenous financial repression, which contrasts interestingly with other cases, such as Kenya or Sénégal, where monetary control was relaxed in response to a boom.

10.1. The Nature of the Shock

Niger started to exploit its uranium mines in 1971, and this new production turned into a major increase in export revenues in the wake of the mid-1970s oil shock, following a large price increase. Therefore, the uranium shock in Niger is made up of two components: there was (i) a resource-discovery shock, of the type which has been much studied in the 'Dutch Disease' literature, and which is outside the scope of the present paper, and (ii) a temporary external shock, owing to the price hike. We now try to identify and describe this external shock.

10.1.1. The Uranium Shock in Nominal Terms

The average f.o.b. price of uranium in Cotonou (Bénin), which is the port through which Niger uranium is exported, went up sharply in CFAF terms by a series of large steps. It nearly doubled in 1975, and made several other jumps in 1976 and 1978. Overall, the price went up fivefold in nominal terms between 1973 and 1979–80, as shown in Figure 10.1.

The CFAF f.o.b. price which Niger gets in Cotonou for its uranium is not directly linked to the world price, as it is in fact a sort of transfer price for the foreign-owned mining firms.[1] It results from a negotiation between the firms and the Government of Niger. But obviously, the relative bargaining strength of the two partners implies that this price is not entirely insulated from world price changes.

The series of the quantity exported is also represented in Figure 10.1. As could be expected from the theory of the optimal exploitation of exhaustible resources (Dasgupta and Heal 1979), output stagnated during the period of the sharp price increases. This is because when the rate of growth of the price of a mineral product is larger than the rate of return on the relevant alternative asset, it is more profitable to keep it stored (in the ground, or otherwise) than to exchange it for other assets. The mining firm will be indifferent between holding the mineral in the ground and holding another asset only if the expected growth rate of the price is equal to the opportunity rate of return. This is known as Hotelling's rule (Hotelling

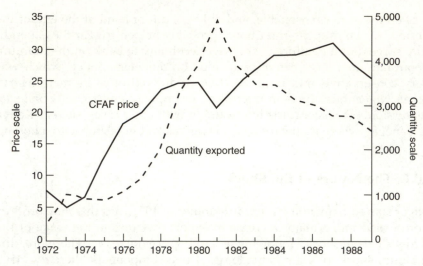

Figure 10.1. Price and quantity of uranium exports, 1972–89

Source: Ministère du Plan, *Annuaire Statistique*.

1931). If the price rises at a slower rate, then the firm will want to extract the mineral as fast as possible, whereas if the price rises at a faster rate, then the firm will want to restrict extraction as much as possible, in order to benefit later from capital gains. However, when dealing with a mining firm in a foreign country, running at any point in time various political risks, we may expect that other considerations will be taken into account. Probably, there is in general a minimum politically acceptable rate of exploitation, since the government may exert pressure on the mining firm to provide a steady flow of royalties because of a liquidity constraint or other capital market imperfections.[2] As will be seen below, this reasoning is not upset by translating these price data into real terms, as the real price series has roughly the same profile as the nominal price series.

Hence, when it became apparent that the growth of the price of uranium was slowing down, the mining firms rushed the extraction, and the quantity exported increased steadily between 1978 and 1981, with peak increases in 1979 and 1981. Then the world market reached a state of glut, and the mining firms became constrained by their outlets. The quantity exported thus started to decline gradually.

This lagged response of output to the price rise, which is roughly consistent with rational inter-temporal substitution behaviour as sketched above, smoothed the change in export revenues. As shown in Figure 10.2, the series of uranium export revenues has a simple hump-shaped profile. It displays a sort of logistic growth until 1980–81, when it reaches a plateau. Then, after 1984, the curve slopes slightly downwards, until 1989.

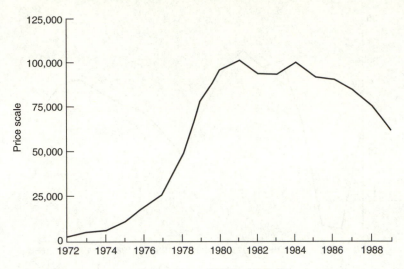

Figure 10.2. Export revenue (m. current CFAF), 1972–89
Source: Ministère du Plan, *Annuaire Statistique*.

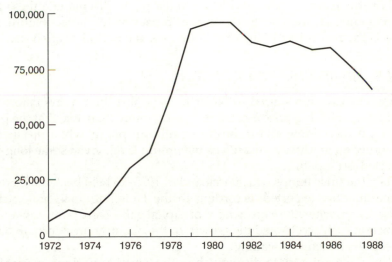

Figure 10.3. Real value of uranium export revenue, 1972–88 (1982 prices)

In order to analyse the macroeconomic consequences of such a shock, we first need to deflate the series in order to express them in real terms. In the case of Niger, this is not a trivial task. The methodology adopted here is discussed in Appendix 10.2. Figure 10.3 represents the real value of uranium export revenue. Moreover, as noted above, the uranium boom in Niger is in fact made of two components: (i) the resource-discovery shock

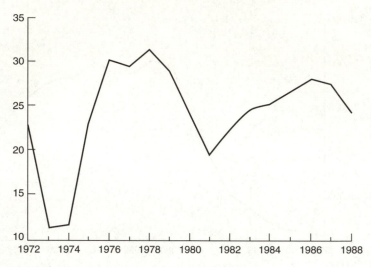

Figure 10.4. Real uranium price, 1972–88 (1982 prices)

and (ii) the external price shock. We must try to disentangle these two components, in order to focus on the impact of the latter. Figure 10.4 depicts the real price of Niger uranium over the period of analysis.

10.1.2. Identification of the Trade Shock

Uranium extraction started in Niger in 1971, just three years before the beginning of the big price escalation. It is therefore plausible that the price shock hit the mining sector during a build-up phase, when production was growing gradually towards its maximum level, given some long-run expected price path.

Then the price jumps which occurred in 1975–76 held back the increase in the quantity exported, according to the Hotelling analysis sketched above. Later, when the expectations of capital gains were fading away, the extraction rush accelerated the growth of the quantity produced, in order to reap the benefits of waiting.

Hence, we must try to distinguish in the actual behaviour of uranium export revenues what is due to the deviation of the price from its expected path, and what is due to the deviation of output from its originally planned path. Moreover, for measuring the price shocks, we should ideally take as a benchmark not the expected price at each point in time, but the price path as it was expected when extraction began.

There is obviously a certain arbitrariness in the type of guesswork involved in the construction of such counterfactuals. We have chosen a rather mechanical approach in order to try to capture as simply as possible the plausible price and quantity deviations from the normal path, without going into too many detailed assumptions.

It is plausible, as noted above, that the mining sector was in the early 1970s in a build-up phase, after the resource discovery. To try to capture the kind of gradual approach to the maximum value that this assumption implies, taking into account that extraction of an exhaustible resource is bound to come to an end eventually, we have simply fitted a regression equation with the actual quantity exported as the dependent variable, and the time trend as the independent variable, over the period 1972–88, with a quadratic specification.[3] The quadratic specification is justified by the fact that extraction cannot go on for ever, unless it is thinly distributed over an infinite horizon, as the unextracted stock of the mineral is finite. The resulting counterfactual quantity path and deviations from the planned path are reproduced in Table 10.1. The deviations are in fact simply the residuals from the regression equation.

Similarly, we had to choose a counterfactual price path, meant to represent the originally expected path. We assume that the management of the mining firms could not have been completely wrong in their long-term expectations when they decided to launch the exploitation of these mines. Hence, they probably got the overall time-profile of the price series right, but not the year-to-year details. In view of the global outlook of the actual series, we constructed the counterfactual price series by fitting a semi-log equation on the actual data, using the log of time as the explanatory variable. The resulting fitted values are represented in Table 10.1, along with the residuals (deviations), for the period 1975–82.

We can see that these series capture the main features that we inferred above from the casual inspection of the series. The deviation of the price path from its counterfactual path is positive during the 1975–79 period,

Table 10.1. Counterfactual quantity and price of uranium exports, 1975–82

	Quantity		Price	
	Fitted	Deviations	Fitted	Deviations
1975	1,501.4	−649.4	21.6	0.3
1976	1,975.5	−925.5	22.4	6.6
1977	2,386.6	−1,032.6	23.0	5.1
1978	2,734.7	−698.7	23.6	7.0
1979	3,019.8	283.2	24.1	4.2
1980	3,241.9	717.1	24.5	−0.2
1981	3,401.0	1,551.0	25.3	−5.5
1982	3,497.2	403.8	25.6	−2.9

Source: Computed from Ministère du Plan, *Annuaire Statistique*, various issue

with large deviations in 1976–77. The negative deviations occur after 1979. On the quantity side, we have negative deviations during the 1974–78 speculative reservation period, with maximum retention in 1976, and positive deviations in the rush-extraction 1979–84 period, with a peak in 1980–81. The end of the period again sees negative deviations, corresponding to the demand-constrained period.

However, these two types of deviation do not play a symmetric role in the analysis. Whereas the price shocks may be regarded as external, the quantity deviations from the planned path must be regarded as the supply response of the mining firms induced by the shock. They must thus be treated differently in the evaluation of the macroeconomic impact of the uranium shock on the Niger economy.

10.1.3. Definition of the Windfall Gains

The interpretation of these deviations from the normal paths must ultimately depend on the questions one has to answer. In particular their relevance depends on the agents whose behaviour we want to analyse. This is especially true of the distinction between the price and quantity paths. For some agents, what matters directly is only the deviation of export revenue from its normal path, rather than that of each series taken separately. There are thus two possible definitions of the windfall gains.

The first alternative is to consider that the extraction slow-down, in the initial phase, is just a form of saving and investment of the windfall gain from the price hike, which is dissaved later in the rush-extraction phase. Then, the appropriate counterfactual quantity path should be the normal path, and the windfall gain should be estimated each year as the counterfactual quantity exported times the excess of the price over the normal price. The production shortfall should then be valued at the actual price to estimate the amount saved 'at the source'.

Formally, one can spell out this decomposition as follows. Let P and X be the actual price and quantity exported; let P^N and X^N be the normal (counterfactual) corresponding variables. Then one can decompose the deviation of export revenues PX from normal export revenue $P^N X^N$ as

$$PX - P^N X^N = (P - P^N)X^N - P(X^N - X). \tag{10.1}$$

The second term on the right-hand side is thus the amount saved at the source, or pre-empted saving, which is positive in the case of an export shortfall, and the first term is the windfall gain. Then $P(X^N - X)$ should be added both to measured income and measured saving and investment in order to provide a consistent accounting framework distinguishing normal export revenue and windfall gain. Formally, if Y is GNP, and R income generated outside the mining sector, we have

$$Y + P(X^N - X) = R + P^N X^N + (P - P^N)X^N. \tag{10.2}$$

Here, we in fact neglect the difference between output and value-added in the mining sector for the moment, to keep things simple. We turn to this point below. The left-hand side of equation (10.2) is, then, the appropriate measure of GNP, including the imputed value of the unextracted mineral. The right-hand side, less R, is the income generated in the mining sector, decomposed into a normal component and a windfall gain. We will refine this decomposition a little more below.

This decomposition is the right one to make if one wants to aggregate all the agents of the national economy into one representative agent. It allows in particular for a precise analysis of the saving behaviour of this agent out of windfall income.

However, in the case of the uranium sector in Niger, this might not seem so interesting, because most of the decisions are made by the foreign-owned mining firms, whose behaviour is not the primary centre of interest in this study. We are much more interested in analysing the reactions of various national agents, such as the government or some representative agent of the private sector, to a sudden change in the income distributed by this sector, or in the money it spends on goods or services produced in the national economy. In this case, the pre-empted saving term must simply be interpreted as forgone income, which must be immediately subtracted from the windfall gain.

There is a fundamental theoretical objection to this second interpretation, for in the Hicksian tradition (Hicks 1939) one should measure changes in income holding wealth constant. As pre-empted saving of a part of the windfall gain is an addition to wealth, it should be added to income. But this point is only relevant if the agent can borrow against this postponed earning to finance current consumption or investment. Otherwise, the present value of the future flow of money must not be treated on an equal footing with the money actually earned. Hence, we will make a distinction between the windfall gain $((P - P^N)X^N)$ and the distributed windfall $(PX - P^N X^N)$, which matters when there is a liquidity constraint. It will prove useful below.

Of course, as the ownership of the mines is shared between the government and foreign capital, this extra income will not accrue directly to the private sector. But this is a problem of income distribution between the various agents, to be discussed later.

On the other hand, one can argue that the entire mineral reserve of the country should be taken into account, and that its re-evaluation by the positive price shock should be added to income. Dasgupta and Heal (1979) discuss this point in more depth. Although this position has some merit, we will neglect it because (i) nobody knows exactly the size of the mineral reserves of the country, (ii) it would make too much of a

Table 10.2. Windfall export revenue (*million 1980 CFAF*)

	Normal export revenue	Windfall export	Pre-empted saving	Distributed windfall
1975	32,340.2	450.4	8,026.6	−7,576.2
1976	44,191.9	12,979.0	15,992.6	−3,013.6
1977	54,987.3	12,052.3	19,753.6	−7,701.3
1978	64,566.3	19,197.6	16,063.1	3,134.5
1979	72,807.4	12,592.6	−6,791.1	19,383.7
1980	79,556.2	−713.2	−17,439.9	16,726.7
1981	85,977.3	−18,671.5	−31,671.4	12,999.9
1982	89,528.3	−10,281.8	−9,699.3	−582.5

Source: Computed from Table 10.1

difference from usual accounting practices, and (iii) it seems likely that the government would face a liquidity constraint if it wanted to borrow on the world market against a windfall gain so computed.

Hence, we have represented in Table 10.2 the series of normal export revenues, corresponding to $P^N X^N$, windfall gains, pre-empted saving and distributed windfall over 1975–82. It is apparent from these series that there are two possible definitions of the uranium shock period. The first one only looks at the windfall gains, and takes 1975–79 as the relevant dates. However, it is evident from the table that this definition would leave out part of the period when distributed windfall was at its highest. In a world of capital market imperfections, it is as important to study what happened to the money flow as to study what the agents made of the income flow itself. Hence, we extend the period of analysis up to 1982. This date corresponds to a major policy regime switch, when the government launched a stabilization programme, soon to be supported by the IMF.

Figure 10.5 represents the series of the windfall gain and the distributed windfall between 1975 and 1982. One can see that there are two different subperiods. In the first one, until 1979, the windfall gain is large, but the distributed windfall is small or negative. In the second period, while the windfall gain goes down, the distributed windfall becomes large.

A similar division into subperiods can be made when these data have been translated from export data, used above, into value-added data. The overall picture does not change drastically, but the differences are worth noticing, especially at the end of the period.

10.1.4. From Windfall Exports to Windfall Income

In order to decompose value-added in the mining sector into a normal component and a windfall component, we assume that at each date the

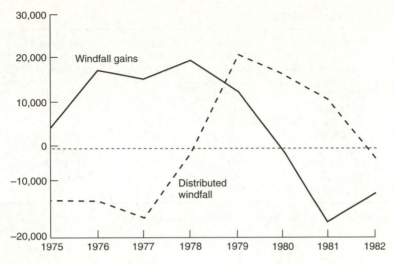

Figure 10.5. Windfalls, 1975–82

ratio of value-added to exports is constant. This assumption is not fully satisfactory as it seems likely that there are decreasing returns to scale in mining, at least in the short run. Then, to try to capture such an increasing marginal cost, one should assume that value-added per unit of export is lower for windfall export, when positive, than for normal export. This assumes quite plausibly that the share of intermediate consumption in output increases with increased production, given the relative prices. But deciding how much lower this ratio should be seems like a somewhat delicate piece of guesswork, so we will not try to do it.

The ratio of value-added to exports is presented in the second column of Table 10.3. One can observe that it decreases sharply between 1975 and 1982. Moreover, there is some rough inverse correlation between this ratio and the level of exports. This is probably due partly to the influence of decreasing returns to scale in mining (with cost increasing both with the size of current extraction and with the size of past extraction, as the remaining unextracted stock becomes smaller and more difficult to exploit) and partly to a change in the relative prices of inputs, in terms of uranium.

This ratio is then applied to the windfall figures computed above, to produce the last two columns of Table 10.3. These value-added windfall (VAW) series look flatter than the export windfall series computed above because of the fall in the value-added ratio. Nevertheless, their overall profiles are similar. The cumulated (undiscounted) VAW over the period 1975–79 now represents 12.9% of 1975 GNP at 1980 prices, whereas the cumulated distributed VAW over the period 1978–81 represents 11.8% of

Table 10.3. Value-added data

	In mining (million current CFAF)	Per unit of exports (ratio)	Windfall (million 1980 CFAF)	Distributed windfall (million 1980 CFAF)
1975	10,600.00	1.0069	453.7	−7,628.4
1976	17,200.00	0.9482	12,306.7	−2,857.5
1977	25,400.00	0.9807	11,819.7	−7,552.7
1978	37,000.00	0.7906	15,177.6	2,478.1
1979	63,100.00	0.7967	10,032.5	15,443.0
1980	67,400.00	0.6999	−499.2	11,707.0
1981	50,600.00	0.4985	−9,307.7	6,480.5
1982	50,700.00	0.5553	−5,709.5	−323.5

Sources: Ministère du Plan, *Annuaire Statistique,* and Table 10.1

1979 GNP at 1980 prices. Using a 10% discount rate, the present value of the VAW represents 10.3% of 1975 GDP at 1980 prices. One may thus expect little effect in the aggregate, as this represents only 1% of 1975 GNP at 1980 prices once it is converted in terms of permanent income.

Now that we have identified the shock, we look at its diffusion through the economy.

10.2. The Propagation of the Shock

Various transmission mechanisms can be imagined for such a shock to be propagated to the economy. Without going into details, one can draw a first line between those effects which are transmitted via the government budget and those which are transmitted via various markets. In particular, the mining sector buys intermediate consumption goods and factors of production, partly on the markets in Niger. This section is devoted to the second type of effect, and government policy is the focus of Section 10.4.

The government share of the value of uranium output is not the only possible source of the impact of the shock on the government budget which one should expect. There are other potential effects as the government taxes the increases in activity induced by the shock (Bevan *et al.* 1989) or finds some fiscal revenues reduced. Hence, to grasp fully the windfall taxes that the government receives it is useful to start first with an analysis of the indirect effects of the shock on the other sectors of the economy.

As a background for this analysis, one can look at the decomposition of export revenue, as estimated by the World Bank (1976) for the SOMAIR

Table 10.4. Decomposition of export revenue (*percentage*)

Export price f.o.b. Cotonou	100.0
Overland transport of uranium port handling and insurance	5.8
Export price ex mine	94.2
Cost of imported inputs (fuel, sulphur, explosives, etc.) delivered to mine	29.3
(of which overland transport costs from depots in Cotonou and Kano)	(7.7)
Total wages, salaries and benefits	7.8
(of which for expatriates)	(3.0)
Interest on loan capital	7.8
Total operating costs	44.9
Depreciation charges	11.4
Total production costs	56.3
Distributable profits	37.3
Distribution of profits	
Profit tax	14.5
Other taxes (royalty, statistical tax, withholding tax)	5.3
Government share in dividends	3.8
Total government take	23.6
(as percentage of distributable profits)	(63.3)
Remains for foreign shareholders	13.7

Source: World Bank (1976)

mining firm. This is reproduced in Table 10.4. According to this estimate, the government takes about 23.6% of export revenue, while about 15% to 20% of it is spent locally as operating costs, either as wages and salaries or as purchases of transport services. Hence, roughly speaking, two-fifths are distributed locally, and three-fifths spent abroad, or in favour of foreigners. One may guess that the latter do not spend much on locally produced goods. Knowing that value-added in this sector accounts for less than 10% of GDP (except in 1978–80), one may thus expect that the shocks in this sector will significantly affect the government, but not so much the rest of the economy, except indirectly via changes in government behaviour. This is confirmed by the following exercise.

10.2.1. Impact on Non-Mining GDP

In order to try to capture the impact of the uranium shock on the non-mining sectors of the economy, we have applied the method used in Chapter 2 to measure windfall income and windfall investment. Since no separate deflators are available for GDP and investment, we have deflated all the series used below by the same deflator, namely the GDP deflator produced by the Ministry of Planning.

Assuming a counterfactual propensity to invest and a rate of return on investment, we have produced simultaneously the series for counterfactual income and counterfactual investment, using the following pair of equations:

$$Y_t^N = Y_t - r^N \sum_0^{t-1}(I_{t-i-1} - I_{t-i-1}^N)$$ (10.3)

$$I_t^N = s^N Y_t^N,$$ (10.4)

where the superscript N stands for 'normal' (or counterfactual), t is the time elapsed since the beginning of the shock, Y is non-mining GDP and I is investment, and r^N and s^N refer to the assumed rate of return and the assumed propensity to invest. The initial value Y_0 is equal to the actual value of GDP in 1975. Windfall income is defined as the difference between actual and counterfactual GDP, and windfall investment is defined likewise as the difference between actual and counterfactual investment.

We tried two values for both r^N (10% and 7%) and for s^N (18% and 19%) without getting any significant values for windfall non-mining GDP, except in 1982, when it represents only 1.76% of non-mining GDP. Windfall investment outside the mining sector only started to become significant at the end of the period, representing at most 38% and 26% of actual investment in 1981 and 1982, respectively. It should thus bear its fruit mainly outside our period of analysis, if at all.[4] As we will see below, the investment boom in the non-mining sector at the end of the period is mainly due to public investment.

Non-mining windfall GDP is presented in Table 10.13 below for the case where the rate of return equals 10% and the propensity to invest equals 18%. In the best case, the cumulated value of windfall investment over the seven years was just above the actual flow of investment in 1982.[5] Converted into an increase in permanent income, the present value of the windfall non-mining GDP amounts to 0.38% of 1975 non-mining GDP in the best case.

The reason for the failure of the uranium shock to make any real impact on the non-mining sector of the economy as a whole during our period of analysis can be understood by looking at the actual propensity to invest of this part of the economy. This series is represented in Table 10.5. One can see that the propensity to invest in the non-mining sector did actually fall significantly in 1976, and started to increase only in 1980, reaching an especially high value in 1981. One could regard this negative response of investment outside the mining sector in 1976 as the dynamic equivalent of the resource movement effect of Dutch Disease theory (Corden and Neary 1982), with investment in the mining sector crowding out investment in the non-mining sector. However, this does not apply, since we will find below that windfall investment in mining is similarly negative for that

Table 10.5. Actual propensity to invest in the non-mining sector (*percentage*)

1975	19.74
1976	16.38
1977	18.70
1978	19.79
1979	19.96
1980	22.26
1981	28.94
1982	24.16

Source: Ministère du Plan, *Annuaire Statistique*

date. This is fairly natural, since this date belongs to the speculative retention phase.

There is no way to check whether the values of this propensity in 1975–79 are not already above normal, since the production of the *Comptes Économiques* (National Accounts by sectors) was suspended from 1969 to 1975. But the fact that this figure increases by nearly 50% between 1978–79 and 1981 suggests that the initial point was probably not very much above normal. Otherwise, there would have been less room for a large increase.

As a result, windfall investment in the non-mining sector, as estimated above, is concentrated at the end of the period, in 1980–82, with the bulk of it taking place in 1981. That year, it amounts to slightly above 11% of GDP and to about 44% of cumulated windfall investment until 1982. Comparing this result with the windfall series described above, we can see that the positive windfall gains of the beginning of the period do not seem to have had any impact on investment outside the non-mining sector, whereas the peak of *distributed* windfall seems to have made a significant impact. This finding suggests that investors outside the mining sector were liquidity-constrained in the first part of the period, and were able to invest only when the money did actually flow.

With such a bunched investment shock, the theory of construction booms (e.g. Bevan *et al.* 1991) leads us to expect a sudden drop in the efficiency of investment. We can get a rough indication on this point by looking at the changes in the ICOR by sector over the period. The ICOR is here defined as investment in year *t* divided by the change in value-added over the subsequent year. This number is thus higher, the lower the growth of output following a given investment. It can become negative when output contracts in a given sector. These series are represented in Table 10.6. Although this is a fairly rough indicator of the efficiency of investment, we can see that the numbers in this table do not contradict this prediction of the construction booms theory.

But although we have shown above that the uranium boom did not

Table 10.6. ICOR by sector

	Mining	Manufacturing	Construction	Trade	Other	Total
1975	0.48	2.63	0.40	0.48	0.31	0.64
1976	0.91	4.17	0.28	0.73	0.46	0.86
1977	1.43	0.80	0.28	0.50	0.48	0.94
1978	1.03	0.65	0.76	0.88	0.65	1.08
1979	8.59	1.40	0.65	0.84	0.41	1.21
1980	−1.93	0.18	1.56	0.57	0.96	2.10
1981	45.09	0.57	−10.03	2.96	0.45	2.66

Source: Computed from Ministère du Plan, *Annuaire Statistique*, various issues

Table 10.7. Allocation of investment among sectors, excluding mining and public administration (*percentage*)

	Tradables		Non-Tradables		
	Agriculture	Manufacturing	Construction and public works	Wholesale trade and transport	Others (utilities and services)
1975	28.9	4.3	1.9	10.4	3.0
1976	28.6	2.9	2.2	11.2	3.3
1977	20.4	0.6	2.9	11.4	3.3
1978	18.3	2.2	6.3	13.8	2.8
1979	16.6	2.0	4.3	11.6	4.0
1980	16.6	2.1	4.6	11.9	6.6
1981	—[a]	1.6	2.4	18.6	—[a]
1982	—[a]	1.7	5.6	7.2	—[a]

[a] There seems to be a break in the investment series for agriculture and 'others', with an incredible collapse. We do not reproduce the resulting figures

Source: Computed from Ministère du Plan, *Annuaire Statistique*, various issues

seem to have any aggregate impact over the non-mining sector of the economy, this does not mean that there was no change in the relative weights of the different sectors over the period of analysis. This appears clearly by looking at the allocation of investment and of labour among the sectors.

10.2.2. Allocation of Production Factors among Sectors

In Table 10.7, we present the shares of investment in the various sectors, excluding mining and public administration. We have tried to classify the sectors into tradables and non-tradables, although this classification could be questioned.

One can observe that the share of investment going to the tradable sectors shrinks, while the share to the non-tradable sectors increases sharply. In the wholesale trade and transport sector, one finds that the share of investment increased by nearly 80% between 1975 and 1981. It more than doubled in the other two non-tradable sectors, while it was cut by half in the two tradable sectors. The main boom year for the non-tradable sectors seems to be 1978.

A major type of investment in productive assets is an increase in herd size (assets on hoof). In fact, for most people in Niger, livestock is the main asset in their portfolio. (Azam (1991b) illustrates some consequences of this fact.) Hence, we cannot get a comprehensive picture of investment in Niger unless we present the evolution of this stock. Table 10.8 presents the estimates of the herd size of the main animals. These figures are known to be fairly inaccurate, as can be expected given that most of the herd is nomadic. Nevertheless, they should not be dismissed, since they probably give some useful information on the changes in the number of heads.

The interpretation of these series is complicated by the fact that we are analysing the period following the 1973 drought, when herdsmen were reconstituting the herd, with some help from the government. In 1974 the government launched a programme for reconstituting the herd. Among the measures were attempts at reducing drastically exports of females. A spectacular move was the *opération redistribution du cheptel* (herd redistribution operation). The idea was to lend five cows or five camels, and ten smaller animals, to 76,000 families regarded as ruined, 80% of them living in the pastoral zone. They were supposed to repay the loan in four years. It seems in fact that this project was drastically scaled down and had very limited impact (SEDES 1987).

Nevertheless, one can observe that there is a fast rate of growth at the

Table 10.8. Herd size (*thousand heads*)

	Cattle	Sheep	Goats	Camels
1975	2,630	2,230	5,395	253
1976	2,800	2,436	5,946	287
1977	2,969	2,640	6,540	367
1978	3,120	2,740	6,700	375
1979	3,257	2,860	6,871	383
1980	3,354	2,973	7,043	391
1981	3,419	3,188	7,118	399
1982	3,472	3,315	7,259	407

Source: Ministère de l'Agriculture

beginning of the series, with rates above 6% in 1975 and 1976, for cattle, followed by a gradual slow-down until 1982, when the rate of growth of the herd size for cattle, for example, reaches 1.6%. There does not seem to be any positive correlation between this series and the uranium boom, as the rate of growth of the herd slows down when the windfall revenues are at their highest.

A similar picture of change in the allocation of factors in favour of non-tradables emerges from the analysis of the data regarding the allocation of labour among sectors. There are no exhaustive data on employment in Niger which take into account the informal sector. But, there are data on the modern sector. These series are known to be somewhat unreliable, since they are based on the declarations by firms of the number of their employees. No attempt is ever made to correct them for the changing fraction of unanswered questionnaires, for example.

It appears from Table 10.9 that employment went down in manufacturing, regarded as a tradable sector, and up in the other sectors. The booms in 1977–79 in the construction and public works sector, as predicted by the theory, and to a lesser extent in the wholesale trade and transport sector, are especially apparent in these series.

However, one must keep in mind that these figures might overestimate the swings in the allocation of labour among sectors, as they only record employment in the formal sector. There probably exists a fringe of firms which change back and forth from formal into informal as the level of activity fluctuates, especially in manufacturing and in construction.

Nevertheless, the overall picture seems to accord with the image given

Table 10.9. Modern sector employment, excluding the public sector

	1975	1976	1977	1978	1979	1980	1981	1982
Tradables								
Mining	n.a.	n.a.	2,315	6,080	3,857	5,851	5,076	7,122
Agriculture	1,025	968	1,682	1,507	1,285	1,649	2,534[a]	1,376
Manufacturing	4,055	5,021	4,597	2,413	2,945	2,745	2,938	1,546
Non-Tradables								
Construction and public works	5,228	7,266	10,716	13,826	17,040	7,716	11,818	5,313
Wholesale trade and transport	4,515	3,433	4,382	6,819	6,301	4,613	5,273	4,659
Other	3,194	3,799	4,533	5,613	4,828	3,419	6,913	5,695
Total	18,017	20,496	28,225	36,258	36,256	26,002	34,552	25,711

[a] This figure is corrected with a 1 and a 2 typed on each other in the 1985 edition, but 2,534 is reproduced in subsequent editions

Source: Ministère de la Fonction Publique et du Travail, Direction du Travail et de la Sécurité Sociale, *Rapport annuel 1985*, Niamey

by the investment data. The latter are produced with an attempt to capture investment in the informal sector, although with little accuracy, by definition.

Therefore, all these data suggest that although the uranium shock did not make any aggregate impact on the non-mining sector of the economy, taken as a whole, at least until the end of our period of analysis, it did affect the structure of production, with the tradable sectors getting a reduced share of inputs, while the other sectors were increasing theirs.

In order to try to confirm the causal link between these empirical observations, we need to try to uncover the transmission mechanisms which have been at work in this case. To start with, we look at relative prices.

10.2.3. Changes in Relative Prices

Unfortunately, the available data are not adequate for a proper analysis of the changes in the relative prices of tradables and non-tradables, let alone those of non-tradable consumer goods and non-tradable capital goods. There are no separate value-added deflators for each sector.

However, we can get some rough indications by looking at some components of the CPI. In Table 10.10 we present the real price of three goods entering the African CPI for Niamey: food, clothing, and dwelling and housekeeping. All these prices are deflated by the CPI. The former two can be regarded as representative of traded goods, and more precisely of agriculture and manufacturing, respectively, while the latter has some links with non-traded goods.

The picture which emerges from this table is somewhat mixed. The price index for clothing goes down, and that for Dwelling goes up, as expected from the theory (see Bevan *et al.* 1991). However, we observe that the price index for food tends to move slightly upwards, contrary to the

Table 10.10. Relative consumer prices

	Food	Clothing	Dwelling and housekeeping
1975	100.0	100.0	100.0
1976	102.7	95.0	100.6
1977	106.6	88.8	90.1
1978	103.3	97.4	102.4
1979	101.8	98.8	118.1
1980	102.0	97.3	119.7
1981	106.6	90.2	112.9
1982	105.9	90.5	112.1

Source: Computed from Ministère du Plan, *Annuaire Statistique*, various issues

theoretical prediction. But this should not be regarded as a partial rejection of this theory.

Two non-exclusive arguments can be used to explain this movement in food prices. First, one can refer to the level of rainfall, presented in Table 10.11, which reached a low point in 1977, and started to decline towards its drought level in 1981 and 1982. This may help support the price of food by reducing supply. The rainfall data have been produced as the average of the series for the towns of Maradi, Niamey, Tahoua and Zinder. The result should be more representative of the economically relevant parts of the country than national averages. In fact, they are probably representative of the climatic condition in the whole relevant area, including southern Niger and northern Nigeria.

Second, we observe that the price of the naira was going up on the parallel market from 1978 to 1982, gaining about 48% between 1978 and 1981 (see again Table 10.11). Taking into account the rate of inflation in Nigeria, this implies that the price of goods from Nigeria, evaluated at the parallel market exchange rate, rose in real terms (that is, compared with the CPI in Niger) by nearly 27% between 1978 and 1981, as shown in the last column of Table 10.11. Since many markets in Niger are in fact integrated with markets in Nigeria, especially in the food sector, this real appreciation of the naira may explain part of the rise of the real price of food seen above (Azam 1991a,b). Azam (1991b) shows in particular that non-tradables have an econometrically negligible role to play in the determination of the CPI in Niger, whereas the impact of prices in Nigeria, at the parallel market exchange rate, plays a crucial part. This predominantly concerns food.

However, for any market in Niger, it is likely that the informal segment is more integrated with the market in Nigeria than the formal one. Even in

Table 10.11. Non-uranium shocks

	Rainfall (mm)	Parallel market exchange rate of the naira	Real price of goods from Nigeria
1975	483.05	245	100.0
1976	496.35	280	104.4
1977	445.33	240	88.1
1978	588.65	200	66.6
1979	479.48	205	75.2
1980	443.25	229	75.3
1981	385.35	295	84.5
1982	319.80	291	84.0

Source: Ministère du Plan, *Annuaire Statistique*, World Bank and BCEAO

the modern agricultural sector, it is likely that the goods which are traded with Nigeria are less capital intensive, in the restricted sense of requiring less machinery and other non-agricultural equipment, than the goods which are traded on the world market. This remark might explain why the level of employment in the modern agricultural sector did not go down, while the share of investment going to this sector was cut, as seen in the above tables.

Hence, we face in fact a fairly complicated shock in Niger. There is a positive shock on the uranium price in the first part of the period, occurring simultaneously with a real loss of competitiveness on cross-border trade with Nigeria, and with no significant aggregate impact on the non-mining sector of the economy. Then, we have a negative price shock on uranium, combined with a positive distributed windfall in the mining sector, and a real appreciation of the naira on the border with Nigeria, at the parallel exchange rate. During this second part of the period, estimated windfall investment outside the mining sector is significantly positive. Relative prices seem to change both between tradables and non-tradables (in favour of the latter) and among tradables as well (in favour of the goods which are more directly in competition with Nigerian goods).[6]

Nevertheless, the dominant diagnosis is that the weight in the economy of non-mining tradables went down, and that of non-tradables went up, as expected from standard Dutch Disease theory. Moreover, it appears that construction and public works expanded relatively faster than the other non-tradables sectors, as expected from constructions boom theory. Table 10.12 confirms this view, by presenting the shares of GDP of each sector. However, it is again evident that the boom in the non-tradables sectors, and especially in construction and public works, responded to the uranium boom with a two-year lag. As shown below, we find the same lag for windfall investment in the mining sector itself.

Table 10.12. Shares of GDP (*percentage*)

	Tradables			Non-tradables		
	Agriculture	Manufacturing	Mining	Construction	Wholesale	Other
1975	49.1	7.6	5.9	2.8	13.9	16.7
1976	51.0	6.1	7.2	2.9	13.9	14.9
1977	50.5	5.1	8.8	3.5	13.7	14.3
1978	46.2	4.2	10.3	4.8	15.3	14.9
1979	42.6	4.1	14.2	5.6	15.6	13.6
1980	42.5	3.7	12.6	6.0	15.8	14.4
1981	41.0	6.0	8.4	6.0	18.9	15.2
1982	42.1	6.1	7.7	5.4	19.1	17.4

Source: Computed from Ministère du Plan, *Annuaire Statistique*, 1986–87 edition

Hence, our task now is to explain simultaneously why non-tradable sectors expanded and tradable sectors contracted or stagnated in such a way that the net windfall effect of the uranium boom on the non-mining sector is nil, in terms of GDP, and largely delayed, in terms of windfall investment. For this, we must first see how aggregate demand behaved and was affected by the policies pursued by the government.

10.3. Aggregate Demand and Saving

All the ingredients for computing total counterfactual GDP are now available. As argued above in equation (10.2), one should add pre-empted saving to measured GDP in order to have a consistent accounting framework for taking into account the difference between measured income and windfall income. However, in a world of imperfect capital markets, this part of income may remain notional, if the agents cannot borrow to mobilize it in the current period. It may thus affect the behaviour of some agents differently from effective current income.

Denoting by Y^N the normal level of income, and by respectively R and R^N the measured and normal levels of non-mining GDP, P and P^N the measured and normal real prices of exports, and X and X^N the measured and normal levels of value-added in the mining sector, we have:

$$Y^N = R^N + P^N X^N, \tag{10.5}$$

$$Y + P(X^N - X) = Y^N + (R - R^N) + (P - P^N)X^N. \tag{10.6}$$

The sum of the last two terms on the right-hand side of equation (10.6) is equal to windfall GDP, which is represented in Table 10.13. For non-mining GDP, we have used the variant with 10% for the rate of return, and 0.18 for the propensity to invest. Using 10% for the rate of discount, the

Table 10.13. Windfall GDP (*million 1980 CFAF*)

	Non-mining	Total
1975	0.0	453.6
1976	518.6	2,825.3
1977	239.1	12,058.8
1978	235.8	15,413.4
1979	962.4	10,994.9
1980	1,840.4	1,341.2
1981	3,871.2	−5,436.5
1982	8,967.9	3,258.4

Source: Table 10.3 and computations from Ministère du Plan, *Annuaire Statistique*

present value of these windfall GDPs is equal to a permanent income increase of 4,305.3 million CFAF at 1980 prices, which is 0.21% of 1975 GDP (at 1980 prices).

To determine the impact on aggregate demand and saving, we need first to complete the calculations made above for non-mining investment, by producing the corresponding series for the mining sector.

10.3.1. Investment in the Mining Sector

For calculating counterfactual and windfall investment in the mining sector, we have applied a different method from that used for the non-mining sector.

We start by computing the ICOR for each year as the ratio of investment in year t to the increase in the quantity exported the year after. This series has a fairly regular profile, except in 1980, when it drops by about 50%, and especially in 1982, when it becomes negative. We thus computed an average ICOR over 1975–81.

Then, using the series of counterfactual exports, estimated above, the series for counterfactual investment in the mining sector was produced. Adding this series to that of counterfactual investment calculated above for the non-mining sector (under the assumption of a 10% rate of return and a propensity to invest of 0.18) produces the series for total counterfactual investment. Then, actual investment minus counterfactual investment is windfall investment. The latter is presented in Table 10.14, along with windfall investment in the mining sector.

It is evident that this series is smoother than that for the non-mining sector. It remains very low at the beginning of the boom period, but starts growing much earlier. It looks much less bunched at the end of the period. Hence, we can reasonably infer that windfall investment in the mining sector played a large part in causing the increase in the weight of the

Table 10.14. Windfall investment (*million 1980 CFAF*)

	Mining	Total
1975	−8,170.0	−2,983.9
1976	229.1	−5,756.4
1977	14,268.2	16,967.8
1978	25,366.2	32,631.7
1979	36,142.7	44,922.6
1980	27,726.1	48,033.4
1981	1,347.8	57,316.2
1982	5,073.4	38,127.6

Source: Computed from Table 10.1 and Appendix 3

Table 10.15. Inventory accumulation (*million 1980 CFAF*)

	Actual	Windfall
1975	11,052.6	−5,022.4
1976	29,937.3	11,835.2
1977	25,915.1	5,105.3
1978	28,696.7	6,393.2
1979	32,526.0	6,443.8
1980	34,400.0	6,580.6
1981	4,128.4	−24,762.9
1982	21,666.7	−6,862.3

Source: Computed from Table 10.12 and Ministere du Plan, *Annuaire Statistique*

non-tradable sectors in GDP and in the allocation of factors that we found above.

Notice that the series for windfall investment in the mining sector is very low in 1981–82, precisely when the corresponding series for the non-mining sector is at its highest. Therefore, a major switch in the allocation of investment between the mining sector and the non-mining sector seems to have occurred at the end of our period of analysis, as if the non-mining sector was getting the funds freed by the mining sector.

To these two types of investment, we must add the accumulation of inventories as a component of aggregate saving. To produce a series of counterfactual inventory accumulation, we have used a method similar to that used for non-mining investment, and hence to that used in Chapter 2. We have taken as the counterfactual propensity to accumulate inventories the average ratio of actual inventory accumulation to GDP over the period 1975–82 (0.0519). This does not seem too outrageous an assumption, since this series does not display wide swings over this period. Multiplying this propensity by counterfactual GDP results in the series reproduced in Table 10.15. Notice that there is a large positive windfall in 1976, and a large negative one in 1981. This is probably an indicator of the 'surprises' faced by firms during these two years. In particular, it seems that aggregate demand was surprisingly low in 1976, and surprisingly high in 1981.

Now that we have investment, inventory accumulation and pre-empted saving, to get the series of aggregate saving we have to subtract the current account deficit of the balance of payments, or foreign saving, to the sum of the above three series.

10.3.2. The Current Account Deficit

It is fairly difficult to imagine a counterfactual for the current account deficit in this case. Its actual values over the 1975–82 period deflated by

Table 10.16. Current account deficit and aggregate windfall saving (*million 1980 CFAF*)

	Actual	Ratio to GDP	Windfall deficit	Windfall saving
1975	3,193.0	0.0101	−4,320.3	4,340.6
1976	8,026.6	0.0215	−548.9	22,620.1
1977	34,376.3	0.0813	24,602.7	39,364.0
1978	56,797.0	0.1262	46,403.3	8,684.7
1979	46,470.6	0.0909	34,504.3	10,071.1
1980	61,137.0	0.1140	48,300.6	−11,126.5
1981	45,245.9	0.0820	31,856.8	−30,974.6
1982	63,753.3	0.1154	50,545.3	−28,979.3

Source: Computed from Ministere du Plan, *Annuaire Statistique*

the GDP deflator, are reproduced in Table 10.16, along with its ratio to GDP. It is apparent that the aggregate propensity of Niger to get indebted abroad was steadily high in 1977–82, on average nearly seven times higher than the 1974–76 average. It was probably too high to be sustainable, since Niger had to launch a stabilisation programme at the end of 1982 (Guillaumont *et al.* 1991). Moreover, in 1971–73, Niger ran a surplus of its current account equal to more than 2% of GDP, which is probably due, at least partly, to the drought, and it reverted to a (small) surplus position in 1984, under the dual influence of the adjustment programme and the drought.

However, it is highly probable that by the time of the price shock, the debt capacity of Niger had already increased substantially, since the size of the uranium reserves was known to be large. Hence, to get a not-too-arbitrary propensity somewhere between the low values of the beginning of the period and the excessively high values prevailing for the second part of the period, we took the average of the values of this propensity in 1974 and 1983 (0.024), which bracket the period of analysis, as our counterfactual propensity. Multiplying it by counterfactual GDP produced the counterfactual current account deficit, which, subtracted from the actual deficit, yielded the windfall deficit presented in Table 10.16.

We are now in a position to compute overall windfall saving.

10.3.3. *Aggregate Windfall Saving*

Aggregate windfall saving is the sum of total windfall investment, windfall inventory accumulation and pre-empted saving less windfall foreign saving. As such, it is extremely sensitive to all the assumptions made in producing the various windfall series. On the other hand, one can refer to the law of averages and hope that the individual errors cancel out in the sum. The results are presented in Table 10.16, along with the current account series.

The behaviour of this series is in fact dominated by that of the pre-empted saving series. We get large positive values during the speculative retention period, and negative ones during the rush extraction phase. Using the 10% discount rate that we have already used above, we can compute the discounted value of this windfall series and compare it to the discounted value of windfall income, computed above. We thus get an average propensity to save out of windfall income of 73.3%. This rather large figure suggests that the temporary nature of the shock was well recognised by the representative Nigerien agent. Performing the same computation with distributed windfall instead of windfall income gives an even larger figure of 193.3%.

However, the overall pattern of this series over time—dominated by pre-empted saving to the point that it reproduces the succession of two subperiods, the first one with large positive values, and the second one with negative values—suggests that the windfall export gains were not dealt with by the Niger economy in the way neo-classical theory would predict.

In the spirit of the 'Ricardian Equivalence Theorem' (Barro 1974), the private agents should have discounted to the present the future benefits resulting, either directly or through the government budget, from the postponed sale of uranium at a higher real discounted price. Then, if they had concave preferences or other incentives to smooth expenditures over time, they should have spread these benefits over the various periods. In order to do this, they should have borrowed for consuming and investing as soon as the boom started.

It thus seems that the agents of this economy either have not correctly perceived the windfall income or, despite their correct perception, have not been able to exploit it optimally. In order to try to resolve this question, we begin by looking at the changes in private and public consumption which occurred during this period.

10.3.4. Consumption

The series of private and public consumption are represented in Table 10.17, both in millions of 1980 CFAF and as ratios to GDP. On average, the latter are 72.04% for private consumption, and 11.04% for public consumption.

The share of public consumption in GDP displays a flat U-shaped profile over the period, losing 2.5 percentage points between 1975 and 1978–79, before almost entirely recovering its previous value by the end of the period.

The share of private consumption in GDP displays a more bumpy U-

Table 10.17. Consumption data

	Private		Public	
	Real (m. 1980 CFAF)	Share of GDP (%)	Real (m. 1980 CFAF)	Share of GDP (%)
1975	243,157.9	76.8	41,403.5	13.1
1976	267,554.6	71.8	44,043.9	11.8
1977	302,489.0	71.5	45,534.4	10.8
1978	331,578.9	73.7	42,606.5	9.5
1979	358,823.5	70.2	62,283.7	9.3
1980	381,700.0	71.2	70,200.0	10.1
1981	376,697.2	68.3	74,311.9	11.7
1982	402,666.7	72.9	72,916.7	12.2

Source: Ministere du Plan, *Annuaire Statistique*, various issues

shaped profile, with an intermediate peak in 1978 and a deep trough in 1981. This series cannot be interpreted in a behavioural sense, like the propensity to consume of the representative household, since we have GDP instead of disposable income as the denominator. But, since fiscal pressure is fairly low and steady in Niger (Chambas 1991), we can already more or less conclude that we should not look into private consumption behaviour to find any striking answer to the questions posed above. The data do not, however, contradict the idea that private agents have not exploited the boom by increasing consumption by anticipation.

It is not possible to compare these propensities to consume with their value in the immediately preceding period because, as we said above, the *Comptes Économiques* were not produced between 1969 and 1975. But we can have a glance at the data produced by the World Bank (1990) to check that there was no exceptional increase in this propensity during the boom. These data show that we have a very high figure for 1974, but that the years 1975–76 are similar to 1970–73 as far as this ratio is concerned.

Similarly, we observe that the series of government consumption is quite uninformative, but points roughly in the same direction. But this remark does not apply to other aspects of government policy, which offer some clues, and to which we now turn.

10.4. Government Policy

Niger is committed to some form of development planning, and 1979 was the starting-point of a Five Year Plan (Charlick 1991). The development problem that the government of Niger had to face in the early 1970s can best be couched in terms of portfolio choice. It owned a valuable asset in the ground, as unextracted uranium mineral, and the basic question was when and how it should be exchanged for other assets with more promising development potential.

To try to characterise the answers given to this question, we look in turn at budgetary and financial policy and monetary policy.

10.4.1. Budgetary Policy

We have already described above the series of government consumption, suggesting that they contained nothing very illuminating for the purpose at hand. A little more can be learned from the public investment series, which is represented in Table 10.18. There is no need for complicated counterfactuals to see that the government is responsible for the investment boom of 1981–82 in the non-mining sector that we saw above. Whereas the share of public investment in GDP fluctuated in a narrow band of two percentage points from 1975 to 1980, it jumped in 1981 to become almost twice the highest share seen before.

This jump can be ascribed partly to a 'grant shock' not directly related to the uranium shock.[7] This appears clearly from Table 10.19. But even if one excludes the public capital expenditures funded by grants, it remains evident that the government increased its capital expenditures dramatically, by more than 85% in 1981, as can be seen from the first column. These data are not, however, fully comparable with our investment data quoted above. But the role of grants remains clear.

Table 10.18. Public investment

	Million 1980 CFAF	Share of GDP (%)
1975	15,780.0	8.8
1976	15,110.0	6.4
1977	23,710.0	8.2
1978	24,550.0	6.8
1979	32,340.0	7.3
1980	47,210.0	8.8
1981	102,390.0	17.0
1982	111,760.0	16.9

Note: To overcome problems related to investments funded by grants, for which the accounting rules seem to have changed, these data are computed as a residual from GFKF data. They include investment by some non-profit organisation, whose share is in fact negligible, and thus are slightly larger than budgetary data, when they can be compared (see Chambas 1991)

Source: Computed from Ministere du Plan, *Annuaire Statistique*

Table 10.19. Public capital expenditures (*million current CFAF*)

	Grants excluded	Grants included
1980	48,100	66,400
1981	89,100	111,500
1982	37,900	67,700

Source: Chambas (1991)

Table 10.20. Government revenues

	Current share of GDP		Share of mining in revenues (%)
	bn CFAF	%	
1975	20.1	8.9	14.0 (WB)
1976	26.3	10.3	n.a.
1977	35.7	11.3	n.a.
1978	45.5	12.6	32.9 (IMF)
1979	58.5	13.2	38.5 (IMF)
1980	77.4	14.4	24.2 (IMF)
1981	76.8	12.8	12.5 (IMF)
1982	73.8	11.1	15.5 (IMF)

Sources: Computed from IMF and World Bank (1976); these data are not exactly comparable with those of Tables 10.17 and 10.18

In Table 10.20, we look at government revenue data. These total revenue data include mostly fiscal receipts, but other resources as well. They have been translated from fiscal years (ending 30 September) into calendar years by assuming a uniform distribution of receipts over each year.

We observe that there is no major swing in the series, but a gradual increase in the share of GDP that the government controls. It is particularly noticeable that the increase in this share corresponds with a one-year lag, as one would expect, to the years when windfall GDP has large positive values (Bevan *et al.* 1989).

The third column of Table 10.20 presents estimates of the share of the contribution of the mining sector to the government budget. It is quite evident that the years of high budget correspond to the years of high contribution of the mining sector.

Chambas (1991) estimated a model where the average tax rate on non-mining income declined during the uranium boom. The tests did not reject this assumption. Hence, it seems that when the contribution of the

Table 10.21. Budget deficit and government saving

	Budget deficit		Government saving	
	Current bn CFAF	Share of GDP (%)	Current bn CFAF	Share of GDP (%)
1975	n.a.	n.a.	20.1	1.3
1976	5.0	2.0	26.3	1.7
1977	4.8	1.5	55.7	2.9
1978	12.0	3.3	45.4	4.6
1979	11.5	2.6	58.5	4.8
1980	22.5	4.2	77.4	5.0
1981	56.4	9.4	76.8	4.2
1982	19.8	3.0	73.8	2.5

Source: Chambas (1991) (deficit) and IMF (public saving). These data, from heterogenous sources, are not perfectly consistent with those of Tables 10.17–10.20

mining sector to the government budget was inflating, this was partly handed over to the private sector as (small) tax cuts. The cuts turned out to be difficult to reverse during the adjustment programme (Guillaumont *et al.* 1991).

Table 10.21 presents the budget deficit in nominal terms and as a share of GDP. Before 1978, it is fairly reasonable. It increases afterwards, but seems to get out of control only in 1981. Unfortunately, this deficit is computed excluding grant-financed investment expenditures and debt servicing (Chambas 1991). Therefore, it might give a distorted picture of the true deficit. Nevertheless, in view of Tables 10.17 and 10.18, it seems safe to regard this diagnosis as qualitatively right. It confirms that the 1981 aid boom was not the only cause of the public expenditure boom which took place in that year. The government saving series which is also represented in Table 10.21 shows again that it was government investment which got out of hand then, and not the other aggregates.

A similar picture emerges from the data on debt. In Table 10.22 we present as ratios to GDP the series of long-term external debt of three agents: central government, non-financial public enterprises and the private sector. As far as the latter is concerned, one can clearly distinguish two periods. Before 1978, its debt is decreasing. It then jumps and start increasing until 1981. A similar path is followed, but on a more modest scale, by public enterprises, as can be seen from the second column of Table 10.22. But it is the first column, representing the long-term external debt of the central government, which has the most striking profile: it grows roughly in line with GDP until 1981, when it jumps to a very high level. This is probably a reflection of the public investment shock described above.

Table 10.22. Long-term external debt (*ratio to GDP*)

	Central government	Non-financial public enterprise	Private sector
1975	9.5	0.3	3.4
1976	10.3	0.4	2.4
1977	7.7	0.5	1.8
1978	9.1	1.5	11.4
1979	8.3	2.7	13.7
1980	9.3	4.2	13.6
1981	16.7	7.9	16.6
1982	20.7	6.4	14.8

Sources: World Bank (1990) and Ministère du Plan, *Annuaire Statistique*

Hence, it is fairly evident that government behaviour did not aim to smooth the path of investment outside the mining sector over time, and that it played the role of a destabilizing shock, drastically increasing public investment and external debt at the time when the uranium boom was over.

It remains to see what mechanism was used at the beginning of the boom to prevent the type of increase in investment which the theory would lead us to expect.

10.4.2. Monetary Policy

In the UMOA, and especially since the reforms of 1975, each government has some influence on the monetary policy pursued in its country. The Comité National du Crédit (National Committee for Credit), where the government is represented by the Finance Minister (and where France has one-eighth of the votes), determines the application of credit control by sector, by firm, and by bank, and proposes to the BCEAO the maximum amount of credit that the latter will offer in the country (Vizy 1989).

In Niger, monetary policy was rather restrictive, and selective, until 1980. The behaviour of the government, which was holding substantial positive net claims on the monetary institutions, was instrumental in making it even tougher.

This can be confirmed by looking at Table 10.23. From the first column, one can see that the central bank increased its holding of foreign assets during the 1976–78 period. Domestic credit was similarly reduced during the 1976–77 boom period. We can see by looking at the third column that the government was pursuing a quite unusual policy, by African standards, by running substantial net positive claims on the monetary institutions. The resulting excessively conservative monetary policy is

Table 10.23. Monetary aggregates (*ratios to GDP*)

	Net foreign assets	Domestic credit	Net government position	Total credit
1975	4.7	9.7	−4.9	14.7
1976	5.7	7.1	−4.8	11.1
1977	7.2	6.3	−4.8	11.2
1978	4.1	9.7	−3.2	12.9
1979	3.4	11.2	−3.3	14.5
1980	0.6	14.0	−2.2	16.1
1981	0.4	15.8	−0.2	16.0
1982	−4.7	18.4	1.3	17.1

Source: BCEAO and Ministère du Plan, *Annuaire Statistique*

Table 10.24. Ratio of net foreign assets to domestic credit (*percentage*)

1975	48.6
1976	80.8
1977	113.0
1978	42.8
1979	30.7
1980	4.4
1981	2.2
1982	−2.6

Source: Computed from Table 10.23

illustrated in Table 10.24 by the ratio of net foreign assets to domestic credit, which increases by more than 100% between 1975 and 1977, and remains high until 1979. It then collapses and reaches a negative value in 1982.

Therefore, as can be confirmed by looking at the fourth column of Table 10.23, monetary policy was fairly restrictive during the uranium boom, with the ratio of credit outstanding to GDP going down in 1976, and starting to grow only when the boom was coming to an end but distributed windfall was large and deceiving. Credit policy was thus probably instrumental in preventing the smoothing of the investment effort during the uranium boom and its immediate aftermath. The mining sector probably crowded out the non-mining one during the boom proper, given the credit ceiling, and then released abruptly both its share of the credit ration and the distributed windfall, triggering an investment shock that the non-mining sector could not absorb.

If this diagnosis is right, then monetary policy can be held responsible for preventing the uranium boom from being propagated in appropriate time to the non-mining sector. This case illustrate how a Friedmanite money growth rule may be inappropriate in economies subjected to sharp shocks, especially when it is enforced by credit ceilings.

10.4.3. Trade Policy

In the case of Niger, there was no spectacular change in trade policy. The country has a deep-rooted commercial tradition (Azam 1991a,b), with a lot of transit trade with Northern Nigeria. Nevertheless, during the period of analysis, various industries were protected by tariff and non-tariff barriers. Among the latter, a fairly uncommon system used in Niger is *jumelage* or product-linking, which is a kind of domestic content rule: importers of some goods that are also produced locally are required to buy locally a given fraction of their imported quantities. This is a way of giving some protection to local producers, with less impact on domestic consumers than with a tariff (Wellisz and Findlay, 1988). This concerns relatively few goods, among them rice. Then, there is the usual mixture of tariff and non-tariff barriers, which makes it difficult to have a synthetic view of the stance of trade policy. The problem with quotas, for example, is that one never knows whether the restriction is binding or not, unless a good estimate of the equivalent tariff is available. This is not the case in Niger.

Nevertheless, we can get some idea about the change in the burden of trade policy by looking at Table 10.25. The first column represents imports as a percentage of GNP. There is no massive change during this period, and this series looks fairly flat. Nevertheless, this share is slightly higher, on average, over the second half of the period. The second column represents import prices as a percentage of the GDP deflator. This series suggests that import prices have a tendency to fall relative to the prices of other goods. It thus seems that many goods entering into the price index

Table 10.25. Trade policy

	Imports (% GNP)	Import prices (% GDP deflator)	Customs duties (% values of imports)
1975	36.96	102.93	24.98
1976	40.84	91.10	26.83
1977	36.09	88.59	20.69
1978	37.37	83.79	19.19
1979	39.48	94.53	17.23
1980	39.07	100.00	19.43
1981	39.53	93.01	17.96
1982	42.15	78.90	18.36

Source: Computed from World Bank (1990) and Ministère du Plan, *Annuaire Statistique*

are not tradable at the margin. This suggests that there was no significant endogenous trade liberalisation during this period. Lastly, the third column presents the average tariff rate, computed as total customs duties as a percentage of the value of imports. One can notice a downward trend in this series, suggesting some endogenous tariff cut during this period. Nevertheless, the change is not massive, and we should not make too much of this observation.

10.5. Conclusion

In the mid-1970s, Niger was facing a rather simple portfolio problem. It owned a valuable asset in the form of unextracted uranium. The main question was how and when this asset should be sold in order to purchase other assets offering better development prospects.

When the boom started, the mining firms held back the pace of extraction, as expected from Hotelling's theory of the optimal exploitation of exhaustible resources. They then cashed in their mineral asset at the end of the boom, thereby creating an important flow of cash into the government budget. The government seems to have realised that this flow of cash was not entirely a flow of income, but was instead a flow of capital in search of a new store of value. Therefore, it tried to invest a large amount just at the end of the boom.

But this resulted in a concentration of the investment effort, which probably had some detrimental effects on the efficacy of these investments (Bevan *et al.* 1987). A better policy would probably have been to start investing earlier on, with funds borrowed from abroad, in the initial phase of the boom, and to use the distributed windfall to repay the debt. However, it is not certain that the international capital market would have backed the government of Niger in such a plan.

The government also played a part in the determination of monetary policy, which was very restrictive in the early phase of the boom. While the flow of windfall income was growing, the private sector was probably prevented by the lack of credit from banking on it for investing. This unduly limited the impact of the boom on the non-mining sector, to the point where we have failed to find a significant value for windfall income in the early phase.

But this result did not prevent the structure of the economy from responding to the boom. It changed in such a way that the weight of the sectors producing non-tradables increased and, correlatively, the weight of the sectors producing tradables was cut to some extent. The consequences of this change were to be felt in the subsequent adjustment phase. The construction and public works sector expanded more than the others, with wholesale trade and transport following behind. This move was probably due mainly to the increase in the investment level by the mining sector, and there were probably some fall-outs outside the mining sector, but on a small scale.

Hence, in the case of Niger, we do not get a good example of a construction boom *à la* Bevan, Collier and Gunning, where the saving–investment behaviour of the national private sector plays a driving role. Here, the monetary and budgetary policies pursued locked the potential benefits of the boom in the mining sector, leaving only limited fall-outs to the private sector. We have a 'construction and public works' boom, led by the investment needs, and the intermediate consumption needs as well, of the mining sector.

Appendix 10.A1
A Simple Model of the Mining Game

Dasgupta and Heal (1979) provided an exhaustive survey of the theory of the exploitation of exhaustible resources, as well as some original contributions. But they did not analyse in game-theoretic terms the potential divergence of interest between the international mining firm and the government of the host country. This is a relevant feature of the real world, and we emphasise here capital market imperfection as a potential cause of such divergence.

We perform this analysis in the simplest possible set-up, by restricting the time-horizon to two periods.

10.A1.1. The Model

Denote by X and X^e the current and future quantity of mineral extracted, respectively, and by S the total available unextracted stock of mineral in the country at the beginning of the period. Then, the extraction programme will have to satisfy the constraint

$$X + X^e \leq S. \tag{10.A1}$$

Let p and p^e be the price at which output is sold at the present date and the future date, respectively. Denote by r the rate of interest on the world capital market, and define

$$W = pX + p^e X^e /(1 + r) \tag{10.A2}$$

as the present value of the extraction programme, which is the value of the mine, since we neglect production costs.

Assume that prior to the opening of the game, the rule for sharing the income stream from the mine, or the shares of ownership, have been agreed upon, and are not negotiable any more. Let $0 < g < 1$ be the government's share, and $(1 - g)$ the firm's share.

We assume that the mining firm is an international firm, with unquestioned creditwothiness, which can lend or borrow freely on the world capital market at the going rate of interest r. Neglecting production costs, it is then natural to assume that the objective function of the firm is to try to maximise its share of the present value of the extraction programme:

$$R = (1 - g)W,   \tag{10.A3}$$

subject to the stock constraint (10.A1) and the non-negativity constraints

$$X \geq 0,   \tag{10.A4}$$

$$X^e \geq 0.   \tag{10.A5}$$

Given $(1 - g)$, this is equivalent to maximising W.

The government has an expenditure programme such that it spends G and G^e in the current and future period, respectively. The price of this good is one in terms of the numeraire. We assume a standard time-separable objective function for the government, with U denoting the instantaneous utility function (assumed increasing, strictly concave and differentiable) and q the rate of time preference. It therefore seeks to maximise

$$V = U(G) + U(G^e)/(1 + q).   \tag{10.A6}$$

In order to highlight the role of capital market imperfections, we will compare the case when the government can borrow on the world capital market at the same rate as the mining firm with the case where it faces an upward-sloping supply curve for funds.

10.A1.2. The Case of a Perfect Capital Market

Let D denote the government debt, which is negative if it purchases foreign assets. For the sake of simplicity, we rule out any initial debt at the opening of the game.

Neglecting any other sources of finance, we can write the government intertemporal budget constraint in the case where the government can borrow on the same terms as the firm as

$$G + G^e/(1 + r) = g(pX + p^e X^e /(1 + r)) = gW.   \tag{10.A7}$$

In this case, the objectives of the government and the firm are convergent. This can be checked by noticing that maximising V (see 10.A6) under the constraints (10.A1), (10.A4), (10.A5) and (10.A7) is equivalent to maximising first W (see 10.A2) under (10.A1), (10.A4) and (10.A5), and second (10.A6) under (10.A7), given maximum W. This problem is recursive.

The solution to this problem leads to the famous Hotelling's rule, as a special case. We have in fact to distinguish three possible solutions:

(i) First, we have the interior solution. This implies first that Hotelling's rule prevails:

$$p = p^e /(1 + r).   \tag{10.A8}$$

Otherwise, the firm and the government would both choose one of the corner solutions, discussed below. When this condition holds, both the firm and the government are indifferent between extracting now or later. The extraction path is indeterminate.

This is not so for the path of government consumption, for maximising (10.A6) under (10.A7), given W, leads to the so-called Keynes–Ramsey (or Euler) condition:

$$U'/U'^e = (1+r)/(1+q),\tag{10.A9}$$

where U'^e denotes the future value of U', the derivative of U. Given W, (10.A7) and (10.A9) determine in general a unique solution for G and G^e. If G is different from gpX, and hence G^e from gp^eX^e, then the gap between revenue and expenditure can be lent or borrowed on the capital market. Notice however that the solution where the extraction path exactly matches the government consumption path is optimal, among others, so that there is no real need for the government to borrow or lend at all in this case.

On the contrary, in the corner solutions, the government must act on the capital market.

(ii) If $p(1+r) < p^e$, then both agents want to keep the mineral asset in the ground, in order to reap the benefit of the expected capital gain in the future. We get $X = 0$ and $X^e = S$ as the optimal extraction programme. The value of the mine is thus

$$W^{c1} = p^eS/(1+r).\tag{10.A10}$$

The maximising exercise by the government again produces (10.A9) as a first-order condition. In this case, where the expected rate of growth of the mineral price is higher than the rate of interest, the government must borrow to finance its expenditure G.

(iii) When we have $p(1+r) > p^e$, both the government and the firm choose to extract the whole stock of mineral now. We have $X = S$ and $X^e = 0$. Then, the value of the mine is

$$W^{c2} = pS.\tag{10.A11}$$

In this case, where the expected capital gains do not pay for the forgone interest earnings, the government gets excess funds in the first period, equal to $gpS - G$. It must lend it on the capital market, for financing next-period expenditure $G^e = (1+r)(gpS - G)$.

In these three cases, the government and the firm can find a peaceful agreement, as they are in fact pursuing the same objective. When they face different financial conditions, their objectives diverge, and a bargaining solution must be adopted.

10.A1.3. The Case of Increasing Country Risk

Assume now that the firm and the government face different borrowing terms. The former still faces an infinitely elastic supply of funds, at the same rate r. One possible reason why the mining firm is not affected by increasing country risk is that it runs businesses in several countries with diversified risks.

On the contrary, the government has all its assets in the country, and hence we assume that the foreign banks will demand a higher interest rate to increase lending, so that the government faces in fact the following supply-of-funds curve:

$$r^G = r^G(D) > r, \; r^{G\prime} > 0 \tag{10.A12}$$

We assume that the firm is neither able nor willing to make arbitrage profits by borrowing in its own name in order to re-lend the money to the government, and thus run the risk of ruining its reputation on the capital market or of being sued in court.

This difference from the model of the previous section is only relevant in the case where the government really has an incentive to borrow, that is, when $p(1+r) < p^e$. We now restrict the analysis to this case, when a conflict arises between the firm and the government. To check this, it is useful first to split the intertemporal budget constraint (10.A7) into two separate budget constraints for each date:

$$G \le gpX + D, \tag{10.A13}$$

$$G^e + (1 + r^G(D))D \le gp^e X^e. \tag{10.A14}$$

Now, maximising V (10.A6) under (10.A1), (10.A4), (10.A5), (10.A13) and (10.A14) is not equivalent to the firm's problem of maximising W (10.A2) under (10.A1), (10.A4) and (10.A5). To check this, notice that there may exist an interior solution even if $p^e > (1 + r)p$, since the first-order conditions for this problem imply that

$$p^e - p(1 + r^G(D)) = r^{G\prime}D. \tag{10.A15}$$

The corner solution with $X = 0$ will only be preferred by the government if

$$p^e > p(1 + r^G(G) + r^{G\prime}G). \tag{10.A16}$$

Hence, unless the expected price rise for the mineral is so high that the expected capital gains more than outweigh the interest cost the government has to pay when it borrows enough to finance its whole expenditure for the first period, the government will object to the mine-value-maximising strategy of extracting no mineral in the first period. There is a whole range of values of the expected growth rate of the price,

$$r < (p^e - p)/p < r^G(G) + r^{G\prime}G, \tag{10.A17}$$

such that the government would rather have both $X > 0$ and $D > 0$.

Therefore, increasing country risk, in the simple sense used here, provides an incentive for the government to try to enforce a smoother extraction plan than the mine-value-maximising one which the firm prefers. A bargaining solution needs to be found to share the burden of filling the gap between the solutions preferred by each agent.

If one selects as a solution concept the classic 'Nash bargaining solution', assuming that there is no outside option other than no mining–no royalties, then the optimal outcome will satisfy

$$\max(1 - g)(pX + p^e X^e/(1 + r))(U(G) + U(G^e)/(1 + q)), \tag{10.A18}$$

subject to (10.A1), (10.A4), (10.A5), (10.A13) and (10.A14). One can check that in this case the optimal outcome is a compromise between the preferred outcomes of the firm and the government. First, the government expenditure path is governed by a new Euler equation, with (10.A9) replaced by

$$U'/U'^e = (1 + r^G(D) + r^{G'}D)/(1 + q). \tag{10.A19}$$

Second, we get a new arbitrage equation, which might be called the 'generalised' Hotelling rule, and which reads for an interior solution:

$$p(1 + gU'W/V) = (p^e/(1+r))(1 + gU''(1+r)W/V(1+q)). \tag{10.A20}$$

Denote by $e^G = r^{G'}D/r^G > 0$ the elasticity of the government rate of interest with respect to the debt level. Then, substituting from (10.A19) and rearranging yields

$$(1 + e^G)r^G(D) = r + (p^e - (1+r)p)(1 + (1+q)V/(1+r)gWU'^e)/p. \tag{10.A21}$$

This equation shows clearly the role of the discounted capital gain factor $(p^e - (1+r)p)$ in determining government debt. For example, assuming that $r^G(0) = r$, then D will be positive provided the following inequality holds:

$$p^e - (1+r)p > pe^G rG/(1 + (1+q)V/(1+r)gWU'^e). \tag{10.A22}$$

The discounted capital gain factor must be high enough to warrant government indebtedness, the more so the higher the elasticity of the interest rate it faces with respect to its level of debt.

Now, returning to the general specification, (10.A19) and (10.A21), combined with (10.A1), (10.A13), and (10.A14), can be used to determine G, G^e, D, and X and X^e.

In this case, there will exist in general a range of values of the discounted capital gain factor such that the government does some borrowing on the capital market but at the same time pushes the mining firm to extract some mineral in the first period, whereas the latter would rather save it in the ground.

Since the equilibrium point of this game is the result of a compromise, we know that the quantity extracted in the first period will maximise neither V nor W. More precisely it can be shown by some tedious calculation that in the Nash bargaining solution of this game, for given values of g, p^e, p, r and S, dV/dX is proportional to $r^G(D) + r^{G'}D - r$ and dW/dX is proportional to $(1+r)p - p^e$. This remark has some bearing on the appropriate way of taking into account the induced change in the quantity extracted as a response to an unexpected price change when defining the windfall gain.

10.A1.4 Conclusion

The capital market imperfection that we have introduced into this model—namely, a simple way to capture the principle of increasing country risk—works like a cost of adjustment term, preventing the model from predicting the sort of all-or-nothing behaviour of the other model. The government thus has an incentive to get a smoother extraction plan than the one the firms prefers. The use of the Nash bargaining solution concept will generally satisfy this claim. So, probably, would any bargaining solution concept, unless it gives full priority to the firm's objective.

Appendix 10.A2
The Choice of a Deflator

The choice of a deflator depends on the type of questions one wants to answer, and on the type of problems one has to face.

The first possible choice is to use an import price index. In this case, the real export price so computed measures the purchasing power of a unit of export on the world market. This is especially useful when one wants to assess the impact of a change in export revenues on the capacity of a country to import, or to finance a target level of imports without increasing its debt. For most countries, a series of unit values of imports is available.

The other choice is to use a domestic price index, in order to assess the impact of a change in export revenue on aggregate demand in the country. Then, the GDP deflator is an appropriate choice. Theoretically, the two choices could be roughly equivalent if the country was a small price-taker on the world market, with the right degree of diversification, and no significant role played by non-traded goods. The weights would differ, but the individual prices would be the same. This price-taker assumption for Niger has been tested elsewhere by the present author without being rejected, at least as far as African consumption is concerned (Azam 1991b).

However, these two types of deflator are Paasches indexes, and as such are sensitive to changes in the composition of the respective aggregates. This is especially important when analysing a period of time when the economy is subjected to shocks originating in policy reforms or in external events. At such a time, major changes in the composition of the aggregates may occur. Therefore it might be the case that one or the other index would go up without any change in the individual prices, if the composition of the corresponding aggregate changed in favour of more expensive goods. The opposite case occurred in Niger after 1981, when the stabilisation programme resulted in a drastic cut in the share of investment in imports, entailing a fall in the import deflator, which does not reflect any major change in import prices, but a simple change in composition.

In the case of Niger, the choice of these price indexes is controversial. Montalieu (1991) has compared the series of import and export price indexes, and hence of the terms of trade, published by various international agencies (UNCTAD, World Bank (1987), IMF, BCEAO, etc.). It turns out that the series diverge widely, especially after 1980. This is worrying because the use of these data can lead to opposite diagnoses regarding the evolution of the terms of trade, or regarding the behaviour of the real price of exports.

In particular, the UNCTAD and World Bank terms of trade series for Niger show a steady deterioration over the period 1966–86, with a flat segment in 1974–79 (Montalieu, 1991), while the BCEAO series displays a slow improvement and a violent hump-shaped movement in 1974–81, with a climax in 1978. Montalieu thus resorted to producing a new series, which is itself a sort of Paasches index. His terms of trade series looks rather like the BCEAO one, with a big bump in 1974–81. In a subsequent edition of the *World Tables* (World Bank 1990), the World Bank changed its import price series dramatically, coming closer to the IMF series. This

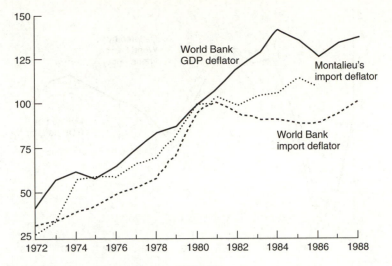

Figure 10.A1. Alternative deflators, 1972–88

Sources: Montalieu (1988); World Bank (1990).

series is represented in Figure 10.A1, along with Montalieu's series and that of the GDP deflator. Now, the import price index goes down after 1981, instead of going up as it did in the 1987 edition of the *World Tables*. But this downturn coincides with a major change in the composition of imports, with the share of investment goods going down strongly, under the influence of a Fund-supported stabilization policy (IMF 1987). Therefore, there is the risk that this downturn is a statistical artefact, rather than an actual change in the relevant prices.

To try to take care of this danger, we have in fact chosen as a deflator the mean of the World Bank's import price index and the GDP deflator. This should dampen the impact of compositional changes on the resulting deflator. The choice of equal weights is only justified by the so-called 'Principle of Insufficient Reason'. However, it turns out that this mean deflator (*MDEF*) comes very close to Montalieu's import price index (*MOPIM*) over the range where the two series can be compared. Regressing the former on the latter yields

$$MDEF = 17.3 + 0.87\,MOPIM \qquad R^2 = 0.96.$$
$$(4.45) \qquad (17.98)$$

This equation confirms that they are very close to each other. A closer scrutiny shows that the mean deflator *MDEF* gives some more weight to the World Bank's import price index than does Montalieu's. While $MDEF = 0.5PIM + 0.5DEF$, where *PIM* is the Bank's index and *DEF* the GDP deflator, regressing Montalieu's deflator on these two variables yields

$$MOPIM = -18.39 + 0.41\,PIM + 0.68\,DEF \qquad R^2 = 0.96.$$
$$(3.13) \qquad (2.69) \qquad (6.26)$$

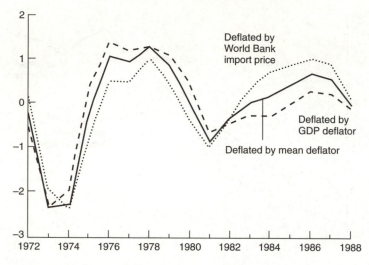

Figure 10.A2. Real price of uranium exports, 1972–88 (normalised)

Nevertheless, *MDEF* seems quite close to Montalieu's index, over the period where they can be compared, and offers the advantage of extending longer in time.

Figure 10.A2 shows the difference that using one or the other deflator makes. Deflating by the GDP deflator irons out the post-1981 mini-boom, whereas using the World Bank's gives the impression that there were two successive positive price shocks in real terms. The second does not seem to have made any impression on the decision-makers in Niger or on any analysts. It contrasts very much with the atmosphere which exists in policy-oriented circles interested in this country, and thus does not seem too reliable.

The choice between these two deflators determines to some extent the interpretation of the post-1981 reduction in the quantity exported. If there was really a second boom, then the cut in output may well have been voluntary, owing to the postponement of extraction to a later date, for the reasons given by Hotelling and invoked above. If there was no boom in fact, then the output cuts are probably due to a demand constraint, or to increased extraction costs entailed by the reduction in the unextracted stock. Obviously, the use of the mean deflator produces an intermediate result, with a second boom after 1981, but much flatter than the first one.

Similarly, the real value of uranium export revenues seems to be high for a longer period when the World Bank's import price series is used as a deflator than when using the GDP deflator. In the latter case, the series looks much more like that of a temporary trade shock, while the former has a longer-lasting plateau. These series are represented in Figure 10.A3. Here again, the mean deflator produces an intermediate result.

It is reassuring to observe that all these series are very close to one another before 1981, and diverge only after that date, since we are mainly interested in the

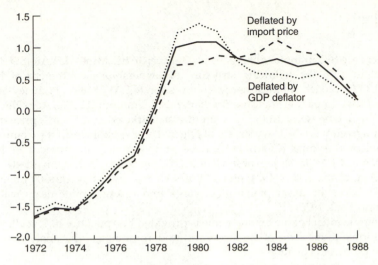

Figure. 10.A3. Real value of uranium exports, 1972–88 (normalised)

study of the first uranium boom (or the unique uranium boom, depending on the deflator chosen). However, the choice made does impinge on the questions of whether the boom was permanent or transitory, whether the price changes were expected or unexpected, and so on.

Appendix 10.A3

Non-mining investment (*million 1980 CFAF*)

	Actual		Windfall	
Rate of return	—	10%	10%	7%
Propensity to invest	—	18%	19%	18%
1975	58,807.1	5,186.1	2,207.1	5,186.1
1976	56,645.8	−5,527.3	−9,038.0	−5,555.3
1977	72,123.0	2,699.6	−2,448.7	2,701.1
1978	79,899.7	7,265.5	3,009.1	7,252.4
1979	87,520.2	8,779.9	4,103.5	8,727.5
1980	104,360.0	20,307.3	15,246.8	20,206.7
1981	146,229.4	55,968.4	50,466.9	55,756.9
1982	123,300.0	33,054.2	27,544.1	32,627.9

Source: Computed from Ministère du Plan, *Annuaire Statistique*, various issues

NOTES

1. There are two uranium mining firms. The Société des Mines de l'Aïr (SOMAIR) had in 1976 the following structure of ownership: Government of Niger (33.33%); French Atomic Energy Commission (CEA) (26.8%); Péchiney-Mokta (15.1%); Compagnie Française des Minerais d'Uranium (11.7%); Agip Nucleare (6.5%); Urangesellshaft (6.5%). Output was marketed by CEA at a price mutually agreed with the Government of Niger. The shareholders of the Compagnie Minière d'Akouta (COMINAK) were at that time: Government of Niger (32.5%); CEA (45%); Japanese OURD (22.5%). SOMAIR had invested US$75 million at the end of 1974, and COMINAK was investing US$200 million in 1975–76 in the development of its large underground mine near Arlit (see World Bank 1976).
2. A simple model of the mining game is provided in Appendix 10.1, spelling out in formal terms some of the theoretical underpinnings of this analysis.
3. The estimated equation is

$$X = -1024.7 + 757.52t - 31.49t^2, \qquad R^2 = 0.76.$$

It implies that extraction should come to an end about 1993. This should not be taken too seriously.
4. In fact, the structural adjustment programme started in 1982–83, changing the conditions for exploiting these investments.
5. The series of windfall investment outside the mining sector resulting from this exercise are presented in Appendix 10.3.
6. See Azam (1991b) for further discussion of the change in the relative price of tradables in Niger.
7. The motivations underlying grants are not always clear cut, and in this roundabout sense these grants might have been related to the uranium shock. Frey (1984) illustrates nicely how grants can in fact be governed by other motives than altruism.

REFERENCES

Adji, B. (1986): *La politique monétaire et le développement économique des Etats depuis la réforme des institutions de l'UMOA (Le cas du Niger)*, doctoral thesis, CERDI, Clermont-Ferrand (unpublished).

Arnoult, E.J. (1983): 'Cross-Border Trade Between Niger and Nigeria', in Elliot Berg and Associates: *Joint Program Assessment of Grain Marketing in Niger*, 2, 1–12, USAID: Niamey.

Azam, J.-P. (1991a): 'Cross-Border Trade between Niger and Nigeria, 1980–87: The Parallel Market for the Naira', in M. Roemer and C. Jones (eds): *Markets in Developing Countries: Parallel, Fragmented and Black*, 47–61, ICS Press: San Francisco.

——(1991b): 'Niger and the Naira: Some Monetary Consequences of Cross-Border Trade with Nigeria', in A. Chhibber and S. Fischer (eds): *The Analytics of Economic Reform in Africa*, World Bank: Washington, DC.

Azam, J.-P. and T. Besley (1989): 'General Equilibrium with Parallel Markets for Goods and Foreign Exchange: Theory and Application to Ghana', *World Development*, 17, 1921–30.

Azam, J.-P. *et al.* (1992): *Ajustement et pauvreté: le cas du Niger*, L'Harmattan: Paris.

Barro, R.J. (1974): 'Are Government Bonds Net Wealth?', *Journal of Political Economy*, 82, 1095–1117.

Bevan, D.L., P. Collier and J.W. Gunning (1987): 'Consequences of a Commodity Boom in a Controlled Economy: Accumulation and Redistribution in Kenya 1975–83', *World Bank Economic Review*, 1, 489–513.

——(1989): 'Fiscal Response to a Temporary Trade Shock: The Aftermath of the Kenyan Coffee Boom', *World Bank Economic Review*, 3, 359–78.

——(1991): 'The Macroeconomics of External Shocks', in V.N. Balasubramanyam and S. Lall (eds): *Current Issues in Development Economics*, 91–117, Macmillan: London.

——(1992): 'Anatomy of a Temporary Trade Shock: The Kenyan Coffee Boom of 1976–9', *Journal of African Economies*, 1, 2, 271–305.

Chambas, G. (1991): 'Ajustement des finances publiques et développement au Niger', in P. Guillaumont *et al.*: *Ajustement structurel, ajustement informel; le cas du Niger*, 179–204, L'Harmattan: Paris.

Charlick, R.D. (1991): *Niger: Personal Rule and Survival in the Sahel*, Profiles/Nations of Contemporary Africa, Westview Press: Boulder and San Francisco.

Corden, W.M. and J.P. Neary (1982): 'Booming Sector and De-Industrialization in a Small Open Economy', *Economic Journal*, 92, 825–48.

Dasgupta, P.S. and G.M. Heal (1979): *Economic Theory and Exhaustible Resources*, Cambridge Economic Handbooks, James Nisbet & Co. Ltd and Cambridge University Press: Welwyn.

Frey, B.S. (1984): *International Political Economics*, Basil Blackwell: Oxford.

Grégoire, E. (1986): *Les Alhazai de Maradi (Niger)*, Editions de l'ORSTOM: Paris.

Guillaumont, P. and S. Guillaumont (1984): *Zone Franc et développement africain*, Economica: Paris.

Guillaumont, P. *et al.* (1991): *Ajustement structurel, ajustement informel: le cas du Niger*, L'Harmattan: Paris.

Hicks, J.R. (1939): *Value and Capital*, Clarendon Press: Oxford.

Hotelling, H. (1931): 'The Economics of Exhaustible Resources', *Journal of Political Economy*, 39, 137–75.

IMF (1987): *Niger: Recent Economic Developments*, SM/87/149, IMF: Washington, DC (unpublished).

Mathonnat, J. and G. Collange (1988): 'L'ouverture financière de la zone franc: financement extérieur et endettement', in P. Guillaumont and S. Guillaumont (eds): *Stratégies de développement comparées. Zone franc et hors zone franc*, 379–411, Economica: Paris.

Montalieu, T. (1991): 'Les sources de variation du solde de la balance des paiements courants du Niger', in P. Guillaumont *et al.*: *Ajustement structurel, ajustement informel: le cas du Niger*, 87–106, L'Harmattan: Paris.

SEDES (1987): *Etude du secteur agricole du Niger*, i and ii, SEDES: Paris.

Sen, A.K. (1981): *Poverty and Famines: An Essay on Entitlement and Deprivation*, Clarendon Press: Oxford.

UNDP (1990): *Human Development Report*, Oxford University Press: New York.

Vizy, M. (1989): *La zone franc*, CHEAM: Paris.
Wellisz, S. and R. Findlay (1988): 'The State and the Invisible Hand', *World Bank Research Observer*, 3, 59–80.
World Bank (1976): *Economic Memorandum: Niger*, Report No. 1109a-NIR, World Bank: Washington, DC.
——(1987): *World Tables, 1987*, Johns Hopkins University Press: Baltimore.
——(1990): *World Tables, 1989–90*, Johns Hopkins University Press: Baltimore.

11

Cameroon

SHANTA DEVARAJAN

During its first two decades of independence, Cameroon had the reputation of being a conservatively managed and moderately successful
economy. Per capita income grew steadily at an annual rate of over 4%.
The country avoided both high inflation and fiscal and current account
deficits. The discovery of oil in 1975, and its production starting in 1978,
stood to alter this pattern of development. On the one hand, the windfall
oil revenues, if invested wisely, had the potential to propel the economy
onto a more rapid growth path. On the other hand, if the experience of
other oil exporters is a guide, these revenues could have turned out to be
a mixed blessing, leaving the economy mired in debt and inflation and
ill-prepared for the post-oil era.

In this chapter we analyse Cameroon's oil era—the period from 1978 to
1985—as a case study of a developing country's response to a temporary
terms of trade shock. Using counterfactual analysis, we examine the effect
of the oil boom on income, consumption, investment, prices and the
budgets of the private and public sectors. We find that, in the aggregate,
Cameroon managed its windfall carefully, saving most of it in foreign
assets. Nevertheless, some troubling signs emerge in looking at the different responses of the public and private sectors, and these may explain the
dramatic downturn in the economy during the oil 'bust' of the late 1980s.

11.1. The Nature of the Shock

Even at the time of discovery, Cameroon was known to have limited oil
reserves, with no more than twenty years' production at current (1978)
prices.[1] The geological structure of the region indicated no new basins of
oil. The 'shock' in terms of windfall income was clearly temporary.

In determining the size of the oil windfall to Cameroon, we take the
actual levels of production and prices up to 1985. After 1985, we consider
a hypothetical profile which would have obtained had oil prices remained
at 1985 levels. In other words, we calculate the oil windfall assuming the
oil bust never occurred. Such an assumption is appropriate if the 1986
price drop was exceptional, so that calculations made in 1978 onwards

using the oil revenues did not include this possibility. Furthermore, despite this overstatement of the *ex post* level of the windfall, we find the portion which was saved to be remarkably high (see below). Had we used the 'true' size of the windfall, the savings rate would have been astonishing.

The hypothetical production and revenue profiles are given in Table 11.1. The post-1985 trajectory was determined by assuming that Cameroon's oil reserves of 100 million metric tons would have been depleted by 1995 (as was believed to be the case in 1978). This required that production decline at 300,000 metric tons per year from 1985 onwards. The resulting net revenue, deflated by the import price index and discounted at 10%, leads to a wealth increase from the boom (in present value) of US$2.6 billion. This figure is equivalent to 54% of Cameroon's GDP in 1978.[2]

A 10% discount rate implies a rate of return to capital of the same level. Thus, had it been fully invested, the oil windfall would have increased permanent income by about 5.4% of GDP in 1978. Sensitivity analysis changes this estimate, but not qualitatively. A discount rate of 5% yields a permanent income increase of 3.8% of GDP, while a 15% rate implies an

Table 11.1. Cameroon: magnitude of the oil windfall

	Production (metric tons)	Net revenue (US$million)	Real net revenue	Present value of (net revenue)
1978	0.1	12.8	12.8	12.8
1979	1.0	107.0	97.5	88.6
1980	1.9	204.5	170.1	140.6
1981	3.4	632.0	454.5	341.5
1982	4.7	738.8	461.8	315.4
1983	5.8	769.1	409.9	254.5
1984	7.0	787.6	411.9	232.5
1985	8.4	862.3	390.3	200.3
1986	8.1	826.2	376.4	175.6
1987	7.8	795.6	362.5	153.7
1988	7.5	765.0	348.5	134.4
1989	7.2	734.4	334.6	117.3
1990	6.9	703.8	320.6	102.2
1991	6.6	673.2	306.7	88.8
1992	6.3	642.6	292.8	77.1
1993	6.0	612.0	278.8	66.7
1994	5.7	581.4	264.9	57.6
1995	5.4	550.8	250.9	49.6
Total	99.8			2,609.4

Source: World Bank, 'Cameroon: Recent Performance and Adjustment to Declining Oil Revenues,' *Country Economic Memorandum*, 6395-CM, 1986 (Text tables 4 and 11)

increase of 6% of GDP. In short, the windfall (in terms of permanent income) to Cameroon was of the order of 4% to 6% of its 1978 GDP.

11.2. Consumption *vs.* Saving

How much of this windfall income was saved and how much consumed? To answer this question, we construct counterfactual savings rates, the difference between these and observed rates being the additional savings attributable to the oil windfall. The savings rates, in turn, will be calculated as the sum of the economy's propensity to acquire domestic assets (gross fixed capital formation or GFKF) and its propensity to acquire foreign assets. We begin with the former.

First, a series for real GFKF must be generated. This will be Cameroon's average propensity to invest (column 1 of Table 11.2) multiplied by the sum of real GDP (at 1978 prices) and the imports made possible by the windfall income. This sum is given in column (2) of Table 11.2.

As for counterfactual GFKF, this is determined along the lines followed in Chapter 2, namely, by multiplying the counterfactual GFKF propensity by counterfactual income. Counterfactual income is actual, non-oil GDP less the contribution of windfall investment to GDP. We assume the latter is 10% of the level of windfall investment (recall that we are assuming that investment has a 10% rate of return in this economy). The counterfactual propensity to acquire domestic assets is taken to be 21%, the country's investment rate before the oil shock. These two estimates, counterfactual income and investment propensity, give us counterfactual GFKF (column 6, Table 11.2). Finally, the difference between actual and counterfactual

Table 11.2. Cameroon: counterfactual growth and capital formation (*billion 1978 CFAF*)

	GFKF/Y (%)	Y + windfall	Actual GFKF	Counterfactual			Windfall GFKF	
				Y	GFKF/Y (%)	GFKF	Cumulative	Annual
1978	21.1	1,094.1	230.9	1,090.6	21.0	229.8	1.1	1.1
1979	22.4	1,206.8	270.1	1,180.1	21.0	247.8	23.3	22.3
1980	23.5	1,350.5	317.4	1,301.9	21.0	273.4	67.3	44.0
1981	24.6	1,592.0	391.6	1,461.4	21.0	306.9	152.1	84.7
1982	23.3	1,689.4	393.6	1,548.4	21.0	325.2	220.5	68.5
1983	25.0	1,723.7	430.9	1,589.9	21.0	333.9	317.5	97.0
1984	25.3	1,838.5	465.1	1,694.5	21.0	355.9	426.8	109.3
1985	25.4	1,972.2	500.9	1,823.2	21.0	382.9	544.9	118.1
Present value								381.8

Source: Author's calculations

Table 11.3. Cameroon: investment rates after the oil boom

	GFKF/Y (%)	Terms of trade (1980 = 100)
1986	30.1	59.5
1987	24.1	65.1
1988	15.7	66.1
1989	11.9	63.1
1990	10.6	66.1

Source: Government of Cameroon, National Accounts

GFKF is taken to be the windfall investment level in Cameroon (column 8, Table 11.2).

Note that the investment rate is quite high and increasing in 1985, the final year of the boom. If the trend continued past that year, Cameroon would have been 'stretching' the investment boom beyond the income windfall. In fact, the opposite happened. The investment rate in Cameroon peaked in 1986 (the year oil prices crashed) and fell precipitously thereafter (see Table 11.3).

A similar procedure is used to obtain counterfactual foreign savings. Cameroon's current account deficit was over 6% of GDP in 1978. We assume that, in the absence of an oil shock, this figure would have been gradually brought down to zero. That is, the country would have tried to reach current account balance by the end of 1985. This assumption is based on the reputation of Cameroonian policymakers for being conservative, as well as the fact that current account deficits cannot be sustained indefinitely. The resulting counterfactual foreign savings propensity is applied to counterfactual income (from Table 11.2) to obtain the level of counterfactual foreign savings. The difference between this figure and observed levels is windfall foreign savings. These are given in the last column in Table 11.4. Note that windfall foreign savings were highly negative towards the end of the period. Despite our relatively austere counterfactual (current account balance by 1985), we find the country running sizeable current account surpluses during this time.

Putting these calculations together, we determine how much of Cameroon's windfall income was saved. The present value of the windfall GFKF stream (up to 1985) is 381.8 billion CFAF; that of the windfall foreign savings trajectory is −40.0 billion CFAF. The difference between these two would be windfall savings, except that it includes the savings arising from extra permanent income, which should be netted out. These additional savings are estimated by applying the difference between the GFKF and foreign savings propensities (i.e. the domestic savings propensity) to each year's additional permanent income. The present value of the

Table 11.4. Cameroon: actual and counterfactual foreign savings (*billion 1978 CFAF*)

	Foreign savings propensity (%)		Foreign savings levels		Windfall
	Actual	Counterfactual	Actual	Counterfactual	
1978	6.6	6.6	71.8	71.5	0.2
1979	10.0	5.6	118.1	66.3	51.7
1980	6.3	4.7	82.6	61.0	21.6
1981	6.2	3.7	91.0	54.8	36.2
1982	5.1	2.8	78.4	43.5	34.9
1983	0.8	1.9	12.4	29.8	−17.4
1984	−4.0	0.9	−68.0	15.9	−83.9
1985	−8.8	0.0	−160.2	0.0	−160.2
Present value					−40.0

Source: Government of Cameroon, National Accounts; author's calculations

resulting savings stream is 22 billion CFAF. The net result is that windfall savings out of windfall income are 399.7 billion CFAF (381.8 + 40.0 − 22.0), or 64% of windfall income. Note that windfall income was calculated assuming the oil boom would persist beyond 1985, whereas the savings computations were made up to 1985 only. Thus, the 64% figure is an understatement. We can safely say that at least two-thirds of Cameroon's oil windfall income was saved.

What do these estimates imply for the path of consumption out of windfall income? By specifying counterfactual domestic and foreign savings propensities, we have implicitly specified counterfactual total savings. If all of the difference between GDP and savings were consumption, the path of counterfactual consumption would be as shown in Table 11.5, column (2). However, we have to subtract inventory accumulation to obtain the 'correct' counterfactual consumption. This is done in going from column (2) to column (3) in Table 11.5. The gap between the observed consumption stream and the counterfactual one is displayed in column (5). Actual consumption grew more slowly than counterfactual consumption in most years. Again, although our counterfactual involves a high level of domestic savings and hence slow growth in consumption (to reach current account balance by 1985), the observed pattern of consumption in Cameroon grew even more slowly, with the gap widening towards the end of the era.

We estimated above that the propensity to save out of windfall income was about 0.64, so the propensity to consume is 0.36. Thus, we would

Table 11.5. Cameroon: actual and counterfactual consumption (*1978 = 100*)

	Counterfactual GDP	Counterfactural consumption	Counterfactual adjusted	Actual consumption	Difference between actual and counterfactual
1978	100.0	100.0	100.0	100.0	0.0
1979	111.5	110.3	112.9	115.7	2.8
1980	127.3	124.6	128.6	126.4	−2.1
1981	146.6	141.8	143.6	149.1	5.5
1982	155.4	148.7	152.4	159.0	6.5
1983	166.1	157.1	162.1	157.5	−4.6
1984	178.8	167.2	173.2	160.3	−12.8
1985	193.4	178.8	185.3	163.6	−21.7

Source: Government of Cameroon, National Accounts

expect consumption expenditure to exceed its counterfactual levels (to the extent that the windfall contributed to higher incomes). Yet, we observed that real consumption was actually lower than the counterfactual towards the end of the period. Bevan *et al.*, who obtain a similar difference for Kenya in Chapter 2, explain it by increases in prices, especially prices of consumer goods. In Cameroon's case, the discrepancy is due to the sharp increase in actual savings after 1983. The rise was so large that consumption was lower in 1984–86 than it would have been in the absence of the oil shock. To understand why this happened, we must go beyond our one-sector view of the economy and consider different types of goods and their prices.

11.3. Traded *vs.* Non-traded Goods

There are two, complementary hypotheses about how prices behave in the presence of a windfall. One is the well-known theory of the 'Dutch Disease', whereby the price of non-tradables is expected to rise relative to that of tradables. Both the resource-movement effect and the spending effect of the Dutch Disease cause this to happen (see, for example, Corden 1984). The other hypothesis is that the price of non-tradable capital goods will rise relative to the price of non-tradable consumer goods. This stems from the notion that temporary windfall income is saved. To the extent that the increased savings lead to higher investment and hence greater demand for capital goods, one would expect the price of non-tradable capital goods to rise faster than that of non-tradable consumer goods (see Chapter 2). The link between these hypotheses is the construction sector, which is both non-traded and a capital good.

In testing these hypotheses for the case of Cameroon's oil windfall, two qualifications must be mentioned. First, in Cameroon (as in many other developing countries), import-competing goods are only imperfect substitutes for imported goods.[3] At the margin, therefore, many of these goods behave like non-tradables rather than tradables (see Benjamin *et al.* 1989; Devarajan and de Melo 1987). In addition, when the import is subject to a quota, the import-competing sector behaves like a non-tradable. Second, in Cameroon's case, windfall foreign savings were at times greater (in absolute value) than windfall fixed investment (Tables 11.2 and 11.4). Thus, the construction-boom effect may not be as pronounced as expected.

The data in Table 11.6 bear out both the hypotheses and qualifications. First, the prices of non-tradable capital goods ('construction') did grow faster than those of private consumption. Furthermore, the gap widened towards the latter years of the period in question. We use private consumption as a proxy for non-tradable consumer goods because of our observation that most import-competing goods are imperfect substitutes. Moreover, consumer goods imports are only 6% of total imports in Cameroon (Benjamin and Devarajan 1986).

However, the prices of both non-tradable consumer and non-tradable capital goods rose more slowly than did the prices of imports (in domestic currency). One reason is the behaviour of the French franc with respect to the US dollar during this period. As a member of the CFA franc Zone, Cameroon's exchange rate is fixed to the French franc (at the time the rate was 50 CFAF = 1 FF). Consequently, fluctuations between the French franc and US dollar affect the domestic currency prices of dollar-denominated goods. In 1981–82 and 1984–85, the French franc depreciated considerably with respect to the dollar, thereby increasing the price of Cameroon's imports.

Another reason for the lack of real appreciation of the CFA franc was mentioned earlier: a significant portion of the windfall income was saved abroad, rather than invested domestically. Nevertheless, note that the non-oil export price index grew much more slowly than did that of construction. Inasmuch as construction is a 'pure' non-tradable and exports are tradables, the drop in this relative price indicates that opportunities for engaging in tradable production were becoming less attractive in Cameroon. Thus, while higher import prices discouraged tradable consumption, there was not a parallel support for tradable production. Put another way, while the real exchange rate in consumption may not have appreciated, that in production did.[4]

Returning to the issue of the construction boom, we note that there might be a lag between the acquisition of tradable and non-tradable capital goods. Quite simply, it is easier to buy imports than build buildings. In Cameroon, however, the reverse occurred. Construction grew

Table 11.6. Cameroon: implicit price deflators *(1978 = 100)*

	GDP	Imports	Private consumption	Public consumption	Fixed investment	Exports	Construction	Equipment imports
1978	100.0	100.0	100.0	100.0	100.0	100.0	100.0	100.0
1979	106.1	108.0	109.0	106.9	119.2	89.9	110.4	130.2
1980	114.2	117.1	118.5	119.0	116.6	101.9	114.7	118.5
1981	126.0	134.4	129.7	129.8	136.2	114.0	130.8	141.9
1982	143.0	159.0	148.5	144.8	147.4	138.6	146.2	148.8
1983	160.7	186.1	165.6	165.5	174.1	153.5	162.7	186.8
1984	181.4	198.4	178.8	189.4	181.1	179.9	195.1	190.9
1985	195.4	228.8	192.4	200.7	193.2	202.4	208.8	211.1

Source: Government of Cameroon, National Accounts

much faster than imported capital goods (Figure 11.1). The latter actually declined in the first two years of the boom and appear to be 'catching up' with construction in the last two years. One explanation for this reversal is the sharp increase in import prices during the early 1980s. The growth in construction, meanwhile, was the result of the ambitious Fourth Five-Year Plan (1977–81), which continued the policy of building large public enterprises. The oil windfall in the early years made it possible to meet some of the Fourth Plan targets. By contrast, the Fifth Five-Year Plan (1982–86) was a more restrained document, calling for only a modest increase in investment. Despite the oil windfall, Cameroon's policymakers were becoming aware of the country's absorptive capacity constraints. Furthermore, many of the Fifth Plan's targets were not being met by 1985, giving credence to the view that the construction boom may have been premature.

The picture that emerges is one of Cameroon's undergoing both the Dutch Disease and construction boom associated with windfalls. The Dutch Disease was milder than observed in other countries because a sizeable portion of the oil windfall was saved abroad. Similarly, the construction boom did not translate into a sharp rise in non-tradable capital goods prices *vis-à-vis* consumer goods prices because import prices were rising quite rapidly at the same time. Finally, the path of the construction boom was such that construction accelerated and then slowed, while imports of capital goods started slowly and then speeded up.

Despite the mild price effects and mixed inter-temporal effects on

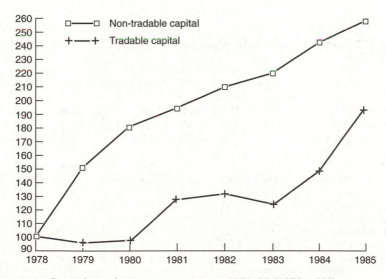

Figure 11.1. Capital goods at constant prices, 1978–85 (*1978 = 100*)

investment goods, Cameroon did succumb to the Dutch Disease where resource allocation is concerned. As Table 11.7 shows, in broad terms, the traditional tradable sector's (agriculture's) share in GDP declined quite substantially during the 1978–85 period, while construction and services gained ground. The one puzzle is manufacturing. If this were a tradable sector, its share of GDP should, as noted above, also have declined; instead, it grew. The reason is that in Cameroon the manufacturing sector is more like a non-tradable than a tradable, since it produces imperfect substitutes for imports (Benjamin *et al.* 1989). Thus, domestic expenditure out of oil revenues caused the manufacturing sector to expand. In addition, recall that the import price index was rising rapidly during this period. To the extent that the manufacturing sector does compete with imports, it enjoyed a small 'boom' of its own (Fardmanesh 1990).

The differential growth rates of these sectors could not have occurred without some factor reallocation. Which factors moved and in which direction? While capital in place is fixed, investment could move according to increased profitability in, say, the non-tradable sector. Similarly, labour is mobile, possibly more so than capital, so it may move to sectors where the windfall-induced boom is temporary. We now investigate these issues.

As data on investment-by-sector-of-destination are not available in Cameroon, we rely on indirect evidence. One source is the sectoral distribution of credit to the economy (Table 11.8).[5] Although the sectoral classification is not the same as in Table 11.7, it is close enough for comparison. Table 11.8 tells the story alluded to earlier. The share of credit going to

Table 11.7. Cameroon: sectoral composition of non-oil GDP (*as percentages of non-oil GDP*)

	1978	1979	1980	1981	1982	1983	1984	1985
Agriculture	30.0	31.8	31.0	31.4	30.6	27.4	24.7	25.2
Manufacturing	10.0	9.6	9.5	11.2	14.2	14.7	15.6	15.9
Electricity, gas and water	1.2	1.4	1.3	1.2	1.4	1.2	1.3	1.3
Construction	4.3	6.0	6.5	6.2	6.3	6.4	6.6	6.5
Trade, restaurants and hotels	16.4	16.6	15.5	14.4	12.8	13.7	15.5	15.4
Transport and communication	7.9	7.1	6.9	6.5	6.8	6.7	6.5	6.5
Public administration	8.1	8.0	7.7	6.9	7.1	7.7	7.7	7.8
Other services	15.1	14.4	15.8	16.3	15.3	17.0	16.4	16.1
Import duties	7.0	5.1	5.9	6.1	5.6	5.3	5.7	5.4

Source: Government of Cameroon, National Accounts

agriculture declined monotonically after 1978. Meanwhile, construction's share rose steadily every year except one (1983). Within the services sector, all subsectors' shares grew with the exception of export trade—further evidence that exporting was becoming unprofitable in Cameroon. Finally, the share of credit going to processing industries has fluctuated, with a two percentage point drop between the endpoints. One reason for the fluctuations is that the processing industries in Cameroon are dependent on the agricultural sector for their raw materials. Variations in the latter's production (due to weather, say) can affect the short-run profitability of the former. Another possibility is that the manufacturing sector built capacity ahead of demand, anticipating the oil-boom-led growth in this sector. A third explanation is that Table 11.8 gives the distribution of credit in value terms. Since investment in the manufacturing sector is import-intensive, and import prices fluctuated during this period, real investment in the manufacturing sector may have been much less variable and, indeed, may have followed a path similar to output in that sector. In fact, as the price of non-tradable capital goods began to catch up with that of tradable capital goods (see Figure 11.2), the value share of the non-tradable-intensive sectors (construction and trade) rose relative to that of the processing industries.

The patterns discerned from Table 11.8 are corroborated by another indicator of investment by destination, the planned and actual distribution of investments in the Fourth and Fifth Five-Year Plans (Table 11.9). Again, the sectoral classification is different. In particular, there is no distinction between the oil and non-oil industrial sectors. Nevertheless, the general pattern is the same: in plan targets and their realisation, there was an increased emphasis on the non-tradable sector at the expense of tradables.

Even when the actual and counterfactual allocation of investment are

Table 11.8. Cameroon: sectoral distribution of credit to the non-oil economy (*as percentages of value*)

	1978	1979	1980	1981	1982	1983	1984	1985
Agriculture	6.3	5.6	6.0	5.5	5.2	4.9	4.8	3.7
Processing industries	26.9	31.8	30.7	31.6	26.6	34.7	23.6	24.2
Construction	7.5	7.8	7.8	9.3	9.9	1.3	11.1	12.6
Retail trade	27.2	27.8	26.5	26.1	28.8	28.8	29.2	29.6
Export trade	10.6	7.6	8.0	6.9	7.3	9.8	7.6	5.4
Services	11.8	8.3	9.5	9.9	10.3	9.0	12.9	12.5
Individuals	7.8	9.4	9.7	8.5	7.3	7.0	7.0	6.9
Non-classified	1.9	1.7	1.8	2.1	4.6	4.4	3.7	5.1

Source: Central des Risques

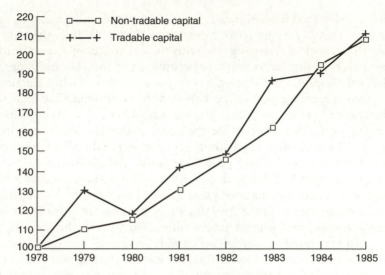

Figure 11.2. Capital goods prices, 1978–85 (*1978 = 100*)

Table 11.9. Cameroon: planned and actual investment (*as percentages of value*)

	Fourth Plan (1977–81)		Fifth Plan (1982–86)	
	Planned	Actual	Planned	Actual[a]
Agriculture, rural development	17.3	13.7	23.7	14.6
Manufacturing, mining and energy	30.9	44.7	16.4	25.4
Commerce, tourism, transportation	6.7	7.9	7.7	8.5
Infrastructure	21.6	22.1	21.1	18.5
Education, training	5.0	2.6	8.8	4.1
Youth, sports	0.4	0.4	1.4	0.2
Health, social affairs	1.7	1.1	4.0	7.0
Urban, housing	12.3	2.6	11.0	7.0
Other	4.1	4.9	5.9	20.2

[a] Actual for 1982–84

Source: Ministry of Planning

compared, the difference (i.e. the additional investment attributable to the boom) is quite close to the shares observed. In Table 11.10, we label investment in agriculture and processing industries as tradables, and everything else as non-tradables. The result shows that the share of additional investment owing to the boom going to tradables is 37.7%—not that different from the observed share in 1978 (32.5%). Hence, we cannot

Table 11.10. Actual and counterfactual investment allocation

	1978	1979	1980	1981	1982	1983	1984	1985
Actual (%)								
Tradables	32.5	37.4	36.7	37.1	31.8	39.6	28.4	27.9
Non-tradable	67.5	62.6	63.3	62.9	68.2	60.4	71.6	72.1
Level (bn CFAF)	234.0	281.8	342.3	430.8	433.3	492.4	537.4	581.9
Tradable	76.1	105.4	125.6	159.8	137.8	195.2	152.5	162.3
Non-tradable	158.0	176.4	216.7	271.0	295.5	297.7	384.6	419.5
Counterfactual (%)								
Tradable	32.5	32.5	32.5	32.5	32.5	32.5	32.5	32.5
Non-tradable	67.5	67.5	67.5	67.5	67.5	67.5	67.5	67.5
Level (bn CFAF)	232.9	258.9	295.6	340.3	360.8	385.6	415.1	449.0
Tradable	75.7	84.1	96.1	110.6	117.2	125.3	134.9	145.9
Non-tradable	157.2	174.7	199.6	229.7	243.5	260.3	280.2	303.1
Difference (bn CFAF)								
Tradable	0.4	21.3	29.5	49.2	20.6	69.8	17.6	16.4
Non-tradable	0.7	1.7	17.1	41.3	52.0	37.4	104.4	116.4
Total difference (undiscounted, bn CFAF)								
Tradable							224.8% (37.7%)	
Non-tradable							371.1% (62.3%)	

Source: Author's calculations

Table 11.11. Cameroon: employment (*in thousands*)

	1980	1984	Growth rate 1980–84 (%)
Private	282.0	360.0	27.7
Public	104.0	135.0	29.8
Agriculture	2591.0[a]	2878.0[b]	11.1

[a] 1981
[b] 1986

Source: World Bank, 'Cameroon: Recent Performance and Adjustment to Declining Oil Revenues,' *Country Economic Memorandum*, 6395-CM, 1986

conclude that in Cameroon a disproportionate share of domestic investment went into tradables.

Data on employment by sector are even harder to come by than investment data in Cameroon. The best estimates are reported in Table 11.11. The figures for the private sector include the parapublic sector. If we consider the private and public sector as those producing manufactured goods and non-tradables, then it is plain that the employment pattern mirrored the output and investment patterns. Employment in manufactures/non-tradables grew by almost 30%, while that in agriculture grew by 11% over a period which includes the oil boom. At this level of aggregation, there are no dramatic reversals of labour-allocation patterns.

A sharper picture can be obtained by a simulation analysis with a computable general equilibrium (CGE) model of Cameroon, which was designed to look at the effects of oil revenues on the economy (see Benjamin *et al.* 1989). The CGE model was calibrated to 1978 data, the first year of oil revenues. An experiment with the model where US$500 million of oil income are spent on the domestic economy reveals the basic Dutch Disease pattern described above. It is assumed that the US$500 million accrue to the government, which is at the margin a net saver. Thus, the economy-wide savings rate goes up, although this is by assumption rather than the endogenous response of the economy to a temporary shock. In the counterfactual simulation, the size of the labour force is held fixed and full employment is assumed. The impact on the allocation of labour across sectors is shown in Table 11.12.

Note that the forestry and cash crops sectors shed labour, while the food crops sector absorbs it. The reason is that the former two are pure tradable sectors (96% of cash crop output is exported), while food crops are essentially non-tradable.

As for wages and salaries, these seem to have followed a curious pattern during the boom period. Overall, wages increased throughout the economy, generally at a faster rate than did prices. This is not surprising.

Table 11.12. Cameroon: effects of oil revenues on the labour market results of simulations with a CGE model

Sector	Percentage change in labour force
Food crops	4.35
Cash crops	−20.69
Forestry	−20.71
Food processing	13.08
Consumer goods	5.24
Intermediate goods	−4.04
Cement and base metals	−4.08
Capital goods	16.70
Construction	61.64
Private services	−0.76
Public services	−15.06
Total	0.00

Source: Benjamin *et al.* (1989)

It is consistent with the Dutch Disease predictions, although it should be noted that Cameroon's labour force is growing very rapidly (the population growth rate was clocked at 3.2% a year). What is unusual, however, is that wages in the rural areas grew the fastest. Over the period from 1979 to 1985, real wages in the rural areas rose by over 30%. The main cause of this was the government's policy of raising rural wages to stem the tide of rural–urban migration. With agriculture losing out to the rest of the economy, rising real wages only squeezed profits from this sector. The diminishing investment in this sector, therefore, is quite understandable.

11.4. Public *vs.* Private Sector

In the case of Cameroon's oil boom, all of the windfall accrued initially to the public sector. The government earned revenues from production-sharing agreements as well as through royalties and profits taxes from foreign oil companies. Significantly, the revenue from production-sharing was not included in the government's regular budget. The money was kept offshore and drawn on to fill capital spending needs. Nevertheless, as shown in Table 11.13, revenue from oil-sector royalties and profit taxes alone grew to become the single largest item in the government's budget. Total oil revenues contributed sizeably to the increase in government

Table 11.13. Cameroon: government revenues (*billion CFAF*)

	1971	1979	1980	1981	1982	1985
Tax revenue	44.7	152.2	210.6	279.3	348.9	598.8
of which:						
Oil royalties			16.2	38.0	77.7	168.4
Income tax	7.2	34.6	50.0	88.6	151.9	274.8
Social security		16.0	18.5	19.5	24.3	43.2
Property tax		4.4	6.1	8.3	9.3	15.1
Tax on goods and services	13.4	32.0	41.3	50.1	56.6	109.8
Import duties	22.3	61.0	88.5	107.2	101.3	148.1
Other taxes	1.8	4.0	4.3	5.4	6.0	7.8
Non-tax revenue	7.3	6.5	18.3	35.2	40.2	62.0
Adjustments		63.7	1.8			
Budget total	52.0	222.4	230.7	314.5	389.1	660.8
Oil revenues		14.0	26.6	110.8	141.5	237.9
(production-sharing)						
Total	52.0	236.4	257.3	425.3	530.6	898.7

Source: World Bank, 'Cameroon: Recent Performance and Adjustment to Declining Oil Revenues,' *Country Economic Memorandum*, 6395-CM, 1986

revenue's share in GDP, which grew from 20% in 1979 to 24% by 1985. Interestingly, non-oil revenues' share of non-oil GDP fell during this period from 20% to 16%. One reason is that revenues from import duties—until then the largest source of government revenue—did not rise as fast as oil revenues during the mid-1980s. The standard Dutch Disease theory would predict the opposite: as the domestic tradable sector contracts, imports grow, increasing tariff revenues. However, in Cameroon, this phenomenon was accompanied by a gradual reduction in tariff rates, as the government found the need for raising revenues and restricting imports less and less compelling.

How was the government's newly-found revenue distributed to the private sector? Table 11.14 gives most of the answers. Even before the oil boom, the Cameroonian government had been known to run fiscal surpluses. This pattern continued after the boom. In short, there were no major attempts to transfer the windfall in lump-sum fashion to the private sector.

The fiscal surpluses before the oil boom were due to the relatively austere capital budget. In 1971, public investment was less than 2% of GDP. The oil windfall permitted a dramatic increase in the capital budget, without threatening the solvency of the public sector. The lion's share of this increase came from 'extra-budgetary' funds—the government revenue from production-sharing agreements with the oil companies. Most of these funds were kept outside the monetary system. Their disbursement remained at the discretion of the President. Not surprisingly, this extrabudgetary account greatly increased the power of the Presidency over the line ministries.

Table 11.14. Cameroon: government expendiures (*as percentages of GDP*)

	1971	1979	1980	1981	1982	1985
Total expenditure	15.3	16.4	15.8	24.8	22.9	26.3
Recurrent	13.8	11.6	10.6	12.2	12.1	16.4
Wages and salaries	7.2	5.8	4.9	5.2	5.0	6.6
Subsidies and transfers	1.3	1.8	1.8	2.0	2.1	4.0
Materials	5.1	3.9	3.6	4.5	4.3	4.7
Interest	0.2	0.2	0.3	0.5	0.7	1.0
Capital	1.5	4.8	5.1	12.6	10.8	9.9
Capital budget	n.a	n.a	1.2	2.3	2.2	2.8
Foreign finance	n.a	n.a	2.3	4.0	2.5	2.3
Extrabudgetary	0.0	0.0	1.7	6.3	6.2	4.8
Total revenue	16.2	20.5	18.0	23.8	24.6	29.1
Surplus/deficit	0.9	4.1	2.3	−1.0	1.7	2.8

Source: World Bank, 'Cameroon: Recent Performance and Adjustment to Declining Oil Revenues,' *Country Economic Memorandum*, 6395-CM, 1986

Another trend was the rise in importance of subsidies and transfers in recurrent expenditure. Their share of GDP has tripled since 1971. A favourable interpretation is that these are reversible commitments. By contrast, wages and salaries and interest on public debt are not. The latter, along with public investment, make up the government's 'exhaustive budget'. This budget, and hence the primary surplus, has remained relatively stable during the oil windfall. Another interpretation, though, is that there is a shift in the government's approach to distributing the oil windfall. Whereas previously the transfer was through the capital budget—and hence a transfer to future generations—the government subsequently increased its expenditure on the current generation. Furthermore, some of these subsidies went towards shoring up inefficient public enterprises—a policy that cannot be maintained in the long run. At the same time, by spending oil money on transfer payments and subsidies, the government was creating a constituency which would oppose a reversal of this strategy when the oil boom turned to bust.

We now consider the relative contributions of the private and public sectors to the boom-induced capital formation and asset accumulation. Recall that the economy as a whole saved about two-thirds of the oil windfall (itself equal to about 54% of 1978 GDP), so that the accumulation of assets—both physical and financial—must have been considerable. What is interesting is how the build-up of these assets was shared by the public and private sectors over time. As Table 11.15 shows, the public sector was responsible for most of the accumulation during the early years of the boom. In fact, in 1981–82, the government's share of windfall capital formation and asset accumulation far exceeded 100%. The private sector's actual investment level was below its counterfactual during these years. Even in the last year of the boom, the government's windfall investment accounted for almost all of the economy's.

The discrepancy between the two sectors becomes even more apparent when we examine their windfall savings rates. The government's rate is extraordinarily high throughout the boom. By contrast, the private sector's windfall savings rate is negative most of the time. Again, this reflects the fact that the private sector's actual level of asset accumulation was below its counterfactual level.

Towards the end of the boom, however, the public and private sectors appear to have become equal partners, at least where asset accumulation is concerned.

This entire pattern of behaviour stands in marked contrast with Kenya's experience, where the government was responsible for only about a quarter of the boom-induced capital formation (see Chapter 2).

A possible explanation for the asymmetry between public and private responses in Cameroon lies in the way publicity about the windfall was treated. Throughout the oil era, the magnitude of the oil revenues was

Table 11.15. Cameroon: boom-induced capital formation and asset accumulation (*billion 1978 CFAF*)

	1979	1980	1981	1982	1985
Actual					
GDP	1,206.8	1,350.5	1,592.0	1,689.4	1,972.2
Govt. revenue	231.4	246.4	376.9	412.6	573.9
Govt. current expenditure	140.0	143.2	194.2	204.4	323.4
Govt. capital expenditure	57.9	68.9	200.6	182.5	195.2
Counterfactual					
GDP	1,180.1	1,301.9	1,461.4	1,548.4	1,823.2
Govt. revenue	212.9	234.9	263.7	279.4	328.9
Govt. current expenditure	136.9	151.0	169.5	179.6	211.5
Govt. capital expenditure	56.6	62.5	70.1	74.3	87.5
Windfall (actual – counterfactual)					
Govt. revenue	18.5	11.5	113.2	133.2	245.0
Govt. current expenditure	3.1	−7.9	24.7	24.8	111.9
Govt. capital expenditure	1.3	6.4	130.4	108.1	107.7
Govt. primary surplus	14.1	13.0	−41.9	0.3	25.3
Total GFKF	22.3	44.0	84.7	68.5	118.1
Total asset accumulation	−29.4	22.4	48.5	33.6	278.3
Govt. shares of					
Windfall GFKF	5.7	14.5	154.0	157.9	91.2
Windfall asset accumulation	−52.5	86.6	182.5	322.6	47.8
Windfall savings rates					
Government	0.83	1.68	0.78	0.81	0.54
Private sector	−5.58	0.08	−2.30	−9.58	−1.51

Note: The counterfactual government revenue and expenditure figures were obtained by applying the 1979 GDP shares (see Tables 11.12 and 11.13) to counterfactual GDP, the latter being obtained from Table 11.2

Source: Authors's calculations

shrouded in secrecy. The Société Nationale des Hydrocarbures, the state-owned oil company, kept even the other ministries in the dark about the size of Cameroon's reserves or their annual throughput. The ostensible reason was that, by hiding the extent of the windfall, the government could resist popular pressure to spend it. However, this could have had the perverse effect of making the private sector think the windfall was greater than it actually was.[6] Its behaviour (of lower than counterfactual investment) in the early years of the boom is consistent with a much larger increase in permanent income. When, by observing the government's behaviour, private agents learned that the windfall was not as large as they had expected, they adjusted, but did so by accumulating foreign assets. Again, this behaviour is rational if the boom turned out to be shorter lived than originally anticipated.

11.5. Conclusions

While almost by definition counterfactual analysis is speculative, this particular application to Cameroon's oil boom yields some unmistakable conclusions. First, the size of the shock was large—equivalent to an increase in Cameroon's permanent income of 4% to 6%. This figure is of the same order of magnitude as Kenya's coffee boom of the mid-1970s. Like Kenya's it was a temporary shock, although the impact on real output was much greater. In fact, in Cameroon, oil production grew from nothing to about 8.5 million metric tons; in Kenya, Bevan *et al.* assume that the impact of the coffee price increase on output was zero.

Second, a sizeable proportion (roughly two-thirds) of the windfall oil income was saved. This is in keeping with the view that the oil boom was temporary, so that income from the boom should be treated as transient rather than permanent.

Third, almost half of these additional savings were used to acquire foreign assets. Whether the government recognised that the country suffered from absorptive capacity constraints is not clear. Nevertheless, it behaved as if it did.

Fourth, Cameroon experienced both the Dutch Disease and the construction boom syndrome, albeit in mild forms. The price of non-tradables (appropriately defined) rose relative to that of tradables, and the relative profitability of exportable activity declined. However, there was an asymmetric response between agricultural and manufacturing tradables. The former suffered the most. The latter, since they are imperfect substitutes for imports and hence behave as 'semi-tradables', had a mixed outcome. The construction boom effect gave rise to an increase in the relative price and output of the construction sector. But the lagged response of the non-tradable capital goods sector (*vis-à-vis* the tradables) did not take place.

Fifth, income from the oil windfall accrued directly to the government. The government, in turn, chose to 'hide' part of this (the income from production-sharing arrangements with the oil companies), presumably so that it could resist the public pressure to spend it. By and large, the government continued to manage its finances in the same manner as before: by running small fiscal surpluses. The public investment programme was accelerated. Much of this was financed by transfers from the hidden, extrabudgetary accounts. In addition, the item which increased the fastest in the government's current budget was transfers and subsidies, including subsidies to public enterprises. While these items can be thought of as reversible, the political and economic significance of oil-revenue-financed transfers may make this a serious problem when the oil boom is over.

Sixth, the behaviour of the private sector was somewhat at odds with that of the public sector. Whereas the latter saved and invested most of the windfall income, the former's actual investment was below its counterfactual level. Furthermore, the private sector's response was to accumulate foreign assets rather than invest at home. One explanation for this asymmetry is that the official secrecy surrounding oil revenues in Cameroon led to the private sector's assuming that revenues were larger than they were, and behaving accordingly. In any event, the dismal performance of the Cameroonian economy after 1986 (GDP declined by 18% from 1986 to 1989) leads one to question whether the government's aggressive investment strategy was prudent. One of the problems facing Cameroon during the oil bust was the recurrent costs associated with investment projects initiated during the oil boom. Had the government saved more of the revenue abroad, or even consumed it, it may not have been facing budget deficits to the tune of 12% of GDP in the late 1980s.

As for lessons to be learned from Cameroon's experience, two stand out. The first is that it is possible for a low-income country to treat a temporary shock as one, that is, for a country to behave as if the income is transient and hence should be, for the most part, saved. Given the experience of Cameroon's African neighbours, this prudent performance is all the more remarkable. The key in this case was the behaviour of the government, which lived up to (some may say surpassed) its reputation for austerity during the boom.

The second lesson has to do with the conduct of economic policy in Cameroon. While the government behaved in an austere manner, its outward rhetoric was considerably more profligate during the oil era. Indeed, it released an ambitious Five-Year Plan in 1987, despite the downturn in oil prices the previous year. Furthermore, there is some evidence that the policy of shrouding the oil sector in secrecy backfired. Both the profligate rhetoric and official secrecy elicited a response from the private sector which made the transition to the post-oil era all the more difficult. The lesson is that a government which already has a reputation for prudent economic policy should behave in as open a manner as possible, so as to send the most accurate signals to the private sector. This lesson applies not just to the oil boom of 1978–85 but also to the difficult circumstances facing Cameroon today.

NOTES

1. Nicod (1983) estimated Cameroon's ultimately recoverable reserves at 100 million metric tons, or 750 million barrels.
2. GDP in fiscal year 1978–79 was 1,146 billion CFAF. The exchange rate that year averaged 238.6 CFAF per dollar. Thus, GDP was about US$4.8 billion in 1978–79.

3. This is true for reasons of both aggregation and quality differences. For instance, Cameroon imports heavy machinery and produces light machine tools, but both are classified as 'capital goods'. The differences in quality are apparent in a variety of consumer goods (such as toilet paper).
4. For an explicit derivation of these two real exchange rates, see Devarajan *et al.* (1993).
5. The data are based on loans reported by the Centrale des Risques.
6. I am grateful to Jean-Paul Azam for suggesting this interpretation.

REFERENCES

Benjamin, N. and S. Devarajan (1986) 'Oil Revenues and the Cameroonian Economy,' in M. Schatzberg and I. W. Zartmann (eds), *The Political Economy of Cameroon*, New York: Praeger.

Benjamin, N., S. Devarajan and R. Weiner (1989) 'The "Dutch Disease" in Developing Countries: Oil Reserves in Cameroon,' *Journal of Development Economics*, January 30, 1, 71–92.

Corden, W.M. (1984) 'Booming Sector and Dutch Disease Economics: Survey and Consolidation,' *Oxford Economic Papers*, 36:359–80.

Devarajan, S. and J. de Melo (1987) 'Adjustment with a Fixed Exchange Rate: Cameroon, Cote d'Ivoire and Sénégal,' *World Bank Economic Review*, 1, 3, 447–87.

Devarajan, S., J. Lewis and S. Robinson (1993) 'External Shocks, Purchasing Power Parity and the Equilibrium Real Exchange Rate,' *World Bank Economic Review* 7, 1, 45–63.

Fardmanesh, M. (1990) 'Terms of Trade Shocks and Structural Adjustments in a Small, Open Economy: Dutch Disease and Oil Price Increases,' *Journal of Development Economics* 34, 1–2, 339–53.

Nicod, M. (1983) 'Prospects for Oil and Gas Production and Reserves through 1990 in the United Republic of Cameroon,' Geneva: Petroconsultants, SA.

12

Trade Shock, Oil Boom and the Nigerian Economy, 1973–83

T. ADEMOLA OYEJIDE

12.1. Introduction

Nigeria attained its political independence from British colonial rule in 1960 and the economy experienced a period of relative calm over the next four or five years. But between 1966 and 1990, the Nigerian economy experienced a series of shocks of varying magnitudes. Not all of these can be classified as trade shocks, temporary or permanent, but neither were all of them necessarily negative. In fact, it is commonly agreed that as a member of the Organization of Petroleum Exporting Countries (OPEC) and as an exporter of the much sought after premium Bonny light crude oil, Nigeria derived a large wealth transfer from the oil price increases which occurred first during 1973–74 and again during 1979–80 (Gelb 1986; Oyejide 1986; Pinto 1987).

This chapter offers an analysis of Nigeria's oil boom associated with these oil price increases and its immediate aftermath in the context of a developing economy trade shocks analytic framework. Given that the economy has been buffeted by a series of shocks over the last twenty-five years, it seems necessary to be both circumspect and specific in determining the duration and magnitude of the trade shock and associated export boom with which this analysis concerns itself. Section 12.2 addresses these issues. Next, the focus turns from the immediate and most direct manifestation of the trade shock (in the form of an export boom) to the mechanisms and channels through which the sharply increased export earnings impacted upon the rest of the economy. In dealing with these matters, Section 12.3 focuses on the windfall income that the boom generated and how this was disposed of through consumption, savings and investment.

Nigeria's oil boom translated into a massive increase in government revenue, given that the crude oil which attracted increased export earnings was public property and the associated taxes also accrued directly to government. The public revenue and expenditure patterns of the boom period can therefore be expected to have significant implications for the way in which the economy as well as its major sectors and subsectors responded to the boom. Section 12.4 presents an analysis of the revenue and expenditure patterns in this context, and Section 12.5 examines the implications of the spending decisions (both in respect of consumption and capital formation) for the movement of the relative prices of tradable and non-tradable goods and for adjustment in the factor markets. Finally, Section 12.6 extends the analysis to the impact of the control regime.

12.2. Nature, Duration and Magnitude of the Trade Shock

The series of trade shocks that accompanied Nigeria's oil boom experience can be described as a mixture of positive and negative shocks. The positive elements of the shock came in two stages, 1973/74 and 1979. Both stages were associated with oil price increases. The per barrel oil price index (Table 12.1) reflects sharp price increase in 1973/74 and again in 1978/79. The negative elements of the shock occurred during 1977/78 and from 1981 onwards; the first was relatively mild and short, whereas the second was deeper and much more long-lasting. As Table 12.1 shows, the negative elements of the shock are reflected largely by volume decline. Thus, the index of oil export volume fell by more than 50% between 1979 and 1983, as OPEC struggled to maintain oil prices, in the face of a softening world oil market fed by increasing non-OPEC supplies, by progressively cutting the production quotas of individual OPEC members.

Table 12.1. Indices of oil price and oil export volume, 1973–83

	Volume of oil exports (index)	Naira oil price per barrel (index)
1973	100	100
1974	110	175
1975	87	175
1976	102	168
1977	99	182
1978	93	178
1979	111	303
1980	91	487
1981	65	528
1982	55	467
1983	54	455

Source: Central Bank of Nigeria (CBN), *Annual Report*, various years

12.2.1. Duration

Oil price and oil export indices provide some pointers regarding the duration of Nigeria's trade-shock-induced oil boom. Additional evidence in the form of movements in such indicators as the barter terms of trade, total export earnings, oil exports and oil revenue offer more convincing proof that the choice of the 1973–83 period is more or less appropriate.

Data on these indicators of trade shock and oil boom are presented in Table 12.2. As this table shows, the barter terms of trade (with base 1980 = 100) moved up rapidly between 1973 and 1977, declined somewhat in 1978 and rose rapidly again before peaking in 1980 and then falling back thereafter until 1983. The real value of exports (at 1973 prices) reflects this general pattern. It rose from N2.5 billion in 1973, peaked at a value of N6.4 billion in 1980 and had declined almost to its starting value at N3.0 billion by 1983. The index of total exports (with base 1980 = 100) started at 39 in 1973 and ended at 48 in 1983. Both oil exports and oil revenue faithfully reproduce this general direction. The visual representation of the movement of the indices of the four selected indicators of trade shock in Figure 12.1 reveals a sharp rise from 1973 followed by slight dips around 1975 and an increase to peak levels around 1980 before a sharp decline, approximately to 1973 levels, by 1983.

Although oil earnings were becoming significant in the late 1960s, the civil war of 1967–70 (which disrupted economic activity nationwide and halted oil-exploration efforts in the war-affected areas in particular) prevented effective and full exploitation of the oil resources. In the immediate post-war period of 1970–72, policy attention focused on reconstruction,

Table 12.2. Selected indicators of the trade shock

	Terms of trade index	Total Exports		Oil exports		Oil revenue	
		Value (N million, 1973 prices)	Index (1980 = 100)	Value (N million, 1973 prices)	Index (1980 = 100)	Value (N million, 1973 prices)	Index (1980 = 100)
1973	21	2,467	39	1,894	31	1,379	29
1974	51	5,676	89	4,878	81	3,873	79
1975	47	4,395	69	3,826	63	3,453	71
1976	44	4,743	75	4,458	74	3,580	73
1977	56	5,471	86	4,633	76	2,943	60
1978	48	3,978	63	3,278	54	2,394	49
1979	64	5,607	88	4,952	82	3,944	81
1980	100	6,359	100	6,059	100	4,896	100
1981	98	4,783	75	4,450	73	3,549	72
1982	81	3,779	59	3,399	56	2,705	55
1983	63	3,039	48	2,748	45	2,014	41

Note: Values converted from current to real using the import deflator

Source: CNB, *Annual Report*, various years

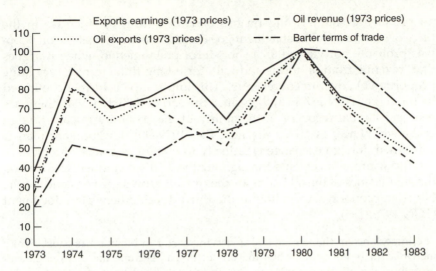

Figure 12.1. Indicators of the magnitude and duration of the oil boom, 1973–83 (*1980 = 100*)

until the sharp price increases of 1973/74 heralded the dawn of an export boom. Correspondingly, a sharp upward movement in most of the oil boom indicators (Figure 12.1) is unmistakable from 1973. But by 1983 almost all of these indicators had more or less returned to their 1973 levels.

The downward movement of these indicators continued beyond 1983, of course. However, policies designed to deal with the problems of the oil bust began to be implemented effectively after 1983; starting with an austerity period (in 1984–85) marked by sharp import compression measures which were followed by more orthodox structural-adjustment measures from 1986 (Federal Government of Nigeria 1986; Oyejide 1990b). The post-1983 developments are excluded from this analysis.

12.2.2. Nature

Was the oil boom viewed as a temporary or permanent phenomenon? Since the boom was immediately manifested in the form of increased oil export earnings and oil revenue, and since the direct beneficiary of the increased oil revenue was the public sector, the perception of the government regarding this question is crucial.

There was an early recognition by the Federal Government of Nigeria (FGN) of the beneficial impact of the oil boom on the Nigerian economy. The federal budget statement of 1974 (FGN 1974a: xv) indicates that 'as an oil producing country, Nigeria has benefited from the increase in the price of petroleum'. The statement goes further, to imply that the oil boom was probably not viewed as a short-term phenomenon, when it argues that 'revenue from oil forms and will, for a long time, form a very large proportion of government revenue'. This implication is further confirmed by the claim (FGN 1974b: 8) that 'since the end of the [civil] war, there has been substantial recovery in the ability of the economy to earn foreign exchange, hence, as far as the next [i.e. 1979–90] development plan is concerned, foreign exchange is unlikely to feature as a major problem'.

Official pronouncements throughout the 1970s continued to focus on the significance of the oil boom for the overall growth performance of the Nigerian economy. According to the third development plan document (FGN 1975: 135),

The importance of the mining and quarrying sector in Nigeria has substantially increased in recent years. Thus the oil sector has become the main engine of growth of the Nigerian economy. Due to the enhanced level of activity in this sector, the Nigerian economy is experiencing unprecedented growth.

By 1980, a note of caution was creeping into appraisals of the oil boom and its impact on the economy. The fourth development plan document (FGN 1980: 41) viewed matters as follows:

Nigeria is entering the Fourth Plan with fairly buoyant financial resources based, as in the Third Plan, on crude oil. But revenue prospects though reasonably bright cannot be regarded as rosy. Although oil prices are at record level, the country's production has already stabilised, so that prospects for revenue increase in the short and medium run now depend mainly on developments on the price front.

But even in the early stages of the oil boom, some government statements attempted to play down the expectations being generated among the public. Thus, the budget address of 1974 (FGN 1974a: xxv) warned that 'although our revenue prospects for the coming year are very bright, Nigeria is not yet a rich country; it is essential therefore that we should continue to husband our resources and spend wisely'. The *Guidelines* issued for the third plan were even more specific (FGN 1974b: 8): 'the upward trend in the net addition to reserves which has been evident for the past few years is likely to terminate in 1976–77 after which revenue accretion takes place at a decreasing rate.' Following the fall in oil exports and revenue during 1977–78, public exhortations took more dramatic forms, such as the following (FGN 1980: xxiii): 'Nigerians must cease to believe and behave as if we are a member of the club of developed nations'.

While the oil boom lasted, what was the focus of government expenditure plans? On this question, official documents suggest two important concerns. First, the budget of 1974/75 makes it clear (FGN 1974a: xxv)

that, 'the Federal Government is as determined as ever to invest the increased resources at its disposal in infrastructures such as roads and social overheads like education and health.' The second recurring theme of government expenditure focus is the diversification of the resource base as a means of avoiding a lop-sided reliance of the oil sector. Accordingly, the third plan document (FGN 1975: 48) asserts that,

The main strategy of the Third Plan therefore is to put the impact of petroleum on the economy on a more permanent footing by internationalising the rapid growth in the sector through the sectoral investment programmes and the policy package articulated elsewhere in this document.

The fourth plan document (FGN 1980: 38) repeats this basic underlying theme thus:

As in the Third Plan period, the basic strategy will therefore be that of using the resources generated by this wasting asset to ensure an all-round expansion in the productive capacity of the economy so as to lay a solid foundation for self-sustaining growth and development in the shortest time possible.

The strategy was also expected to lead to a rapid diversification of the economy away from its over-dependence on the petroleum sector.

Two broad conclusions, at least, may be drawn from this review of official documents. One is that the oil boom generated by the trade shock of 1973/74 appears to have been viewed largely as a permanent phenomenon until around 1977. Second, the sharp decline in oil revenue between 1976 and 1978 provided an important lesson which forced the government to give some recognition (however vague) to the short-lived nature of the oil boom phenomenon. References to a 'wasting asset' and the need to transform its resources into some 'permanent' form by quickly expanding the economy's productive capacity and building up its infrastructure are important clues to the gradually changing perception of the trade shock and resulting oil boom as temporary events generating windfall incomes which, if wisely expended, could create a future stream of permanent income.

12.2.3. Magnitude

The trade shocks which Nigeria experienced during 1973–83 generated a large export boom. The magnitude of the resources transferred to the Nigerian economy as a result of this boom can be estimated by comparing real actual exports with counterfactual exports during this period. Real actual exports are the observed exports expressed in 1973 prices. Counterfactual exports are derived on the basis of the assumption that, in the absence of an export boom, exports would have grown during 1973–83 at their average historic (1960–65)[1] growth rate of 9.08% per annum. The

Table 12.3. Actual and counterfactual exports, 1973–83 (*N million, 1973 prices*)

	Actual exports	Counterfactual exports	Windfall exports	Present value of windfall exports
1973	2,467	1,660	807	807
1974	5,676	1,811	3,865	3,514
1975	4,395	1,975	2,420	2,000
1976	4,743	2,154	2,589	1,945
1977	5,471	2,350	3,121	2,132
1978	3,978	2,564	1,414	876
1979	5,607	2,796	2,811	1,587
1980	6,359	3,050	3,309	1,698
1981	4,783	3,327	1,456	679
1982	3,779	3,629	150	64
1983	3,033	3,959	−920	−355
Total				14,949

Source: CBN, *Annual Report*, various years

difference between actual and counterfactual exports is referred to as windfall exports. Values of windfall exports are further discounted at the rate of 10% to derive their present values.

Table 12.3 presents the result of this exercise. The present value of the stream of windfall exports over the 1973–83 period amounts to N14.949 billion. This figure is equivalent to almost 606% of Nigeria's total exports value in 1973.

A similar exercise was conducted with respect to the gross domestic product. A comparison of actual real GDP (at 1973 prices, using the GDP implicit deflator) with counterfactual GDP (estimated by applying the average annual growth rate of GDP during 1960–65 period) yields a windfall GDP series for 1973–83 (Table 12.4). The present value of this series adds up to N62.189 billion, which is equivalent to approximately 566% of Nigeria's 1973 GDP. Assuming a 10% rate of return on capital, the investment of this oil windfall income would have increased permanent income by N6.2 billion, or almost 57% of the country's total income in 1973.

12.3. Consumption, Savings and Investment

The windfall income that emanated from the oil boom was obviously allocated over time partly to investment and partly to consumption. An attempt to determine how much and what proportions of the windfall income were consumed/saved and invested requires the construction of counterfactual series for consumption and investment.

Table 12.4. Actual and counterfactual income 1973–83 (*N million*)

	Actual GDP (current prices)	Actual GDP (1973 prices)	Counterfactual GDP (1973 prices)	Windfall income (1973 prices)	Present value of windfall income
1973	10,991	10,991	8,161	2,830	2,830
1974	18,811	17,124	8,647	8,477	7,706
1975	21,779	18,050	9,161	8,889	7,346
1976	27,572	19,833	9,707	10,126	7,608
1977	12,520	21,297	10,284	11,013	7,524
1978	35,540	20,524	10,896	9,628	5,978
1979	43,151	22,060	11,544	10,516	5,936
1980	49,755	22,150	12,231	9,927	5,095
1981	56,602	23,613	12,959	10,654	4,949
1982	60,483	23,947	13,730	10,217	4,333
1983	63,293	22,029	14,547	7,482	2,884
Total					62,189

Source: CBN, *Annual Report*, various years; Federal Office of Statistics, *Economic and Social Statistics Bulletin*, 1985

Starting with consumption, actual real consumption is taken as the sum of actual private and public consumption spending valued at 1973 prices. Counterfactual consumption is derived from counterfactual income by applying the average consumption/income ratio observed during 1960–65. Windfall consumption is generated as the difference between the actual and counterfactual series. As before the present value of the stream of windfall consumption is estimated using a 10% discount rate. Table 12.5 shows the results. The present value of the stream of windfall consumption expenditures over the 1973–83 period was just over N39 billion.

Windfall consumption was thus quite high. But this should be related to income. One way of doing this is to compare the trends in the growth of both income and consumption over the period under consideration. Table 12.6 provides the data for this exercise. The most striking result is that, while real income increased twofold between 1973 and 1983, the index of counterfactual consumption rose from 100 in 1973 to just 178 in 1983. But actual real consumption increased more than threefold over the same period. Thus, actual consumption increased much more rapidly than both counterfactual consumption and actual real income.

How much of the windfall income was saved and invested? An answer to this question required the construction of counterfactual investment expenditures. This is accomplished by deriving counterfactual investment (or gross fixed capital formation) from counterfactual income using the historic (1960–65) average investment/income ratio and then comparing the result with actual real gross fixed capital formation (GFKF) to generate

Table 12.5. Actual and counterfactual consumption, 1973–83 (*N million, 1973 prices*)

	Actual consumption	Counterfactual income	Counterfactual consumption	Windfall consumption	Present value of windfall consumption
1973	6,837	8,161	6,937	−100	−100
1974	11,158	8,647	7,350	3,808	3,462
1975	13,311	9,161	7,787	5,524	4,565
1976	13,584	9,707	8,251	5,333	4,007
1977	14,306	10,284	8,741	5,565	3,801
1978	16,960	10,896	9,262	7,698	4,780
1979	15,689	11,544	9,812	5,877	3,318
1980	16,332	12,231	10,396	5,936	3,046
1981	20,523	12,959	11,015	9,508	4,435
1982	21,391	13,750	11,688	9,703	4,115
1983	21,693	14,547	12,339	9,354	3,606
Total					39,035

Source: CBN, *Annual Report*, various years; FOS, *Economic and Social Statistics Bulletin*, 1985

Table 12.6. Growth trend of income and consumption, 1973–83 (*1983 = 100*)

	Actual income (1973 prices)	Actual consumption (1973 prices)	Counterfactual consumption
1973	100	100	100
1974	156	163	106
1975	164	195	112
1976	180	199	119
1977	194	209	126
1978	187	248	134
1979	201	229	141
1980	202	239	150
1981	215	300	159
1982	218	313	168
1983	200	317	178

Source: Tables 12.4 and 12.5

windfall investment. Table 12.7 displays the data and results of this comparison, including the present value (at a 10% discount rate) of the stream of windfall expenditures on gross fixed capital formation. This present value sums to N22.794 billion over the 1973–83 period.

Windfall gross fixed capital formation represents only one of the two components of the economy's savings; it reflects the economy's propensity to acquire domestic assets. The second component of savings corresponds to the economy's propensity to acquire foreign assets.

Table 12.7. Actual and counterfactual gross fixed capital formation, 1973–83 (*N million*)

	Real GFKF	Counterfactual income	Counterfactual GFKF	Windfall GFKF	Present value of windfall GFKF
1973	2,505	8,161	1,132	1,374	1,374
1974	2,862	8,647	1,200	1,662	1,511
1975	4,707	9,161	1,271	3,436	2,840
1976	6,584	9,707	1,347	5,237	3,935
1977	7,409	10,284	1,427	5,982	4,086
1978	5,372	10,896	1,511	3,861	2,397
1979	4,447	11,544	1,601	2,846	1,607
1980	5,091	12,231	1,697	3,396	1,743
1981	5,521	12,959	1,798	3,723	1,737
1982	4,567	13,750	1,907	2,660	1,128
1983	3,148	14,547	2,018	1,130	436
Total					22,794

Source: CBN, *Annual Report*, various years; FOS, *Economic and Social Statistics Bulletin*, 1985

To estimate windfall foreign savings, actual and counterfactual foreign savings are compared. The construction of counterfactual foreign savings requires an assumption regarding the current account deficit as a ratio of gross domestic product. The historic average (during 1960–65) of this ratio is 5.04%, and this is the rate adopted for constructing the counterfactual. It is applied to counterfactual income to generate counterfactual foreign savings. As Table 12.8 shows, the present value (discounted at 10%) of the stream of windfall foreign savings totals −N3.917 billion during the 1973–83 period. This implies a large net increase in foreign indebtedness, since the oil boom seems to have permitted an increased capacity of the economy to accumulate debt.

The difference between these two components is windfall savings after the savings generated by the additional windfall income have been deducted. The additional windfall income gives rise to savings that are estimated by applying the economy's historic (1960–65) average domestic savings rate to the stream of windfall income and discounting at 10%. The discounted value of this amounts to 6.222 billion over the 1973–83 period. Thus, total windfall savings are N20.489 billion (22.794 + 3.917 − 6.222).

It is now possible to go back to the original question: how much of the windfall income was saved and how much was consumed? Table 12.9 pulls the different pieces together and shows that consumption spending accounted for just over N39 billion (or almost 63%) of the windfall income, and another N20.5 billion (or 33%) of the windfall income was allocated to

Table 12.8. Actual and counterfactual foreign savings, 1973–83 (N million, 1973 prices)

	Actual foreign savings	Counterfactual foreign savings	Windfall foreign savings	Present value of windfall foreign savings
1973	−5	408	−403	−403
1974	−2,929	432	−3,361	−3,055
1975	−21	458	−479	−396
1976	162	485	−323	−243
1977	432	514	−82	−56
1978	1,421	545	876	544
1979	−393	577	−970	−548
1980	−1,233	612	−1,845	−947
1981	1,651	648	1,003	468
1982	1,921	688	1,233	523
1983	1,235	727	508	196
Total				−3,917

Source: CBN, Annual Report, various years

Table 12.9. Allocation of windfall income, 1973–83

	Present value (N billion)	Proportion (%)
Income	62.189	100.00
Consumption	39.035	62.77
Savings	20.489	32.95
GFKF	(22.794)	(36.65)
Foreign debt	(−3.917)	(−6.30)
Extra savings	(6.222)	(10.00)
Inventory accumulation	2.665	4.29

Source: Tables 12.3–5 and 12.8

savings. Inventory accumulation took the residual value of N2.7 billion (or just over 4%). This result seems to conflict with repeated government pronouncements to the effect that the fundamental strategy of Nigeria's third and fourth development plans was to use the resources generated by the oil boom to ensure an all-round expansion in the productive capacity of the economy. The observed behaviour reveals a strong bias towards allocating a large proportion (over 60%) of the windfall income to consumption rather than investment spending directed at expanding the economy's productive capacity. Gross fixed capital formation over this period was only 37% of windfall income, but over 17% of GFKF was financed by foreign debt. Further analysis of this issue, as well as a more detailed examination of the sectoral content of the investment spending which actually occurred, requires a review of the pattern of revenue and investment expenditure, to which attention is turned in the Section 12.4.

12.4. Revenue and Expenditure Pattern

The Nigerian oil boom transferred resources immediately and directly to the public sector. The resulting windfall income was subsequently allocated between consumption and investment spending through the fiscal mechanisms of government revenue and expenditure processes. The sectoral pattern of the corresponding resource-allocation and spending decisions ultimately impacted on sectoral prices and factor movements.

12.4.1. General Trends

As shown in Section 12.2 above, an important manifestation of Nigeria's oil boom was a sharp increase in oil revenue accruing directly to the government. Thus, oil revenue became a dominant portion of total government revenue, rising to well in excess of 80% during 1973–83. The character of the oil boom and its overall impact on the economy are closely related to the size of the resulting massive increase in revenue and its allocation in expenditure terms. The data presented in Table 12.10 provide some indications of these relationships. The data and the discussions that

Table 12.10. Revenue and expenditure components, 1973–83 (*as percentages of GDP*)

	Revenue	Total expenditure	Recurrent expenditure	Capital expenditure	Debt servicing	Debt servicing as a percentage of recurrent expenditure	Surplus/ deficit
1960–65	8.4	10.9	n.a.	n.a.	0.8	12.6	−2.5
1973	15.4	13.9	8.8	5.1	0.8	9.7	1.5
1974	24.1	16.3	8.1	8.2	0.7	8.8	7.8
1975	25.3	27.3	12.6	14.7	0.9	6.9	−2.0
1976	24.5	28.5	13.8	14.7	1.2	9.0	−4.0
1977	25.7	27.1	11.7	15.4	0.6	5.0	−1.4
1978	21.4	29.0	8.7	20.3	1.3	15.1	−7.6
1979	28.4	18.0	8.8	9.7	0.8	12.8	9.9
1980	30.6	23.6	8.1	14.8	2.7	33.8	7.0
1981	22.4	19.0	9.0	10.0	1.4	16.1	3.4
1982	19.4	20.5	8.0	12.5	1.7	21.0	−1.1
1983	17.3	18.4	8.3	10.1	1.8	21.1	−1.1

Source: CBN, *Annual Report*, FOS, *Economic and Social Statistics Bulletin*, 1985

follow cover only federal government revenue and expenditure patterns; figures for local and state government are less reliable and are excluded. Revenue as a proportion of GDP rose sharply from the 1960–65 annual average of 8.4% to 15.4% in 1973, and even more sharply, to an average of 25%, over 1974–77, before peaking at almost 31% in 1980. Thereafter it fell back to 17.3% in 1983.

This general trend masks significant differences in sectoral changes and changes over time. For example, boom induced change in total revenue (i.e. in comparison with corresponding counterfactuals) amounted to about 64% during 1973–76; this increased to 67% in 1977–80 and fell to 56% during the 1981–83 period. Direct and other taxes accounted for these increases; in fact, this revenue source showed increases of over 83% during each of the three periods indicated above. In comparison, revenue from indirect taxes (which impacted directly on tradables) suffered large boom-induced declines, which averaged 75% during 1973–76, 63% in 1977–80 and 52% between 1981 and 1983.

Total expenditure as a proportion of GDP exhibits the same broad pattern although there was a two- to three-year lag before expenditures caught up with the rising revenue. This is reflected in the surplus/deficit column of Table 12.10. Thus, the traditional (i.e. 1960–64 average) deficit of 2.5% of GDP gave way to surpluses during 1973 and 1974 and again between 1979 and 1981, the twin peaks of the boom period. It is worth noting also that public debt charges as a proportion of GDP and of recurrent expenditure rose significantly during the boom period. Starting from a historic average of less than 1% of GDP in the early years of the boom, the ratio rose to 1.2% in 1976 and averaged close to 2% of GDP during 1980–83. As a proportion of recurrent expenditure the increase in debt servicing is even more dramatic; compared with an average of 12.6% during 1960–65, the ratio fell to an average of less than 8% in 1973–77 and then rose sharply to an average of 20% during 1978–83, with a peak value of almost 34% in 1980.

Recurrent expenditure as a percentage of GDP was remarkably stable— at an annual average of about 8.5%—during most of the boom period. However, 1975–77 proved to be an exceptional subperiod during which this ratio rose to an average of 12.7%, or as much as 49% above the norm. It may be inferred, therefore, that a significant part of the above-average increase in expenditure was allocated to capital expenditure.

12.4.2. Capital Expenditure

This brings the analysis to the role of the development plans in allocating capital expenditures during the period of the oil boom. A series of five-year national development plans has served as the framework for public expenditure allocation in Nigeria since the first was launched in 1962. The

Table 12.11. Distribution of public capital expenditure (*percentage*)

	3rd Plan 1975–80	4th Plan 1981–85	Actual 1975–80
Tradables	31.0	31.7	20.8
Agriculture	6.6	12.8	7.1
Mining and quarrying	8.2	9.4	5.0
Manufacturing	16.2	9.5	8.7
Non-tradables	69.0	68.3	79.2
Public utilities	31.3	26.2	36.9
Education	7.5	10.8	10.2
Health	2.3	4.4	2.0
Other services (including defence)	27.9	26.9	30.1
Total	100.0	100.0	100.0

Source: CBN, *Annual Report*, various years; FGN, *Third National Development Plan*; FGN, *Fourth National Development Plan*

first national development plan covered 1962–63 to 1967–68, with an extension to 1969. Compared with the subsequent boom-influenced ones, this plan has a capital expenditure component of N2.2 billion. The second plan was originally designed for the 1970–74 period and was aimed at reconstruction following the civil war of 1967–70. It had a capital expenditure component of N3.2 billion.

The third and fourth plans were the ones most directly influenced by the euphoria associated with the oil boom. The third plan covered 1975–80 and was originally designed with an overall capital expenditure of N30 billion, out of which the public sector was allocated N20 billion. It was subsequently revised to N53.3 billion, since finance was not expected to constitute a binding constraint. The fourth plan of 1981–85 was even more ambitious, with a total capital expenditure of N82 billion, including a public sector component of N70.5 billion.

As shown in Table 12.11, the two plans which more or less cover the oil-boom period had a clear bias for non-tradables in terms of the planned allocation of capital expenditure. In both cases, proposed allocation to tradables was less than half that to non-tradables. The actual sectoral allocation of capital expenditure during 1975–80 was even more heavily oriented towards non-tradables, which accounted for almost 80% of the total.

This strong bias of the public sector investment projects no doubt had a significant influence on the sectoral distribution of overall gross fixed capital formation in the economy. Table 12.12 indicates that non-tradables accounted for 66.5% of total gross fixed capital formation during 1975/76 and that this share declined mildly to 63.6% by 1979/80. Building and

Table 12.12. Sectoral allocation of gross fixed capital formation 1975–80

	1960/65	1975/76	1977/78	1979/80
Non-tradables	75.5	66.5	63.9	63.6
Building and construction	n.a.	64.9	62.8	62.4
Land improvement	n.a.	1.6	1.1	1.2
Tradables	24.5	33.5	36.1	36.4
Transport equipment	n.a.	14.1	15.2	16.5
Plant and machinery	n.a.	19.4	20.9	19.9
Total	100.0	100.0	100.0	100.0

Source: FOS, *Annual Abstract of Statistics*, various years

construction alone accounted for 65% in 1975/76 and 62% in 1979/80. Correspondingly, the share of tradables (i.e. transport equipment and machinery) increased marginally, from 33.5% in 1975/76 to 36.4% in 1979/80.

Nigeria's public sector investment portfolio during 1973–83 was dominated by resource-based activities such as iron and steel, pulp and paper, aluminium smelter, vehicle assembly plants, machine tools, petroleum refineries and petrochemicals. In particular Nigeria concentrated heavily on steel plants, which gulped more than US$6 billion during this period. Concentration of public sector investment on such large, capital-intensive projects contributed to the marked excess-capacity creation and inefficiency generally associated with this type of investment. Thus, the incremental capital/output ratio of Nigeria's resource-based industry investment was as high as 39.2, while 'the actual and potential production costs of the two Nigerian steel plants were two to three orders of magnitude higher than those of competitive world producers' (Auty 1989: 358, 369).

12.5. Relative Prices and Factor Shifts: Dutch Disease *versus* Construction Boom

The behaviour of sectoral prices and factor shifts normally reflects fundamental pressures of demand in the economy relative to the volume of sectoral outputs or supply. In the presence of a windfall induced by a trade shock and exports, this behaviour can be explained in the context of two complementary theoretical frameworks. One of these has been developed around the 'Dutch Disease' syndrome (Corden and Neary 1982; Corden 1985); the other is the 'construction boom' theory (Bevan *et al.* 1989). A brief description of both theories and the testable hypotheses with which they are associated is given below and followed by an attempt to test them against the Nigerian oil boom experience.

Models of the Dutch Disease phenomenon have been analysed to identify basic hypotheses relating to the effects of an export boom, particularly on the relative size of sectors, sectoral prices and the real exchange rate. The rapid expansion of the resource sector in a resource-exporting country affects the overall economy through a network of interactions. The resource sector uses factors, particularly labour and capital, which, if not brought in from abroad, must be withdrawn from other sectors of the economy. Expansion of the resource sector creates additional income, which generates expenditures. The effects of these expenditures depend on the types of goods on which the increased income is spent. The resulting spending pattern affects demand and supply conditions in the product market. The sector's withdrawal of factors also impinges on the economy's factor markets. Thus expansion of the resource affects not only relative product prices but also factor prices and the exchange rate. The effect on the exchange rate occurs because the exports of the expanding resource generate an inflow of capital, the spending of which affects the real exchange rate.

The total impact of a resource boom is a combination of several effects. The magnitude of each may vary depending on the inter-sectoral substitution relationships in both production and consumption. For instance, the movement of resources as a result of the boom causes the price received by the traditional export goods sector to fall relative to the price of domestic goods, and the domestic output of this sector is reduced. In the same way, the relative price of importables falls and the quantity of import-competing goods diminishes. However, the non-tradables sector is not homogeneous, and some of these goods may have elasticities of substitution (in consumption) with import-competing or exportables goods which are quite high. In such cases, a resource boom may be expected to reduce the output of those non-traded goods for which imports are close substitutes, all else being equal.

In summary, the general effects of a resource boom on the traditional export goods sector (in many cases agriculture) and the import-competing goods sector (primarily manufacturing) include lost competitiveness in both exportable and importable goods sectors, as revealed by falling relative prices; loss of relative shares (of total output and employment) by the exportable and import-competing sectors; an upward trend in the real wage rate in the tradable goods sector; and upward trend in the general price level; and currency appreciation.

Construction boom theory modifies the basic hypotheses of the Dutch Disease theory by arguing that, if the windfall generated by an export boom is perceived as temporary, there will be a disproportionate increase in the demand for non-tradable capital goods compared with non-tradable consumer goods; hence the price of the former is likely to rise relative to that of the latter. Thus, in testing the hypotheses associated with these two theories, it is necessary to decompose non-tradables into their capital and consumer components, while the tradables are disaggregated into those which are protected (e.g. by the trade regime) and those which are not.

Previous studies (Pinto 1987; Oyejide 1986, 1987) which have examined the Nigerian oil boom experience in the light of the Dutch Disease theoretical framework uphold at least some of its major hypotheses, including significant shifts against non-oil tradables and appreciation of the real exchange rate. Starting with sectoral shifts and how these have affected non-oil tradables relative to non-tradables, Table 12.13 offers some insights. Compared with the 1960–65 (pre-boom) sectoral shares, Table 12.13 reveals marked changes in the structure of the Nigerian non-oil economy. It is clear, for instance, that the agricultural sector declined sharply in terms of its sectoral share of non-oil GDP up to 1981 and that, with the advent of the oil glut, it was beginning to recapture some of its lost share by 1983. On the positive side, the other major non-oil tradable, manufacturing, made some gains; its sectoral share more or less doubled between 1960/65 and 1983. This gain probably reflects the fact that, unlike the agricultural sector, the manufacturing sector enjoyed the benefits of protection by the trade regime. As predicted by the Dutch Disease theory, sectoral shares of non-tradables (such as building and construction, distribution and services) increased sharply.

The relative gains and losses in sectoral shares are further demonstrated in Table 12.14. Using 1960/65 sectoral shares as the norm, this table shows that only the agricultural sector sustained large losses in terms of its sectoral contribution to GDP. These losses amounted to approximately 50% of its share before the oil boom. Protected manufacturing made sectoral-share gains of between 22% and 70% above its 1960/65 shares. Protection of the manufacturing sector through tariff policy made

Table 12.13. Sectoral distribution of non-oil GDP (*percentage*)

	1960–65	1975	1977	1979	1981	1983
Agriculture	62.5	32.2	30.2	30.6	27.5	37.1
Manufacturing	5.7	7.0	6.5	6.9	7.6	11.7
Utilities	0.5	0.4	0.4	0.5	0.8	1.1
Building and construction	9.0	16.2	16.9	14.9	15.6	7.8
Transport and communication	4.0	4.1	4.4	5.0	6.2	4.7
Distribution	12.2	26.0	28.0	29.5	30.1	20.8
Services	5.2	12.1	10.6	9.7	9.8	15.4

Source: FOS, *Economic and Social Statistics Bulletin*, 1985

Table 12.14. Boom-induced gains and losses in relative sectoral shares of non-oil GDP (*percentage*)

	1975	1977	1979	1981	1983
Agriculture					
Actual	32.2	30.2	30.6	27.5	37.1
Counterfactual	62.5	62.5	62.5	62.5	62.5
Gain/loss	−30.3	−32.3	−31.9	−35.0	−25.4
Manufacturing					
Actual	7.0	6.5	6.9	7.6	11.7
Counterfactual	5.7	5.7	5.7	5.7	5.7
Gain/loss	1.3	0.8	1.2	1.9	4.0
Building and construction					
Actual	16.2	16.9	14.9	15.6	7.8
Counterfactual	9.0	9.0	9.0	9.0	9.0
Gain/loss	7.2	7.9	5.9	6.6	−1.2
Distribution					
Actual	26.0	28.0	29.0	30.1	20.8
Counterfactual	12.2	12.2	12.2	12.2	12.2
Gain/loss	13.8	15.8	17.3	17.9	8.6
Services					
Actual	12.1	10.6	9.7	9.8	15.4
Counterfactual	5.2	5.2	5.2	5.2	5.2
Gain/loss	6.9	5.4	4.5	4.6	10.2

Source: Table 12.13

manufactured goods imperfect substitutes for imports; since the sector was more or less non-tradable, increased domestic spending of the oil boom boosted the manufacturing sector's relative share of non-oil GDP. However, most of the sectoral share lost by agriculture accrued to building and construction (whose sectoral share more or less doubled, except for 1983), distribution and services. The oil boom clearly had sectoral-shift effects that are consistent with the predictions of the Dutch Disease model.

How well do the movements of sectoral prices and the real exchange rate reflect the prediction of the Dutch Disease and construction boom theories? Table 12.15 offers some answers. The real exchange rate declined almost continuously throughout the 1973–83 period. This means that the naira generally appreciated in terms of its external value. The appreciation of the real exchange rate led to a significant loss of competitiveness by the non-oil tradables, particularly agricultural exports. The domestic price of agricultural exports rose sharply between 1973 and 1974 and fell equally sharply over the following year. Subsequently it rose more gradually, until it peaked in 1978 at almost twice its 1973 level. Then it fluctuated erratically around a downward trend and ended at 16% of its 1973 level in 1983. The import price grew higher and at a steadier pace, so that by

Table 12.15. Exchange rate and sectoral prices, 1973–83 (*1973 = 100*)

	Real exchange rate	Agricultural export price	Building and construction (implicit deflator)	Services (implicit deflator)	Import price
1973	100	100	100	100	100
1974	94	135	104	100	117
1975	83	91	109	101	136
1976	69	113	118	108	158
1977	70	128	116	114	140
1978	66	197	124	121	156
1979	65	196	133	128	172
1980	61	137	139	133	190
1981	55	156	144	140	210
1982	56	143	151	146	232
1983	48	160	159	151	257

Source: CBN, *Annual Report*, various years; FOS, *Economic and Social Statistics Bulletin*, 1985

Table 12.16. Relative prices, 1973–83 (*1973 = 100*)

	NT capital/ export	NT capital/ import	NT capital/ consumer
1973	100	100	100
1974	77	89	100
1975	120	80	108
1976	104	75	109
1977	91	83	102
1978	64	79	102
1979	68	77	104
1980	101	73	105
1981	92	69	103
1982	106	65	103
1983	99	62	105

Note: NT = non-tradable
Source: Table 12.15

1983 it had increased 150% over the 1973 level. Price indices for non-tradables (building and construction representing capital goods, and services representing consumer goods) also grew steadily over the 1973–83 period and were generally in between those of imports and exports in terms of levels.

A comparison of relative prices (see Table 12.16) provides a better handle for examining the behaviour of sectoral prices in relation to the predictions of the Dutch Disease and construction boom models. The former model predicts that the price of non-tradables would rise relative to that of tradables in response to resource-movement and spending effects; while the latter expects the price of non-tradable capital goods to rise relative to the price of non-tradable consumer goods as most of the temporary windfall income is saved, thus inducing higher investment and increasing the demand for capital goods.

Table 12.16 shows that the price of non-tradable capital goods did increase relative to that of agricultural exports during certain parts of the 1973–83 period. Thus this relative price responded to the boom with a two-year lag after the first shock in 1973/74 and almost simultaneously on the second occasion in 1979/80. In comparison, the price of non-tradable capital goods rose more slowly than the domestic price of imports, with the gap widening considerably over the period. In spite of the overall appreciation of the naira over the entire 1973–84 period, the domestic currency depreciated gradually against the dollar, particular towards the end of the period. This increased import prices considerably between 1978 and 1983 and probably contributed to the widening gap between import prices and the price of non-tradables noted above. The upward trend in the price of imports can also be traced to the foreign exchange controls and the import regime that characterised this period (see Section 12.6). The behaviour of non-tradable goods prices relative to those of imports and exports seems to imply that, although relative price movements penalised the production and hence discouraged the expansion of non-oil exportables, they were generally much less adverse in relation to the production of importables and import substitutes. This result is quite consistent with the conclusions reached on the basis of the analysis of sectoral-share changes reported earlier.

In spite of the relatively low rate of savings out of windfall income shown above, a comparison of the price of non-tradable capital with that of non-tradable consumer goods indicates clearly that a construction boom occurred in Nigeria during the 1973–83 period. In fact, the behaviour of this relative price (column 4 of Table 12.16) indicates that a construction boom occurred first during 1974–76 and again between 1979 and 1980. In essence, therefore, the predictions of both theories regarding the movement of relative sectoral prices are largely confirmed by the Nigerian experience in the 1973–83 period.

12.6. Trade, Exchange Rate and Credit Control

The Nigerian economy shifted almost completely into a rigid control mode during the 1967–70 civil war. Although the oil boom emerged soon after the war ended, the war left a legacy of stringent controls over many aspects of the activities of private economic agents. In any case, since oil earnings accrued directly to the government, the boom-induced increase in revenue provided the means of implementing a direct-control-based 'commanding heights' strategy of economic development which was first enunciated in the second development plan.

The control regime had a large coverage in terms of facets of economic activities. But its scope and stringency varied considerably over the 1973–83 period. In terms of stringency, a clear pattern is discernible. As the government's foreign exchange revenue situation improved rapidly following the oil price shock of 1973/74, many of the existing controls (e.g. on foreign trade and domestic prices) were relaxed. However, the fall in oil export earnings that occurred during 1976–78 generated a predictable response, heralding a return to more stringent controls. This period of tightened controls was followed by another period of liberalisation, which accompanied the second spurt of oil export earnings increase during 1979–80. Finally, stringent controls grew rapidly between 1982 and 1983, following the world oil market collapse that began mid-1981.

The stringency and scope of the control regime must be qualified by another important consideration. Nigerian regulatory controls are notoriously porous so that many rules that appear on the statute books are routinely ignored in practice. Thus, large-scale smuggling make nonsense of import controls since prohibited items are prominently displayed on market stalls and a large and active parallel market renders the nominally rigid exchange control regulations largely ineffective.

In spite of these qualifications, it is useful to gain an insight into the impact of Nigeria's control regime during the 1973–83 period. For this purpose, the following analysis focuses on controls relating to foreign trade (primarily imports), exchange rate and credit allocation, which are, by and large, those with the most significant macroeconomic effects.

12.6.1. Import Control

Import protection, in its various forms, has constituted an important instrument of trade policy in the management of the Nigerian economy since 1960. The general trend of import protection has been dictated by the predominant policy objective during the different economic policy experiments in the period. Thus in the first half of the 1960s, when the revenue-generating objective was predominant, tariffs were the main instruments of import control and their rates were generally low. From the second half of the 1960s, industrialisation via an import-substitution strategy had priority of place in the set of policy objectives. Hence, a system of discriminatory tariffs (with generally high tariff rates and a built-in escalation structure) was established.

The economic dislocation caused by the civil war of 1967–70 brought in

Table 12.17. Growth and structure of imports, 1960–83

	1960–65	1973–76	1977–80	1981–83
Total imports				
% of GDP	15.6	14.0	20.6	19.7
Consumer Goods				
% of GDP	7.4	4.4	5.9	8.1
% of total imports	47.4	31.4	28.6	41.1
Capital goods				
% of GDP	4.3	5.8	10.0	6.4
% of total imports	27.6	41.4	48.5	32.5
Raw materials				
% of GDP	3.9	3.8	4.7	5.2
% of total imports	25.0	27.1	22.8	26.4

Source: CBN, *Annual Report*, various years

its train serious balance of payments problems. This development led to the emergence of quantitative restrictions (QRs) on imports designed quickly and sharply to compress imports as a tool of balance of payments management. This policy stance of using QRs, including a generous dose of import prohibition, as a means of managing the balance of payments in periods of crisis became the norm throughout the post-civil-war period until late 1986. Hence, even during the oil-boom period, policymakers were quick to resort to a combination of tariff hikes and QRs whenever there was a downturn in oil export earnings and therefore a shortfall in foreign exchange supply. This became particularly rampant after 1982 following the world oil market collapse and the accompanying external payments crisis (Oyejide 1990a).

The boom-induced upsurge in imports was moderated by the import control regime described above. This had the effect not only of reducing the growth of imports of specific periods but also of altering their structure. Table 12.17 presents data illustrating aspects of these changes. Total imports as a proportion of GDP averaged almost 16% during 1960–65. This average was only 14% during 1973–76 in spite of the oil boom, which was due partly to the delay in liberalising imports after the civil war and partly to the lag in response even after the foreign exchange situation had markedly improved. In fact, the twin peaks of the imports/GDP ratio occurred in 1978 (23.1%) and 1981 (22.8%), in both cases some time after the peak of the oil boom. The 'catching-up' both in terms of import liberalisation and response to the oil boom shows up during 1977–80 when the imports/GDP ratio averaged almost 21%, from which it subsequently fell, to average just under 20% in 1981–83.

Imports of consumer goods and raw materials exhibit roughly the same

Table 12.18. Boom-induced change in imports, 1960–83

	1973–76	1977–80	1981–83
Total imports			
Change in value (Nm.)	−131	1,831	2,356
% change	−4.4	22.6	20.1
Consumer goods			
Change in value (Nm.)	−556	−652	562
% change	−61.2	−28.0	11.3
Capital goods			
Change in value (Nm.)	382	2,194	1,181
% change	31.0	55.9	45.7
Raw materials			
Change in value (Nm.)	43	290	611
% change	5.3	15.6	20.7

Source: CBN, *Annual Report*, various years

pattern as total imports. But imports of capital goods show a much quicker response to the oil boom; this was, no doubt, assisted by an import control regime that had a marked bias in favour of capital goods (Oyejide 1990a). As a result, the structure of imports changed significantly: capital goods imports gained at the expense of consumer goods as their share rose from 28% during 1960–65 to 41% in 1973–76 and 49% during 1977–80, before falling to 33% in 1981–83. The share of consumer goods fell sharply, from 47% during 1960–65 to 29% in 1977–80, before rising again, to 41% in 1981–83.

Boom-induced gains and losses for total imports and the three broad components, computed by comparing actual values with counterfactuals (based on 1960–65 import/GDP ratios), are shown in Table 12.18.

These figures demonstrate that, in spite of the boom, imports of consumer goods during 1973–76 and 1977–80 were substantially below what they would have been if the import/GDP ratio of 1960–65 had been maintained. Consumer goods imports suffered 'losses' averaging 61% and 28% respectively over this period. This is reflected also in the loss of 4.4% by total imports. Gains were recorded by capital goods and raw materials over the three periods; these gains were particularly large in the case of capital goods (31% to 60%) but more modest (5% to 21%) in the case of raw materials. These results are clearly consistent with what one might expect from the prevailing import control regime.

12.6.2. Foreign Exchange Control

The naira replaced the pound as the Nigerian currency on 1 January 1973 with an official exchange rate of US$1.52. Through the 1973–83 period, exchange control regulations remained in force in various forms. Nigerian residents could not import or export more than N50 in national currency and could not own, deal in or trade in gold. They could also not own foreign currencies or foreign securities or maintain bank balances abroad. A foreign travel allowance, ranging from N500 to N1000, was permitted per person per year, depending on the availability of foreign exchange. Foreign remittances and capital transfers abroad were subject to prior approval, while proceeds from invisibles and exports had to be surrendered in exchange for local currency at the official exchange rate.

This rate moved up and down as the oil boom intensified or subsided (see Table 12.19). Thus, the nominal rate appreciated by almost 7% within a year and then descended from that peak to reach US$1.54 in 1977 and 1978. Following the second oil boom it appreciated sharply again, by over 19%, between 1978 and 1980, to reach US$1.84, from which it dropped rapidly to US$1.34 in 1983, thus recording a 27% depreciation.

Movements in the parallel market exchange rate more or less reproduce the same pattern, although divergence between the two rates widened considerably over time. Thus, while the lowest points of the official and parallel market exchange rates occurred in 1974 and 1983, the parallel market premium increased significantly, from a range of 20% to 30% during 1973–76 to a range of 42% to 52% in 1977–80 and then to one of 32% to 82% during 1981–83. Exchange control regulations clearly kept the official rate at a much higher level than the underlying market conditions justified.

Table 12.19. Official and parallel market exchange rates, 1973–83 (*US dollars per Nigerian naira, end of period*)

	Official rate	Parallel market rate	Parallel market premium (%)
1973	1.52	1.20	21
1974	1.62	1.21	25
1975	1.60	1.12	30
1976	1.59	1.12	30
1977	1.54	0.74	52
1978	1.54	0.90	42
1979	1.79	1.02	43
1980	1.84	1.07	42
1981	1.57	1.07	32
1982	1.49	0.81	46
1983	1.34	0.24	82

Source: Pick's Currency Year Book, 1973–84

12.6.3. Credit Control

During the 1973–83 period, banking system credit in Nigeria was control-led through the use of a range of instruments, prominent among which were interest rate ceilings, ceilings on aggregate credit, cash reserve and liquidity ratios and prescribed percentages for sectoral credit allocation. This elaborate credit control system enabled government not only directly to control the total amount of banking system credit available to the economy but also to determine how much of that credit was allocated to itself and other sectors of the private economy without significantly alter-ing the structure of nominal interest rates.

A look first at the major monetary aggregates and their movements over the period provides a useful background. Table 12.20 offers the appropri-ate data. Compared with the pre-boom (1960–65) period, the ratios of the major monetary aggregates show dramatic changes during the boom period. But it is significant that, with the exception of the net foreign assets/GDP ratio, whose value doubled compared with the pre-boom norm, all other ratios for 1973–76 were well below their 1960–65 values. However, these values were quickly exceeded as the money supply dou-bled between 1973–76 and 1981–83 while the total credit/GDP ratio in-creased more than sixfold over the same period. A substantial part of this increase in total credit was accounted for by government, which was transformed from a negative net credit position of −2.2% during 1973–76 to 18.1% in 1981–83. The upsurge in the net foreign assets/GDP ratio was short-lived; this ratio fell from 13.2% in 1973–76 to 8% in 1977–80 and 2.6% in 1981–83.

The boom-induced changes in total bank credit and its two broad com-ponents are computed using deviations from the pre-boom (1960–65) levels; the results are displayed in Table 12.21. Actual total credit during 1973–76 averaged 31% less than the corresponding counterfactual value. This was reversed sharply during 1977–80 and 1981–83, when the actual value of total credit exceeded the counterfactuals by 68% and 82%, respec-tively. Increases in banking system credit to the government accounted

Table 12.20. Monetary aggregates as percentages of GDP, 1973–83

	1960–65	1973–76	1977–80	1981–83
Money supply	10.2	8.8	15.5	17.2
Total credit	6.6	5.4	20.5	36.5
To private sector	6.8	7.6	12.8	18.4
To government	−0.2	−2.2	7.7	18.1
Net foreign assets	6.6	13.2	8.0	2.6

Source: CNB, *Annual Report*, various years

Table 12.21. Boom-induced changes in credit, 1973–83

	1973–76	1977–80	1981–83
Total			
Value (Nm.)	−310	5,650	181,145
%	−31.1	68.0	82.1
Private			
Value (Nm.)	180	2,457	7,038
%	11.8	47.3	63.3
Government			
Value (Nm.)	−490	3,193	11,106
%	−92.5	102.6	101.1

Source: CNB, *Annual Report*, various years

Table 12.22. Sectoral credit allocation, 1973–83 (%)

	1973–76	1977–80	1981–83
Tradables[a]			
Prescribed	69.75	66.00	66.66
Actual	60.03	55.48	54.53
Non-tradables			
Prescribed	30.25	34.00	33.33
Actual	39.97	44.53	45.47

[a] Tradables include agriculture, mining, quarrying, manufacturing, foreign and domestic trade

Source: CBN, *Annual Report*, various years

for most of this upsurge; the public sector took N3.2 billion of the N5.7 billion increase in total credit in 1977–80 as well as N11.1 billion out of the N18.1 billion increase in total credit during 1981–83.

In addition to the regulatory instruments that were used to allocate bank credit to the private and public sectors, credit control also extended to detailed specification of the proportion of the total credit that should be allocated to each of sixteen subsectors of the economy. The intention behind this element of the credit-allocation policy was to provide special incentives to the 'production' sectors of the economy. Hence, total annual allocation to the tradable sectors exceeded 60% each year during the 1973–83 period.

As Table 12.22 shows, however, actual credit allocation was not always in accordance with the prescription of the monetary authorities. Stipulated penalties notwithstanding, the banks actually allocated a declining proportion of credit to the tradable sectors favoured by the monetary authorities. Thus, the share of credit provided to tradables fell from an average of 60% in 1973–76 to about 55% in 1977–80 and in 1981–83. Compared to the prescribed proportions, this showed a deviation that widened from −10% in 1973–76 to over −12% in 1981–83. In this same way, actual credit to non-tradables was higher than the prescribed proportions; whereas the prescribed ratio was in the 30% to 34% range during the 1973–83 period, the actual ratio rose from an average of 40% in 1973–76 to just over 45% during 1981–83.

Various elements of the Nigerian control regime were apparently driven by different policy concerns during the 1973–83 period. Changes in the scope, coverage and stringency of import controls reflected an underlying import-substitution, industrialisation policy stance which was often overridden by periodic attempts to tackle balance of payments problems. Credit control and the use of direct credit allocation instruments also reflected policies to favour certain sectors. In spite of the plethora of control instruments, however, large-scale smuggling and the porosity of other regulatory mechanisms rendered the control regime much less effective than a mere examination of the rule book would imply. Hence, the fundamental effects of the trade shocks and oil boom were not significantly deflected by the control regime.

NOTE

1. All counterfactuals are constructed using 1960–65 average ratios. Political turmoil culminating in the civil war that ended in 1970, and the subsequent reconstruction efforts which occurred until 1972, render any other period between 1965 and 1973 unsuitable. It should be borne in mind, however, that this may impart an upward bias to the estimated windfalls.

REFERENCES

Auty, R.M. (1989) 'The International Determinants of Eight Oil-Exporting Countries' Resource Based Industry Performance', *The Journal of Development Studies*, 25 (3, April): 354–72.

Bevan, D., P. Collier and J.W. Gunning (1989) 'The Kenyan Coffee Boom of 1976–79', mimeo.

Corden, W.M. (1985) 'Booming Sector and Dutch Disease Economics: Survey and Consolidation', *Oxford Economic Papers*, 36 (3): 359–80.

Corden, W.M. and J.P. Neary (1982) 'Booming Sector and De-Industrialization in a Small Open Economy', *Economic Journal*, 92: 825–47.

Federal Government of Nigeria (1974a) *Recurrent and Capital Estimates of the Government of the Federal Republic Nigeria, 1974–75*, Federal Ministry of Information, Lagos.

——(1974b) *Guidelines for the Third National Development Plan 1975–80*, Central Planning Office, Lagos.

——(1975) *Third National Development Plan 1975–80*, Central Planning Office, Lagos.

——(1980) *Fourth National Development Plan 1981–85*, Federal Ministry of National Planning, Lagos.

——(1986) *Structural Adjustment Programme*, Government Printer, Lagos.

Gelb, A. (1986) 'Adjustment to Windfall Gains: A Comparative Analysis of Oil Exporting Countries', in J.P. Neary and S. van Wijnbergen (eds) *Natural Resources and the Macroeconomy*, Basil Blackwell, Oxford.

Oyejide, T.A. (1986) *The Effects of Trade and Exchange Rate Policies on Agriculture in Nigeria*, Research Report 55, International Food Policy Research Institute, Washington, DC.

——(1987) 'The Oil Boom, Macroeconomic Policies and Nigerian Agriculture: Analysis of a Dutch Disease Phenomenon', IFPRI Workshop 27–29 May Annapolis, Maryland.

——(1990a) 'Impact of Price Based and Quantity Based Import Control Measures in Nigeria', Seminar on Trade Liberalization Experiences, IEDES, Université Pantheon-Sorbonne Paris I, January 1990.

——(1990b) 'Adjustment with Growth: Nigerian Experience with Structural Adjustment Policy Reform', International Conference on Policy-Based Lending, Institute for Development Policy and Management, University of Manchester, September 1990.

Pinto, A. (1987) 'Nigeria During and After the Oil Boom: A Policy Comparison with Indonesia', *World Bank Economic Review*, 1 (3): 419–46.

13

Multiple Trade Shocks and Partial Liberalisation: Dutch Disease and the Egyptian Economy

NEMAT SHAFIK

13.1. Introduction

To understand the economic consequences of the Egyptian foreign exchange windfall it is necessary to disentangle the effects of multiple trade shocks that coincided with a partial liberalisation programme. Egypt experienced a number of different trade shocks during the late 1970s, each of which had its own characteristics. Moreover, after many years of public-sector-led import-substitution industrialisation, the Egyptian government launched an effort to revive private investment in the economy in 1974. This was accompanied by a series of reforms which affected exchange rate regulations, the financial system, and the trade regime. This liberalisation programme, the *infitah* or 'open-door policy,' was not in response to the windfall income; in fact, many of the reforms preceded the windfall. But the evolution of the reform effort did respond to the changing external circumstances associated with the boom and the impact of the windfall was mediated through these policy changes.

The analysis that follows will evaluate the economic implications of these changes in the control regime in the presence of a foreign exchange windfall. Section 13.2 analyses the nature of the trade shock and the state of expectations for the different sources of growth in national income. The consequences for aggregate consumption and savings behaviour are discussed in Section 13.3 and the effects on the government budget are the subject of Section 13.4. Section 13.5 considers the consequences of the trade shock for private sector savings behaviour and Section 13.6 looks at the evolution of aggregate capital formation in both the public and private sectors. The implications for the labour market are analysed in Section 13.7 and the evolution of relative prices in the goods market is presented in Section 13.8. Section 13.9 describes the control regime—foreign exchange controls, the financial system and trade policy. Section 13.10 considers the overall impact of the control regime on the ability of agents to adjust to the windfall. Some general conclusions are presented in Section 13.11.

13.2. The Nature of the Trade Shock

The foreign exchange bonanza experienced by Egypt was caused by the combination of a sharp increase in petroleum prices and an increase in production volumes during the 1970s. Although Egypt had been producing oil on a small scale for decades, the country did not become a net oil exporter until 1977.[1] Egypt's terms of trade improved somewhat after the first oil shock in 1973, but there was no significant windfall until after 1975, when export volumes had increased (Figure 13.1). In 1976, revenues from oil exports rose by 123%. Production volumes doubled in the late 1970s with new discoveries and the return of the Sinai fields after the signing of the peace treaty with Israel. Oil export volumes increased by 56% in 1975, 42% in 1976, 26% in 1977 and 17% in 1978. Production increased fairly steadily between 1979 and 1984 at a rate of about 9% per year. This quantity shock after 1975 was compounded by the price shock in 1979. Thus the increase in transitory income was delayed. The windfall associated with oil accrued largely to the government since domestic private sector activity was limited to providing services to the petroleum industry.

In addition to the oil windfall, the economy experienced a number of other shocks during the same period. The most important one derived

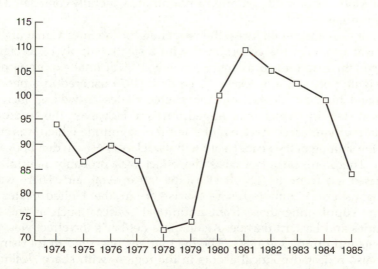

Figure 13.1. Terms of trade index, 1974–85 (*1980 = 100*)

from the remittances of migrant labour working in the oil-exporting countries of the Middle East. As with petroleum exports, Egyptian labour had been migrating to the Gulf for decades, albeit in considerably smaller numbers. Demand for Egyptian migrant labour increased sharply in the 1970s fuelled by the oil boom and higher wages. Although no comprehensive figures on the number of migrants from Egypt are available for the entire period, estimates are that the numbers rose from 100,000 in the early 1970s to over 1 million in the early 1980s, and to possibly double that number by the late 1980s.[2] This massive emigration represented between 5% and 10% of the labour force. Most of the demand was for labour in the non-tradables sectors of the oil-exporting countries, particularly construction and services (Serageldin *et al.* 1983).

The tradability of Egyptian labour was facilitated by a number of policy changes. Emigration was made a constitutional right in 1971. Exit visas were abolished in 1973 and replaced by travel permits available at one's place of work. The issuing of passports was also decentralised so that they could be, in principle, obtained at any police station within twenty-four hours. Remitting earnings abroad back to Egypt was made more attractive with the establishment of the 'own exchange' market, which effectively legalised the parallel market for the private sector. In addition, the state exempted migrants from paying taxes on income earned abroad and abolished a law requiring migrants to transfer a minimum of 10% of earnings to Egypt at the official exchange rate (Ibrahim 1982). The volume of the resulting remittance income was large (see Table 13.1), sometimes exceeding revenues from petroleum exports, and ranged from 22% to 43% of total export earnings. Moreover, because remittances are both in cash and in kind, the officially reported amounts are generally considered to be underestimates.

Besides oil and remittances, the reopening of the Suez Canal after the 1973 war provided the government with a steady supply of foreign exchange which amounted to approximately 10% of total export earnings. The signing of the Camp David Accords in 1979 ushered in a period of sustained high aid flows from the United States as well as increased political stability, which encouraged tourism. However, this increase in US aid partly replaced Arab aid of a similar magnitude which was cut off after the signing of the peace treaty with Israel in 1979 (van den Boogaerde 1990). Therefore, on a net basis the effect was probably neutral with increased aid from the US offset by the fall in Arab aid. There was an analogous effect with tourism—tourists from the United States and Europe supplanting those from traditional sources, such as the Arab countries and Eastern Europe. Again, on a net basis the effect was probably neutral during the 1980s. The fluctuations observed in tourism revenue also reflected political events in the region, with sharp declines in periods of regional conflict.

Table 13.1. Magnitude of trade shocks—levels and growth rates (*m. US$*)

Shock	1974	1975	1976	1977	1978	1979	1980/81	1981/82	1982/83	1983/84
Oil	187	289	644	720	802	1,878	3,179	3,329	2,807	2,957
Growth rate		0.55	1.23	0.12	0.11	1.34	0.69	0.05	−0.16	0.05
Remittances	189	366	755	897	1,761	2,445	2,855	1,935	3,165	3,931
Growth rates		0.94	1.06	0.19	0.96	0.39	0.17	−0.32	0.64	0.24
Aid	140	361	598	931	1,202	997	1,402	1,464	1,172	1,428
Growth rate		1.58	0.66	0.56	0.29	−0.17	0.41	0.04	−0.20	0.22
Suez canal	0	85	311	428	514	589	780	909	957	974
Growth rate			2.66	0.38	0.20	0.15	0.32	0.17	0.05	0.02
Tourism	265	332	464	728	702	601	712	611	304	288
Growth rate		0.25	0.40	0.57	−0.04	−0.14	0.18	−0.14	−0.50	−0.05

Notes: Oil export revenues only reflect Egypt's share, not that of foreign companies; the category 'aid' reflects official loans and grants

Source: World Bank

Table 13.2 presents a taxonomy of the different shocks experienced by the Egyptian economy, providing a disaggregation in terms of (i) whether the public or private sectors were the primary beneficiaries and (ii) the duration of the windfall gain for individual agents and for society as a whole. The oil price shock of 1973 is not included in Table 13.2 since it had insignificant effects on the economy as export volumes were low. The quantity shock associated with oil occurred after 1975, when volumes increased. The price shock of 1979, which coincided with the higher volumes, resulted in a 134% increase in export revenues. The increase in revenues from higher production levels stabilised by the mid-1980s. Given knowledge about reserves and the extent of exploration, the increase in foreign exchange revenues associated with the quantity shock was perceived as temporary.[3] This was exacerbated by the rapid increase of domestic demand because of subsidised energy prices and rising incomes. Agents in Egypt could observe the declining world price during the 1980s which signalled the end of the world oil price boom. Therefore, in the absence of major new discoveries of petroleum reserves, the international signals were fairly clear that the price boom in the oil market was on the wane and that Egypt's windfall was a temporary one. The government's strategy was clearly one of exploiting oil resources as rapidly as possible to finance diversification of the economy, particularly towards industry.

Remittances are linked to the oil price through the demand for labour in the oil-exporting countries. However, remittance income has tended to be more stable than the price of oil because of structural labour shortages in the Gulf. Thus, in terms of aggregate income, the increase in remittance flows represented an upward shift in permanent income. For the individual migrant, however, the remittances were a temporary increase in income which would usually be used to finance major purchases (such as housing) or for investment (in land or a business). An analysis of migrant spending of remittance income based on household survey data found that 54% was spent on housing and 21% on land.[4] Except for the poorest

Table 13.2. Taxonomy of shocks

Shock	Beneficiary	Expected duration	
		Individual	Society
Oil quantity (1975)	Public	Temporary	Temporary
Oil price (1979)	Public	Temporary	Temporary
Remittances (1979)	Private	Temporary	Permanent
Aid (1979)	Public	Permanent	Permanent
Suez Canal (1975)	Public	Permanent	Permanent
Tourism (1979)	Public/Private	Permanent	Permanent

migrants, the share of remittance income devoted to consumption was fairly low (about 32%). Migrants in the top 20% income quintile devoted over 80% of marginal budget shares to investment. Thus, income from tradable labour was spent largely on investments in non-tradable assets. Whereas the migrant's use of remittance income reflected his/her perception of its temporariness, society as a whole experienced an increase in permanent income.

The increase in foreign exchange earnings from aid, the Suez Canal and tourism can be considered as Egypt's 'peace dividend'. These were revenues which were permanent as long as there was no war between Israel and Egypt and relative stability in the region. Barring any major political changes, agents would probably assume that these increased revenues represented a rise in permanent income.

The above discussion implies that the only truly temporary shock experienced by the Egyptian economy was that associated with oil. The magnitude of this shock is analysed in Table 13.3, where the effects of the price and quantity shocks are disaggregated. The oil-production figures reflect only the Egyptian share, not that of foreign partners. Egypt's total oil reserves are estimated to be about 600 million metric tons, which, if depleted at the rate of 44 million metric tons per year, would last until the year 2000.

Table 13.3. Magnitude of the oil shock (*m. US$*)

	Price shock		Quantity shock		Total windfall	
	Real net oil income	Present value	Real net oil income	Present value	Real net oil income	Present value
1975	962	795	552	456	1,513	1,251
1976	1,131	850	1,219	916	2,350	1,766
1977	1,266	864	1,689	1,154	2,954	2,018
1978	1,169	726	1,850	1,149	3,019	1,875
1979	2,228	1,257	1,740	982	3,968	2,240
1980	4,666	2,394	1,791	919	6,457	3,313
1981	6,019	2,808	2,047	955	8,066	3,763
1982	5,848	2,480	2,339	992	8,187	3,472
1983	5,510	2,124	2,633	1,015	8,143	3,140
1984	5,990	2,099	3,083	1,081	9,073	3,180
1985	6,038	1,924	3,296	1,050	9,334	2,974
Total		18,322		10,669		28,991

Notes: For the quantity shock, real net oil income was derived as [change in quantities produced since 1974 × 1974 oil price]/import price index. Oil production only includes the Egyptian share; partners' shares are excluded. Present values were calculated using a 10% discount rate. The windfall real net oil income is calculated as [(oil production × oil price) − quantity shock]/import price index

Source: World Bank data and author's calculations

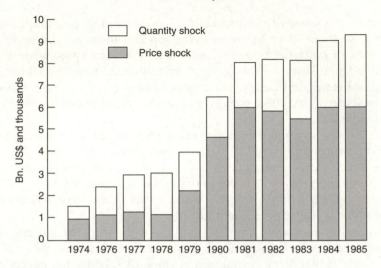

Figure 13.2. Magnitude of the oil shock, 1975–85

The price shock counterfactual is constructed assuming that the price and volume of oil production were maintained at 1974 real values and levels. Real net oil income was derived using an import price index and the present value of the oil revenue and calculated using a 10% discount rate. The present value of the oil price shock is US$18.3 billion, which is greater than Egypt's GDP of US$15 billion in 1977 when it became a net oil exporter.

The quantity shock counterfactual is based on the assumption that production volumes in 1974 were maintained. Increases in production volumes above the level of 7.5 million metric tons annually are defined as the quantity shock. The real revenue that resulted from the quantity shock and the net present value are presented in Table 13.3. The net present value of the quantity shock is US$10.7 billion, which is two-thirds of Egypt's GDP in 1977. The quantity shock was particularly important between 1976 and 1978, when volumes were increasing rapidly and prices were relatively stable, but after the 1979 price increase most of the wind-fall came from the oil price shock. The total windfall to the Egyptian economy was about US$29 billion in net present value terms. About two-thirds of the windfall could be attributed to the price shock and one-third could be attributed to the effects of increased production volumes (Figure 13.2).

The price and quantity shocks estimated in Table 13.3 were used to explore various counterfactuals for the windfall period 1975–85. Actual income was defined as real GDP in 1980 prices plus the price windfall from Table 13.3. Counterfactual income was defined as real GDP in 1980

Table 13.4. Actual and counterfactual income and savings (*m. real 1980 LE*)

	Savings/ GDP	Actual income	Windfall income	Windfall savings	Present value of windfall income	Present value of windfall savings	Windfall savings rate
1975	0.07	9,847	1,513	122	1,513	122	0.08
1976	0.11	10,737	2,350	615	2,136	559	0.26
1977	0.12	12,003	2,955	786	2,442	649	0.27
1978	0.14	12,968	3,019	1,145	2,269	861	0.38
1979	0.12	14,247	3,968	937	2,710	640	0.24
1980	0.11	15,740	6,457	1,094	4,009	679	0.17
1981	0.10	16,370	8,066	1,081	4,553	610	0.13
1982	0.16	18,247	8,187	2,181	4,201	1,119	0.27
1983	0.17	19,513	8,143	2,549	3,799	1,189	0.31
1984	0.16	20,724	9,073	2,397	3,848	1,017	0.26
1985	0.17	22,185	9,335	2,798	3,599	1,079	0.30

Source: World Bank data and author's calculations

prices minus the export volume effect in Table 13.3. This counterfactual level of income was that which could be considered 'permanent' had the temporary oil windfall not occurred. The resulting estimates of income appear in Table 13.4.

13.3. Consumption and Savings Behaviour

To understand the impact of the windfall on the economy, actual and counterfactual estimates of consumption and savings are presented in Tables 13.4 and 13.5. Actual savings rates rose after 1974, reflecting the effects of the quantity shock associated with increased oil export volumes. While there is no major increase in savings rates associated with the 1979 oil price shock, saving rates were markedly higher over the 1975–1985 period as a whole compared to other periods. This implies that savings rates were responding to a temporary, albeit long, windfall which began with an oil quantity shock in 1975, was reinforced by an oil price shock in 1979 and subsided with the oil price collapse in 1986.

Counterfactual consumption was calculated on the assumption that consumption and savings rates remained at 1975 levels. The resulting counterfactual levels were calculated as a share of counterfactual income. Windfall savings were calculated as the difference between the counter-factual and actual levels of savings. The results in Table 13.4 indicate that a substantial portion of the windfall was saved (as high as 38% in 1978 and

Table 13.5. Actual and counterfactual foreign savings (*m. LE*)

	Actual		Counterfactual	
	Current account deficit	As a share of GDP	Current account deficit	Windfall foreign dissavings
1975	662	0.07	417	246
1976	329	0.03	419	−90
1977	612	0.05	452	160
1978	706	0.05	497	209
1979	1,290	0.09	514	776
1980	1,022	0.06	464	558
1981	1,537	0.09	415	1,122
1982	2,516	0.14	503	2,013
1983	1,441	0.07	569	872
1984	2,119	0.10	583	1,536
1985	3,421	0.15	643	2,779

Source: World Bank and author's calculations

averaging 24% for the entire period). This may reflect the fairly high levels of consumption in the year chosen for the counterfactual—aggregate savings were only 7% of GDP in 1975. But the savings rates in the previous years, 1971–73, were similar, ranging between 6% and 8%.

Counterfactual foreign savings are presented in Table 13.5, based on the assumption that the current account deficit remained at 5% of counterfactual GDP over the period. The average current account deficit as a share of actual GDP for the 1970–73 period was 5%. Windfall foreign dissavings are calculated as the difference between the actual current account deficit and the counterfactual current account deficit. The data indicate substantial foreign dissavings during the windfall period, with the exception of 1976. Egypt drew on foreign savings particularly heavily during the end of the 1980s. The windfall made it possible for Egypt to run a current account deficit that was on average two to three times the norm.

This accelerated foreign dissavings reflected the increased perceived creditworthiness of Egypt, possibly based on the perception that the windfall would persist and on growth in often politically motivated official credits. Egypt's experience is broadly consistent with the view that creditors tend to lend procyclically, rather than countercyclically. Instead of saving the windfall income abroad, Egypt public sector accumulated a substantial foreign debt of approximately US$50 billion by 1988.[5] However, unlike other heavily indebted countries, Egypt borrowed largely from official creditors and often on very concessional terms: 80% of Egypt's long-term debt was owed to official creditors, mainly bilateral, and the average maturity of Egypt's total loans between 1980 and 1985 was twenty-five years, at an average interest rate of 7.5%.

13.4. The Government Budget

Egypt is a classic 'high-absorbing' country with limited oil reserves and a rapidly growing population. Thus it is not surprising that the government's propensity to spend its windfall income was high, especially after decades of being subject to a foreign exchange constraint. Table 13.6 presents the actual and counterfactual government budget for the period 1974–87. The counterfactual assumes that the pattern of revenues and expenditures as a share of GDP in 1974 prevailed throughout the period. The resulting counterfactual budget was constructed by applying 1974 government budget shares to counterfactual income. The windfall to the government budget is derived as the difference between the actual and the counterfactual budget. Table 13.6 gives an indication of the magnitude of the windfall to the government budget. For much of the 1980s, the windfall almost doubled the government's revenues and expenditures when compared to the counterfactual. Over the entire period, the government tended not only to spend its entire windfall, but to overspend it. Deficits continued to be substantial (and to increase over time) during the entire windfall period. The major source of windfall revenue was oil, which was reflected in the public sector surplus. Other important sources of government revenue during the boom were trade taxes in the years 1974–79, which increased with higher levels of importation under the more liberal trade regime, and increasing business profits, which grew with the re-emergence of the private sector after the introduction of the open-door policy in 1974.

Although the government's windfall revenue came largely from tradables, its expenditure was on both tradables and non-tradables. By the early 1980s, when windfall revenues were substantial, government expenditure on investment was the most rapidly growing part of the budget. The largest share of this public investment (about half) went to public sector industry, much of which was protected and oriented towards the domestic market. Thereafter, the most important area for public investment was infrastructure—particularly transport and communication, electricity and, to a lesser extent, housing (see Figure 13.3).

The government's wage bill did not increase by a large amount, despite the fact that about one-third of the labour force is nominally employed in the public sector as a result of the government's policy of guaranteeing employment for all graduates. The absence of a further increase in government employment was a reflection of the low and declining real wages

Table 13.6. Summary of government budget (m. LE)

	1975	1976	1977	1978	1979	1980/81	1981/82	1982/83	1983/84	1984/85	1985/86
Actual (in nominal terms)											
Total revenue	1,524	2,015	2,755	3,306	3,684	7,373	8,322	9,749	10,371	11,312	12,792
Indirect taxes	692	907	1,416	1,421	1,672	2,355	2,821	3,282	3,714	3,930	4,067
Foreign trade	400	538	979	920	905	1,329	1,573	1,644	1,920	1,907	1,808
Direct taxes	330	416	551	726	870	1,824	1,702	1,918	1,649	1,993	2,453
Business profit	195	278	387	538	656	1,506	1,578	1,788	1,486	1,800	2,131
Public sector surplus	364	574	652	1,012	875	2,700	2,950	3,553	2,830	2,740	3,212
Total expenditure	3,015	3,280	4,169	5,559	7,097	10,555	13,205	14,497	16,804	18,477	21,637
Current expenditure	1,352	1,670	1,701	2,037	2,495	3,691	4,722	5,416	6,586	7,630	8,384
Subsidies	622	434	650	710	1,352	2,166	2,909	2,054	1,988	2,007	2,989
Investment	900	980	1,549	2,311	2,547	3,766	4,541	5,020	5,518	6,556	8,261
Overall deficit	−1,491	−1,265	−1,414	−2,253	−3,413	−3,182	−4,883	−4,748	−6,433	−7,165	−8,845
Actual (as a share of actual GDP in nominal terms)											
Total revenue	0.29	0.30	0.33	0.34	0.29	0.45	0.48	0.47	0.43	0.40	0.39
Indirect taxes	0.13	0.13	0.17	0.15	0.13	0.14	0.16	0.16	0.15	0.14	0.12
Foreign trade	0.08	0.08	0.12	0.09	0.07	0.08	0.09	0.08	0.08	0.07	0.05
Direct taxes	0.06	0.06	0.07	0.07	0.07	0.11	0.10	0.09	0.07	0.07	0.07
Business profit	0.04	0.04	0.05	0.05	0.05	0.09	0.09	0.09	0.06	0.06	0.06
Public sector surplus	0.07	0.09	0.08	0.10	0.07	0.16	0.17	0.17	0.12	0.10	0.10
Total expenditure	0.58	0.49	0.50	0.57	0.56	0.64	0.76	0.70	0.70	0.65	0.65
Current expenditure	0.26	0.25	0.20	0.21	0.20	0.22	0.27	0.26	0.27	0.27	0.25
Subsidies	0.12	0.06	0.08	0.07	0.11	0.13	0.17	0.10	0.08	0.07	0.09
Investment	0.17	0.15	0.19	0.24	0.20	0.23	0.26	0.24	0.23	0.23	0.25
Overall deficit	−0.29	−0.19	−0.17	−0.23	−0.27	−0.19	−0.28	−0.23	−0.27	−0.25	−0.27
Counterfactual (in nominal terms)											
Total revenue	1,167	1,314	1,551	1,889	2,381	2,400	2,533	3,219	3,741	4,419	5,038
Indirect taxes	478	538	635	774	975	983	1,038	1,319	1,532	1,810	2,064
Foreign trade	228	256	303	369	465	468	494	628	730	862	983
Direct taxes	247	278	329	401	505	509	537	682	793	937	1,068
Business profit	141	159	187	228	288	290	306	389	452	534	608
Public sector surplus	333	375	443	539	680	685	723	919	1,068	1,262	1,438

Total expenditure	2,042	2,300	2,715	3,308	4,169	4,201	4,435	5,636	6,549	7,737	8,820
Current expenditure	935	1,053	1,243	1,514	1,909	1,923	2,030	2,580	2,998	3,542	4,038
Subsidies	404	455	537	654	825	831	877	1,115	1,295	1,530	1,744
Investment	588	662	782	953	1,201	1,210	1,277	1,623	1,886	2,228	2,540
Overall deficit	−876	−986	−1,164	−1,419	−1,788	−1,802	−1,902	−2,417	−2,809	−3,318	−3,782
Windfall government budget											
Total revenue	357	702	1,205	1,417	1,302	4,973	5,789	6,530	6,630	6,893	7,754
Indirect taxes	214	369	781	647	696	1,372	1,783	1,963	2,182	2,120	2,003
Foreign trade	172	282	677	551	440	861	1,079	1,016	1,190	1,045	825
Direct taxes	83	137	223	325	365	1,315	1,165	1,236	856	1,056	1,385
Business profit	54	119	200	310	368	1,216	1,272	1,399	1,034	1,266	1,523
Public sector surplus	31	199	210	473	195	2,015	2,227	2,634	1,762	1,478	1,774
Total expenditure	973	980	1,454	2,251	2,927	6,354	8,770	8,861	10,255	10,740	12,817
Current expenditure	417	617	458	523	586	1,768	2,692	2,836	3,588	4,088	4,346
Subsidies	218	−21	113	56	527	1,335	2,032	939	693	477	1,245
Investment	312	318	767	1,359	1,346	2,556	3,264	3,397	3,632	4,328	5,721
Overall deficit	−615	−278	−249	−834	−1,625	−1,381	−2,981	−2,331	−3,624	−3,847	−5,063
Memorandum items											
GDP deflator	51	57	63	70	85	100	101	110	119	132	144
Actual GDP (nominal)	5,218	6,727	8,344	9,795	12,705	16,497	17,320	20,781	24,170	28,504	33,132
Permanent GDP (real 1980)	8,333	8,387	9,049	9,948	10,279	8,794	9,182	10,715	11,510	12,251	12,820
Permanent GDP (nominal)	4,275	4,814	5,683	6,924	8,727	8,794	9,283	11,797	13,709	16,195	18,461
Windfall income	1,513	2,350	2,955	3,019	3,968	7,262	8,127	8,165	8,608	9,204	9,427
Private sector windfall	1,156	1,648	1,750	1,602	2,666	2,288	2,338	1,635	1,978	2,311	1,672
as a percentage of total	0.76	0.70	0.59	0.53	0.67	0.32	0.29	0.20	0.23	0.25	0.18

Notes: Private sector windfall is calculated as the difference between windfall come and government windfall revenue. Because of the switch to a fiscal year in 1980, windfall income (which is on a calendar-year basis) is calculated as the average of two years after 1979

Source: Ministry of Finance, World Bank data and author's calculations

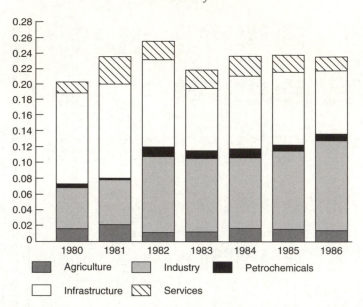

Figure 13.3. Composition of government investment in real terms, 1980–86 (*share of GDP*)

paid by the public sector and increased employment opportunities in the private sector.

The consumer subsidy bill also absorbed a large proportion of the windfall revenue. Almost half of this subsidy bill went to cover the costs of maintaining artificially low domestic prices for imported wheat and flour. In addition, domestic energy prices for most consumers were a fraction of world prices during the period and represented a loss of potential export revenues to the public sector.[6] By the end of the windfall period, current expenditures became more important as some of the subsidies were phased out. Investment, however, continued to absorb a large portion of windfall revenues.

The resulting government deficit was largely financed domestically through the banking system and through the social security surplus. The government was able to avoid rapid inflation by accumulating arrears, exploiting money illusion among savers and sacrificing the enforceability of foreign exchange controls.[7] Egyptian savers continued to hold domestic assets, despite their negative real returns, because of restrictions on immediate conversion of Egyptian pounds into US dollars, some risk associated with the parallel market owing to periodic crackdowns on foreign exchange dealers, and high transactions and insurance costs associated with holding other types of assets (such as gold or real estate). There was also some apparent money illusion over the period, in part, perhaps, because of poor information and the lack of access to the formal financial system of some parts of society.

The government's savings rate was negative throughout the boom period, but was less so over time. This did not reflect greater pass-through of the windfall to the private sector—the memorandum items at the bottom of Table 13.6 show how much of the windfall went to the private sector (defined as windfall income minus government revenue). The numbers are quite high in the early years, when between three-quarters and two-thirds of the windfall went to private agents. But by 1980/81, the private sector share of the total windfall falls sharply as government spending levels 'ratcheted up', accustomed to the higher levels of revenue. This growth in spending was driven by investment—which accounted for over 50% of expenditures after 1977.

Government savings and debt accumulation are depicted in Table 13.7. A counterfactual has been constructed on the assumption that the government's savings as a share of counterfactual GDP remained at their 1974 level of 6% (derived from a deficit of 20% of GDP minus an investment rate of 14%). The resulting debt associated with the windfall was substantial and rose steadily over the boom period.

13.5. Private Savings Behaviour

Unlike the public sector, which consumed the windfall (and more), the private sector saved a fairly high proportion of the windfall (Table 13.7). The private sector savings rate out of counterfactual income averaged 40% over the entire period—which was about three times the savings rate from 'permanent income.' In the earlier period 1975–79 much of this private savings stemmed from transfers of the windfall from the public sector. But after 1979 the proportion of the windfall passed from the public to the private sector fell from levels averaging 65% (1975–79) to about 25% (1980–85).

The way in which private agents saved domestically changed dramatically over the period. Private agents were permitted to hold foreign exchange accounts in Egypt under Law 64/1974 and Law 97/1976. As a result of these changes associated with the open-door policy, there was a shift in asset holding out of Egyptian pounds (LE) and into foreign exchange, largely US dollars which were held abroad by the domestic banking system. Private foreign exchange deposits held in the domestic banking system grew by over 50% per annum on average between 1978 and 1982. The resulting 'dollarisation' of the economy served to shift investment inter-temporally.[8] This was in response to the higher returns to foreign assets in the context of low, often negative, real interest rates on savings held in Egyptian pounds, rising world interest rates, growing

Table 13.7. Actual and counterfactual government savings, debt and private savings (*m. LE*)

	Government (windfall) savings	Net accumulated savings (debt)	Government savings rate	Net present value of government savings	Private savings rate
(a) Actual					
1975	−591	−591	−0.11	−537	0.18
1976	−285	−876	−0.04	−236	0.15
1977	135	−741	0.02	101	0.10
1978	58	−683	0.01	40	0.13
1979	−866	−1,549	−0.07	−538	0.19
1980	−141	−1,690	−0.01	−80	0.12
1981	−489	−2,179	−0.03	−251	0.13
1982	−35	−2,214	0.00	−16	0.16
1983	−322	−2,535	−0.01	−136	0.18
1984	−762	−3,297	−0.03	−294	0.19
1985	−597	−3,894	−0.02	−209	0.19
(b) Counterfactual					
1975	−649	−649	−0.67	−590	0.75
1976	−402	−1,051	−0.21	−332	0.47
1977	−24	−1,074	−0.01	−18	0.28
1978	−112	−1,186	−0.04	−76	0.42
1979	−1,104	−2,290	−0.28	−686	0.52
1980	−574	−2,864	−0.08	−324	0.25
1981	−1,024	−3,889	−0.11	−526	0.24
1982	−618	−4,507	−0.06	−288	0.33
1983	−960	−5,466	−0.09	−407	0.40
1984	−1,550	−7,016	−0.12	−597	0.38
1985	−1,474	−8,490	−0.10	−517	0.40

Note: Government savings are defined as total revenues minus total expenditures plus public investment. Private savings are calculated as the residual of total savings from Table 13.4 and government savings. Counterfactuals assume 1974 government saving rate (deficit plus investment), which was equivalent to −6%

Source: World Bank and author's calculations

domestic inflation, a depreciating parallel exchange rate and uncertainty.[9] By the mid-1980s, foreign exchange deposits accounted for 40% of total liquidity (El-Erian 1988). Deposits in LE also grew, although at a much slower pace, despite the negative real interest rates.[10] This shift in favour of assets denominated in foreign exchange meant that the monetary authorities' control over domestic liquidity was reduced, tax revenue capacity was weakened and the efficacy of exchange rate policy was diminished.

Reliable estimates of the size of Egyptian private sector asset holdings

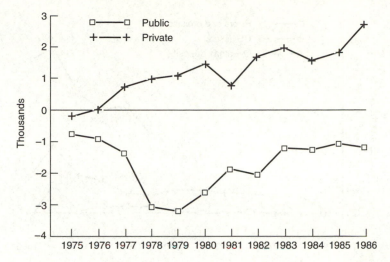

Figure 13.4. Net foreign asset position, public and private sectors, 1975–86

abroad are not available. The net foreign asset positions of the public and private sectors in Egypt based on data from the IMF's *International Financial Statistics* are presented in Figure 13.4. The graph confirms that the private sector tended to accumulate foreign assets after the windfall whereas the public sector maintained a negative net foreign asset position throughout the period. Data available on cross-border bank deposits of non-banks resident in Egypt are available after 1981. These indicate the degree to which agents accumulated foreign assets during the windfall and began to draw down foreign assets when the oil price fell in 1986 (IMF, *International Financial Statistics*). An additional crude proxy of private foreign assets is net errors and omissions in the balance of payments, depicted in Figure 13.5, along with US liabilities to Egypt. Here too, the evidence points to increased foreign asset holding by the private sector during the windfall period. Thus, the private sector was better able to smooth the windfall income over time by accumulating foreign assets.

13.6. Aggregate Capital Formation

How much of the windfall was invested? Figure 13.6 depicts capital formation as a share of GDP in the public and private sectors over the windfall period. Although the public sector remained the primary investor in the economy, both the private and public sectors experienced considerable growth during the windfall period. This was especially the case

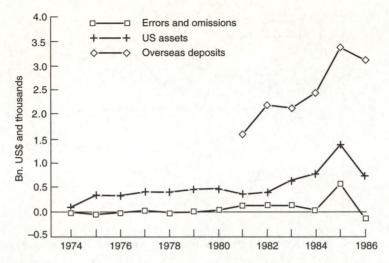

Figure 13.5. Capital flight: balance of payments, errors and omissions, 1974–86

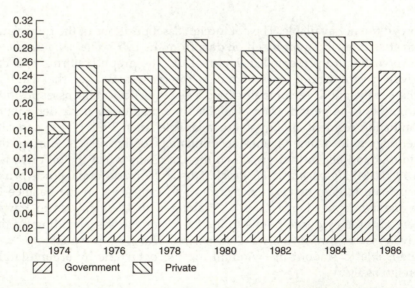

Figure 13.6. Real government and private investment, 1974–86 (*share of GDP*)

between 1982 and 1984, when the aggregate investment rate was 30%. With the collapse in the price of oil in 1986, however, private investment virtually ceased, although the government was able to maintain public capital formation above 20% through continued borrowing.

The investment attributable to the windfall is presented in Table 13.8. Counterfactual investment was derived as the sum of counterfactual

Table 13.8. Actual and counterfactual investment (*m. LE*)

(*a*) *Actual*

	Savings	As a share of GDP	Current account deficit	As a share of GDP	Investment	As a share of GDP
1975	706	0.07	662	0.07	1,368	0.14
1976	1,202	0.11	329	0.03	1,531	0.14
1977	1,419	0.12	612	0.05	2,031	0.17
1978	1,842	0.14	706	0.05	2,548	0.20
1979	1,656	0.12	1,290	0.09	2,946	0.21
1980	1,744	0.11	1,022	0.06	2,767	0.18
1981	1,662	0.10	1,537	0.09	3,199	0.20
1982	2,885	0.16	2,516	0.14	5,401	0.30
1983	3,345	0.17	1,441	0.07	4,786	0.25
1984	3,213	0.16	2,119	0.10	5,331	0.26
1985	3,697	0.17	3,421	0.15	7,119	0.32

(*b*) *Counterfactual*

	Savings	Windfall savings	Current account deficit	Windfall foreign dissavings	Investment	Windfall investment
1975	583	122	417	246	1,000	368
1976	587	615	419	−90	1,006	525
1977	633	786	452	160	1,085	946
1978	696	1,145	497	209	1,193	1,354
1979	720	937	514	776	1,234	1,713
1980	650	1,064	464	558	1,114	1,622
1981	581	1,081	415	1,122	996	2,203
1982	704	2,181	503	2,013	1,207	4,194
1983	796	2,549	569	872	1,365	3,421
1984	816	2,397	583	1,536	1,399	3,933
1985	900	2,798	643	2,779	1,543	5,577

Source: World Bank data and author's calculations

domestic savings (from Table 13.4) and counterfactual foreign dissavings (from Table 13.5). The final column, which shows the investment associated with the windfall, gives an indication of how important the boom was for capital formation in the economy during this period. Relative to the 'normal' levels of investment, the foreign exchange windfall enabled an increase in capital formation of often several orders of magnitude. For much of the first half of the 1980s, the windfall enabled a doubling, and in some years a tripling, of the normal rate of investment in the economy.

13.6.1. Public Investment

Much of the public investment that did occur went towards the rebuilding of Egypt's decaying infrastructure. The social returns to this infrastructure investment, although difficult to quantify, appear to have been fairly high. Egypt's infrastructure had been neglected for decades and there is some econometric evidence that it had significant crowding-in effects on private investment (Shafik 1992). This crowding-in of private investment as a result of public investment in infrastructure was accompanied by crowding-out in financial markets, where government borrowing resulted in rationing to private borrowers. Public investment in infrastructure also fuelled inflation of non-tradable prices, particularly of land and construction, for all agents in the economy.

Public investment in tradables, largely agriculture and petroleum, did not grow substantially. However, capital formation in non-financial public enterprises did increase. Because the activities of these public enterprises were highly protected, their output is largely non-tradable. Unlike the investment in infrastructure, where the economic returns may have been high, the returns from these public enterprise investments were very mixed. Some, such as the petroleum companies, were profitable, but many public industries generated negative economic rates of return (Hansen 1988). Estimates by the World Bank for the period 1973–1983/84 indicate that the marginal productivity of capital in public sector industry was approximately 5%, the ICOR was 19 and the total factor productivity gains were only 1.37% (World Bank 1987: 24–6).

13.6.2. Private Investment

The recovery of private investment after 1974 depicted in Figure 13.6 was partly in response to the liberalisation and investment incentives associated with the open-door strategy, but was also strongly motivated by increased demand associated with the foreign exchange boom. Although the rate of private investment in Egypt appears fairly low compared to industrial countries, it is about average for low- and middle-income countries, where private investment's share of GDP is around 10%. Moreover, in Egypt's case, it is important to consider the historical context: all medium- and large-scale private sector firms were nationalised during the 1960s. Also, the official statistics for private investment tend to underestimate capital formation in the smallholding agricultural and informal sectors because of measurement problems. Therefore, in terms of other developing countries and in Egypt's own historical terms, the recovery of private investment was significant.

Data on the sectoral disaggregation of private investment as a share of total private investment are available up to 1982 because of a special

Table 13.9. Sectoral private investment as a share of total private investment, 1974–82

	Agriculture	Industry	Housing	Construction	Finance	Transport	Services
1974	0.08	0.19	0.50	0.01	0.02	0.12	0.08
1975	0.05	0.24	0.43	0.01	0.01	0.24	0.02
1976	0.04	0.35	0.27	0.04	0.01	0.04	0.21
1977	0.09	0.36	0.24	0.05	0.01	0.04	0.20
1978	0.07	0.36	0.19	0.11	0.01	0.07	0.19
1979	0.09	0.38	0.22	0.12	0.01	0.07	0.12
1980	0.09	0.42	0.09	0.09	0.02	0.08	0.21
1981	0.24	0.24	0.36	0.01	0.01	0.04	0.09
1982	0.16	0.20	0.49	0.05	0.04	0.03	0.03

Note: Numbers may not sum to 1.00 in any particular year because of rounding of figures
Source: Shura Council (1985)

report prepared for Parliament in 1985. The figures, reported in Table 13.9, provide insights into the relative profitability of different economic activities. Table 13.9 excludes the booming petroleum sector, which absorbed a large share of total private investment as a result of investments in services to the oil industry after 1974. The first column shows not much change in the sectoral share of agriculture, except for a sharp rise in 1981–82 which probably reflects growing private investment in capital-intensive land-reclamation projects in response to government incentives. However, aggregate data on private investment in agriculture are likely to be unreliable in an economy in which most of the agricultural sector is based on small peasant holdings. Within the agricultural sector, there was a shift away from tradables, such as cotton and rice, towards non-tradables, particularly the import-substituting, protected livestock sector and goods produced for home consumption (Commander 1987). The sectoral share of industry rose from an all-time low of 1% of total private investment in 1968 in the wake of the nationalisations to an all-time high of 42% in 1980.

Private investment in housing as a share of the total experienced an enormous decline—from absorbing 50% of total private investment in 1974 to as little as 9% in 1980. This decline in housing investment is in relative, not absolute terms. In fact, the level of private investment in housing grew considerably based on censuses from 1976 and 1986. The desirability of investment in housing was caused in part by government policies, in particular rising inflation and government subsidies to building materials and housing loans.[11]

The figures for private investment in construction give some indication of the boom in construction activity with the *infitah*. In addition to increased private demand for construction, the boom was fuelled by

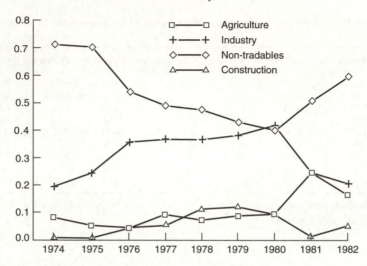

Figure 13.7. Sectoral private investment shares, 1974–82

government contracting of large-scale projects, largely in infrastructure, to the private sector. Prior to the open-door policy, the private sector was restricted to small-scale projects, and large contracts were awarded exclusively to public sector construction companies.

To evaluate the behaviour of private investment more directly in Dutch Disease terms, the sectors have been aggregated in Figure 13.7. Agriculture and industry have been entered separately as potentially tradable, construction has been disaggregated and the non-traded sector consists of transport, finance, housing and services. Only two observations from the 1980s are available, so the results must be considered tentative, especially given the lags in the investment process.[12] The available evidence shows that in the early part of the windfall, from 1974 to 1980, the agricultural and industrial sectors gained relative to non-tradables. However, after 1980, when oil revenues became substantial, both agriculture and industry experienced declining shares of private investment and non-tradables' share rose sharply. The construction sector experienced some increase in its share of private investment from 1977 to 1980, declined in 1981, and was on an upward trend thereafter.

13.7. Labour Movements and Wages

In addition to the spending effect which results from a windfall, there is a resource-movement effect which results from the rising marginal product of labour in the booming sector. Assuming that labour is inter-sectorally mobile, workers are expected to move out of the lagging and non-tradables sectors into the booming sector. The effect on real wages is indeterminate since wage-earners consume non-tradables. In the case of an oil boom, or any other type of enclave-based boom, there is no major effect on labour markets because of the small number of fairly skilled labourers needed in the industry.[13] The existence of income from remittances also had consequences for labour movements and real wages.

The growth in employment was substantial during the windfall period, particularly in non-tradables. Overall labour force growth was 2.4% over the same period (Assaad and Commander 1990). Employment in the construction sector grew by 9.5% per year between 1973 and 1982, and employment in services grew by 4.6%. In the import-substituting manufacturing sector, employment grew by 2.9%, reflecting the expansion of capital-intensive industry. In contrast, employment in the tradable agricultural sector fell by 1.1%, despite an 11% increase in real wages in the sector over the period. The excess demand for labour in the agricultural sector was often met by female and child labour which was frequently underreported or unreported (Commander 1987). Much of the male agricultural labour shifted to urban construction, where wage growth was even greater than that which occurred in agriculture.

The growth in employment was fuelled by the public sector, which expanded by over 3.5% per annum between 1973 and 1982, providing over half of the net increase in employment (Handoussa 1992: 5). This was not wage-induced, but reflected the policy of guaranteed employment of all graduates and the non-pecuniary benefits (such as status, job security, free medical care and privileged access to subsidised goods and services) associated with government employment. This growth in public employment during the boom effectively served as a mechanism for transferring some of the public sector's windfall to private citizens. The demands of public sector employment were often minimal, providing substantial scope for second jobs. As the windfall subsided, the government was forced to reduce its annual recruitment of graduates from about 110,000 to fewer than 30,000 (Handoussa 1992: 6). This was achieved not by eliminating job guarantees for graduates, but by increasing the queuing time prior to appointment to between five and six years. Employment in the formal private sector, defined as firms with over ten workers, also grew by 4.5%, but still constituted only 3% of total employment (Assaad and Commander 1990: 11). Open unemployment during the period ranged between 3% and 5% (p. 12).

The sectoral distribution of labour did shift away from tradables in favour of non-tradables in response to the windfall, as evidenced by the data in Table 13.10. The data include both public and private formal sector employment, and thus underestimate small-scale and informal sector activities. If counterfactual sectoral employment shares were hypothesised

Table 13.10. Sectoral labour force as a share of total labour, 1974–88

Year	Agriculture	Industry	Housing	Construction	Electricity	Utilities	Trade and finance	Transport	Services
1975	0.44	0.12	0.01	0.05	0.004	0.005	0.10	0.04	0.22
1976	0.42	0.12	0.01	0.05	0.005	0.006	0.11	0.04	0.23
1977	0.42	0.12	0.01	0.05	0.005	0.006	0.11	0.04	0.24
1978	0.40	0.13	0.01	0.05	0.005	0.006	0.11	0.04	0.24
1979	0.39	0.13	0.01	0.06	0.006	0.006	0.11	0.04	0.24
1980	0.37	0.12	0.01	0.06	0.005	0.006	0.12	0.04	0.26
1981	0.36	0.13	0.02	0.06	0.005	0.006	0.11	0.04	0.28
1981/82	0.39	0.14	0.02	0.04	0.006	0.006	0.10	0.05	0.26
1984/85	0.37	0.15	0.02	0.03	0.006	0.006	0.10	0.05	0.27

Note: After 1981/82, data on the labour force in the petroleum sector are included under industry

Source: Shura Council (1985) and Ministry of Planning

to be the same as in 1974 (for the sake of consistency with other counter-factuals), the windfall seems to have resulted in a clear shift in employment along Dutch Disease lines. The most significant changes were in agriculture, industry and services. The steadily declining share of the agricultural sector can be explained in part by technology and growing mechanisation in agriculture over the period. It is difficult to disentangle the historically declining trend of agricultural employment from that associated with the windfall. The evidence from the other sectors is perhaps more interesting. The rising labour shares of non-tradable industry and services are significant and the labour force in the construction sector virtually doubled during the boom. Most of the other sectors experienced very little change in their labour share—including the booming petroleum enclave, where expansion was very capital intensive.

Table 13.11 considers the evolution of average wages across sectors for selected years using 1970 as the base year. Not surprisingly, the sector in which wages were growing most rapidly was the booming mining sector. But petroleum employed a very small fraction of the labour force—less than 1%—and did not have many spillover effects on the rest of the economy.

The only other sectors in which wages consistently rose more rapidly than the index of total wages were agriculture and construction. The explanation for the rapid increase in wages in both the agricultural and construction sectors in Egypt was the petroleum-based construction boom. In the case of the construction sector, the boom resulted in an increase in the relative price of non-tradables, particularly non-tradable capital. The domestic construction boom associated with the windfall fuelled higher prices which were driven in part by rising labour costs, which increased fourfold between 1970 and 1980 (Table 13.11). In the case of agricultural wages, the explanation lies in the migration of large num-

Table 13.11. Index of average wages by sector, selected years (*1970 = 100*)

	1970	1975	1977	1982	1984	1985
Agriculture	100	136	267	444	630	890
Mining	100	172	284	620	914	780
Manufacturing	100	130	181	445	606	617
Construction	100	140	191	411	718	733
Transport	100	161	174	372	483	593
Finance	100	109	136	323	411	469
Services	100	139	167	320	486	510
Total	100	132	184	418	580	620

Source: CAPMAS, *Employment, Wages and Hours of Work*, various issues; cited in Zaytoun (1991)

bers of rural labourers to urban construction and, perhaps more importantly, to the construction sectors of the neighbouring oil-exporting countries. A recent survey of emigration found that 35.8% of returned migrants
during the period 1974–84 worked in the construction sector while
abroad.[14] An increasing number of these international migrants came
from rural areas. In the early 1970s, when emigration was largely to Libya,
only 30% of Egyptian migrants were from rural areas. By the late 1980s,
when Iraq emerged as a major labour importer, over 50% of Egypt's
migrants came from rural areas. This increase in rural emigration for
construction put substantial upward pressure on agricultural wages.

13.8. The Goods Market: Did Relative Prices Change?

A number of price indices for the Egyptian economy are presented in
Table 13.12. The indices are labelled according to whether they would be
considered tradable (T) or non-tradable (NT) or both. Analysis of the price
effects of the foreign exchange windfall in Egypt is complicated by the
existence of widespread subsidies alongside hidden indexation. For
example, the official index of petroleum and fuel prices in the wholesale
price index shows no sign of the 260% increase in world energy prices in

Table 13.12. Price deflators (*1974 = 100*)

	GDP (T/NT)	Imports (LE official) (T)	Capital goods imports (LE) (T)	Other services (NT)	Construction (NT)	Housing (NT)
1974 wiggle	100	100	100	100	100	100
1975	110	76	114	112	156	100
1976	124	73	121	113	186	99
1977	137	74	130	133	211	100
1978	151	84	140	152	235	101
1979	185	100	157	173	267	103
1980/81	224	120	176	199	320	101
1981/82	244	120	176	233	370	102
1982/83	264	128	192	244	408	112
1983/84	294	133	199	277	433	119
1984/85	320	140	212	314	473	130
1985/86	361	172	270	346	515	142

Note: There is a break in the import price indices in 1980/81 because of a change from a
calendar-to a fiscal-year basis

Sources: World Bank and CAPMAS, *Statistical Yearbook*, various issues; *Pick's Currency
Yearbook*, various issues, IMF, *International Financial Statistics*

1973/74 and the 60% increase in 1979/80 because of subsidies to domestic consumers of energy. However, private firms established under the investment-promotion legislation enacted in 1974 were generally required to pay world prices for their energy. The index for construction may also be an underestimate since there was a large parallel market for cement and other building materials during the period. At times, the parallel market price of cement was as high as 225% of the official selling price.[15] Similarly, the housing index, a frequently used proxy for non-tradables, displays very little movement over the period because rents have been fixed in perpetuity in Egypt since the 1960s. However, the 'key money', a one-off illegal payment required before moving into a rented dwelling, has risen steadily in response to growing demand for housing. This infla-tion in *de facto* housing costs caused by rising key money payments is not reflected in the official price index for housing.

The price indices provide strong evidence of Dutch Disease and con-struction boom effects during the boom, with prices of non-tradables, particularly non-tradable capital, rising relative to tradables. Prices in the construction sector rose faster than any other price in the economy. Ser-vices prices, also a non-tradable, increased relative to the aggregate price level. The relative price of tradables, as measured by the import price index and the price of capital goods imports, fell relative to the GDP deflator. Figure 13.8 depicts relative prices of services (non-tradable) to all

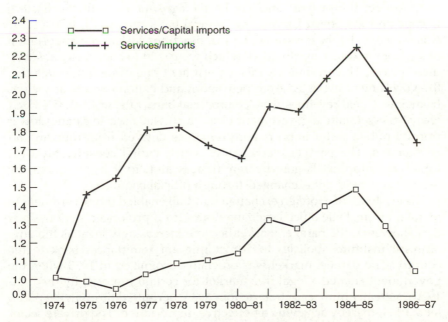

Figure 13.8. Relative prices of non-tradables to tradables, 1976–86/87 (*1974* = 1)

importables and to imports of capital goods. The shift in relative prices in favour of non-tradables is apparent during the windfall.

Evidence on agricultural land prices from survey evidence also reveals the rise in non-tradable prices in the economy. In a survey of 1,000 rural households in three villages in Egypt, Adams (1991: 719) found that the average price of a feddan of agricultural land increased by 500%, from LE 2,000 to LE 12,000, between 1980 and 1986. This reflected rates of return on agricultural land that averaged about 9.5% over the same period. In contrast, rates of return on most small-farmer crops in Egypt, most of which were tradable, were negative during the windfall period (Adams 1986). These negative rates of return to much of tradable agriculture reflected, among other things, the low procurement prices imposed by the government for selected crops.

13.9. The Control Regime

13.9.1. Foreign Exchange Controls

The foreign exchange regime in Egypt prior to 1987 has been described as one in which a number of different 'pools' served the foreign exchange needs of different borrowers. There were a few relatively unimportant and highly overvalued exchange rates that were used only for accounting purposes on transactions such as barter agreements with the Eastern Europe and the Soviet Union. The 'central bank rate' of LE 0.70 = US$1 was used only by the government for transactions such as the importation of key commodities, mostly food, which were sold to consumers at subsidised prices. The revenue for this government rate came from rents that the government extracted from petroleum and cotton exports as well as from Suez Canal revenues. The 'commercial bank rate' of LE 1.35 = US$1 was also essentially a government rate which was used to finance lower priority public sector imports with revenues derived from tourism and remittances. The parallel market rate, which varied considerably over time, was supplied largely by remittances and, to a lesser extent, by tourism revenues not exchanged through official channels.

The existence of a foreign exchange windfall enabled the government to maintain unrealistic official exchange rates for a prolonged period. Over time, however, the parallel market became increasingly legal as the government instituted policies to attract migrant remittances back to the country. The parallel market was officially recognized in 1973 when the government created a legal free market for certain imports. By the mid-1970s, a greater number of transactions were permitted through the parallel market, thereby achieving an effective depreciation. The private sector was permitted to import though the 'own exchange' system established in

1974/75. Egyptians were permitted to hold foreign currency accounts under Law 97 of 1976 and to engage in foreign exchange transactions.

Subsequent policies attempted to restrict the parallel market because the government experienced foreign exchange shortages in the mid-1980s. These attempts, which included various import bans and restrictions on private foreign exchange accounts, were fairly unsuccessful at reducing the foreign exchange constraint. By May 1987, some public sector transactions were also conducted at the parallel market exchange rate after an exchange rate reform which was agreed with the International Monetary Fund. Subsequent reforms have effectively unified the exchange rate at the parallel market price.

13.9.2. The Financial System

Between the nationalisations and the end of 1974 there were four public sector commercial banks, two specialised public sector banks, and two offshore banks. After the 1974 liberalisation, there were forty-three commercial banks, thirty-one business and investment banks, twenty-one specialized and two offshore banks by 1984.[16] The plethora of financial institutions was in response to the growing needs of the private sector and, perhaps more importantly, to the highly profitable structure for banking services provided by the central bank's schedule of fees and commissions. The schedule was originally designed to protect the profitability of the public sector commercial banks, which would, in theory, lend on the basis of developmental rather than profitability objectives. However, the government managed the public sector banks on a more or less commercial basis from their inception. Because profitability became an important criterion in evaluating the performance of the public sector banks, there is no evidence that they distributed loans in any more or less socially desirable way than do the private banks. With the *infitah*, private banks could take advantage of the approximately 6% margin over their cost of funds allowed for by the central bank's regulations.[17]

Egypt, like many developing countries, used central bank administered interest rates which were below market levels for loans in domestic currency.[18] Real rates of interest on domestic loans were negative throughout the windfall period. Loans in foreign currency are at world market rates.[19] Not surprisingly, this spawned considerable arbitrage, since private agents preferred holding LE-denominated debt to that in foreign currencies whereas they preferred assets denominated in foreign exchange over LE.

Subsidised interest rates for agricultural and industrial loans were intended to encourage investment in these sectors. In practice, these especially low rates meant that banks, both public and private, preferred making loans to the more lucrative commercial sector rather than to higher-risk projects in agriculture or industry. While a 6% margin is generous for 'safe' lending such as short-term trade transactions, banks would require much higher returns to embark on the kinds of long-term investments in manufacturing that the government sought to encourage. Thus, the government's interest rate policy had the effect of discouraging investment in tradable agriculture and industry in favour of commercial transactions.

In addition to financing trade, the banks were heavily involved in exporting capital abroad. A report of the Central Auditing Authority found that only 42% of total Law 43 bank deposits were invested in local projects; the remainder were held with correspondent banks abroad.[20] This was made possible by the financial liberalisation brought about by the government's interest in attracting the foreign exchange earnings of migrant workers. Through Laws 64/1974 and 97/1976, the government permitted the holding of foreign exchange domestically and facilitated transfers from abroad through 'free accounts for non-residents' available through bank branches located near large concentrations of migrant workers (see IMF 1990: 141–3). Egyptian migrants were also encouraged to subscribe to special bond issues on favourable terms (Serageldin *et al.* 1983). These foreign exchange accounts were also made available to domestic residents through both the public and private sector banks. Thus, the structure of interest rates and financial regulations served to discourage investment in potentially tradable agriculture and industry. However, the expansion of the financial system and the possibility of holding foreign exchange accounts encouraged savings, particularly foreign savings, because of the low returns offered on domestic assets.

During the mid-1980s, new financial institutions emerged that sought to circumvent the central bank's low administered interest rates on domestic assets. These were so-called Islamic financial funds, which operated like venture capital firms or mutual funds, paying depositors on the basis of the profitability of their portfolio, rather than with a fixed rate of interest. These funds were unregulated and uninsured, but were able to mobilise substantial savings with exceptionally high rates of return, ranging from 20% to 40%. Many savers began shifting their domestic assets away from the formal banking system towards the Islamic funds.

The Islamic funds played an important role in buying foreign exchange from migrant workers and in holding domestic assets accumulated during the windfall. Although no balance sheets were published, it was widely believed that their investments were concentrated in currency speculation, gold, real estate and a small number of industrial projects. As the size of their holdings grew (some estimated their total assets were valued as high as US$5 billion), the government became increasingly concerned about their activities. In 1988, reporting requirements and a regulatory structure were imposed on the Islamic funds, triggering numerous bankruptcies. This episode in parallel financial markets resulted in massive losses for depositors, many of whom were small savers. But it also caused a major change in the expectations of Egyptian savers and investors.

13.9.3. The Trade Regime

The import regime in Egypt was liberalised substantially after the launching of the open-door policy. The private sector import-licensing system was abolished in 1975 and a negative import list of twenty-eight commodities was established in its place. In 1977 this was modified with the introduction of an open general licensing system. Reductions in import duties and a broadening of exemption from duties were instituted in 1980. The increased openness of the economy was reflected in the growth of imports from about one-quarter of GDP in the early 1970s to about one-half of GDP in the early 1980s. Exports also grew, from 15% of GDP in 1972/73 to 44% by the late 1970s; however, this largely reflected gains in the petroleum sector.

Although the trade regime was fairly liberal during the windfall period, the industrial sector could still get protection through tariffs and quotas, often on an *ad hoc* basis. This was facilitated by an amendment to Law 43/1974 which allowed investments which produced import substitutes to reap the gains of the incentives and subsidies under the *infitah* legislation originally intended exclusively for export-oriented activities. Many private investors obtained guarantees of quantity controls as preconditions to their investing (see Shafik 1992). These factors, combined with the entrepreneurial learning, growing confidence and lags inherent in the investment process, meant that by the early 1980s, private investors began to shift from importing commodities to domestic production of import substitutes under protection.[21] In general, the private sector tended to invest in those areas where tariffs were high or where there were quantity restrictions on imports—such as construction materials, luxury goods, clothing, engineering and assembly operations.

In the Egyptian case, the protection to industry was not instituted specifically in response to the foreign exchange windfall, but had existed since the 1960s as part of the government's encouragement of import substitution. Within the industrial sector, there existed a tremendous range of effective protection across industries and between individual firms. A World Bank study of domestic resource costs and effective protection in 1983 found that private sector firms within the same industrial sector had effective rates of protection that ranged from negative to highly positive values (World Bank 1983). In general, the study found that food products had negative rates of effective protection whereas textiles, metals and engineering and building materials showed positive rates of protection in ascending order. However, there was considerable variation in domestic resource costs within industries and between individual firms within an industrial sector.

The availability of protective tariffs for the industrial sector became particularly useful when the combined effects of the foreign exchange windfall and the *infitah* facilitated greater investment in both the public and private sectors by affecting demand, costs and mark-ups. Interestingly, the effective protection given to the private sector was higher than that for the public sector, reflecting the private sector's ability to set its output prices at the levels implied by the structure of tariffs. By the mid-1980s the government began to revert to a more restrictive trade regime—a negative import list was reinstated and an 'Import Rationalisation Committee' was established. These restrictions on imports were in large part a response to the slowdown in the foreign exchange windfall.

13.10. The Control Regime and the Windfall

The previous analysis of the windfall and counterfactuals provides strong evidence on the existence of Dutch Disease and construction boom effects in Egypt. Relative price movements indicate a rise in the price of non-tradables relative to tradables and they show an increase in the price of non-tradable capital goods relative to other prices during the windfall period. This is evident in the data on both output prices and wages. The movement of capital and labour also indicate fairly classic Dutch Disease effects, with the non-tradable sectors gaining relative to tradables. The construction sector experienced some of the most extreme shifts, with a doubling of investment and employment alongside a fourfold increase in prices. There also emerged a parallel market for construction materials and a widespread deterioration in building standards to save on costs.

While the real economy largely followed the pattern identified by construction boom theory, the control regime sometimes served to suppress these effects. Specifically, the rise in the price of the booming sector was offset by substantial domestic energy subsidies. The decline in the price of tradables was counteracted by the granting of protection to the industrial sector, which became a *de facto* non-tradable. The rise in the price of non-tradables such as housing was constrained by the policy of fixed rents. The boom in construction prices was restrained by government subsidies in the form of credit and inputs to respond to a perceived shortage of housing and infrastructure.

Some of these policies existed prior to the windfall and were not part of a concerted effort by the government to avoid relative price changes during a temporary boom. The initial motive behind the liberalisation of the control regime was not the foreign exchange windfall. However, the existence of a foreign exchange boom provided momentum and a new rationale for the reform process. For example, the opportunity cost of the subsidy required to maintain domestic energy prices at artificially low levels increased in proportion to the rise in world oil prices during in the 1970s. The increased demand for housing was manifested in rapid growth in the amount of 'key money' required to occupy a fixed-rent dwelling. In rural areas, land prices rose rapidly as returning migrants sought to translate their temporary windfalls into fixed assets. The number of firms interested in taking advantage of the availability of protection for industrial investments increased substantially. And an open financial system became more important when the economy had to smooth windfall income inter-temporally. In general, the control regime was better at repressing construction-boom effects when the activity was exclusively in public hands, such as energy pricing and the trade regime. Where the private sector played an important role, such as in housing, construction and foreign exchange and financial services, demand spilled over into parallel markets.

Just as the boom facilitated an economic opening, the bust resulted in efforts to restrict imports, control foreign exchange markets and restore government price controls. Parallel markets—in goods, foreign exchange and financial services—were repressed. These recidivist tendencies made it more difficult for the economy to manage the downside of the windfall.

13.11. Conclusions

Unlike foreign exchange booms which are concentrated in one particular sector, the windfall in Egypt affected the economy through a variety of channels and its consequences were the result of the actions of both private and public agents over a fairly long period of time. The public sector's use of the oil windfall implied a perception that the shock was a permanent one. There was little public sector saving, although there was an increase in public investment, some of which was financed by borrowing. The returns to this increase in public investment were mixed. Some of the windfall was also used to sustain a growing subsidy bill from artificially low prices for certain foodstuffs and energy and to maintain an overvalued official exchange rate. Private sector consumers were the major beneficiaries of the subsidy programme, although the public sector also consumed subsidised energy; the public sector was the sole beneficiary of the overvalued exchange rate. In general, the government was not very successful at shifting the boom inter-temporally nor at investing the windfall income optimally.

The private sector increased both its consumption and its savings and investment during the windfall period. High consumption levels in part reflected the permanent nature of some of the windfall for the private sector. However, individual migrant labourers experiencing a temporary windfall did have a higher propensity to invest their remittance income than did non-migrant households. Private capital formation rose rapidly in response to the combination of the windfall and investment incentives. Private firms also took advantage of the government's willingness to provide protection for rent-seeking purposes. Private production decisions reflected a shift in favour of using tradable inputs to make non-tradable outputs. This was in response to the extremely profitable opportunities offered under the open-door policy's incentive structure and served to concentrate the boom, especially in terms of the demand for non-tradable capital goods. Although the relative size of the private sector did expand as a result of this protection, the firms which evolved were uncompetitive by international standards. Nevertheless, unlike the public sector, the private sector did save some of its windfall income, particularly in the form of foreign assets. This was made possible by the changes in the control regime adopted by the government to attract the foreign exchange earnings of migrant workers. This was the one area in which the policy response to the shock contributed to improved management of the temporary foreign exchange windfall.

These private savings, most of which were held in foreign exchange, helped to shift the boom inter-temporally. What was damned as 'unnationalistic capital flight' in the 1970s and 1980s became a source for investment financing during the 1990s.

NOTES

1. Oil seepages were discovered near the mouth of the Gulf of Suez in early Roman times, but the first significant modern discoveries were not made until 1909. Despite these early discoveries oil development in Egypt lagged behind that in the better endowed Gulf countries (Ikram 1980).
2. The available estimates vary, but all show an upward trend over the 1970s and early 1980s. Fergany's estimate based on survey data is that there were not more than 200,000 migrant labourers in 1976. This rose to 1.2 million in 1985 (Fergany 1988, cited in Assaad and Commander 1990). Amin and Awney (1985) estimate that as many as 1 million Egyptians were working abroad in the early 1980s, which constituted between 9% and 10% of the labour force. Commander (1987: 125) reports that approximately 5% of the labour force was abroad in the mid-1970s and 9%–10% by 1981/82.
3. For example, Dervis *et al.* (1984) writing in the early 1980s were concerned about inter-temporal choices about growth given finite non-renewable resources. The Egyptian government's own plans reflected its awareness of limited oil reserves and the need for future diversification.

4. Adams (1991) uses household survey data to explore differences in migrant and non-migrant expenditure patterns. He estimates counterfactual income and expenditure of migrant households econometrically and then compares the actual levels with those of non-migrant households. His results provide strong evidence against the view that migrants consume the bulk of their remittance income.

5. Roughly half of this accumulated debt has since been forgiven by Egypt's creditors though the Paris Club.

6. Domestic petroleum prices in Egypt averaged one-third of the world price during the windfall period. The exception to this was private sector firms established under the investment promotion legislation, Law 43, who were required to pay world prices for their energy to offset preferential treatment on taxes, customs, duties, etc.

7. For a detailed analysis, see Giugale and Dinh (1990).

8. For a more detailed analysis of the portfolio aspects of Dutch Disease in Egypt, see de Macedo (1982).

9. El-Erian's (1988) econometric analysis shows that the most important determinants of currency substitution in Egypt over the 1979–86 period were expectations of exchange rate depreciation and political uncertainty.

10. Foda (1982: 23) explained this growth of deposits in domestic currency as resulting from the expansion in the money supply, the increased use of banks by the public, the tax-exempt status of deposits and the shortage of readily accessible alternative investments.

11. The government's subsidies to the housing sector were intended to address the perceived housing shortage, but actually fuelled the construction of housing units that were inflation hedges and would remain empty. During the 1980–86 period an average of 211,000 new housing units were constructed each year in urban areas. In rural areas the annual average was 171,000 per year during the 1975–86 period. Yet 17% of the urban units and 14.5% of the rural units were empty at the end of 1986. This implies that, using a conservative estimate of US$5,000 per unit, there are US$9 billion of idle, unproductive assets held in the form of empty housing in the Egyptian economy. Note that the fixed rental, pro-tenant laws discouraged the rental of unfurnished units, despite the fact that there is substantial unfulfilled demand for housing. These controls mean that the monthly rent for a large flat in Cairo's most expensive residential neighbourhood can be roughly the same as the cost of two cups of coffee in a local hotel. Handoussa (1987) provides a useful summary of the evolution of investment in housing.

12. Attempts were made to extend the private investment series beyond 1982 by deriving private investment as the residual from total and government investment. Because of different categorisations used, it was not possible to arrive at a plausible time-series.

13. In Egypt's case, only 0.2% of the labour force was employed in the petroleum sector. This proportion remained constant during the windfall (Shura Council 1985; Ministry of Planning).

14. Assaad (1991), citing results from the Egyptian Emigration Survey carried out in 1985 under the auspices of the National Population Council.

15. Interview, Suez Cement Company, Dec. 1987.

16. For a survey of the evolution and operations of the banking system, see Foda (1982).
17. This is in contrast to the approximately 2% margin for banks in most developed countries on loans to regular clients.
18. The government committed itself to liberalising interest rates in 1991.
19. The interest rate on loans in foreign exchange reflects international prices. Most institutions lend foreign exchange at approximately 2% over six-month LIBOR for the short and medium term.
20. The public sector banks also tended to hold their foreign exchange holdings abroad. Foda (1982: 6) also found that banks in Egypt were net placers of assets abroad, implying a fair degree of liquidity in foreign exchange.
21. Shafik (1989) provides a number of examples of firms that made this transition from importing to domestic production under protection.

REFERENCES

Adams, R. (1991) 'The Economic Uses and Impact of International Remittances in Rural Egypt', *Economic Development and Cultural Change*, 39(4), July.
——(1986) *Development and Social Change in Rural Egypt*, Syracuse: Syracuse University Press.
Amin, G. and E. Awny (1985) 'International Migration of Egyptian Labour', IDRC Report MR 108c, May.
Assaad, R. (1991) 'Structure of Egypt's Construction Labour Market and its Development Since the mid-1970s', in H. Handoussa and G. Potter (eds) *Employment and Structural Adjustment: Egypt in the 1990s*, Cairo: American University in Cairo Press.
Assaad, R. and S. Commander (1990) 'Egypt: The Labour Market through Boom and Recession', mimeograph, World Bank, May.
Central Authority for Public Mobilization and Statistics (CAPMAS) (various years) *Statistical Yearbook*, Cairo.
Commander, S.J. (1987) *The State and Agricultural Development in Egypt Since 1973*, London: Ithaca Press.
Corden, M. (1984) 'Booming Sector and Dutch Disease Economics: Survey and Consolidation', *Oxford Economic Papers*, 36, pp. 359–80.
de Macedo, J.B. (1982) 'Currency Diversification and Export Competitiveness: A Model of the Dutch Disease in Egypt', *Journal of Development Economics*, 11, pp. 287–306.
Dervis, K., R. Martin and S. van Wijnbergen (1984) 'Policy Analysis of Shadow Pricing, Foreign Borrowing and Resource Extraction in Egypt', World Bank Staff Working Paper Number 622.
El-Erian, M. (1988) 'Currency Substitution in Egypt and the Yemen Arab Republic: A Comparative Quantitative Analysis', *IMF Staff Papers*, 35(1), March.

Fergany, N. (1988) 'In Pursuit of Livelihood: A Field Study of Egyptian Migration', Centre for Arab Unity Studies, Beirut (in Arabic).

Foda, A.S. (1982) 'Banking Sector Survey', mimeograph, report to the United States Agency for International Development, Cairo, June.

Giugale, M. and H. Dinh (1990) 'Money, Inflation and Deficit in Egypt', PRE Working Paper 553, World Bank, December.

Handoussa, H. (1987) 'The Impact of Foreign Aid on Egypt's Economic Development: 1952–1986', paper presented to a conference on Aid, Capital Flows and Development, Taillories, France, September.

——(1992) 'Crisis and Challenge—Prospects for the 1990s', in H. Handoussa and G. Potter (eds), *Employment and Structural Adjustment: Egypt in the 1990s*, Cairo: American University in Cairo Press.

Hansen, B. (1988) *The Political Economy of Poverty, Equity and Growth: Egypt*, (unpublished).

Ibrahim, S. (1982) in M. Kerr and S. El-Yassin (eds), *Rich and Poor States in the Middle East*, Boulder, & Colo.: Westview Press and American University in Cairo Press.

Ikram, K. (1980) *Egypt: Economic Management in a Period of Transition*, Washington, DC: World Bank.

IMF (1990) *Exchange Arrangements and Exchange Restrictions*, Annual Report, Washington, DC: International Monetary Fund.

Neary, J.P. (1980) 'Non-Traded Goods and the Balance of Trade in a Neo-Keynesian Temporary Equilibrium', *Quarterly Journal of Economics*, 93(3), 403–29, November.

Neary, J.P. and S. van Wijnbergen (1986) *Natural Resources and the Macroeconomy*, Oxford: Oxford University Press.

Penwell Publishing Company (1988) *Energy Statistics Sourcebook*, Tulsa, Oklahoma.

Serageldin, I., J. Socknat, Stace Birks, Bob Li and C. Sinclair (1983) *Manpower and International Labour Migration in the Middle East and North Africa*, Oxford: Oxford University Press.

Shafik, N. (1989) 'Private Investment and Public Policy in Egypt', D.Phil. thesis, Oxford University.

——(1992) 'Modelling Private Investment in Egypt', *Journal of Development Economics*, 39, 263–7.

Shura Council (1985) 'Investment Policy', mimeograph, Financial and Economic Affairs Committee Report (in Arabic).

van Wijnbergen, S. (1984) 'Inflation, Employment, and the Dutch Disease in Oil-Exporting Countries: A Short-Run Disequilibrium Analysis', *Quarterly Journal of Economics*, 99, pp. 233–50.

van den Boogaerde, P. (1990) 'The Composition and Distribution of Financial Assistance from Arab Countries and Arab Regional Institutions', IMF Working Paper No. 67, July.

World Bank (1987) 'Arab Republic of Egypt: Issues of Trade Strategy and Investment Planning', mimeograph, December.

——(1990) *World Tables 1989–90*, Baltimore and London: Johns Hopkins University Press.

——(1990) *World Debt Tables 1989–90*, Washington, DC: World Bank.

Zaytoun, M. (1991) 'Earnings and the Cost of Living: An Analysis of Recent Developments in the Egyptian Economy', in H. Handoussa and G. Potter (eds), *Employment and Structural Adjustment: Egypt in the 1990s*, Cairo: American University in Cairo Press.

INDEX